*Positive Social Behavior
and Morality*

SOCIAL AND
PERSONAL INFLUENCES

Positive Social Behavior and Morality

SOCIAL AND PERSONAL INFLUENCES

ERVIN STAUB
DEPARTMENT OF PSYCHOLOGY
UNIVERSITY OF MASSACHUSETTS
AMHERST, MASSACHUSETTS

Volume 1

ACADEMIC PRESS   New York   San Francisco   London   1978
A Subsidiary of Harcourt Brace Jovanovich, Publishers

Figure 8.1 on page 340 is from Donnenwerth, Gregory V., & Foa, Uriel G. Effect of resource class on retaliation to injustice in inter-personal exchange. *Journal of Personality and Social Psychology*, 1974, **29**(6), 785–793, Fig. 1. Copyright 1974 by The American Psychological Association. Reprinted by permission.

ACADEMIC PRESS, INC.
111 Fifth Avenue, New York, New York 10003

United Kingdom Edition published by
ACADEMIC PRESS, INC. (LONDON) LTD.
24/28 Oval Road, London NW1 7DX

Library of Congress Cataloging in Publication Data

Staub, Ervin.
    Positive social behavior and morality.
    Social and personal influences

    CONTENTS: v. 1.   Social–personality determinants.
    1.   Social psychology.   2.   Altruism.   3.   Helping
behavior.   4.   Interpersonal relations.   I.   Title.
HM251.S755   301.1   77–92246
ISBN   0–12–663101–8

PRINTED IN THE UNITED STATES OF AMERICA

Contents

Preface   xi

Acknowledgments   xv

chapter 1

Positive Behavior, Morality, and Human Nature   *1*

Prosocial Behavior: Definition, Significance,
and Relationship to Morality   2

Prosocial Acts and Altruistic Motives   6

Morality and Human Nature   10

Sources of Morality   13

Genetic Origins of Altruism   25

Social Evolution in Contrast to Biological Evolution   32

Prosocial Behavior in Animals   34

chapter 2

*Personality, the Situation, and the Determination
of Prosocial Behavior*   *39*

Why People Behave Prosocially   42

Self-Gain   42

Personal Values and Norms   43

Empathy and Identification with Other People   44

A Theoretical Model for Predicting Prosocial Behavior   45
Personal Goals and the Activating Potential of Situations   45
Goal Conflict and Conflict Resolution   49
The Measurement of Goals and Activating Potentials   51
Other Personality Influences on Goal Activation and Behavior   54
Perceptual Tendencies   54
Competence   55
*A Person's State of Well-Being and the Connection
between the Self and Others*   57
Justification Processes   58
Supporting Research   58
Classes of Influences on Prosocial Behavior   69

chapter 3

Determinants of People Helping Other People in Physical Distress

73

The Early Research of Latané and Darley   74
The Influence of Others   77
*Defining the Situation, Defining the Appropriate Response,
and Communicating Expectations about Appropriate Behavior*   77
*Diffusion of Responsibility and Normative Explanations
of Helping Behavior*   88
Stimulus Characteristics That Affect Helping   105
Variation in Ambiguity   105
*The Degree of Need, the Cost of Helping,
and the Opportunity to Escape*   106
Spontaneous (or Impulsive) Helping   114
Temporary States of the Actor, Stimulus Overload,
Urban–Rural Helping, and Personality   116
Summary of Situational Influences   121
Personality and Helping Others in Physical Need   122
Moral Reasoning and Helping Behavior   125
The Influence of Combinations of Personal Characteristics
and of Situations   127
Personality and the Influence of the Number of Bystanders on Helping   131
The Personalities of Helpful Individuals   132

chapter 4

Observing and Causing Harm to Others: Affective, Cognitive, and Behavioral Consequences

135

Empathy and Prosocial Behavior   135
Physiological Arousal in Response to Another's Suffering   136

The Reinforcing Effect of Reducing Another's Pain or Distress   138
Perceptual–Cognitive Set, Empathy, and Helping   140
Individual Differences That Affect Empathic Reactions   144
Demonstrating the Influence of Empathy on Prosocial Behavior   146
Empathy-Related Issues   148

Just World, Devaluation, and Aggression   150
Research on the Just-World Hypothesis   156
Conditions Affecting Devaluation   159
Devaluation and Helping Others   168

Harmdoing Trangression, and Their Consequences   170
Questions and Problems; Research and Theoretical Issues   172
Proposed Explanations of the Effects of Harmdoing   176
Comparing the Effects of Observing and of Causing Harm   184
Alternative Explanations   189

Conclusions, Issues, and Limitations of Research   192
Can Violence Be Constructive?   195

chapter 5

Prosocial Behavior in Response to Varied Needs   *197*

Social Influence   198
The Effects of Exposure to Others' Deeds and Words   198
Research on Modeling and Verbal Communications by Models   201
Attributions about Models' Motives as a Determinant of Imitation   205
Verbal Communications That Specify Behavioral Rules   208
The Effects of Vicarious Reinforcement   211
Summary of Modeling and Verbalization Influences   213
Reactance and Prosocial Behavior   214
Verbal Requests, Reactions to Helping, Self-Attribution,
and Later Positive Behavior   217
Changes in Self-Perception and Positive Behavior   219
Additional Studies of Reactions to Help Giving and Positive Behavior   223

Stimulus Influence   225
Degree of Dependence and Need   225
Sex Differences in Reactions to Dependence   230
Internal versus External Sources of Dependence   233
Additional Studies on How the Degree of Need
and the Degree of Cost Influence Helping   236
The Meaning and Validity of Research   241

Decision Making, Personal Norms, and Helping Behavior   242
Schwartz's Decisional Model   242
Specific Norms versus General Orientations   247
An Additional Decision-Making Model   250

Individual Characteristics and Helping Behavior   253
Sex Differences and Helping Behavior   253

Morally Relevant Characteristics and Positive Behavior   258
The Capacity for Control, Competence, Social Desirability,
and Other Nonmoral Characteristics   270
Issues for Future Research   275

chapter 6

Orientation to the Self and Others: The Effects of Positive and Negative Experiences, Thoughts, and Feelings

277

The Effects of Success and Failure, Moods, and Self-Concern
on Positive Behavior   278
Competence   278
Success and Failure   282
The Effects of Positive Experiences   290
The Psychological Consequences That Mediate the Effects
of Positive and Negative Experiences and States   295
Preoccupation with the Self and Self-Concern   297
Sense of Potency   299
Benevolence to the Self and to Others: Strengthened or Weakened Bonds   300
Sense of Well-Being and Hedonic Balancing   302
Individual Differences in Sense of Well-Being, Characteristic Moods,
and Levels of Self-Esteem   308
Self-Esteem and Prosocial Action in Everyday Interactions   311

chapter 7

The Connection between Self and Others: Similarity, Attraction, and Common Group Membership

313

Conditions That Affect the Bond between the Self and Others   315
Similarity in Attitudes, Opinions, and Personalities   315
Prior Experience with Another Person   318
Common Group Membership: Race, Sex, Nationality, and Other Criteria   320
Shared Humanity and Orientation toward Other Human Beings   328
Personality and the Bond between Self and Others   330
Variations in the Bond between the Self and Others   332

chapter 8

Exchange and Reciprocity in Positive and Negative Behavior

335

The Nature of Social Exchange   336
Reciprocity and Equity in Social Exchange   340

Beliefs about and Preferences for Reciprocity 343
Indebtedness, Help Seeking, and Reactions to Receiving Help 344
Reciprocity in Behavior 350
Generalized Reciprocity 355
Perceived Intent of a Benefactor (or Harmdoer)
and Its Effect on Reciprocity 357
Conditions That Affect the Attribution of Prosocial Intention 361
Personality Differences in Making Attributions and in Reciprocity 367
Reciprocity between Friends and Transactions in Prosocial Behavior 369
Reciprocity in Everyday Life 371
Trust in Other People 374

chapter 9

Cooperation and Intimate Relationships: Further Explorations in Human Transactions 381

Determinants of Cooperation 385
Inducing Cooperation and Its Consequences 389
The Development and Maintenance of Intimate Relationships 394
Relationships: Their Formation and Nature 395
Self-Disclosure 399
Principles of Interaction in Extended Relationships 409
A Model of Interpersonal Relationships 412

chapter 10

Summary and Conclusions: The Determinants of Positive Behavior 417

Limitations of Our Knowledge: Future Goals 417
How Does Positive Behavior (Or Its Absence) Come About? 422
Moving from Perception to Action 424
The Influence of Cultures 429

References 433

Subject Index 465

Preface

This is the first of two related volumes on positive social behavior and morality. This volume is concerned with the wide range of influences that lead people to behave in a positive fashion toward other people or inhibit them from behaving positively; that is, with how varied forms of positive behavior are determined. The second volume is concerned with how the tendency to behave positively, the personal characteristics that make positive behavior more (or less) likely, develop through socialization, through the influence of peers, and through the child's varied experiences (Staub, 1978b, which will be referred to herein as Volume 2). Although the two volumes are related and enlarge upon each other, the material in them is organized in such a way that each can be meaningfully read independently and that each represents an independent whole.

I feel as if I had started writing this book in the ancient past. I first began thinking about it and doing some preliminary writing in 1969. The field was young at that time, and I was younger and more energetic; perhaps this explains why I planned to review all the existing research and theories about positive social behavior and positive aspects of morality. I did not foresee the immediate future. The explosion of research and writing in the 1970s about the various topics related or relevant to the theme of this book—the word explosion is not, I believe, an exaggeration—made comprehensiveness a nearly monumental task. Once I started writing the book in earnest (after several intervening projects), I stayed with this ideal of comprehensiveness in dealing with most (although not all) of the topics in the book. I resorted to increasing selectivity near the completion of the book, primarily as I was revising already written chapters and was considering for inclusion material that had been published after the original draft was completed. This selectivity is evident in the presentation of literature published in 1977 and is even more so with material published in the early months of 1978.

I had also planned to derive from the existing research literature principles about influences that affect the occurence or nonoccurence of positive behavior and about how the tendency to behave positively toward others develops. To some extent it was possible to do this. My original desire for this inductive approach led me frequently to review research projects in some detail, since I wanted to provide the reader with enough information to be able to join with me in evaluating the findings, in integrating them, and in deriving principles from them inductively.

As I reviewed and tried to integrate existing literature, I became aware of both unanswered and unasked questions. It seemed both necessary and inevitable to raise questions and issues, to propose theoretical assumptions, and to state goals for future research. The necessity to theorize, speculate, and develop conceptions also arose due to the limitations of existing research. Most of us would agree that our knowledge is limited in most areas of psychology. It is inevitable that this would be so in an area that has received attention primarily in the last 10–15 years. Nevertheless, a surprising amount of knowledge has, I believe, accumulated in the domains that this book explores. I hope this book contributes to advancing this knowledge.

He and She. A brief note about the use of "he" and "she" in this book. I laboriously included in my manuscript "he" and "she" in most sentences in which I used a third-person pronoun, as well as "him" and "her" and "herself" and "himself," whichever was appropriate. My copy editor—about whom I know only that she is a woman and that she lives in California—conscientiously erased all the feminine pronouns, leaving the masculine ones. At about this time I read a column by Tom Wicker, the New York Times columnist. He described various proposals to deal with the issue, providing examples of some of the most exquisitely convoluted language I have seen anywhere, examples that I certainly did not want to follow. Wicker suggested that when we first make a general reference to the race (of humanity) we use "whatever awkward formulation may be necessary to include both camps." Then writers can proceed to use pronouns referring to their own sex. I shall follow this suggestion.

I hope this book at least implicitly communicates my belief in his and her common humanity and equal rights, including the right to kindness and consideration and to equal well-being. Unfortunately, having stated this, I am still left with following tradition by using the masculine pronoun in the book. Here is *my* suggestion for the future: that we all write in Hungarian, which has a single third-person pronoun (ö) for he, she, and it.

Acknowledgments

I would like to thank various people whose positive influence on me gains expression, I hope, in this book. Several people influenced me while I was a graduate student at Stanford, and they continued to do so later as colleagues and friends. Walter Mischel had an important influence on my thinking about psychology, and my association with him led me to want to do research and writing in psychology. Eleanor Maccoby also has strongly affected my way of thinking about psychology. Al Hastorf and Al Bandura were important sources of knowledge and inspiration. During his term as Visiting Professor at Stanford, Arnold Lazarus taught me, in clinical work, a greater appreciation of human complexity. Perhaps it is not surprising, given these varied intellectual influences, that I came to regard social, personality, and developmental psychology as strongly interrelated, at least as an ideal, if not as a reality. Furthermore, during my graduate school years, conversations with Perry London about his attempts to study characteristics of "rescuers," people who, during World War II, saved Jews and other minorities persecuted in Nazi Germany, made me wonder about the willingness of human beings to sacrifice themselves for others, as well as about their willingness to close their eyes to the suffering of others.

In beginning my independent research in my first job at Harvard and later, in beginning to write this book, my colleague and friend, Robert Rosenthal, was always a willing listener, a source of ideas, and a generous source of encouragement. Lane K. Conn, also a colleague and friend at

Harvard, was an important source of both ideas and support. He contributed to my personal growth in ways that, I hope, have found some expression in this book. Many students collaborated with me in research that I discuss or refer to in this book. I am grateful to all of them. Dan Jaquette and Sumru Erkut at Harvard and Helene Feinberg at the University of Massachusetts made particularly important contributions. Lynne Feagans was a highly competent, reliable, and hard-working research assistant while we conducted at Harvard some of my early research on helping and sharing behavior.

I am grateful to the many people, both children and adults, who participated in my research. My early research with children was conducted primarily in Watertown, Massachusetts. After 1971, much of my research with children was conducted in Amherst, Massachusetts. I am grateful for the extensive cooperation given me by teachers, by principals (particularly Mr. John Dalton, Mr. Michael Greenebaum, and Ms. Nancy Morrison), and by the superintendent of the Amherst schools, Mr. Donald Frizzle.

Finally, I am grateful to the National Institutes of Mental Health. Grant No. MH23886 supported the research that my students and I have been conducting since 1973 and enabled me to spend time and energy on research and writing.

Positive Social Behavior and Morality

SOCIAL AND
PERSONAL INFLUENCES

Positive Behavior, Morality, and Human Nature

chapter 1

Human beings can be extremely cruel, selfish, and inhuman in their treatment of other human beings. The myriad manifestations of human aggression and selfishness in everyday life, together with the mass destruction brought about by war, led Sigmund Freud to believe that human beings are aggressive by nature. The same phenomena led Konrad Lorenz to apply hypotheses drawn from studies of instinctual aggressive behavior in animals to man; he concluded that man also is aggressive by nature. But manifestations of human kindness, goodness, love, and willingness to sacrifice for others are everywhere. Different observers have been inspired, in their thinking about man, by different parts of this total vista. Are people cruel or kind? Obviously, they can be either, or both. What makes them behave kindly rather than cruelly toward others? What leads them to behave in a manner that benefits other people? How is the tendency to behave either way acquired? Although in their research psychologists have emphasized forms of prosocial acts that are either dramatic or simple or both, such as helping others in physical distress, donating possessions to others, and sharing with others, this book is concerned with the whole range of positive social behaviors. Positive acts within intimate relationships—behavior that leads to or maintains friendship, love, and marriage—are part of what will be examined.

Prosocial Behavior: Definition, Significance, and Relationship to Morality

Positive social (or prosocial) behavior is simply defined as behavior that benefits other people. To behave in such a way a person has to understand another's needs, desires, or goals and act to fulfill them. However, even this seemingly simple definition can be problematic. How does one determine whether an act results in benefit? If someone who has long been depressed works up the courage to commit suicide and then is saved by another—does he benefit? By what standards of judgment? Did missionaries who bore great material and physical deprivation to save souls necessarily produce any benefits? The complexity of the judgment is demonstrated by the controversy about giving food to deprived nations: Some argue that, although this may alleviate short-term suffering, it allows further population growth without creating self-sufficiency and thus leads to even greater human suffering in the long run (Greene, 1975).

Although the beneficial consequences of an apparently prosocial act, or of an act that was intended to be prosocial, are often clear, they are sometimes questionable. Unneeded help can upset rather than benefit the recipient. In studies of prosocial behavior, psychologists have tried to circumvent these issues by setting up situations in which a certain action is defined as prosocial. They then study the conditions that determine whether this action will be forthcoming. Usually, the need and the required beneficial act are intended to be unambiguous and are probably (although not certainly) perceived by subjects as acts that would produce benefits. The less clear the benefits, the more judgmental processes enter; such processes are also involved in the assessment of the intention underlying prosocial acts.

Behavior that has consequences for the welfare of other human beings or for the social group is guided by proscriptive and prescriptive moral values and principles. Proscriptive values and standards prohibit action that would harm others ("Thou shalt not"). Usually people perform prohibited acts to satisfy a need or impulse, or to bring about material or social advantage. Prescriptive values and principles tell people what they ought to do ("Thou shalt"). Much of prescriptive morality is prosocial in nature; it prescribes behavior that will benefit other people. Such behavior usually involves self-sacrifice on the part of the actor; the sacrifice may be of time, effort, material possessions, physical welfare, and sometimes life itself.

The importance of prohibitive morality is obviously great. The consequences of people freely acting according to their immediate self-interests without regard for others would make the functioning of a social group impossible. This applies not only to behavior that physically harms others, but also to theft and dishonesty of various forms—in general, the violation of others' rights. The laws that protect us express this; they incorporate prohibitions necessary for the protection of the welfare of individuals and the group.

Prosocial behavior is also crucial for the functioning of the social group and for the welfare of its individual members. Although prescriptive morality is not usually expressed in laws, in a number of European countries and now also in some states (e.g., Vermont), helping others in certain kinds of extreme need is required by the law; refraining from giving help is a criminal offense.

At the most basic level, social groups are based on cooperation, on the willingness of members to work with one another and share the benefits of mutual labor. In some hunting and gathering societies (Cohen, 1972), cooperation was necessary for survival and probably advanced the development of the social organization. On another level, cooperation is involved in the mutual satisfaction of needs in intimate relationships in our everyday lives. By cooperating with others each person benefits, and thus the behavior of each person can be considered prosocial.

Prosocial behavior may be classified according to the degree of self-sacrifice involved (cost to the actor) and according to the degree of benefit an act produces (utility for the recipient). When people cooperate, the cost to the actor may be low relative to his gain, since there is benefit or utility for the actor as well as for others. However, the amount of gain for the participants may be different. Although a larger ratio of effort to gain for one person than for another may be considered a condition of inequity and may result from differential power and exploitation, such inequity may also be due to unselfishness and self-sacrifice; a person may willingly agree that another's gain relative to the other's efforts is to be greater than his own.

There are individuals in every society who cannot contribute sufficient work and services to be compensated according to their needs. Old people, young people, the ill, and the infirm have to be taken care of by society or they will suffer and die. In some societies individual members of the society—families, rich people, or others specifically designated by the community—care for those who need help. In the United States it is primarily the government and social agencies that do so, but they rely on the contributions of members of society (taxes and donations to charity). Societies vary in the extent to which they help members who cannot help themselves. For example, in the United States old people do *not* seem to be well cared for, but a tremendous amount is actually done, nevertheless, to provide needed help, as evidenced by old-age homes, welfare, and medicare.

Prosocial behavior is also extremely important at the individual level, when one person acts to benefit another who needs help. This kind of prosocial behavior has been the major focus of research, and examples abound. The need may be small—a person may need help carrying a package or changing a flat tire. If asked for a dime, many people freely give it, particularly when the reason for the request seems to be a good one (Latané & Darley, 1970). Most hitchhikers seem to get a ride. The need may also be extreme, such as when someone's life is in danger. Although it often happens that people do not help someone who desperately needs help—Latané and Darley (1970) have described some shocking examples—at other times they risk their lives to save others. And among friends, lovers, and members of close-knit groups, there are usually long-standing and persistent commitments to one another's welfare and to the mutual satisfaction of needs and the fulfillment of goals.

The Carnegie Hero Commission awards dozens of medals for heroism each year to people who attempted to and usually did save the life of another. Some of these awards are posthumous, the hero having died in the attempt. A 42-year-old Carnegie hero with whom I talked saved a woman from drowning in the ocean 10 days after he had had both a gallbladder operation and an appendectomy. Hundreds of people were on the beach; why was it he, a person who was still weak from an operation, who dived into the water to save this woman? Other examples of heroism can be found in the study by London (1970) of those Christians in Nazi-occupied Europe who rescued Jews and others who were persecuted and thereby saved their lives.

Another form of behavior that some consider prosocial is a willingness to die for one's group (tribe, nation). This willingness can arise from a desire to protect the group from attack or danger (Campbell, 1965), or, unfortunately, from a desire to promote the less-justified interests of the group, as in wars of conquest, which seem to have aroused voluntary, enthusiastic participation by members of societies throughout human history. This willingness can be an important source of security for the group. The willingness, in the face of opposition and at great personal cost, to promote causes that benefit some members of the social group is also important, both for those whose interests are promoted and for the evolution of society. The actions of those who fought for the abolition of slavery in the early 1800s, as well as of some civil rights workers in our time, serve as examples (Tompkins, 1965; Rosenhan, 1970).

Psychologists have just begun to explore domains of behaviors that may be considered prosocial. What determines whether people help others in *physical* distress has been extensively explored. My associates and I have been studying how people respond to someone who is upset or unhappy, to a person's *psychological* distress (see Chapter 2). Rheingold, Hay, and West (1976) reported that very young children point to, show, and give objects to other people, a behavior Rheingold *et al.* called sharing. Such behavior may really be an expression by the children of their desire to have someone share their perspective. Certain reactions to these behaviors can be regarded as prosocial. An important human need—and an important opportunity for prosocial behavior—may be the desire to be understood by others, to have other people share one's perspective.

This book focuses on prosocial behavior, but it is also concerned with intentions, values, empathy, and other internal processes and characteristics of individuals that might mediate action. The primary focus is on action, because of its significance for individuals and for the social group; a person is helped by action, not by a belief that one ought to act. Values, empathy, and other internal processes are important, however, as motivators of prosocial action. They are also important because consistency or inconsistency between values, beliefs, and personal goals on the one hand, and behavior on the other, is likely to have a strong effect on a person's emotional experience and self-concept. Preliminary findings of studies based on extensive self-observation by many subjects suggest that an important dimension that people use to evaluate themselves is how moral they are (Epstein, 1973). Research using the semantic differential technique also suggests that people use the concepts of goodness and badness to evaluate events and objects. Self-evaluation and feelings of satisfaction and happiness might be importantly affected by a person's adherence to internalized moral values, by the degree to which they are translated into action. Self-evaluation appears to affect, in turn, future behavior toward others. People are also likely to be evaluated along these dimensions by other people, the nature of the evaluation affecting behavior toward them.

The examples of prosocial behavior considered clearly show that a person's willingness to assume responsibility for the welfare of others and to behave prosocially toward them is important both for the individuals who are directly affected and for the social group as a whole. It is questionable whether societies could function at all, whether people could live together in groups, without a minimum of such helpfulness. But even if they did (see Benedict, 1934; Turnbull, 1972), the climate of interaction among members, the mistrust of those whose help could not be counted on, and the resulting hostility among the members would make life barely tolerable.

In addition to prosocial behavior's significance for society, the study of prosocial behavior is having significant effects on psychology. Advances in knowledge and theory about prosocial behavior are beginning to balance the historically one-sided focus of psychological theorizing and research. The two major theoretical influences on psychologists have been Freudian theory and homeostatic-drive theory. Both assume that man's behavior aims at satisfying his needs and gratifying his impulses. Neither theory provides for the existence of behavior aimed at benefiting others; such behavior would have to be conceived of as indirectly aimed at the satisfaction of the actor's needs.

The study of prosocial behavior and morality has begun to demonstrate that there is a positive side to man, and it has begun to provide theories, or at least to modify existing ones, to explain it. It may have been partly because of the direction provided by previously dominant theories, partly because of the questions raised by clinical psychologists who were dealing with human suffering, and partly because of theoretical difficulties in accounting for positive social behavior using dominant theories that psychologists focused their attention on behavior leading to the satisfaction of the actor and on man's attempts to cope with his environment and the associated stresses, anxieties, and defenses. In this realm also the study of positive social behavior provides an extension and balancing within the domain of psychological knowledge.

Prosocial Acts and Altruistic Motives

Probably the first psychologists to study "moral" behavior extensively were Hartshorne, May, and Maller (1929), who wrote:

> Without knowledge of actual tendencies and habits, knowledge of motives would be of small use. Furthermore, it is easier to pass from deeds to their causes, than from motives to their possible results. A man may be of great service to his society while solely working for himself. It is equally true that he may be a great nuisance while devoting himself heart and soul to the good of his neighbor. The neighbor may prefer to be let alone. Our sole standard by which we rate any behavior is for the moment its utility in the given situation. We assume that the man of socialized motive is the one who seeks to discover what the utility is and then produce it [p. 8].

As already suggested, the tendency to behave positively toward others is of great importance, regardless of motive. For example, the social value of a person behaving positively toward others in order to enhance his own welfare is great in comparison to a person attempting to gain similar benefits by aggressive means (Staub, 1974a). However, the values, intentions, or motives of the actor are also of great importance. To predict later behavior it is often necessary to understand what motivated a prosocial act; if the act was motivated by selfish intent it is less likely that the person would act prosocially under different circumstances. To increase a tendency to act prosocially, one must increase prosocial motivation. We cannot assume, however, a straightforward connection between motives and actions. An important task is to explore this connection (see Chapter 2). Finally, understanding the development of moral values, prosocial intentions, positive affective orientations toward others, and the interrelationship of these factors is also important in its own right.

Although definitions vary, the term *altruism* is usually used to refer to behavior resulting in substantial benefit to the recipient, behavior that demands great self-sacrifice from the actor and is intended to benefit only the recipient, not the actor. Leeds (1963) stated three criteria that determine whether an act ought to be called altruistic:

1. The act is an end in itself and is not directed at self-gain.
2. The act is performed voluntarily.
3. The act results in good.

In contrast to such definitions of positive behavior as either altruistic or not, I regard it most meaningful to recognize that there can be varied motives for positive acts, and specific acts may vary in the *degree* to which they are altruistically motivated.

It is usually assumed that a conflict exists between self-interest and the interest of others, between egoism and altruism; in order to act altruistically, one has to act contrary to one's self-interest. Comte (1875), in introducing the term *altruism*, suggested that in order to act in others' behalf individuals need to overcome self-interest and develop a concern for others' welfare. Partly in this spirit, it was for a time directly stated or implied that for an act to be altruistic no reinforcement of any kind should result for the actor. However, for most psychologists, this is an unreasonable motivational assumption: Psychological theories assume that behavior is influenced by its consequences, both real and anticipated. If behavior that demands various sacrifices is not reinforced in any way, it would extinguish over time. As people develop concern for others' welfare, they are likely to learn to gain satisfaction from promoting others' goals and reducing others' needs. Consequently, rather than experiencing conflict between the interests of the self and others, people may often identify one with the other.

An actor may behave prosocially to gain material rewards for his act or to gain social approval and praise (or avoid social disapproval and even ostracism). Acts motivated by such intentions might be considered only minimally altruistic. An actor's motive may be considered altruistic when he expects that as a result of his prosocial act he will feel good (gain self-reward) because he acted according to his values and principles (thus he maintains a positive self-concept) or when he expects empathic reinforcement (a reduction of the distress he felt as a result of vicariously experiencing another person's distress or an increase in his own positive feeling by vicariously experiencing the positive feelings of another that would result from his prosocial act). When a person behaves prosocially out of altruistic intentions, purely to benefit another, he is still likely to have some anticipation of, and certainly the experience of, such reinforcement.

Some of these considerations are implied, although not specified, in a definition of altruism by Bryan and London (1970). According to them, altruism refers to "those behaviors intended to benefit another but which appear to have a high cost to the actor with little possibility of material or social reward [p. 200]." According to this definition, internal reinforcement is possible when someone performs an altruistic act.

Issues of definition can be argued extensively. Severy (1974) suggests, for example, that an act ought to be called altruistic if a person immediately responds to the recognition of another's need with behavior that is designed to be helpful. Any prior consideration of reinforcement makes the act nonaltruistic, although subsequent reinforcement does not alter the definition. As Krebs and Wispé (1974) note, however, we do not really know whether human beings are able to do anything without expectations of gain. Most acts are preceded by a history of experiences, in the course of which people learn to evaluate the consequences for themselves of various forms of conduct, including prosocial acts. A person may not consciously deliberate about the various rewards and costs inherent in a prosocial behavior that is required to alleviate another's need, partly because of intuitive understanding or expectations formed through previous experiences.[1]

Even personal motives for helping can vary. I shall repeatedly consider differences in motivation arising out of different value orientations. A person may want to benefit another because of concern about others' welfare and the desire to enhance others' welfare. A person may also act prosocially out of a sense of obligation to help other human beings, even if the helper has no wish to benefit the person in need. A desire for justice can sometimes lead to help (e.g., for someone who had been unjustly treated) but not at other times. Many variations in motives that may enhance or decrease positive behavior are possible.

Additional distinctions may be drawn with regard to the kind of external benefits or rewards that may motivate prosocial acts. A person may expect strong social disapproval for not helping someone in need, and praise and acknowledgment for doing so. Alternatively, a positive act may be motivated by the hope of establishing or maintaining friendship, intimacy, or mutual trust and benevolence. Certainly, such varied social reasons for behaving positively have different meaning and will have different personal and social consequences.

Many prosocial acts are probably the result of mixed motives, including selfish ones. Furthermore, two levels of intentions may be distinguished. As long as a person voluntarily engages in prosocial behavior (his help is not coerced, and it is not accidental), one might argue that this person intends to benefit another. However, if we ask why he intends to do so, at this second level of intention the answer may vary. The reasons for wanting

---

[1] Sometimes people may motivate themselves to make sacrifices for others by thinking about the possible gain that their behavior will procure for them, even when the chances of such gain are very small. In our culture at least, most people learn that they ought to look out for their own welfare. Although they also learn contrary values, looking out for their own welfare may contrast with making important sacrifices to help others. At times, people may justify self-sacrificial acts by imagining that material gains will follow, that they will be rewarded by God, or that they will gain fame and honor. A cartoon that appeared in the *New Yorker* showed a man who was lying on the ground, being ignored by several pedestrians. Then a little boy walked up to him and asked, "Can I do something for you?" The man raised his head, smiled at the boy, and said, "I am a millionaire, and you are the first person who asked me whether I needed help. I will give you a $5000 reward!" Such fantasies might not be uncommon and might motivate helping.

to help may range from the expectation of external reward to adherence to a principle and/or the desire to gain various internal (self) reinforcements.[2]

The emphasis on altruistic motives for prosocial behavior may be peculiar to Western civilization or to "advanced" civilizations. Cohen (1972) writes that the idea of unselfish helpfulness is an alien one to most social groups; it is assumed that when you do things for other people you do it for self-gain, and denying this would make others regard you as an untrustworthy person. According to Cohen, hunting and gathering societies are characterized by mutual cooperation and the obligatory sharing of food. However, balance is achieved in production and distribution by the esteem and power accorded to the person who contributes the most. Thus, giving to others becomes a form of prestige seeking. Obviously, this is also true to some degree of our own contemporary society.

Giving can even be a form of revenge:

> I have witnessed a Hare Indian near the Arctic Circle of Canada in a near frenzy of decision making because he had killed a moose and was plotting how to give it away for both prestige purposes and revenge against those who had up to now slighted him. This latter quality is well documented by Redington (1968) in his description of a Beaver Indian who after making a splendid kill of three moose "could not resist capitalizing" on it and therefore gave some very good meat to the leader of a competing faction in the band with whom there was an agreement *not to share* food [Cohen, 1972, p. 44].

The degree to which people intend to benefit themselves by benefiting others certainly varies in instances of prosocial behavior. Unfortunately, determining a person's reasons for his actions is very difficult, if not impossible. Intention cannot be judged on the basis of the act itself, since there seldom are characteristics of the act that unequivocally indicate whether the beneficial consequences were a by-product of behavior performed to accomplish other goals, and what the other goals might have been. The attribution of intent by other people is the result of an inferential process; on the basis of characteristics of the act (possibly including what the actor says), surrounding conditions, and knowledge of the actor's personality, assumptions are made about the actor's intention. Usually it is impossible to ascertain the accuracy of these assumptions. Since altruistic intentions are socially valued, actors are motivated to present their intentions as altruistic, and thus their reports might not be reliable. The characteristics of this inferential process are discussed at a later point (Chapter

---

[2] Independent evaluation of a person's values, beliefs, or motives might suggest whether in general his intentions in helping another are more or less altruistic, but this still would not provide reliable evidence of his intentions in any specific instance.

8). Whatever their accuracy, inferences about other people's intentions are extremely important, because they strongly affect behavior toward those people. For example, the attribution of altruistic motives by a recipient is itself an important determinant of reciprocal prosocial acts.

In this book *prosocial behavior* refers to behavior benefiting others; both the benefits produced and the sacrifice demanded of the actor may greatly vary in degree and kind. A prosocial act may be judged altruistic if it appears to have been intended to benefit others rather than to gain either material or social rewards. Altruistic prosocial acts are likely to be associated, however, with internal rewards (and the expectation of such rewards) and with empathic reinforcing experiences.

Morality and Human Nature

Morality and human nature have long been of concern to philosophers. A number of psychological conceptions of human nature seem to be related to earlier, philosophical views. The examination of these conceptions highlights both the assumptions of psychologists who do empirical research on the development of moral values and the determinants of moral behavior and their neglect of certain important issues—for example, the manner in which moral values of a social group develop and change.

Morality is a set of rules, customs, or principles that regulate people's conduct in relation to other people, conduct that affects human welfare. Several stages of morality have been distinguished by philosophers; these stages may characterize both individuals and cultures. The most primitive level of morality is *prerational* or *group-enforced morality*, in which moral rules are adhered to because of the fear of negative consequences for deviation and because of the expectation of positive consequences for adherence. The highest level of morality has been conceived of as *personal, rational, reflective,* or *autonomous morality*. The adjectives indicate that the moral standards or values belong to the individual—they are not simply taken over from others—and are the result of rational examination and reflection. The autonomously moral individual may hold beliefs about right and wrong conduct that are different from those of his society. An important intermediate stage is proposed to be *internalized morality*. It is characterized by individuals who learn the moral values and standards of their culture and accept them as their own; they internalize them. This acceptance may be irrational rather than the result of rational examination. Tradition-oriented societies may be characterized by either group-enforced or internalized morality, or both. Riesman (1950) suggested the existence of *other-directed morality,* when other people's conduct rather than traditional values serve to determine what is right and wrong. Such morality may arise in cultures that Mead (1970) described as *configurative*. In configurative cultures individuals are guided by tradition and by parents, who usually transmit tradition, but they also model themselves on their peers and learn their standards from them. Individuals who act according to demands of the group may move to a possibly irrational kind of inner direction (unconditional acceptance of group values) and then to a more rational determination of action as they become autonomous moral agents. The notion of other direction may usefully and accurately point to the influence of peers and the environment on a person's values, and to one of the ways that morality may change. The variations in levels or types of morality may characterize either societies or individuals in their orientation to moral values and standards. Although it is often implied that these different orientations result in different action, the relationship between moral cognition and action should be regarded as complex. The existing evidence will be presented later (Chapters 2, 3, 5; Volume 2).

It is at the level of autonomous morality that moral philosophy appears to play a role. According to moral philosophy, the standards of society are not necessarily *the* moral standards. There are several reasons for this. First, moral rules seem to vary across cultures.[3] For the Siriano Indians of eastern Bolivia, food is extremely scarce. They tend to hide their food from others, and they would rather eat all their food at once than share it. Since not sharing is generally practiced, it must be considered an acceptable form of conduct. In contrast, other social groups living under similar conditions of food scarcity, such as certain tribes of Bushmen in Australia, have developed highly cooperative ways of dealing with scarcity; they share the available food. The acceptance of slavery in some societies but not in others is another example of varying moral rules. Second, some of a society's rules may be unjust, immoral, or unnecessarily incapacitating of human life (for example, rules permitting slavery). Third, standards of society often admit to exceptions and may be in contradiction with each other: for example, a society may hold that killing is wrong but that killing an enemy in war is right.

In philosophy, morality is often regarded as equivalent to values that carry a sense of obligation (in contrast to nonmoral values, which do not imply obligation). These values usually refer to the effect or consequence of conduct on individuals or the group. Philosophers have put forth two different approaches to morality. One approach is that the consequences of an act are the basic criteria of morality; one should act to maximize

---

[3] Certainly, practices vary. However, there may be some uniformity in the realm of certain very basic values and rules. The value placed on human life and prohibition of murder of a member of one's own social group may be such a basic rule. It is true, of course, that different societies allow different exceptions, but that does not change the fact that the rule exists. (For example, committing murder to avenge dishonor is typical in some societies but not in others.)

beneficial consequences, to bring about the greatest possible ratio of positive to negative consequences. The second approach suggests that moral conduct has to be based on certain basic rules or principles. Advocates of this approach propose a variety of principles and different virtues, that is, human characteristics or dispositions that would embody morality.

Justice was regarded as a basic virtue by Plato and has been so regarded by many others. Kant proposed the *categorical imperative* as the basic rule of morality: You should "act only on that maxim which you can at the same time will to be the universal law." Or, one ought to act in a certain way only if one is willing to have everyone else act that way in a similar situation. Other, more specific rules applicable to various situations can presumably be derived from this basic one. A traditional (both classical and religious) set of virtues is made up of prudence, justice, fortitude, and temperance (Dieper, 1966). Some of these characteristics do not themselves appear to be "moral." Their significance seems to lie in that they are necessary for moral action. Prudence, for example, involves the capacity to judge or evaluate the consequences of action. Only when these consequences are correctly evaluated can a moral value or principle be appropriately applied to action. Fortitude and temperance may also enhance the likelihood that a person will act morally. Some philosophers have suggested that the basis of morality lies in benevolence—the desire to do good rather than evil—and justice—the distribution of good to affect the greatest number of persons (Frankena, 1963).

The classical Greek conception of morality emphasized moral judgment, the ability to decide what is right and what is wrong. Moral judgment was regarded as an essentially rational phenomenon. Moral philosophy in general seeks to determine what the basic moral values are and relies primarily on the use of reason. However, it has long been recognized that the will, regarded as a motive force that impels man to action, also has to be considered as part of morality. More generally, the idea that feelings are importantly related to morality because they connect thought and action has become widespread; feelings were considered in the writings of Augustine. Most psychologists believe that the affective elements, such as feelings of guilt for not doing the right thing or anticipation of satisfaction for doing the right thing, motivate moral action. Action itself, adherence to moral values and principles or norms of conduct, is another element of morality. Deciding what is the right thing to do and doing it are far from being the same thing. From a scientific point of view, it is important to understand both processes; from the point of view of societies and their members, action is crucial.

Complications arise when one attempts to make judgments about the morality of specific acts or persons. According to some psychologists (Kohlberg, 1969), the morality of an act is determined by a person's perceptions of and beliefs about the right conduct and by that person's reasons for acting or not acting in a particular way. However, even if we could know what a person really thought, human thought, reasoning, or judgment can be strongly affected by self-serving motives, both conscious and unconscious. Consequently, a person may apply moral standards to a situation in a manner that eliminates the necessity for taking action on behalf of another person. Moral standards and reasoning can also be used to justify action that promotes self-interest but harms others. One guide to the complexities of the issue is legal custom: Circumstances surrounding an act, the character of the actor, potential gain for the actor, and other aspects of the situation are all considered in attempting to make a reasonable judgment about the intent underlying a harmful or illegal act. Certainly a person who always says but never does the right thing will soon be suspect.

A number of questions and issues emerge from this brief discussion. Where do the moral values or standards held by a social group come from? How are societal standards acquired by specific individuals? Is man capable of going beyond the standards of society and developing autonomous standards that are different from societal standards, and how does this development take place? What is the relationship between moral cognition, affect, and conduct? What determines each, and how do they in turn affect one another? What is the interrelationship among different aspects of an individual's morality? These and other questions are considered in different parts of this book (and in Volume 2).

Sources of Morality

Human Beings Inherently Capable of Goodness.   What is the source of morality? Human nature, God, and society were most often regarded as the source.

Varied conceptions of morality originated with Plato.[4] He described the Socratic method of developing virtue, which consisted of two parts. The negative part aimed at the elimination of all preconceptions from the mind: conventions, values, concerns with career, and so on. The aim of the positive part was to find out about human nature through self-examination, if possible in the company of others in order to pool the reactions of several minds. This process was thought to lead to the knowledge of virtue. This conception implied the validity of self-consciousness and included belief in a monitor within the person that would prevent action that is contrary to the laws of human nature. Socrates' saying, "Knowledge is virtue," implies that knowing what is right leads to the right action.

---

[4] In contrast to the practice throughout the book to provide the exact source of ideas and research findings that are presented, in the historical overview of philosophical and psychological conceptions of human nature and morality that follows—frequently these are conceptions that certain authors expressed in varied works or that are commonly associated with their name—exact sources will not always be provided.

An important implication of this Platonian view is that human nature has within itself the elements of man's goodness. Another implication is that morality is rational, and that man can become moral through self-examination that leads to understanding. A third, less direct implication is that man can be corrupted by circumstances; this is suggested by the emphasis on man's divesting himself of societal convention if he is to reach self-knowledge. Finally, the conception of an internal monitor foreshadows the conception of conscience; both are internal guides to the right action.

The notion that human nature is good can be found repeatedly in the writings of later philosophers and also of psychologists. Most of these writings hold that man can be good if certain conditions are fulfilled. The use of reason in self-examination appeared to be such a condition for Plato. Thomas Aquinas, who relied heavily on the classical writers, particularly Aristotle, and considered the importance of will as a motive force in determining human action, also believed that the combined use of reason and will work toward the perfection of each person. He believed that it is natural to do good, so when man fails to follow his reason and does not do good, his action is unnatural (and sinful). Among later writers, the naturalists also believed that human nature is or could be good. According to "optimistic" naturalism, if man lives according to natural law, which is good, he will have no evil. The influence of the environment is important. If the environment allows it, then it is possible for men, "barely by the use of their natural faculties," to bring their ideas and their conduct, and hence the institutions by which they live, into harmony with the universal natural order (Locke, 1939). Evil in man was accounted for by certain human institutions and customs that were contrary to natural law; under such circumstances, undesirable human actions were inevitable. Clearly, in this view, man was potentially good. Rousseau's noble savage lived outside societal convention and was therefore good. (The notion of returning to nature and the simple life has been repeatedly romanticized in the course of human history.) Man's reason was regarded as a powerful and effective instrument for changing both the individual and the world.

The notion that human nature is good or that man will develop to be good under the right circumstances has also been implied by several contemporary psychologists. The notion of self-actualization propagated by Rogers and Maslow implies that under circumstances that allow and lead man to actualize his own nature he will be both psychologically healthy and good.

How a person becomes self-actualized is not a simple matter. The environment must not be too restrictive; the circumstances must be right. Self-examination, self-knowledge, and productivity all seem to be involved in self-actualization. According to Maslow (1965), in the course of self-actualization man reaches the point where he fulfills his deficiency needs (his biological needs and needs for security) and can devote himself to the fulfillment of higher needs such as love and creativity. Presumably a loving person will be "good." Maslow strongly condemns the view that man's nature is evil. Man does have an inner core, which, "as much as we know of it so far, is definitely not 'evil,' but is either what we adults in our culture call 'good' or else it is neutral [Maslow, 1965, p. 309]." He suggests, as proof, that "uncovering therapy lessens hostility, fear, greed, etc., and increases love, courage, creativeness, kindness, altruism, etc., leading us to the conclusion that the latter are 'deeper,' more natural, and more basic than the former [p. 309]." Clearly, in Maslow's view, man's inner core is good. Moreover, Maslow suggests that with greater firmness of personality identity and sense of selfhood, which are associated with self-actualization, there are more self-transcending and unselfish thoughts and as a by-product also greater positive unselfish love. In fact, Maslow (1965) believes that our knowledge about man implies a "naturalistic system of values, a by-product of the empirical description of the deepest tendencies of the human species and specific individuals [p. 312]."

Fromm (1941) also stresses self-actualization and man's potential for good.[5] Fromm rejects authoritarian ethics, which denies man's capacity to know what is good or bad and determines ethical values and conduct by reference to a higher authority, such as God, the church, or society. He suggests that in such a system obedience is the main virtue and disobedience is the main sin. Fromm refers to humanistic ethics, where only man can determine the criterion of virtue; the sole criterion is man's welfare. All organisms have an inherent tendency to actualize their potentialities. Man's virtue is the set of qualities that is characteristic of the human species, and man is virtuous if he unfolds his qualities. Virtue is identical with the actualization of man's nature. The science of man, psychology, is the theoretical science on which virtue is based, because it points to or identifies man's nature.

According to Fromm, man's virtue is potency, the productive use of his powers. A productive orientation in man (one of several character types described by Fromm) involves both reproductive functioning (learning, memory, and so on) and generative functioning, a creative type of approach in one's life. Love and work are components of this. Love, moreover, implies both self-love and love for others, as well as responsibility and care toward objects of love. Jonah is mentioned by Fromm as a man of justice, but not of charity—he did not love his fellowman.

Fromm assumes, then, that human nature includes all that is necessary for virtue, that no external imposition of morality (rules and regulations) is necessary, and that in fact obedience to imposed rules inhibits man's development of his virtue. Some of the roots of this view can be found in the

---

[5] The discussion that follows is based on Fromm's early views, some of which he has since modified (see, for example, Fromm, 1973).

philosophical views that have been mentioned. Other roots in philosophy are identified by Fromm. For example, an important characteristic of productive man is activity, the value of which was emphasized by Aristotle. Spinoza wrote that each thing endeavors to persevere its being, to become what it potentially is. Fromm also derives some of his thinking from Freud (with whom he disagrees in his conception of human nature), who suggested that love and work were characteristics of the mature, healthy individual.

Fromm suggested that the science of man, psychology, is an important guide to morality because it points to what is man's nature. Having suggested this, Fromm wrote as if psychology had already established what man's nature is. In a less confident fashion, the importance of psychology for contributing to the goodness of man has been implied by Maslow and Rogers. If self-actualization results in man's being good, psychologists have an important contribution to make by studying and specifying the conditions that allow or will lead to self-actualization. All three writers have adopted the view that man is basically good, and they have attempted to base it on psychology rather than on philosophy. Their writing represents a social philosophy, a psychological humanitarianism, that has little scientific support as yet.

Is it possible to specify testable hypotheses to evaluate their views? First, the processes that lead to self-actualization would have to be specified. However, it would probably be impossible to create for a whole group of individuals the life conditions that are necessary for these processes to operate. Moreover, it is questionable that such life conditions could be regarded as merely providing an opportunity for the unfolding of man's nature, rather than as representing a form of socialization that shapes personality. An alternative would be to specify the nonmoral characteristics of individuals who have achieved a measurable degree of self-actualization, find such persons, and then evaluate their moral characteristics. On the basis of the view of Rogers, Maslow, and Fromm, this may be possible, since the outstanding characteristic seems to be "activity," a productive and creative approach to life. Love toward other human beings could not be regarded as a defining characteristic of self-actualized individuals. This approach would not help determine whether these characteristics are part of the biological potential of man that needs to be actualized; it would only help determine the existence of a relationship between a productive approach to life and "goodness." If such a relationship is found the reason may be that a productive life leads to satisfaction, even happiness. Evidence exists that temporary feelings of satisfaction enhance, whereas dissatisfaction or failure decreases prosocial behavior (Chapter 6). Also, to draw conclusions about the meaning of a relationship between actualizing tendencies, satisfaction, and prosocial behavior, one would have to show that the relationship exists in a variety of cultures. Otherwise it may just mean that in our society self-actualizing tendencies are defined as desirable, enhancing the satisfaction of those who achieve them. Obviously, testing these views is no easy task.

Kohlberg's (1969, 1976) currently influential "cognitive-developmental" theory of moral development also assumes that being morally good rather than "bad" is the fundamental potential of human beings. The theory makes assumptions similar to those of Socrates, as presented earlier, and incorporates other conceptions that were developed by Plato. In Kohlberg's view, extensive opportunities for experience, for assuming varied roles in relationship to other people, result in the development of progressively more advanced moral reasoning. Experience results in reorganizations in people's thinking about right and wrong, each reorganization representing a new stage. Moral reasoning at each of these stages is advanced over the previous stage, *more* moral than before. That is, with experience people naturally move from a primitive form of morality—where right is what is defined as right by those in authority and is rewarded by them, whereas wrong is what is regarded as wrong by authorities and is punished—to the most advanced, autonomous stage of morality, in which people hold their own principles of what is right and wrong. The content or type of reasoning employed at each stage is specified by the theory. The last stage is characterized by beliefs in justice and in the sanctity of human life as the bases for judging right and wrong conduct.

Thus, the theory assumes that, by nature, human beings are potentially good and, without direct instruction or inculcation of tradition and simply through experiencing varied roles in interaction with other people, will progressively evolve higher levels of morality. The unfolding of innate potentials and the content and characteristics of stages are not presented as assumptions about man's nature but as theory derived from empirical evidence. Though some issues and some evidence related to the theory will be considered at varied points, the theory itself and the relevant research will be discussed in Volume 2.

Humans as Self-Seeking Creatures: Morality Externally Imposed.   The assumption that man is inherently evil has also been long present in philosophy, and its influence extends to present-day psychological theory. It was promoted by many religious thinkers, who believed that man was basically sinful. In the sixteenth century, man came to be considered as willful and rebellious against God's order. The strongest, and a non-religious, expression of a pessimistic view of man's nature came from Thomas Hobbes (1650/1962). Hobbes believed that phenomena were subject to scientific laws and accounted for man's thought, action, and even society in terms of mechanistic materialism. He described man as hedonistic, motivated to seek pleasure and avoid pain, a view that goes back to early (pre-Socratic) Greeks. He thought that good and bad are determined by individual aspirations and that what is good for one man may be evil (e.g., undesirable) for another. In general, he regarded life as a war, man against man, or as a race in which the object is to get ahead and stay ahead of others. Man seeks as much power as possible for the purposes of hedonistic gratification, and this power then serves the goal of self-aggrandizement at the expense of others. According to Hobbes, a strong external authority, such as a strong state, is necessary to control with terror "our natural passions, that carry us to partiality, pride, revenge, and the like." Without such a strong external authority men would rob one another and would thereby gain not only spoils, but also honor. That is, even others' respect could be gained through behavior that harms others if man's self-serving tendencies were not restricted by external authority. The pessimistic view of man's nature gained expression at a later time in social Darwinism, the view that life consists of man struggling against man, and the strongest survive. This view was derived by Spencer and others from Darwin's theory of natural selection, according to which those who are best adapted to cope with their environment will survive, and evolution is based on the survival of the best members of the species. (However, Darwin's writings include other ideas that suggest that man will help his fellow man in need.)

This pessimistic view of man's nature is represented in one of our most influential psychological theories, psychoanalysis. According to Freud, the sexual and aggressive impulses are the basic impulses in human nature. Morality derives from the necessity to restrict the amoral, self-seeking character of man. Freud (1930) thought that man developed ethical norms in order to make social life possible. A system of taboos and norms was established to inhibit the expression of antisocial impulses and thereby protect the individual and the group from the dangers of man's impulses. On the other hand, Freud thought that society develops too-restrictive norms and standards, overly inhibiting the expression of basic impulses. The individual may then develop an overly strict conscience—superego—in the course of internalizing societal standards. Such unnecessary restrictions of basic human impulses could lead to psychological illness. Man is caught between his own instinctive impulses and restriction by social norms, and the best result can only be an imperfect compromise.

Although he held a pessimistic view of man's nature, Freud placed great importance on man's self-understanding. According to psychoanalysis, self-understanding and insight into the causes of one's behavior, which are often repressed and consequently unconscious, are important for psychological health and maturity. However, self-understanding also has implications for morality. Freud and Jung have similar views on this point. Jung (1966) also believed that in man's nature there are desires, needs, and impulses that are contrary to moral values. He referred to this part of man's nature as the shadow, or the dark side of man. These impulses may be hereditary, part of man's natural inclinations that he learns to control through social experiences; they include impulses such as aggression, incest, and adultery. For Jung, the process of individuation, an individual's development of himself, meant at least in part that the shadow of man, which is usually unconscious, becomes conscious. Knowledge of one's negative inclinations is good, because then these inclinations can be considered and evaluated. Many of them may be permissible upon careful evaluation because they do not really conflict with important values. Others may be controlled better if they are known than if they direct behavior without being known.

The psychoanalytic view and Jung's analytic view both regard man or part of man as inclined to harm others; morality, rules, and regulations by society are necessary in order to protect individuals and society from the consequences of these negative inclinations. Self-examination is important. The difference between Freudian and Jungian views of self-examination and the earlier views mentioned, such as Plato's, is that the former refers to bringing into consciousness "repressed" motives, whereas the latter refers to a rational examination of the meaning and purpose of life. In contrast to moral philosophers who regarded certain basic principles as the cornerstones of morality, both Hobbes and Freud have relativistic views. The moral values used to maintain control over man's negative impulses are not regarded as predetermined in some manner or as self-evident or derivable from rational considerations. In Freud's pessimistic view of man's nature no true altruism exists, and behavior that seems to be altruistic is likely to be the result of reaction formation (Anna Freud, 1963) to neurotic needs. Obviously, this is a highly restricted and—I hope the subsequent chapters demonstrate—the incorrect view.

Partly following Freud's lead, partly generalizing from observations of instinctual aggressive behavior in animals, and partly using examples of human aggression as evidence, a number of writers have argued that aggression in man is instinctive (Lorenz, 1967; Ardrey, 1961). Lorenz, for example, reported his extensive observations of apparently instinctual aggressive behavior in animals manifested in the defense of their territory against members of their own species, or elicited under other circumstances. He then argued that man's makeup also includes instinctual aggression. Instincts are usually regarded to be species-specific behaviors that are elicited by specific stimuli or a range of stimuli. They are apparently not learned, although experience, opportunity to interact with the environment, is necessary for the unfolding of instinctual behavior patterns. However, the scientific community in general regards as highly questionable the ideas that in man such complex behavior patterns as aggression would be instinctual, that such behavior would appear without learning, or that they would be elicited by specific, genetically determined stimuli. This does not exclude the possibility that aggression has a genetic origin; the possibility that altruistic behavior is genetically determined is, in fact, discussed later in this chapter.

Another influential psychological theory, *homeostatic-drive theory*, does not state explicitly that man's nature is self-seeking, but clearly implies it. The notion of homeostasis (Cannon, 1932), or internal balance, is well supported by evidence. It is related to the fact that man's biological makeup causes cyclical imbalance to develop in man's internal chemical–hormonal state, resulting in psychological states such as hunger, thirst, and sexual desire. This cyclical imbalance is simply a function of the passage of time. The resulting psychological conditions or "drive states" activate the organism; the goal of this activity is to reduce the drive or imbalance and achieve homeostasis. The notion of drive, based on homeostasis, has become the cornerstone of behavioristic learning theories, the dominant theories in psychology from about the mid-1920s to the mid-1960s. Moreover, drive conceptions, which were originally derived from knowledge about the physical or primary needs of the organism where evidence for homeostasis is rather clear, were extended to other areas of human functioning. The motivation for approval, affiliation, and achievement, as well as other motives that guide man's social behavior and relationships with others, were regarded as secondary needs also guided by drive and drive reduction. The notion that the goal of behavior is to redress an internal imbalance appears to have been extended by the conception of an optimal or habitual level of internal arousal (or external stimulation). According to some writers, organisms seek to achieve the optimal level of arousal (Hebb, 1955); other writers believe that organisms seek to deviate from it to a slight degree (Fiske & Maddi, 1961; Hunt, 1965). The drive conception and related notions imply that man is self-seeking because his behavior is motivated by drive reduction —by the satisfaction of his own needs, desires, and impulses.

Clearly, there are many examples of people suffering deprivation of biological needs in order to satisfy a higher-order need, such as creative activity or consistency with their belief or faith. Although biological needs are part of human nature, it is likely that only under conditions of deprivation would they help us predict man's behavior toward his fellow man, and, even then, they are not the exclusive determinants. However, to the extent that a person experiences some form of internal imbalance related to the satisfaction of his own goals or needs, he might be less likely to attend to the goals or needs of another. Nevertheless, to the extent that "secondary" needs can be a source of imbalance, there is no reason to believe that the satisfaction of other people's goals and needs cannot become a secondary need and thus a potential source of imbalance and the motivator of goal-directed behavior.

The conceptions discussed in this section imply that man is self-seeking and morality has to be imposed from the outside. This imposed morality may originate in the state or in society as a whole. Another "external," *imposed* source of morality is religious law. Such laws circumvent the usual rationale for moral rules and values, which is the respect for the welfare of other humans. Religions promote morality because respect for God demands adherence to His laws. Although religious morality does, of course, include standards of morality relevant to human welfare (after all, presumably that is an underlying reason for the existence of religions), it also includes arbitrary standards that demand obedience. (This, of course, can also be the case with societal rules and standards and conventions that are regarded as morally relevant but really are not. For example, sexual conduct does not in itself seem to be morally significant. It has moral significance only to the extent that it affects others' welfare.) "Humanitarian" thinkers object to any kind of prescriptions for moral conduct that are external to concern with man alone. Fromm (1941) suggests that authoritarian morality is usually based on feelings of weakness and awe of authority, and that usually the content of morality is determined by what is good for the authority.

Philosophers of the Enlightenment also regarded religious laws or respect for God as the basis of morality, as a form of authoritarian ethic. They approached the study of man through man; human nature, and universal standards applicable to man that could be derived from human nature on the one hand, and the universal condition of man living in social groups on the other hand, were regarded as appropriate nonauthoritarian sources of morality. Several contemporary views are relevant to the conception that morality derives in some manner from the universal condition of men interacting with other men.

Morality Arising from Society and the Conditions of Social Living. To understand the origins of morality, we must consider the consequences of people living together in social groups, with perhaps certain uniformities in the influence of social existence regardless of the nature of social organization, and variations due to different social organizations.

Hobbes himself, and Enlightenment thinkers such as Adam Smith, suggested the development of some kind of a balance that controls man's selfishness. Hobbes believed that in a model system forces could be set up to lead each man, for his own selfish reasons, to contribute to social stability and the common good. Adam Smith suggested, a century later, that the natural law in the field of economics was that each man acting in his own interest in the end benefits society as a whole. Pope, in the Federalist Papers, suggested that a social system could be devised to counteract man's folly by a skillful counterbalancing of man's separate impulses.

David Hume was one of the foremost expositors of the view that man's selfish motives could lead to the development of a positive social order. Self-love, he thought, would give rise to justice and greed would give rise to honesty because of man's ability to judge that in the long run the practice of such virtues would bring him more gratification than a more direct expression of his passions. It is in the self-interest of men living in social groups to behave according to certain values or principles that may be regarded as moral. This view represents a beginning of the conception that morality derives from humans living in social groups, and that rules that regulate conduct in a manner that enhances the welfare of individuals and the group evolve or may be created.

An extreme position that might have had its origins in such thinking has been presented by Emile Durkheim (1961). In his view, society—the social order—is the paramount source of morality. Morality is the totality of definite rules originated by society. Morality has three elements. The first element is discipline. One meaning of discipline is regularity, the capacity for restraint and self-mastery. This is crucial for certain aspects of social life and it is necessary for happiness, as well as for the capacity to be involved with specific tasks and situations. Discipline also leads people to follow the authority of moral rule, which is essential.

The second element of morality is attachment to the social group. Moral rules prescribe behavior that has impersonal goals; an act is not moral if consideration of adverse consequences has determined it. One must obey moral rules out of respect for them, and for that reason alone. According to Durkheim, society constitutes a being *sui generis*, of special character, and it is the object of moral goals. There are no genuine moral ends except collective ones. Sentiments of personal sympathy, acts of charity directed toward individuals, do not constitute intrinsic elements of moral temperament. They have moral value only to the extent that a moral state (sentiment for the group) is associated with them. According to Durkheim, history demonstrated that morality is related to the social structure of the people practicing it. Individuals also tend to approximate the moral type that is best for their social system.

The third element of morality is autonomy, which implies the rule of reason in morality. Morality is imperative; obedience to the authority of rules is imperative. Nevertheless, we do not regard an act as completely moral except when we perform it freely, without any coercion. The concept of autonomy is an attempt to resolve this contradiction; it refers to the understanding of the world and the ordering of conduct in relation to our understanding. We can investigate and come to understand the reasons for the moral rules that we received from others.

This leads to Durkheim's important assumption that morality is based on the scientific study of social order. Morality is founded on the nature of society. By achieving the most complete and clear awareness of the reasons for our conduct, we develop an autonomy that the public conscience expects of every genuinely and completely moral being. Durkheim's view of autonomy as rational acceptance of what is taught by society seems quite different from other views of autonomy, which suggest that an individual develops principles of his own that may be contrary to societal standards (presumably when these are unjust). However, Durkheim seems to have believed that moral standards can be "perfect" if they truly reflect the nature of a society. If so, no higher principles would seem possible. We can check the extent to which the moral order is founded on the nature of society, that is, the extent to which it is what it ought to be. We can also determine the nature of the imperfection and the change that is needed, with the help of a science of morality, which is based on the science of society. Durkheim believed that, in relying on the authority of reason rather than on external authority such as God, man would become more sensitive to injustice and would turn against traditions divorced from reason's influence. Ideally, there should be channels available to bring about the change that would bring social institutions and moral rules into greater harmony.

It is worth noting the apparently great problems created by the lack of such channels to bring about change in moral rules so that they reflect the nature of social institutions. However, sometimes the goal has to be the bringing of social institutions into harmony with existing moral values. It is an interesting question whether Durkheim would have thought that this ought to be done, since he believed that the nature of moral rules ought to be derived from the existing institutions.

Some writers believed that a science of man would define moral values; Durkheim believed that a science of society would do this. However, certain questions arise from this belief. It would seem that Durkheim's views allow for injustice, even under the best conditions. The nature of social organization may be such that it deprives some people of privileges; Durkheim does not specify what kinds of social organizations demand this and make it acceptable. For example, serfs were an integral part of the feudal system. Did the feudal system provide a just social order because the fit between moral rules and social organization was appropriate? What criteria can we use to determine this? The idea that a relationship exists between the nature of social institutions and the moral order of society, and the implication that the latter cannot be changed without the former, seem important. But the elevation of the group over the individual and the derivation of justice and morality from the nature of existing institutions open the way to questionable moral positions leading to practices restricting individual rights and freedom.

Durkheim also makes a distinction somewhat similar to that between prohibitive and prescriptive morality. He suggests that morality has two aspects; that of duty, what one ought to do, which involves discipline, and that of the good, which is a matter of inspiration and feelings for others. He suggests that at times of change a society is less characterized by clear-cut moral laws, and therefore the dutiful aspect of morality is less important. At such times, man's aspiration for the good, his passion for causes, and his potential for doing things for others should be engaged so that his morality is maintained through active exercise of at least one aspect of it. Corresponding to these two aspects of morality, duty and the good, there are men characterized by inclinations more to one than to the other. Self-discipline, order, and the fulfillment of duty characterizes one kind; less discipline, consequently less reliability, but engagement in doing good for others, emotional expression toward others, and passion in good causes characterize the other kind. Again, whole societies may differ along this dimension. Fully integrated societies (perhaps Rome at the time of Augustus would be such a society) were characterized by fulfillment of duty and relative lack of tolerance for deviation even in the service of what was thought to be good. At other times morality is in flux, and rules are less clear-cut and less imperative. Then the engagement of man for good causes is important. Maybe our society at present is in the latter state.

The conceptions that morality is a result of human beings living together and that the pursuit of enlightened self-interest can lead to the development of a positive social order can also be related to contemporary theories in psychology. One such theory, usually referred to as *exchange theory* (Homans, 1961; Thibaut & Kelley, 1953; Gergen, 1968a), suggests that people interact in a manner that leads to gain for all parties involved in the interaction (see Chapter 8). Unless a certain minimum benefit is derived for each party, the interaction will cease, and no benefit will come to anyone. Therefore, it is of mutual advantage to arrive at a relationship based on the exchange of benefits. Once such a relationship develops it comes to be guided by norms, expectations about how each party will behave. These norms often acquire an obligatory character; they come to be regarded as right, particularly when they guide the relationships of a large number of people, such as members of a social group. The pursuit of self-interest thus leads to the development of norms, standards, or principles that guide action.

Related to the views of Enlightenment philosophers and those of Durkheim are some currently propagated views. Lerner states that justice "plays a central and necessary role in the well-being, if not the survival, of any society . . . the form which justice takes is eventually shaped by what is wise and necessary for the collective well-being [Lerner, 1975, p. 10]." The implication is that the degree to which equality, equity, or other principles represent justice, and the ways these principles are defined and applied, are a function of the nature or characteristics of a society. In different societies, and for different purposes, different forms of justice may be most functional. For example, Nadar (1975) suggests that when people have limited relations to each other and/or scarce resources, they develop principles of conflict resolution by which they can speedily resolve conflict and assign blame. Under conditions of greater relatedness, they need and will have procedures that maintain the continuity of human relationships. Deutsch (1975) notes that good interpersonal relations are better served by a guiding principle of equality than by principles of equity. When there is a greater degree of continuity and intimacy in the relationship among interacting individuals, equality may be a more adaptive principle of justice than equity.

Here several important questions arise. How are the moral values and standards of a culture determined? What is the relationship between them and the institutions of the society? We know little about these matters. How does societal morality change? Such changes presumably reflect changes in life conditions that give rise to changes in the institutions of society (see Turnbull, 1972). Perhaps cultural or societal crises also influence them. An example is the crisis of the Vietnam war, an unsuccessful war that did not seem necessary for the welfare of the society. Unfortunately, our knowledge of how morality changes is minimal.

There may be certain universal elements of social living, and there may also be special elements that emerge from the nature and organization of a specific society. Social-exchange theory deals, to some extent, with the question of how the condition of humans living in social groups affects the development of both group and individual moral norms. Cognitive developmentalist theory (Piaget, 1932; Kohlberg, 1969) suggests that the development of individual morality is a function of experience in social living. Interaction with others spurs an "advance" in the moral reasoning of individuals. A question that has not been raised by other psychologists, but is considered important by cognitive developmentalists, is how autonomous morality develops. The cognitive developmentalists believe that discrepancies can arise between the morality of society and that of an individual because the individual acquires moral concepts not from socializing agents teaching standards of the society, but from his own life experiences, his varied interactions with other people. Other approaches, which view moral development as the learning and accepting of societal standards by individuals, have not addressed the question of autonomy. They do not specifically consider whether it is possible to develop a personal morality that is in contradiction with societal morality (although a deficiency in learning societal standards has been discussed) and how that would come about. There are, of course, alternatives to the cognitive developmental view; there are many and conflicting moral standards that an individual can be exposed to in a culturally advanced society through reading philosophy and literature, and through exposure to socializing agents whose views and practices vary. Individual morality may develop out of a combination of all these modeling and tuitional experiences and the person's own life experiences. Autonomous moral values and principles may result from the integration of these varied influences, or they may be generated in the course of resolving conflict among them.

Genetic Origins of Altruism

The preceding section dealt with conceptions of morality and human nature formulated by philosophers and psychologists. Geneticists and biologists are also concerned with the origins of morality and altruism. A number of psychologists and biologists have proposed that altruism is genetically determined, and they have attempted to use the theory of evolution (or their extension of it) to show at least the possibility that this can be so. Others have attempted to demonstrate that altruism is present in animals —some for the purpose of demonstrating that it is instinctual in nature, in the hope of arguing by analogy that altruism in man is also genetically determined. Whether these goals are successfully accomplished, research on prosocial behavior in animals seems instructive about prosocial behavior in man. An examination of the literature gives us the opportunity to consider the meaning and value of conceiving of "human nature" as the origin of particular behavioral tendencies.

Before serious interest in altruism arose, a few writers suggested, as I noted earlier, that aggressive behavior in man has an instinctual origin. Instinctive behavior in animals has two basic characteristics. First, it is transmitted by heredity; though it does not require "learning," it does seem to require prior experience as well as the opportunity for its performance at certain critical periods in life. Second, instinctive behavior often has specific eliciting stimuli, such as color, shape, or pattern of movement of another animal (or of an object). Few psychologists assume that man has instincts of this kind—hereditarily programmed behavior patterns of such great specificity. The dominant psychological view is that aggression does not have a simple hereditary basis in man. Various theorists, including psychologists, argue that a "critical period" exists in the development of attachment by children to parents or caretakers (Bowlby, 1969), and they tend to regard this as the most specifically programmed characteristic human beings possess. In a number of species there seems to be such a critical period, although not highly fixed, in the development of attachment between young animals and other members of the species.

A number of writers have considered the possibility that altruism is part of man's biological makeup. Altruistic behavior, although it may endanger the life of the actor, unquestionably has survival value for the species. Therefore, some reasoned, it is likely to have been favored by natural selection. Holmes (1945) argued that altruism is the result of evolutionary development that comes to be represented in the genetic makeup of the species. He regards a mother's care of her infants as the prototype of altruistic behavior. A basic question has been how natural selection, which operates at the level of the individual, could have increased the chances that the genes of altruistic individuals would be transmitted more frequently than the genes of less altruistic individuals, so that the frequency of genes promoting altruism would increase in the population.

First, I would like to consider what it would mean if altruistic or prosocial behavior had a genetic component—the connection between genes and specific behavior. Genes are the active ingredients of the chromosomes, which direct the cells to produce certain chemicals necessary for behavior to occur. The environment acts on the organism to cause certain changes in the composition or quantity of these chemicals; these changes in turn affect behavior. Such changes can be temporary, or they can be the result of learning and therefore relatively permanent. Thus, biochemical processes, tied to the genes but affected by environmental conditions, are involved in the determination of behavior.

In human beings, most behaviors—other than simple reflexes—are probably affected by a combination of genes, rather than controlled by a single gene, that is, the influence of genes on behavior is polygenic. Furthermore, in human beings, genes, rather than directly controlling specific social interactive behaviors, are likely to create a predisposition that enhances the probability that certain kinds of learning will take place, given appropriate environmental (experiential) conditions. This learning may be emotional, furthering the likelihood that certain kinds of behaviors will be performed. For example, the precondition for the development, under appropriate circumstances, of both attachment to other people and empathy with others may be provided by man's genetic makeup—both in turn enhance the likelihood of prosocial action.

The discussions about the genetic origins of altruism center on the question of whether altruism *could* have become part of man's genetic makeup in the course of biological evolution through the mechanism of natural selection, without providing evidence that it has or has not. Such discussions must show, minimally, that altruism has survival value, that altruistic acts enhance rather than reduce the likelihood that the actor's genes will be transmitted.

Three ways have been proposed through which altruism might have become part of man's genetic makeup: group selection, kinship selection, and the development of reciprocal altruism. Group selection has been discussed by a number of writers (Haldane, 1932; Wright, 1945; Wynne-Edwards, 1962), some arguing for it, and some arguing against it. Williams (1971) has strongly, and to many writers convincingly, argued against its plausibility (see Campbell, 1972).

Kinship selection means that a person engaging in an altruistic act, even a self-sacrificial one, contributes to the survival of closely related individuals, so the reproductive potential of any altruistic gene that he and his relatives have is increased. In engaging in a self-sacrificial act, the probability that he dies without an offspring would be smaller than the likely genetic gain, because of the higher probability that the kin whom he benefits also has the altruistic gene. Group selection and kinship selection are conceptually similar, but kinship selection is a more acceptable view, because of the greater commonality of genetic makeup among close relatives. The applicability of the kinship selection model to the evolution of altruistic genetic makeup among humans is limited to groups small enough so that the probability is high that when a person helps another in need he would be helping a close relative (Hamilton, 1964). Kinship selection might re-affirm and help to explain close family ties and self-sacrificial behavior among family members. But does it offer an explanation of the evolution of a genetic basis of altruism applicable to unrelated individuals? This will be considered later.

Campbell (1965) argued that man's genetic makeup has a dual "selec-tive" system, egoism and altruism, with a resulting fundamental ambival-ence. Consequently, both self-serving and altruistic tendencies may be irra-tional and "amoral," rather than the latter being an externally imposed moral tendency. As the basis of his argument Campbell refers to realistic group conflict theory and the finding that intergroup conflict increases in-group solidarity and loyalty to the group (as well as hostility to the out-group). He suggests that this is not predictable from the individualistic hedonism of modern learning theory (which he considers as a strategy of de-liberate initial oversimplification that was taken too seriously). The in-creased loyalty to the group even results in the willingness to sacrifice one's life for it. Both this and the concentrated defensive and offensive efforts of the group made possible by the willingness for altruistic self-sacrifice increase the likelihood of survival of the group. "The tremendous survival value of being social makes innate social motives as likely on a priori grounds as self-centered ones [p. 301]." Campbell points out that although the early interpreters of Darwin derived their political views from his view of individual competition (social Darwinism), Darwin (1871) actually emphasized the survival value of group life and the probability that man's moral sense and group loyalty had instinctive bases.

In a subsequent article, Campbell (1972) reviewed evidence and reason-ing presented by geneticists and reversed his position, concluding that it is unlikely that through natural selection altruism could have become part of man's genetic makeup:

> Let us suppose that mutations have produced a heterogeneity within a social group so that there are some individuals with genes predisposing a self-sacrificial bravery, which furthers group survival, and others with genes predisposing a self-saving cowardice. Let us suppose that due to the presence of the bravery genes in some individuals the group as a whole survives better. This increases the average reproductive oppor-tunity for both the brave and the cowardly among the group members. The net gain for the brave is reduced to some degree because of the costs of risks they incur. (That is, some of the brave die in the course of being brave and sacrificing for others. The net gain for the cowardly has no such subtraction. They will not die in the course of attempting to help others.) Thus, while all gain, the cowardly gain more and their genes will gradually become more frequent as a result. There is no way in which the altruistic genetic tendency could increase relative to the cowardly, to say nothing of becoming predominant if there is a self-sacrificial component to the bravery [p. 25].

A limitation of Campbell's discussion is that he focuses on the possibility of a genetic basis of altruistic behavior that demands extreme self-sacrifice, a serious risk to the actor's life, without considering the possibility of a genetic component in altruistic and prosocial behavior that is less dangerous to the actor.

A further input in the dispute comes from Wilson (1975), a major proponent of sociobiology, the genetic basis of social behavior. Primarily on the basis of animal behavior that appears altruistic (see later in this chapter) he argued that altruistic behavior among both animals and humans has a genetic basis. He stressed kin selection as the basis of the evolution of altruism, since "if the genes causing the altruism are shared by two organisms because of common descent, and if the altruistic act by one organism increases the joint contribution of genes to the next generation, the propensity to altruism will spread through the gene pool [pp. 3–4]." That is, even if the altruist sacrifices his life in the course of propagating the life of a kin, the likelihood of the transmission of the altruistic gene will be increased and will provide the basis of the spread of altruistic disposition in the whole population.

Campbell (1975) reiterated his position, arguing that "evolutionary genetics shows that when there is genetic competition among the cooperators (as for humans but not for the social insects), great limitations are placed upon the degree of socially useful, individual self-sacrificial altruism that biological evolution can produce [p. 1123]." According to Campbell, the portrait of biologically based social personality remains one of "predominantly self-serving opportunism." He does note that the selfishness that is biologically favored includes many characteristics that we happen to think of as altruistic, such as parental care and altruism in relation to the young. Since genetic transmission takes place through offspring, they will be protected.

Trivers (1971) discussed the manner in which altruistic interaction among unrelated individuals might have become part of man's genetic heritage. He concentrated on situations in which one individual engages in an altruistic act that involves some measure of self-sacrifice and where the recipient engages in an act of altruism at some cost to himself to benefit the first altruist; these two acts may be temporally separated. He called the interaction *reciprocal altruism*. In later chapters, I shall discuss contemporary research on the determinants of such interactions, and I shall refer to the interaction as *positive exchange behavior*. Shapiro (1974) gives the following examples of reciprocal altruism:

> Let us take a relatively small group of people. In this group, there are, say, five hunters from each of the five unrelated families in the group. Let us imagine that the main food source consists of dodo birds and that the average probability of a hunter catching a dodo bird is low, so that

he catches a dodo only once every 5 days. Let us also suppose that an average dodo bird will last a family for 5 days but really only lasts at most 2 days because of spoilage. Let us also suppose that a single dodo will suffice all five families for one day and that the total probability of any hunter's catching a dodo every day is unity. Then it would appear that those genetic variants that have a predisposition to share food will be more fit than those that hoard food. The sharing individuals' reproductive potential will increase, and this altruistic quality will be selected for. Another illustration concerns two individuals, who are unrelated neighbors, who are continually fishing each other's children out of the river, preventing them from drowning. In each of these situations the costs to the altruists of performing these behaviors is very low compared to the benefits they received from, in the two examples mentioned above, not starving and not losing their children. Such behaviors are genetically egoistic in that they increase the net reproductive potential of the actors, and they are also altruistic in virtually any definitional sense of the word [p. 7–8].

Trivers (1971) listed three conditions for the evolution of reciprocal altruism: (a) a large number of situations in which actors can be altruistic; (b) a large number of interactions involving a relatively small group of individuals; and (c) a distribution of symmetrical situations where the actors are in roughly equivalent roles as recipients and altruists in their turn. Furthermore, he proposed certain biological, behavioral, and situational parameters that are prerequisites for these three conditions: a long lifetime for individuals; a localized existence and high need for interdependence (because of common predators, scarce food supply, and the like) resulting in a small, stable group size; an absence of a dominance hierarchy; and the providing of aid in fighting with other groups. These are conditions thought to have existed during the middle Pleistocene, between 200,000 and 600,000 years ago. There is evidence suggesting that in Tanzania cooperative hunting behavior developed during this period.

There is impressive evidence (see Chapter 8) that reciprocity guides human interactions to an extensive degree, and that preference for and a tendency toward reciprocal interactions exist in a variety of cultures (Gouldner, 1960; Gergen, 1968a; Staub, 1972a). Trivers' thesis suggests that there might be a genetic predisposition toward reciprocal interactions, particularly of a positive kind. Trivers (1971, 1974) proposed not only the possibility that reciprocal altruism is selected for, but also the possibility that the tendency to enforce altruism and moral behavior in others is selected. These tendencies benefit the group but have no genetic cost to the individual. Moreover, the tendency to retaliate against those who do not act according to reciprocal altruistic trade-off arrangements, and moralistic aggression in general, would also be genetically promoted.

One may argue that the *capacity* of human beings for altruism *must* be genetically based—that genes that *permit* the development of personal characteristics that lead to altruism, rather than genes that *code* for altruistic behavior, must exist (Greene & Barash, 1976). As Wilson (1976) notes, it is "virtually inconceivable" that human beings could be socialized into the patterns of altruistic behavior existing among baboons, orangutans, or other animals, and vice versa. Further, if the capacity for altruism is genetically based, individual differences in this capacity are probable. Kin selection as a mechanism of transmission implies such individual variation. Given apparent variation in human characteristics at birth and some evidence from sophisticated twin studies (Freedman, 1965) for the genetic basis of such variation, including variation in social responsiveness, there could certainly be a genetic basis of individual variation in the *potential* for altruistic behavior.

In response to Campbell's (1975) views, many arguments were offered as to what processes, beyond those described by Wilson and Trivers, could have led to the development of altruistic disposition in humans. One suggestion is that females, who have greater power in selecting or at least encouraging males with whom to mate, would tend to select cooperatively or altruistically inclined males (Blaney, 1976). Another proposal involves "artificial selection," posited by Darwin. In our society artificial selection may take the form of special honors and advantages provided to heros and altruists of various kinds, and the suggestion is that these honors more than make up for the genetic loss that altruists expose themselves to in the course of their self-sacrificial acts (Ghiselin, 1976). It also seems that altruism in old people—for example, women who no longer have the capacity for reproduction—would contribute to the survival of a group, without the loss of the genes of the altruist. Thus, group selection based on altruism by the old may have occurred.

It is difficult to question the existence of at least parental self-sacrifice in humans. Several writers (Hogan, 1976; Messick, 1976) argued that altruism toward kin is a very genuine form of altruism. Messick notes that if the unit of analysis is the individual—rather than the clan, or a group of kin—then self-sacrifice for the sake of kin would have to be regarded as altruistic rather than selfish, even though it contributes to the propagation of one's own genes. Individuals may lose their own lives but may further the survival of their genes.

If altruistic disposition toward kin has evolved, what stimulus configurations would elicit altruistic acts? Messick (1976) suggests that the important cues may be of an emotional nature, such as affection, love, and empathy. Close and frequent association with kin would have led to the selection of such cues as "altruism mediating stimuli." If that were so, altruistic dispositions could then have been directed to individuals who were not kin, but elicited such internal reactions. The quality of altruistic acts may then vary as a function of the intensity of the internal experience.

How much value has the discussion about genetic bases of altruism for the understanding of individual behavior? Most writers (Campbell, 1975;

Wilson, 1976) stress that their analysis of the genetics of altruism applies to the species, not to individual human beings. Individuals vary tremendously in the likelihood that they would act prosocially. If a number of genes exert influence on prosocial behavior, the amount of influence would vary across individuals depending on the degree to which a person possesses the controlling genes and might, in fact, be normally distributed around some moderate degree. However, if individuals vary in the genetic influence on their prosocial behavior, what is the nature of this influence? Most likely, sensitivities or susceptibilities to environmental conditions that might lead to the acquisition of a prosocial orientation would vary, some reacting more or learning more from them than others. Thus, genetic differences would manifest themselves through differential susceptibility to experience (Wiggins *et al.*, 1976). For example, experience might lead to the development of greater empathic capacity—a greater ability to experience another's emotion vicariously—among individuals whose genetic makeup is more prosocial. Let us assume that in the future it becomes possible to examine and test the characteristics of genes and to provide biochemical evidence for individual differences in altruistic potential. Then, additional research could specify whether people with differential gene composition require different experiences, in amount and kind, for their prosocial disposition to be fostered. (Alternatively, we may be able to demonstrate differences in potential for prosocial responding early in life, perhaps by identifying primitive empathic responsiveness; see Volume 2.) Until, and if, such developments take place, we have to focus on cultural conditions and personal experiences as the origins of positive behavior.

Social Evolution in Contrast to Biological Evolution

Campbell (1975) proposed that biological natural selection did select for altruism in human beings, but only at about the level of altruism among the social vertebrates. However, this level is below the *biosocial optimum*, the level functionally adequate for society. Consequently, social norms evolved to move the level of altruism higher. Norms promoting altruistic conduct develop in the course of social evolution: they attempt to balance genetically based selfishness. The optimal balance seems to be a compromise between the greatest good for a particular person and the greatest good for the social group as a whole.

Campbell (1975) suggested that social evolution acts to select features of the social environment on the basis of their utility for the system, or their social adequacy. The mechanism of social evolution is thus similar to that of natural selection at the biological level. Thus, features of the social system such as rules of social organization, inhibitory moral norms, and beliefs in transcendant gods may have been subject to a systematic selection process. Others note that social evolution is probably not as blind as biological evolution, that human decision makers apply their intelligence in policymaking, in the choice of cultural actions, and that they thereby shape the evolution of their culture (Boehm, 1976). That culture develops in a manner that maximizes its functional adequacy is an appealing notion. Very little is clear, however, about this process. First, what does the term *adequacy* mean in relation to culture (Boehm, 1976)? Does it refer to the capacity to survive in relationship to other cultures, to the existence of equilibrium within the culture, and in turn to the capacity of members of the social group for biological reproduction? At least from a nonevolutionary perspective, adequacy of a culture must also have something to do with the emotional well-being of its members. Second, by what processes do cultures evolve? Third, what is the relationship between the external environment —for example, abundance or scarcity of food in the ecology, hostile or friendly neighbors—and the institutions of the culture, such as the kind of governing bodies that exist and the manner in which food is gathered, shelters are built, and lines of communications among members are maintained? How are these, in turn, related to morality? Durkheim's conception was that morality is implied by the social institutions, and a science of morality would specify the proper moral rules given the nature of a society's institutions. To what extent is morality the result of the social institutions that represent a culture's adaptation to ecological conditions, and to what extent does the moral system affect adaptations? We must be dealing with an interrelated system in which each element can be affected by, and in turn can affect, the other elements.

It seems probable, as I implied earlier when noting different adaptations to similar conditions of scarcity in food, that although limitations are set by the ecology—not all possible cultural evolutions will be effective— varied moral and institutional adaptations to similar ecological conditions are possible. For the survival and growth of a culture, it is essential to have institutions and rules that provide effective guidance for the utilization of resources, as well as sufficient flexibility to permit the development of different adaptive modes in response to changing conditions.

In addition to ecological conditions and the social institutions and moral systems that arise, a duality in human nature may be a fourth element affecting the continued evolution of cultures. If such a duality exists, is it between aggression and altruism, or between selfishness and kindness? More likely, it is between dependence, submission to, and/or identification with others' interests and personal ascendance, the inclination to promote the self in varied ways. To what extent is such a duality biologically determined, and to what extent is it the result of the conditions of human existence? Certainly, dependence on and submission to caretakers are inevitable experiences in childhood and can lead to identification with others; these can become aspects of the growing child's personality. Beyond such biologically determined facts of *experience* as the complete dependence on caretakers in early life, human beings have long struggled with the rights of the state, of society as a whole, versus the rights of the individual

(Messick, 1976). They have frequently attempted to establish a compromise that would protect individual rights while maximizing the common good. Man's biologically established dispositions, his biologically determined experiences such as childhood dependence, and the conditions of social existence may jointly give rise to varied orientations toward the self and others.

To place social or cultural evolution in its proper perspective, it should be noted that changes in religion, governmental forms, and many other social and moral institutions can be extremely rapid (Goldschmidt, 1976). The industrial revolution changed ecological conditions and wrought tremendous changes in an amazingly short time. The change from autocracy to democracy can be very fast, as we know from American history. Societies always change, and the rate of change is particularly great now. As the nature of the physical and social environment changes, the techniques, capacities, values, and personal characteristics that are necessary or useful to deal with them change. To the extent that systems of socialization keep up with the requirements of different personal characteristics for optimal adaptation, or to the extent that people's beliefs about such requirements change, there will be different characteristics that are valued, different goals set for child rearing (by the culture and by parents), and different techniques of socialization employed or different contents of socialization stressed. Consequently, there will be continuous change in socialization emphasis, as well as different forms of learning and adaptation to the culture by individuals once they progress beyond parental socialization, as they continue to be socialized by the culture.

Depending on the flux in the system—the extent of ongoing change in institutions, customs, ideals, and values—a great deal of conflict can be generated at the societal or personal level. We are now experiencing rapid technological changes, as well as changes in values and cultural emphasis on the potential of human beings. This implies to us, among other things, the possibility of increased sensitivity, considerateness, and investment in relationships by men who are assumed to have been traditionally limited in these qualities. It also implies meaningful, genuine, open relationships among men and women. It implies opening the horizons for achievement, opportunities for instrumental competence and creativity and power for women. Finally, there is an orientation toward the self, in the sense that we believe that we must be true to ourselves. These sometimes conflicting ideals and expectations lead to the disruption of traditional patterns, the seeking of new adaptations to a social world that is in the process of being created.

Prosocial Behavior in Animals

In contrast to the theoretical approach just discussed, the attempt to show that altruism has a genetic origin has also taken an empirical form. A number of experiments have attempted to demonstrate the existence of altruism in animals; for most of these researchers altruism means prosocial behavior that is not learned or reinforced. Thus, to show that altruism exists in animals one needs to demonstrate that a helpful behavior is *not* maintained by some form of reinforcement. To show that altruism is genetically based one needs to establish that it is not learned. The *lack* of learning or reinforcement is exceedingly difficult to establish; it amounts to proving the null hypothesis. Even if both are demonstrated, generalization to man would be questionable.

In an early study, Nissen and Crawford (1936) observed and recorded interactions among chimpanzees. Their observations clearly demonstrated that chimpanzees share food. However, much of the sharing was the result of solicitation by other chimpanzees. Such sharing might be reinforced by getting rid of the presumably unpleasant stimulus of begging. The sharing that was unsolicited seemed mostly reciprocal: An animal would give food to another and would later get food from the recipient. As is the case with observational studies, we do not know what experiences led to such behavior. The existence of delayed reciprocal sharing in monkeys is of substantial interest, but it certainly may have developed in the course of interaction among monkeys. Neither a genetic explanation nor the assumption of altruism seems justified.

Nissen and Crawford also examined sharing behavior of a more systematic kind. In one study, they put two monkeys into adjoining cages. One monkey had both food and tokens, another monkey had only a vending machine in which a token yielded a grape. In a second study, each monkey had a vending machine, but only one had food and tokens. In both studies the "rich" monkey shared tokens and also some food, often in response to begging, but sometimes without any solicitation. The investigators noted that positive response to begging occurred more frequently among animals who had previously established an intimate relationship.

Rice and Gainer (1962) did an experimental study on helping behavior in rats. In one experiment rats were exposed to a rat that had been placed on a platform. When the platform was raised in the air, the rat on it wiggled and squealed in distress. The rats were also exposed to a styrofoam block that was raised up in the air. The animals were taught to push a button to lower the platform, and they pushed the button more frequently when another rat emitting distress cues was on the platform than when the platform held the block. In another experiment Lavery and Foley (1963) found that rats exposed to white noise pressed a button to terminate the noise more frequently than did animals exposed to the distressed squealing of another rat. Thus, the intensity of the noises rather than their quality as distress sounds may have made the squeals aversive.

An experiment by Church (1959) also explored rats' reactions to another rat's distress sounds. He trained rats to press a lever in order to receive food pellets. Once this behavior was well learned, the rats witnessed another rat in an adjoining cage receiving electric shocks. The distress sounds produced by the other rat completely eliminated lever pressing, for a short period at least. Moreover, rats who had previously experienced electric shocks reacted to these distress sounds more strongly.

In another experiment, Masserman, Wechkin, and Terris (1964) taught rhesus monkeys to pull one of two chains to get food. When a red light appeared, pulling one of the chains provided a food pellet; when a blue light appeared, pulling the other chain did so. Then, whenever the monkeys pulled one of the two chains, a monkey that had been placed in an adjoining cage, visible to the experimental monkey, would get a high-intensity shock. When they pulled the other chain, the other monkey did not get shocked. Under these conditions, 2 out of 15 monkeys in the experiment stopped pulling either chain, and 10 tended to forgo the food that was available when they pulled the chain but also delivered a shock, showing a preference for the other chain. Monkeys who had previously experienced shocks responded more in this manner. The monkeys who starved themselves—pulled neither chain—were among these. Monkeys that were previously housed in the same cages with the shocked animals showed significantly greater preference for the no-shock chain than other monkeys.

In this experiment, the monkeys did not have to forgo food to forgo hurting another monkey. Under these conditions, they responded to the other's distress and learned to pull the lever that produced no harm. As with the squealing rats, the distress cues of shocked monkeys might have produced distress in the experimental monkeys. The finding that prior experience affected the behavior of both rats (Church, 1959) and monkeys shows, minimally, that the animals' responses to distress cues were neither just a function of innate sensitivity to noise nor a purely genetically determined reaction. Prior experience with aversive stimulation might have increased fearful reaction by animals exposed to another's distress cues. However, the increase in the response to distress cues as a function of prior relationship with the animals in distress makes it likely that the subjects' responses were, at least in part, vicarious and empathic in nature.

Several experiments by Miller and his associates (Miller, Banks, & Ogawa, 1963; Miller, Caul, & Mirsky, 1967) explored the communication of affect between monkeys. Monkeys learned to push a button to avoid the administration of a shock to themselves and to a second monkey. The only clue that shock was coming was the facial reaction of the second monkey to a signal light previously associated with shocks. The experimental monkey could not see the signal. Thus, monkeys were responding to facial characteristics of another monkey. Monkeys that grew up in isolation (Miller, Caul, & Mirsky, 1967) did not push the button more often at times when the signal light was visible to the other monkey, in comparison to between-signal periods. Nor did experimental monkeys push the button in response to the facial expression of partner monkeys that had grown up in isolation. Apparently monkeys that had been isolated were deficient in both sending and perceiving distress cues (or in acting on cues that they perceived). Nonisolated monkeys that observed other monkeys' facial expressions not only pushed the button more often when the signal light appeared, but also responded physiologically at such times with increased heart rate, which indicates increased emotionality. Clearly, monkeys can perceive and use as a cue the affective reactions of other monkeys; this might be an important precondition for prosocial behavior. The Miller, Caul, and Mirsky (1967) study does not, however, demonstrate that monkeys actually behave prosocially, because the experimental monkeys, as well as the other monkeys, were receiving shocks following the signal, and both physiological and behavioral reactions might have been due to that.

Animals—like people—can behave horribly toward other members of their species. Rats who smell a "foreigner" in their midst attack and tear the intruder apart. Yet the research findings that have been reviewed here show that animals can be affected by other animals' distress and that they can and do behave in a positive, helpful manner toward other animals. The findings suggest that positive behaviors—sharing food, responding to another's distress, and denying oneself rewards—are more frequent, at least among monkeys, when the other animal is well known to the experimental monkey. The influence of past aversive experiences and of prior interactive experiences indicates, minimally, the highly important role of *learning* in the development of positive responsiveness to other animals. How the reaction to another's distress is motivated, to what extent it is a reaction to the physical properties of distress stimuli, as in the Lavery and Foley (1963) study, to what extent it is a conditioned fear response caused by an animal's past experiences with distress, and to what extent it is an empathic response, a vicarious experience of distress evoked by the other animal's distress, are as yet unclear. Past experience and surrounding conditions are likely to affect the extent to which these motivations enter into the picture.

Observational, anecdotal, and descriptive information (Carpenter, 1964; Hebb & Thompson, 1954; Hornstein, 1976) also suggest that animals can be highly responsive to the need of members of their own species, and even to humans. Monkeys scratch one another's backs. Although this action is often reciprocal and is also rewarded when the scratching monkey finds lice, which monkeys eat, in the other animal's fur, it is clearly prosocial behavior. Howler monkeys have been noted to help their young move across spaces difficult for the young to cross, to adopt orphans whose mothers had been killed or lost, and to come to the defense of members of their group who are attacked. One of a pair of gorillas in captivity has been observed cleaning and/or soothing the other's wounds, this following the observation of the other doing this for himself at a previous time. Porpoises apparently surround a pregnant female to protect her from assault, possibly sexual, by aroused males. Wilson (1975) reviewed many examples of seemingly altruistic behavior in animals and noted that members of various species will endanger themselves to save others—usually their offspring or relatives. Consider females of some bird species. Ducks and partridges feign injury when a predator approaches and act as if they were hurt and therefore easy to capture. They apparently try to entice the predator away from their off-spring in their nest. Once they are some distance from the nest they attempt to escape, sometimes successfully, other times not. Among chimpanzees, according to Wilson, the hunters share with other animals who beg food and communicate the location of food to others or directly lead them to it.

Some of the above animal behaviors are probably genetically controlled in a relatively direct fashion. Certainly, self sacrificial behavior is genetically controlled in the social insects (Campbell, 1975). However, we have as yet no experimental evidence or sufficiently methodically conducted observations to demonstrate the nature of genetic control over self sacrificial behaviors that have been observed in animals, or the manner in which genetic influence, experience, and learning jointly effect such behaviors. As I noted earlier, it is difficult to establish that certain behaviors are genetically controlled; however, it is not impossible. There is acceptable evidence, for example, that certain forms of aggressive behavior among animals (Lorenz, 1967), as well as variations in aggressiveness among different strains of mice or different types of dogs, are genetic in origin (Wiggins *et al.,* 1976).

With regard to some of the animal behaviors that were observed, it seems justified to regard them as not maintained by immediate, direct, external reinforcement. Certainly, material reinforcement has often been absent. The available evidence suggests that empathic responsiveness might be a motivator of response to another animal's distress. It is interesting that both experimental studies and observations suggest that positive relatedness enhances prosocial behavior. For example, Yerkes and Yerkes (1935), who observed sharing of food among monkeys, noted that sharing depends on the nature of the relationship between donor and recipient. "Ordinarily there must exist friendly relationship, sympathy, . . . as a condition of food sharing. Between antagonistic individuals we have never seen the sharing of foods or other prized and strongly desired possessions [p. 1024]." Hornstein (1976) views the evidence as suggesting that among animals, as among man, a bond of "we" has to exist, an experience of the other organism as part of one's in-group, in order for a positive response to occur. At any rate, as humans do, so animals also respond differentially to other members of their species as a function of prior experience with them.

The animal literature strongly suggests that, whatever the extent to which organisms possess the genetic potential to learn to respond prosocially to other organisms, the most useful and reasonable approach is to explore the social origins of prosocial reactivity, individual differences as the consequence of opportunities for learning, and the determination of prosocial behavior by the individual characteristics that developed and the social conditions that exist.

Personality, the Situation, and the Determination of Prosocial Behavior

chapter 2

How are social behavior in general and prosocial behavior in particular determined? Psychologists have long believed that a person's personality in combination with the surrounding conditions determine that person's behavior. However, an adequate conceptual model of how the two combine is still lacking. One purpose of this chapter is to attempt to provide such a model.

Two basic concepts that psychologists traditionally used in designating individual differences are the concepts of *trait* and *motive. Trait* refers to distinguishable and relatively enduring ways in which individuals differ. Traits are descriptive; a person might be more or less helpful, more or less aggressive. These characteristics are inferred from behavior. *Motive* refers to a goal or end state that is valued by a person. Certain conditions in the environment (external or internal) of the person may activate a motive. A motivated state might be inferred from a heightened level of arousal or activation and/or from behavior that is goal-directed.

Each of these two concepts implies consistency, similarity in behavior over time and across situations. The assumption of consistency has been one of the cornerstone assumptions in traditional theorizing about personality. How can we talk about individual differences or hope to predict behavior if we cannot point to stable, enduring characteristics of people?

However, even the most avid promoter of trait theory and an ideographic approach to personality, Gordon Allport (1961), clearly recognized the limitations on consistency in behavior. He believed that several important sources of inconsistency exist. Personality traits may contradict one another; the environment constantly changes, activating one trait, then another; usually several traits act together. Considering motives as the units of analysis, every motive is relevant to and active under a specific set of conditions, so that similarity in behavior would only be expected under those conditions. Furthermore, an important characteristic of normal, healthy individuals is their adaptability to their environment. People who cannot adapt themselves to circumstances in a reasonable fashion are usually regarded as maladjusted. Thus, the degree to which we can expect consistency, in the sense of similar behavior across varied circumstances, has to be limited.

The justification for assuming consistency in behavior has been repeatedly questioned (see Bem & Allen, 1974). Walter Mischel (1968, 1969) reviewed evidence that led him to conclude that consistency is in the eye of the beholder, that consistency is not real but is illusory. We are motivated to believe that the world around us is predictable, so we perceive our own behavior and that of others as consistent. Mischel concluded that a fair degree of consistency does exist in cognitive functioning. People's performances on varied intellectual and cognitive tasks tend to be reasonably highly correlated with each other. But consistency in interpersonal and social behavior is low. Mischel points out that correlations in behavior under different circumstances, or between personality test scores and behavior, seem to reach a maximum of about .30. Greater consistency in behavior is found only when the situations in which behavior is tested are highly similar. But when the characteristics of situations vary, behavioral similarity declines. Mischel's reasoning clearly implies that a person who is helpful at one time need not be expected to be helpful another time.

As I have said, it has long been assumed that behavior is a function of the situation, the person, and the interaction between the two. A situation may be highly forceful and may powerfully activate the need for survival, the need to avoid ostracism, or some other important need or goal that most people share, at least in a particular culture. If the satisfaction of the need demands particular behaviors, such a situation may lead most people to behave in the same way. However, most situations do not exert such powerful influences. Bowers (1973) reviewed experiments that examined how situations and personality interact in affecting behavior. He found that the interaction effects usually accounted for more of the variance than either the situation alone or personality alone. He also suggested that consistency is created when people seek out or shape situations. In one study, for example, Kelley and Stahlesky (1970) found that some subjects who believed people in general to be competitive rather than cooperative behaved competitively from the start in a game (a prisoner's dilemma game). Their behavior resulted in competitive reactions by their partners. By their own behavior they apparently brought about the competitive behavior they expected. A substantial body of research, which is reviewed later (Chapter 8), shows reciprocity in human interactions; by what we do, we shape others' reactions to us.

Although the concept of interaction has a long history (Ekehammer, 1974), most personality research has related a single measure of some personal characteristic to behavior; situation–personality interactions have rarely been tested. The writing of Mischel (1968, 1969, 1973) and of Jones and Nisbett (1971), who also questioned consistency, gave rise to controversy and renewed vigorous interest in an interactionist approach. Ekehammer points out that classical approaches to interactionism tend to be more theoretical than current approaches; the current "movement" involves collecting empirical evidence. However, the still limited research on interaction has been primarily demonstrative, in that the influence of some personality characteristic and of some situation on behavior have been jointly considered, without specification of the classes of personality characteristics and situations important in determining particular types of behavior. Moreover, most studies explored the influence of a single personality characteristic in conjunction with some situational variation. We need to consider the joint influence of a variety of personality characteristics in interaction with situations if we are to improve our understanding of how behavior is determined and our ability to predict it.

The underlying assumption in the reasoning that follows is that consistency in behavior is limited. Most behavior is determined in a complex manner. Varied personality characteristics, their combination, and their activation by characteristics of the situation all determine whether a person behaves prosocially in a specific instance. With the proper specification of the most important personality characteristics, relevant situational influences, and their manner of interaction, reasonably accurate predictions about behavior in specific settings becomes possible.

I do *not* mean to suggest that consistency in behavior is nonexistent. Recent findings (that will be reviewed later) provide evidence of both consistency and stability (e.g., consistency over time) in prosocial behavior (Chapter 5; Volume 2; see also Mussen & Eisenberg-Berg, 1977 and Rushton, 1976). Block (1977) suggested that although consistency in behavior across laboratory situations has been limited, with other data sources both consistency and stability have been found. Longitudinal research reported by Block showed a moderate to high degree of stability in dependence and other personal characteristics. These characteristics were evaluated by extensive observations of interaction with peers in childhood and by in-depth interviews and other means of data collection dealing with the same individuals in adolescence and in young adulthood. An important aspect of such research is the collection of extensive samples of data, not just a few instances of behavior. In laboratory research investigators usually expose participants to circumstances that, in the investigators' view, have certain properties and would instigate particular kinds of behavior. However, the subject's perceptions of the situation are rarely determined; they are only deduced from the subject's behavior. Consequently, apparent inconsistency in behavior across several situations may result from differences in what the situations mean to the experimenters and to the subjects. Moreover, most situations have varied elements and make varied demands on people, even if some similarity in the components of different situations can be identified. All aspects of a situation are relevant to prosocial behavior. When many samples of behavior are taken, the influence of certain personality characteristics, mainly motivational, may become apparent. Across many situations additional determinants may, in a sense, average out, and the influence of important motives will gain expression. This also implies that people are consistent primarily in domains of activity that are important to them (Bem & Allen, 1974; Staub, 1979).

The theoretical model schematically presented later in this chapter specifies personality characteristics that are important in affecting prosocial behavior and the nature of personality–situation interaction. I have progressively elaborated this model in other writings (Staub, 1974a, 1976a, 1978a, 1979; Staub & Feinberg, 1978). Some aspects of this model are relevant to the determination of any kind of social behavior, and others are specific to prosocial behavior. The determination of prosocial behavior, or "moral behavior" in general, can be understood, in part, by understanding the manner in which social behavior is determined. However, prosocial and moral behavior also have unique aspects and unique determinants. The model will only be applied to the interpretation of the research reviewed in later chapters when the nature of the research design and/or findings make it clearly relevant. On the whole, the research will be examined inductively, and generalizations will be derived from the findings. The model provides a framework for viewing research on the determinants of prosocial behavior, but its major purpose is to guide future research.

Why People Behave Prosocially

Briefly, I shall first describe the major classes of motivators of prosocial behavior that have been proposed. The concepts presented here are elaborated in later chapters.

Self-gain

I have already implied that one reason for prosocial behavior is a person's expectation of gain or avoidance of loss. Often the action is the result of acquiescence to external pressures. Social norms are one important kind of external influence. Norms are expectations that people will behave in certain ways. They are generally-held rules that tell a person what behavior is expected in various situations, based on agreement or consensus among members of a group (Staub, 1972a; Thibaut & Kelley, 1959). People adhere to social norms presumably in order to be regarded as members of the group in good standing, to gain praise and positive recognition, and to avoid disapproval, ostracism, and other negative consequences.

Generalized expectations about behavior are derived from societal values. These values are statements of ideals; social norms specify the behavior necessary to carry out these ideals. Values have been defined as prescriptive or proscriptive beliefs (Rokeach, 1973) or as beliefs "upon which a man acts by preference [Allport, 1961, p. 454]." Values specify conditions or states of affairs that are desirable or undesirable. In specific instances a person may have to derive the socially appropriate or "right" behavior from societal values and from social norms, which are guidelines that have to be applied to the specific instance. Various kinds of competence, including intellectual competence, may contribute to the capacity to construct specific rules from more general ones. Experience with helping situations that leads people to construct specific rules of action makes new occasions for helping easier to deal with, since there are already available rules and/or the past experience can help people in constructing better ones.

Considerations of self-interest guide people not only to adhere to social values and norms, but also to benefit others in the hope of being rewarded. There is an interesting confluence here of possibly quite basic human characteristics and social norms. First, when we benefit other people, usually (but not always) we generate positive feelings toward ourselves, and because the others like us they will presumably be more likely to engage in behavior to benefit us. Second, there are strong social norms that prescribe reciprocity in behavior, so people are also likely to return benefits because they are expected to do so. These and other processes of social exchange are considered in great detail in later chapters.

Personal Values and Norms

In the course of socialization, growth, and development, most people accept some societal values and norms as their own and/or construct their own values and norms. Subsequently these values and norms guide their behavior. A personal norm is a person's expectation that he will engage in certain kinds of behavior, presumably derived from personal values and beliefs. Adherence to personal norms is motivated by self-reactions: positive self-evaluation—contributing to a positive self-image—and other forms of self-reward and the generation of positive emotions as a result of acting according to the norm; and negative self-evaluation, self-punishment, and the generation of negative emotions, including guilt, upon deviating from the norm.

There are many specific values and related norms, both social and personal, that seem relevant to prosocial behavior. They include norms that prescribe help for other people as well as values and norms related to maintaining justice, equity, and reciprocity. Different value orientations apparently exist (Hoffman, 1970b; Staub, 1974a, 1976a); there are different configurations of values and related norms, which have different implications for prosocial behavior. We may distinguish between a value orientation characterized by concern for other people's welfare and another one characterized by concern for doing what is right. The former may lead people to focus on the welfare of others and to minimize their distress and enhance their well-being. The latter implies concern about adherence to norms and a focus on discharging one's duty. Although both value orientations may give rise to a sense of obligation, in one case the obligation is to other people, in the other it is to norms and rules. These two value orientations do not exhaust the possibilities; others, including less prosocial ones, are certain to exist. Each of Kohlberg's (1969, 1976) stages of moral development can be regarded as a different value orientation—as values and norms organized around a different guiding principle.

Empathy and Identification with Other People

The vicarious experience of another person's emotions, that is, the experience of some emotion because another person experiences it, has been regarded as a motivator of prosocial behavior. Either experiencing or anticipating another's distress can motivate action aimed at eliminating the distress. Anticipating another person's positive emotions can lead to behavior that will promote their welfare.

Many writers (Schantz, 1975) consider role taking to be identical with empathy. Affective role taking refers to the capacity to perceive the feelings of others and the probable or actual consequences of events on others' feelings. However, a person's having the capacity to take others' roles does not guarantee that he will take another's role in a specific instance. Neither does it guarantee that, having taken another's role and having understood the other person's feelings, the role taker will experience parallel feelings. Role taking may be a precondition for but not a guarantee of experiencing empathy or activating prosocial values or goals. Accurately perceiving and/or understanding another's feelings of distress or joy does not exclude the possibility that the observer will experience the opposite emotion, for example, experience joy in another's suffering. Or does it? There are varied levels of role taking. A person may understand that another suffers, may enter into it and appreciate the feelings of the other person, may even have an understanding of the elaborate thoughts and feelings involved. As role taking becomes more elaborate the cognitive representations of another's condition may give rise to parallel emotions. But whether this is so and the extent to which such in-depth role taking can give rise to sadistic pleasure are unknown.

It is generally assumed that people have different capacities and different tendencies to respond empathically under activating conditions. How do these qualities develop, and how are they "stored"? It has been postulated that empathy may develop out of primitive emotional reactions that are present at an early age (Simner, 1971), and out of conditioning experiences of varied kinds (Aronfreed, 1976) and their cognitive elaborations (Hoffman, 1975a, 1976). Also, individual differences in beliefs, values, and related norms may determine whether people will react empathically. For example, a value orientation that emphasizes concern with other people's welfare may lead to interpretations of others' distress and needs that arouse empathic emotional reactions. The distinction that has been traditionally maintained between empathy and values is probably unjustified—at least it has been too strongly drawn. Particular values and value orientations are likely to form a cognitive network; these interrelated cognitions are applied to the interpretation of the world. The current cognitive theories of emotion (Arnold, 1960; Lazarus, 1966; Leventhal, 1974; Schachter & Singer, 1962) certainly imply that such interpretations both give rise to emotions and determine the nature of the emotions. Unfortunately, research on empathy has been limited, in amount and kind, because of the difficulty of measuring empathic reactions. (The concurrent evaluation of physiological reactions and subjective emotional experience is the most adequate but least frequently used measure of empathy.) It is therefore difficult to demonstrate that certain conditions give rise to empathy. No one has attempted to evaluate values and empathic capacity independently, to establish a relationship between them, and to elucidate the manner in which each affects behavior.

Empathy implies a certain kind of identification with other people. The extent to which various conditions lead to identification without the experience of empathy is of interest. Identification with other persons implies the adoption of their goals and desires—to a degree as if the goals were one's own—and subsequent attempts to fulfill these goals. Such a conception, variants of which have been proposed by Hornstein (1976) and Reykowski (1975), raises fundamental questions about the relationship between self and others, and the varied bonds that can exist (see Chapters 6, 7).

A Theoretical Model for Predicting Prosocial Behavior

Personal Goals and the Activating Potential of Situations

Psychologists have long emphasized motivational constructs as the keys to understanding the causes of behavior and predicting behavior. The names of the constructs have varied: *Drive, need, reinforcement, reward value,* and other terms have been used. The purported properties of these constructs have also varied. A primary characteristic of human behavior is its purposefulness. I assume that personal motives or goals—the construct I shall use to denote motivation—direct behavior. I am also assuming that many other personality characteristics that need to be considered are mainly important in determining whether personal goals are activated and/or their satisfaction pursued. The word *goal* implies a preference for certain outcomes or end states or an aversion to certain outcomes. It also implies a striving toward or away from these outcomes. The word *personal* implies a special individual character. Nonetheless, there is likely to be enough similarity among goals of different individuals for people to be grouped on the basis of communality in goals. Mischel (1973; Mischel & Mischel, 1976) argued that people are highly idiosyncratic in the outcomes they value. However, for each individual there is probably a range of similarly valued outcomes. Minimally, a person who values diminishing others' physical pain is likely to hold this value for varied sources of pain. Moreover, certain classes of outcomes are valued to some degree by many, perhaps even by most, who live in the same culture: positive evaluation and approval rather than negative evaluation and disapproval (the latter might be regarded as a negative goal, something to be avoided), physical safety, the enhancing of material gain, and so on.

Prosocial values, norms, and beliefs and the tendency to react empathically to others' needs increase the value or desirability of a related set of outcomes and thus contribute to a prosocial goal. Depending on the nature of the values, the extent to which empathy is involved, and so on, the specific character of the goal may differ. For some people the desired outcome might be to improve the welfare of others, and for other people acting in a helpful manner might itself be the desired outcome. Variation in the nature of personal goals is likely to be found in most domains, not only in prosocial ones. Some individuals characterized by a strong achievement goal may want to do the best job they can when the goal is activated, whereas others may want to experience success. These and other achievement goals may primarily gain expression in hard work and in attempts to do well in varied activities.

Most personal goals are likely to have an associated network of cognitions. It is of these cognitions, in a sense, that the goal consists. A person who regards helping others as a personal goal might evaluate other people positively and might think of others' welfare as something desirable and good, of others' distress as bad. Consequently, that person would want to help another in distress. Thus, a cognitive network refers to a way of thinking, a set of cognitions related to a goal. Given the existence of such a cognitive network, as I noted, contemporary cognitive theories of emotion suggest how it might lead to emotional arousal that motivates action. It is also possible, however, to want very much to do something without having a variety of thoughts related to that activity or its outcome. That is, the inclination to reach a goal can be primarily emotional.

Two properties of personal goals, the desirability of (or aversion to) certain outcomes, and a set of cognitions that is usually associated with them, have been noted. A third property may be the arousal of tension upon activation of the goal. This tension continues to exist until the goal has been reached or some other resolution of the goal has occurred. One such resolution may be the deactivation or abandonment of a desired outcome. The notion that tension is aroused and maintained in conjunction with goal activation was proposed by Lewin (1938; Deutsch, 1968) and has been currently extended by Horrstein (1976) to the realm of prosocial behavior. The primary function here of this construct is to represent a motivational force that maintains goal-directed behavior and has certain other behavioral manifestations, such as an increase in the intensity and/or persistence of behavior as a desired goal is approached. The limited evidence that is available about tension systems and their properties supports the concept. An example is the well-known Zeigarnick (1927) effect. Consistent with Lewinian assumptions, Zeigarnick found that interrupted tasks are remembered better than completed ones. Tasks that are interrupted nearer their completion—nearer to reaching the outcome—are remembered better than tasks interrupted further from completion (Deutsch, 1968). The latter finding provides support for another Lewinian concept, that of a goal gradient.

It is important, I think, that even if certain people have similar goals, the *range of applicability* of their goals can vary. For example, some people may apply their concern about others' welfare only when physical need is involved. Others may apply such concern only to people of certain kinds, perhaps people whom they think of as similar to themselves, or coming from the same ethnic or racial background. The range of applicability may be narrow or it may be broad. Situational influences may, moreover, widen or narrow the range. We have to develop measurement devices that will determine not only the existence and intensity of various personal goals but also the specific ranges in which they are applicable (Staub, 1979).

Earlier I discussed the difference between motives (or goals) and traits. Let us say that for one person a strong personal goal is to defend himself from physical or verbal attack by other people. This goal might be served by different types of action. Some people may defend themselves by avoiding all kinds of situations in which they might be attacked. Others might counterattack on the slightest provocation in order to diminish the likelihood of further attack (Staub, 1971c).

People may follow habitual strategies to satisfy their goals: habitual modes of dealing with existing circumstances; habitually seeking out or creating particular circumstances in which their goals can be satisfied; and perhaps dealing with these circumstances in habitual ways. However, people are frequently able to change their plans or strategies for action when their habitual modes of satisfying their goals do not work. I am suggesting that goals are more basic than habitual behavior patterns. The trait concept, as usually employed, refers to persistent characteristics of individuals. With regard to consistency in behavior, it does not distinguish between habitual behavior and motivation for certain outcomes as the basis for persistence. This is a source of confusion.

It is important to distinguish between the goal or desired end state, and habitual ways of attempting to reach the goal. Personal goals and habitual modes of behaving are not always easy to distinguish, however. Bem and Allen (1974) found that people are capable of accurately reporting how consistent they are in categories of behavior such as conscientiousness and friendliness. Self-reports of consistency in these realms were significantly related to several indices of relevant behavior. This was found even though the meanings of conscientiousness or friendliness were largely defined by the experimenters. Correlations with behavior might have improved had the range of applicability of these "traits" been defined by the subjects. Bem and Allen thought of these behaviors as representing traits, but the possibility clearly exists that they actually tapped goals. Some people were conscientious in academic work, whereas others were conscientious in keeping order in their living quarters, but few were conscientious in both areas. These findings may be easily understood as the result of different goals, the degree to which subjects valued either academic success or order in their surroundings.

In a particular situation an important determinant of a person's behavior is the kind of goals the situation activates. The goals activated are determined by the nature of the situation (the goals the situation may potentially activate) and the nature and characteristics of the persons in that situation (the kind of personal goals they possess). A particular situation may *potentially* activate both the goal of helping a person in need and a person's need for achievement and the desire to perform well on some task. One person might have a strong prosocial goal and a weak achievement goal, and another might have a strong achievement goal and a weak prosocial goal. Assuming that the activating potential of the situation is about equal for these two goals, these two people will behave quite differently. A third person may have equally strong prosocial and achievement goals, thus resulting in goal conflict. However, an achievement goal may support and intensify the prosocial goal rather than create a conflict. This in fact happened in an experiment conducted by Feinberg (1977), which was the first attempt to test elements of this model. In Feinberg's study, people characterized by a strong achievement goal, rather than primarily focusing their attention on a task, made more of an effort to help others in psychological distress than did people characterized by a weak achievement goal. Clearly, several goals that are activated can support one another rather than give rise to conflict.

An illustration of how personal goals affect helping behavior and how personality and the situation must interact for help to occur is provided by the retrospective analysis of an extreme form of helpful behavior (Staub & Feinberg, 1978). This example draws on a report by London (1970). He conducted extensive interviews with "rescuers," people who were involved in an underground system set up to save the lives of Jews and other persecuted individuals in Nazi Germany. London concluded that the rescuers possessed three characteristics: a strong conscious identification with moral parents, adventurousness, and a sense of marginality in relation to the community. Presumably, strong moral identification led to personal values promoting helping behavior, thus to the motivation to help. The costs of helping in this situation were potentially extremely high; if the rescuers were discovered by Nazi authorities, the loss of life was probable and loss of liberty was certain. A sense of adventurousness, gaining satisfaction from dangerous activities and perceiving them as exciting—which apparently led these individuals to participate in other dangerous activities—seems important. Adventurousness might have enhanced the likelihood of acting on prosocial goals (see below) and might also have been an additional goal that could be satisfied by helping. The third characteristic, a sense of marginality, might have kept rescuers from accepting the definition of their environment of the persecution of Jews and others, a definition that would have minimized the perception of the need or at least the justification for involvement.

Goal Conflict and Conflict Resolution

Does the concept of a prosocial goal have any advantage over the independent consideration of the varied motivators discussed earlier—values, empathy, and so on? After all, we still have to recognize the varied elements that enter into a prosocial goal, because they are likely to make different outcomes desirable and, having different networks of associated cognitions, they affect the nature of the motivation to seek these outcomes. Thus, we need to think in terms of a "family" of prosocial goals. However, the present conceptualization explicitly recognizes that prosocial behavior has to be understood in the context of social behavior in general. Usually circumstances activate varied personal goals. Other goals may either add to or diminish the influence of prosocial goals. Because we need to consider the combined influences of varied motives if we are to understand and predict social behavior in general and prosocial behavior in particular, it is desirable to use a motivational construct that is applicable to varied motives.

The study of conflicts among goals that are activated in specific situations has been surprisingly neglected. Although psychoanalytically oriented writers, and Dollard and Miller (1950) when translating psychoanalytic concepts into a behavioral framework, recognized the importance of goal conflict, they stress the role of conflict between approach and avoidance tendencies toward a *single goal*. Usually multiple goals are activated by circumstances. The manner in which one or another comes to predominate, and the extent to which they mutually inhibit one another, need to be considered.

The relative importance of a specific personal goal varies over time and as a function of the circumstances affecting a person. For example, during the academic year students may rank-order the importance of their personal goals quite differently than they would during summer or Christmas vacation. Furthermore, some degree of prior activation of a personal goal, in a different situation, may enhance its importance and increase the likelihood of its being activated in a new situation. Recent satisfaction of some goals may reduce their influence on a person's behavior and may affect their ranking in that person's hierarchy of goals; this may not be true of other goals. As with other motivational constructs, an important issue is to what extent measures of personal goals under "neutral" conditions (when they are not activated) enable us to predict behavior when the goal is activated. Taking into account the kinds of variations in the importance of personal goals that I have already noted would probably improve the accuracy of prediction.

To make accurate predictions we have to measure (a) the intensity and/or relative importance of personal goals and (b) the activating potential of situations for personal goals. We also need some conception of conflict resolution if we are to predict behavior when several conflicting goals are activated in the same situation. The relative strength of an activated personal goal will be a function of the intensity or importance of the personal goal relative to other goals and of the intensity or strength of the activating potential of the situation for the various goals.

Given activating potentials identical in strength, the behavior that is performed may be the one that serves the satisfaction of the strongest personal goal. Usually, however, the strengths of activating forces vary. There is little empirical evidence to guide us in determining how the strength of an activating potential and the strength of a personal goal jointly determine the intensity of the activated goal. We may, by analogy from expectancy-value theories, make tentative assumption that the intensity of an activated goal will be a function of the multiplicative relationship between the intensity of the personal goal and the intensity of the activating potential (see also Lewin, 1938; Deutsch, 1968). Thus, the greatest product that results from this multiplication may predict which personal goal will direct behavior. When the activated strengths of two or more goals are nearly equal, however, action toward any goal may be inhibited and/or several processes may enter into conflict resolution. Justification processes may lead to a reevaluation of the activating potential of the situation (e.g., the degree of need for help) or of the applicability of the personal goal to the situation (e.g., "I have no particular obligation to help this person because of his race or because of his responsibility for his problems"), or to other cognitive changes. These processes are discussed in detail in subsequent chapters. Conflict resolution may also occur early, by a different process: As one goal is activated, the activation of the other is suppressed by various attentional, perceptual, and cognitive processes. The foregoing discussion of the influence of activated goals and of conflict resolution can also be extended to the resolution of conflict between a positive and a negative goal. For example, the desire to help someone may conflict with the desire to protect oneself from danger, as in the case of a fire.

The Measurement of Goals and Activating Potentials

To predict prosocial behavior and evaluate the proposed model, we have to develop ways to measure personal goals and the activating potentials of situations. Three approaches may be used to measure personal goals. First, as in Rokeach's (1973) measure of the hierarchy of values, people may simply be asked to *rank-order their goals*. Values themselves can be used, in fact, as a measure of the hierarchy of personal goals, since values imply the desirability of certain end states or outcomes, and thus are similar to goals. As one would expect with goals, values are relatively stable. The reliability (test–retest) of rank-ordering values on Rokeach's measure (where a subject rank-orders each of 18 values relative to all the others) was about .73 with a 3- to 7-week interval, and .63 with a 1½-year interval. Obviously, one would expect some but not extreme stability, since values and goals may change over time and with the circumstances of testing. The less time elapsed between the measurement of the hierarchy of goals and the evaluation of the influence of some goals on behavior, the greater may be the accuracy of prediction. A limitation of this method is that the ranking of personal goals (or values) provides only some overall, relative information about them. To give helpfulness a high rank says little about the exact nature of the outcomes that are important to a person. It also says little about the range of applicability of outcomes.

A second approach would be *to measure the network of cognitions* related to particular personal goals. Knowing the nature and extensiveness of the network may lead to better predictions about whether and when goals will be activated.

Three dimensions of thought (and feeling) seem important here: (*a*) a positive orientation toward other human beings based on positive evaluation of them and positive feelings about them; (*b*) concern about the welfare of other human beings; and (*c*) a sense of personal responsibility for others' welfare. The importance of the last two components is suggested by findings of research that explored situational influences on helping, and research that examined personality correlates of helping behavior. Both kinds of research are thoroughly reviewed in subsequent chapters.

The first component is likely to be important, but it has been generally neglected in research and theory (Staub, 1975a, 1976b). In one study Wrightsman (1966) found that the subjects' evaluation of human nature was related to their trust and trustworthiness in a laboratory game. Christie's test of Machiavellian orientation has many items testing beliefs about human nature and human beings. Scores on this test were found to be associated with prosocial behavior (Staub, 1974a). A test Midlarz (1973) developed to measure trust also measured this basic orientation toward others, that is, the extent of positive regard for others. Scores on this test were significantly related to the acceptance of another's need as real when there were reasons to question it, and to the resulting helping behavior. These three dimensions may define a prosocial goal of a relatively broad range of applicability.

I have implied in the preceeding discussion that a family of personal goals of a particular kind may exist. However, the primary members of the family may be few. In the case of prosocial goals, two types of value orientations may give rise to two primary prosocial goals, and even these two can frequently be related to each other, even occur together. The value orientation that I discussed above emphasizes concern about the welfare of other human beings. Another value orientation focuses on duty and obligation toward other people, but these are based on societal rules, religious laws, or abstract moral principles that prescribe positive behavior rather than on concern about persons to be helped (see Volume 2; Hoffman, 1970b; Staub, 1979). The prosocial goal that this value orientation gives rise to is likely to focus on somewhat different outcomes and have somewhat different affective elements associated with it than the one discussed above.

A third approach to measuring prosocial goals is *to evaluate the degree to which they have been aroused* under activating conditions. We should evaluate the cognitive–emotional consequences of activating conditions that participants are exposed to in experimental studies. Do they arouse thoughts and feelings related to others' welfare, values and norms that would guide relevant behavior, and the desire to pursue outcomes related to others' welfare? By using pairs of identical experimental conditions and measuring the cognitive–emotional effects of treatments in one group and the behavioral effects in a separate group the cognitive–emotional and behavioral effects could be compared.

To make accurate predictions about behavior from personal goals, the activating potential of situations also has to be evaluated. Frederiksen (1972) suggested that we need a "systematic way of conceptualizing the domain of situations and situational variables before we can make rapid progress in studying the role of situations in determining behavior [p. 115]." Others have noted that we need to consider the meaning and significance of situations for people (Mischel, 1976). The present model clearly indicates the interrelatedness of situational and personal characteristics.

Activating potential is an element of the situation, but an element that is perceived and reacted to by persons.

How does one determine whether a situation has an activating potential for a prosocial goal, or for an achievement goal, or for some other goal? One way may be to make up situations that activate either specific goals or combinations of specific goals that conflict with or support one another, and ask other people to evaluate these situations. Do they also think that certain goals are activated, that certain types of actions are reasonable or desirable or preferable in these situations? Even better, we may expose people to these situations and see how they behave.

However, according to this theoretical model, neither would provide very sensitive information. A situation that potentially activates a certain goal is likely to activate that goal only in people who possess the goal. Thus, circumstances that provide the opportunity for achievement would activate the goal to achieve in different people only to the extent that the goal is important for them. Accordingly, it seems necessary to consider personal goals and the activating potential of the situations for them in relation to each other and thus to validate measures of each, at least partly, in relation to each other (see Footnote 1 on page 54). Thus, situations that are perceived as relevant to certain outcomes and goals and/or elicit certain kinds of behavior should do so to a greater degree in people who possess those goals to a greater degree—all other things equal (such as goal conflicts and the existence of other personality characteristics that affect behavior, which will be discussed later). We may progressively specify dimensions of stimulus situations that are relevant to the activation of various goals, and we may think of particular situations in terms of their location along those dimensions. The degree of another's distress or need for help is an obvious dimension in terms of its relevance to the activation of a prosocial goal.

Research on the manner in which people perceive others and the dimensions they employ in describing other people shows that implicit personality theories influence the perception of other people (Schneider, 1973). Personal needs of subjects (such as nurturance, achievement, and endurance) as measured by the Edwards Personal Preference Schedule were found to be significantly related to the dimensions along which the subjects perceived and/or described other people (Cantor, 1976). Cantor developed rules of inference for evaluating the correspondence between personal needs and the perceptual dimensions that people employed in describing others, on the basis of rules that were spontaneously used by a group of clinicians in attempting to match needs and perceptual dimensions. The accuracy achieved in matching personal needs and perceptual dimensions was substantially greater by college freshmen who were instructed to use these rules, in comparison to others who received only instructions to match. Two rules were used: "Rule 1: If a person places a strong positive value on some characteristic in other people, he or she is likely to have a need corresponding to (similar to) that characteristic. Rule 2: People appraise others in terms of whether those others will be receptive to them and will fulfill their needs [Cantor, 1976, p. 523]." As needs influence how others are perceived, so they are likely to influence how elements of situations other than people are perceived. Principles that specify how needs lead to varied perceptions—or "rules of correspondence" —are likely to improve our ability to identify how personal goals lead to activation.

Psychologists are just beginning to attend to the extremely important problem of the measurement of situations. Although there has been a great deal of interest in an interactionist view, theories about the aspects of individuals and of situations that are particularly important to consider, although not absent (see Ekehammer, 1974 and Mischel, 1973), have been minimal. Using concepts similar to those suggested by Murray (1938), who emphasized needs, and Rotter (1954), who emphasized the value of outcomes, as well as ideas in some ways like those of Lewin (1948), the present conception proposed basic dimensions along which personality and situations interact. A number of writers have suggested that person measures and situation measures should be in the same units (Murray, 1938; Rotter, 1954). The concepts of personal goal and goal-activating potential of a situation are consistent with this view.[1] They imply a relational classification of situations, a classification in relation to individual differences in the relevance of goals. Comparable units of measurement for personal goals and activation potentials can thus be specified.

Other Personality Influences on Goal Activation and Behavior

Perceptual Tendencies

What perceptual tendencies contribute to the activation of prosocial goals? The capacity for role taking, which was discussed earlier, may be an important one. Sometimes another person's need is so obvious that no special skill or sensitivity is needed to perceive it. This is usually the case in emergency studies when a person is faced with another's strong physical distress. At other times the need is subtly expressed, and a well-developed

---

[1] In the preceding discussion, I suggested not only a relational *classification* of situations, but also a relational *measurement* of personal goals and activating potentials. This makes them nonindependent predictors of behavior. Though in reality they are intertwined, it may be advantageous to separate them for measurement, or to measure them both independently and in relation to each other. For a further discussion of measurement, see Staub, 1979.

role-taking capacity is needed to perceive it, particularly to perceive it accurately. Role taking affects not only perception but also the manner in which what is perceived is then processed. Role taking varies in kind (perceptual, communicative, affective) and not all kinds are, of course, equally involved in the activation of prosocial goals.

The likelihood that a person will take another's role might itself be increased by prosocial values or cognitions that increase sensitivity to others' welfare. Providing people with different perceptual orientations— instructing them to observe another person and imagine what an experience would be like for that other person, telling them to imagine what it would be like if they themselves were to have that experience (imagine self), or telling them just to watch the other person—results in different degrees of physiological reaction, emotional experience, and/or behavior (Stotland, 1969; Aderman & Berkowitz, 1970; Aderman *et al.*, 1974; Chapter 4). Prosocial values and empathic capacity may, in everyday life, lead to such differences in perceptual orientation. That is, values, empathy, and role taking are likely to be related to one another. There are, in fact, research findings that show that a positive relationship exists between certain types of role-taking capacities of persons and their level of moral reasoning (see Volume 2).

Another relevant perceptual–cognitive tendency is the speed with which one can make judgments about events. People seem to vary in this (Denner, 1968). If a person suspends judgment about the meaning of events, the opportunity for taking action may pass.

Competence

Competence is probably a crucial determinant of whether a person will take action to attain a personal goal. A lack of the subjective experience of competence may also inhibit the activation of personal goals.

Competence refers to a class of related variables, in particular the belief in one's ability to influence events, to bring about desired outcomes —a notion similar to the locus-of-control concept proposed by Rotter (1966; see also Lefcourt, 1979). Belief in one's ability to influence events and bring about desired outcomes seems important in leading people to initiate action and actively pursue goals, except when the required action is easy and straightforward.

The possession of plans or strategies for action in various situations and the capacity to generate plans seem to be other important aspects of competence (Mischel, 1973). When the behavior that is required is completely clear, specified by the need or the existing circumstances, such competence may not be needed. However, the kind of action that would be helpful is frequently unclear, and the ability to generate plans is therefore needed. Schwartz (1970b, 1977) suggested that awareness of the possible consequences of one's behavior for other people is an important determinant, in combination with other characteristics, of helping behavior. Awareness of consequences may be the result of joint variation in role taking, in a person's sense of his ability to exert influence over events, and in the capacity to generate plans. It is the combination of these characteristics that would lead people to consider the consequences of their behavior and to realize and appreciate its potential beneficial consequences.

Another aspect of competence is the possession of behavioral skills and/or the belief that one possesses the skills needed for prosocial action on a particular occasion. One has to swim in order to pull someone out of a raging river. One has to have certain interpersonal skills and/or the belief that one possesses them in order to attempt to and actually help persons distressed about some aspect of their lives.

Competence thus contributes to a person's expectations of success in reaching a desired outcome (Rotter, 1954; Mischel, 1966), which may determine whether that person will take action to reach that outcome. In essence, competence contributes to a feeling of control. The feeling of control over aversive events increases tolerance for them and diminishes both the physiological arousal they produce and their negative effects on task performance (Glass & Singer, 1972; Staub et al., 1971; Staub & Kellett, 1972). Lack of control produces a sense of helplessness (and/or lack of hope), which reduces the likelihood that subsequent attempts to take action and exert influence will be made (Lefcourt, 1973, 1979; Seligmen, 1975). Lack of competence, subjective or objective, may not only diminish attempts to reach the outcomes implied by personal goals, but may also diminish the likelihood that goals are activated, since a goal activated but not pursued is likely to create distress. If competence is lacking, the person's attention to activating stimuli may be minimized, a desire to avoid the activating stimuli may be created or contributed to, and justification processes may be activated.

Related to competence, to some extent an outcome of variation in competence, is a person's *action tendency*—the capacity to take initiative, to engage in action under ambiguous or difficult conditions. Variation in subjective or objective competence is certainly not the only determinant, however, of action tendency; independence, impulsiveness, courage, adventurousness, and anticonformity may all contribute to the tendency to initiate action consistent with one's goals. Depending on the circumstances, some of these characteristics may be more important than others. In one study, for example, we found a significant positive correlation between the ranking by subjects of the importance to themselves of the value *courageous*—a term that was defined as standing up for one's beliefs—and their entering an adjoining room in response to mild sounds of distress coming from the room (Staub, Erkut, & Jaquette, in Staub, 1974a).

Other issues are related to competence. People may vary in their concern about looking incompetent, and in the extent to which they are willing to attempt helpful action even if their actual or subjective competence is not strong. Moreover, some people may evaluate themselves in terms of their willingness to initiate action or assume responsibility, either when other people need help or in many situations. Taking initiative, assuming responsibility, may be a personal goal for them.

A Person's State of Well-being and the Connection between the Self and Others

Prosocial goals are one indication of a person's connectedness to other people. However, a variety of other influences can affect the connection between the self and others. One of them is the relationship a person has to a person or persons who need help. The length and nature of this relationship or, if the relationship is minimal, the beliefs this person has about the characteristics of the other person are important in determining the degree and nature of relatedness, the likelihood of identification with this person, and the probability of empathic reactions (Chapters 7, 8, and 9).

A second influence is the state of self—a person's well-being, the extent of preoccupation with the self. Concern about evaluation by other people, negative mood, and a temporarily negative self-esteem all lead people to turn inward, which interferes with feeling connected to others, particularly to strangers. A positive state of well-being has the opposite effect (Chapter 6).

A third influence is the state of the other person. The degree and nature of the other's need are important. A person may need help because his state of welfare deviates in a negative direction from the usual, customary, expected state; that is, he may need help to eliminate distress or deficiency. In contrast, a person may also need help to achieve positive goals, to improve a satisfactory state of affairs. Usually some kind of balancing between one's own state of well-being and that of another person is likely to take place. Equity, the concept of a *just world,* and a concept I am introducing—*hedonic balancing* (see Chapter 6)—all relate to this process.

One's own state of well-being probably affects both the temporary rank of prosocial goals in one's hierarchy and one's attention to stimuli, such as the need of another, that may activate these goals. The nature of the connection between the self and others may also affect the activation of other goals, such as the desire for friendship, approval, or intimacy. If prosocial goals are activated, variation in the connection between self and others may determine whether helping another is regarded as a self-sacrifice, so that it diminishes the self, or whether sufficient identification with the other person results for the goals of others to be perceived as interrelated, even identical, with one's own.

Justification Processes

There are many activating conditions under which people will not help others. Frequently people engage in cognitive activities of some kind to minimize the activating potential of the situation. They may decide that the need for help is low, that the person in need does not deserve help, or that the importance of their own conflicting goals is so great that they cannot reasonably be expected to help. Or, they may draw on values and beliefs that justify not helping. These and other justifications permit one to minimize activation, deal with activation in a manner that reduces conflict, or deal with the fact that one has not helped (see Chapter 4). The term *justification* may be used in a general sense, to refer to the use of cognitions that inhibit the activation of some goal or deactivate goals. Thus, justifications may inhibit the activation of goals that would conflict with prosocial goals and may thereby contribute to helping (e.g., "I don't need to try to do well on this task—it is a poor task," or "I know how to do it anyway").

One condition that presumably frequently leads to justification is the high cost of helping (Piliavin & Piliavin, 1975; Schwartz, 1977). The perception of injustice or inequity that another person experiences and that one cannot (or will not) correct is another. Cost is usually an undifferentiated variable in research on helping behavior; it is used as a summary variable for time, effort, risk of safety, sacrifice of one's own positive goals, the possibility of appearing foolish, and so on. Although some of these may best be summarized as costs, others are best regarded as independent influences that are in conflict with those that would lead to helping.

Supporting Research

The concepts of personal goals, goal activation, and goal conflict and the role of competence in determining the execution of goals are basic elements of this theoretical model. The significance of the connection between the self and others and the role of justification processes have been derived from the existing literature and are considered in detail in the following chapters. The basic concepts are applied to the interpretation of the research data when possible. Unfortunately, much of the research has explored only situational influences on helping. Few research strategies aimed at evaluating the interactive influences of situations and personality, and even fewer studied the combined influence of several personality characteristics.

A limited amount of directly relevant evidence does exist, however. In one study, Schwartz and associates (1969) first gave subjects the opportunity to cheat in solving multiple-choice vocabulary problems. Then they placed the subjects in a situation that provided an opportunity to help another person. In the second situation the task involved putting a puzzle together, and the other person made requests for help. Before these two activities took place, three personality characteristics were measured: the need for achievement, the need for affiliation, and the level of moral reasoning (Kohlberg, 1969). Schwartz and associates made differential predictions about the relationships between personality characteristics and behavior in the two situations. They expected a strong need to achieve to be related positively to not cheating, because the desire for excellence cannot be satisfied by getting the right answers through cheating, but related negatively to helping, because helping would interfere with solving the puzzle. They expected the need for affiliation to be unrelated to cheating, which is an impersonal activity, but related positively to helping, which involves a positive interpersonal interaction. And they expected more advanced moral reasoning to be related positively to both honesty and helping, since both can be regarded as moral behaviors. The hypotheses were confirmed by the data. However, the two behaviors, cheating and helping, were unrelated to each other.

These researchers considered the activating potential of each of two situations with regard to three values or motives, and they measured individual differences in these values or motives. By doing so they were able to predict the relationship between these personal motives and behavior.

In another study, Liebhart (1972) measured some form of a prosocial motive or goal of male German high-school subjects (grade 11–grade 13) by administering a projective test of "sympathetic orientation" previously used by Lenrow (1965). The subjects' disposition to take instrumental action to relieve their own distress was measured by a Likert-type scale that Liebhart devised. Subjects with a sympathetic orientation helped more quickly in response to sounds of distress—a bang followed by cries and moans—from an adjoining room if they were also disposed toward instrumental action. This finding supports the idea that when personality characteristics that make assisting others a desirable goal are activated, an action-oriented person is more likely to help.

In a study I conducted with my associates (Staub, Erkut, & Jaquette, as reported in Staub, 1974a), a subject's response to sounds of distress and his rendering of help to a distressed person were found to be affected by the characteristics of the situation and of the personality of the subjects. Subjects whose level of moral reasoning was more advanced (Kohlberg, 1969) or those who held themselves responsible for others' welfare (Schwartz, 1970b) helped more, but only when the experimenter had previously indicated that it was permissible for the subjects to interrupt work on their task. When this was the case, subjects were presumably less concerned about disapproval for interrupting their work. People who held prosocial values, such as helpfulness or equality—as indicated by their ranking of these values on Rokeach's (1973) measure—were more helpful, at least in the permission condition. Values that conflicted with helping, such as ambition, reduced helping. The negative influence of valuing ambition was particularly clear when the experimenter told subjects that they were working on a timed task and asked them not to interrupt their work, a condition that would be expected to activate ambition or achievement.

A factor analysis of measures that expressed positive values about people or about helping produced a strong factor with a high loading of most of the measures on this factor.[2] High scores on this factor indicated a prosocial orientation. The measures that indicated prosocial orientation including high ranking of prosocial values, feelings of personal responsibility for others' welfare, positive evaluation of human beings, and nonmanipulativeness. These scores were related to most of the helpful actions that subjects had opportunities to perform, and the relationship was relatively unaffected by situational variation.

Still other relevant evidence comes from a study reported by Gergen and associates (1972). Members of an undergraduate class were told that the psychology department needed help with various projects. Students could indicate, on a mimeographed sheet, their willingness to aid with five ongoing projects—counseling male students from a nearby high school, counseling female students from the same school, working on a faculty research project on deductive thinking, working on a research project on unusual states of consciousness, or collating and assembling materials for use by the class. In the class session preceding the request for help the students had completed a battery of personality tests measuring a variety of characteristics or traits.

Gergen and associates found significant relationships between personality characteristics and volunteering, but they emphasize that different personality characteristics were significantly related to helping with different tasks. Moreover, the pattern of correlation differed for males and females. The findings are consistent with the present model; people selected tasks that satisfied some personal goal or led to a desirable outcome. For example, need for nurturance in males was significantly related to their willingness to counsel other males ($r = .41$), but it was not significantly related to volunteering with other forms of help. Note that this relationship can be predicted from the previously described rules of correspondence between personal needs and the perception of—and presumably also the orientation to—other people that Cantor (1976) proposed. People who need counseling may be nurturant and/or responsive to nurturance. Sensation seeking as a personality characteristic was positively related to helping with research on unusual states of consciousness, but

---

[2] We conducted a factor analysis that was reported in Staub, 1974a. The statements here describe, however, a subsequent factor analysis of the same data.

negatively related to volunteering for research on deductive thinking; the difference between the two correlations was significant. The correlations between personality and volunteering showed a similar kind of specificity among female subjects. Gergen *et al.* stressed that helping behavior is determined by situational payoffs. People will have different payoff preferences that affect their movements toward particular social contexts. Gergen and associates discourage the notion that certain trait dispositions or individual differences will be found to account for variability in prosocial behavior.

Several issues need to be noted. First, helping behavior was not measured in this study. Rather, the subjects' stated intention to help was evaluated, in a group situation. The relationship between measures of the intention to help and actual helping is poor, as I shall demonstrate in later chapters. For the purposes of considering the theoretical meaning of the data, however, this is not a prohibitive problem. Second, the subjects were not confronted by someone's distress or by an immediate or serious need demanding attention. Given this situation, combined with the fact that the class consisted of 72 people who could help, the students in the class presumably did not feel an obligation to provide substantial help with most of the five tasks. The present theoretical model clearly suggests that the students would select tasks to help with that would be satisfying and meaningful from the standpoint of their personal goals.

A third important consideration also enters. No attempt was made in this study to evaluate personality characteristics relevant to helping—the kinds of characteristics that enter into or might be components of a prosocial goal. Only a high degree of motivation for prosocial behavior—and only under certain conditions—can be expected to lead to any generality in helping behavior or in the expressed intention to be helpful. An "irrelevant" characteristic, such as sensation seeking, would be expected to add to the influence of a prosocial goal at some times but to detract from the influence at other times. Such a characteristic, when considered by itself, can be expected to lead to helping only when the helping behavior satisfies that characteristic—that is, for accidental reasons. However, given the existence of a strong prosocial motivation, a positive relationship between such motivation and several helping acts can be expected under certain specifiable conditions.

Two studies (Feinberg, 1977; Grodman, 1978) represent the first attempts to test some aspects of the model I have described. Feinberg (1977) administered a large number of personality tests to female subjects. Some tests measured characteristics that would promote prosocial behavior: prosocial values, a positive evaluation of other human beings, interpersonal sensitivity, affiliation, and nurturance. Some of these presumably contribute to a prosocial goal, and others are characteristics that may motivate prosocial behavior but represent other goals—for example, affiliation. Other tests measured components of an achievement goal. Separate factor analyses of the two groups of tests provided a strong prosocial factor and a strong achievement factor. On the basis of factor scores subjects were divided into high and low groups on each factor. A third variation was experimental. The subjects were exposed to a female confederate who at one point began to talk about her distress related to her boyfriend. She confided that after an intense relationship that included talk about marriage he suddenly broke up with her and was unwilling to discuss the reasons for the breakup. To some subjects she said the breakup occured the day before (high need), and to others she said it occurred a year before (low need). The confederate was induced to talk about her distress because of its relationship to a story that was part of the experimental material. Although her words were nearly identical in both cases, the confederate acted and was perceived as greatly upset only in the high-need condition. It was expected that subjects with a strong achievement motivation would try to do well on the task, whereas those with a strong prosocial motivation would be helpful. Specific predictions were derived for different combinations of personality characteristics.

Four kinds of data were obtained:

1. Verbal communications by the subjects to the confederate—how much and what kinds of things they said. These ranged from minimal verbal reactions to questions about what had happened, stories about similar experiences, expressions of sympathy, and so on.
2. Nonverbal responses of the subjects to the confederate—the subjects' looking at the confederate, leaning toward her, or smiling. These acts were contrasted to task orientation, which included looking at the task, working on it, and so on.
3. Ratings of the subject and/or of her behavior by the confederate and by the experimenter or an observer who witnessed the interaction from behind a one-way mirror.
4. Responses on a postexperimental questionnaire indicating the subjects' feelings about the confederate and about various aspects of their experience.

The manner in which, nonverbally, the subjects oriented themselves to the confederate and to the task was coded by observers looking through one-way mirrors. Analyses of variance of subjects' nonverbal reactions showed that, on several measures, there was a significant degree of need–prosocial goal interaction.[3] When the situation was one of high need, high-

---

[3] "Interaction" refers to two or more influences, such as personality or experimental conditions (in this instance the degree of experimentally created need for help and the level of prosocial goal that characterized the potential helper), that modify each other's influence. As the subsequent example indicates, subjects who had a certain level of prosocial motivation tended to behave one way when the need was high, another way when the need was low.

prosocial subjects looked at or worked on the task much less than did low-prosocial subjects; when the low-need situation was in effect, high-prosocial subjects looked at or worked on the task more than low-prosocial subjects did. In high need, high-prosocial subjects oriented themselves toward the person in need rather than toward the task. High prosocial subjects with low achievement orientation looked at and worked on the task least in the high-need situation (Table 2.1). Thus, with regard to nonverbal interaction, Feinberg's findings tend to agree with the model's predictions.

The participants' responses to some of the items on a postexperimental questionnaire give meaning to the nonverbal data, as well as to some of the findings reported later in this chapter. The high-prosocial subjects expressed more of a feeling of obligation to the experimenter to do the task than did low-prosocial subjects. Moreover, high-prosocial subjects expressed less desire to help the experimenter and more desire to help the confederate in the high-need condition than in the low-need condition. Perhaps these subjects felt an obligation to help the experimenter, to do what they agreed to do, but in the high-need condition their desire to help the confederate became dominant.

The analyses of verbal communications showed that high-achievement subjects tended to speak more than low-achievement subjects. On several verbal dimensions there were significant prosocial-by-achievement interactions: That is, the two goals modified each other's influence. Subjects in the *low*-prosocial and *high*-achievement group were more verbal than subjects in other groups. For example, their total verbal responses were substantially greater (Table 2.2). Also, in several specific categories of seemingly helpful verbalizations (such as problem-directed questions), these subjects spoke more than those in other groups. Though they were verbally helpful, low-prosocial high-achievement subjects attended to the task (rather than to the confederate) to a substantial amount in the high need condition (Table 2.1). The amount of talking by high-prosocial subjects was moderate in the high-need situation, substantially less than that of low-prosocial high-achievement subjects in either need condition, but somewhat more than that of subjects with other personality combinations.

Table 2.1
Nonverbal Responses by Subjects: Looking at Work and Writing[a][b]

Achievement orientation	Low Need		High Need	
	Low Prosocial	High Prosocial	Low Prosocial	High Prosocial
Low	77	93	99	58
High	71	76	125	68

[a] Data from Feinberg, 1977.
[b] Duration, following the distress stimulus, in number of seconds.

Table 2.2

*Total Verbal Responses: Cell Means of Analysis of Variance by Need,
Prosocial Goal, and Achievement Goal[a][b]*

Achievement orientation	Low Need		High Need	
	Low Prosocial	High Prosocial	Low Prosocial	High Prosocial
Low	11.23	12.30	11.82	14.24
High	25.8	11.00	26.75	14.38

[a] Data from Feinberg, 1977.
[b] Frequency of units of verbal responses.

How clear an index of help is the amount of talk? A purported helper may monopolize the interaction and thereby limit a distressed person's opportunity to express feelings. Thus, a great deal of verbalization directed to a person in distress may show less sensitivity, and may be less helpful, than a moderate amount.

How does one determine what behavior is really helpful? External criteria can be wrong. We have little or no empirical guidance in this— even psychotherapists of different schools disagree on what behavior directed at their patients is helpful. The subjective experience of the person to whom help is directed is one important criterion. The impressions of a "bystander" are also relevant. Feinberg had the experimenter or an observer, as well as the confederate, rate the behavior of the subject on a variety of dimensions. On some dimensions their ratings were similar and thus "reliable," so the combined ratings were used as dependent measures in analyses of variance. The raters knew, of course, the degree of need the subject responded to, but they did not know their personalities. Analyses of subjects relating their own experiences, presumably to help the confederate, showed a need–prosocial goal interaction. High-prosocial subjects related their experiences more under high need, less under low need, than low-prosocial subjects. Both high need and high achievement resulted in greater expression of "sincere sympathy." A major dependent variable was the subjects' expression of willingness to continue the interaction with the confederate at a later time. The confederate at some point indicated that she did not want to keep the subject from working on the task. She expressed satisfaction from having had the opportunity to talk and indicated her interest in continuing the conversation. Analyses of the ratings of the subjects' expressed willingness for future interaction again resulted in a need by prosocial interaction. Low-prosocial subjects were more willing under low need and high-prosocial subjects were more willing under high need. Finally, high-achievement subjects were rated significantly friendlier than low-achievement subjects.

Some further ratings from the postexperimental questionnaire are relevant. Although there were varied significant influences on these ratings, a tendency by low-prosocial, high-achievement subjects in the high-need group to report dislike of the confederate, to judge her cold, depressed, and unemotional, may help us understand the findings. High-prosocial subjects rated her positively, particularly in high need.

Clearly, high-achievement orientation tended to manifest itself in this study by people making efforts to respond to the confederate, both verbally and in other ways. Feinberg refers to the review by Stein (1973) of the literature on achievement orientation in women: Those with high achievement will strive for success in sex-typed activities. Involvement in interpersonal relations and giving help to another woman in distress seem such activities. The greater responsiveness by the high-achievement women tended to occur in both high- and low-need situations; it was not elicited only by the confederate's distress. A high prosocial orientation resulted in differentiated responding, in greater attention to and work on the task in the low-need situation, and more interest in and attention for the confederate in the high-need situation.

The data did confirm specific predictions. For example, subjects low in both prosocial and achievement goals tended to be minimally helpful. There were varied indications of conflict and/or discomfort among subjects high in both prosocial and achievement goals. For example, they smiled a great deal at the confederate in the high-need condition, much more than subjects with other combinations of personality characteristics. Since the confederate's distress was great, a great deal of smiling at her seems inappropriate. That subjects perceived this to be so is indicated by significantly less smiling, overall, in high than in low need.

High-prosocial, low-achievement subjects were expected to be unconcerned with the task and to be the most helpful. These subjects worked primarily on their task and helped the confederate little when her need was low, presumably fulfilling their obligation to the experimenter. When, however, the confederate's need was high, they talked to her a moderate amount and showed a great deal of attention to her and little attention to their task. On the postexperimental questionnaire they expressed less desire to help the experimenter in the high- than in the low-need conditions and more desire to help the confederate. They expressed liking for the confederate and the feeling that they were liked by her, in contrast to the low-prosocial high-achievement subjects. The difference was greatest in the high-need condition.

High-prosocial, low-achievement subjects seemed responsive to their circumstances, and responsively helpful. Both the low-achievement, high-prosocial subjects and the high-achievement, low-prosocial subjects appeared helpful in the high-need condition, but in their own ways, the former attentive and moderately verbal, the latter highly verbal and unattentive to the confederate while attending to the task. The greater liking of the confederate by low-achievement, high-prosocial subjects may indicate that their helpful behavior was more in tune with their motivation, their desire to help, than the helpfulness of low-prosocial, high-achievement subjects, who appeared responsive to varied situational pressures. The latter seemingly attempted to satisfy all existing demands.

The findings clearly show the complexity of human interactions. However, they also show that despite its complexity behavior is predictable on the basis of the situation and personality, and they provide some support for the model. Low need was, in essence, not a need but a control condition: The confederate reminisced about a distressful event but was not distressed. Consequently, a prosocial goal was not activated. When it was activated, in high need, high-prosocial subjects were responsive to the distressed person in varied ways. Finally, the findings suggest that it is important to be careful in establishing what conditions are likely to function as activators of what goals. In this study, another's request for attention—through expressing distress or describing past distress—seemed a more potent activator of the women's achievement goals than performance on a task. We will have to measure the activating potentials of situations for varied goals and/or develop rules of correspondence that specify what kinds of behavior may satisfy a motive or a combination of varied motives given a certain set of stimulus conditions.

Grodman (1978) used the basic procedure that Feinberg developed, with some improvements, primarily in processing the data. The categories that were used to classify the subjects' verbal behavior were somewhat different and more elaborate. Because of the difficulty of determining what kinds of reactions are helpful to a person in psychological distress, Grodman had both observers and the confederate make more elaborate ratings of the subject's behavior, immediately after the interaction was concluded. Moreover, independently of other data analyses, naive judges listened to tapes of the complete interaction between the confederate and the subject and rated the subject's global helpfulness. These ratings allowed consideration of the whole interaction, both what the subjects said and the affects expressed by their voices.

Grodman first administered to female subjects a large number of personality measures, similar to those used in the two studies just discussed (Staub *et al.,* reported in Staub, 1974a; Feinberg, 1977), to measure prosocial orientation. These included the measures that had high loadings on the prosocial factor in Feinberg's study, and a few others. Factor analysis again provided a prosocial factor, with most of the same tests as in the previous study loading high on this factor. (The following tests had high loading: Schwartz' [1970b] ascription of responsibility, Berkowitz and Lutterman's [1968] social responsibility, the Machiavellian scale [negative: Christie & Geis, 1968], and some of Rokeach's values.) Subjects were divided into high and low prosocial groups on the basis of their factor scores. They were exposed, several weeks after the administration of the personality tests, to a distressed confederate. Feinberg's high-need condition was used. Grodman included two types of experimental variations in her study. First, the subjects were told either that they would again meet the person working in the same room with them on the experimental task—that at a later time they would discuss and have to draw some conclusions about several "case histories"—or that they would not need to meet this person again. The second variation was in the cost of helping. In a high-cost condition the subjects were told that feedback about their personalities, based on the personality measures they filled out, would be available to them. It was indicated to the subjects, as they started to work on the task that "activated" the expression of distress by the confederate— the evaluation of the personalities of people described in passages taken from short stories (Staub, 1974a)—that information on this task was relatively unimportant for the experimenter but quite valuable in providing feedback to the subject. No feedback was mentioned in the low-cost condition. In the high-cost condition, by responding to and interacting with the confederate, the subjects would give up the opportunity to work on the task and thereby diminish the value of the feedback to themselves.

In this study the subjects were exposed to another person's relatively intense psychological distress. This was expected to activate their prosocial goal, as measured by prosocial orientation. One of the consistent findings was that, in comparison to low-prosocial subjects, high-prosocial subjects acted in ways that appeared more helpful. Frequently, the difference was substantial. On a few measures of help, variation in the cost of helping had a significant influence; less help was given in the high-cost condition than in the low-cost condition. More frequently, there was an interaction in the influence of cost and prosocial orientation in addition to the effect of personality. In these cases usually the difference between high- and low-prosocial subjects was small in the high-cost condition; high-prosocial subjects still helped numerically more, but not significantly so. In the low-cost condition, low-prosocial subjects helped about as much as subjects in the high-cost condition, whereas high-prosocial subjects helped substantially more. Expecting or not expecting to meet the distressed person had relatively little effect on the subjects' behavior.

The consistency of Grodman's findings is quite impressive. High-prosocial subjects looked at the task less than low-prosocial subjects ($p < .01$), whereas high-cost subjects looked at the task more than low-cost subjects ($p < .01$). High-prosocial subjects smiled more at the confederate ($p < .01$). An analysis of variance of the sum of all the positive (helpful) verbalizations by subjects again showed a significant prosocial effect ($p < .05$), as well as a cost by prosocial interaction ($p < .01$). Similar findings were obtained when verbalizations were factors analyzed and the analyses of variance were based on scores on two emerging factors of positive verbalizations. Analyses of what the subjects said in response to the confederate's expression of the desire to talk after the experimental session showed a generally more positive attitude by high- than by low-prosocial subjects ($p < .001$). Moreover, high-prosocial subjects agreed sooner to meet the confederate ($p < .005$) and also to a definite meeting place ($p < .03$). The ratings of global help by independent raters who listened to the taped interaction again showed substantially more help by high-prosocial subjects ($p < .002$) and a personality by cost interaction ($p < .05$). That is, high prosocial subjects were primarily more helpful when the cost was low (Table 2.3).

Ratings by the confederates following their interactions with subjects showed that they perceived high-prosocial subjects as substantially more helpful than low-prosocial subjects, in varied ways. (Naturally, the confederate had no information about the subjects' personality scores.) High-prosocial subjects were perceived as more responsive, more sympathetic, less nervous, and less shy. On all these ratings except shyness, there was a personality by cost interaction. Analyses of ratings in response to the question, "If it were a life situation, do you think she would have done a good job making you feel better?" showed significant prosocial ($p < .002$), cost ($p < .01$), and prosocial by cost ($p < .05$) interaction effects. Ratings by the observers also supported these findings. The confederates' (and observers') ratings are valuable because even though they were trained participants they responded to the total behavior of the subjects.

Postexperimental responses by subjects to a questionnaire were consistent with other findings. High-prosocial subjects liked the confederates substantially more than low-prosocial subjects, with a significant personality by cost interaction. The former believed more than the latter that they

Table 2.3
Global Ratings of Help Provided by Subjects [a] [b]

Cost condition	Future meeting .	
	Expected	Not Expected
	Low prosocial motivation	
Low	2.1	2.0
High	2.0	2.5
	High prosocial motivation	
Low	3.1	3.1
High	2.7	2.3

[a] Data from Grodman, 1978.

[b] Numbers in the cells represent averages of ratings by judges who listened to tape recordings of the interaction between subjects and confederates and rated helpfulness on a 4-point scale, ranging from 1 = very helpful to 4 = very helpful.

could be helpful. It was more important for subjects in the high-cost than in the low-cost condition to do well on the test. Surprisingly, subjects in the high-cost condition reported stronger beliefs than those in the low-cost group that their finishing the test mattered to the experimenter, perhaps in justification of their less help.

As mentioned, the expectation of meeting the confederate had relatively little influence. Subjects who expected to meet the confederate looked more at her, but after the confederate said she would later like to talk more, they made more attempts to disengage—mainly the subjects low in prosocial orientation—and said more negative things than subjects who did not expect to meet the confederate. It seemed that under the conditions that existed in the experiment, the expectation of future involvement with the distressed person led to some attempts by subjects, mainly those less prosocially oriented, to distance themselves.

As we provide less restricted opportunities for action and study interpersonal, interactive behavior—as we approximate real-life circumstances, when personal goals can be manifested and satisfied in varied ways—behavior becomes more difficult to predict. In Feinberg's and Grodman's studies, the confederate's behavior had to be affected by the degree and nature of the subject's responsiveness. The confederate's instructions allowed her to proceed with her story beyond a certain point only if the subjects responded and thereby made it appropriate to continue. Moreover, when the subject asked for more information, made comments that required responses, these were provided. Naturally, some subjects behaved in a way that required more responsiveness by the confederate than others. Thus, to some degree the interaction between the subject and the confederate was *transactional*, as it usually is in real life. In an unpublished study of psychological distress that I conducted (Staub, 1969) using somewhat similar procedures to those just described, there was a substantial positive relationship between the amount the subjects and the confederate talked. This again shows the interdependent nature of the behavior of a person in need and the behavior of someone attempting to help. Whether people give help, share, act in a friendly and positive manner, and do favors for one another is to an important degree a function of the ongoing interaction between individuals. Requests for help and acts by a potential recipient that elicit or inhibit help are important but frequently neglected determinants of positive conduct (Staub, 1973; Staub & Noerenberg, 1978; Staub & Feinberg, 1977b).

Classes of Influences on Prosocial Behavior

Subsequent chapters extensively analyze the determinants of prosocial behavior, of specific positive acts and prosocial interactions. What environmental conditions and personality characteristics enhance or decrease the likelihood of people behaving prosocially, and in what combinations? How do these conditions exert their influence? Why do people act prosocially? Many categories of influences on prosocial behavior will be considered.

The Situation. The *social influence exerted* is an extremely important element of a situation. People exert powerful influence on one another. Another element of the situation is the *nature of the stimulus* for prosocial behavior. Such stimuli may differ along many dimensions. A stimulus may clearly indicate that some form of prosocial behavior is needed; a person may clearly be in physical distress, in psychological distress, hungry, and so on. But the stimulus may also be ambiguous. Other relevant stimulus variations are the degree of need for aid and the cost of helping. Another aspect of the situation is the nature of the *conditions surrounding the stimulus.* For example, if you travel on a bus and somebody is crying, you can physically get away from it by getting off the bus. On the other hand, if your boyfriend or husband is extremely upset, it is difficult to remove yourself physically. You may continue to be exposed to it until you take some action.

Temporary States of Potential Helpers. Another influence on prosocial behavior is how people who are in a position to help feel at the time someone needs help. Do they feel good or bad, competent or incompetent? Is their momentary self-esteem high or low? Is their attention and concern strongly focused on themselves, or are they "free" to attend to others?

Relationship to Potential Recipients of Help. The kind of relationship a person has to others may be very important in determining whether that person will help them. Prior interactions or information about others, as well as mutual obligations and social or personal norms that are applicable as a result of these obligations, may determine the nature of the bond that exists.

Personality Characteristics. A whole variety of personality characteristics are important in determining prosocial behavior, mainly in combination with the influence of situations. In addition to prosocial behavior that is under the control of eliciting stimuli, people often seek out opportunities to engage in prosocial acts. The determinants of this behavior are also important to consider.

Psychological Processes. Our understanding of the determinants of positive social behavior, our ability to predict it, and our capacity to employ socialization practices that would enhance the likelihood that people will behave prosocially would all be enhanced if we knew why certain conditions lead to more or to less helping—if we knew what internal processes they evoke that mediate helping. Obviously, even if a mediator of prosocial behavior such as empathy is aroused, action does not necessarily follow, because of conflicts among goals, low expectation of success, and other conditions that might make the goal of providing aid inactive.

Unfortunately, it is difficult to infer internal processes from external conditions. Usually any one situation might activate a variety of processes. Someone's need for help might remind a bystander of values and norms promoting help or it might activate empathy or other internal processes. As I noted, our confidence in drawing conclusions about mediators of prosocial behavior would increase if we could independently demonstrate that a certain internal reaction was actually aroused and affected the probability of action. With regard to empathy, for example, this could be done by demonstrating that the presence of a person in need produced varying degrees of phsysiological arousal in observers, suggesting emotional reactions of varying intensity. Then one would have to determine what emotions they experienced. Some might be afraid, others might simply be excited, still others might report feelings similar to what the person in need seemed to experience, suggesting the presence of empathy. If the observers who appear to experience empathy are the ones who are more helpful, that would increase confidence in inferring an association between empathy and prosocial action. If these individuals tend to be more helpful only when the arousal of empathy in them can be demonstrated but not at other times, one would have reason to believe that the experience of empathy mediated helping, that the degree to which empathy is aroused is likely to increase helping. In practice, such methodology is difficult to carry out. However, the more we are able to measure internal processes, the greater our ability will be to draw firm conclusions about what psychological processes motivate prosocial behavior.

Methodologies to determine the extent to which personal characteristics actually lead to the arousal of internal processes that may motivate behavior have been suggested at various points in this chapter. The way events are perceived and processed by people, which is to an important degree a function of their personality, must ultimately determine their psychological experience and the resulting behavior.

It used to be assumed that conscience is unitary. If people developed conscience to a greater degree, then they would always behave morally; if they developed it to a lesser degree, they would behave less morally. It is now clear that this position is not tenable. Behavior is multidetermined. The type of demands that a particular form of prosocial behavior puts on a person is likely to influence his behavior. In order to behave prosocially one way, a person might have to give up valued possessions. To behave prosocially in another way, a person might have to sacrifice time, to exert effort. Sometimes a person has to forgo the satisfaction of various personal goals in order to aid someone, but at other times no such conflict exists.

Sometimes one has to put aside personal safety to help. In some situations prosocial actions demand decisiveness, fast judgments, and initiative. In other situations it is entirely clear what action is required; one may face a specific request. Depending on these different demands the determinants of prosocial behavior might vary. The extent to which similar or different influences and internal processes determine different types of prosocial action needs to be evaluated.

Determinants of People Helping
Other People in Physical Distress

There are two reasons for considering prosocial behavior in response to physical distress before considering other types of prosocial behavior. First, physical distress is one of the most basic conditions of human need. A person whose life is in danger is unquestionably a person in extreme need. Second, the avalanche of research on prosocial behavior was initiated by research on physical distress.

The apparent lack of concern by witnesses to the tragic murder of Kitty Genovese in New York, and similar occurrences, led social psychologists Latané and Darley (1970) to explore what inhibits people from intervening in emergencies. Kitty Genovese was a young woman who, going home about 3:00 a.m. one morning in 1964, was attacked and stabbed by a man. In response to her screams for help, lights were turned on in apartments and people looked out their windows. Some shouted "Leave that girl alone"—and then all apparently returned to their beds. The attacker ran away, came back, and stabbed her again. Again there was commotion and again the attacker left, only to come back a third time and complete the murder. Some time after it was all over one person called the police, after he checked with his lawyer about the advisability of doing so.

This was not the only time that a number of people witnessed someone's distress and no one attempted to help. Latané and Darley (1970) described other cases that had been reported in the media in the United States. I learned of a number of similar cases during travels through Europe, in conversations with people or through reports in the media.

One report in an Italian newspaper described how an infuriated husband caught his wife sitting in a car with a man, presumably her lover, and dragged her to the nearby lakeside, where he drowned her in front of about 100 passive bystanders. (The man ran away.)

The Early Research of Latané and Darley

Why do people not intervene? Is it apathy, the alienation that results from living in big cities, as some commentators on the Kitty Genovese murder proposed, or are the reasons different? To answer these questions Darley and Latané started a research program exploring the influence of the number of persons present on both the likelihood of a person in distress being helped and, more generally, the likelihood that people would take action in emergencies.

In their first experiment their subjects were in a setup often used by social psychologists, a number of cubicles connected by an intercom system. Ostensibly, the subject was participating in a group discussion, but all other participants except the subject were simulated by tape recordings. Every person could talk without interruption for 2 minutes; the microphones of the other participants were inactive during this time. Each subject was made to believe that a certain number of others persons were present: either just one other person, the "victim" who later needed help; two others; or five others. The first time the victim had a chance to talk he mentioned, with embarrassment, that he was prone to seizures. The next time he spoke, he started to speak calmly, but speech became increasingly more difficult for him; he became loud and incoherent and obviously was having great difficulties. He called for help and seemed to need help desperately. The researchers hoped to find answers to these questions: Would people attempt to help by going to find the experimenter and reporting the victim's distress to him? How would the speed and likelihood of help be influenced by the number of people that subjects believed to be present? It was found that the number of bystanders exerted a powerful influence. With an increase in the number of people who the subject believed could help, both the probability that the subject would help and the speed with which help was given decreased. The larger the number of bystanders believed to be present, the greater was the decrease.

To explore this phenomenon further, Darley and Latané conducted a variety of other experiments. In one of these a male subject was ostensibly participating in market research, working on a questionnaire either alone, with another subject, with a nonresponsive confederate (who did not react during the emergency), or with a friend. The young woman who had instructed the subjects on the task was working next door: She climbed up on a chair, then fell down and screamed. The chair fell over, and she started to cry for help, shouting that she could not move, could not get "the thing" off her foot. Of subjects who were alone, 70% helped; 40% of pairs of strangers helped; and 7% of subjects who were with a passive confederate helped. In comparing groups, a correction was used for the number of people who were in a position to help, a procedure always followed when several bystanders were together. In the case of a pair of strangers, two persons rather than one were in a position to help, and, computing a hypothetical baseline of expected help on the basis of subjects who were alone, 91% of the pairs should have helped. Subjects who were alone helped significantly more than pairs of strangers, who in turn helped significantly more than the subjects with the passive confederate. Pairs of friends helped 70% of the time. With correction for the number of people in a position to help, this was significantly less than help by lone subjects, but significantly more than help by pairs of strangers. The presence of another person reduced initiation of helping behavior, more so when he was unresponsive, and less so when he was a friend.

The two studies described so far differed in that in one case the bystanders presumed to be present were not visible or in communication with the subject, whereas in the second study they were visible. Both the presumed and the actual presence of others reduced helping behavior. Latané and Darley (1970) proposed two explanations for these findings: *diffusion of responsibility* and *pluralistic ignorance*. In their discussion they also considered concern about negative evaluation by other bystanders as a possible inhibitor of action.

The concept of diffusion of responsibility suggests that people feel responsible for helping others. However, when other people are present, the feeling of responsibility gets diffused. Every single person feels less responsibility to act. The concept of pluralistic ignorance applies to a greater degree to the situation when bystanders are together. When a number of people witness an emergency together, each looks around to see how the others react. However, people learn not to show their feelings in public. Male college students in particular would not want to show concern or anxiety in front of others. As a result, each person sees other people looking unconcerned, as if there were nothing to worry about and nothing to react to. The result is that people define the situation as a nonemergency, where no action is needed, so they do nothing. Darley and Latané mention a third reason for the inhibiting influence of other people—many persons are concerned about negative evaluation or disapproval by others, perhaps for appearing foolish (by initiating action when no action is required) or perhaps for being incompetent (in the course of attempting help).

Latané and Darley proposed a decision-making model of helping in an emergency. First, one must notice that something is happening. Second, one has to interpret the stimulus. Third, if one perceives the stimulus (noise from another room, for example) and interprets it as an emergency, one must then assume responsibility for providing help. Fourth, one must decide what to do, what sort of action to take. And fifth, one must actually carry out the action decided on. Several other writers have proposed decision-making models (Schwartz, 1977; Bar-Tel, 1976). Schwartz, for example, specified individual characteristics and situational elements that enter into decision making and the sequence of steps involved in the decision making that leads to action or inaction. His model is discussed in Chapter 5, in conjunction with relevant research. Unfortunately, research that would elucidate the steps in a sequence of decisions is not available in the realm of helping people in physical need. The determinants that are discussed later in this chapter are likely to contribute to each of the decisions in the sequence.

Before examining determinants of helping others in physical distress and the processes that are involved, I should note that Latané and Darley (1970) explored the influence of the number of bystanders in additional experiments and showed fairly wide generality of the inhibiting influence of others. In one experiment self-help was also involved. While the subjects were working on a questionnaire, smoke started to fill the room through a vent. Three naive subjects initiated action by reporting the smoke much less frequently than a lone subject did, and the presence of two passive confederates in the room with the subject further decreased the likelihood that action would be initiated. In this experiment, reliable observations through a one-way mirror also showed that subjects who were with others *noticed* the smoke later. Significantly more lone subjects noticed the smoke in the first 5 seconds than subjects who were in the company of others. Thus alertness to environmental events declines in the presence of others. In another experiment Latané and Darley demonstrated that a confederate stealing a six-pack of beer from a liquor store was somewhat more likely to be reported to the owner when a single customer was in the store than when more customers were present.

In the rest of this chapter, Darley and Latané's proposed explanations for bystander inaction are examined within the broader framework of exploring the determinants of helping others in physical distress. Their independent variable, the number of other bystanders present, is presumably one of many forms of social influence that can affect helping. Their explanations of the inhibiting effect of this variable can also be considered as part of broader explanations. Responsibility for action may be both diffused, probably in a large variety of ways, and focused on a person. Although the presence of others may lead to pluralistic ignorance, the broader issue is how various influences affect the perception and interpretation of stimuli that have the potential to evoke help. The discussion that follows focuses first on social and situational determinants of helping, because that was the primary focus of past research, and then on the influence of personality.

Latané and Darley's writings and the writing of most other researchers (e.g., Staub, 1974a) imply that, when bystanders do not help a person in need, they are inhibited by circumstances. This view is likely to be incomplete. For one thing, in certain field experiments, it was found that many subjects preferred to escape from a situation in which someone needed help, if escape was easy (Staub & Baer, 1974). Some people might have relatively weak prosocial values or goals, and their egocentric values may enable them to avoid intervention with perhaps little conflict. I recognize that this cannot be a welcome view for idealistic researchers of prosocial behavior (like myself) and for idealistic readers. And sometimes bystanders act in what appear to be intentionally harmful, destructive ways. In incidents reported in the media, bystanders have urged persons to jump from tops of buildings and to engage in other self-destructive or violent acts. Although explanations such as the influence of mobs (Huston & Korte, 1976), perhaps acting through deindividuation (Zimbardo, 1969), have been proposed, they do not seem complete. Despite such behavior, however, it has been increasingly noted that, although they are often inhibited, sometimes unconcerned, and sometimes truly vicious, bystanders often do attempt to help a person in distress.

The Influence of Others

Defining the Situation, Defining the Appropriate Response, and Communicating Expectations about Appropriate Behavior

Other people can have tremendous influence on our behavior. As discussed, the presence of a stranger inhibits action, and that of a passive bystander does so even more. The manner in which people exert this kind of influence on one another may be clarified by examining other ways that people influence one another by what they say and by what they do.

The presence of people who are passive might affect behavior because their passivity may lead others to create a negative definition of the stimulus, to decide that there is no reason to be concerned. People probably also strongly influence one another by actually saying something that defines the meaning of the event. Furthermore, people influence others by communicating to them, behaviorally or verbally, what they regard as reasonable or appropriate behavior and thus implying or explicitly stating the kind of behavior they expect. What one person says or does might affect the behavior of another either because the latter comes to interpret the stimulus or judge the appropriate response in a certain way or because he complies with the other person's expectation of proper behavior.

In one study Bickman (1972) explored the influence of an explicit verbal definition of a potential stimulus for help on subsequent helping behavior. He had female subjects participate in an "ESP experiment." The subject was told that two others participated at the same time. One of the others (the victim) was supposedly in the same building, in another room. Some subjects were told that a third person was also in the same building; others were told that she was in a different building. Subjects could communicate through an intercom system. Immediately after a tape-recorded emergency sequence was played, a confederate, acting as the other bystander, defined the meaning of what they heard.

The emergency consisted of the victim saying through the intercom, "Wait a minute. I think something is falling off the bookcase. I'd better fix it." This was followed by sounds of the victim getting on a chair. She then cried out, "It's falling on me." A scream and a loud crash followed, and nothing more was heard of the victim. In one condition, the *no-emergency* interpretation, the confederate said, "Hey, what happened? Subject 1, something must have fallen on the intercom. Hey, Subject 3 [who was the subject], what do we do now? Oh, yeah, you can't answer [because the intercom was not open for this person]; well, I guess she will tell the guy it's not working. We had better wait for him to tell us what to do next." Obviously, this interpretation implied that nothing needed to be done. In the *possible-emergency* interpretation the subject heard the confederate say: "What happened? Hey, Subject 1, are you OK? Why don't you answer? It sounds like the whole bookcase fell. Hey, Subject 3, what do you think? Oh, yeah, you can't answer. I hope it's nothing serious. I hope she is OK." In the *certain-emergency* interpretation the confederate said: "What happened? Hey, Subject 1, please answer me, are you OK? Are you all right? She is not answering; something must have fallen on her. She is hurt. Hey, Subject 3, she must have gotten hurt."

In the certain emergency, there was substantially more helping than in the possible-emergency interpretation; in the possible-emergency interpretation there was substantially more helping than in the no-emergency interpretation. Interpretations provided by another person about the meaning of the stimulus strongly affected behavior.

This is further illustrated in another study (Staub, 1974a). In all conditions of this study, a female subject and a female confederate were working on their tasks in the same room, the subject facing the door of another room, the confederate with her back to it. At some point a crash, cries of distress, and calls for help were heard from the other room. Five seconds after the sounds started the confederate said, in the *positive-definition* condition, "Gee, that sounds pretty bad. Maybe we should do something." She stayed in her place, however, not initiating action, but following the initiative of the subject. In the *negative-definition* condition the confederate turned her head and said, "Gee, that sounds like a tape recorder. Or, perhaps it's another experiment. But at any rate, it does sound like a tape recorder." In other conditions the confederate defined the distress sounds positively, and then did one of several additional things. In one condition she jumped up, hurried to a door leading out of the room (but not to the adjoining room), and said, "I'd better go and get the experimenter." In another condition she did the same and said, "I'd better go get the experimenter. You'd better not do anything; I don't think we are supposed to go into that room." Or she said, "I'd better go and get the experimenter. You go into the other room and see what happened."

Subjects helped significantly more in the positive-definition than in the negative-definition condition. When the stimulus was defined as an emergency and the appropriate behavior for the subject was defined as going into the other room, all subjects helped. The frequency of help was significantly greater than in the positive-definition condition, in which the confederate defined the sounds as distress sounds but did not start any action and did not tell the subject what to do. The way the stimulus and the appropriate reaction to it were defined by one person affected the behavior of the other person.

In another study (Staub, 1971a) with kindergarten children, the experimenter modeled helping behavior. While the experimenter interacted with the subject there were sounds of mild distress coming from the adjoining room, as if another child had fallen off a chair. The experimenter immediately went into the other room, came back, then told the subject that the child in the other room fell off her chair and she helped her. In the *no-modeling* condition there were no distress sounds at this point. Afterward, while the subject worked on a task alone, sounds of a crash and of severe distress from the adjoining room were heard. Modeling significantly increased helping behavior, in the form of either reporting what happened to the experimenter on her return or going into the other room and thus directly taking some form of action. Modeling in this study may be regarded as the experimenter defining for subjects both the meaning of the stimulus and the appropriate reaction.

The evidence thus suggests that what people say and do, as well as their unresponsiveness to a stimulus, powerfully affect the response of others to apparent emergencies. Why and how does this happen? First, social comparison processes are likely to be involved. Usually social reality is somewhat unclear. We rely on other people's reactions, in part, to define for us the meaning of events. We look at other people, we see what they think about an event, and make up our minds about its meaning—partly on the basis of the others' reactions. The importance of other people in the definition of reality can be very great. Nisbett and Valins (1971) argued that, depending on the extent to which our definition of reality is similar to or different from that of other people, we make attributions about ourselves as either mentally ill or normal and healthy individuals. Other people make attributions about *us* on the same basis. Therefore, it is important to check our definition of reality against that of others; people are likely to be strongly motivated to be in agreement with others. Another reason for the powerful effect of other people is our concern about their reaction to us—whether they will evaluate us positively, negatively, as competent or incompetent. To avoid negative evaluation people try to behave in a manner that is consistent with other people's expectations of them. Such expectations are sometimes implied, other times communicated with various degrees of clarity by what people say, do, or do not do.

Thus, social comparison may lead to a definition of reality consistent with the definition others hold. However, we may also comply with others' definition despite our own divergent interpretation of events. Festinger (1954) suggested that the tendency to engage in social comparison increases as a function of perceived similarity. Smith and associates (1972) hypothesized on this basis that a subject's behavior would be more affected if a similar rather than a dissimilar bystander did not react to another's distress. A female experimenter who administered instructions to the subjects started to act as if she was experiencing pain, then staggered out of the room, bumping into a filing cabinet in an adjoining room. Similarity was manipulated prior to this experience by varying the agreement between the confederate's written attitudes and opinions on contemporary issues and those of the subject. Of lone subjects, 65% helped, and of persons with dissimilar confederates, 35% helped; but only 5% of those who were with a similar, nonreactive bystander initiated help. The difference between the last two groups was significant, that between the first two marginally significant ($p < .06$). Thus, similarity enhanced the confederate's influence over subjects, either in getting them to define the situation as not an emergency or in causing them to model his behavior out of compliance.

We know that people comply with others' expectations to a very great degree. Milgram's research provides an extreme demonstration of this (1963, 1965b). He had subjects participate in a learning task, in which they were assigned, by a procedure that appeared random, the role of teacher, and a confederate had the role of the learner. Subjects were instructed to administer increasingly severe electric shocks when the learner made mistakes: The stated purpose of the experiment was to investigate the effect of pain or stress on efficiency in learning. Many subjects (70%) proceeded to administer shocks up to the limit that was possible, even though there were signs on the machine that indicated that shocks at the upper limit were not only very painful, but also dangerous. Many subjects administered these extreme shocks even when they heard the learner protest, call out in agony, and shout that he had a bad heart and did not want to continue the experiment. However, with an increase in pain cues (feedback), the percentage of subjects who proceeded to administer the strongest shocks progressively declined. Some of the subjects wanted to stop administering shocks but continued when the experimenter insisted. Thus, administering the shocks was a matter of compliance. Rosenhan (1969) found that about 50% of his subjects went through the sequence of shocks and administered the most intense shocks available even when they observed a model who discredited the experimenter. This model asked the experimenter what authority he had to conduct the study. The experimenter's unwilling responses indicated that he was an undergraduate who was conducting the study without the direct supervision of a professor. The model referred to the shock administration as "frying" people and refused to continue. Nevertheless, 50% of the subjects in this condition obliged and administered the most intense shocks, in contrast to 80% in a no-model condition.

Such unreasonable compliance is not entirely out of character with other findings on compliance. Nonetheless, it does seem possible that in the Rosenhan experiment some of the subjects might have felt bad about the humiliation that the experimenter experienced and tried to compensate him by accepting his authority. Although this would be a strange kind of "helping" behavior, the real-life example of private individuals trying to help former President Nixon pay his delinquent tax bill might be another manifestation of this kind of sympathy.

The evidence shows that by what they say, by what they do, or by their inaction people affect others' reactions to emergencies. They do this by affecting the interpretation or perceived meaning of the stimulus, whether it is an emergency or not, by affecting the assessment of appropriate reaction to it, or by producing compliance with their interpretation and with their implied expectation about how to react. It is difficult to differentiate to what degree each of these happens.

Are the Effects of Interpretation and Compliance Separable?   Some experimental findings suggest that the interpretation of the stimulus itself is affected, which in turn affects behavior. In the study where Bickman (1972) varied interpretations of the emergency, half the subjects were told that the person who later provided the interpretation was in the same building; the other half were told that he was in a different building. Beforehand, subjects had been told that they would not meet this person. This, combined with their fellow "subject" being in another building, made it unlikely that the subjects were greatly concerned about how the other person would react if they did not comply. Nonetheless, the confederate's interpretations significantly affected the subjects' behavior.

In another experiment Darley and associates (1973) exposed subjects to a crash and sounds of distress presumably coming from the adjoining room. The subjects were engaged in sketching a model horse and either faced one another or worked back to back. The experimenters reasoned that any cue that another person was concerned about the sounds would lead subjects to take the sounds seriously and define them as an emergency. Subjects who did not face one another could not have any cue as to the other's concern.

However, subjects who faced one another would be likely to notice some startle reaction to the sounds. Because a startle reaction is spontaneous, subjects would consider it an important cue and would view the sounds as something to be concerned about. The experimenters found that 80% of lone subjects, 75% of pairs who faced each other, but only 20% of pairs who sat back to back helped. The presence of another person did not significantly reduce helping when subjects faced each other. The experimenters viewed this finding as evidence that it is the definition of the stimulus itself that is affected by another's presence and then inhibits helping, not compliance with others' definitions. They reasoned that, as in the case of conformity research (Asch, 1952; Allen & Levine, 1968), "any signals which break the uniformity of the group's apparent indifference to the emergency may free the individual to consider the possibility that the event is in fact an emergency and act accordingly [Darley *et al.*, 1973, p. 396]." Actually, in conformity research, a single confederate's deviation from the group may increase deviation by subjects because of the lessened pressure toward compliance. In the Darley *et al.* experiment the consequences of the startle response and of the exchange of nonverbal cues by subjects who saw each other apparently led to a *mutual* definition of the stimulus as one to be concerned about, perhaps making the issue of compliance for subjects in that group irrelevant.

Other evidence for the importance of definition is provided by one of the conditions of a study described earlier (Staub, 1974a). The confederate, who was in the same room with the subject, defined sounds coming from the adjoining room as distress sounds, then said that she was going to get the experimenter. Before she left she also told the subject not to go into the other room because "I don't think we are supposed to." Under these conditions, helping was not inhibited. The frequency of subjects going into the adjoining room was between the frequency in the positive-definition and the "maximum-positive-influence" groups (where the confederate told the subject to go into the other room), not significantly different from either. Having defined the situation as one where help was needed, the added opinion of the confederate that they should not help directly did not inhibit intervention, suggesting that definition was primary and concern about the disapproval of the "other subject" was secondary.

Another side of the issue concerns the independent effect of compliance in helping situations—whether people act contrary to their own definition of a situation to comply with others. Although the research findings make such compliance appear likely, little direct evidence exists. The demeanor of subjects in Milgram's (1965b) studies suggests compliance rather than a definition of the situation identical with that of the influence agent. Findings of a study by Latané and Darley (1970) also seem relevant. They had two confederates play with a Frisbee in a waiting room of Grand Central Station in New York City. One of the confederates threw the Frisbee to a bystander. This person entered the game and threw it back. Then it was thrown to another person; soon a number of people were involved. Latané and Darley were interested in the factors that determined whether people would participate. In one condition a third confederate was present; when the two players threw the Frisbee to him, he loudly protested their Frisbee game. This protest substantially reduced the likelihood that others would get involved, regardless of the reason this person gave as to why they should not play Frisbee. Because of the confederate's negative reaction, other people might have come to view Frisbee playing as an inappropriate activity in the waiting room; his protest affected their interpretations. However, in one condition, the confederate left the waiting room after voicing his criticism. After he left, other people joined in the game to about the same extent as in the other conditions. This suggests that people complied with the expressed wish of this other person, perhaps because they feared abuse or confrontation, perhaps out of respect for his wish.

Concern about Negative Evaluation. In a further study that provides information about the extent to which social influence might affect the definition of events or lead to compliance, Beaman and associates (1974) attempted to explore the influence of "evaluation apprehension" on helping. It is a widely held assumption (Latané & Darley, 1970; Staub, 1974a) that concern about evaluation by others—for example, fear of disapproval or negative evaluation for appearing foolish or acting incompetent—is an important inhibitor of helping behavior. Concern about others' negative reactions might have two components: fear of open disapproval (public abuse and humiliation) and fear or concern that the other person will evaluate us negatively, think of us badly, without necessarily saying so. Evidence that concern about an experimenter's negative reactions diminishes helping behavior is presented later (see also Staub, 1971b, 1974a), but direct evidence that fear of negative reactions by fellow bystanders inhibits helping is sparse.

In their study, Beaman *et al.* had a male subject sit in a room; a female who was ostensibly a subject (actually a confederate) was in an adjoining room. It was made reasonably believable to the subjects that, because of a bad lock, the door of the adjoining room could not be opened from the inside. Thus, the confederate could not get out of her room. There was a one-way mirror between the two rooms. In one condition, the subject's room was illuminated so that the confederate could see the subject, but the subject could not see her. This was the evaluation apprehension condition (EA). In another condition, the confederate's room was illuminated but the subject's room was not (social comparison, SC), and in a third condition both rooms were illuminated (EA + SC), so that the subject and confederate could see each other. In a fourth condition there was no confederate; the subject alone was involved. The confederate always remained passive during the emergency, which consisted of another female confederate fainting while both the subject and the confederate watched her on separate video screens. In the evaluation-apprehension condition, helping behavior was not reduced (75%) in comparison to the alone group (80%). The subject did not know what the other person was doing but did know that she could not help—and even though he could be observed by her, he frequently initiated help. Social comparison, witnessing the other's inactivity, marginally reduced helping (55%), presumably a definitional effect. The combination of social comparison and evaluation apprehension resulted in significantly less help than social comparison alone (25%). The findings suggest that people are not concerned that whatever they do will be judged negatively; rather, they are concerned that deviation from others, in judgment and/or expected action, will be negatively evaluated. Being observed reduced helping only when it deviated from the other person's apparent definition of the event, her lack of any reaction to the distress cues. Although these findings are instructive, the special conditions of this study should be noted: Since the other person could not leave the room, responsibility for helping was focused on the subject. As the discussion in a later section shows, being the only person in a position to help while being observed by another person tends to *increase* helping, since normative pressure for help would be strong in such a situation.

One question about evaluation apprehension is this: What are the types of behavior that people particularly fear will be negatively evaluated? Deviation from others' definitions of events, from their apparent expectations of how one will behave, seems to be one such behavior. Probably assuming a position of leadership without legitimate authority is another. This might inhibit people from taking charge and initiating action when others are present. Any deviation from conventional social norms and from conventional forms of behavior might cause strong fear of negative evaluation, resulting in an inclination to do nothing, which results in less public exposure than doing something. Tangentially relevant, because it shows the state of mind that contemplating an unusual behavior might create, is Milgram's (1974) description of his attempt to walk up to a person in the subway and ask for his seat. Standing in front of this person and about to ask, he apparently felt paralyzed and had to retreat. Urged on by one of his students, he finally performed this act, but he found this extremely difficult to do, as did his students. Many times when the meaning of a stimulus or the appropriate behavior is not entirely clear, people might find it similarly difficult to expose themselves and perform what *they* might consider deviant acts.

The study conducted by Beaman *et al.* suggests that simply being observable does not substantially reduce helping. It is surprising that, considering the apparently widespread belief that fear of negative evaluation and criticism by others reduces helping, experimental evidence is so minimal. What is the source of the belief, then? Probably it is subjective experience. Most of us have experienced subjective paralysis similar to that described by Milgram, particularly in ambiguous situations. Sometimes, knowing the inhibiting influence of social situations, one can push oneself to overcome this. It certainly seems rational to act on the basis of principles similar to the one implied by a second-grade boy during one of our experiments (Staub, 1970b). Having actively attempted to help in response to distress sounds, this boy, one of the few to express suspicion, said afterward, "I thought that might be a tape recorder [the distress sounds], but I wasn't sure and I didn't want to take any chances."

Assuming that people are inhibited by what others might think about them and by how others might evaluate them, how much reason do they really have for being so inhibited? Do other people in fact evaluate them negatively if they initiate helping action when actually none is needed?

In a study referred to earlier in this chapter (Staub, 1974a) the confederate varied both her verbal definition of sounds of distress coming from an adjoining room and her behavioral response to the situation. After the emergency was over the experimenter put the subject and the confederate (who was still acting in the role of a subject) into separate rooms and asked them to fill out a questionnaire. The subjects were asked to describe the feelings they had and to evaluate the other person's reactions and personal characteristics. They were asked to indicate how flustered or composed the other person was. When the confederate just verbally defined the sounds, whether as distress sounds or as a tape recording, people thought that she was composed rather than flustered. When she took some form of action, they thought she was more flustered. Very reasonably, subjects judged the confederate as more active when she actually took action. When the confederate gave only a verbal definition, regardless of its content, her behavior was judged significantly more appropriate than when she jumped up and initiated indirect help. But all the means on this last rating were between scale points 1 and 2 on a 5-point scale, where 1 was "very appropriate" and 5 was "very inappropriate." Thus, taking action was judged fairly appropriate, not inappropriate. Subjects were also asked how concerned the confederate was. The confederate was judged as very concerned, except when she defined the sounds as a tape recording. Subjects were also asked to judge a variety of other characteristics of the confederate, such as the degree to which she was likable or strong. The behavior of the confederate did not affect these ratings. This evidence suggests that people do not evaluate others negatively when the others "overreact" to a situation in a helpful manner.

It is possible, of course, that the subjects did not judge the confederate negatively when she initiated help because they knew that most people judge helping as a good thing and, knowing that the experiment was about helping, they might have thought that the experimenter judged helping positively.

An interesting sidelight to this issue is the discussion generated by the presentation of these data in an undergraduate class I taught at Stanford University. The students strongly, and seemingly unanimously, argued that people do judge the actions of others harshly. To quote one student: "Well, but in a society where one's worth is so often based on one's performance, what you're suggesting is that we go on the assumption that other people will make allowance for the possibility of our making a mistake. And our experience is that often that allowance is not made." The students insistently asked why people so commonly believed that others would react negatively if the assumption was not based on reality. Even though the class was relatively large and students are frequently inhibited in front of many other students, this issue led to passionate expression of opinions. Students strongly expressed the feeling that unless one is careful one will be negatively evaluated. Although this is not the place to try to deal with the question of origins in detail (see Volume 2), extensive instruction of children by adults in the rules of proper social behavior may lead to overconcern about evaluation by others (Staub, 1971b, 1974a) and to feelings of shame about inappropriate public behavior.

Ambiguity and the Interpretation of Events.   An issue surrounding this discussion is that social and even physical events are often ambiguous and lend themselves to varied interpretations. Before they respond to events, for most people the ambiguity has to be sufficiently reduced. Sometimes events that are unclear are also threatening or upsetting for various reasons, even to the degree that people deny their reality and engage in "motivated misperception."

A clear example of the difficulty people can have in interpreting an event is provided by this paragraph by Baron and Byrne (1976; see also Baron and Byrne, 1977, pp. 375–376) showing reactions to a sudden, dramatic event.

> A few years ago, two of the authors were on the University of Texas campus the day a student carried guns and ammunition to the top of the highest tower on campus and then systematically shot down several dozen random individuals on the sidewalks and pathways in range of his rifle. Some of those who were hit heard the shots when they began and some had actually seen bodies lying about. Rather than take cover, many in this situation simply continued about their business and thus came under fire themselves. Of those who were only wounded, or who were lucky not to be hit, several described their reactions at the time in terms of confusion about what was going on. Some thought the rifle shots were sounds made by construction workers. The dead and wounded were perceived as actors in a fraternity stunt. And the gun

powder smoke blowing from the tower was attributed to a fire. One wounded student described his confusions about what was going on and his feeling that he would look foolish if he altered his plans and stopped walking toward the student union where he intended to eat lunch. Hiding behind a wall in response to the sound of construction, or the sight of actors lying on the sidewalk, would be a social disaster.

An experiment by Denner (1968) further demonstrates interpretational difficulties. He dealt with personality differences in the way people perceive and report an unusual event. Denner measured variation in subjects' speed in perceiving and/or reporting small stimulus changes, using a leveling–sharpening task and the autokinetic light test. Some people reported apparent movement of the light quickly, others did so more slowly. Some reported slight changes in geometric forms very fast, others did so only after larger stimulus changes. In a second session, as the subject left an experimental room and entered another room, he saw a man with his hand in a lady's handbag. Upon the subject's entry, the man smiled in an embarrassed fashion, pulled his hand out of the bag, and left the room quickly. The question was whether subjects would report this event to the experimenter or later mention it while talking into a tape recorder about their experiences in the experiment. Subjects who were slow in reporting stimulus changes were also significantly less likely to report what they saw and/or reported it at a later point in time. Denner suggests that subjects who were slow to report stimulus changes continued to wonder about the meaning of what they saw and were concerned about being somehow misled or taken in. The possibility that variation in the perception and definition of social events can be a function of perceptual decision-making style is important. In addition, people in general are likely to vary in the ease or difficulty with which they decide what is going on as the characteristics of the situation vary, making what is happening more or less clear.

Many complex, unclear social situations also create conflict. If people were to get involved, they might have costs that they did not bargain for. As a result they might be motivated to perceive events in such a way that no intervention is necessary.

A study by Latané and Darley (1968) provides an example. Subjects filling out a market research questionnaire were told that two children were waiting in the adjoining room to participate in a market research study. The experimenter expressed hope that the children would not be too noisy. After the experimenter left, the older child asked for the toy the younger child was playing with. The younger child refused to give it to him. The older child asked again, and the younger child refused. The older child said, "I'll beat you up if you don't give it to me" and the younger child said "No." The older child started to beat the younger child. When the younger child said, "OK, OK, it hurts, I'm going to give it to you," the older child said, "No, now it's too late. I'm really going to beat you up."

He went on beating the younger child. Then the younger child said, "No, it really hurts, oh, look, I'm bleeding. Help. Please help."

What did the subjects do? One out of 11 went out of the room and told the first person he encountered about the children. The rest did nothing. Afterward they were asked what they thought was going on and all had some kind of interpretation that made intervention unnecessary. For example, some thought that the children might have turned on the television, and others thought the voices were coming from a tape recorder.

Of course, the subjects were right. Nobody really needed help. What is of interest here is how and why they came to their conclusions. Darley and Latané added another condition in which the subjects heard the same tape, but were told that an adult was in the room with the children. Again, subjects did not intervene, but they did not afterward report disbelief in what they heard. Only when *they* felt responsible were the subjects motivated to see no need for intervention, but not when another adult was responsible for supervising the children.

Diffusion of Responsibility and Normative Explanations of Helping Behavior

The Conception of Normative Influence.   Latané and Darley (1970) proposed that each person's feeling of responsibility gets diffused when other people are present, so helping behavior is reduced. A feeling of responsibility for others' welfare is likely to be an important determinant of helping behavior whether others are present or absent. Is that the case? What determines whether a person feels responsible for another? Responsibility for others' welfare presumably originates from existing societal values and norms, and from personal values and standards.

Norms refer to generally held expectations about how people will behave in a social group. Berkowitz and Daniels (1963) hypothesized that a widely held societal norm is the norm of social responsibility, according to which people should aid others who are dependent on them. They wrote, "The perception of the dependency relationship presumably arouses feelings of responsibility to these others, and the outcome is a heightened instigation to help them achieve their goals [p. 430]." One goal might be to be free of distress. Norms imply that a person will be rewarded for behaving in the expected fashion and might be punished for not adhering to the societal expectation. Darley and Latané discuss, in fact, diffusion of responsibility and diffusion of blame together, as resulting from others' presence.

If adherence to social norms is motivated by expectation of external rewards and external punishment for deviation, the presence of others might be expected to *enhance* norm-prescribed behavior. The more concerned people are about others' reactions the more they might obey norms, at least in public. As I noted earlier, in contrast to—or in addition to—social norms, the personal, individual norms that result from internalizing societal values and norms may motivate helping behavior.

There is evidence that the presence of other people increases adherence to social norms, as one would expect. Children cheat less (Hartshorne & May, 1928) and they share more (Liebert & Poulos, 1971) when they are under surveillance. In one study, when people knew that their behavior could be or was being observed, they helped another person more in manipulating small metal objects, even though they had to endure electric shock each time they touched one of the objects (Midlarsky, 1971). In light of the aforementioned reasoning and these findings, shouldn't the frequency of helping *increase* in others' presence? Seemingly it should, and that is one reason why the decrease in help when others are present is a surprising finding. In fact, sometimes others' presence does increase helping (Staub, 1970b; Horowitz, 1971; see later in this chapter).

One might reason, however, that when several bystanders are present, a condition of *mutual surveillance* exists. If a bystander feels that intervention is needed, he might still reason that as long as the others who are present do not act, they cannot blame him for inaction; and potential blame by outsiders seems less potent because it is shared by those present.

Having proposed the diffusion of responsibility explanation, which seems to refer to a norm, Darley and Latané (1970) proceeded to reject the value of norm-centered explanations. There are a number of contradictory norms that apply to any one situation, they reasoned, and thus one cannot really predict which norm will determine behavior. Also, some of their research demonstrated that people do or do not behave helpfully as a function of the cost of helping and other influences, and thus they often act contrary to helping norms. However, just as the existence of helping behavior is no evidence for the influence of norms, lack of helping or modification by other determinants is no contrary evidence. Behavior is clearly multidetermined, and when we investigate any possible influence on prosocial behavior we must ask under what conditions, to what degree, and with modification by what other influences it affects behavior. It should be clear from the discussion in the previous section, for example, that often people are likely to act not according to *generalized* expectations about behavior embodied in norms, but according to *specific* expectations implied or communicated by other people who are present, even if the specific expectations are contrary to normative expectations.

Situational and Other Modes of Focusing Responsibility. A host of experiments attempted to evaluate the diffusion of responsibility hypothesis by examining the effect of conditions that focus responsibility on a person. In one experiment, Korte (1969) had a person overhear an asthmatic attack of the experimenter. The subject was led to believe that another person in another room also witnessed it. Furthermore, the subject was led to believe either that the other person was in a position to help or that he was tied down by electrodes for the purpose of measuring his physiological reactions to some stimuli. When responsibility was focused on the subjects by the circumstances (the other person was not in a position to help), subjects helped somewhat more ($p < .07$). In two studies Bickman (1971, 1972) compared subjects' reactions to an emergency when that emergency was overheard by another person. In one condition the second person was in the same building with the subject and the victim. In a second condition, the other person was in another building and presumably not in a position to help. When circumstances focused responsibility on subjects they helped significantly more. In one of Bickman's studies (1972) this finding was replicated with different interpretations of the emergency provided for the subjects.

Ross (1971) attempted to focus responsibility on subjects by exposing them to emergencies while they were with two children (a 4- and a 6-year-old who were confederates of the experimenter). Other subjects were alone when exposed to an emergency, still others were in groups of three. Ross studied reactions to two emergencies. In one, subjects heard a workman fall and emit sounds of distress; in the other emergency, smoke filled the room. Ross assumed that children are less capable of helping others than are adults and that the smoke coming into the room would make the adults responsible for helping the children. Findings were similar with the two emergencies. Of the subjects who were alone, about 80% initiated action; only about 20% of those in the group of three strangers initiated action. Surprisingly, only about 50% of the subjects who were with the two children acted, regardless of the kind of emergency. In attempting to explain these findings, Ross suggested that although children place re-responsibility on the adult they are also models of nonresponsiveness. In another study (Ross & Brabend, 1973) subjects were either with a nonresponsive sighted confederate or with a nonresponsive blind confederate when they witnessed one of the two emergencies. The presence of a blind person presumably focused responsibility on the subject to respond to smoke filling the room. The presence of both blind and sighted nonresponsive confederates reduced help for the injured workman. The presence of a sighted confederate reduced reaction to the smoke, but the presence of a blind confederate slightly increased reaction ($p < .08$). The subjects' feeling of responsibility was also shown in that four of nine subjects who responded to the smoke took the blind confederate from the room with them. Again, the subjects' behavior was probably affected not just by the channeling of responsibility but also by the fact that the blind person did not react, although he could hear the sounds of distress and possibly smell the smoke. Obviously, blindness does not eliminate the cue value or definitional power of a person.

Schwartz and Clausen (1970) replicated the original epileptic attack experiment conducted by Darley and Latané (1968). Again, subjects were made to believe that other people were in different cubicles. In one of the conditions, one of the others was presented as a premedical student who worked in a hospital emergency ward. Presumably his competence made him responsible to help with an epileptic fit and thus reduced the subjects' responsibility. The study showed that for females the presence of other bystanders resulted in a substantial reduction in helping, and the presence of this competent other resulted in a further substantial reduction. Surprisingly, males were unaffected by the treatments; they helped to an intermediate degree in all conditions. Schwartz and Clausen speculate that males might have been affected by the presumed presence of females in other cubicles. However, in Darley and Latané's original study (1968) mixed groups of males and females were also present. Nonetheless these studies indicate that when conditions focus responsibility on a person, that person is likely to help. When circumstances focus responsibility away from a person, helping decreases.

A field experiment also provides some evidence for this conclusion. Piliavin and Piliavin (1972) found that when a person collapsed on the subway and had blood trickling from his mouth, he was helped less than when he simply collapsed. However, subjects helped less in the former condition primarily when a confederate, dressed in white to look like an intern, was sitting close to the victim. People in this case probably felt they could do much less to help the bleeding person, and therefore had much less responsibility to help, than their medically competent fellow bystander.

Not surprisingly, there is some indication that people who have roles or positions that focus responsibility on them, and people whose jobs involve helping others, tend to be helpful. Formal research is minimal on this point, but Midlarsky (1968) reports that firemen, policemen, and other people in help-related professions engage in rescue efforts at times of natural disasters (such as tornadoes, cyclones, and earthquakes) to a greater degree than do members of the general population. In part, one may regard this as a response to formalized, job-related responsibilities. It may also result from training, past experience, and the resulting competence to help. There are other, anecdotal reports indicating that being in a position of responsibility leads people to respond to someone's need to a greater degree. Sometimes the origin of responsibility may be that one created or caused another person's need, a situation that is discussed at length in Chapter 4.

In a book that vividly and dramatically re-creates a number of the heroic incidents that led to the awarding of the Carnegie Hero Medal to individuals, Markowitz (1973) describes several incidents where conditions focused responsibility on the hero. In one, a lion got loose in an animal shelter and the manager of the shelter single-handedly went to the rescue. The manager might have felt responsibility because he was in charge of the shelter and thus responsible for what was happening there, and because he agreed that the lion be temporarily housed at the shelter, even though proper facilities were not available.

An interesting issue is the relationship between responsibility and commitment. Frequently people get involved in helping others by getting gradually committed; they may take some initial action (sometimes when the seriousness of the need is not yet recognized and the potential difficulty and cost of helping are not known) and then remain engaged. The gradual involvement may lead to increasingly greater commitment to, and in turn feelings of responsibility for, the welfare of others.

Several heroic rescue efforts that are described by Markowitz (1973) exemplify these issues; the brief discussion here foreshadows more detailed examination of the influences and processes involved (e.g., relatedness to the victim) in later chapters. In one incident, a game warden and another person volunteered to go down a cliff, at night, tied to a rope held by others, in order to rescue a person at the bottom of the cliff. They could not reach the person on their first attempt, so the two returned to the top of the cliff. But it was the exhausted game warden, not someone fresh or less tired, who made a second effort and saved the person, apparently with extreme effort and bravery. In still another incident, a pleasure boat with a family aboard—parents and children—got stuck on a sandbar. A young man from the crew of an excursion boat that passed by was willing to give up his wages for the day to stay with the family until the tide came and lifted the boat. When this did not happen and they had to swim for miles to save themselves, his spirit, leadership, and physical effort saved the family. The man whose life and family he saved had this to say about him: "He never showed fear, not even the slightest concern for his own safety, but was continually swimming and encouraging us to help and directing us to work in the direction of the island. His great courage and optimism kept up our hope when there was little reason to have any [Markowitz, 1973, p. 229]." The hero died 5 years later in a car accident; the car he was in had been in a drag race just prior to the accident. Perhaps we can here surmise adventurousness, satisfaction gained from exciting, demanding, or unusual experiences, as a *contributing* motive.

I am giving these examples to suggest a process of involvement that probably frequently occurs in helping others. Experimental research is needed to elucidate and verify this process. External conditions or personal characteristics focus responsibility on a person. The existence of some kind of relatedness to a person in need may contribute to the feeling of responsibility. A person's initial involvement in the helping process, which can result from environmental conditions or can be due to personality characteristics or prior relatedness that led to self-selection, may lead to increased feelings of responsibility.

One heroic incident that carries this argument one step further involved a mine accident. When part of a mine collapsed, a miner was pinned down underground. A tunnel had to be dug to reach him. This took a long time, and the first exhausted team of rescuers was replaced by another team. Two members of the first team voluntarily remained. One was a member of the mine rescue squad, the first one to get to the scene. The other person was a German, as was the man pinned down underground, but there is no indication in Markowitz's report that he was a friend of the injured miner. However, he was the first person to get close enough to the endangered man to find out, in their native language, his position and circumstances. This information guided further rescue efforts. Later he climbed down the deep, narrow tunnel that led to the injured man. Their common national origin might have created some identification, and his initial involvement may have led to a feeling of special responsibility and/or commitment.

An experiment that provides information about the influence of a person's position of responsibility and of that person's characteristics was conducted by Firestone *et al.* (1975). In this study male subjects formed five-person problem-discussion groups. One person, a confederate, who had earlier noted that he was a diabetic, became agitated in the course of the discussion. He said that he was having a diabetic reaction and needed sugar, that he might pass out and could not get the sugar himself. As he was expressing increasing urgency in this manner, he was looking toward the leader of the group. Whether someone left the room to get sugar, and the latency of this reaction, was noted by observers.

Each of the groups had a leader. In the *emergent-elected* condition the members "elected" the leader. The experimenter always counted the votes, but the name he announced was that of the person who, on the basis of his participation in a preceding 5-minute discussion period, was voted by judges as having the highest leadership potential. The observers served as judges. In the *pseudo-elected-leader* condition the person whom the judges scored lowest on leadership potential was announced as elected leader. In the *appointed-leader* condition an arbitrary criterion was used in appointing a leader. Of the emergent-elected-leader groups, 84% (11 out of 13) sent someone for help, compared with 46% for appointed leaders and 23% for pseudo--elected leaders. The difference among the three groups in frequency of help, as well as in reaction time, was highly significant.

When the groups with appointed leaders were divided into those whose leaders had high leadership potential and those whose leaders had low leadership potential, the former groups helped significantly more than the latter. In many groups whose leader had low leadership potential, the leader was overthrown. A person other than the original leader took charge and initiated helping activity, usually by sending someone to get sugar or to find the experimenter. The person who ended up as a leader was invariably one with a high leadership potential. When the person who was formally in charge of a group showed leadership during the discussion, rescue efforts were more frequent and faster. Individuals who established de facto leadership tended to take charge even when they were not formally in charge, and formal leadership by someone who was not exerting or developing actual leadership inhibited helping efforts.

A formal leader who does not take action may have a definitional influence on others. Other members may experience diffusion of responsibility, or they may be constrained because they do not want to preempt the leader's position by initiating help. It is unfortunate that a control group without a leader was not included in the study. A comparison between such a group and the arbitrary-leader condition could have established the extent to which the leadership role focuses responsibility on people to initiate help. The findings do show that imposing a position of leadership on a person does not necessarily lead to the assumption of leadership in helping others. Certain personality characteristics that are apparently also relevant to helping behavior led some individuals to demonstrate leadership in the discussion. Initiative, self-assertiveness, and low self-concern may be such characteristics. A contrasting possibility is that those knowledgeable about the topic or comfortable in group discussion became leaders in the discussion, and then their position of leadership led them to assume responsibility in the helping effort.

Verbal Focusing of Responsibility.   In some studies, responsibility for someone's welfare was verbally focused on participants. In one of these studies (Staub, 1970a), the experimenter told either first-graders or kindergarten children that she was leaving them in charge; she asked them to take care of anything that happened. These vague instructions increased helping behavior by first-graders in response to sounds of distress from an adjoining room. They did not increase helping by kindergartners, but increased their denial that they heard anything. Since some of the children plugged their ears with their fingers, it is unquestionable that they did hear. Presumably, uncertainty about what to do and lack of competence inhibited these young children from helping. Because responsibility had been focused on them, they feared blame for not helping, which led to denial. Focusing responsibility also affected behavior in a Milgram-type experiment. Tilker (1970) had subjects observe a confederate administering shocks of increasing magnitude to a presumed learner. In a similar study, Kaufman (1968) found that regardless of the exact task subjects had—whether they were supposed to learn how to supervise the learner (how to administer shocks) or to learn how to act as a recorder of events—they rarely attempted to stop the administration of shocks. In Tilker's study, when the observer was made responsible for what happened to the learner, he interfered more often. Interference by telling the confederate to stop administering shocks or by contacting the experimenter was particularly frequent when the feedback about the learner's reactions to the shocks, evidence of his pain, was stronger.

In summary, both situational focusing and verbal focusing of responsibility on people affect their helping behavior. When responsibility is focused on them, people are more likely to adhere to societal values and norms prescribing help for others, or to act according to the specific expectations of those who have focused responsibility on them. Conditions that focus responsibility on a person may also activate relevant personal values and norms or relevant personal goals.

An interesting example of verbal focusing of responsibility in a life situation was shown in the film *Nine Heroes* broadcast on public television (PBS). Each segment of this nine-part movie told the story of a person who received a Carnegie Hero Medal for saving the life of another. In one segment, people describe how they stood in front of a burning building. Some children were still in the building, and these people—even members of the fire department—turned to a man known for acts of bravery and asked expectantly, "Are you going in?" His prior role in the community and his reputation for bravery made others turn to him in a manner that clearly focused responsibility for action on him.

Verbal communications that create responsibility have resulted in substantial degrees of intervention of other types. In one study (Moriarty, 1975), some people at Jones Beach, New York, were asked by a confederate to watch the confederate's belongings for a few minutes. Other people were asked for a match. In both cases the confederate left the scene for a few moments. When another passerby later picked up the confederate's radio and started to walk away with it, 29% of the subjects, all of whom were in the no-commitment condition (who were asked for a match), appeared not to notice the incident. Of the remaining subjects, 95% of those who were asked to watch intervened, whereas only 20% of those who were not asked intervened and stopped the thief, a highly significant difference. These findings were replicated in a substantially different setting, an Automat cafeteria in New York City during the busy lunch period. People who were asked to watch another person's suitcase intervened substantially more frequently to stop a thief than people who were not asked.

Moriarty (1975) explained these findings by the concept of commitment, which refers to "a prior decision to help should the occasion arise [p. 374]." He proposed that commitment eliminates the conflict that arises and immobilizes people when they try to decide whether or not to act. Once the decision is made, conflict is minimal and responsiveness is greater. The conception I have presented so far focuses on a feeling of responsibility that would result from the agreement to watch over another person's belongings. Having such a feeling of responsibility does minimize conflict, because it makes the decision to help easier. Obviously, the two interpretations have much in common, but they differ in emphasis. One emphasizes the primacy of a feeling of responsibility, the other, of the decision to help.

There are various conditions that focus responsibility on a person. If a person is the only witness to another's need for help or the only one of several witnesses who is in a position to help, he may be regarded as the subject of *circumstantial* focusing of responsibility. Having a position, status, or authority that confers leadership on a person may be regarded as leading to *positional* focusing of responsibility. Special competence, personal characteristics that are needed for helping, may lead to *ability*-induced responsibility. A job or formal role—that of a doctor or policeman—may give rise to *role*-dictated responsibility. Prior relationships to persons in need can lead to *relationship*-induced responsibility. Once someone has already taken some steps to help another person, a special form of relationship-induced responsibility, which may be called *commitment*-induced responsibility, can take hold. Personality characteristics may lead to a sense of *personal* responsibility for other people's welfare. The more a sense of personal responsibility can be developed through socialization and experience, the more widespread helping behavior is likely to be.

Do Norms Affect Helping Behavior?   There are several problems with the way that social norm explanations are usually applied to behavior, specifically to helping behavior. First, the existence of specific norms is usually not measured but assumed. There is little formal evidence, in fact, that people believe that others expect them to help or that one ought to help others. Most such evidence is indirect. For example, people's reactions to norm violations can serve as evidence of their belief in the norm. Writers of letters to the editor of the *New York Times* were outraged about the people who witnessed the murder of Kitty Genovese and did not help. Some asked for their names and addresses so that they could be exposed to the public wrath that they deserve.

Second, although helpfulness might generally be valued, beliefs about the kind of help that is expected, the degree to which people are expected to help others, and the manner in which norms that prescribe helping behavior apply under various circumstances vary from person to person. Conceptions of the range of applicability of a societal or personal norm may vary greatly. We know nothing about such differentiations, even though they could be measured.

Although some of the research findings that have been reviewed might be considered evidence for normative influences on helping, it is difficult to draw firm conclusions about internal processes (concern about adherence or deviation from norms) from research manipulating external conditions. A reasonable way to demonstrate the influence of norms on a global, cultural level would be to show that there are behavioral differences between cultures that correspond to differing values or beliefs in relevant norms.

However, cross-cultural studies of values (Almond & Verba, 1963) and helping behavior (Berkowitz, 1966; Feldman, 1968; Whiting and Whiting, 1975) have been few and limited.[1] Moreover, the cross-cultural research that does exist has not related behavioral differences to differences in values or beliefs in norms. Another meaningful way to demonstrate the influence of norms is to measure individual differences in values related to helping or norms about helping behavior and demonstrate a reasonable correspondence to these norms in people's behavior under both private and public conditions.

In an experiment that attempted to examine the influence of subcultural differences in values or norms on helping behavior, Horowitz (1971) used the epileptic-fit paradigm. The subjects in the study were males. Some were members of social groups (campus fraternities) and others were members of a service group (a campus organization that engaged in charitable activities and activities related to community betterment). Some were made to believe that they were alone with the victim, and others were told that there were three additional bystanders. Half the subjects were asked to include, in the course of a discussion to be conducted over an intercom, comments about the effects that membership in their group had on their ability to cope with college life; the other half were not asked to do this. This treatment aimed at varying the salience of the group's norms. Service-group members helped the victim significantly more often. Norm salience increased helping behavior in both groups, presumably because of an increased feeling of identification by subjects with their group. More important, there was little difference between the behavior of subjects in the two groups when the subjects thought themselves alone. But the presence of others substantially decreased helping behavior by social-group members, whereas it *increased* helping by service-group members, under both norm salience conditions. A marginally significant interaction in the subjects' post-experimental reports of their feelings of responsibility, which corresponded to behavior, showed similar effects. Given their own values and beliefs, service-group members may have thought that others expected them to help a person in need and therefore felt more responsibility when others were present (and thus they were under public surveillance), instead of experiencing diffusion of responsibility. A related explanation is that the presence of others functioned as an activator of their prosocial goal and associated norms of conduct. Unfortunately, although Horowitz's report shows that the victim was supposed to belong to an "accounting group," it does not indicate what groups the other presumed bystanders belonged to. If subjects thought that the other bystanders were members of their own group, then

---

[1] There have been many recent cross-cultural studies of cooperation and competition among children, but these behaviors were tested under restricted conditions, on specialized games (see Chapter 9; Volume 2).

not only their own values but their knowledge of the other bystanders' values and presumed expectations would have affected their behavior.

Other research attempted to demonstrate the relationship between personal values and beliefs and helping behavior. Most of this research is reviewed later, when personality influences are considered. Some findings by Bickman and Rosenbaum (1977) suggest that verbal influence that is consistent with a person's prior attitudes or internalized norms has greater effect than verbal influence that is inconsistent with or contrary to personal orientation. These researchers found that communications by a confederate to a person, the subject, who was standing behind a shoplifter in the checkout line of a supermarket, had different effects with students and nonstudents. Students, who subsequently expressed much more lenient attitudes toward shoplifting than nonstudent adults, were more influenced by a communication that defined the shoplifter's behavior as a crime but discouraged reporting it. Following such a communication, fewer of these students reported the shoplifter than students in a control group. Nonstudents, on the other hand, were more affected than students by a communication that defined the shoplifter's behavior as a crime and encouraged reporting it.

Schwartz (1970, 1977) developed a model according to which helping behavior is determined by belief in prosocial norms combined with a sense of personal responsibility for others' welfare and awareness of the consequences of one's actions for others. Schwartz and Clausen (1970) gave subjects a paper-and-pencil test that measured the assumption of responsibility for others' welfare. They found that those who scored high on the test were generally more helpful than those who scored low. When subjects witnessed an emergency (an epileptic seizure) alone, which focused responsibility on them, there was little difference in helping by subjects scoring high or low on this test. When other people or a competent other or both were present—conditions that reduced helping by females—subjects who scored high on this test were more helpful. Conditions can focus responsibility and enhance everybody's helping, but people who believe in their personal responsibility seem to remain more helpful when circumstances allow the diffusion of responsibility. People who value helpfulness and believe that it is their responsibility to help others want to behave according to their beliefs, not only out of concern about the reactions of others, but also because of their own self-reactions. The degree to which prosocial norms became personal—and internalization is probably a matter of degree rather than an either/or affair—determines the degree to which people are likely to follow norms when external surveillance does not exist. To repeat, the justification of inferring the influence of norms on behavior is substantially enhanced when personal norms are first evaluated, and a relationship is shown between the degree to which individuals hold such norms and their behavior under conditions that are expected to activate the norms.

Conditions That Limit the Influence of Other People. Are there conditions that minimize or negate the influence of other people on a person's helping? Probably when the situation is crystal clear (if it ever is) people are *less* influenced by others, because they can arrive at an unequivocal definition of the event by themselves. Some suggestive support for this comes from studies by Clark and Word (1972, 1974), who varied the ambiguity of an emergency. In one study they found that the presence of others, even of a passive confederate, did not reduce helping when the need for help was unambiguous. In a second study they found no difference between single and pairs of subjects when the stimulus was entirely clear and visible, or when the stimulus was highly ambiguous. In the latter case there was a generally low frequency of helping. In a medium-ambiguity condition there was a marginally significant tendency for pairs of subjects to help less. This gives some support for the idea that certain conditions minimize social influence.

Other experiments also show that the presence of others does not necessarily decrease helping and might even increase it. Relative certainty about the need for help might exist when a distressed person is visible, or when it is possible to face others and monitor their reactions (Darley, Teger, & Lewis 1973). Piliavin, Rodin, and Piliavin (1969) found that the number of bystanders did not affect the reactions of bystanders to staged emergencies in New York City subway trains. According to Darley, Teger, & Lewis (1973), subway riders usually face one another and would be able to see one another's startle reactions. Another factor is a victim's visibility. The resulting low ambiguity is likely to contribute to a positive definition of need and minimize or eliminate a bystander effect. The lack of diffusion of responsibility in subway emergencies seems a reliable effect, replicated by Piliavin *et al.* in other studies (1975). A positive relationship holds between the number of people in a compartment and indices of help, probably reflecting the greater probability of help when more people are present.

Another influence on helping behavior in the Piliavin *et al.* (1969) study, however, which will soon be discussed at greater length, might have been that the subjects were in an express train, which had its next stop only $6\frac{1}{2}$ minutes after the emergency was staged. The extended exposure, with only minimal opportunity for escape from the situation, might have exercised strong normative pressure on subjects. Similar conditions existed in the other subway studies.

These findings suggest (but do not prove) that when circumstances permit an onlooker to define a stimulus as a person clearly in physical distress, other forms of social influence (such as diffusion of responsibility) are not likely to affect behavior. Further support for this conclusion comes from the finding (Staub, 1974a) previously described that after a confederate defined sounds coming from the adjoining room as distress sounds, both verbally and by initiating indirect help (going to get the experimenter), a verbal instruction to the subject not to go into the adjoining room did not decrease helping behavior. Perhaps once a stimulus is defined in such a way that it activates internal processes, such as norms or empathy or a prosocial goal, that promote helping, inhibiting social forces are less effective. However, alternative explanations of this last finding also exist: In the study just mentioned, the inhibiting verbal instructions were often late, starting after the subject had already begun to move toward the adjoining room, thus their inhibiting influence was smaller (see Staub, 1974a).

Only two experiments found an increase in helping behavior in the presence of others. One of these experiments, in which members of service groups helped more when they believed that others witnessed an emergency, I have already described (Horowitz, 1971).

In the other experiment (Staub, 1970b), I explored the hypothesis that the presence of others will increase helping among young children. Another's distress is likely to cause anxiety and discomfort in an observer. There is fairly widespread evidence, however, from studies of rats, other animals, and human beings, that the presence of another member of the same species reduces anxiety (Bovard, 1959). The presence of another might increase a person's willingness or ability to approach the anxiety-producing distress stimulus. To adults, unfortunately, other people are sometimes a source of anxiety because of concern about negative evaluation by them. However, young children are relatively unconcerned about evaluation by their peers. I found that pairs of children in kindergarten, first grade, and second grade who were exposed to sounds of distress coming from an adjoining room were more likely to help than was a single child. This finding did not hold for children in the fourth and sixth grades. Younger children often communicated their reactions to the distress sounds to one another, saying such things as, "Gee, you know, I am scared" or "That sounds like a baby crying." Older children rarely did this. Both younger and older children sometimes responded inappropriately, with smiles. Younger children, however, usually said something that would correct the impression that they regarded the sounds amusing, but older ones did not. A definitional process counteracting pluralistic ignorance might have enhanced helping by pairs of younger children. Concern about their peers' reactions apparently exerted an influence on fourth- and sixth-grade children.

Other evidence, as well as reasoning about the influence of varied numbers of bystanders, has also been proposed. Morgan (1978) found that the latency of response to persistent, repeated knocks on a door of the room where subjects worked was unaffected by variation in the number of bystanders when the cost of "helping," that is, of opening the door, was minimal. One subject, groups of 2–3 subjects, and groups of 5–7 subjects helped about equally fast when the importance of their task was deemphasized. When, however, cost was higher, that is, the problems subjects worked on were presented as tests of ability and subjects had a time limit, the latency of response increased with increased group size. Morgan explains the findings in terms of concepts similar to those emphasized by Piliavin and Piliavin (1972), which are discussed extensively later in this chapter. In Morgan's view, diffusion occurs as the costs of intervening for the actor increase and the benefits of intervening for the actor decrease. Latané (1976) suggested that the extent to which people feel responsible to act in a particular situation and to behave according to a norm depends on the force of the stimulus divided by some power of the number of individuals who are present. Using his model, Latané could accurately predict variation in bystanders' help for a person who dropped some objects and the extent to which people deviated from leaving a 15% tip in a restaurant as a function of the number of individuals in the group.

Any conditions that affect helping behavior in general, such as the cost of helping, may have a greater effect with an increase in the number of bystanders, which diffuses responsibility. Involvement with one's own goals, the ambiguity of the stimulus, and temporary psychological states may all have greater power in reducing helping when the number of bystanders increases. This notion is also supported by findings of Gaertner and Dividio (1977), whose white female subjects showed no difference in their response to the plight of a white and a black victim when they were alone, but they helped the black victim less than the white victim when they believed that other bystanders were present (see Chapter 6). A further statement may be also reasonable: When any conditions (external or internal) focus responsibility more on a particular person, other conditions that may diminish helping are less likely to be influential.

Rules of Appropriate Social Behavior as Determinants of Helping. In the above study (Staub, 1970b), I also found that as the age of the children increased, helping behavior first increased and then decreased. Sixth-graders helped only about as much as kindergartners. I had assumed that with increasing age helping would increase, because as children grow older they learn that they are expected to help and they become more competent. They may also learn to react more empathically. To learn why helping behavior decreased, the experimenter conducting the study asked older children the reasons for their behavior.

A number of them indicated that they thought the experimenter would be angry or upset with them if they went into the other room. One said, "I thought I was not supposed to go into the other room," and another said that he thought someone "would get mad." When the experimenter asked who that would have been, the child said, "You." These and other comments suggested that sixth-graders were concerned more about acting properly, about not doing something that might be regarded as socially inappropriate (e.g., going into a strange room) than about acting according to important societal values that promote helping others in need.

To explore the hypothesis that children feared disapproval for going into the adjoining room, I conducted two experiments (Staub, 1971b). In one experiment seventh-grade boys and girls, while drawing pictures, heard sounds of distress from a 7-year-old girl in an adjoining room. Some children had been told beforehand that they may go into the adjoining room if they needed more drawing pencils (permission group). Others were told nothing about entering the adjoining room (no-information group). Children in the permission group attempted to help significantly more often than those in the no-information group. No difference in behavior was observed between boys and girls. In one case, the relevance of permission was particularly obvious; a girl listened intently to the distress sounds, then broke the points of her drawing pencils, jumped up, and ran into the adjoining room. This suggested that some children who received permission might still have felt inhibited, believing that they were only justified in going into the other room to get more drawing pencils. In the second experiment seventh-grade girls were the subjects. They heard sounds of distress, including calls for help, from another seventh-grade girl in an adjoining room. Some of the girls received prior permission to enter the adjoining room— they were told that when they finished their task, or if they wanted to take a break during the task, they could play with some games in the adjoining room. Other girls received no information about the permissibility of entering the adjoining room; still others (the prohibition group) were told not to go into the other room because a girl in that room was working on the same questionnaire as the subject, and the experimenter did not want the two of them to talk to each other and exchange information. Again there were significant differences between groups. Children in the permission group helped significantly more often than children in either the no-information or the prohibition group; there was no difference between the last two groups. In the permission group, 10 of 11 girls actively attempted to help by going into the adjoining room. In the prohibition group only 3 of 11 and in the no-information group only 4 of 11 did so. The findings of the two experiments suggest that children feel that it is inappropriate to go into an adjoining room in a strange environment, and that they fear disapproval for doing so. Having no information about the permissibility of entering the other room seemed to function as a prohibition.

These findings indicate that rules of proper social behavior affect children's behavior. Presumably, such rules include not going into the other room in a strange situation, not interfering with others' business, and doing what one is told. These rules seem less important than morally relevant rules, such as norms that prescribe behavior that has consequences for other people's welfare. But children learn rules of proper social behavior across a wide variety of settings. They are taught to obey these rules extensively, so these rules may become dominant over what might be regarded as more important, morally relevant rules. Moreover, when proper social behavior is unclear, concern about disapproval and negative evaluation may inhibit the initiation of any action.

Given these findings, I decided to investigate whether adults' helping would also be inhibited by such implicit rules of appropriate action, and replicated the last study with adults (Staub, 1971b). As an adult female subject sat in a room working on a task, she heard sounds of distress from the adjoining room. The sounds came from an adult female who had apparently fallen off a ladder and hurt herself. Beforehand, the experimenter either told the subject that she could go into the other room to get herself a cup of coffee (that she had just plugged in the pot and it would be ready in a little while); or made no reference to going into the other room; or told the subject not to go into the other room. To ensure credibility, in this last condition the experimenter first said that she had just plugged in a pot of coffee. She then added that it would be better if the subject did not go into the other room because the person in there was working on a timed task and should not be interrupted. She said that she would get the subject a cup of coffee in a while. How did this affect behavior? Subjects in the permission group and in the no-information group helped frequently. Having no information apparently did not function for adults as an implicit rule prohibiting entry into the other room, as it had for children. However, helping behavior was substantially reduced in the prohibition group.

In this experiment, the subjects were given the experimenter's definition of appropriate behavior, not an interpretation of the distress cues. Subjects might have complied with the expectation expressed by the experimenter, no matter what they thought about the distress cues. Alternatively, prohibition might have resulted in motivated interpretation of the stimulus as not an emergency. Having been prohibited entry, the subjects were in a state of conflict, which they could resolve by defining the stimulus as not an emergency. It is not clear whether this happened, but a couple of subjects in the prohibition group said afterward that they thought the sounds of distress might have been the timed task that the person in the other room was working on. Another possibility is that the communication by the experimenter created a conflict of a different kind. The prohibition condition might have activated both the goal of helping the person in distress and the goal of helping the experimenter do her job. Subjects might have thought that by not going into the other room they were helping the experimenter.

In another experiment (Staub, Erkut, & Jaquette, described in Staub, 1974a), which aimed primarily at exploring the influence of personality characteristics on helping, the effects of varying the permissibility of entering the adjoining room were again explored. Male subjects were used. There were several procedural changes in varying permissibility, and a substantial change in the nature of the distress sounds. Here live male confederates attempted to create the impression that they had stomach cramps by making a series of moans and groans. In this study permission enhanced attempts to help in comparison to both a no-information and a prohibition condition. Given the milder distress sounds, the importance of helping apparently did not supercede rules of appropriate behavior or conflicting motives that inhibited helping behavior, but permission decreased the force of the inhibition.

In another study Ashton and Severy (1976) exposed female undergraduates to sounds representing a mild, medium, or severe emergency. They either gave subjects permission to leave their room ("If you should have a question or want me") or prohibited leaving by telling subjects that it was important for them to stay in their place and pay attention to the experiment. No control group was included. Variation in the permissibility of leaving the room had a highly significant and substantial effect on helping behavior.

In other studies, which have implications for the development of prosocial behavior and are considered in more detail in Volume 2 of this work, children were exposed to sounds of distress from an adjoining room, following interaction with either a warm and nurturant or a neutral adult experimenter (Staub, 1971a; Weissbrod, 1976). Nurturance increased subsequent helping behavior, perhaps by decreasing children's concern about disapproval for entering a strange room.

The earlier discussion suggested that people are affected by general norms that prescribe helping behavior, and it showed that these general norms might be changed by specific expectations communicated by another person. The series of experiments just discussed showed that children, and probably adults as well, are concerned with general rules of proper social behavior, *unrelated* to helping norms. They are also concerned with definitions of appropriate behavior made by another person in specific situations. Such rules and definitions probably affect all kinds of social behavior.

The Inhibiting Effect of Self-Concern.   A variety of conditions in an emergency can have relatively similar consequences. An ambiguous stimulus for help, the presence of other people, the ambiguous reactions of others, rules of appropriate behavior that conflict with helping—all could contribute to greater self-concern on the part of an observer. Rather than focusing on the stimulus for help and on the fate of the person in distress, people may wonder about their *own* role, the kind of impression they will make, and the consequences of initiating action. As a result they may suspend judgment and simply not arrive at a definition of the situation; the internal processes that would mobilize them might not be activated. Even if they arrive at a definition, their self-concern would decrease the likelihood of their mobilization for action. There is probably a tremendous difference in such a situation between the experience of a person before initiating action and after. Before initiating action a person is likely to be in conflict, distressed; afterward, if help is initiated, the conflict is resolved, attention is focused outside the self, and the person's experience is likely to be much more positive.

Stimulus Characteristics That Affect Helping

So far I have discussed social influences on helping. However, other aspects of the situation also affect helping. An important one is the nature of the stimulus for help. The characteristics of the stimulus are likely to determine how it is perceived and interpreted.

Variation in Ambiguity

As already mentioned, a stimulus for help may be extremely clear or extremely ambiguous. In two studies, Clark and Word (1972, 1974) found that when the stimulus was extremely clear the frequency of help was very high (nearly 100%) whether one or two people were present. To minimize ambiguity, Clark and Word (1974) let subjects hear both the sounds of a workman falling and the workman's voiced distress; subjects also *saw* the man lying on the ground, with an electrical wire touching him. As the experimenters increased the ambiguity of the situation, subjects were not able to see the distressed person, or they heard only the sounds of a crash but neither saw the victim nor heard distress sounds; in this case, there was a progressive and substantial decline in attempts to help. When a stimulus is unambiguous, interpretational difficulties are absent; conceptual conflict in deciding what behavior is appropriate might be minimal. As a result self-concern may not be aroused and attention may focus on the person in need, activating internal processes such as values and empathy. Translating the motivation to help into action may be less difficult when the stimulus is clear.

One problem in arriving at conclusions about the effects of ambiguity by itself is that although variation in ambiguity might be intended in an experimental situation, the subjects' perception of the severity of distress might be affected instead. This may have happened in the experiments carried out by Clark and Word. Separating ambiguity and severity might be an extremely difficult task.

In another study, Yakimovich and Saltz (1971) had a workman fall off a ladder in front of a building. Subjects could look out their windows and see him. In this situation the frequency of helping was relatively low. When the workman also called for help, the frequency of help was substantially greater. High frequencies of help in some other experiments might have been due to unambiguous distress cues. As indicated earlier, in the study by Piliavin, Rodin, & Piliavin (1969) the confederate who collapsed on the

New York City subway under several treatment conditions almost always received help. The only exception occurred when the confederate was hugging a bottle and appeared drunk. In several conditions of other subway studies, the frequency of help was high (Piliavin & Piliavin, 1972; Piliavin et al., 1975). There are several reasons for the high frequency of help in this situation, one of them being that the visibility of the distressed person minimized ambiguity of need.

In an unpublished study (Staub & Clawson, 1970), we found that when sounds of distress coming from an adjoining room were made particularly credible through the use of an excellent sound system, much pilot work on the distress sounds, and an initial scream produced by a live confederate (a tape recorder then took over), the frequency of help was extremely high. In all experimental conditions—a subject alone, a subject in the company of one or two others, each member of a group working on a task alone, or all members of a group working together so that the interaction already in progress might decrease the possibility of pluralistic ignorance—the frequency of help was close to 100%.

We have seen that the stimulus to help can be ambiguous; ambiguity about how to provide help also affects helping behavior. Again, the less ambiguity there is the more likely a person is to come to another's aid. In one of their treatment groups Schwartz and Clausen (1970) had the person who was later to have an epileptic attack inform others through an intercom that in case of any problems he had some pills in his coat pocket. This knowledge significantly increased subsequent attempts to help. A number of investigators have suggested that a feeling of competence increases the likelihood of helping. Much of the research, however, provided positive or negative information about a person's performance or competence on some task, and thus dealt only with the subject's feeling of competence, not with actual competence. The findings show only that momentary feelings affect a person's willingness to help. Midlarsky (1968) notes, however, that in a natural disaster people who have had previous experience in a similar situation and know what to do are more likely to help. Knowing what to do may well decrease the arousal, anxiety, and disorganized thinking and behavior produced when help is called for. Greater competence may also reduce the cost of helping (Clark & Word, 1974). For all these reasons, an existing desire to be of help would be more likely to lead to action.

The Degree of Need, the Cost of Helping, and the Opportunity to Escape

Information inherent in the stimulus for help may also indicate the nature of the need and its degree—how important it is for the distressed person to receive help, the possible consequences if help is not given (further pain, physical deterioration, even death)—and the benefits that help may produce. The greater the need for help, the more motives that promote helping may be activated. Social norms as well as personal values are presumably more imperative when someone's need is great, and empathy with the sufferer might be evoked to a greater degree.

These speculations suggest that as the degree of need for help increases, the social and personal rewards inherent in helping also increase. The social and personal costs of not helping also increase—the probability of negative reactions from others if one remains inactive, and feelings of guilt and other forms of self-punishment that result from deviation from personal values. What is also suggested, of course, is that as need increases the probability that help will be given also increases. As we will see, however, complications arise, partly because when the need is greater, the potential costs of helping may be or appear to be greater.

A clarification of the distinction between the concept of need and the concept of dependence, elaborated by Berkowitz and his associates, might be useful (Berkowitz, 1972; Berkowitz & Daniels, 1963). Berkowitz and his associates explored variation in helping behavior as a function of variation in the degree of dependence of one person on another for help. In their research, the dependent person experienced no distress or disadvantage; instead, by being helped he could gain material and social rewards for himself. Dependence was varied by the extent to which the person needed the help of another if he was to acquire the benefits that were available. Help could only be provided by one particular person. Thus dependence consisted of the need for help to acquire a benefit and exclusive reliance on one other person. In the present context, degree of need refers to the degree to which a person's state of well-being deviates in the negative direction from some average or usual state of well-being.

Few experiments have explored the effects of varying degrees of need on helping behavior. In one experiment, which varied the nature or origin of need and probably affected the perception of its degree, Piliavin, Rodin, & Piliavin (1969) staged emergencies on the New York City subway. A confederate staggered forward, collapsed, and remained supine on the floor, looking at the ceiling until he received assistance or until the model who was part of the experimental team intervened. In one condition the victim carried a black cane; in another, he smelled of liquor and carried a liquor bottle in a brown bag. The frequency of help was extremely high (62 of 65) when the victim carried a cane, regardless of whether he was black or white; the frequency of help was lower and help was slower in coming when the victim appeared drunk. Members of the victim's race tended to help more when the victim was drunk, but not when the victim carried a cane. Helping behavior was affected by the apparent source of distress; but the exact reason for the difference in helping is unclear. It may have been due to different perceptions of the degree of need, or to the cost of helping (a drunk may get abusive, may throw up, and so on), or to a devaluation of the drunken victim that made helping less obligatory, or to other factors. With regard to devaluation, research on helping in response to nonphysical distress shows that when a person seems responsible for his condition of need, when he brought it on himself, he sometimes receives less help (Chapter 4). Such derogation of a person, negative evaluation that might lead to the feeling that he deserves his suffering and one is not obligated to help him (Lerner & Simmons, 1966), can also occur with a drunken person.

In a subsequent study Piliavin and Piliavin (1972) varied the degree of need more directly. Again, emergencies were staged, this time on subways in Philadelphia. The confederate either simply collapsed, or collapsed and let a red fluid ("blood") trickle from his mouth. When blood trickled from the victim's mouth, he was helped significantly *less* often. However, as I have pointed out, an examination of the group means suggests that this difference was primarily due to the treatment condition in which a confederate dressed either as a medic or as a cleric sat nearby the collapsed victim and did not help. Others might have expected such a person to initiate help, and when he did not their own initiative was inhibited. The number of subjects in each treatment condition of this study was too small and too variable (the researchers had to discontinue the experiment) to show this interaction effect statistically.

The investigators regarded the variations in conditions, between an invalid with a cane and a drunk, and between victims who did or did not bleed, as creating differences in the costs of helping. It is as likely or perhaps more likely that the actual effect was to create perceived variations in need, or in both need and the cost of helping.

Piliavin *et al.* (1975) attempted to demonstrate the effects of the cost of helping in still another study. A young white male who was carrying a cane collapsed on the New York City subway. In one condition he had a large red birthmark on his face, in another condition he had no birthmark. The birthmark was expected to create disgust and thereby increase the cost of helping. But although the birthmark probably did increase the discomfort of others in approaching this person, and therefore the cost, other consequences are also possible. For example, a person's similarity to those in need appears to lead to empathy and/or identification and increased helping, as Chapter 7 will show; dissimilarity can decrease helping. Physical characteristics may lead people to perceive another as similar or dissimilar. The influence on helping of the presence of a bystander who wore a medical coat in some conditions ("intern") but not in others ("no intern") was also explored. Unmarked victims (low cost) received help significantly more often than marked victims (high cost), and when the "intern" was present there was a tendency for people to help less ($p < .08$). As regards the speed or frequency of helping, when the cost was high the presence of the intern reduced helping, but when the cost was low such a difference was not found. When an intern was there, cost affected helping; when there was no intern, cost had no effect.

It seems, then, that when people are disinclined to help, either because the cost is high or because the characteristics of the victim are such that they do not lead to, and even inhibit, identification with the victim, the presence of a person with special competence decreases the willingness to help. Perhaps high cost or dissimilarity decreases the *desire* to help, and the remaining motive to help is that of fulfilling an obligation and/or abiding by social norms. When it comes to fulfilling an obligation, the person most competent, and in a sense obligated by his profession, ought to do it. When a medical person was not present, the presence of a birthmark did not affect helping; the need for help was unambiguous, apparently great, and people responded to it. It is somewhat surprising that the presence of the intern had no effect in the low-cost condition, when the victim had no birthmark. Perhaps the reason is that the intern did nothing, and the clarity of the need made other people respond.

Piliavin and associates (Piliavin, Rodin, & Piliavin, 1969, 1975; Piliavin & Piliavin, 1972) progressively elaborated a model to explain people's reactions to emergencies. The major assumptions of the model are as follows: An emergency, such as the suddenly occurring distress of another person, creates varying degrees of arousal in bystanders. The greater the arousal, the more unpleasant it is, and the more motivated a person will be to reduce the arousal. Thus, the greater the arousal the more likely it is that the person will make some response to the emergency. The observer's behavior will be a function of his desire to reduce his own arousal with as little cost and as much reward to himself as possible. That is, the response will be determined by "the outcome of a more or less rational decision process in which he weighs the costs and rewards attendant upon each of his possible courses of action [Piliavin & Piliavin, 1972, p. 6]."

The costs are of two kinds: costs of helping and costs of not helping. Costs of helping include physical and material costs, time, embarrassment, and feelings of inadequacy if help is ineffective. Costs of not helping include self-blame, public censure, and in some situations prosecution as a criminal. Rewards for helping are both internal and external. Rewards for not helping include all the rewards for activities that would be interrupted if one were to help. "Basic to these are rewards associated with personal freedom and lack of involvement, conditions which have recently been conceptualized by Brehm (1966) as minimizing reactance [Walster & Piliavin, 1972, p. 181]."

Piliavin and Piliavin (1972) specified, on the basis of these considerations, how bystanders would respond in emergencies having various levels of costs of helping and not helping. Table 3.1 presents reactions most likely to occur when the level of arousal is relatively high.

"Holding arousal constant, as costs for not helping increase, the probability of helping increases. Similarly, as costs for direct helping increase, the probability of direct intervention decreases and the likelihood of indirect help, justification for not helping, or flight increase [Walster &

Table 3.1
Matrix of Most Probable Responses for Varying Combinations
of Costs Associated with Helping [a, b]

		Net costs for helping	
		Low	High
Net costs for not helping	High	Direct intervention	Indirect intervention
	Low	Wide variation: Response a function of personality	Running away or apparent ignoring

[a] From Piliavin and Piliavin, 1972.
[b] A relatively high level of arousal is assumed.

Piliavin, 1972, p. 180]." Piliavin *et al.* (1975) note that when the cost of helping is low there are "no restraining forces to offset the driving forces set up by the arousal state [p. 430]" and direct intervention is the most efficient response. When the cost of helping is high people may seek to help indirectly, or they may attempt to redefine the situation and thereby lower the cost of the person's not receiving help. Redefinition can take varied forms, such as minimizing the victim's need or deciding that the victim is undeserving. Redefinition is a justification process; such processes are considered in Chapter 4. No research on emergencies actually attempted to measure justification. In the model presented by the Piliavins and their associates personality characteristics would affect helping when the costs of both direct and indirect help are low. It does seem reasonable that personality characteristics would have the strongest effects under these conditions, when the situational influence is weaker.

However, other assumptions seem more questionable. First, under most conditions the degree of arousal itself is jointly determined by the circumstances and by the person's personality. Murphy (1937) found, in the course of extensive observation of nursery-school children, that children who became visibly upset in response to another's distress, and who also acted to relieve that other's distress, experienced emotional arousal of shorter duration than children who did not act on the other's behalf. The reduction of one's own negative state would presumably reinforce helpful behavior. Probably some people learn to minimize the arousal created by another's distress by responding relatively fast. Others might minimize their arousal by interpretive strategies that minimize the need for intervention. Furthermore, it is questionable whether such an "economical" model can adequately account for helping behavior, since it reduces a variety of dimensions of situations and the internal characteristics of individuals that determine the response to those dimensions to two types of costs. Can variations in ambiguity of need, in social influence, in degree of need, in conditions focusing responsibility on a person, in empathic reactions, and so on be adequately translated into cost factors? Do external and internal sources of costs exert equivalent influence? Are they better conceptualized jointly than examined independently? Would they not have to be assessed independently for us to understand the degree, nature, and comparability of their influence? Would not external conditions and personality jointly determine arousal, the activation of other mediators of behavior, and finally the behavioral reaction?

The model emphasizes the "selfish" nature of helpful conduct; this is more an ideological or philosophical view than an empirical one. If empathic distress induces helping, the motivation may be regarded as self-oriented, and the behavior may be thought of as in the service of reducing one's own vicarious distress. Alternatively, empathic distress may be regarded as other-oriented, since it is the consequence of another person's experience. In Aronfreed's view (1968; 1976), for example, empathy and sympathy are altruistic bases of conduct. Such differences in conceptions can also be applied to behavior motivated by the desire to adhere to norms that prescribe prosocial conduct. People may enjoy, even welcome, the opportunity to help others, or they may identify with others' goals, adopt those goals, and proceed to help with their attainment. This again can be viewed as highly unselfish, altruistic behavior, since a person expends effort and energy for the sake of others, or it can be viewed as selfish behavior, in that satisfactions are gained from the help one provides for others.

A final issue is the relatively limited evidence of the influence of costs on helping people in physical distress. It is highly probable, as much of the preceding discussion indicates, that as the cost of helping affects other types of helping behavior (see Chapter 5) so it affects helping others in physical need. Procedures of experiments that were discussed did not convincingly vary costs, neither did they separate the costs of helping and the costs of not helping. For example, it might be more costly to help a bleeding person than to help someone who is not bleeding, because the blood might soil one's clothes and because help by a medically incompetent person might do more harm than good and the "helper" might have to account for the harm that is done. The need of a bleeding person also appears greater, however, so both social and personal norms would increase the cost of not helping. Unfortunately, the two types of costs are intermingled to an unknown degree. The differentiation and separate examination of variables that may enter into costs of helping and of not helping appear necessary in order to disentangle their influence.

In a study that varied degree of need Ashton and Severy (1976) exposed female undergraduates to an emergency that consisted of sounds of something falling and verbal reactions by a victim, all coming from an adjoining room. The subjects were exposed to emergencies of low, medium, or high severity; the taped sequences representing these levels were selected on the basis of ratings of eight tapes by a group of 110 pilot subjects. The participants who were exposed to the medium- and high-severity tapes helped more than those who were exposed to the low-severity tape. Ashton and Severy attempted to verify a prediction divergent from that proposed by the Piliavin model. The latter suggests that arousal is a monotonic function of the perceived severity of an emergency, and that the response is a direct function of the degree of arousal. Ashton and Severy proposed, in contrast, that according to the Yerkes and Dodson (1908) law, which describes an inverted-U-shaped relationship between arousal and performance, the strongest response would occur at medium ranges of severity. The analyses of the data showed both a significant linear increase in helping from low to high severity and a significant quadratic component, suggesting some form of curvilinearity. Both models received some, although not clear, support.

Other research that demonstrates both how helping behavior is affected by the degree of a person's need and the complexity of the issue was conducted by Staub and Baer (1974). In the first of a series of studies, just as a passerby started to cross an intersection, a male confederate (*a*) collapsed on the side-street that the passerby was crossing; (*b*) grabbed his knee and collapsed holding his knee; or (*c*) grabbed his chest over his heart and collapsed holding his chest. Surprisingly, the frequency of approach to the distressed person was equal in the first two conditions, and significantly greater than in the third condition. About 50% of passersby helped in the first two conditions, but no one stopped in the third condition. This was not only surprising, but also upsetting, since a person with a bad heart would presumably need help more urgently and to a greater degree than would a person with a bad knee. Possibly, we thought, people perceived the cost of helping a person with a bad heart as very high. The degree of involvement demanded of them might be extensive; such a person might even get worse while they were trying to help him, and they might be held responsible for his misfortune.

It is possible that when the potential cost of helping is great people will be less likely to help—even when the need for help is great—*if* they can easily escape from the presence of the distress cues. When, however, escape is not easy or possible, because of the nature of surrounding conditions or the manner in which people are confronted by the distressed person, people will be as likely or more likely to help when the need is great, and the degree of perceived cost will have less effect. This reasoning was suggested in part by the findings in the Piliavin, Rodin, & Piliavin (1969) study of extremely high frequencies of help for a physically handicapped person.

Although several explanations of this phenomenon have already been suggested, I would like to suggest another one: The emergencies were staged in express trains, which stopped 6½ minutes after the victim collapsed. It was difficult for onlookers to escape the distress cues. When helping behavior was not forthcoming, a number of passengers did escape by leaving the compartment, the only way that escape was possible.

In our second experiment (Staub & Baer, 1974) a male confederate appeared from a side street and walked toward a passerby, either on the same side of the street, or crossed over and walked toward him or her on the other side of the street. When he was about 40 feet from the passerby, he grabbed either his chest over his heart or his knee, and collapsed, holding his chest or his knee. After three attempts to get up he remained on the ground. Subjects approached the victim and asked about his problem significantly more often when he appeared to have a heart problem. They approached him significantly more often when he was on the same side of the street, in their path, so that escape was difficult, than when he was on the other side of the street.[2]

When escape was more difficult, people helped more. They might have done so because of the greater social costs of not helping, the greater fear of social disapproval of either bystanders or the distressed person himself for obviously avoiding him. A few people did this anyway; some simply passed him, some left the sidewalk and made a big circle around him, and some crossed to the other side of the street. If the subjects continued on their path they got nearer to the person on the same side of the street than to the one on the other side. An alternative or additional reason for the difference in help might have been that greater physical proximity had greater impact or force, leading to a greater activation of personal values and norms, which made it a desirable goal to help.

Of the people who passed on the other side of the street, a number of them glanced at the victim once or twice, then hurried on without looking at him again. A few of these individuals turned at the next corner and disappeared. Apparently, some people minimized their exposure to the distress cues in this manner. "Milgram (1970) suggested that people in large urban areas are so frequently exposed to others' needs that they have to protect themselves if they are to maintain a private life. As a form of self-protection, some people may use maneuvers that minimize their involvement with other people's needs [Staub & Baer, 1974, p. 283]." Clearly, there may be important individual differences. Some people may defend against

---

[2] Awareness of ethical issues in research has changed greatly over the last decade. However, even in 1969–1970, when these studies were conducted, we were greatly concerned with not *harming* anyone. We kept in touch with the police so that they would not be unnecessarily summoned to help in our staged emergencies. We also debriefed subjects and discussed the reasons for such a project with them.

exposure to stimuli relating to other people's needs and in that way limit the impact of those needs on themselves. However, when circumstances make escape costly, sustained exposure is likely to focus attention on the person in need, activating processes that contribute to helping.

The greater degree of helping offered to the person with the apparent heart problem was a clear reversal of the finding of the first experiment. The slight difference in the procedures of the two experiments may have been responsible, or the difference in the appearance of the two confederates. The one in the first experiment was strong and vigorous, whereas the one in the second experiment was obviously overweight. We replicated the conditions of the first experiment with a small number of subjects, using the second confederate; a slightly greater degree of helping in the bad heart condition resulted, suggesting that the procedural differences were not responsible. A large number of undergraduates watched films of the performance of the bad heart condition by the two confederates, and the second (overweight) confederate was significantly more often judged to have a heart problem. The appearance of the second confederate was consistent with people's conception of a person who has a heart problem, so he was helped more. A lack of "fit" between a person's needs and his other characteristics might reduce helping reactions.

It seems likely that our procedure for producing variation in the opportunity for escape resulted primarily in variation in the perceived costs of not helping (whether the costs were external or internal). These experiments and others make it appear that the degree of need for help affects helping behavior, but other factors such as the characteristics of the stimulus person, the context, and the competence of other potential helpers, have an effect on helping behavior.

Spontaneous (or Impulsive) Helping

The Piliavins and their associates have proposed that "there will be (a) special circumstances that give rise to and (b) specific personality types who engage in rapid, impulsive, noncalculative irrational helping or escape behavior following observation of an emergency [Piliavin *et al.*, 1975, p. 430]." Piliavin (1976) presented a variety of studies in which impulsive helping was supposed to take place, as defined by either average latencies of help in at least one condition of 15 seconds or less or 85% or greater frequency of help. What conditions lead to impulsive helping? Piliavin specifies four conditions that appear at least somewhat related to impulsive helping; in combination they are significantly associated with impulsive helping: (a) The victim must be visible, or there must be clear cries for help; (b) the victim must not be perceived as part of an experiment; (c) the subject must be moving or at least standing; and (d) there must have been a prior meeting between the bystander and the victim. Other conditions that lead to impulsive helping behavior are rapid onset of need and perceived time pressure for help.

Impulsive helping in Piliavin's view is high-probability and/or high-speed helping when rational calculation of costs does not take place. An example par excellence of impulsive helping is provided by Markowitz (1973, p. 75): A passerby sees a boy who is falling out of a sixth-story window, runs over, and catches him. The phenomenon of impulsive helping appears to exist. Some environmental conditions may induce impulsive helping in many people. Under other conditions, perhaps when some of the situational influences are not active and/or when costs associated with helping seem high, fewer people may engage in impulsive helping. What may the cognitive decision-making processes in impulsive helping be? Are there any? There probably are, but perhaps decision making does not have to deal with the resolution of conflict. The costs involved in helping may not be considered by the actor, and self-concern may not be activated. The circumstances may arouse only prosocial motivation, and strategies of action that promote help.

Are most people impulsive helpers under the conditions specified? Are people who have a generalized tendency to be impulsive, to react fast to any kind of sudden or attention-getting stimulus, more likely to be impulsive helpers? General impulsivity may be insufficient. In one study (Staub, Erkut, & Jaquette, as described in Staub, 1974a) we found that male subjects who heard sounds of discomfort and distress from an adjoining room reacted faster to the sounds if the subjects appeared impulsive on a measure administered to them earlier, but they did not necessarily help more. Subjects were earlier administered Kagan's Matching Familiar Figures Test, a measure on which they were supposed to match one figure with the only identical one of six other figures that varied only in small details. The individuals who made fast (and thus more frequently erroneous) responses on this test responded faster to the distress sounds—by interrupting their work, standing up, and so on—but they did not help more. Perhaps they would have helped more if the distress sounds had been more intense or if the victim had been visible. I would expect, however, a combination of prosocial motives and impulsiveness to be necessary for impulsive helping to occur.

In closing this brief discussion of impulsive helping, I would like to suggest that an important determinant of such helping is the lack of certain types of decision-making processes. We are likely to be dealing with a continuum, ranging from conditions (external and internal) that clearly focus responsibility on a potential helper and demand fast response of a specific kind, which lead to a short circuiting of decisional processes, to those that evoke uncertainty, conflict, and complex affective reactions and/or decision making. Lack of an elaborate decisional process does not mean, however, that the behavior is "irrational." In fact, in addition to prosocial motivation that enables people under certain external conditions to make a rapid or instantaneous decision to help, prior experience that led to the availability to people of plans or strategies for action or enables them to speedily construct such plans probably increases the likelihood of this type of help. Consequently, *spontaneous* helping may be a better label than impulsive helping, since the latter has the connotation that the behavior is not controlled by reason.

Temporary States of the Actor, Stimulus Overload, Urban–Rural Helping, and Personality

As Chapter 6 shows, in research on helping with tasks or sharing material possessions with other people, evidence has accumulated showing that momentary moods and current levels of self-esteem—in general people's current psychological states—affect their helpfulness. For example, good feelings promote prosocial behavior and bad feelings hinder prosocial behavior. These differences result from moods that are presumably highly temporary, since they are experimentally created by immediately preceding experiences. Helping people in physical distress also appears to be affected by the temporary states of potential helpers, although there is only minimal research evidence to show this. Preoccupation with the self or with an activity, a temporary feeling of relatedness to another person, and other internal conditions produced by experiences preceding exposure to a stimulus for help, or concurrent with it but unrelated to it, might all be included here. These conditions are considered in the brief discussion that follows, but differences in their meaning and consequences, particularly between temporary states of an actor and temporary connections to other people, are considered in Chapters 6 and 7.

Latané and Darley (1970) reported a study by Allen who found that people were more helpful in subway stations than at the airport to a young man who had his foot in a cast, hobbled along on crutches, and fell down. Interviews with bystanders showed that people who frequently traveled by plane and were thus familiar with airports helped as much as subway riders. This suggests that the difference in the frequency of help was due to people being in a relatively unfamiliar environment at the airport, this making them less relaxed and less comfortable. These findings seem relevant to mood, but also to the earlier suggestion that when conditions arouse self-concern (and thus people feel less relaxed and less comfortable), people attend to others' needs less and help less.

Latané and Rodin (1969) reported that when two friends heard sounds of distress from an adjoining room, they were more likely to help than were two strangers. Furthermore, incidental findings of Latané and Darley

(1970) indicated that when subjects arrived early for an experiment and waited with others who were later to be their fellow bystanders in witnessing an emergency, they were more likely to help. One cannot rule out the possibility of the influence of personality in the latter instance, where a tendency toward responsible action might be manifested both in arriving early and in helping. But a likely explanation for both sets of findings is that familiarity with the environment and with other people in it makes people more relaxed and comfortable, which enhances helping.

In other research Darley and Batson (1973) had seminary students as their subjects. The students had to deliver a lecture from prepared notes. The lecture was to be either about the parable of the Good Samaritan or about job opportunities for seminary students. The students prepared for their lecture in one building. Some were told that they were late and had to hurry to the other building where they were to deliver their lectures. Others were told that they had plenty of time to get there. On their way to the other building the students had to pass by a person who was lying on the ground in a doorway, coughing, with his eyes closed. The seminary students who were told to hurry to their lectures stopped significantly less frequently than those who had time. Darley and Batson found that this happened regardless of the kind of lecture they had to deliver; even when their lecture was about the Good Samaritan, the seminary students who had to hurry helped less. However, a reanalysis of the data (Greenwald, 1975) showed that students who were to deliver a lecture about the Good Samaritan, and were presumably thinking about kindness and altruistic self-sacrifice, did help more frequently than those who were to lecture about job opportunities.

We do not know, of course, to what extent those who did not help noticed the distressed person and thought about helping him but decided against it because they were motivated to carry out their task. Although the hurried seminary students' behavior may have been due in part to motivational conflict, it seems a likely possibility that, because of their preoccupation with their task or with the fulfillment of their obligation, they perceived less and processed the stimulus of the distressed person less. Thus even though "on several occasions a seminary student going on his way to give his talk on the Good Samaritan literally stepped over the victim as he hurried on his way [Darley & Batson, 1973, p. 107]," helping behavior was not activated.

A number of studies have shown that some form of stimulus overload, which presumably is stressful and demanding, affects subsequent prosocial behavior. Sherrod and Downs (1974) created an overload condition by having female subjects simultaneously perform two tasks and listen to distracting background sounds. In a perceived control condition the participants were told that they could turn off the distracting sounds if they so desired. In a no-overload condition the background sounds consisted of "soothing auditory stimuli." The subjects performed on the tasks equally in the three conditions. Afterward they were asked to work on some problems as a favor for a confederate who ostensibly had nothing to do with the experiment. Significant group differences were found in helping, as well as a significant linear trend (progressive increase across the three conditions), but only with the amount of time that subjects worked as the dependent variable, after those with extreme time scores were dropped. The no-overload condition led to significantly more help than the other two conditions. Although the magnitude of the difference between no overload and perceived control, and perceived control and overload, was similar, the difference between the latter two groups did not reach significance. The ratings of the background noise, of the experiment, and the experimenter did not differ across conditions. Sherrod and Downs suggest that perceived control affected the nature of the relationship between the actor and the environment, allowing participants the feeling that they were Origins (in control) rather than Pawns (controlled)—that is, that they had the power and capacity to exert influence. This increased their willingness to help. Extending this line of reasoning, the stressful stimulus overload may have produced feelings of helplessness. One cannot account for its effect by assuming a high task motivation that diminished attention to, or the motivation to help, another person. Overload reduced the willingness to extend effort for another person *following* the experience of overload. It was the psychological state that resulted that diminished subsequent helpfulness.

The need for help in the preceding study did not involve physical distress. In another study, Weiner (1976) varied stimulus overload and explored the effects on reactions to physical distress. Overload was created by "simultaneous tasks, that presented varied demands and sensory bombardment." High overload demanded frantic activity in contrast to the leisurely work required of the low-overload subjects. In addition to overload, the effects of variation in the background of the subjects, whether they were reared in rural or in urban areas, were examined. Finally, measures of cognitive complexity were administered. After the participants were exposed to all the novel stimuli of their tasks, there was a repeated exposure— a retrial period—during which the emergency occurred. During this time the subjects could check their previous responses. At this time a woman, looking for someone, entered the room. She tripped on the threshold and fell; moaning, and clutching her right ankle, she remained on the floor until the subject helped her or 1 minute had passed.

Low-overload subjects helped significantly more than those exposed to high overload. There was a significant interaction between background and how the subjects reacted to overload. Rural subjects helped about the same amount in both conditions. Urban subjects helped more in the low-overload condition, and about the same amount as rural subjects in the high-overload condition. Urban subjects helped significantly more in the low-overload than in the high-overload condition. Overall, regardless of conditions, rural subjects helped less. These findings are based on analyses of scaled helping reactions, indicating differences in the magnitude of help. An analyses of the frequency of helping reactions (based on a somewhat inadequate dichotomization, between those who did not respond or verbally responded by inquiring about the need for help but did not leave their seat and took no helping action, and those who attempted some form of help— I use the term *inadequate* because the verbal reactions would presumably have led to helping action if the victim's verbal responses called for it— showed significantly more help by urban than by rural subjects, but there was no difference due to overload. Thus, overload affected the magnitude but not the frequency of help. The dominant response of rural subjects to the emergency was that of ignoring it.

Scores on Baron's Complexity Scale were significantly positively related to both the scaled and the dichotomized measures of helping. Further analyses indicated substantially greater cognitive complexity of urban than of rural subjects. When the influence on helping of variation in cognitive complexity was eliminated in a covariance analysis, the main effect of urban–rural differences in helping behavior disappeared. The other effects, however, including the interaction between residence and overload conditions, remained. Weiner suggests that rural subjects may consider a total stranger an outsider, not a member of their reference group, and therefore help such a person less. Urban subjects, growing up in a more varied and complex environment, are more likely to include strangers in the in-group. These differences may be mediated by cognitive complexity; greater complexity affords a more expansive view of the world and leads to a more inclusive reference group. People low on cognitive complexity attempt to deal with their environment by withdrawing from it and thereby minimizing involvement with it.

Stimulus overload primarily affected the *nature* of the help given, (what Weiner called the *magnitude* of help), but not its frequency. Subjects in the high-overload condition were more likely to seek indirect help by going to find the experimenter, whereas those in the low-overload condition were more likely to attempt to help the victim directly. Perhaps the experience of stress, tension, and discomfort reduced the subjects' willingness in the high-overload condition to face the interpersonal demands of interacting and dealing with a person in distress. It may be that people do seek more superficial forms of interpersonal involvement when they attempt to cope with some form of excessive stimulation (Milgram, 1970).

These findings may serve as a step toward clarifying Milgram's (1970) findings and suggestion that people in rural areas help more than those in cities. Although Milgram's discussion emphasized the stimulus overload that people in cities have to deal with, the implication to many researchers was that people reared and/or living in rural areas are more helpful. Other psychologists have also reported research findings showing urban–rural difference. For example, Merrens (1973) reported that more help was given by people in midwestern cities and towns than by those in New York City in some activities (for example, asking the location of the post office) but not in other activities. Korte and Kerr (1975) found that greater help was given on several measures in small towns in eastern Massachusetts than in Boston. On the other hand, several authors found no rural–urban differences (Lesk & Zippel, 1975; Schneider & Mockus, 1974; Krupat & Coury, 1975). Krupat and Coury (1975) suggested that in their study, where helping was measured by the return of lost letters, the density of passers-by was a more critical factor in helping than was the setting.

Weiner's (1976) study suggests that people who grow up in rural and urban areas may develop different individual characteristics, such as the degree of their cognitive complexity. These differences in turn lead to differences in how they deal with particular stimulus conditions. To understand and predict differences in helping, it becomes necessary to analyze how the personalities of rural and urban individuals differ, and how these differences affect a person's response to particular experiences, under particular stimulus conditions. Rural individuals may be less helpful at times because certain conditions and experiences are novel to them and they have no existing plans for dealing with them; the circumstances call for decision making. Under other circumstances they may show less avoidance of another's need, greater willingness to process the meaning of an event—unlike some subjects in the Staub and Baer (1974) study, who turned into a side street and thereby avoided further exposure to a person who had collapsed on the street—having had less experience with unpleasant demands and excessive stimulus overload than urban subjects.

A feeling of relatedness to another person arising from information about or experiences with that person immediately preceding exposure to a stimulus for help might also be considered a temporary state. In later chapters it is repeatedly shown that when subjects expect to meet another person later, or when they are made to believe that they are similar to another person in attitudes or in personality, the other person is likely to be more positively evaluated, devalued less when conditions might lead to devaluation, and helped more. To some extent this finding is similar to that described in Chapter 1, where positive relatedness was found to be important in prosocial behavior among animals. It may also help us develop hypotheses about the determinants of prosocial behavior among intimates. Reasons for such reactions are considered in Chapters 4 and 7. In essence, when some form of relatedness is created toward another person, a number of processes contributing to prosocial behavior are likely to be activated to a greater degree. The tendency to take the other's role, perhaps because the other person's reactions are expected to be similar to one's own, and the likelihood of empathy with such a person, might be greater. Hornstein

(1972) argues, from a Lewinian perspective, that such conditions of relatedness and similarity make one react to others as one would react to oneself; one adopts the other's goal and thereby a need or goal state is created that leads to "promotive tension" for helping.

Again, in the realm of helping people in physical distress, relevant research is rare. Liebhart (1972) found that an "interpersonal orientation" treatment, which involved showing the subjects photographs of a person who later had an accident in the adjoining room, did not enhance attempts to help. However, this treatment does not seem to be a powerful means of inducing a feeling of relatedness to another person. When the subjects, male German high-school students in the eleventh to thirteenth grades, were already acquainted with the victim, the interactive effects of a sympathetic orientation and of instrumental capacity in enhancing helping behavior (both evaluated by paper-and-pencil personality measures) were greater, suggesting that familiarity did have an effect.

It is unfortunate that direct evidence about the influence of temporary states of potential helpers on helping others in physical distress is so limited. Such temporary states are important in affecting other forms of prosocial behavior, and also seem important in the domain of physical need.

Summary of Situational Influences

Can we proceed, as Frederiksen (1972) suggested, with a "systematic way of conceptualizing the domain of situations and situational variables [p. 115]"? We might begin a classification of situations by specifying the dimensions along which situational characteristics empirically relevant to helping vary. The location of a particular situation along such dimensions might help us specify the degree of force of the situation in leading to helping behavior or in inhibiting helping behavior and the likelihood of the influence of various kinds of personality characteristics.

I shall now summarize the preceding review of the literature by describing such dimensions. Most of these dimensions are also relevant to helping when the stimulus is not physical distress; to evaluate the extent of relevance is one goal of subsequent chapters. For a few of these dimensions the evidence is more substantial in domains of helping other than that of physical distress. The following are conceptual dimensions: Different types of stimuli can fall on the same stimulus dimension, and the same kind of stimulus may be located on different dimensions. Variations in the location of stimuli along these dimensions can specify their activating potential for prosocial goals. Variation along some dimensions may also affect the involvement of personality characteristics other than goals, such as competence or speed of decision making about the meaning of an event, or may activate a goal that conflicts with a prosocial goal.

1. The degree to which the nature of the stimulus for help, surrounding conditions, and social influence provide an unambiguous definition of someone's need for help.
2. The degree to which circumstances require self-initiated rather than responsive help. Sometimes stimuli clearly indicate not only the need for help, but also the kind of action that is required and a distressed person's desire to be helped. A potential helper may even receive a specific request to do something. At other times, decisions need to be made, and initiative is required in helping.
3. The degree of need for help.
4. The degree of impact of the stimulus for help. The degree of exposure to it, and the ease or difficulty of getting away from it are strong determinants of impact.
5. The material costs of helping. (The social costs and the cost of not helping are also important, but they are summary dimensions, and some of the dimensions that determine them are listed separately.)
6. The degree to which responsibility for help is focused on a particular person rather than diffused among a number of people.
7. Situational rules and social influence that indicate that initiating the action needed might be disapproved or approved.
8. The degree to which social conditions focus attention on a task, or create an obligation to someone other than the person in need, or focus attention on the self (when somehow self-concern is aroused), thereby reducing attention to the stimulus for help.
9. The existence of a relationship to the person in need, and the degree and kind of relationship.
10. Psychological states either created by experiences concurrent with the need for help or existing prior to it; positive or negative moods or internal states.

Variation in all these dimensions may be expected to affect the degree to which social norms or personal goals that promote prosocial behavior are activated or empathic reactions are aroused.

Personality and Helping Others in Physical Need

A variety of experiments found no relationship between various personality characteristics and helping (Latané & Darley, 1970; Yakimovitch & Saltz, 1971; Darley & Batson, 1973; Staub, 1971b). For example, Latané and Darley (1970) administered to their subjects, who later overheard someone having an epileptic fit, measures of social approval, authoritarianism, alienation, Machiavellianism, and social responsibility. Scores on these measures were unrelated to the reporting of the epileptic seizure to the experimenter. Korte (1970) also found several personality measures un-related to subjects' reactions to the experimenter's asthmatic attack, al-though an autonomy scale that appeared to tap a person's unconven-tionality (Huston & Korte, 1976) differentiated between those who in-tervened and those who did not. I found (Staub, 1971b) that a measure of need for aproval was unrelated to subjects' reactions to a crash and sounds of sobbing and crying coming from the adjoining room.

The lack of predictive power of scores on personality tests is not uniquely characteristic of helping behavior:

> The attempts that have been made to demonstrate the relationship between personal dispositions and social behavior have often focused on only one personality variable at a time (Singer & Singer, 1972), and/or studied the influence of a personality characteristic on a single behavior, in a single setting. On the whole, the attempts to demon-strate how personal dispositions affect social behavior have not proved very satisfactory [Staub, 1974a, pp. 321–322].

Although in Chapter 2 I noted literature that leads to more optimistic conclusions and advanced conceptual reasons for more optimistic conclu-sions, the conceptual and methodological problems that besieged the helping studies that were cited (and research in other areas) are worth examining.

In most of the previously mentioned experiments on helping, a variety of experimental treatments were employed. However, often only the overall relationship between personality scores and helping was evaluated; the in-teractive effects of treatments and personality were not examined. One reason for this might be an insufficient number of subjects in studies, which is not surprising, since often the purpose of the research is to explore ex-perimental hypotheses, and personality measures are "thrown in" for good measure. With such an approach the selection of the personality tests does not seem to receive as much attention as does the design of the experi-mental treatments. In general, the characteristics of the helping situation have rarely been analyzed. Such an analysis might indicate the importance of perceptual or decision-making tendencies, or of competence in specific areas, for helping to occur in that particular situation. A reasonable theoretical basis, combined with an analysis of the situation, might be ex-pected to lead to more success in selecting personality characteristics that would predict helping in a particular situation. The analysis that I am re-ferring to implies the scaling of stimulus situations along certain dimen-sions, perhaps those described in the preceding summary. One method for doing this might be the following: First, a group of subjects would be used similar to the group to be used in the actual experiment. Second, these subjects would receive detailed descriptions of the events that are to take place in the experiment, including exposure to the stimulus for help. Third, the subjects would be asked what kinds of goals might be activated in the situation, what areas of competence might be involved in helping, and so on (see Staub, 1979).

A further problem has been that the available measures for determining personality are often inadequate. Consequently, the use of multiple measures for evaluating individual differences on a particular dimension, or the development of new, theory-based measures, would be important.

Finally, very few of the studies have approached the evaluation of personality–behavior relationships by considering the *combination* of personality characteristics that might be necessary or important in a particular situation to enhance helping. According to the model described in Chapter 2, a prosocial orientation as well as other personal goals that may be satisfied in the situation and competence in various areas are minimally necessary to consider.

There is little experimental evidence that demonstrates the influence of personality on helping others in physical distress, but there is enough to generate hope.

In a study (Staub, 1974a) that had many of the strategical–methodological faults that were just criticized, I found that subjects who had Stage 5 scores on Kohlberg's test of moral reasoning (1969) were significantly more helpful in response to sounds of distress from another room than were subjects with lower scores.[3] Stage 5 subjects are considered to have "principled" morality in the sense that right and wrong are defined by rational consideration, not by group definition. The principle guiding Stage 5 reasoning is that interaction among members of society is to be guided by social contract. [Neither in this experiment, involving 108 female subjects (Staub, 1974a), nor in another large experiment, soon to be described (Staub, Erkut, & Jaquette), involving 130 male subjects, have we found subjects reasoning about moral dilemmas at Kohlberg's highest stage (Stage 6), in which reasoning is presumably guided by principles of justice and the sanctity of human life.] In this experiment, where the treatments consisted of a confederate reacting differently to sounds of distress coming from an adjoining room, we were unable to statistically analyze treatment by personality interactions, because we did not have a sufficient number of subjects in each group. Several other personality measures, including Schwartz's measure of responsibility and Rotter's internal–external scale, turned out to be unrelated to helping in this study; however, a reasonable evaluation of personality influence without a sufficient number of subjects to evaluate interactions is not possible.

---

[3] In relation to my proposed model of social behavior (Chapter 2), Kohlberg's measure of moral reasoning might best be regarded as a measure of value orientations, specific stages indicating different values or principles as well as a hierarchy or organization of component values.

Moral Reasoning and Helping Behavior

In another study that related Kohlberg's test of moral reasoning to helping behavior, McNamee (1972) confronted subjects with a person who was having a bad reaction to psychedelic drugs. The subject faced interpersonal influence of two kinds: the definitional influence of the experimenter, who refused to help, and the implicit demand by the experimenter to proceed with the experiment. About to enter a room to be interviewed, the subject was interrupted by a young man who told the experimenter that he was scheduled to participate, but was unable to because he had had a bad drug trip. The young man then asked the experimenter for help. Not only did the experimenter provide no help, saying that he was a researcher, not a therapist, that he had no experience with drugs and did not know any place to call, but he also seemed annoyed about the cancellation and asked the young man to call to reschedule the appointment. Then the confederate slowly left the room.

The subjects' reactions were coded as (*a*) no intervention to help, (*b*) statements of sympathy or support, (*c*) offer of information about a place to get assistance, and (*d*) offer of personal assistance, such as taking the distressed person home. With the three helpful reactions combined, 11% of Stage 2, 27% of Stage 3, 38% of Stage 4, 68% of Stage 5, and 100% of Stage 6 subjects offered assistance. These are impressive numbers and show a powerful relationship between moral judgment and helping behavior in this situation.

Unfortunately, the moral judgment dilemmas were administered to subjects soon after their experience with the distressed person. It would be highly surprising for a person's thinking about moral issues to be unaffected by such a powerful immediately preceding experience. Having helped or not helped someone in need might have started different directions of thinking about morality, about good and evil, about responsibility toward other people, in part justifying, in part explaining one's own behavior. The moods and motivational dispositions created by the total complex of the stimulus and the subject's response to it are likely to have affected moral reasoning.

It is possible to distinguish between a person's competence to reason about morality at a certain "level" (the highest stage at which he is able to perform) and the kind of reasoning that he normally engages in under varied conditions in everyday life. There is the implication in the literature on moral reasoning (Kohlberg, 1969; Turiel, 1969) first, that a person's reasoning about moral dilemmas represents his maximum capacity at that point in his development—he cannot reason at a more advanced level—and second, his response on a test is equivalent to the reasoning he employs in everyday life. However, even in laboratory testing there is a great deal of stage mixture (Turiel, 1969) in moral reasoning, and in everyday life thinking characterized by "earlier" stages rather than by a person's best current capacity might be evoked by specific circumstances. In other words, would not even the most "principled" individuals think about some morally relevant situations in terms of the consequences to themselves of acting one way or another? The answer to this question is probably yes. From an early age on, we are all exposed to varied cultural and philosophical views of morality, many of which we might have in our repertoire. Although we might normally prefer to think in certain ways about moral dilemmas, under specific circumstances other ways of thinking may come to predominate because of activation by the circumstances. Sometimes a specific mode of reasoning about right and wrong might serve the function of rationalizing our actions, whether positive or negative.

With regard to the McNamee (1972) study, it is possible that the thoughts of subjects who helped, even if they normally reasoned at a lower stage, were elevated to the realm of generalization about the obligations of human beings to one another, the importance and sanctity of human life, and the like. In contrast, others who normally reasoned at an advanced level but did not help might have come to think about morality, at least temporarily, in a more self-oriented rather than other-directed fashion.

The foregoing discussion has several implications. First, we do not know to what extent performance on measures of moral reasoning represents the "best" performance that a person is capable of and to what extent it indicates a person's preference for a particular mode of reasoning. Second, it is widely recognized that a discrepancy frequently exists between the manner in which people think about a particular situation, and their conduct. The discrepancy may be overestimated, however, because it is based on data about the relationship between performance on a paper-and-pencil test under "neutral" conditions and people's behavior under complex, real life or life-like conditions. Surrounding conditions probably affect not only the relationship between thoughts and action but also how people think. This is recognized by the concept of justification processes. Situational influences, a person's own temporary psychological state, and other conditions may affect the nature of a person's thinking, including moral reasoning, and whether a particular stage or mode of reasoning is employed to support prosocial action or to decide against it.

We now have some evidence of varied influences on moral reasoning. The content of moral dilemmas, the nature of the issues they deal with (Levine, 1976; Urbach & Rogolsky, 1976), the identity of the protagonist— whether stranger, best friend, or mother in one study (Levine, 1976)—were all found to affect the level or stage of reasoning that people employed in laboratory testing. Haan (1975) found discrepancies between subjects' reasoning about hypothetical dilemmas and about an actual situation of civil disobedience. A discrepancy between a person's actions and ideology resulted, for example, in reasoning at lower stages about the actual situation than about the hypothetical dilemmas. In this study 20% of the subjects reasoned at a lower stage about the actual situation than about the hypothetical dilemmas, but 46% reasoned at a higher stage. Although these data call into question the assumption that reasoning about hypothetical dilemmas represents a person's maximum competence, they have to be interpreted with caution. The data were collected following an actual case of civil disobedience—the activities of students in the Free Speech Movement at Berkeley—which was certain to generate extensive discussion prior to testing.

The Influence of Combinations of Personal Characteristics and of Situations

In conjunction with the theoretical model presented in Chapter 2, several experiments were described that dealt with the combination of personality characteristics and situational influences on helping. One experiment provided evidence that the combination of sympathetic orientation and tendency for instrumental activity can increase attempts to help others in physical distress (Liebhart, 1972).

A large-scale experiment that I and my associates conducted (Staub, Erkut, & Jaquette, as described in Staub, 1974a) attempted to study the influence of several types of personality tests on reactions to a sequence of interrelated stimuli for help. In this experiment male undergraduates, while working on a task, heard sounds of distress from an adjoining room. The sounds were made by a male confederate and were supposed to indicate that the victim had severe stomach cramps. If the subject responded during a 135-second period to these distress sounds, which fluctuated in intensity, by going into the adjoining room, the confederate told him he had a stomach problem and asked whether he could lie down on the sofa that was in the subject's room. This was always permitted. If the subject did not enter the adjoining room the confederate opened the door, asked if he could lie down on the sofa, and told the subject about his stomach problem. This was followed by a sequence of actions in which the confederate always reacted to the somewhat varied behavior of the subject in a manner that allowed the confederate to perform the next part of the sequence, which provided another stimulus for help, in the planned manner. Thus, a number of behavioral reactions of the subjects could be evaluated. For example, if the subject offered a particular form of help when the victim was lying on the sofa, the latter would say, "Let me just lie here for a while." Some of the major opportunities for help that were offered were the following: (*a*) the original distress sounds in the adjoining room; (*b*) the confederate saying, after he lay on the sofa for a while, that he did not want to bother the subject and would go to another floor where he could lie down on another sofa for a longer time, thus providing an opportunity for the subject to get rid of the interruption if he wished or to show his concern either by trying to stop the victim or by offering to help him go there; and (c) on his way out of the room, the confederate asking the subject to do something for him—either to call his roommate (in another part of town) who would come to fill the victim's prescription for pills for his stomach problem, or to go to Harvard Square to get the prescription filled, since that would be faster.

In the usual laboratory experiment, my own and others', tape-recorded distress sounds were used. If subjects attempt to help the "distressed person" they discover the tape. The purpose of the procedure in this study was to enable us to evaluate reactions to a real person in distress, the degree of sacrifice people are willing to make when there are several avenues for help available that vary in effort but also in the utility of help. In other words, we wanted to study helping behavior under more true-to-life conditions. Our purpose was also to study variation in aid as a function of certain experimental influences, personality characteristics, and their interaction.

Before the subjects were exposed to the distress sounds we varied the experimenter's communications to subjects about the permissibility of entering the adjoining room from which the distress sounds would originate. The subjects either received no information, or they were told that they might go into the adjoining room to get a cup of coffee, or they were told that their task was a timed task, that they should not interrupt their work on it, and they received a stopwatch to time themselves.

About 3–6 weeks before the experiment the subjects were administered a large number of personality tests. The tests were selected on the assumption that several types of personality characteristics are related to helping. Which characteristics and combinations of characteristics affect helping is a function of the kind of demand the circumstances, including the stimulus for help, will place on a person. We administered a variety of tests to measure subjects' prosocial orientation, which was conceptualized at that time as a "concern about the welfare of others, a feeling of responsibility for others' welfare, and a belief in moral and prosocial values [Staub, 1974a, p. 322]." We expected a prosocial orientation to contribute to providing assistance under all circumstances, although its influence would be affected by the experimental treatments. We also thought that when a person was faced with a direct request for help, primarily his prosocial orientation and conflicting goals that might have been activated would determine helping; and when he was faced with sounds of distress coming from an adjoining room his speed in making judgments about events and his tendency to take action rather than remain passive would also contribute to helping behavior. Unfortunately, we knew of no measures of the ability to make fast judgments about social events. Therefore, we used a reaction-time test, and

Kagan's Matching Familiar Figures Test, a test of a cognitive style. We found neither test to be associated with helping behavior. (However, impulsivity on Kagan's test was associated with the speed of reacting to the distress sounds by looking up or standing up.) Similarly, there seems to be no good measure of action orientation; probably, as discussed earlier, action orientations that are demanded by a situation need to be specified. We used Rotter's (1966) measure of internal–external control (a tendency to feel that one can affect one's environment in contrast to a sense of inability to control or affect events) as an index of competence that would increase the tendency to take action.

The findings supported several expectations. First, subjects in the permission group helped more by going into the other room when they heard distress sounds than subjects in the other two groups, who did not differ. The experimental treatments did not, in themselves, affect others forms of helping. One might reason that once the situation had changed, as it did substantially when the confederate entered into it, the treatments lost their relevance. However, this assumption does not seem justified if the following experimental conditions by personality interactions are considered. Subjects who scored high on Kohlberg's measure of moral reasoning (Stage 5 versus lower stages) helped more, as indicated by their entering the adjoining room, by their taking the action that resulted in the prescription being filled faster, and by an average of all helping acts—but only in the permission group. In the other two groups, level of reasoning made no difference. Apparently when released by the experimenter from their implicit "contract" to work uninterruptedly on their task, subjects with a social-contract orientation helped more. On several other single measures of prosocial orientation a similar interaction with treatments was found, but only affecting the speed of subjects attempting to get the prescription filled. For example, subjects who scored low on a test of Machiavellian orientation were most helpful in this manner in the permission group. These and a variety of other measures of prosocial orientation were correlated with some form of assistance in some treatment conditions but not in others. Significant correlations were found with measures of responsibility for others' welfare (Schwartz's Ascription of Responsibility (*AR*) for others' welfare to the self or away from the self), with a measure of responsibility in one's general conduct (Berkowitz & Lutterman, 1968), and with the values of helpfulness and equality. Less aid was associated with the values of comfortable life, cleanliness, and ambition.

The relationship between behavior and the subjects' ranking of cleanliness and ambition is interesting. Subjects who ranked cleanliness as important for them were less helpful in all the treatment groups in a number of ways. Contemporary college students who rank "clean" as an important value may be traditional in their value orientation, concerned with order and duty but not with others' welfare. Some support for this idea comes from the type of values that cleanliness was positively related to, such as religiosity. Cleanliness was negatively related to most of the measures of prosocial orientation. High ranking of the value of ambition was negatively related to subjects' willingness to help actively by getting the prescription filled fast, but primarily in the prohibition condition. When a timed task activated their ambition, these subjects were less willing to discontinue their work.

Measures of prosocial orientation were related to one another. A factor analysis showed that most of these measures clustered together, loading high on the same factor. Scores of a "composite prosocial orientation" were computed on the basis of subjects' scores on each of the measures that loaded high on this factor. (The following statements best represent the factor analysis noted in Footnote 2, Chapter 2, p. 60). The resulting scores correlated significantly with most of the measures of helping behavior in most of the experimental conditions. Thus, when the index of prosocial orientation was based on a thorough test of its probable components, including tests of values, moral reasoning, and personal responsibility (and whatever else these tests measured—the actual meaning of self-reports of behavioral orientation, included in some of the measures, is unclear) stable relationships resulted with a variety of consecutive helping acts, unaffected by the treatment conditions.

How did action orientation affect helping? Variation in internal–external control had relatively little influence. The interaction between treatments and high and low scores on the control measure was significant in the subjects' actively helping the distressed person by going into the adjoining room and by filling his prescription. External subjects, those whose test responses indicated that they do not feel they have control over events, responded less to the distress sounds in the control group than did subjects in the other conditions, whereas internal subjects responded more in the permission group and less in the prohibition group than did external subjects.

The value placed on courage in acting according to one's beliefs might also be regarded as an index of action orientation in responding to distress sounds from an adjoining room. The more highly subjects ranked that value the more helpful they were in responding to distress sounds, but not in other ways.

As in some of our other studies (Chapter 2), these data provide support for the proposed model of how prosocial behavior is determined. They also show the need for specifying the potential activating components of the situation and the kinds of demands these components place on people, as well as the need for specifying personality characteristics relevant to the situation. With regard to prosocial orientation, its components need to be specified, not only conceptually, as I did in Chapter 2, but also empirically. How strongly related are the different components; for example, concern for others, prosocial values, and a sense of personal responsibility? Will under certain conditions one or another be more important in affecting behavior? As discussed in Chapter 2 just as personality characteristics need to be carefully scaled, we need to develop methods of scaling situations along dimensions that are relevant to helping behavior.

Personality and the Influence of
the Number of Bystanders on Helping

As described earlier, Schwartz and Clausen (1970) found that subjects who scored high on a measure of personal responsibility for others' welfare (AR) were generally more helpful in response to another person's apparent epileptic fit. The difference between people with high and low scores was slightly greater when an increase in the number of bystanders apparently diffused responsibility. Girls helped less when more people were present, but high scorers were relatively unaffected by the number of bystanders.

In another study discussed earlier, Horowitz (1971) found that subjects who were members of a service group were more helpful than members of social fraternities. This was particularly true when subjects believed that other bystanders were present, which increased helping by members of the service group but decreased helping by fraternity members. When circumstances focus responsibility on people, many are likely to help regardless of individual characteristics; but when circumstances allow the diffusion of responsibility, individual characteristics enter. Certain characteristics lead to a sense of personal responsibility.

In a study that seems consistent with the model I presented, Wilson (1976) showed that the influence of bystanders is modified by the personality of a potential helper. A large number of undergraduates, while participating in an interview, received a sentence-completion test designed to measure safety and esteem motives. Individuals who were characterized as safety oriented gave answers that showed them to be

> highly anxious, mistrustful, passive, and dependent. They have strong feelings of personal incompetence, uncertainty, insecurity, inefficacy, and view the world as an unpredictable and therefore uncontrollable place. Esteem-oriented persons, in contrast, are less anxious. They are achievement oriented, assertive, and striving for competence and efficacy in interpersonal relations. They have strong feelings of personal adequacy, and believe that they can master situations in realistic and functional ways [Wilson, 1976, p. 1079].

On the basis of their responses, persons were selected who scored in the top 15 percentile on one motive and the bottom 15 percentile on the other motive; a third group was composed of individuals who scored in the middle range on both motives.

Subsequently, the subjects took part in one of three experimental conditions. In one condition subjects were alone; in another, they were with two passive confederates; in the third, they were with one helpful and one passive confederate. Participants heard a crash in an adjoining room and sounds of distress (which indicated that the experimenter's foot was hurt) lasting for 20 seconds. Treatments affected helping. Persons who were with the two passive bystanders helped substantially less than those in the other two groups. The difference in helping by subjects with different motivational orientations was substantial. Esteem-oriented subjects showed a high level of helping across all three treatment conditions. When there was one help-- ful confederate, participants in all three conditions helped frequently. Both safety-oriented and middle-range subjects helped substantially less than esteem-oriented subjects when they were with two passive bystanders. Apparently people who feel competent and self-confident take action despite the presence of passive bystanders, a condition that inhibited helping for most people. (Unfortunately, no separate analyses were presented in this study for males and for females.) It seems reasonable that individuals with a strong safety motive would be self-oriented, whereas people with esteem motives would be more other oriented. Thus, in addition to differences in action tendency and resistance to external influence, the subjects may have differed in their prosocial orientation.

Other Studies of the Personalities of Helpful Individuals

Although there is little additional experimental research that contains information about the personalities of individuals who do or do not help others in physical distress, a number of research projects provide such information through interviews with helpers, ratings of the characteristics of both helpers and nonhelpers, and knowledge of the difference in helping behavior associated with group membership in organizations.

In one experiment, kindergarten children were exposed to sounds of distress from an adjoining room (Staub, 1971a). The effects of variation in prior nurturance by an adult experimenter and of modeling of helping behavior by the experimenter were explored. Teachers' ratings of several characteristics of these subjects were also available: initiation of activity, need for approval, expression of positive affection, and competence. The ratings were highly related to one another, apparently representing a single dimension of judgment, probably positivity–negativity. Only ratings of boys' initiation of activity were significantly positively related to helping, whereas ratings of girls' need for approval were significantly negatively related. However, in general, boys who were judged positively tended to be more helpful, whereas girls who were judged negatively tended to be more helpful. These findings suggest the possibility of a rating bias. Active, self-assertive girls might be more likely to initiate aid for another child in distress, but such girls may be judged negatively by teachers. The findings also suggest, more clearly for boys than for girls, that the tendency to be action oriented in everyday life contributes to helping in emergencies.

The interview study by London (1970) of rescuers, people who were involved in an underground system for saving Jews and other persecuted individuals in Nazi Germany, was described in Chapter 2 to demonstrate the match between personality and situational characteristics that may be important for helping to occur. Strong, conscious identification with moral parents, presumably a source of moral values and prosocial goals, adventurousness, and a sense of marginality in relation to their community were characteristics of these rescuers. Even if people do possess characteristics that are required for helping, when helping is potentially extremely dangerous special circumstances that lead to involvement may be required for help to occur. Most of the rescuers got involved in order to help a specific person they knew; then, once involved, they continued their rescue activities. Similarly, circumstances that led to gradually increasing involvement characterized the experience of people who fought for the abolition of slavery in the first part of the nineteenth century (Tomkins, 1965).

Finally, the relationships between age, sex, race, and helping behavior have been explored in emergency and other situations. All three are summary variables. Variation in any one of them can be associated with variations in a whole host of personal characteristics, social norms that are applicable, and other relevant influences. These characteristics are considered in later chapters, with a focus on understanding the reasons for any influence they may have.

Observing and Causing Harm to Others: Affective, Cognitive, and Behavioral Consequences

chapter 4

This chapter will extensively explore the types of cognitive and affective reactions that can follow from observing harm that another person suffers and from causing harm to others. How do people think and feel when they observe or have caused harm to another person, what internal processes are activated, and how do these in turn affect behavior toward a suffering victim? A knowledge of conditions and personality characteristics that lead to cognitions and affects that may enhance positive behavior or to cognitions (such as justifications) and affects that may diminish subsequent positive behavior is central to the understanding of people's reactions to others' needs, whatever the nature of the needs.

Empathy and Prosocial Behavior

Observing another person's suffering can evoke empathy—a parallel experience of distress—and can motivate the observer to help. Piliavin *et al.* (1969, 1975) proposed that empathic distress motivates help (or escape) for selfish reasons, in that people desire to reduce their own distress. Others consider empathy to be an altruistic basis of helping, because affect in the helpers is evoked not by anything happening directly to them but by another person's fate (Aronfreed, 1969, 1976; Hoffman, 1975a). This is my view also. As I noted earlier, empathy has been regarded as an important motivator of prosocial behavior. Prosocial acts may also be motivated by the anticipation of another person's increased well-being and the positive emotions that follow—that is, by anticipated vicarious positive emotions. Thus empathy may motivate positive acts to benefit a person who is not experiencing distress.

Unfortunately, no attempts have been made to show that empathy is evoked in people who are exposed to others' distress in emergencies, primarily because of methodological difficulties in demonstrating the experience of empathy and its influence on behavior. Consequently, there is no direct evidence that empathy does motivate help in emergencies. There is a substantial body of research dealing with the capacity to take the point of view of another (role taking). However, as I have noted, although role taking may be required for an accurate perception of others' emotions and thus may be a precondition for empathy, the capacity for role taking does not guarantee that a person will experience empathy. Research on role taking is reviewed in Chapter 5 of this volume and in Volume 2.

A substantial body of earlier research explored *predictive empathy*, the ability to predict others' reactions to events or describe how others' would feel under certain circumstances. This line of research was discontinued, in part because of methodological criticism (Cronbach, 1955) and in part because of the trend toward research on role taking, which used different methodologies. Several criticisms were provided, but one issue that seems to underlie these criticisms, in my view, is relevant to role taking and empathy. In predictive empathy studies, people could and probably frequently did make judgments about others on the basis of their own characteristics— projecting how they themselves would feel, what they would think, how they would act under varied circumstances. The studies usually did not differentiate between judgments based on projection and judgment based on perception. However, empathic reactions to others are frequently based on past experience, on one's own feelings and knowledge of the feelings of others under various circumstances—when someone is ill in a family, when a person experiences disappointment in a love relationship, and so on. Empathic reactions can also be based on the actual observation of facial and bodily expressions, what a person says, and how a person acts. Frequently these various sources provide the same information. Sometimes they may not. Personal experience may suggest that the death of someone's mother would lead to great sorrow, but the person in question may view his mother's death as a blessing, because it terminated great suffering. Thus some sources of information may be misleading on specific occasions. Consequently, false empathy may result.

Physiological Arousal in Response
to Another's Suffering

A basic step in demonstrating that people experience empathy is to show that they respond emotionally to others' emotional experiences. However, a similarity in the quality of the emotional experience also has to be shown. A variety of experiments have indicated that observing another person's pain results in the observer's physiological arousal.

Lazarus *et al.* (1962) have shown that the observation of a film of a primitive puberty rite—an operation performed on an adolescent's penis and scrotum with a piece of flint—has produced much greater physiological arousal in observers than the observation of a film about farming. Arousal was indicated by increased galvanic skin response (GSR) and heart rate. Other films—particularly those segments that showed people being hurt in a series of sawmill accidents (Lazarus *et al.*, 1965)—also resulted in increased heart rate and GSR. These findings coincide with everyday experience. Seeing a movie can arouse the intense physiological as well as emotional reactions that the specific actor we identify with appears to experience.

In a number of studies participants watched other people receive electric shocks and show painful reactions to the shocks. The person who presumably received the electric shock—and did so voluntarily—was a confederate. This is a somewhat limited analogue for the suffering of other people, but it is one of the empirical demonstrations available to us. How did observers react? There is evidence that they reacted with physiological arousal: increase in GSR, increase in heart rate, and increase in other indices of arousal.

In an experiment that attempted to demonstrate vicarious conditioning (Berger, 1962), subjects watched another person receive an electric shock (regarded as an unconditioned stimulus) and jerk his arm upon receiving the shock, which was supposed to indicate his discomfort. After a number of trials, subjects responded to a signal indicating the onset of the shock with physiological arousal (measured by GSR) greater than that of subjects who did not expect the signal to be followed by electric shock although they saw a similar arm movement by the "performer," or of subjects who saw no movement. Aversive-conditioning studies clearly indicate that when people receive electric shocks they show physiological reactions to a signal preceding the shock. Berger's study showed that the same process of conditioning occurs in response to another person's experience, suggesting that people respond vicariously to another's pain itself.

A number of other experiments have shown that people respond with physiological arousal when they observe a person receiving electric shocks and experiencing pain (Bandura & Rosenthal, 1966; Craig & Lavery, 1969; Geer & Jarmecky, 1973). Geer and Jarmecky (1973) varied the intensity of shocks that the confederate was apparently receiving. The confederate acted as if he was experiencing intense pain in the severe shock condition and less pain in the mild shock condition. The more intense shocks resulted in stronger physiological reactions on the part of observers. Observers responded with maximum arousal in the early trials when the shocks were intense, but showed some increase in arousal over trials with less intense shocks. Thus, reactions to others' discomfort may sometimes be strong initially, but at other times they may increase with repeated exposure to suffering.

The development of empathic reactions is examined in Volume 2 of this work. There is evidence, however, that people who were themselves first exposed to electric shock responded with greater physiological arousal to the shock-induced pain of others than people who did not have the same experience (Craig, 1968). Moreover, the intensity of the electric shocks previously received and the intensity of those witnessed combined in determining the level of physiological reaction (Ogston & Davidson, 1972). These findings are consistent with everyday experience: People frequently respond more empathically to others' experience when they themselves have had similar experiences.

It is clear that physiological reactions, presumably indicating emotional reactions, do occur in people who witness others' discomfort or pain. The predominant emotion of observers is thought to be distress. Unfortunately, the quality of emotion experienced by observers was rarely evaluated. Some people may react with positive emotions to others' pain or to signals indicating that others will experience pain. A past history in which a person's pleasure was dependent on or associated with others' pain can lead to such "sadistic" reactions. Moreover, many people may respond to others' distress with positive feelings under certain special conditions. Bandura and Rosenthan (1966) found, in fact, that some of their subjects reported feelings of satisfaction upon observing another person receive shocks. Bramel, Traub, and Blum (1968) found that subjects who had been insulted by another person increased their liking for him if they thought he had suffered and decreased their liking for him if they thought he had been happy. These subjects would not be likely to experience empathy for the other person if they saw him suffer. Other research findings also show that a person who is insulted or harmed is likely to experience positive emotions while observing the suffering of the harmdoer (Staub, 1971c). Hartman (1969) found that delinquents who had been insulted administered more electric shocks to the person who insulted them after they saw a movie in which somebody was severely beaten than after other experiences. Nondelinquent subjects in the same condition administered fewer electric shocks than did the delinquents. Observing pain and suffering, which normally reduces aggression, functioned as an instigator of aggression for the delinquents. To determine whether arousal is the result of empathy or of other emotions, we need to evaluate not only the intensity of the emotional reaction but also the kind of emotion experienced. We have to ask people how they feel and/or devise other methods of evaluating the quality of their affect.

The Reinforcing Effect of Reducing
Another's Pain or Distress

There is evidence that the reduction of others' distress can act as a reinforcer. Weiss and his associates (1971) had subjects observe someone receiving electric shocks that apparently produced pain. These subjects were supposed to push a button to reactivate an apparatus. In one experimental condition, pushing the button also shut off the electricity, eliminating further pain of the victim on that trial. In another condition (partial reinforcement), pushing the button to reactivate the apparatus shut off electricity some of the time but not always. In a third condition, pushing the button had no effect on shock administration. When pushing the button discontinued the shock on each trial, over trials subjects came to respond, to push the button, significantly faster than subjects in the other two conditions. Partial reinforcement resulted in some increase in speed, less than continuous reinforcement, but more than button pushing that did not eliminate the shock. There was also a trial by treatment interaction; the difference in the speed of the three groups increased over trials.

In another series of studies by Weiss *et al.* (1973), the subjects observed someone receiving painful and continuous electric shocks while performing a motor activity, a tracking task. Ostensibly, the study was to explore the effects of stress on complex motor skills. Female confederates were used with female subjects and male confederates were used with male subjects. In the first study of the series, Weiss *et al.* again found that altruistic reinforcement —button pushing by subjects eliminating shock—led to increased speed of responding over trials. In a second study, the researchers varied the magnitude of the effect of pushing the button. In one group it eliminated shock completely. In another group it reduced shock magnitude. In a third group it did nothing. Again, the latency of pushing the button decreased when button pushing eliminated shock. Latency also decreased, but to a smaller degree, when pushing the button reduced shock. Very little change in speed occurred over trials in the group where pushing the button had no effect on the shock. In a third experiment the authors had a 100%-reinforcement group, a 33%-reinforcement group, and a no-reinforcement group. Again, the same relative differences were found. The elimination of another's pain acted as a reinforcer of the button-pushing response. Weiss *et al.* concluded that people learn an instrumental response that reduces another's pain and altruistic reinforcement seems to have all the properties of other kinds of reinforcement.

Geer and Jarmecky (1973) measured not only physiological reactions to another person's pain, but also differences in observers' attempts to eliminate the pain as a function of its degree and the responsibility of the subject. Incorrect responses on a problem-solving task resulted in either a mild or a painful shock for the person observed. The subjects were asked to pull a switch when they heard a noise, either to terminate the shock or—as a control—to provide a measure of their reaction time.

Both the victim's receiving stronger shocks and the focusing of responsibility on subjects to eliminate the victim's pain resulted in greater physiological reactions; both also increased subjects' speed in pulling the switch. Subjects in the responsible condition apparently responded with the maximum speed possible from the very beginning. Why was there such a difference between findings of this and of other studies? These subjects knew from the beginning of the experiment that another person would receive painful shocks, and that they not only could but were expected to do something about it.

Why did reducing another person's pain function as a reinforcer? The findings reviewed earlier suggest that many observers of another's pain may experience empathic emotional reactions. The elimination of the other's continued distress may have resulted, on each occasion, in empathic reinforcement, reinforcement due to reduction in the observer's vicarious distress. Other possibilities also exist, however. People may have reacted to the demand characteristics of the situation. Once they saw that their behavior reduced pain they thought they were expected to do so; they saw it as the socially desirable thing to do. The adequacy of this explanation is lessened by the fact that the behavior of the participants was so sensitive to the differences in the experimental conditions. Would people feel that it was less expected of them to eliminate pain when the pain was somewhat milder? It is certainly possible, however, that under some conditions subjects had more difficulty figuring out the effects of their behavior, so that treatments varied in how clearly they implied expectations about behavior or focused responsibility on the subjects.

Another possibility is that button pushing was reinforced to different degrees as a function of how much impact it had, how great a change it produced. When we do something that has no significant consequences we will not try to do the same thing better. But if our behavior has important consequences, whatever the nature, we may show learning, reinforced by our feeling that we are influential, are "agents" (Deci, 1975; 1979).

Finally, the observation of another's suffering may have activated personal norms that prescribe help for people who suffer; acting according to these norms would be reinforcing. Such reinforcement could be regarded as altruistic in nature, since it results from prosocial action, but it is not empathic. I am distinguishing between two types of arousal, one produced by empathy and the other produced by the activation of values and related norms and a sense of obligation to promote others' welfare. These two sources of arousal have not been differentiated in research, although presumably they can be differentiated. If the arousal is not empathic, the observer will not experience an emotion parallel to that of the sufferer. I do believe, however, that empathy and certain value orientations probably correspond, that the former may result from interpretations of events that are based on the latter (see Chapter 2).

Perceptual–Cognitive Set, Empathy, and Helping

Certain conditions lead people to respond empathically to others. The nature of the circumstances and individual differences in personality probably act jointly to determine when this will happen.

Stotland (1969) proposed that a person's perceptual orientation determines how that person processes the experiences of another. In a series of experiments, Stotland and his associates varied the instructions they gave to male subjects who were engaged in observing a male confederate (presented as another subject). These instructions were expected to induce varied perceptual orientations and thereby induce or inhibit empathy in the observers.

The confederate was directed to put his finger on a "diatherm" machine. Then he apparently received either a mild, warm, pleasant sensation or a strong, hot, painful sensation that made him jerk his hand away. Some observers were told, "Watch this person and see how he reacts." They were asked to focus their attention on muscle movements, on the details of this person's reactions. This "watch him" orientation was expected to make observers feel removed, less attentive to the confederate's subjective experience, and therefore unlikely to respond empathically. Other subjects were asked to imagine what the confederate's experience was like and how he felt. This "imagine him" orientation was expected to induce subjects to look at the confederate's experience from his perspective. In a third condition, observers received an "imagine self" orientation. They were to imagine themselves in the confederate's role, to imagine how they would feel and react. In a number of the experiments the degree of similarity between the confederate and the observer was varied. On the basis of personality measures the subjects had previously filled out, the subject and the confederate were presented as more or less similar. The physiological reactions of subjects while they observed the confederate were the primary data in this research. The findings were complicated, but they showed that, in comparison to the "watch him" orientation, both "imagine self" and "imagine him" orientations resulted in significantly greater—although not in identical patterns—amounts of physiological arousal on the part of observers in response to the confederate's experience. Perceived similarity to the confederate also increased empathic reaction, as measured by physiological arousal. (This was more true of firstborn than of later born subjects.) The subjects' descriptions of the quality of their subjective experiences supported the idea that they had experienced empathy.

A number of subsequent experiments have confirmed that "watch him" and "imagine him" orientations lead to different reactions and/or behavior. In one study, Aderman, Brehm, and Katz (1974) found that people who observed another person receiving electric shocks but were unable to help devalued this person when they had a "watch him" orientation. Those observers who had an "imagine him" orientation devalued the person significantly less, or not at all.

Regan and Totten (1975) considered the phenomenon that individuals (actors) tended to interpret their own behavior more in terms of situational influences, to report that circumstances induced them to act as they did, whereas observers tended to explain the same behavior in terms of the characteristics or dispositions of the actors. The "divergent perceptions of the causes of behavior" by actors and observers were originally proposed by Jones and Nisbett (1971) and received a fair amount of experimental support. Regan and Totten (1975) elaborated on one possible cause of this difference, that actors and observers process the available information about the causes of the actors' behavior differently. They suggested that the "adoption of an empathic set by observers would increase the likelihood that they would provide relatively more situational and less dispositional attributions for the actor's behavior [p. 852]."

Female undergraduates in this study observed a videotaped "get-acquainted" conversation. Half the group saw both participants in the conversation and were asked to focus their attention on one of them; the other half saw only the person they were asked to attend to. Half the subjects received instructions based on Stotland's "imagine him" orientation. They were asked to empathize with "Margaret," to imagine how she felt, how she reacted to what she heard. The other half were simply asked to observe Margaret. The instructions for these subjects were intended not to minimize empathy, as with Stotland's "watch him" instructions, but neither to promote nor to inhibit it. Differences in the tapes had no effect, but observational set had a significant effect. "Imagine" instructions resulted in more situational and less dispositional judgments about the reasons for Margaret's behavior. Regan and Totten suggest that an "empathic orientation" may do more than facilitate the sharing of emotional responses of another person; it may alter the observer's perspective and "highlight the causal sequence of situational cues. In fact, emotional experiences may be shared precisely because situational aspects are more salient for the empathic observer [p. 855]."

The findings imply that under certain circumstances people with an empathic observational set may be less judgmental or evaluative. In explaining negative behavior, for example, they may emphasize the influence of circumstances on a person rather than the person's characteristics. Negative judgments about and evaluations of another person can often inhibit positive behavior toward that person. An empathic perceptual set would decrease the likelihood of this happening.

One problem with research on observational sets is that, except in the original studies of Stotland, physiological reactions of subjects were never measured. Nor was the subjective emotional experience of observers evaluated. Stotland's research findings were not definitive enough—and it is doubtful that any single set of findings can ever be so definitive—to justify a belief that instructions attempting to induce empathic observational sets necessarily induce emotional reactions in the observer that are parallel to those of the observed.

One study attempted to show that varied perceptual orientations, which presumably affect empathy, will in turn affect helping behavior (Aderman & Berkowitz, 1970). Male subjects heard a tape recording in which someone asked a friend to help him take notes for a term paper. The friend, who had the skill to help, (a) provided the help, (b) provided the help and was also thanked for it, or (c) did not provide help. Some subjects were instructed to imagine how the person who asked for the help felt (imagine him). Others were told to imagine how they themselves would feel in his place (imagine self). The attention of other subjects was focused on the person who was asked to help; again, some were told to imagine how he felt and others were told to imagine how they would feel in his place. Following the story subjects noted how they had felt while listening to the tape recording. Then the experimenter asked the subjects to score some data, while they were presumably waiting for the resumption of the experiment. They were told that an analysis of these data was to be included in a talk the experimenter was to give. The amount of data scored in a 10-minute interval provided the measure of help. The findings, as in the Stotland experiments, were complicated. In two "imagine him" conditions—when they attended to the person who asked for help but did not receive help, and when they attended to the person who helped and was thanked for it—the subjects scored more data than in other groups. Although the ratings of affect were complicated, subjects in the former condition tended to report the most negative affect (anger, sadness, unpleasantness), whereas those in the latter condition reported the most positive affect. If an empathy interpretation is applied, the findings suggest that vicariously experiencing the emotions not only of someone who needs help but also of someone who experiences positive consequences upon helping can increase later prosocial behavior.

Interpreting this research in terms of the influence of empathy on prosocial behavior is difficult, for several reasons; the authors themselves point out some of them. First, no "watch him" or "observe him" or control conditions were included to provide a basis for comparison. Second, no physiological measures were taken. Third, the extent to which reports of affect and helping behavior influenced one another is unclear. Admittedly, research on empathy is difficult and cumbersome because the measurement of empathy may interfere with other experimental procedures, such as the independent measurement of behavior. And fourth, subjects were asked to help the experimenter, not the person whose fate presumably aroused empathy.

Although clear evidence of the influence of empathic orientation on helping is not yet available, the nature of the evidence we do have makes it appear likely that an empathic orientation would increase helping. Moreover, the evidence that perceptual–cognitive orientation affects the meaning and impact of an experience is strong. In addition to the studies that used the Stotland paradigm, others by Lazarus and his associates support such conclusions. Having shown that exposure to others' harm produced strong physiological reactions—which they considered threat reactions (Lazarus et al., 1962)—Lazarus and his associates reasoned that the manner in which people attend to and process the events they see will determine their reactions to these events. The appraisal of events determines emotional reactions. Appraisal is presumably affected by the stimulus itself, by external influences, and by a person's characteristic manner of processing information or dealing with events ("defensive" strategies).

Speisman et al. (1964) also used the film of the crude surgical operation performed on the genitals of a male adolescent of a primitive Australian tribe. In one condition (trauma) the film was accompanied by a sound track that emphasized the harmful features—pain, mutilation, possibility of disease. In another condition (denial) the sound track's theme was that the operation did not produce harm and the boys happily looked forward to it. In a third condition the sound track presented the detached attitude of an anthropologist (intellectualization). A silent version of the film was also included. Both denial and intellectualization significantly reduced physiological arousal. Moreover, there was a treatment by personality interaction. Subjects who were judged, on the basis of personality measures, to have defensive orientations of the kind that were incorporated into their treatment procedures, were the ones who responded most to their treatments. In another study (Lazarus & Alfert, 1964) the denial orientation was presented to subjects before they saw the film. The previously cited findings were replicated. This treatment significantly reduced physiological reactions in comparison to those aroused by a film without any preceding comments. Moreover, the significant effect of denial was due to the behavior of subjects who were judged, on the basis of paper-and-pencil tests taken before they saw the film, to be disposed to denial defenses. To show the generalizability of their findings, Lazarus et al. (1965) demonstrated that giving observers intellectualization and denial orientations to a film that depicted sawmill accidents resulted in lower heart rate and GSR while they watched the film.

When people observe the harmful and/or painful experiences of others, they react emotionally. Their emotional reactions are strongest when they view segments of films in which others' experiences are most harmful. Lazarus (1966) and his associates assume that people identify with the individuals whose experiences they observe. As a function of how observers assess what is happening, which can be affected by perceptual orientations that are provided to them and by their own perceptual tendencies, their reactions will vary. Lazarus (1966) suggests that "the dynamics of vicarious and direct threat are indeed comparable [p. 51]." As the basis of this conclusion he offers Alfert's findings (in Lazarus, 1966) of a high correlation between subjects' reactions to a part of the film about sawmill accidents, and their reaction to expecting to receive a painful shock themselves.

Individual Differences That Affect Empathic Reactions

Many conditions can affect a person's perceptual–cognitive orientation, the manner in which he interprets an event, and emotional reactions to that event. As I noted in Chapter 3, the nature of a stimulus and social influences can strongly affect behavior in emergencies, partly because they can affect how a person interprets an event—and in turn whether that person reacts empathically to the fate of another person. Either real or imagined similarity to another person may be important; so may be knowing another person well. Such conditions may lead to real or imagined awareness of the subjective experience of that person. Knowing nothing about another or believing that he is different may inhibit or diminish empathy.

In addition to such situational and experiential factors, persistent individual characteristics may affect empathic responsiveness. Examples of such characteristics are role-taking capacity and modes of interpretation of events. Differences in such characteristics may be "defensively" based, in that some people habitually minimize their experience of stress, threat, and distress. They do this by perceiving and interpreting events in such a way that their involvement is minimized. Differences may also arise from varied views of other human beings and varied personal values and goals. There is evidence, for example, that people vary in their perception and evaluation of other people as hostile (Loew, 1967; Slavson, 1965; Staub, 1971c).

Another dimension of individual difference is the degree to which people are physiologically labile. Some people are simply less responsive physiologically, and consequently emotionally, than others. For example, a defining characteristic of psychopaths appears to be deficiency of affect (Maher, 1966). However, there is a controversy about the origin of this deficiency. Some believe that it is due to psychopaths' tendency to overreact physiologically to stimuli; consequently they adapt to arousal and particular stimuli become less capable of producing affect (Schachter & Latané, 1964). Others believe that psychopaths tend to underreact physiologically; House and Milligan (1976) found some evidence for this position. Young male subjects, from a prison population, who scored high on the Minnesota Multiphasic Personality Inventory (MMPI) Pd (Psychopathic deviate) scale, considered an indication of psychopathic personality, were compared to low scorers in their physiological reactions to observing another person receive electric shocks. Subjects who scored high on the Pd scale reacted significantly less, as shown by a skin resistance measure, than low-scoring subjects. Moreover, high-anxiety subjects, as measured by another derivative scale from the MMPI, responded significantly more to the modeled distress of a person receiving shocks than low anxiety subjects. This study demonstrates that there are individual differences in physiological reactions to another's distress. It is likely that individual differences exist in physiological reactivity in general, so that some people respond less than others to stimuli having emotional significance. This in turn contributes to individual differences in the degree to which people respond empathically to others' experiences. Systematic study is needed of individual differences in both perceptual–cognitive orientation and physiological reactivity. In considering such differences, it seems that a very high level of emotional reactivity, combined with an empathic personal orientation, may not be most conducive to helping others under all conditions. Sometimes such a combination of characteristics may result in a very intense vicarious emotional response, which interferes with effective intervention.

Demonstrating the Influence of Empathy
on Prosocial Behavior

It is difficult to demonstrate convincingly the mediating influence of empathy on helping. Unless attempts to do so follow careful methodology, it is usually possible to find alternative interpretations. For example, even if substantial evidence showed that "imagine" orientations enhanced helping, one could argue that the instructions point to the "humanness" of the person whose experiences an observer is supposed to imagine, and thereby make the observer feel responsible for that person's welfare. Thus the conclusion could be drawn that relevant social norms and a personal feeling of responsibility, rather than empathy, induced helping.

How can the influence of empathy on helping be demonstrated? Measures of physiological reactions in response to another's experience can indicate whether an emotional reaction is present. Asking people to describe the nature of their emotions may, unfortunately, interfere with the emotional reaction itself; it may modify the reaction, and may influence the manner in which subjects subsequently act. Asking people after they responded behaviorally how they felt may be an inaccurate measure of their original affect, since both the memory of earlier affect and the willingness to report it can be affected by the intervening response. One effective method may be to expose two groups of subjects to every experimental treatment and measure their physiological reactions. In one group the quality of the subjects' feelings would be assessed at some point during and/or immediately after a potentially empathy-producing experience, whereas in the other group behavioral reactions would be measured. If the same conditions produced the strongest empathic reactions and the most help, then it is likely that empathy motivated helping. Another procedure might focus on using indirect measures, such as facial and bodily reactions, to ascertain the quality of emotion during and/or immediately after the observation of other people in need. Such measures may be most useful, however, in conjunction with other kinds of measures.

In one study (Hamilton, 1973) facial expressions of preschool, second-, and fifth-grade subjects tended to correspond to the expressions of models in happy and sad films. In another study (Buck, 1975) preschool children watched a series of slides that were expected to have emotional impact. By watching the children's reactions only, both the children's mothers and undergraduate observers were able to distinguish between children who watched pleasant slides and those who watched unpleasant slides. However, large individual differences existed among children in their "sending ability." Sending ability was significantly related to teachers' ratings of the children's "activity level, aggressiveness, impulsiveness, bossiness, sociability, etc., and negatively related to shyness, cooperation, emotional inhibition and control [p. 644]." Other studies showed that accurate adult senders have smaller physiological reactions to emotion-arousing stimuli, are more outgoing and sociable, and have higher self-esteem than inaccurate senders (Jones, 1960; Buck, Miller, & Caul, 1974). Do facial and bodily reactions to emotional stimuli indicate empathy, and would individual differences in these reactions provide an index of empathic responsiveness? Although they may do both, such reactions seem to have broader implications about personality; by themselves they may not be adequate measures of empathy. They may have to be used in conjunction with other indices.

The findings indicate that people who show greater facial and bodily reactions to slides presenting emotionally laden material are generally less responsive physiologically. Is there, then, a negative relationship between facial and physiological reactions in response to specific experiences of other people? On the one hand, people may differ in the intensity of their affect, including empathy. On the other hand, the relationship between the quality of affect, the intensity of affect, and nonverbal expressions of affect is likely to be both complex and variable.

If we had measures of individual differences in empathy and could demonstrate greater help by more empathic individuals, particularly if we could also demonstrate the arousal of empathy in specific instances, our confidence in empathy as a mediator of help would be increased. Using this approach we could also examine the relationship between empathy and other presumed motivators of help. As I noted in Chapter 2, a certain value–norm–goal orientation, which focuses on the importance of the welfare of other human beings, should lead to the tendency to interpret events in a manner that gives rise to empathic emotions. This kind of research could also show to what extent individual differences in role-taking capacity are related to individual differences in empathic reactivity.

One experimental study attempted to demonstrate differences in empathic emotion in response to different experimental treatments, and to relate such differences to differences in prosocial behavior (Krebs, 1975). In one condition of this study, the male subjects observed another person (a confederate) who presumably received electric shocks, gained rewards, or had neutral experiences on different trials. A signal light of a different color preceded each of these events. In a control condition the confederate responded to the lights with the same bodily reactions as in the experimental condition, but this happened for "neutral" reasons, without reference to electric shocks or rewards. To enhance variation in empathy, half the subjects in each condition were told that the confederate was similar to them, whereas the other half were told that he was different. The similarity manipulation was elaborate. Subjects were told that the other person's performance on personality scales was similar or dissimilar to theirs. Moreover, while the subject was observing, the confederate indicated that his field of study or profession was one that would be either highly valued or devalued by the subject—as determined by the subject's prior responses on the Allport–Vernon–Lindzey scale of values. After a series of trials in which the lights appeared and were followed by varied consequences, the subjects had an opportunity to determine how much money the confederate would receive ($2 was the maximum amount) or how strong a shock he would receive. A roulette wheel was used to determine whether the confederate was to receive money or the shock, but the confederate decided how much. Altruistic decisions (more money, less shock) were made at a sacrifice to the subjects themselves (who would themselves receive correspondingly less money or more shock).

Participants exposed to similar persons showed the strongest physiological reactions to the confederate's experiences, and they also engaged in the most altruistic behavior. These subjects also reported feeling more discomfort than subjects in other conditions while they waited for the confederate to receive the shock. Since these reports were provided after subjects made decisions about amounts of shock, a desire or tendency for consistency may have been at work. Groups did not significantly differ in their reported feelings while the confederate was waiting for a reward.

The experimental treatments affected both empathic reactions and altruistic behavior. Unfortunately, Krebs did not report the relationships between measures, whether observers who showed greater physiological reactions also acted more altruistically and reported feelings parallel to those of the confederate. Although this study comes closer than most other studies to the criteria for adequately demonstrating that empathy increases helping behavior, a strong relationship between empathic experience and positive behavior within groups would have been important further evidence.

Empathy-Related Issues

Cumulatively, the research findings do suggest that empathy is a likely determinant of helping. In addition to the research mentioned in the preceding section, there is a body of research that relates to how empathy develops, as well as to how a connection between empathic emotions and instrumental acts to help others may be learned. In the course of discussing this research in Volume 2, I shall discuss whether empathy develops through conditioning or through the development of role-taking skills or in still other ways—for example, through the elaboration of primitive empathic reactions (Hoffman, 1975a). In my view primitive emotional reactivity (which may not be empathy), conditioning, and role taking, as well as the learning of values and beliefs that lead to perceptual–cognitive orientations that contribute to empathy, are all involved.

Although the research findings indicate that empathy is involved in helping, research is still needed to demonstrate this influence unequivocally. A further issue is the nature of empathic emotion. Lazarus (1966) suggested that empathic "threat" and direct threat have similar consequences. However, the construct *empathy* has not yet been adequately defined. Are there differences in the correlates of empathic emotion when a person experiences an intense emotional reaction and when a feeling is not accompanied by a substantial degree of arousal? Does one reaction lead to helping more than the other? Is the subjective experience in one case very different from that in the other case? Is it possible that certain individuals tend to have empathic reactions more like their own direct emotional experiences, whereas for others empathic reactions are different from their own emotional experiences? The relationship between empathy and instrumental acts associated with it may also affect the degree of arousal in empathic reactions. A person who has learned to respond to empathic emotions by attempting to help another person may have different emotions than someone who has not learned to make such a connection.

Also in need of attention is the validation of currently available personality measures that purport to measure individual differences in empathy (Feshback & Roe, 1968; Hogan, 1969). We need evidence that these measures relate to individual differences in emotion that includes both physiological and feeling components. They may measure differences primarily in cognition, or in sensitivity to others, or in feelings that are not accompanied by arousal, that is, feelings limited in intensity.

The importance of empathy and other mediators of helping behavior is further enhanced if we consider that they are likely to inhibit or reduce aggressive behavior. The assumption that empathy would inhibit aggression is consistent with the line of reasoning that led to the expectation of a positive relationship between empathy and prosocial behavior; others' distress may negatively reinforce aggression through the empathic distress it produces in the aggressor.

In one study, Feshbach and Feshbach (1969) examined the relationship between children's empathy and teachers' ratings of aggressive behavior. Empathy was measured by the technique developed by Feshbach and Roe (1968). Children were shown sequences of slides, each depicting something that happened to a child and produced some affect. The index of empathy was provided by children's descriptions of how they themselves felt immediately after they saw a sequence of slides. More frequent reports by children that their feelings were similar to those of the child observed in the slides resulted in higher empathy scores. Then the children were asked to describe what happened and how the observed child felt, as a measure of their social comprehension. Feshbach and Feshbach related aggression to empathy at two age levels, 4–5 and 6–7. In prior research Murphy (1937) found a positive correlation between sympathy (children helping others) and aggression in nursery-school children. Murphy suggested that both these behaviors may be indices of the young child's social maturity, as indicated by frequency of interaction with peers. Following this reasoning, Feshbach and Feshbach expected the relationship between empathy and aggression to be positive among the younger children. They also expected empathy to inhibit aggression among older children.

Feshbach and Feshbach found a positive relationship between empathy and aggression for the younger boys but a negative relationship for the older boys. Although the magnitude of the relationship for the older children was not substantial, the reversal was significant. However, no correlation was found between empathy and aggression for girls. Moreover, empathy scores were not substantially greater for the older children. Changes in empathy with age may be slight, or, perhaps more likely, the measure of empathy employed in the study was insensitive. The correlation between social comprehension and empathy scores was not reported. A positive relationship between empathy and social comprehension could be expected, since the children had to perceive the meaning of the situation depicted and the feelings of the other child before they could experience emotions appropriate to the situation depicted in the pictures. In fact, the children may have reported experiencing an emotion that seemed appropriate for the observed situation without actually experiencing the emotion. Whether empathy or comprehension was actually measured, the findings do suggest that one of the two relates to boys' aggressive behavior. The items that were used in the aggression measure were not described, so we do not know whether aggression meant inflicting injury or harm on others or acts that were primarily instrumental in nature.

Anecdotal evidence and case studies in the clinical literature (Slavson, 1965; Staub & Conn, 1970; Staub, 1971c) indicate that aggressive delinquents have difficulty in role taking and in considering others' motives, needs, and desires. They also tend to interpret others' actions as potentially hostile. As a consequence they may experience relatively little empathy; this lack of empathy may contribute to aggressive behavior.

Although an examination of research on the instigators and determinants of aggression suggests that empathy is likely to inhibit aggression (Staub, 1971d), experimental evidence is as yet minimal. In addition to empathy, values such as generosity and kindness may decrease aggression. However, other values, such as justice, may decrease aggression under some circumstances but increase it under others.

Just World, Devaluation, and Aggression

There is much suffering in the world. People are discriminated against, they are mistreated, and they have bad luck. They experience physical and psychological distress. How do witnesses deal with others' suffering when they cannot alleviate it or choose not to try to alleviate it? The research and theory on this issue highlight perceptual, cognitive, and emotional processes and are an important source of information about internal processes that contribute to helping as well as to not helping.

Lerner (Lerner & Simmons, 1966; Lerner, 1971) proposed the "just world" hypothesis to explain how people deal with those whose suffering they witness:

> People must believe there is an appropriate fit between what they do and what happens to them—their outcomes. It was reasoned that if people did not believe they could get what they want and avoid what they abhor by performing certain appropriate acts, they would be virtually incapacitated. It seems obvious that most people cannot afford, for the sake of their own sanity, to believe in a world governed by a schedule of random reinforcements. To maintain the belief that there is an approximate fit between effort and outcome the person must conclude it is a relatively "objective" belief—one that applies to everyone (Festinger, 1954). If this is true, then the person who sees suffering or misfortune will be motivated to believe that the unfortunate victim in some sense merited his fate [Lerner & Simmons, 1966, p. 203].

According to Lerner (Lerner & Simmons, 1966; Lerner, 1971; 1975; 1977), people find the suffering of innocent people—those who have done nothing to bring about their own suffering—unacceptable. Witnesses reason that if innocent people can suffer, they themselves can suffer without cause. To defend themselves from this possibility they have to engage in a defensive psychological act; if they cannot attribute the cause of others' suffering to their actions, they must attribute it to their character. Thus, the innocent victims will be negatively evaluated, devalued, so the observers' belief in a just world can be maintained. On the other hand, if people bring about suffering by their own actions, an appropriate fit exists, and belief in a just world can be maintained. Devaluation of the person is not necessary. "There seem to be two senses in which people are considered to be deserving. They are seen as deserving if they have behaved in an appropriate or commendable fashion." Similarly, they are seen as deserving punishment if they have behaved cruelly, badly, or stupidly. "And in another sense [they] are considered deserving if they are personally good and desirable [Lerner & Simmons, 1966, p. 204]." If they suffer without having acted badly or stupidly, then it might be that they are undesirable as persons.

There are important questions related to this hypothesis. What is the empirical support for it? What are the exact conditions under which people would devalue another person? Does devaluation inhibit the activation of empathy or other components of a prosocial motivation in response to the devalued person's need? Will it actually lessen the likelihood that the person will later be helped if in need?

Anecdotal and other types of information do suggest that "people have a strong desire to live in a just world [Rubin & Peplau, 1973]," and writers other than Lerner have also emphasized this. Heider (1958), for example, wrote that justice is an "ought force that people consider inherent in their environment." I suggested that at an early age children learn a "norm of deserving," an expectation that one ought to have rewards that one has earned and thus deserved, but not undeserved rewards (Staub, 1968; 1973). Equity theorists have emphasized the importance to people of a balance between their own efforts and outcomes, and a similar ratio of their own and others' efforts to outcome (Homans, 1961; Walster et al., 1973; 1978).

These conceptions relate to deserving, to justice and injustice. They imply that if people defend themselves against the sight of injustice, they do so not only because they are afraid that in an unjust world bad things can happen to them, as Lerner suggests, but also perhaps because they learn and further develop a belief–value system in which the notion that the world is just has a central position. Evidence of injustice threatens such a belief system and is resisted. This also implies that we are likely to find important individual differences in reactions to injustice. Many people are likely to hold the belief that the world is just only to a limited degree. For some, this belief might have less centrality in their belief or value system than for others. Some people probably agree with Job's view, as stated by Rubin and Peplau (1975), that "the world is not a just place at all, but rather a place where rewards and punishments are often unfair and capricious. . . . An unbiased glance about us will reveal countless instances of innocent people suffering, wicked people reveling, and, more generally, fate playing mischievous and arbitrary tricks with our lives [p. 66]."

However, Walster and Walster (1975) have noted that "equity researchers have documented that under the right conditions, both exploiters and their victims tend to be capable of convincing themselves that the most unbalanced of exchanges is in fact perfectly fair [p. 34]." Many people may actively attempt to maintain a belief in justice. However, devaluation of victims is only one of the possible reactions to injustice. People can react with concern, compassion, and empathy to the fate of an innocent victim, which is probably an alternative to and might be incompatible with devaluation. Ideally, of course, that is how people would react; that is how "logically" they "should" react, given the innocence of a person who suffers. Because of its potential consequences, understanding whether devaluation of an innocent victim occurs and what leads to it is extremely important.

A number of authors in *Sanctions of Evil*, a book edited by Sanford and Comstock (1971), suggest that evil perpetrated on others most often starts with and is made possible by devaluation of the victims. It becomes permissible to harm others, to discriminate against them, even to murder them, because of the undesirable character ascribed to them. Duster (1971), for example, writes about the psychological conditions for guilt-free massacre:

> The most general condition for guilt-free massacre is the denial of the humanity of the victim. You call the victims names like gooks, dinks, niggers, pinkos and japs. The more you can get high officials in government to use these names and others like yellow dwarfs with daggers and rotten apples, the more your success. In addition you allow no human contact. You prevent travel or you oversee the nature of contact where travel is allowed. You prevent citizens from going to places like China, Cuba, and North Vietnam, so that men cannot confront other men. Or on the homefront, if contact is allowed, or if it cannot be prevented, you indicate that the contact is not between equals; you talk about the disadvantaged, the deprived. You make sure that the culture and customs of the target populations are seen as having no value to your own group and you inculcate this attitude either by laughing at those cultures and customs or by destroying them [p. 27].

According to a number of authors in *Sanctions of Evil*, making others appear different and worse than oneself is a primary condition, a necessary although probably not sufficient condition, for the perpetration of evil. Historical events support this proposition; we need only look at the manner in which Jews in Nazi Germany, blacks in America, and mistreated groups in other places were presented to the dominant culture. It seems important to explore the conditions that lead people to devalue others and the consequences of devaluation, derogation, and negative evaluation on subsequent behavior toward victims.

An experiment by Bandura, Underwood, and Fromson (1975) presents clear empirical evidence of how describing people in negative terms enhances aggression against them, and it specifies some conditions under which this happens to greater and lesser degrees. In this study male subjects acted as supervisors who were to punish a "group of decision makers" in a nearby room when a red signal indicated that they reached an "inadequate" decision. The punishment was an electric shock that ranged in intensity from level 1 (mild) to level 10 (painful). The subjects were free to select any shock level for punishment on the 10 of 25 trials when the decision was inadequate. Subjects in an individual responsibility group believed that the level of shock they selected would be administered to one member of the decision-making group. Those in a diffused-responsibility group believed that the shock levels set by three participating supervisors would be automatically averaged. Seemingly inadvertently, the subjects overheard through an intercom an exchange between the experimenter and his assistant. The exchange implied that the questionnaires filled out by the decision makers provided information consistent with the impression these people made on the person who recruited them. One group heard the decision makers described as "perceptive, understanding" and characterized by other "human" personal qualities (humanized condition). Another group heard them described as an "animalistic, rotten bunch" (dehumanized condition). Yet another group heard no evaluative remarks made about the decision makers (neutral condition).

Subjects who heard the derogatory comments set significantly higher shock levels, both in the individual-responsibility condition and (to an even greater degree) in the diffused-responsibility condition, than those who heard no comments. Subjects who heard complimentary comments set lower shock levels than those who heard no comments. Individual responsibility resulted in subjects setting significantly lower shock levels in both humanized and dehumanized conditions, but not in the neutral condition (Figure 4.1).

In this study correct responses by the decision makers frequently followed punishment. In a second study, all subjects had individual responsibility for setting shock levels. In one group punishment was functional; it led to correct decisions on the next trial. In another group punishment was dysfunctional. The effects of humanization and dehumanization of victims were replicated. However, when punishment was dysfunctional, the increase in shock to dehumanized victims was substantial, even greater than in the functional group. When punishment did not work, shock levels were increased to near maximum intensity for devalued, dehumanized victims but not for people in the other two conditions.

Bandura and his associates (Bandura, 1973; Bandura *et al.,* 1975) suggest that internalized moral codes do not necessarily lead to moral conduct, because "reprehensible" behavior can be made "personally or socially acceptable by construing it in terms of high moral principle [Bandura *et al.,* 1975, p. 254]." In fact, subjects engaged in "self-disinhibiting justifications" for giving punishment to a significantly greater degree in the dehumanized

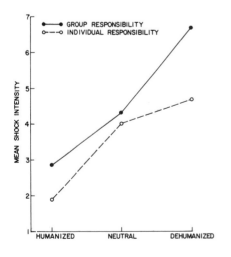

Figure 4.1
Shock levels set by subjects under varied conditions of responsibility and dehumanization of recipients. (From Bandura et al., 1975.)

condition than in the other groups. Such justifications took varied forms. Subjects engaged in (*a*) ascribing culpability to the performers (e.g., "in many cases poor performance is indicative of laziness and of a willingness to test the supervisor, and people are basically evil and have to be put in their place"); (*b*) extolling the benefits or necessity of punishment (e.g., "it gets more efficiency out of the group and although punishment is looked down upon, that is not going to influence me because I've seen it work"); (*c*) attributing punitive behavior to situational or role requirements (e.g., "as an acting supervisor it was my job to punish poor performance and if doing my job as a supervisor means I must be a son of a bitch, so be it"); (*d*) displacing responsibility (e.g., "I administered shocks because I was told to"); (*e*) minimizing the painful consequences of their actions (e.g., "it would not hurt them too badly"); (*f*) disavowing conscious involvement in the activities (e.g., "I was reacting mechanically to the lights"); and (*g*) emphasizing the prevalence of punishment (e.g., "everyone is punished for something every day"). (See Bandura *et al.,* 1975, p. 261.) Some subjects did not justify aggression but repudiated punitiveness. This happened significantly more with humanized recipients of punishment than with neutral or dehumanized ones. In both studies subjects who justified punishment set more intense shock levels.

These studies clearly show that describing people in negative terms disinhibits aggression directed at them. They also show that diffusion of responsibility not only diminishes helping but also increases aggression. In general, diffusion of responsibility seems to lead to less adherence to valued social conduct. It seems to contribute to a condition of deindividuation (Zimbardo, 1969) that diminishes a sense of personal responsibility for the welfare of other human beings.

Other research has also showed that deindividuating conditions enhance aggression. Diener, Dineen, and Endersen (1975) found that pointing out to subjects that they themselves were responsible for the consequences of their behavior led to less aggression than telling them that "of course" the experimenter would be responsible for the consequences of their behavior. Varying the subjects' "cognitive set," by presenting their activities as gamelike, resulted in more aggression than presenting the activities as similar to those of real life. In this study the subjects entered a dimly lit room, where they found a "role player" sitting on the floor. They could do various things to this role player with materials available in the room for throwing, hitting, and so on.

Bandura's findings and his theorizing (Bandura, 1973) suggest that people frequently use moral concepts to justify behavior motivated by varied personal desires or needs or by external pressures. Our capacity to moralize—to apply principles such as justice or fairness—for self-serving purposes, and the tendency of even well-meaning human beings to do so, is one of the dangerous human characteristics. It enables humans to inflict harm on others for what seem to be the noblest reasons. That this "adjustment" in thinking takes place will also be demonstrated by further findings reviewed in this chapter. (Note also the adaptability of level of moral reasoning to circumstances, discussed in Chapter 3.)

Research on the Just-World Hypothesis

In a number of experiments Lerner and his associates explored one type of situation that was expected to lead to devaluation. Groups of subjects, whose stated task was to observe the behavior of another person, observed a female confederate engage in a learning task. When she made mistakes she received electric shocks. Lerner and Simmons (1966) presented several hypotheses in their original study. They proposed that less devaluation will occur when the person observing a confederate receive shocks knows that the confederate will receive no additional shocks (endpoint condition). When the person observed will continue to receive shocks after a break during which she is evaluated by the subject (midpoint condition), the need for subjects to defend themselves from the possibility of an unjust world will be greater; thus their devaluation of her will be greater. When the confederate has suffered for a period of time and during a break the observers can decide about her subsequent fate, if they can decide that she should receive a reward and thus she will in some sense be compensated for her suffering, devaluation will be less (reward condition). Lerner and Simmons also thought that observers would not devalue the confederate if they decided that she should get a reward but she nonetheless received shocks; having acted positively toward the victim they will not devaluate her (reward–decision condition). They hypothesized that a "martyr" condition, in which the confederate was willing to suffer altruistically so the observers could gain some benefit, would lead to the most devaluation. This is a counterintuitive hypothesis. In this condition the would-be learner did not want to experience the shock, but was persuaded to do so in order to enable other people who came to the experiment (the subjects) to act as observers and thus earn credit for their psychology course. Lerner and Simmons reasoned that when a victim behaves kindly, makes a self-sacrifice, the injustice of her receiving electric shocks is particularly great. To deal with the injustice and to maintain their belief in a just world, subjects devalue this person to a greater degree.

The measures of devaluation consisted in part of the subjects' evaluation of the victim and in part of the difference between their evaluation of the victim and their evaluation of themselves prior to the start of the experimental procedures.

On the whole, the subjects tended to evaluate the victim most negatively in the martyr condition, less negatively in the midpoint condition, and significantly less negatively in the endpoint or reward conditions. The reward condition led to the most positive evaluation. In the reward–decision condition, when the confederate was to receive electric shocks despite the observers' recommendation of a reward, strong devaluation occurred, contrary to the authors' expectations. All other findings supported Lerner and Simmons' reasoning. To the authors' surprise, however, there were no significant differences among treatment conditions in the degree to which the observers judged the confederate similar to or different from themselves.

It is of interest that in the reward and reward–decision conditions, where the observers could determine by a secret ballot after the first series of learning trials whether the learner should be in the negative-reinforcement, positive-reinforcement, or control condition for the next series of trials, all but one subject voted for positive reinforcement. When the opportunity existed, subjects attempted to provide the person who had suffered with a positive experience.

Before the subjects were told about the purpose of the experiment, they were asked to make written comments about it. Forty subjects made positive comments about the experiment, and 25 made negative comments. The subjects who negatively evaluated the experiment rated the confederate substantially more positively. This suggests that injustice can be dealt with either by rejecting the person who suffers the injustice or by rejecting the system that perpetrates it; either the victim or the system may be perceived as responsible. This also suggests that reaction to another's suffering may be a function of role taking; the evaluation of the parties involved—the sufferer and the perpetrator—would be determined by which role was taken. Finally, the findings in the reward condition may be interpreted as showing, as do other data, that the ability to affect another person's fate in a positive manner enhances liking for that person.

In subsequent research Lerner (1971) explored whether both males and females devalue an innocent victim, since in the original study only female subjects were included. To the midpoint condition was added a "denatured" condition, in which subjects were told that the learner was an actress who was not actually receiving shocks; she was simply acting as if she were. Subjects were asked to judge how college students observing this person would evaluate her. The denatured condition was used to explore the possibility that there was something inherently obnoxious in the behavior of the confederate receiving electric shocks, and she was devalued for that reason, not because she suffered innocently. Subjects did not devalue the actress, but again devalued the victim in the midpoint condition.

In another experiment, Simons and Piliavin (1972) used a variety of role-playing conditions. The subjects were asked to judge how other people would evaluate someone receiving electric shocks in a midpoint- or endpoint-type situation. These researchers also found that people devalued another person only when they believed that she was actually getting shocked.

In a second study Lerner (1971) wanted to determine whether subjects who were committed to the helping professions would behave similarly to others in devaluing victims. He used a midpoint condition, a denatured condition, and a reward condition in which the subjects were told that although the person receiving electric shocks did not know it she was going to receive $30 at the end of the experiment. The knowledge of impending compensation of the victim for her suffering was expected to decrease or eliminate devaluation. Lerner found that only in the midpoint condition did subjects devalue the victim. In a third study Lerner wanted to examine whether in the martyr condition a feeling of responsibility by subjects for the martyr's suffering contributed to her devaluation: The martyr agreed to receive electric shocks so that the subjects could get experimental credits. In this study, sociology rather than psychology students were the participants. However, when assembled in a group, they were told that some members of the group were sociology students and others were psychology students. The martyr agreed to undergo the shocks to help the psychology students receive credit. Thus, the subjects, all sociology students, would presumably not feel responsible. Several other conditions were also included in the study. The sociology students also devalued the martyr, and the midpoint effect was replicated. There was no devaluation in a $30 reward group, but some devaluation occurred in a $10 reward group. Lerner concluded that the determinant of reaction to a victim was apparently the degree of injustice seen in the victim's fate. The less deserved or compensated the victim's suffering was, the more likely it was for devaluation to occur.

In the study just discussed, the subjects were asked to rate the confederate and to rate the characteristics of average college students, on varied dimensions, before and after the shocks were administered. The difference between the ratings of the confederate and of students before and after the shocks was used to measure devaluation. It was found that how female subjects rated the confederate varied in the different treatment groups. Males, on the other hand, gave the same ratings to the confederate in all conditions, but they changed their rating of the average college students. In the midpoint condition, for example, rather than evaluating the suffering person negatively, males evaluated average college students more positively. Thus the difference in the rating was the same for males and females.

Obviously, then, the difference measure that Lerner used has no unequivocal meaning. Unfortunately, the study gives no indication why males, after observing someone receiving electric shocks, came to feel more positive about average college students. Perhaps by doing this they reaffirmed that, despite what they saw, people are worthwhile and likable. Their cognitive activity seems opposite to that suggested by the just-world hypothesis, at least in that it elevates rather than reduces the quality of other human beings.

Conditions Affecting Devaluation

Responsibility of the Victim.   The just-world hypothesis says that *innocent* victims will be devalued. People who have done something to deserve their suffering experience a relatively just situation, and observers would not need to devalue them as persons.

That victims who are in some sense "guilty," who have brought about their own suffering and are thus responsible, would be evaluated more positively than innocent victims is counterintuitive. The research that has been reviewed showed that female victims were devalued, by female subjects at least. But are people devalued more or less if they are perceived as truly innocent? Relevant to the issue is the phenomenon called *defensive attribution*. In a study by Walster (1966), for example, subjects received a written description of an incident in which a person buys an old car and parks it on a hill. The hand brake apparently fails, and the car rolls down the hill, causing an accident. The more severe the consequence of the accident, the more responsibility is attributed by subjects to the owner of the car. According to Piaget (1932), beyond a certain age (about 8 years) children judge responsibility, or lack of it, as a function of the intention of the actor, not as a function of the consequences of the act. But this research shows that, in fact, the attribution of responsibility for accidents by adults is affected by the severity of consequences. This is called defensive attribution because of the interpretation of the phenomenon. People do not like the idea that chance brings about undesirable outcomes; if such things can happen by chance to other people, they can happen to themselves. This is similar to the defensive conception of the just-world hypothesis. (If other people can suffer innocently, the observer can suffer innocently, and so victims are devalued to make their suffering more deserved.)

When a person causes harm or experiences a need, it might be important for other people to determine the degree to which that person is responsible. Attribution of responsibility might, in turn, affect behavior toward the person. It might also be important for people to determine the degree to which a person who suffers is responsible for his suffering, and they might, in fact, be motivated to perceive such a person as responsible, as having caused the suffering, whenever the circumstances allow them to do so. Having found a person responsible, would they not devalue him more than an "innocent" sufferer?

In the Lerner studies the victim participated in a learning task and got shocked for her mistakes on the task. She might be perceived as not truly innocent, since her mistakes caused her suffering. An unpublished study by Piliavin and Simmons provides data supporting this view. They compared subjects' reactions to a person who made mistakes on a task and got shocked with subjects' reactions to someone who received shocks but could not conceivably be thought of as having brought about her own suffering; she was truly innocent. Only in the former case was the victim devalued. In Lerner's studies the victim may have been devalued because she was perceived as at least somewhat responsible for her suffering.

In a study by M. Stein (1973), fifth- and sixth-grade girls saw, on video-tape, other children play a bowling game. Some observed a child who voluntarily played the game, and others observed someone who had been assigned to play. Stein intended to vary responsibility this way. While playing the game the children either earned money, received feedback, or received electric shocks. The player who received electric shocks was devalued relative to the players in the other two groups, but only the difference with the feedback group (regarded by Stein as a neutral condition) was significant. Variation in responsibility for participation (voluntary versus assigned) had no effect. The shocked child was perceived as less deserving of the outcome (of receiving shocks) than the children in the other two conditions; the experimenter was perceived as less nice when she shocked the player than in the other two conditions. Children can apparently perceive another as not deserving of suffering, evaluate her negatively, and evaluate the person who inflicted the suffering negatively, all at the same time.

In another study, subjects learned about, but were not exposed to, the immediate suffering of another person. Stokols and Schopler (1973) called this *situational detachment*. Female subjects participated in a study that was ostensibly about sexual beliefs and beliefs related to women's liberation. In the first session they read information about someone who became pregnant as a result of having been raped by a man whom she had dated only for a week and thus did not know very well (no responsibility), or about someone who became pregnant as a result of carelessness in using contraceptives (responsibility). The consequences were either relatively mild (an abortion without complications) or quite serious (a lot of physical pain, social ostracism, and emotional trauma). Subjects evaluated the person who was responsible for her own suffering slightly more negatively. They also expressed substantially more sympathy for the person who was raped (the innocent victim?) and they considered her fate to be the result of bad luck. Regardless of responsibility, however, subjects evaluated the person who suffered severely much more negatively. It was also found that subjects who expected the victim to be their partner in a later discussion evaluated her substantially more positively. A number of studies have shown that expected future interaction leads to less devaluation of a victim (see Walster, Berscheid, & Walster, 1970).

Godfrey and Lowe (1975) also questioned whether the devaluation of innocent victims was the best explanation of Lerner's findings. They suggested that observers actually engage in an attributional analysis of a victim's reasons for his or her behavior. If the victim's willingness to undergo electric shock, for example, is seen as the result of extrinsic motivation, stemming from coercion, the victim is seen as weak and yielding and is therefore devalued. If, however, the victim seems to be intrinsically motivated—either strong external pressures are absent or the victim indicates a belief in the study's worth—people make a "belief inference" and will not devalue the victim.

Godfrey and Lowe employed the Lerner and Simmons procedure. They used four conditions. In a "volunteer" condition the victim actually volunteered to receive the shocks. She expressed her dislike of being shocked but her belief in the study's worth. In the "good reasons" condition the victim was randomly selected but also expressed belief in the study's worth. In this condition the victim could not be seen as responsible for her fate. The "random" condition was a replication of the midpoint condition, and the "unwilling" condition a replication of the "willing martyr" condition. Only in the last two conditions, when the victim appeared to accept the shocks for extrinsic reasons, was devaluation expected. Although there was no control condition to serve as a basis of comparison, evaluation of victims was significantly more positive in the first two conditions than in the last two conditions. Only when victims could be seen as weak, yielding to external pressure, and thus responsible for their unwanted suffering were they devalued.

People who suffer are negatively evaluated and those who suffer more are evaluated more negatively. It seems, however, that innocent victims are not devalued more than those who are responsible for their suffering. On the contrary, although the evidence is not extensive, findings of the Simmons and Piliavin, Stokols and Schopler, and Godfrey and Lowe experiments suggest that responsibility for one's own suffering might lead to *greater* devaluation. There are several possible explanations. First, devaluation of those who act in a faulty, reprehensible, weak, or stupid manner and thereby bring about their own suffering results in more balanced cognitions. Such persons can easily be seen as unattractive or unlikable. Second, observing another's suffering can lead to concurrent experiences of empathy and sympathy, as well as to feelings that one ought to intervene. Thus vicarious negative affect, feelings of guilt, and uncertainty about what one ought to do are likely to make the observation of another person's suffering very distressing. Devaluation might diminish both feelings of guilt and vicarious distress and might help the observer make a decision not to intervene (because there is no need to). Many observers of others' suffering may, whenever they cannot help or choose not to help, make their own situation easier to handle by devaluing the victim. (An interesting research question is whether devaluation has physiological effects; for example, does it result in decreased arousal during the observation of a person's suffering following an opportunity to devalue?) Devaluing someone is probably easier to accomplish when the victim can be held responsible for his own fate, when he acts in a manner that can be regarded as reprehensible. When people are faced with a person's suffering but they have no information about the circumstances leading to that suffering, it may again be relatively easy for them to devalue the sufferer. A victim's membership in groups that are subject to prejudice may also make devaluation easier. When, however, the observer has information about the manner in which the suffering came about, he is less likely to devalue the sufferer if he thinks that the sufferer did not bring about his own suffering.

On the basis of various findings (e.g., Staub & Baer, 1974) I suggested in Chapter 3 that in certain emergency situations many people try to escape from the presence of the distressed person. One reason for this may be that they are trying to avoid or diminish empathic involvement. Another reason may be the desire not to get involved, not to have to endure the efforts demanded by helping others. This may also motivate escape under non-emergency conditions when someone needs aid. Probably escape can also take a psychological form, justification, one aspect of which is devaluation. A possibly frequent manner of dealing with other people's need may be "motivated devaluation" of those who need help, which reduces the necessity for intervention. As in the case of physical escape from a stimulus for help, it is possible that unless external conditions, or internal conditions such as values, make devaluation difficult people deal with others' needs by devaluation or other justifications of inaction, particularly in conflictful situations. The complete innocence of another person or conditions that strongly activate empathic reactions may make devaluation minimal. The relative ease of devaluation that is suggested here for those who bring about their own suffering or problems might explain why such people are helped less than those who do not appear responsible. Actually, however, the giving of less help to people who are "responsible" for their need is not as widespread as is suggested in the literature (Bar-Tel, 1976; see Chapter 5).

I am not implying that innocent people are never evaluated negatively. Observers may devalue a sufferer who is innocent, partly to maintain belief in a just world, partly to decrease their own involvement with another's suffering, partly to minimize conflict with social influences that encourage cruelty and aggression toward innocent people, and for other reasons. Moreover, people frequently accept and "use" communications that describe others in negative terms with little validation from other sources.

Nonetheless, some of the findings supporting the just-world hypothesis can be interpreted in still other ways. It is apparent that it is aversive for people to see others suffer, and more suffering is more aversive (Geer & Jarmecky, 1973). Furthermore, anything that is associated with a person's own suffering might also become aversive. Straightforward classical conditioning principles seem to apply here. Persons whose suffering causes one's own suffering might become aversive and therefore negatively evaluated. This process is in a sense circular—seeing them suffer makes us suffer, and this leads to dislike of the sufferer. The everyday observation that people avoid those who have many problems confirms this. Our own aversive reactions might be caused, moreover, not only by others' past suffering but also by their anticipated future suffering. In Lerner's midpoint condition devaluation might have been greater than in the endpoint condition because the victim's total suffering (already seen and anticipated) was greater. In the martyr condition, there is the issue of the responsibility of the martyr, and there is also her greater suffering. When she found out that she was to receive shocks, this person protested; she did not want to participate. Observers might assume that she was therefore suffering more than person to whom shocks did not matter. Moreover, her compliance after first refusing to participate implicates this person, makes her more responsible for her fate. The combination of more responsibility and greater suffering might account for the greater devaluation of the martyr.

Perceptual Set. The observers' perceptual set or orientation toward others may also affect devaluation. Aderman, Brehm, and Katz (1974) noted that in Lerner's experiment subjects were asked to *observe* someone receive punitive shocks. They argued that this "observe" instruction was similar to the "watch him" orientation that Stotland (1969) and others employed; consequently it was likely to minimize empathic involvement with the person receiving shocks.

Aderman and his associates conducted a study in which subjects observed another person receiving electric shocks. Just as in Lerner's experiment, a learning task was used. Either several subjects observed the victim together (Lerner's procedure), or single individuals observed the victim by themselves. Subjects were given a "watch him" orientation or an "imagine self" orientation. In a third group the experimenters used Lerner's instructions, which they believed would produce an "observe him" orientation, similar in meaning to the "watch him" orientation. They used a modified midpoint condition—the learner receives a series of shocks, evaluations are taken, and then the learner is to receive a few more shocks. The "imagine self" orientation resulted in significantly less devaluation than either the "watch him" or the "observe him" orientations, which had similar effects. It seems, then, that the reaction to a suffering victim depends in part on the perceptual-cognitive orientation that is taken. Given certain orientations people are likely to respond more sympathetically, more empathically; they will not devalue the other person.

Here a question pertinent to much of the empathy research arises: If a role-taking orientation lessens devaluation (and therefore increases helping), what environmental conditions and what personality characteristics determine the kind of orientation a person will assume? In these studies the orientation was produced by telling people what stance to take in observing someone. In everyday life sometimes others exert influence on us, other times there are no external agents to guide our perceptual orientation.

What then determines the kind of orientation a person will assume? Personality, the relationship to the other person, and other factors are probably involved.

In the Aderman *et al.* study a person who was alone while observing the victim was less likely to devalue her than were people who observed together. Here, as in the emergency and aggression studies described earlier, the findings indicate that responsibility for other people's welfare is focused to a greater degree on a single observer. Could it be that conditions that minimize personal responsibility for others' welfare lead to devaluation of victims and to other justifications of their suffering, and in turn diminish help for them or increase aggression directed at them?

Relationship Variables.   Several other conditions decrease the devaluation of suffering persons. One is expected "fate similarity." In one experiment (Sorrentino & Boutilier, 1974) some observers were made to believe that they themselves might later participate as learners and receive electric shocks. This led them to evaluate the victim positively. In another study (Chaikin & Darley, 1973) participants were less likely to evaluate the victim of an accident negatively if they expected to be placed in a role similar the victim's. A related finding is that expected fate similarity increases help for another person, at least under high stress, when the role is highly unpleasant, when the subject expects also to receive electric shocks. Expecting dissimilar fate reduced helping under high stress (Dovidio & Morris, 1975). Sometimes if one devalues the character of a person even though one might later be in his or her position, one also exposes oneself to negative evaluation. Moreover, expecting to fill the same role is likely to lead subjects to assume an "imagine self" orientation, which is likely to lead them to respond empathically.

Expected future interaction also diminishes negative evaluation of other people. In the Stokols and Schopler (1973) study, subjects who expected to interact with the person who was raped evaluated her less negatively. There is evidence from a variety of other studies that harmdoers devalue their victim less when they expect future interaction with this person (Walster, Berscheid, & Walster, 1973). People might regard an expected interaction as an opportunity for starting a friendship, a relationship. As a result, they may take the other's role and feel concern about her interests. The range of applicability of prosocial values may also be more likely to be extended to this person. Walster, Berscheid, & Walster (1970) suggested that devaluation is less likely to occur in the case of expected future interaction because, since one's negative evaluation can be tested in the course of the interaction, it may be proved invalid. As a result, negative evaluation might be an ineffective strategy for dealing with the presence of injustice. Finally, the expectation of interacting with a person whom one thinks of negatively is probably unpleasant (since the actual interaction with an unattractive, disliked person would be unpleasant), and devaluation may be minimal because of this consequence for the self. Most generally, however, expected fate similarity, expected future interaction, and other kinds of similarities (in personality and attitudes, for example) affect the bond to another person and the degree of identification with that person (see Chapter 7).

Individual Differences. I suggested earlier that belief in a just world may vary, affecting the need to devalue innocent victims. It is primarily people who strongly believe that the world is just, or who give this belief a central position in their belief system, who need to devalue other people.

One research study attempted to measure individual differences in belief in a just world and to relate these measurements to the evaluation of "innocent victims" (Rubin & Peplau, 1973). In this seminaturalistic study the subjects were young males whose draft priority was to be determined by the national draft lottery in 1971. The number drawn for each birthdate determined the likelihood of induction. In groups of five to eight the subjects watched the lottery drawings on television. They filled out several personality measures before the lottery (including a just-world scale). After the group members' birthdates had been drawn, each person made evaluations of all the other group members and filled out several additional personality measures. The relationship between each person's own fate, his draft priority relative to the other members of the group, and each person's evaluation of the others were examined.

In this study subjects tended to like and feel sympathetic toward those who drew numbers that made induction likely. At that time inductees were likely to be sent to Vietnam. The authors point out that the subjects might have thought that those with bad draft numbers had several avenues of potential escape, such as failing physicals or being classified as conscientious objectors, and this might have affected their views. These individuals waited together for several hours and came to know one another to some degree. The more fortunate ones observed the others' reactions to their bad luck. The earlier discussion of the effects of expected future interaction clearly suggests that these circumstances would make negative evaluation more difficult. Furthermore, given that bad luck was determined by lottery, attribution of responsibility to the victims was difficult and the "innocence" of victims was apparent.

Nonetheless, subjects who scored high on the just-world scale were significantly more likely to evaluate those who fared badly in the lottery negatively in comparison with medium- or low-scoring subjects. Even among the high-scoring subjects, however, about as many rated less fortunate others positively as rated more fortunate others positively. There was about as strong a tendency to report sympathy for unfortunate victims as among subjects medium or low on the just-world scale. However, high-scoring subjects resented unfortunate others substantially more, and they preferred them less as companions in a future discussion. Thus, the findings provided strong support for the effects of individual differences in regarding the world as a just place on reactions to others' fate. Almost all findings were similar for subjects whose own fate was in the less fortunate half of the group and for those whose own fate was in the more fortunate half.

The difference between Rubin and Peplau's findings and those of Lerner might be due, according to Rubin and Peplau, to regional differences. Lerner's original research was conducted in Kentucky, whereas their study was on the East Coast. This implies the existence of differences between students in the two locations, perhaps in the degree of their belief in a just world. The passage of several years between these studies might also have affected the students' belief in a just world.

A number of Rubin and Peplau's subjects who had a strong belief in a just world rated others with bad luck positively. The factors that resulted in generally positive evaluation of victims might have brought this about. However, we have to consider the possibility that people who share a similarly strong belief in the just world vary in other characteristics—for example, in their capacities for empathy, compassion, and mercy. A belief in justice can be tempered by mercy and compassion.

Rubin and Peplau informally report data about characteristics associated with varying degrees of belief in a just world. This information was based on questionnaires administered to 90 women and 90 men undergraduates at Boston University. Belief in a just world was strongly positively related to belief in God, to religiosity, and to self-reported church attendance. It was also strongly positively related to the subjects' authoritarianism as measured by a brief questionnaire, and to a tendency to be internal on a locus-of-control scale—that is, to believe that one has control over events. Belief in a just world was associated with justification of both race and sex discrimination, as evidenced by such comments as, "The problems of blacks in the United States are to a large extent due to their unstable family structure." Finally, self-report items indicated that the greater the belief in a just world, the less the inclination to participate in social action such as demonstrating, picketing, or contributing money to political or social causes. This makes sense: In a just world there is no need to take action to improve society or the plight of its victims. As suggested earlier, the devaluation of other people, which seems to be enhanced by a belief in a just world, leads to acceptance and under some conditions active propagation of their suffering.

Individual differences in belief in the just world and the correlates of this belief again point to differences in value orientations. As before, *value orientation* refers to variations along a dimension that is fundamental for some persons, probably produced by a set of interrelated values that characterizes a person's orientation toward other people and society. In Chapter

2 I referred to Durkheim's distinction between responsible people and good people, and Hoffman's distinction between humanistic and conventional orientations. Another dimension that is discussed in Volume 2 is the proscriptive–prescriptive dimension, which involves emphasis on not doing what is wrong versus doing what is right. People who strongly believe in a just world might be conventional. They seem to be characterized by an orientation toward rules that are supposed to guide conduct and determine the nature of society, rather than by an orientation toward persons and their welfare. This dimension of variation is related to the ones proposed by Hoffman and Durkheim and reflects my distinction between prosocial orientation and duty orientation (Chapter 2; Volume 2; Staub, 1979).

An interesting aspect of belief in the just world was pointed out by Zuckerman (1975). Those who believe in a just world should derive a feeling of deserving from helping others; they should gain the expectation that in turn some need of their own will be satisfied. Zuckerman thought that people scoring high on the just-world scale would be more helpful, in varied ways, at a time of some need of their own than people scoring low on that scale. Their behavior would be guided by the belief that people who behave deservingly (or are deserving individuals because they have high personal worth) are rewarded.

When contacted on the telephone and asked in one study to help by participating in research, in another study to help by reading to a blind student, undergraduates who at the beginning of the semester scored high on Rubin and Peplau's just-world scale volunteered more help than those scoring low. However, this greater helpfulness was in evidence only when the request came a few days prior to an exam, not when it came several weeks before the exam. In a third study a request was made just prior to the exam; again, greater belief in a just world was associated with more help. The effects were equal for men and for women.

An unfortunate confounding of this study is that the person who called to ask the favor always knew the identity of the student. In two studies this person indicated some connection to a current instructor of the subjects. In one study the caller was a graduate student in social psychology; in another the caller was the reader for the blind student, the latter taking a social psychology course from the same instructor as the subject. At the time of testing, the subjects in both studies were enrolled in a social psychology course. In the third study, the subjects may have feared public exposure. It is possible that students scoring high on the just-world scale feared retaliation for not volunteering help, particularly near their exam periods, rather than expecting that their goodness would be rewarded. Such an explanation is consistent with the characteristics of people scoring high on the just-world scale (an acceptance of the status quo and of power relations).

A final issue that I want to introduce in this section is the effect of responsibility of an *observer* for another person's suffering. Observers may feel responsible, to some degree, when they quietly stand by and watch another person suffer without intervening. Sometimes they may have directly contributed to another's suffering. How does such responsibility affect the observers' evaluation of a victim?

In an experiment by Lerner and Matthews (1967) either the subject herself or another person, a presumed subject but in reality a confederate, was to receive shocks. In one condition the subject picked a piece of paper out of a hat, which determined that she would not receive shocks; this automatically made the other person receive the shocks. Even though the decision appeared to be based on chance, some subjects perceived themselves as responsible for the other's fate. In another condition the other person picked a paper out of a hat, again with the result that the other person rather than the subject was to be shocked. In a third condition the draw was independent and the subject pulled the no-shock and the other person pulled the shock designation. The victim was devalued most when the subject picked the piece of paper and (in an objectively minimal sense) was responsible for the other's fate. Evaluation of the victim was intermediate when their fate was independently determined, each picked a paper from the hat. When the confederate's pick determined that she would receive the shocks, she was evaluated most positively. In this condition, however, in addition to the subject not being responsible for the confederate's fate, the confederate also saved the subject, in some sense, from having to receive shocks.

Devaluation and Helping Others

Some of the data of this study also had bearing on the important question of the likelihood that people will help a person they have devalued. Following their evaluation of the confederate, the subjects learned that the confederate was afraid of shocks and hated to wait for them alone. Even though the subjects could have waited by themselves for the next part of the experiment, they chose to wait with the confederate. This happened with high frequency even among subjects who were "responsible" for the confederate's negative fate and devalued her. Perhaps, as with children (M. Stein, 1973), a number of different reactions were aroused at the same time, and several concurrent attempts were made to resolve them. For example, the subjects may have felt guilty for having caused the other's fate, and attempted to minimize their guilt by helping her. Furthermore, since every aspect of this situation was known to both the experimenter and the purported victim, subjects may have felt that they were expected to be helpful, that it was socially highly desirable to be helpful, and so they acted accordingly. The conditions of this experiment allow no clear conclusion about reasons for the subjects' behavior.

Nonetheless, the findings raise the possibility that the assumptions of

Lerner (1974) and of equity theorists that derogation is a form of restoration of equity, and that following derogation no help will be forthcoming for the derogated individual, may be incorrect. Lerner (1974) theorized that "once the rejection is accomplished, the observer can again rest easy—his world is just, and he need not feel impelled to act to establish justice [p. 344]." If this assumption is incorrect, what is the relationship between derogation and subsequent behavior toward a victim?

Research findings of Lerner and his associates (reviewed earlier) as well as those of Mills and Egger (1972) indicate that when a victim is compensated for his suffering derogation is reduced or eliminated. Perhaps compensation makes people believe that equity or justice has been created, and this minimizes the need for devaluation. Will prior devaluation of persons who suffered increase aggression against them? The discussion early in this chapter and the findings of Bandura, Underwood, and Fromson (1975) suggest that it *may* do this; intense negative evaluation and derogation of them by *other* people have that effect. Will devaluation reduce later positive behavior toward victims? If one considers devaluation strictly as an equity-restoring device, one would expect this to be so. If, however, the hypothesis I presented earlier is correct—that devaluation sometimes serves the function of reducing a person's discomfort about being exposed to another person's suffering—different predictions may be made. Derogation may be a useful but incomplete way of dealing with others' suffering. When better means are available people will turn to them; they may therefore be kind and helpful to the person who suffered. To some extent, whether or not this happens may depend on the intensity of the other's suffering and the amount of time that passed. When another person suffers greatly, and much time passes after his suffering, devaluation may take hold and reactions to that person may be determined by it. When suffering is less and/or little time has elapsed, people may avail themselves of the opportunity to be helpful, even if they originally devalued the victim.

In addition to the findings of Lerner and Matthews (1967), an experiment by Kenrick, Reich, and Cialdini (1976) provides support for this view. Groups of female subjects were exposed to an experimental procedure similar to Lerner and Simmons' (1966) martyr condition. In a control condition, following mistakes on the learning task the victim heard a buzzer. In the experimental group, the victim both heard the buzzer and received apparently quite painful electric shocks. Some subjects then evaluated this person on a variety of dimensions; the index of devaluation was again the difference between these ratings and the subjects' prior ratings of "the average female college student." Subsequently the subjects were told that the learner would receive compensation for her substantial effort, and they were asked to recommend how much compensation (from $.50 to $5) this person should receive. In another group the sequence of providing this person with compensation and rating her characteristics was reversed.

The person who suffered was devalued, in comparison to the learner who did not suffer. Moreover, subjects recommended significantly more compensation for the person who suffered than for the one who did not suffer, whether compensation preceded or followed devaluation. There was no significant difference in the evaluation of victims as a function of whether evaluation occurred before or after compensation, only a weak tendency for less devaluation following compensation. This may be interpreted as evidence for the view I advanced, that help may follow even after devaluation occurred. In previous studies, when compensation diminished devaluation subjects usually knew that the victim would be compensated while they were observing her suffering. This may have reduced the observers' own distress; they may have felt that justice would prevail. In this study they did not know that compensation would follow, and they may have diminished their own discomfort and empathic suffering by devaluing the victim *while they were observing* her suffering. Consequently, when the information that she would be compensated was presented to them, the victim was already devalued. Nonetheless, since devaluation is a less adequate way of dealing with suffering, when the opportunity arose subjects favored compensation.

The preceding discussion suggests that varied and somewhat paradoxical reactions can follow the observation of another person's suffering and/or the devaluation of a sufferer—possibly greater aggression, but also greater positive behavior than behavior directed at someone who did not suffer or was not devalued. The extent this is so, and the conditions determining these reactions have only been sparsely explored.

Harmdoing, Transgression, and Their Consequences

Research has also been done on the effects of harmdoing on prosocial behavior. If a person actually causes harm to other people, how are that person's subsequent thoughts, feelings, and behavior affected? Does prior harmdoing (and thus responsibility) affect how victims are evaluated? Does it affect subsequent prosocial behavior? Toward whom, and for what reason? Such questions have both theoretical and practical significance. In everyday life it commonly occurs that we intentionally or unintentionally cause psychological distress or material damage to others. We may feel that we caused harm, or we may be accused of having caused harm. It is not only Erica Jong's heroine in *Fear of Flying* whose family members habitually accuse one another of suffering from "such a headache" because of some behavior of another family member. When relatives and friends cause one another psychological, material, and even physical harm, the situation must be dealt with to maintain equilibrium in the relationship or even the existence of the relationship. On a wider scale, those members of a society who have suffered injustice may blame other members; or other members may blame themselves for having caused injustice or harm to others. Clearly, such feelings associated with harmdoing have been involved in the relationships among blacks, whites, Indians, and others in our society. How are their attitudes and behavior affected? Unfortunately, existing research has explored the effects of harmdoing only under limited circumstances, in simple situations. However, the findings do provide some ideas that can be used for contemplating more complex situations and varied forms of harmdoing.

Having caused harm might have several kinds of psychological effects on the harmdoer, or it might have multiple effects. Harmdoing may lead to a feeling of concern about the harmed person, or to concern and distress because the harmdoer has not acted according to personal values or ideals (internal reactions). The harmdoer may also feel concern about aversive social consequences—negative evaluation or retribution by the harmed person or by others (external or social reactions).

A large number of studies have evaluated varied consequences—behavioral, cognitive, and affective—of different types of harmdoing. The behavioral consequences that have been examined include the willingness of a harmdoer (*a*) to help his victim at a later time, (*b*) to help someone who witnessed his harmdoing, (*c*) to help a third person, or (*d*) to promote a worthwhile cause. In most studies a direct request for help was made, and thus compliance is involved. In some instances, however, an opportunity for help was provided without a specific request, under relatively anonymous conditions, so the people who helped were more likely to do so for internal rather than for social reasons. The cognitive consequences of harmdoing that have been explored include the harmdoer's evaluation of the victim and the harmdoer's evaluation of his responsibility for the harm. Additional affective, cognitive, and behavioral consequences have been explored, to some degree: self-punishment following harmdoing, mood and self-esteem, and the degree of disorganizing effect on task performance. Rarely have several dependent measures been used in the same study so that the relationship between evaluation, action, and other consequences could be determined.

Having a person cause harm to others has been accomplished in a variety of ways in the studies conducted. Most frequently the subjects caused harm accidentally. A neglected consideration is that the consequences might be due not only to the causing of harm but also to the harmdoer's reaction—perhaps feelings of shame and lowered self-esteem—to his apparent incompetence. Here again, the influence of internal reactions in contrast to concern about social consequences is an issue.

In one study, the subject was enticed by a confederate to push a button, which caused a machine thought to be needed by the experimenter to blow up; in other studies the subject knocked down a table or chair (previously arranged by the experimenter to collapse upon being touched), scattering carefully arranged index cards or slides on the floor; in still others the subject performed poorly on a task (sometimes after preliminary examples of the task had misled the subject to set unreasonably high standards of performance) and thereby deprived another person of the opportunity to win desired rewards. In some cases the harmdoing involved intentionality, since the subject had an opportunity to decide whether to do something that would cause harm to another person. In still other experiments subjects followed experimental instructions and administered shocks to another person.

Before some of this research is examined in greater detail in conjunction with the theories that were offered to explain the findings, I will present certain generalizations about the consequences of harmdoing or transgression. On the whole, harmdoing increases subsequent compliance with requests for positive behavior, whether the harmed person, an observer, or a stranger makes the request, and whether the help benefits the harmed person or a good cause. Although no research has focused on this issue, there is some evidence that harmdoers also comply with requests that lead to behavior that is not prosocial in nature.

One study (Regan *et al.*, 1972) found that harmdoing increased help for others without a direct request or surveillance. In other studies, primarily when no opportunity existed for helpful behavior or compensation of the victim, following the harmdoing victims were negatively evaluated and/or attempts were made by actors to minimize their own responsibility for the harm. Little is known about preferred or dominant modes of responding when several avenues for responding are available.

Questions and Problems; Research and Theoretical Issues

Some researchers (Freedman, 1970; Freedman *et al.*, 1967) suggest that it is not specifically harmdoing that is followed by such consequences as I just noted, but more generally the transgression of societal values and norms that prohibit lying and cheating, as well as causing harm to others. However, in research where subjects were induced to lie, their behavior also caused harm. Whether lying itself has consequences independent of but similar to the consequences of being an agent of harm cannot be determined from existing research. Freedman, Wallington, and Bless (1967) conducted an experiment that served as the prototype for several others. While a subject was waiting to participate in the experiment, another subject (actually a confederate) told the subject what the test was like and how to do well on it. Then, before starting the test, the experimenter told the subject that it was important that participants have no prior information about the test and asked whether the subject had heard anything about it. Had the subjects admitted their knowledge, they would not have been able to participate. They would have lost the time they invested and presumably they would not have been paid. Most subjects faced by this conflict lied, clearly harming the experimenter by providing misleading experimental results. Subsequently, more of the subjects who had lied agreed to participate in another experiment without pay, in response to a request by the experimenter—twice as many as those in a control group.

This experiment can be used to highlight several issues. First, an element of intentionality was clearly involved; the subject had a choice about lying. Second, the effects of transgression were evaluated only by the verbal agreement of the subjects immediately following participation. We do not know how many would have actually helped with the other experiment. Assuming that committing a transgression made their experience an unpleasant one, there is a good chance that the subjects might have wanted to avoid having anything more to do with whatever would remind them of it. In one experiment Freedman and associates (1967) found evidence of such avoidance even in the immediate verbal compliance of subjects. In this experiment the subject "caused" the collapse of a table on which there was a large pile of index cards. The cards had been arranged in alphabetical order and, when they fell, the order was destroyed. The cards had belonged to a graduate student who was working on his dissertation. The subjects later agreed to spend more time, compared with those in a control group (who had done no harm), working on a project without pay, interviewing people to help this graduate student. However, this was only true if, while working on the project, they would not meet the person they harmed. Such a differentiated reaction might increase confidence in the validity or meaningfulness of verbal compliance, but not in the likelihood of the verbal promise actually being carried out. Subjects may have thought the idea of having to face the person whom they harmed so distasteful that they would not even verbally agree to help him. Unfortunately, a number of experiments suggest that agreement to help does not correspond to actual helpfulness. Bryan and Kazdin (1971) found that few of the subjects who agreed to donate blood actually did so. Schwartz (1970) reports that although people agreed, when they were interviewed at a place where they donated blood, to participate in a program of activities leading to bone marrow donation, they avoided the interviewer when they saw him there on a subsequent occasion. This gives reason to believe that, whatever their reasons for the initial agreement, they were not inclined to follow through with it. Verbal agreements might reflect transitory psychological processes, including variation in the need to get out of a situation without further conflict.

This last point leads to another issue. To what extent is a person's verbal agreement to help evidence of weakened resistance to demands placed on him, and to what extent is there a genuine desire to help for internal reasons? Harmful acts can range from those a person has reason to believe nobody will know about to those that have been witnessed. It is hard to decide where the first of Freedman *et al.*'s experiment fits on this dimension. Although only the confederate, who was not present when the experimenter questioned the subjects, actually knew about the subjects' transgressions, subjects may have feared that their lying might become publicly known. In most other experiments the harmdoing occurs in front of witnesses; afterward subjects face a request. They may comply for purely social reasons, to balance the negative image that they created by a positive one. They may feel that others will judge them badly because they acted contrary to social values that prohibit harming others or because of their incompetence. It is also the case, of course, that people may act not out of compliance or out of the desire to produce a positive image, but for private reasons; they may be motivated by internalized values and beliefs, and by a desire to create a positive self-image.

Unfortunately, most research employed a compliance paradigm—that is, subjects were faced with a direct request. In some cases it is particularly clear that subjects' behavior was due to weakened resistance to demands. In one of the first studies on harmdoing Darlington and Macker (1966) had subjects converse with a subject–confederate before participating in an experiment in which the subjects could win money. The confederate indicated in the course of the conversation that he badly needed the money. The amount of money each person would win depended on the other's performance on a task. Although the confederate "performed" well, the subject himself "performed" poorly, so the confederate gained little money. Subsequently, subjects were asked to donate blood. A person passed through the room where the subject was waiting and asked him, as part of an ongoing donation drive, to donate blood. If the subject did not volunteer in response to the description of the opportunity to donate, two more prods were used in which, with increasing directness, the subject was asked to donate. Subjects who had deprived the other person of winning volunteered significantly more often than control subjects, who had not harmed the other person. However, the difference emerged only after the third prod.

An important question, then, is the extent to which harmdoing leads to weakened resistance to pressure, or the extent to which subsequent helping behavior is performed for private rather than for social reasons. It is difficult to determine when and to what extent private or social reasons are influential. The first task might be to show that each of them can be influential.

In a relevant study by Carlsmith and Gross (1969), subjects were in a teacher–learner situation, administering either loud noises or electric shocks when the learner made mistakes. Afterward, while the subject was filling out a questionnaire, either the learner or an observer asked the subject to help him with a socially useful activity—making telephone calls and talking to people about saving California redwoods. If the subject agreed, he was asked to make 50 phone calls. Although only about a quarter of the subjects who delivered noise agreed, three-quarters of those who delivered shocks agreed. Also, compliance by subjects was greater when the observer, rather than the victim, made the request. Perhaps subjects were inclined to minimize contact with the person they harmed. Or perhaps they were concerned about how they were evaluated by a witness to their harmdoing.

Other research findings show more clearly that social reasons are at work in bringing about compliance following harmdoing. Carlsmith and Gross (1969) and Wallace and Sadalla (1966) included unwitnessed transgression conditions in their studies and found that these conditions, presumably most conducive to the arousal of guilt feelings (as subsequent discussion shows), did not lead to increased compliance. Aronfreed (1960) reported similar findings with children. In these studies, and probably in many others, compliance seems to have been motivated by social considerations. If so, would subjects who have done harm subsequently comply with any demands (possibly even engage in behavior that has harmful consequences), or are these social goals served only by compliance with demands for behavior that has beneficial consequences?

Brock and Becker (1966) varied the amount of damage subjects did to a machine, which either exploded in a display of fireworks or simply broke down. Subjects who did a great deal of damage tended to accede to the experimenter's request to sign a petition advocating increased tuition for themselves. Wallace and Sadalla (1966) used a machine that smoked slightly; the experimenter made a diagnosis that the machine was broken. Subjects who broke the machine were significantly more willing than others to sign up for an experiment in which they would receive painful electric shocks. Although these studies indicate that harmdoers are more willing to impose harm on themselves, neither study demonstrates clearly that harmdoers would be more willing to inflict harm on others.

To what extent do people who are made to appear incompetent but do not cause harm show the same compliance as those who do cause harm? Research by Isen, Horn, and Rosenhan (1973) found that children who failed on a task shared less of their material rewards with others than did those who succeeded, and somewhat less than those in a control group, except when their failure was known to the experimenter, in which case they shared more. The explanation suggested by the researchers, that the children wanted to improve their image, which had been tarnished by failure, may also apply to the effects of compliance following harmdoing.

The findings that have been reviewed and others show that one of the effects of harmdoing is increased compliance with the demands of other people. Furthermore, concern about social consequences seems to be a motivator of compliance. There is some evidence, however, that harmdoing increases responsiveness to others even without direct verbal demands, and that harmdoing causes internal reactions in addition to concern about social consequences. In a field experiment by Regan *et al.* (1972) subjects did not actually cause harm, but they were told that they had. A confederate went up to a woman in a shopping center and asked her to take a picture of him. As she kindly complied and tried to do so, the camera failed to respond. In a "control" condition the confederate made the subject feel that she had nothing to do with the camera's failure ("The camera acts up sometimes"). In a "guilt" condition, the confederate communicated to the subject that she must have done something to ruin the camera. Afterward, another confederate passed by the subject. This confederate was carrying a grocery bag, and pieces of candy were dropping out of a hole in the bag. Of the women who had been made to feel that they were responsible for the camera's failure, 55% called this person's attention to the hole in the bag, but only 15% of the women in the control condition did so. It is not known how the women, who were trying to be helpful and had only briefly handled the camera, felt upon being told that they had ruined it. Nonetheless, the findings are interesting, not only because subsequent helpfulness occurred without a request, but also because on the basis of research on the effects of mood on prosocial behavior, contrary predictions could be made. Generally, research findings show that success and feeling good enhance helpfulness; failure and feeling bad sometimes decrease helpfulness. In this case, however, failure and the bad feelings that probably ensued increased helpfulness, perhaps because "failure" resulted in harm for another person. (For a discussion of other "exceptions," see Chapter 6.)

Additional issues, and research that shows the effects of harmdoing on how victims are evaluated, are discussed in conjunction with proposed explanations of the harmdoer's reactions in the next section.

Proposed Explanations of the Effects of Harmdoing

Guilt and Harmdoing. What are the psychological consequences of having caused harm to others, which in turn affect the harmdoer's behavior? Freedman and associates (Freedman, 1970; Freedman, Wallington, & Bess, 1967) suggested that harmdoing and transgression in general lead to feelings of guilt:

> I have made the assumption that the effect produced is produced by some internal feeling that is common to any situation in which there has been transgression. The problem now is to specify the characteristics of this internal feeling. . . . I also know from other work that it causes subjects to tend to minimize their wrongdoing or to deny that they did anything wrong. . . . What shall we call an internal state that has all of the properties mentioned [Freedman, 1970, pp. 151–159]?

Freedman concluded that the internal state could be called guilt.

Freud and many other writers have suggested that transgression leads to feelings of guilt. When people do something that deviates from their values and standards, they are assumed to experience negative emotions, feelings of distress. This distress can be minimized in a number of ways. In the case of harmdoing, one way is to compensate others; another way is self-punishment. Many young children in fact learn that when they do something wrong some form of self-punishment, including self-derogation, will lead to their parents' forgiveness. "Repent, sinner," and repentance leads to forgiveness.

What specific evidence supports this explanation? In a recent study Wallington (1973), using the procedures of Freedman *et al.* (1967), induced subjects to lie to the experimenter. Wallington assumed that this would lead to guilt, which brings about depression. Subsequently, on a "decision task" subjects were supposed to put dots into a matrix. Transgressors were expected not to perform as well as subjects who had not been induced to lie, because depressed people are less efficient. Transgressors were also expected to report more negative mood on an adjective checklist and to make more negative statements on a self-evaluation measure. Finally, on a task that involved self-administration of shocks, they were expected to punish themselves and administer stronger shocks. Subjects were told that the strength of the shocks did not matter to the experimenter.

In the transgression condition the subjects did perform significantly worse on the decision task, and they gave themselves highly significantly stronger shocks than people who had not lied. There was no difference in self-reported mood and self-description. Advocates of guilt theory suggest that altruistic behavior in general, and altruistic or prosocial behavior following harmdoing in particular, are self-punitive in character. The reason people engage in such behavior following harmdoing is that by expending effort, through the self-sacrifice that is demanded of them, they punish themselves.

It has long been assumed that guilt is an internal experience, a reaction to deviation from one's own values. Consequently, guilt should be aroused under private conditions when nobody knows about one's deviant acts. There is some evidence, however, that private transgression does not increase compliance or prosocial behavior in response to a request, or that it does so to a lesser degree than does public transgression. Carlsmith and Gross (1969) found that subjects who administered shocks to others in such a way that their behavior was not known were less likely to agree afterward to make telephone calls to preserve the redwoods of California. Wallace and Sadalla (1966) had similar findings.

In an early experiment by Aronfreed (1960) in which children caused a machine to break down, an attempt was made, using projective story completions, to evaluate whether the children felt guilty. There was no indication that children experienced guilt in an unobserved condition, where presumably nobody would know what happened. Although these "failures" do not preclude the possibility that guilt affects reactions to harmdoing, they raise questions about the sufficiency of a guilt explanation, and the conditions under which guilt is aroused.

Equity and Inequity.   Another attempt to account for the variety of consequences of harmdoing was made by Walster and her associates (1970; 1973). They proposed that equity theory, as they formulated it, provides the best explanation. Because equity theory is important in considering exchange, reciprocity, and varied forms of positive behavior, I shall examine it in some detail.

Walster and her associates (Walster *et al.*, 1970; 1973; 1978; Walster & Walster, 1975; Walster & Piliavin, 1972) suggested a set of propositions. First, "individuals will try to maximize their outcomes, when outcomes equal rewards minus costs [Walster *et al.*, 1973, p. 151]." This is a straightforward statement that people will pursue their self-interest. Walster *et al.* also suggested, however, that if all people pursued their own self-interests, unchecked by consideration for others, social disaster would result. We would be at each other's throats all the time. They proposed that "groups can maximize collective reward by evolving accepted systems for equitably apportioning rewards and costs among members. Thus groups will evolve such systems of equity and will attempt to induce members to accept and adhere to these systems [Walster *et al.*, 1973, p. 151]." They continued with a further proposition, that "groups will generally reward members who treat others equitably, and generally punish (increase costs for) individuals who treat others inequitably [Walster *et al.*, 1973, p. 15]." Essentially this says that it is a social value, a social norm, for people to behave equitably toward others. Walster *et al.* include here the proviso that what is equitable and what is inequitable vary tremendously from culture to culture. Certainly it also varies from individual to individual.

Equity is defined as the equivalence of the ratio of inputs and outcomes: $O_a/I_a = O_b/I_b$, where O stands for outcome, I stands for input, and subscripts represent different individuals. Presumably, whether a situation is equitable can be determined for a single person if the appropriate ratio of inputs (costs) to outcomes (rewards) can be evaluated according to existing standards in society. Walster *et al.* emphasize equity between individuals, especially between individuals who stand in some relationship to one another and provide some of the outcomes for one another. Inputs and outcomes can be positive and negative. An outcome can be money, reward, favors, and the like. Any kind of effort, as well as positive characteristics of the person, prestige, or capital, can be inputs. To give consideration of positive as well as negative inputs and outcomes, the following formula is used to compute equity (Walster *et al.*, 1978):

$$\frac{O_a - I_a}{(|I_a|)^{k_a}} = \frac{O_b - I_b}{(|I_b|)^{k_b}}$$

where $|I|$ designates the absolute value of a's and b's inputs. The exponents

k_a and k_b have the value $+1$ or -1, depending on the sign of a's and b's inputs and their gains (Outcomes — Inputs). For example, $k_a = \text{sign } (I_a)$ $\times \text{sign } (O_a - I_a)$. (For elaboration, see Walster *et al.*, 1978) The value of each term is a function of how individuals define it. A participant and an observer might define values differently, and therefore perceive the relationship between two people as more or less equitable.

Walster *et al.* suggest that, as a consequence of socialization experiences, individuals become distressed when they find themselves participating in inequitable relationships. The more inequitable the relationship, the more distress they feel. From the perspective of this book, people who accept the value that they should behave equitably, and who violate this personal value, will feel distressed. This is no different from violating any other personal value, which would also produce distress. Walster *et al.* (1973) propose that "individuals who discover they are in an inequitable relationship attempt to eliminate their distress by restoring equity. The greater the inequity that exists, the more distress they feel, and the harder they try to restore equity [pp. 153–154]."

In realms unrelated to harmdoing, there has been extensive research and theorizing about equity (see Berkowitz & Walster, 1976; Walster *et al*, 1978) since the pioneering influence of Adams (1965). Adams himself showed that people who are made to believe that they are overpaid for some job they are doing will work harder, increase their productivity, presumably in an attempt to create equity. People who are made to believe that they are underpaid decrease their productivity.

In one research paradigm, investigators had a subject and another person—either a confederate or an absent "partner"—work on some task. In some instances the two performed equally well; in other instances one did better work than the other. Then the subject was given the opportunity to divide some reward between the two of them. Alternatively, a subject was asked to divide rewards among other people whose performance on a task varied, or to rate their merit as a function of performance and other information. Research findings showed variation with age in the extent to which children based reward distribution on equity or on equality. Lane and Coon (1971) found that 4-year-olds took more of the reward for themselves regardless of whether their partner's performance was better than, worse than, or equal to theirs; 5-year-olds predominantly divided rewards equally, regardless of performance, in this and in other studies (Lerner, 1974a). Morgan and Sawyer (1967) found that 8- and 12-year-olds tended to divide rewards equally. Research findings do show, however, that children have a sense of the meaning of differences in merit and are capable of rewarding a better performer to a greater degree (Lerner, 1974a; Walster & Walster, 1975).

A variety of generalizations can be made with regard to the manner in which equity operates in studies using methodologies of the kind I have briefly described. First, the tendency to divide rewards equitably develops with age, so that adults tend to follow equity principles in dividing rewards. Second, people tend to favor themselves, in various ways. They frequently give themselves somewhat more than they deserve. When there is a surplus of reward, more than what all the participants deserve, subjects tend to take more of the surplus for themselves. There is a sex difference, moreover. Men follow equity principles to a greater degree, and women are more likely to divide rewards equally—perhaps because they respond empathically to a person who does poorly on a task (and deserves less).

For example, Leventhal and Anderson (1970) found that kindergarten boys and girls tended to favor themselves and take about half of the reward when their performance was inferior to the performance of another child. They also distorted the results and minimized performance difference. When their performance was superior, boys tended to take more than in the equal or inferior performance condition, usually more than half the reward, whereas girls again took about half. In this study there is evidence of children favoring themselves, of sex differences, and of the fact that equity does influence the behavior of preschool children in some ways. Sampson (1975) had 3- to 12-year-old children indicate, in doll play situations, how they would allocate rewards to dolls that did equal or unequal amounts of work. With increasing age boys tended to allocate rewards in an increasingly equitable fashion, in relation to the amount of work done. Girls tended to allocate rewards equally regardless of age. Leventhal, Popp, and Sawyer (1973) argued that whether children follow a principle of equity or equality is likely to be a function of circumstances. That circumstances affect which of these (or other) principles guide behavior is likely to be true of both children and adults. These researchers found that when kindergarten children were to divide rewards for distribution to other children, a small difference in performance led to a fairly equal distribution; a large difference led to a more equitable distribution, the superior performer being favored. An interesting sex difference was found when the discrepancy in performance was large. Boys showed a strong tendency to give the first reward—a "seal"—to the superior performer, whereas 17 of 22 girls gave the first seal to the inferior performer. This was found even though both boys and girls favored the superior performer, although boys favored the superior performer to a greater degree. In research with adult subjects there is further evidence that men tend either to attempt to gain an advantage over others (e.g., they are exploitative; see Lane & Messe, 1971) or to distribute rewards as a function of quality of performance. Women favor equality, perhaps because they seek "harmonious relations" (Vinacke, 1969; Walster & Walster, 1975).

Equity and Harmdoing.   One area of relevance for equity theory is harmdoing, which is

> a situation in which inequity is produced in the relationship between
> two individuals . . . harm-doing shall be defined as the commitment

of an act which produces an inequitable relationship between the members, such that the actor's outcome/input ratio becomes greater than that of the other members of the relationship [Walster *et al.,* 1970, p. 181].

These authors believe that the distress that people experience as a result of harmdoing derives from two sources: (*a*) distress about the possibility of retaliation and (*b*) self-concept distress, which arises because they have violated their concepts of how they should behave. Walster *et al.* do not mention distress that might arise from social consequences other than retaliation (such as negative evaluation by others) and they do not seem to include these consequences in the concept of retaliation distress. With regard to self-concept distress, it seems similar to, but more specific than, the conception that harmdoing induces guilt. Freedman (1970) proposed that distress following harmdoing arises because the person violated an internal standard. Walster *et al.* essentially present the same view but specify the particular internal standard that has been violated (i.e., that one should behave equitably or maintain equity in one's relationships with other people). Although Freedman (1970) and Walster *et al.* (1970) have presented their views as alternative explanations of the consequences of harmdoing, clearly there is an important conceptual similarity: the assumption that deviation from an internal standard leads to distress. Furthermore, several of the avenues that they describe for reducing distress are the same.

The just-world hypothesis may be regarded as a partial derivative of equity theory. When people suffer, their negative outcomes are cognitively balanced by the perceiver with negative inputs that are attributed to them. The relevance of equity theory to the just-world hypothesis will become clearer when the manner in which equity can be restored is examined.

What are the ways in which harmdoers attempt to reduce their distress? According to Walster *et al.* (1970; 1973) there are two major ways to restore equity following harmdoing: (*a*) by restoring psychological equity and (*b*) by restoring actual equity. One can restore actual equity by compensating the victim, by increasing his outcomes. The harmdoer can also restore actual equity by punishing himself, decreasing his own outcomes. Self-punishment may be accomplished either by self-abasement or by self-injury. The clinical literature provides anecdotal evidence that people who feel guilty for real or imagined wrongdoing, including harmdoing, sometimes harm themselves, but there is little experimental evidence. The finding of Wallington (1973) that subjects who lied to the experimenter administered more shocks to themselves supports this notion. The finding of Brock and Becker (1966) that subjects who damaged a machine were willing to sign a petition for increased tuition, and the finding of Wallace and Sadalla (1966) that subjects who broke a machine were more willing to sign up for an experiment in which they were to receive electric shocks, can be interpreted in this fashion. To me, however, the view that decreased resistance to compliance with any kind of demand follows public knowledge of one's harmdoing is a more convincing interpretation of the last two findings. Altruism is considered by Walster *et al.* (1970) as a form of self-punishment, because effort has to be expended.

Psychological equity can be restored by derogating the victim. Derogation establishes equity because it implies that although the outcome of the victim is negative, his real input was also negative. He suffered harm, if not because of his actions, at least because of the kind of person he is. Derogation does not restore actual equity, but Walster *et al.* claim that it restores equity from the standpoint of the harmdoer. This view is reminiscent of Lerner's as presented in the just-world hypothesis.

Another way of restoring psychological equity is to deny responsibility for the act. If a person is not responsible, then that person's own negative input is irrelevant. Blaming another person—for example, citing the orders of the experimenter or of one's superiors—is one way to deny responsibility. This was a method favored by Nazi war criminals who claimed that they acted on the orders of powerful others and that they had to obey to avoid harm to themselves. It is hard to know, of course, to what extent this served the purpose of minimizing responsibility in the eyes of others, and to what extent this was an expression of their true feelings. The equity view suggests that they would have been motivated to believe this. Finally, psychological equity can be restored by minimizing the suffering of the harmed person. If the outcome of the victim was not really negative, no inequity exists.

There are several factors that determine the selection of equity-restoring techniques. One factor is the adequacy of the technique, its capacity to exactly restore equity to the relationship. Berscheid and Walster (1967) did an experiment in which women from a church auxiliary participated. A fellow parishioner told the subjects that it was very important for her to win a certain amount of the rewards that were available. Preliminary examples of the problems that the subjects had to solve to win rewards led the subjects to believe that their tasks would be easy. On that basis, they set high goals for themselves. The rewards that both the other person and the subjects themselves received were based on the extent to which they reached their goals. The actual tasks were much more difficult than the preliminary examples. Subjects fell short of their stated goals, and as a result deprived the other person of the reward.

In a second game, subjects had a chance to compensate the deprived women at no cost to themselves. In general, there was a very strong inclination to compensate. There were also significant differences depending on the amount of compensation that was possible. When this amount was about equal to the amount of which the subjects had deprived the other person, subjects compensated significantly more than when the amount of compensation (the number of books of trading stamps the other person would gain) was much larger or much smaller than the amount they deprived her of. This finding was replicated by Berscheid, Walster, and Barclay (1969). This experiment differs from many others in that subjects *were not asked* to do anything for the person whom they had harmed. Nevertheless, when given the opportunity, they behaved in a manner that would benefit her.

In another study Walster and Prestholdt (1966) provided information that led social work trainees to make a mistake in their diagnosis of a patient's condition and to recommend incorrect therapy to a psychiatrist on the basis of that diagnosis. Subsequently, they received evidence that their diagnosis was incorrect, and they were provided with an opportunity to volunteer free time to help the patient with some therapy. When the misdiagnosis was private, there was a greater tendency to volunteer help, whereas when the misdiagnosis was public, there was a greater tendency to justify the error, to insist despite the evidence that the diagnosis was correct. Walster and Prestholdt suggest that commitment to a harmful act is likely to decrease the willingness for compensation.

Walster *et al.* (1970) proposed that another determinant of the method of equity restoration is the desire to maximize the outcome-to-input ratio, for both others and oneself. The better the outcomes that some action can bring about the more likely it is to be selected to restore equity. On this basis self-punishment seems the least likely method to be used, because it does not maximize outcomes.

A number of experiments have shown that harmdoing leads to the type of reactions that Walster *et al.* believe produce psychological equity. For example, harmdoers come to derogate their victim (Berkowitz, 1962; Davidson, 1964; Davis & Jones, 1960; Glass, 1964; Sykes & Matza, 1957; Walster & Prestholdt, 1966). As in the Lerner and Matthews (1967) study that was discussed, when people have reason to believe that they are responsible for the harm another person suffers, and they are asked for an evaluation of the victim, they devalue the victim more than people who did not inflict harm. When people expect future interaction with a person whom they harmed they are less likely to derogate that person. Ross (1965) led students to cause their partners to receive painful electric shocks in order to avoid such shocks for themselves. When they believed that the partners were to work with them again only once, they derogated them more than when they believed that they were to work together on many tasks.

According to Walster *et al.* (1970, 1973), the credibility or correctness of derogation of the victim is more difficult to maintain in the case of contact with him, which makes the use of derogation less likely when future contact is anticipated. Similarly, the more public justification (particularly derogation of the victim) has to be, the less likely it is that it will be utilized, because justification has to be adequate to survive critical appraisal by others. However, as I suggested earlier, expected future interaction may also lead to taking the other person's point of view and thereby to the experience of empathy.

Comparing the Effects of Observing
and of Causing Harm

Several other experiments provide information about how people react to both causing and observing harm. They also provide additional opportunities to evaluate support for the guilt and equity interpretations.

Judith Regan (1971) had female subjects monitor low-voltage, nonpainful electric shocks that were administered to a rat. In the experimental groups the rat received much stronger shocks than were intended. In the responsible condition strong shocks were administered when the subject was looking not at the voltage indicator, which was her task, but at the rat. Had she been checking she would have noticed a change in voltage and could have regulated it. The experimenter communicated to the subject that this ruined all her efforts in the project. In the witness condition the rat received the strong shocks when the subject was looking at the voltage indicator, although the experimenter also administered at least one strong shock when the subject turned from the monitor to the rat. The subject was told, in this group, that what happened was not her fault, but was due to equipment problems. In a control group the equipment broke down, but the rat did not receive strong shocks. Responsibility enhanced subsequent prosocial behavior, the donating of money for a cause. However, the *observation* of harm enhanced it even more. In the responsibility condition those subjects who looked at the dial of the voltage regulator most of the time were less affected by the responsibility manipulation than those who looked at the dial less. The former donated less. Possibly these subjects differed in the degree of responsibility they felt for what happened.

Half the subjects were interviewed before the request for donation. It was assumed that talking about the experience would have a cathartic effect or that it would provide an opportunity for the subject to experience repentence. Either of these would reduce the feeling of guilt and subsequent compliance with a request. The interview did reduce subsequent donations, but only slightly. It reduced to a greater degree donations by those subjects who talked more about themselves in the course of the interview. Had Regan described the content of what people said, we could evaluate whether they used any of the specific equity-restoring techniques that Walster *et al.* (1970; 1973) proposed, such as minimizing their own responsibility, or whether they primarily expressed their feelings and presumably experienced catharsis, which would indicate guilt reduction. The findings only indicate that the effect of observing or being made responsible for harm (to the rat and to the experimenter) can be dissipated to some extent by verbal self-expression.

Freedman (1970) mentioned another experiment by Carlsmith and others, in which people who cheated on a task had an opportunity to confess what they had done. Confession was expected to reduce guilt. Subjects who confessed complied less with a request than people who did not have the opportunity to confess.

The review of research findings and theories suggests that observing another person's suffering and causing harm to another may have similar consequences. Are these findings best explained by the same theoretical concepts? The central question may be this: How does variation in responsibility by a person for another person experiencing harm affect the first person's thoughts, feelings, and behavior? Several experiments show that some modes of reactions to observing and to causing harm are similar.

In the study conducted by Regan (1971) subjects were *more* likely to donate money if they witnessed harm, but they were not made to feel responsible for it. In another experiment Rawlings (1968) had some subjects make errors on a perceptual discrimination task; the errors resulted in their partners receiving electric shocks. Others engaged in the same task while their partners received random electric shocks, ostensibly to test the effect on task performance. Thus subjects either caused or only observed another person receive electric shocks. In a third group both subjects and their partners received shocks of the same magnitude, and in a fourth group neither received shocks. Afterward, with different partners, the subjects engaged in another task. Both the subjects and their partners were to receive electric shocks for mistakes made on the task, but the subjects could determine what portion of the shock each of them would receive. The subjects were to be the instructors on a concept formation task. When learners made mistakes they would receive shocks; because this presumably enhanced learning, the instructors also received a shock. The longer the shock was for one of them, the shorter it was for the other. Before each trial subjects could set a dial indicating how much of the shock they would take and how much the partners would take.

Observing another person receive electric shocks in the first part of the study and causing the other person to receive electric shocks had equivalent effects. Both increased the duration of the shock that subjects set for themselves in the second part of the study in comparison to subjects in two other groups in which both subject and partner, or neither, received shocks in the first part. Rawlings suggests two explanations. First, observing another person's suffering made subjects aware of the violation of a norm that people should not be made to suffer. This resulted in subjects experiencing anticipatory guilt, which later led to helpful behavior. Second, having observed another person receiving shocks, people experience sympathy. Having thus been sensitized to another person's suffering, they took more of the suffering on themselves.

Other experiments also found that causing harm and observing it have similar effects. In an experiment by Cialdini and his associates (1973) a stack of cards was knocked off a chair either by the subject or by the experimenter. Afterward, whether the subject or the experimenter caused the accident, subjects responded more to a request that they make telephone calls for a good cause than did others in a control group.

Observing harm to others without the opportunity to help the harmed person leads to justification. Responsibility for harm seems to lead to justification of a greater degree. Lerner and Matthews (1967) found that people who believed that they caused harm to another devalued the other person more than people who had no reason to feel that they caused harm. Brock and Buss (1962) found, in two experiments, that participants who believed that it is wrong to administer shocks to people in psychological experiments, but who were then themselves led to do so, minimized the other's suffering and denied their own responsibility. Presumably acting in ways that are contrary to one's values and harm someone makes it more imperative to justify one's behavior and therefore leads to more derogation and more denial of responsibility.

As we saw in analyzing the just world concept, responsibility by victims for their own suffering resulted in greater devaluation of victims whose suffering people observed. Contributions, however minimal, by victims to their own suffering also appear to decrease the guilt of the people who inflict the suffering. Brock and Buss (1964) found that when subjects who were induced to administer electric shocks to another person in a teacher–learner situation were told that the confederate was randomly selected as the learner, they reported feeling more guilt following the administration of the shock and judged the harm greater than when they were told that the learner–teacher selection was determined by prior information that indicated that the subject would be a better teacher. In the latter, high justification condition, the subjects may have felt that the victim was responsible for his fate and thus felt less responsible for making the victim suffer.

The motivation for helping behavior, and for devaluation and other types of justification, may differ in the cases of observing and causing harm. For one thing, when one causes harm, concern about evaluation by other people and the desire to improve a tarnished image may be relatively important motives; when one observes suffering that one did not inflict, these motives are not as strong. In addition, observing another person's distress may create empathy, or it may activate certain values including concern about "other equity" (discussed subsequently)—that people should not suffer innocently. All these may motivate attempts at positive behavior. When a person feels implicated, feels responsible for another's distress, feelings of guilt and distress arising from having caused harm or having created inequities may result. Having caused harm may give rise to more self-oriented than other-oriented processes; however, it would also motivate attempts to help. Such help may be forthcoming more from a feeling of obligation and from a desire to maintain a positive image in one's own and in others' eyes than from a desire to benefit the other person. When the opportunity to help the victim is physically or psychologically absent, these feelings and the resulting justification processes may minimize the likelihood of empathy or sympathy. Similar inhibition of empathic reactions may result from having created harm that appears so great in magnitude that alleviating the suffering is difficult or impossible. Given that the feeling of responsibility to undo the other's distress is great, and that the kinds of psychological processes that motivate it are somewhat different from those evoked by observing harm, it becomes more likely that people will minimize their distress and discharge their responsibility by creating equity through devaluation.

Weick and Nesset (1968) speculate that there are several types of equity. They called one type *comparison equity;* this involves the comparison of one's inputs and outcomes with those of other people. Comparison equity is involved when there is an interaction between people, in the course of which they affect one another's outcomes. In addition, there are *own equity* and *other equity*. In own equity, one's personal state of equity is evaluated on the basis of internal standards derived from past experience, independently of equity in relation to others. Similarly, others' states of equity can be evaluated in comparison to existing standards. The just-world hypothesis implicitly involves other equity. There is a standard that specifies that people should not suffer and what suffering is, and people consider others' inputs and outcomes relative to that standard. Standards that determine the kinds of input that make suffering equitable also seem to exist. It is likely that, in our own culture as well as in others, depending on the status of a person or other characteristics, what is equitable for one person is evaluated differently from what is equitable for another. The standards used to evaluate different types of equity probably derive both from cultural values inculcated in children in the course of socialization and from personal experience, in interaction with others and in the kind of outcomes that a person is accustomed to achieving for certain degrees of effort. For example, a person who has to extend great effort to gain particular outcomes will probably develop different standards for own equity than someone who gains the same outcomes with ease.

Several theorists have been concerned with the meaning of justice (Lerner, 1975; Deutsch, 1975; Walster & Walster, 1975). Certainly equity is only one conception of what is just; equality is another dominant conception. Equity points to people receiving what they deserve. Equality suggests that people should have equal outcomes, regardless of differences in inputs. Walster and Walster (1975) suggest that equality can be viewed as a special case of equity rather than as something separate. When our humanity is regarded as the basic input, all should have equal outcomes. In the case of equity, other, variable inputs usually are considered as the proper bases for determining outcomes.

A basic question involves which inputs are valuable and should lead to differential outcomes. Different societies, a single society over time, and different subgroups in a society may vary in what inputs they regard as deserving valued outcomes. Changes in what is regarded as just come primarily from a redefinition of what inputs are valuable—for example, today's society holds the ideal that maleness or whiteness does not make a person more deserving than femaleness or blackness. In addition to cultural variations, there are individual variations in what each person considers valued inputs and deserved outcomes. Specific circumstances may, moreover, motivate people to vary their standards. This contributes to their ability to deal with observing and causing harm to others when helpful intervention is difficult. For example, a person may decide that negative inputs, such as mistakes on a learning task, deserve negative outcomes, such as electric shocks.

The cognitive developmentalists (Piaget, 1932; Kohlberg, 1969) assume that in the course of experiences with other people individuals discover the "logic" of human interactions—for example, that reciprocity guides such interactions. The wider the range of a person's experience, the more he will learn from it. However, what people learn from their experience is likely to be affected by instructions they received from parents and others.

When people have caused harm or were made to believe that they caused harm, their willingness to help somebody other than the person they harmed, when they were not under surveillance, may result from a form of own equity. They might desire to balance the harm that they caused with the good that they will do. Two issues need to be considered. First, the different forms of equity are probably not completely independent. For example, what a person regards as equitable in relation to another person would depend on his standards for own equity and other equity. Second, as noted earlier in the chapter, there is apparently a special consideration for the self that keeps people from acting completely equitably. Lane and Messe (1972) explored the last issue by examining whether people are more concerned with own equity than with comparison or other equity. In an experiment they varied levels of input, both in terms of the amount of time subjects worked and their performance. The amount of reward for the work was also varied; it was sufficient for the amount of work, insufficient, or oversufficient (very generous). Upon completion of the task each subject was asked to divide the available reward between himself and another person, who worked on the task under conditions identical to the subject's. Compared to the sufficient-reward condition, where subjects tended to distribute the rewards equally, in the insufficient condition subjects tended to take relatively more for themselves. When they could not create equity for both another person and themselves, in terms of the standards of equity that they probably held, they treated themselves equitably. Subjects also took more for themselves in the oversufficient condition. Possibly they rewarded the other subject according to his input, equitably, but what was left they took for themselves. Standards of equity and self-interest seem to act jointly to guide behavior.

Causing harm to others might be a situation in which concern about all three forms of equity is aroused. Causing harm leads to inequity in relation to the victim. It leads to inequity in the victim's relationship to the world, in other equity, if he did not bring about his suffering by his own negative input. Finally, it leads to inequity in terms of the actor's own equity, because his negative input is not balanced either by his own positive input or by his own negative outcome.

In summary, there are a number of reasons for distress being generated as a result of a person's observing and causing harm to others. These reasons include empathic reaction to others' suffering, the violation of the value that people should not suffer and one should not cause suffering, and the violation of values and beliefs related to equity. An expanded conception of equity is based on the assumption that people are concerned with justice for themselves, for other people, and in their relationships with others.

The concept of responsibility is important for the understanding of helping behavior and related processes. The subjective experience of responsibility—for having caused harm or to relieve harm—and defenses against experiencing responsibility appear to have influence on people's thoughts about, affective responses to, and behavioral reactions to others' needs. In the few studies that made comparisons possible, a victim received about equal help whether subjects only observed his suffering or caused his suffering. In one study, when the subject's responsibility or fault for the suffering of an animal had been especially stressed, this reduced subsequent prosocial behavior unrelated to the victim (Regan, 1971). Devaluation and other justification of a victim's suffering has been greater when the subject was responsible for the harm another suffered than following the mere observation of another's harm. This is presumably due to the different psychological processes that follow observing and causing harm, as is discussed above. The analysis of research on the just world hypothesis indicated that the responsibility of a *sufferer* for his or her fate results in more devaluation than suffering "innocently." The evidence that, when responsibility to help a distressed person is focused on bystanders their helping behavior is substantially greater, is also strong (Chapter 3).

Alternative Explanations

Cialdini, Darby, and Vincent (1973) have proposed that suffering and harmdoing cause a negative state. They do not attempt to specify what psychological processes bring about this negative state and what its nature is. The main purpose of people's behavior, once they experience that negative state, is to reduce it or eliminate it, through altruism or by other means. Once the negative state is reduced, people are less likely to do anything for others.

Both guilt theory and equity theory assume that people tend to reduce a negative state in ways that are commensurate with how it was aroused, in some manner balancing violations of standards that concern themselves with others' welfare. In contrast, Cialdini *et al.* assume that the negative state can be reduced in many ways, all having the same effect. Their study involved three conditions: (*a*) Subjects accidentally knocked down a set of cards containing information for another person's thesis; (*b*) The experimenter accidentally knocked down the cards; and (*c*) Subjects participated in control conditions. Compared to control subjects, the experimental subjects were more likely to agree to a subsequent request that they make telephone calls—to help an investigation of study habits—whether they caused the accident or the experimenter did. Before the request was made, some experimental subjects were exposed to an experience designed to reduce the negative state that was presumably created by the accident. In one condition subjects worked on a task for a short time and then unexpectedly received a $1 reward for having done well on the task. In another condition they received positive social reinforcement in place of the monetary reward (the experimenter told them that they did a good job on the task). These positive experiences reduced the number of telephone calls that the subjects agreed to make to about the level of the control subjects. Cialdini *et al.* assumed that the positive experiences reduced the negative state that motivated compliance. In their view harmdoing and observation of harm are not necessary precursors of compliance; any experience that generates a negative state should have the same effect.

I believe that there may be alternative explanations for the findings of Cialdini *et al.* The helpful behavior of the experimental subjects in the two conditions may have been motivated in different ways. Those who knocked down the cards may have complied with the request to improve their image or to create equity. Those who saw the experimenter knock the cards down may have been helpful to make the experimenter feel good. The intervening positive experiences could have made the subjects feel good about themselves and thereby reduced their need to improve their image. The positive experiences could also have made the subjects feel that they helped the experimenter by their good performance; this also could have reduced the need to help more. The intervening positive experiences could also have had a definitional effect, in that the experimenter's behavior may have communicated to the subject unconcern about the harm. However, if clear evidence existed that a person was seriously harmed by some behavior, public reassurance might be less effective, because to a greater degree internal reactions might be activated arising from the violation of personal values and standards related to concern about the victim's welfare.

Some findings of McMillan support the view of Cialdini *et al.* that a positive experience reduces compliance. McMillan's findings can be also interpreted as showing, however, that following certain kinds of harmdoing compliance with requests is motivated by concern about evaluation by other people. When concern diminishes, for example, as the result of increased self-esteem, compliance diminishes. McMillan (1971) had subjects receive illicit information about answers on a test, a procedure similar to that used by Freedman *et al* (1967). After subjects worked on the test they were asked to help the experimenter score the test. There was weak indication that people who received positive feedback about their performance on the test helped less than those who did not receive such feedback. These findings support the interpretation advanced earlier, that compliance following transgression indicates concern about the self more than concern about other people. This is likely to be particularly so when the harm is relatively small.

The findings of both Cialdini *et al.* and McMillan, in combination with those that are reviewed in Chapter 6, suggest that in many such transgression studies the subjects may not believe that significant harm has been caused, or their feelings of empathy and concern for another person are not evoked because of how the harm was created. Research that is reviewed later shows that positive experiences of many kinds usually increase subsequent help for people in need. However, they also reduce the willingness to comply with unappealing demands.

Still another explanation, specifically of the effect of harmdoing on compliance, has been proposed by Brock (1969):

> An individual who has affected the fate of another person *in a certain magnitude* will repeat that magnitude of control over the other person (or a person in a similar role) if an opportunity to do so presents itself. The assumed dynamic construct, the motive to behave consistently, in similar situations, is akin to cognitive consistency needs that are central postulates of current theorizing in social psychology. . . . what has been called transgression was primarily sensed by the individual subject as his control over the fate of another [p. 143].

The manner in which we try to affect the fate of the other person, negatively or positively, is a function of how we are inclined toward that other person, negatively or positively. Brock also suggests that this attempt to maintain fate control is directed not only toward other persons whose fate we have affected, but also toward people in similar roles. This is an interesting notion, and it is worth further exploration. Keating and Brock (1976) do present some rather complex data that can be viewed as support for the theory. However, the applicability of this theory to various harmdoing situations needs examination and clarification. Would it apply when a person barely touches a table and it collapses or when a woman is accused of ruining another person's camera? In such situations the subjective experience of most people might be an inability to control anyone's fate, others' as well as their own, in contrast to a sense of power over the fate of others. Moreover, a crucial question remains: What determines whether a person will then be positively or negatively inclined toward others? The theories previously presented imply a desire to balance an act that was deviant with some new behavior. In Brock's view, the motivation is to maintain consistency.

Conclusions, Issues, and Limitations of Research

I would again like to emphasize that varied reactions are possible to either observing or causing someone's suffering; these include derogation of the victim as well as devaluation of those who caused the harm, guilt if one himself caused the harm, empathic reactions, distress due to deviation from one's values, embarrassment, or shame. With regard to harmdoing, the reactions depend on the manner in which harmdoing came about (voluntary or accidental, for example) and on external pressures that operate on a harmdoer, the behavioral alternatives that are available following harmdoing, and characteristics of the harmdoer.

Compliance with requests following harmdoing appears mostly externally motivated by the desire to gain approval, to diminish disapproval, or to repair a negative image created by having caused harm. There is only limited evidence that behavior following harmdoing is sometimes internally motivated, and if such behavior is internally motivated, we know little about what processes operate—personal norms, values, empathy, guilt, the desire to benefit another person, and so on. Some findings suggest that internal motivation of an unspecified nature is active; see the Regan *et al.* (1972) field study. Heilman and associates (1972) also found that subjects who accidentally overturned a table and caused harm reported the harm to a greater extent if the harm was greater and if it was rectifiable, even though they probably believed that it could not be discovered that they had caused the harm. However, the same conditions did not increase the subsequent willingness to comply with a request. Thus, when seemingly internally motivated reporting of harm occurred, no compliance followed. There is little *direct* evidence of guilt as a motivator of positive behavior following harmdoing, or of equity distress. However, equity principles can sometimes explain positive behavior or cognitive activities following harmdoing. For example, people balance the amount of harm they caused with the amount of benefit they try to create. When accidentally caused harm is rectifiable and external pressure for positive behavior is limited, internal motivation to at least report the harmdoing or to rectify it by some action may be greatest.

The interrelationship among varied types of reactions by people to their own harmdoing is as yet minimally specified. Some reactions may be less adequate ways of dealing with a particular situation than others; derogation may therefore be followed by positive behavior when the opportunity for the latter becomes available. People certainly respond differently as a function of their personal characteristics. Sometimes, having dealt with the existing circumstances one way may make it unnecessary for them to deal with it another way. Katz *et al.* (1973) found that subjects reacted with more guilt, in a teacher–learner situation, if the victim received more shock. There was no correlation, however, between guilt feelings reported by subjects and the amount they derogated the victim.

Some important conclusions may be drawn from the research and theory presented in this chapter. First, concern about justice (the desire to maintain belief in a just world) can have a constraining effect, limiting help for other people, rather than leading to active attempts to help. Second, there are a variety of psychological processes, which I called justification processes, by which people can deal with others' distress and/or with circumstances under which helping another person may be desirable. Some of the conditions, and one personality characteristic—the belief in a just world—that make such justification processes more or less likely to occur have been specified. Circumstances that make it difficult to intervene in another person's behalf, and experiences that are likely to produce guilt and distress either for having produced harm and inequity or for not having helped are likely to give rise to various justifications. Justification processes can be defined broadly as cognitive activities that inhibit or deactivate prosocial goals. Conditions in addition to those specified, including goal conflicts, may give rise to justification. Since justification is part of the manner in which a person thinks about events, it must be important in guiding conduct. Unfortunately, the extent to which this is so and the circumstances that increase or diminish the likelihood that justification affects behavior have been only minimally explored. Devaluation of a sufferer did not, for example, diminish later compensation of the sufferer.

Most of the theories that have been proposed to explain the phenomena discussed in this chapter assumed that people experience distress, particularly in response to having caused harm to someone. Unfortunately, internal states that were produced by harmdoing or by the observation of others' suffering have not been directly evaluated. Little attempt has been made to measure the experience of guilt feelings and thoughts about violation of standards of equity or other standards. We have, therefore, only minimal evidence that these internal processes were activated and mediated subsequent behavioral reactions. Primarily, we have to rely on inference.

A related issue is that individual differences in internal standards or in empathic capacity and the effects of such individual differences on reaction to witnessing and causing harm have not been explored. Demonstrating relationships between such individual differences and cognitive, emotional, and behavioral reactions to harmdoing and witnessing harm is one of the important ways of demonstrating the mediating role of these variables. If we had evidence, for example, that people who believe in principles of equity to a greater degree react more in ways predicted by equity theory, our confidence that beliefs in equity mediate their behavior would increase.

The measurement of personality differences and the examination of how they affect reactions to others' distress and to having caused harm to others becomes even more important in light of the interpretation of the research findings that I proposed. People may respond to another's suffering to a greater degree with empathy and the activation of their prosocial goals, or with feelings of guilt and distress due to their responsibility for inequity, as a function of whether they observe or have caused another's distress. We may find that similar variations follow from individual differences in personality. Differences in experience, or in personality characteristics, or in their combination may in turn affect the likelihood that another's distress is dealt with by empathy and the activation of prosocial goals, by repeated attempts to help and the rejection of injustice, or by various forms of justification that reduce responsibility or guilt.

Another issue is that in the studies discussed alternative avenues for responding to another person's distress or to having caused harm were usually lacking. In some studies people could respond first by devaluation, then by compensation, or vice versa. Under many life circumstances people are less constrained by circumstances and can choose whether to help a distressed person or deal with the circumstances by means of varied justifications or do both to different extents. The nature of the circumstances and the characteristics of the person must determine which of these consequences follow.

Much of the research that has been reviewed in this chapter deals with these important phenomena in somewhat peripheral and often artificial ways. As an initial step, this is acceptable and perhaps necessary. But these phenomena and their explanations should be tested in more meaningful, interactive, transactional contexts. I started the discussion of harmdoing by pointing to its ecological significance. It is frequent and to some degree inevitable in human relationships that we harm our friends, colleagues, and lovers. Researchers, having laid the groundwork for the exploration of prosocial behavior and having provided data with which to begin the building of theory, will have to deal with the difficult task of exploring such behavior where it occurs most—among friends and intimates. I shall consider prosocial behavior in more transactional and interactional relationships in Chapters 8 and 9.

Can Violence Be Constructive?

Most of us—at least most social scientists who study prosocial behavior—consider aggression harmful and undesirable, not only for victims but for the perpetrators, the community, and society. This chapter dealt with some aspects of aggression, since harmdoing frequently involves aggression, and did so in research where participants were induced to administer electric shocks to other people. Is aggression or violence always harmful, or can it have constructive consequences?

Having caused accidental harm to another person can result in intense emotional reactions, genuine regret, and concern for the harmed person; it can create a personal bond. Having caused harm can then give rise to attempts to help that are not motivated by feelings of obligation, and thus will not be aversive to the helper. Again, the circumstances under which the accidental harmdoing occurred, its nature, and the personality of the harmdoer—as well as the reactions of the victim—would determine what happens. I am suggesting, however, that any interpersonal experience that gives rise to strong emotion has the potential to create a bond rather than hostility or devaluation.

Such reactions can follow from aggressive confrontations. Averill (1977), in collecting descriptions of anger-provoking experiences, had one person describe such a confrontation. The cause was seemingly trivial—a student in a dorm fed another student's dog contrary to the owner's expressed wishes—but it resulted in a confrontation with knives. The confrontation was resolved, however, by extensive discussion, sharing of world views, and an intense interpersonal experience.

Retaliation in response to aggression by another person can also be constructive (see Chapter 8). It may decrease further aggression (Staub, 1971c) and establish equity in the inequitable relationship that followed the original aggression (Berscheid et al., 1968).

Finally, Walster and Walster (1975) note that usually it is the power of particular groups in a society that determines what characteristics and behaviors are regarded as valuable and deserving of valuable rewards. It is in the interest of the powerful to maintain the status quo, which usually serves their interests. Moreover, frequently only the use of power will alter the manner in which the less powerful can redefine equity and so gain more valued resources. Unfortunately, the powerless tend to accept the definition by society (and thus by the powerful, who shaped society's definition) of what is just and equitable. Even social reformers tend to deviate in only small degrees from what is generally accepted in the culture, demanding modest changes. Although the minority can try to persuade, passively resist, or sabotage, unless they have real power, it is unlikely that they can substantially redefine justice. Frequently, such redefinitions occur in the course of a social upheaval.

The implication of this view is that some forms of aggression may be necessary to increase the rights and benefits of those who are not treated justly. Such a view raises more questions than it resolves with regard to issues of morality. When is aggression justified? How much aggression, and of what kinds? How can one know that aggression will lead to desirable rather than only to destructive consequences? These are just a few of the questions one may ask.

Prosocial Behavior in Response to Varied Needs

The determinants of varied forms of prosocial behavior are considered collectively in this chapter because the independent variables that were explored and their effects are quite similar. However, I shall continue to be concerned with the extent to which certain influences have different effects as a function of the type of prosocial behavior. The different forms of prosocial behavior considered in this chapter include helping others with tasks, helping others in various types of need, doing favors, sharing, and donating possessions for charity. Researchers have frequently explored determinants of such behavior under conditions that provide no opportunity for give and take; the helping behavior under study is not part of an ongoing relationship between individuals. The determinants of interactive types of prosocial behavior are considered in Chapters 8 and 9. In most of the research, subjects had an opportunity to reduce a negative state, to alleviate an undesirable condition. At other times a person needed help in order to gain a desirable reward, to achieve a positive goal. As in the case of helping people in physical distress, the research is organized here according to classes of determinants: social influence, the influence of the stimulus condition, and personality characteristics. Temporary states of actors are considered extensively in Chapter 6, where the connection between the self and others is discussed.

Much of the research explored in this chapter deals with the influence of modeling and of varied verbal communications on prosocial behavior. These are social influences that can activate both external and internal motivators of help. An important difference exists between the verbal influence in this research and that used in research discussed in Chapter 3. In studies dealing with physical distress the stimulus representing the need for help existed independently of verbal communications about it. In these studies, the need for help is communicated through and is embedded in the verbal communication or the behavior of models. Usually no independent stimulus for help exists.

Social Influence

The most frequently studied form of social influence has been modeling, the exposure to the positive or negative example of someone, followed by the opportunity to behave prosocially. In another group of experiments subjects were directly asked to do something. A direct request represents a demand; it communicates an expectation. It is of interest to see under what conditions and what forms of requests lead to prosocial behavior.

The Effects of Exposure to Others' Deeds and Words

Since the influence of modeling has been studied extensively, we might ask how and why modeling affects prosocial behavior. We know that modeling does influence behavior, both prosocial and other kinds. The demonstration that modeling influences prosocial behavior is an extension of the demonstration of this same fact in other behavioral domains.

How does modeling affect people? First, through the observation of others people may learn something that will continue to exert an influence on them. The long-term influence of modeling is discussed in conjunction with socialization in Volume 2 of this work. There is little convincing evidence that a single brief observation of the behavioral example of another person does have this kind of effect, that it leads to learning, to persistence and generalization of changed behavior. The influence of a model may be situation-specific, the effect of the behavior of one person on others in a specific setting. Much of the research demonstrated this effect but did not elucidate *why* people are affected by the example of others.

In Bandura's conception (1969, 1971, 1977) the observation of a model is sufficient for learning to take place. In most of the research on prosocial behavior, learning how to perform the behavior was not an issue, because the form of the observed behavior was very simple. For example, children were asked to give gift certificates that they had earned to charity. All they had to do was to put the gift certificates in a box. Not even kindergartners would have difficulty doing this. Modeling can also affect the probability that the observed behavior will be performed. According to

Bandura, the major determinant of this is the expectation of reward for performing the behavior. Thus, the example of a model might indicate to the observer that positive or negative consequences can be expected if the behavior is performed. Vicarious reinforcement, seeing the model reinforced for his behavior, would most clearly provide such information. However, a model's high status (which suggests that the model is a successful person) and other characteristics are also likely to increase the expectation that the behavior will lead to positive consequences. The behavior of a prosocial model may also communicate to observers that this is the expected, desirable behavior, and failing to behave that way might have aversive consequences.

Although learning a new form of behavior and performing it can be separated, change in the probability of the performance of a behavior itself represents a form of learning. Clearly, when modeling brings about durable and/or generalized change in the probability that a certain behavior will be performed, learning has occurred.

Bandura and Walters (1963) also specified other effects of modeling: disinhibition and inhibition. When a person desires to behave a particular way, but believes that others disapprove of that behavior and the consequences of such action would be negative, the example of a model performing the behavior without negative consequences would indicate that the behavior is acceptable in that particular setting, thus enhancing the likelihood of its performance. If someone feels that a certain form of prosocial behavior might be inappropriate in a particular setting, the observation of such behavior by a model might lead to disinhibition. Aggressive behavior increases following observation of a model, even when the model is not rewarded (Hoffman, 1970a). Children normally learn that aggression is not acceptable, that it is likely to be punished. When they see that it is not punished in a particular setting, aggression is disinhibited. On the other hand, someone not behaving prosocially in response to an apparent need, particularly when the cues are ambiguous, is likely to inhibit the prosocial behavior of others.

Giving permission to children to enter another room, which increased their later attempts to help another child (Staub, 1971b), might be regarded as a demonstration of disinhibition. Permission was verbally provided, but a similar result would probably have been produced by an appropriate model (another child, perhaps) entering the adjoining room.

Why does modeling have an influence on prosocial behavior? Krebs (1970) summarized the possibilities suggested by a number of writers: "At the most elementary level, models make behavioral alternatives salient: They draw attention to particular courses of action and increase the salience of social norms [p. 268]." There are many ways to react to an event and many standards of behavior that might seem relevant in any particular situation. When another person behaves prosocially, this behavior makes norms that prescribe prosocial behavior appear more salient, particularly relevant.

This effect of exposure to another person's behavior may be a very basic and important one. Although there is no independent evidence that would demonstrate that modeling works through this particular avenue, the speculations of William James (1890) on the operation of the will may be instructive in considering how modeling may increase the salience of norms and behavioral alternatives. James suggested that usually there are many and often conflicting thoughts and desires occupying people's attention. When all except one thought is eliminated, this thought, having no interference, will naturally come to be expressed in action, assuming that action is implied in it. When conflicting interpretations, values and standards, and behavioral alternatives are called forth by a particular situation, the example of a model might focus attention on one, leading observers to focus on it and consequently act upon it. Perhaps this is one way to view "behavioral contagion" (Wheeler, 1966), an increased tendency to initiate social behavior when others do it. Sometimes what might appear to be the disinhibition of some form of behavior is explainable in this manner. Macauley (1970) noted that people are much more likely to approach a Salvation Army collection table when other people are present. Sometimes models may lower restraints against public behavior, disinhibit it, but at other times they may increase the salience of a form of action in the manner implied by James. Although this discussion suggests that another person's behavioral example can eliminate conflicting alternatives, sometimes it can simply make the observer aware of the relevance of a particular value or norm, without resolving (or perhaps even creating) conflict.

Krebs (1970) also suggests that models "supply information about what is appropriate in various situations by setting an example, by helping to create a normative standard, and by helping to supply a definition of the situation [p. 268]." The behavior of a model might define the meaning of an event and might indicate what standards of conduct are relevant or appropriate. The model provides a definition of the appropriate behavior in the situation. That is, someone's example can define a situation as one in which a particular behavior is appropriate or expected, at least by the person whose example is seen. Clearly, these suggested effects of modeling are all forms of social influence, identical with those that appear to affect reactions to people in physical distress.

Krebs' third suggestion is that models "supply information about the consequences of courses of action [p. 268]." The behavior of the model may contain information about the likelihood of external or internal rewards or punishments. By indicating what behavior is appropriate, models already imply different consequences. The addition of clearly visible consequences may enhance the power of models to induce imitation.

The effect of someone's behavioral example and the information it communicates to observers might be summed up in the following manner: It can make norms, values, and behavioral alternatives salient, specify the expectations of other persons as well as situational rules, and imply or clearly indicate the probable consequences of certain acts.

Research on Modeling and Verbal Communications by Models

Many experiments show that observing a model increases prosocial behavior. In an early study, Bryan and Test (1967) had a person stand on the side of the road beside a car with a flat tire. In a modeling condition the same person was standing there, but at a point earlier on the road another person with a flat tire was being helped by someone. The observation of the model significantly increased the frequency of drivers who stopped. Although in this and other studies the effect of modeling was usually significant, often it was not substantial. That is, although more people helped, the percentage of helpers was still low. In studies of donating, particularly with children, the amount that is donated is often low, although enhanced by modeling (Bryan & Walbeck, 1970a, 1970b; Grusec, 1972; White, 1972). In another study Bryan and Test (1967) set up a Salvation Army collection table. They noted donations 20 seconds after a model donated, versus donations made during the subsequent 20 seconds, which served as a control period. Observation of a model increased donation. Bryan and Test (1967) suggest that the behavior of the model increased salience and provided information about positive consequences. In addition, bystanders might have compared themselves with the model and experienced shame for not behaving prosocially. Krebs (1970) also interprets these and other studies as showing that modeling can increase the salience of behavioral alternatives and of prosocial norms. However, in this and most other studies there is no direct evidence about the motives or internal processes that are aroused in observers—for example, that thoughts about standards or norms or societal expectations arise as a result of exposure to a model.

Observing a person who acts as a negative model, who does not help or share, usually decreases helping behavior (Wagner & Wheeler, 1969). However, under certain circumstances observing a negative model might even increase attempts to aid others. This seems to happen when the model blatantly violates prosocial norms and/or conceptions of fairness and equity. Macaulay (1970) found that a positive model increased donations at a Salvation Army collection table. However, a negative model—someone who came to the table, looked, and then said, "Oh, I don't give for that"—did not decrease donations. Instead, people donated slightly more than in the control period. In a study that attempted to explore reactions to harmdoing, Konecni (1972) had subjects witness one of several events. In one condition, while a confederate was walking down a street, another confederate bumped into him, knocked some books out of his hand, and then just continued on his way. Subsequently, when subjects saw another confederate drop some papers, they helped pick them up significantly more than subjects in a variety of other conditions who were not exposed to such a blatant violation of appropriate social behavior. Observing a person who does not do something that might be regarded as highly desirable and normatively correct apparently may enhance rather than decrease prosocial behavior. The more blatant a violation, the more forceful a reminder of the obligation to help others it might be, and the more likely it is to produce anger about injustice and a desire to be just, and/or create sympathy with the victim.

In Chapter 3 the inhibiting effect in emergencies of the presence of inactive confederates (who obviously function as negative models) was discussed. In most of those studies positive modeling effects were not explored, presumably because once a person receives help from a model the observer has no opportunity to help; the need for help ceases to exist. In one study, (Staub, 1971a) kindergarten children observed an adult model respond to sounds of a child's mild distress coming from an adjoining room. Subsequently, they were substantially more likely to respond to sounds of severe distress from the adjoining room than children who were not exposed to the model. In one of the Milgram (1965) experiments subjects were asked to administer increasingly severe shocks to a "learner." Two confederates were also present; one refused to continue administering shocks when the shock level was low, and the other refused to continue when the shock level was higher. This substantially decreased the number of subjects who completed the whole sequence of shocks. This finding is consistent with other findings on compliance showing that even when a single person refuses to comply the power of the group in eliciting compliance substantially decreases (Asch, 1951). In Rosenhan's (1969) study also the behavior of a model decreased subjects' willingness to administer shocks. Although earlier I emphasized the fact that despite a negative model many people still complied and administered the most intense shocks, the negative model did decrease the frequency of compliance with the experimenter's demand to administer these shocks.

Solomon and Grota (1976) proposed that a helpful model would increase helping in low-level emergencies when the person who is requiring aid is in no immediate danger and there is no overwhelming need for an immediate response. In high-level emergencies, like most of those discussed in Chapter 3, bystanders would take into account the high cost of helping, in part due to the possibility of continued demands on them, and might diffuse responsibility to the model, rationalizing their failure to act on the grounds that the victim is already receiving help. These researchers observed the effects of a male model who either helped another male pick up some pencils and papers he had dropped in a supermarket, or responded to this person after he dropped the same material but also appeared to be in distress, apparently from stomach cramps. They did find a significant inter-action between modeling and the nature of the need. More bystanders in the low-level emergency helped after the model initiated help, but more bystanders initiated help in the high-level emergency when no model was present. Solomon and Grota's counterintuitive hypothesis is interesting, but clearly requires more evidence. Sometimes greater need and the pres-ence of a helper may create a condition in which the motivation to escape from the stimulus for help is aroused and the opportunity for escape is en-hanced (Staub & Baer, 1974).

Krebs suggested that in some studies models exerted their influence by providing information about the appropriateness of certain behavior. In one early study (Blake *et al.*, 1955) each subject was asked to donate money for a present for a retiring secretary. They were asked to write the amount of their contribution on a sheet of paper on which other people's names and their donations were already listed. Corresponding to the amounts already listed, subjects donated more or less. In another study subjects who were asked to volunteer for an experiment were less likely to do so if they were asked in a classroom rather than in private (Blake *et al.*, 1955). The inter-pretation was offered that others in the classroom who did not volunteer served as negative models. However, in asking a person when he is alone one exerts a more powerful social influence on him, which might explain the difference. Such a view is consistent with Latané's (1976) theory of social impact. According to this theory the impact of an influence source gets diffused as a function of the number of individuals who are present; the larger the number, the greater the diffusion.

There are a number of studies that show that modeling has specific effects, suggesting that under certain conditions a person's behavioral example might set the standard, and indicate appropriate conduct. The evi-dence is clearest on this point with adult models and child observers. Lie-bert and Fernandez (1970) used multiple models. The several models that a child observed each donated the same amount to needy others. The chil-dren tended to match the models in their donations. Additional studies have shown that observing a model significantly affects children's donations (Rosenhan & White, 1967; Bryan & Walbeck, 1970a,b; Harris, 1970, 1971; Presbie & Coiteux, 1971). In some studies the model's behavior had fairly specific effects, affecting only behavior closely corresponding to the model's. For example, Harris (1970) found that children who either had an adult share with them or observed an adult donate to charity tended either to share with the adult or to donate to charity but did not show increase in the prosocial behavior that they did not observe. In another study, how-ever, Harris (1971) found that children who observed a model donate to one charity showed at least some generalization effect, in that they subse-quently donated at least marginally significantly more to another charity than children who did not observe a model. Midlarsky and Bryan (1972) found, moreover, that observing generous or greedy models not only increased children's subsequent donating behavior but significantly affected donating behavior of a different kind a week or more later.

In a number of studies by Bryan and his associates (Bryan & Walbeck, 1970a,b; Bryan, 1972, 1975) the observation of models who won gift certificates for high scores on a bowling game and then either donated the certificates to needy children or kept them for themselves significantly affected the subsequent donations by children of gift certificates they won while playing the game. The observation of generous and selfish models respectively increased and decreased children's donations. Surprisingly, however, verbal statements by the model about the desirability of donating to needy others (usually for the March of Dimes) did not affect the children's donations. Neither statements about what a good thing it is to share nor statements about what an undesirable thing it is had any effect on donations. Findings of this research suggest that children know about values and beliefs promoting sharing and donating. Although hearing a model say that donating is a nice thing to do or uttering other such normative statements did not affect subsequent donating behavior, children did evaluate the person who said such things more positively than a neutral model, and they evaluated the person who extolled the virtues of keeping the rewards for oneself (as Bryan and his associates put it, the virtues of selfishness and greed) more negatively than the neutral model. Children also expressed the desirability of sharing when they subsequently instructed another child. Furthermore, they evaluated models who shared more positively than selfish ones.

Rushton (1975) attempted to replicate Bryan and Walbeck's design with some "improvements" in the procedure, which he expected would change the outcome and produce an effect for "preaching." He found no verbalization effect immediately following the exposure to the model. On a 2-month retest, subjects exposed to generous models continued to share more than those exposed to selfish models. Moreover, preaching had a highly significant effect: "Models who preached selfishness produced less giving than those who preached generosity or neutral messages," whether the retest situation was highly similar to or somewhat dissimilar to the original test situation. Furthermore, the effects of modeling and preaching interacted. Selfish behavior when the model expressed generous sentiments, and selfish sentiments when the model behaved generously, both reduced donations in comparison to the conditions that included no selfishness. Thus, verbalization did not have a social-influence effect; it did not affect behavior in the immediate setting but exerted a long-term influence. In contrast, the models were judged less attractive immediately following the subjects' exposure to them either if they behaved selfishly or if they preached selfishness.

In the studies by Bryan and his associates the modeling and verbal communications were combined. They were either consistent (the models either donated and communicated the desirability of donating rewards, or they behaved selfishly and provided reasons for not donating) or inconsistent (the models' actions and verbalizations were in conflict). Not only did verbalizations have no effect on children's prosocial behavior, but hypocrisy, inconsistency between words and deeds, also had no effect. However, there is evidence that inconsistency decreases the subsequent effectiveness of the model as a social-influence agent. For example, when a selfish model who preached charity later praised children for donating, this decreased the amount they donated (Midlarsky *et al.*, 1973).

Attributions about Models' Motives as a Determinant of Imitation

Does the behavior of a model supply more information to the children than verbal statements alone? It seems to be so when children have to learn some behavior or when verbal statements are nonspecific in nature and thus do not contain information about how much is to be donated. In Bryan's research the verbalizations were always combined with behavioral examples, and thus they did not need to have such an informational component. Presumably they were intended to serve a motivational function. In these studies, the verbal statements were normative; they communicated the "right" conduct. Children were told that it is good to share, that sharing was a nice thing to do. Such statements may result in psychological reactance (Brehm, 1966; Staub, 1975a,b; see under Reactance and Prosocial Behavior, this chapter). Normative verbal statements might make children (or adults) feel that force is being exerted to influence their behavior, that their behavioral freedom is being limited; this arouses opposition. When they observe a model's actions both children and adults may feel to a greater degree that they are free to decide what to do. The model's behavior implies what the right thing to do is, but it does not exert social influence that is powerful enough to induce resistance rather than compliance. However, the effects of modeling as well as of accompanying verbalizations may strongly vary as a function of the kinds of motives or intentions they imply about the model's conduct, the apparent reasons for the model's behavior.

Hornstein (1970) described an experiment in which he varied the reasons for a model's prosocial behavior. Subjects found a wallet on the street. It apparently had been found earlier by another person who intended to return it to the owner. This person wrote a brief note to the owner, put it into the wallet, and then lost the wallet himself. In the neutral condition, the note simply said, "Dear Mr. Irwin, I found your wallet. Everything is here, just as I found it." In the "contrary to social pressure" condition the note communicated that social pressure had been exerted on the finder not to return the wallet but he was returning it nonetheless. The note said,

"When I found it everyone who was around, including my best friend, said that I should keep it and I was stupid if I returned it. I disagreed with them, so here it is." Obviously the writer exercised choice; he returned the wallet because he considered it right to do so. In the "consistent with social pressure" condition the note said, "When I found it everyone who was around me, including my best friend, said that I should return it, and I was stupid if I kept it. I agreed with them and here it is." This model simply acted according to social expectations. In a "contrary to personal experience" condition the model did not do what other people had done to him, but again acted out of his conviction: "I want you to know that I have lost my wallet twice and no one ever sent mine back to me. That is why I am sending yours back." And finally, in the "consistent with personal experience" condition the note said, "I want you to know that I lost my wallet twice and both times someone simply mailed it back to me. That is why I am sending yours back." This model was also acting according to the standards of conduct that others set for him.

In the neutral model condition a high percentage of the subjects (61%) returned the wallet. Whenever the original finder seemed to make a choice to act independently and apparently out of consideration for the recipient or for what is the right thing to do, contrary either to his past experience or to social pressure exerted on him, the return rate was about equal to that in the neutral condition. When the model was simply being consistent with his past experience or acting according to social pressure, the return rate was substantially lower, about 20% in each condition.

Hornstein concludes that people are influenced not simply by a model's behavior, but by the motives attributed to the model. Presumably in the neutral condition they attributed positive motives to his intended prosocial act. It cannot be determined from the data whether the exercise of his own volition or the high standards of conduct that the model invoked, or both, were important in leading to the high rate of return of the wallets in some of the experimental groups.

The concept that people follow the example of a model as a function of the values that the model implicitly communicates has also been proposed by Epstein and Rakosky (1976). They discussed the possibility that the observation of aggressive models will lead to imitation when certain values are implicitly communicated in the course of modeling—that "aggression works, that admirable people engage in it, and that it defines the very essence of manliness." Although their findings were complicated, internal analyses showed that when a model who administered strong shocks to an "opponent" was perceived positively subjects imitated aggressive behavior to a significantly greater degree than when the model was perceived negatively.

In studies of children's donating, prosocial models may be perceived positively. Free choice and prosocial motivation were presumably attributed to the models. When normative statements were made by the models, the results were similar to those of Hornstein's "consistent with social pressure" condition. Appropriateness and consistency with societal expectations might have appeared to be the reasons for the model's behavior, rather than a desire to be generous in order to benefit the recipient or on account of important personal values.

In the studies by Bryan and Walbeck (1970a,b) the verbal communications to children stated the desirability of donating or not donating to other children. Following exposure to the model the children were left alone, to provide them with opportunities to donate when they believed that they were unobserved. The investigators in these and similar studies (Rosenhan & White, 1967; Harris, 1970) hoped to demonstrate that modeling does not simply make children adhere to demand characteristics communicated by the model, but affects their intrinsic desire to donate. The children played a game, won rewards, and had the opportunity to donate the rewards. Believing that they were unobserved, they presumably felt free not to donate. First, one may question to what extent the children felt "safe" in such a setting, whether their behavior was actually unaffected by concern about social evaluation and adult reactions. Second, because of the normative nature of the verbal statements, they may simply have assumed that the model donated in order to comply with social norms. They may have felt pushed to comply with the invoked norms themselves, but the verbal communication may not have made generosity appear more desirable. An alternative possibility is that children ignored the verbal communication that preached charity. In everyday life they must have heard many times that a certain form of behavior is "nice," "good," "desirable," and such statements might lose their power to exert influence.

Several studies have shown that when parents point out to children the consequences that their behavior might have for other people, as a primary means of socialization, this leads to the development of internalized moral values in the children (Hoffman & Saltztein, 1967) and to the tendency to show consideration toward other children and act helpfully in interaction with them (Hoffman, 1963; Hoffman & Saltztein, 1967; Hoffman, 1975c). This research and experiments that attempted to use such verbal communications to enhance children's tendencies to behave prosocially (Staub, 1971d; Staub & Fotta, 1978; Staub & Jancarino, 1975, in Staub, 1975b; Staub & Feinberg, 1977a; Staub, 1975a,b) are discussed in Volume 2 of this work. However, one study by Midlarsky and Bryan (1972) that used procedures somewhat similar to the other studies by Bryan will be considered here.

In this study an adult model played a game, won rewards, and either donated some of the rewards or kept them all, while administering verbal statements to the observing child. Then the child played the game and could donate his or her winnings. At a later time the child received rewards for participating and could again donate some of the rewards to needy children. In one modeling condition the model pointed out the positive consequences of donating for the recipient. In another condition the model pointed out both the material loss for himself and the possibility of negative consequences—embarrassment, discomfort from being helped—for the recipient. Prosocial exhortations significantly enhanced prosocial behavior in comparison to selfish exhortations, not only immediately after the exhortations but also on the delayed test of donations. An important problem with this study is the lack of a no-verbal-communication control group. Consequently, we do not know to what extent negative exhortation reduced sharing and/or positive exhortation enhanced sharing. As Rushton's (1975) study showed, statements that justify selfishness can reduce children's willingness to give up desirable possessions.

Verbal Communications That Specify Behavioral Rules

Grusec and Skubicki (1970) found that a verbal communication that directly instructed children to share enhanced subsequent donations made by girls who had previously interacted with a nurturant model, although it did not enhance donations by girls in other treatment groups and by boys. In another study, Grusec (1972) found stronger effects. Verbal communication by itself had an effect on young girls (7-year-olds) and on older boys and girls (11-year-olds) equal to the effect of modeling, and only among young boys did it have less effect than modeling. Grusec expected that verbal communication would affect the donations made by older children because they would have already learned the virtue of sharing and the norm of social responsibility, and therefore a simple verbal statement would be sufficient to induce sharing. Younger children have been found to share less than older ones, and often very little is shared (Handlon & Gross, 1959; Midlarsky & Bryan, 1967; Staub, 1973, Experiment 2), so Grusec did not expect that a verbal communication would induce sharing in this group.

The stronger than expected effect of verbalization might have been due to the nature of the adults' verbal statements. Same-sex models, who were supposed to play a game before the child did but were called away before they actually played the game, said, "Well, I guess they expect us to share our marbles. Probably that's what we'd better do. I guess if I have one out of every two, that would be fair. I hope I get a lot of 70s and 80s (scores that led to winning marbles) and then there would be a chance to share." This statement, rather than stating a normative ideal in an impersonal fashion (it is good to share), communicated a specific expectancy about behavior in that situation. Not only was the expectancy to share communicated, but a rule for the amount that seemed appropriate (fair) was also included. Thus, the children received highly specific guidance. The final statement by the model further implied that he or she would like to share, suggesting an expectation of positive internal (rather than external) consequences by the model. Children were admonished to follow a specific but worthy situational rule, not a general, often-preached ideal. These findings were replicated and extended by Rice and Grusec (1975).

White (1972) also found that modeling increased children's donations to a worthy cause. In addition, instructions by the model to donate in the model's presence resulted in substantial donating behavior. The children who had been told to donate also donated substantially more just after the modeling experience, once the model left, than children in other modeling conditions. Moreover, although the amount they donated on a delayed posttest decreased, it was not different from the amount that children who observed a model without receiving such instructions donated (contrary to White's interpretation of these data); in the latter group, children donated about the same amount on the immediate and delayed posttests.

In another study White and Burnam (1975), with fourth- and fifth-grade girls as subjects, examined the effects of models donating differing percentages of their winnings, as well as the effects of "permissive" and "constraining" instructions, on children's donations to needy orphans in Tucson, Arizona. At first the opportunity to play a game and to donate winnings was public; the model was still present. Then the children played the game privately and again had the opportunity to donate. Modeling had a significant effect when the donations were public and had complicated interaction effects with grade and instructions when donations were private; no meaningful conclusions can be drawn about the effects of different percentages having been donated. Constraining instructions resulted in significantly more donations under both conditions. The permissive instructions consisted of telling children that they could donate but did not have to, whereas the constraining instructions consisted of a specific demand to donate: "What I'd like you to do is to give some of the pennies you win to them each time you win five." Of substantial importance is the result of covariance analysis. When the amount that children donated under private conditions was adjusted for the amount they donated the first time, under public conditions, the only significant effect that remained was for grade level, with older children donating more than younger ones. Children who had responsibility focused on them to donate by the constraining instructions, the exposure to the model, and the surveillance that they experienced later continued to be affected by the conditions that induced their original prosocial behavior. They were probably also affected by the fact that they behaved generously when they first had the opportunity to do so. When I consider the development of a tendency to behave prosocially, in Volume 2, I present arguments that focusing responsibility on children to behave prosocially and having them actually engage in prosocial behavior are important sources of learning to be prosocial.

Poulos and Liebert (1972) attempted to differentiate the influences of modeling, verbalization, and surveillance by adults on children's willingness to donate rewards. They assumed that all three influences would enhance sharing because of the information inherent in them: Modeling and verbalization would inform children about the appropriateness of donating and surveillance would suggest immediate consequences of the behavior. Second- and third-grade girls could win tokens (for correct answers on a task) that could be exchanged for prizes. They were told that they could donate tokens to children at another school who would not have the opportunity to play. Verbalization—an adult saying, "I think it would be good to give some tokens"—significantly enhanced children's donations. Modeling—the children observing the adult share four tokens and say, "I think I will give four"—significantly interacted with verbalization. The children who were exposed to neither modeling nor verbalization shared less than children who were exposed to either or both. Surveillance—the adult remaining in the room with the children—significantly interacted with verbalization. When the adult remained in the room after telling the children that it would be good to share, children shared significantly more than in the other three conditions. Furthermore, the effects of modeling and surveillance were additive. When exposed to both, children donated more than the combined amount in the modeling–no surveillance and surveillance–no modeling groups. Presumably due to their nature, both modeling and the verbal statement by the adult appeared to define appropriate behavior in the experimental situation. Children were exposed to a specific act of the model underlined by an accompanying verbal description of the act, or to a brief, specific verbal statement promoting donations in that specific situation.

It is of substantial interest, I believe, that only when either the action or the words of the model set a standard did surveillance by the adult increase children's donations. As I suggested in Chapter 3, given a person's knowledge of certain societal norms, the presence of other people would be expected to increase that person's adherence to them. The specific expectations of another person also affect behavior. In the Poulos and Liebert (1972) study, when the adult's words or actions specifically indicated that the adult believed in a prosocial norm and specified relevant expectations, children acted accordingly. Fouts (1972) also found that the presence of an "audience," an adult experimenter, did not itself increase the work done by 10- and 11-year-old children, who by pulling a lever caused a penny to drop into a box. All the money in the box was to be used to "send food to the poor, starving children in Africa and China."

There is an additional element to consider. In most of the studies with children that have been reviewed, the subjects played a game or worked on a task and *won* rewards. Then they had an opportunity to share the rewards with, or donate the rewards to, other children. I have proposed (Staub, 1968, 1973) that children's willingness to share rewards will be reduced when they feel that they have earned and thus deserved them, when they feel that they have a legitimate and socially respected claim to them. Such a belief is, of course, applicable to adults, but it might exert its greatest influence on young children who have not yet learned to place a high value on sharing with others. This conception is supported by equity considerations, and by the just-world hypothesis and research generated by it (Long & Lerner, 1974). Having earned and thus believing that they deserve the rewards might also explain why children often share or donate very little in control groups in which the opportunity to donate is mentioned but no additional social influence is exerted.

I hope that the presentation of these data and the surrounding discussion imply to others, as they do to me, that the effect of verbal influences depends on their content or nature, among other things. Clear communication of an expectancy and a behavioral rule may lead children to conform to the demands of the situation, possibly to follow the rule for extrinsic reasons, to gain approval and avoid disapproval. Having acted prosocially is, however, likely to increase later prosocial behavior (see Volume 2). Beyond specifying behavioral rules, verbal communications can make it appear desirable to donate for intrinsic reasons. For example, Grusec's (1972) model expressed the hope that sharing would be possible and thereby placed a value on it.

The Effects of Vicarious Reinforcement

An important reason for the influence of models on observers' behavior is assumed to be that a model's example affects the observers' expectations about the consequences prosocial behavior would have for them. Recent theory does not assume or imply, as early theorizing did, that positive consequences of prosocial behavior have to be material or external (brought about by other people). Rather, it clearly acknowledges the possibility that modeling might enhance the expectation of self-reward of different kinds (Masters & Mokros, 1974; Bandura, 1977). The actions of a model who engages in a behavior that involves self-sacrifice might by themselves imply that some reward can be expected. A number of experiments, furthermore, have explored the consequences of various types of vicarious reinforcements on subsequent imitation.

In many studies of donating behavior in children, observing a model enhanced donating by children, but observing a model who was reinforced for donating did not result in any additional increment in subjects' donations (Harris, 1968; Elliott & Vasta, 1970; Presbie & Coiteux, 1971). Harris (1968) found no difference between the behavior of children who saw a model receive praise for her prosocial behavior and the behavior of children who observed a model who was not praised. The children may have had no reason to expect external reinforcement themselves, because the person who praised the model was absent when the children donated. Prosocial behavior does seem to increase, however, when a model experiences reinforcement that places a value on or suggests intrinsic satisfaction with acting prosocially. Elliott and Vasta (1970) had children observe a prosocial model and a model who received reinforcement for donating. In a third condition the children observed a model who was reinforced with an explanation of the reinforcement to the effect that someone who donates is a good person. Modeling with reinforcement and explanation resulted in more sharing behavior than either modeling alone or modeling with reinforcement, which did not differ.

Some studies explored the effects of affective self-reinforcement by models. Midlarsky and Bryan (1972) used both contingent self-reinforcement, in which the model reinforced herself on donating, and noncontingent self-reinforcement, in which the model reinforced herself on winning trials on a bowling game before donating. In the contingent modeling condition the model would say, for example, "It feels good to give money. Giving to the poor makes me feel good. I like to give money." In the noncontingent affect condition the model would make such statements as, "I won. Wow. I won again. This is a great game." The model's effectiveness increased when she appeared to experience positive affect upon donating. A greedy model's effect in decreasing sharing behavior was also enhanced by expressing positive affect on keeping rewards. Affect statements by the model amplified the effect of modeling: the intrinsic consequences to the model affected observers' behavior. In another study Bryan (1971) found that the expression of positive affect by a model, particularly immediately upon donating rather than after some time, significantly increased donating by first- and second-grade children.

Hornstein (1970) had similar and dissimilar models experience varied feelings about returning a lost wallet. The similar model left a letter, written in perfect English, in the wallet. The dissimilar model wrote, in broken English, that he was a "visitor to this country." Of those subjects who read a letter by the similar model expressing either positive feelings or no feelings about returning the wallet, 60% returned the wallet. Expressing negative affect substantially reduced this kind of helping behavior. When a similar model does not enjoy a prosocial act observers are less likely to engage in the behavior. The prosocial example of a dissimilar model was followed *less* when he expressed positive affect or no affect, and resulted in somewhat more prosocial behavior when he expressed negative affect. The last findings might further support the previously suggested phenomenon that the counternormative behavior (or motives) of one person may increase the normative behavior of others. It also suggests that this phenomenon is more likely to occur when someone who does not act (or feel) as he ought to, or acts as he ought not, is perceived as different from oneself. People may try to distance themselves from those whom they perceive as dissimilar and/or perhaps unattractive (which might often be related) by acting differently.

Summary of Modeling and Verbalization Influences

I have reviewed some of the research that explored the influence on children and adults of observing models' behavior; of knowing why the models behaved as they did; of hearing models make verbal statements that specified situational rules the models had adopted, that referred to societal ideals, that indicated the consequences of the behavior for the recipients of prosocial acts, or that pointed out the affective consequences for the models. Sometimes the models' verbal statements specified or implied the reasons for their behavior, the intentions or motives underlying it. Observers' perceptions of these intentions or motives may be a primary determinant of the model's influence on observers' behavior. Although any generalization from this research has to be tentative, one might conclude that alerting a person to expectations by an adult or to a behavioral rule, or to the value of the behavior for the recipient or for the actor, is more effective than implying that one should follow general societal dictates. Moreover, similarity to or difference from the model may determine whether an observer will identify with the model, which in turn can determine the meaning of the model's behavior. External reinforcement given to a model might not increase children's willingness to sacrifice possessions that they value because they make a reasonable discrimination—if the person who provided the reward is not present, they cannot expect to be rewarded themselves. Affective self-reinforcement by models does not have this limitation.

I have discussed findings of many studies on the influence of modeling and verbalization, ignoring certain differences that might have modified that influence. First, one cannot assume that behavior and verbalization by a model will affect children and adults equally and/or that the processes by which the influence of the model's behavior and verbalization are exerted will be identical. However, the existing research indicates that there are important similarities; no research identifies differences. Furthermore, the recipients of prosocial behavior, together with the nature of their needs, were varied in the studies. In studying children's donations, for example, the would-be recipients included the March of Dimes (Bryan), children at another school who would not be able to play the game and win rewards (Poulos & Liebert), poor children for whom toys would be bought from donations (Grusec), and orphans. The particular objects that were to be donated included marbles, tokens, and gift certificates. The subjects probably had varied feelings about particular recipients. What are the conceptions of children about the March of Dimes or about poor children? How do children feel about other children who are needy, in contrast to children whose status is similar to their own but who simply lack the opportunity to win rewards? Many and contradictory hypotheses might be made about the influence of such factors on children's sharing and donating, and empirical research that explores their influence would be useful. To the extent that children donate for internal rather than completely external reasons, the range of applicability of their prosocial values, which would be a function of their perception of and feelings about potential recipients, would influence their behavior.

Another potentially important source of variation in the effectiveness of verbal communication should be considered. Most of us are aware that, in everyday life, the way somebody makes a request or suggests the desirability of certain forms of action to us substantially affects our reactions, regardless of the merit of the case. The exact words that are used in experimental studies and the degree to which verbal communications have a true-to-life quality, are likely to affect how seriously the messages are taken. Certain appeals evoke humanitarian reactions in us, concern about other people, whereas others seem false, or sound like slogans. Clear-cut statements of expectations, and perhaps statements that point to the human consequences of our actions, might have less of the latter quality and may be more effective.

Reactance and Prosocial Behavior

I have already suggested that prosocial behavior is likely to be decreased by psychological reactance, an oppositional tendency created by the desire to maintain or reestablish one's freedom of action or to eliminate any threat to freedom. Although any strong force exerted on a person may result in psychological reactance, prosocial behavior, because of its very nature, may be particularly sensitive to the arousal of reactance. On the one hand, prosocial behavior often demands self-sacrifice, and a person's inclination to promote his self-interest and satisfy his own needs could lead to resistance to donating or sharing possessions, or to helping others. Given an already existing resistance, social forces that attempt to influence behavior in a manner that makes people feel that their freedom of choice is diminished might be particularly likely to arouse reactance. In addition,

> morally relevant behaviors carry the implication of ought and ought not. When through verbal or other means the desirability of such behavior is communicated, automatically cultural norms and standards that make such behavior obligatory are invoked, thus limiting behavioral freedom and producing reactance. The nature of an influence attempt may determine whether and to what extent this will happen [Staub, 1975a, p. 11].

There was relatively little discussion of reactance in Chapter 3, when emergency studies were considered. This is partly due to the nature of the experimental treatments, which were less likely to induce resistance. People were not told to help, but were usually exposed to cues indicating the presence of a person who seemed to need help. Presenting a person with a suddenly emerging, usually serious physical need of another person is probably less likely to create reactance than the primarily verbal stimuli for help used in the studies reviewed in this chapter. Moreover, in an emergency the obligation to help that is imposed by moral norms is so strong that most people may not question it once the situation is adequately defined for them. Part of the reason for this may be that in comparing their own state of well-being with that of the person in need, the discrepancy is usually substantial. Therefore, they may feel less imposition due to the need for self-sacrifice. Strong psychological distress may evoke reactance, particularly in a continuous relationship if one party frequently experiences distress and thereby demands the attention of the other. However, the research in Chapter 3 dealt with sudden events, when the people in need and those in a position to help were strangers.

The concept of psychological reactance and the related concept of an oppositional tendency, which I use in discussing children's tendencies to act contrary to influence directed at them, may be rather widespread characteristics of people, particularly in our society. Apart from any genetically based inclination toward self-assertion, our society stresses individual freedom— freedom of choice and self-determination. For many people an important aspect of this is freedom from being influenced or dominated by other people. Just as people vary in their perceived locus of control, and in the importance of such control for them, they can be expected to vary in their desire to protect themselves from control by other people, and in their perceived capacity to do so.

Although reactance is probably a frequent inhibitor of helping behavior, the concept lends itself to overuse in explaining lack of helping behavior. I will try to inhibit my tendency to do this, even though I have regarded reactance for some time as an inhibitor of help and a psychological state that is likely to be produced by various, particularly powerful social-influence procedures (Staub, 1971d, 1975a,b; Staub & Feinberg, 1978). However, many other conditions and psychological processes can also inhibit helping. To return to the example about psychological distress among people in a continuous relationship (as well as in other cases when continuous or elaborate demands are placed on a helper), the expected cost of helping, which people might be unwilling to expend, has to be differentiated from psychological reactance created by the limitation of freedom due to extended sacrifices. Are they separable? Since it is very difficult to demonstrate that people actually experience reactance, to measure this psychological condition directly—and researchers have not attempted direct measurement—prior specification of conditions that would lead to reactance would increase confidence in a reactance interpretation. A measure of individual differences in the tendency to experience reactance would also be useful.

The different kinds of verbalization that were discussed are likely to induce reactance to different degrees. Invoking social norms might induce strong reactance, because the norms that are invoked have an obligatory character. Certain circumstances, in contrast—for example, children having earned their rewards—appear to grant freedom of action. Consequently, the obligation may be resented. On the other hand, when a particular situational rule is laid down, when the appropriate behavior is clearly defined, particularly for children, the issue of decisional freedom may not even arise for them, and its lack may not be resented.

A study conducted by Jones (1970) contains information relevant to the suggestion that under certain circumstances people do not feel that they have any decisional freedom and thus experience no reactance. Jones either gave subjects no choice about their participation in a second part of an experiment or presented the second part to them as optional. During the second part of the study, subjects were presented with someone's need for help and a request for help. When this person's dependence on the subject's help was high (he needed 250–300 people out of a subject pool of 700 to help him complete his dissertation research), subjects who had no choice helped him substantially more than those who were free to decide about participating. In the low-dependence condition (only 10–20 people were needed), subjects who had choice helped more. The findings are somewhat surprising, considering that the help was to be provided not during the second part of the experiment, to which the variation in choice to participate directly applied, but at a later time. Nonetheless, because the request was presented during the second part of the experiment, subjects may have experienced variation in their freedom to decide about helping the person who was dependent on them. If so, Jones's hypothesis can explain the results: When people do not feel free to refuse a request for aid, greater dependence results in more help, but when they do feel free to refuse, greater dependence increases the threat to their freedom and leads to reactance and to refusal to help.

The studies by Grusec (Grusec & Skubicki, 1970; Grusec, 1972) found that verbalizations are more likely to increase donations by girls than by boys. Differences in the effects of verbal statements on boys and girls, with the latter responding more to them, have also been found in studies attempting to influence other types of behavior (Staub, 1972b) or attitudes (Hovland & Janis, 1959). These differences may in turn be due to differences in reactance, as well as to other causes. Grusec (1972) found, for example, that boys paid less attention and remembered fewer statements than girls. Boys may usually be less "manageable" than girls; they may more frequently disobey verbal instructions and get away with it. As a result they may become less concerned about the consequences of not acting the way adults ask them to.

It is possible, however, that boys respond to verbal statements with more reactance and opposition than girls. This possibility is supported by the findings of research in which we attempted to explore the influence of inductive verbal communications combined with participation in prosocial activity on the later prosocial behavior of children (Feinberg & Staub, 1975). I shall review in Volume 2 this and related studies in detail, but one finding is relevant to this discussion. In one condition fifth- and sixth-grade boys who were making toys for poor, hospitalized children in two training sessions had the beneficial consequences of their activities for the recipients of the toys pointed out to them. These boys made very few additional toys when subsequently asked to do so in the days immediately following the treatment sessions; they made fewer toys than children in any other experimental group. However, those boys who were asked to make additional toys 10 days after the second training session expended substantially more effort in making toys, at least as much or more than boys in other experimental groups. The elaborate discussion of the positive consequences of the behavior may have created reactance, which dissipated over time. Girls, in contrast, responded positively to such verbal statements both when the posttest was immediate and when it was delayed. Furthermore, Bernstein (1975) provided an elaborate description to seventh-graders of the kinds of needs that poor, hospitalized children have. This elaborate description significantly reduced the number of puzzles the boys made for hospitalized children in comparison to a control group in which the description of the need was minimal.

Verbal Requests, Reactions to Helping, Self-Attribution, and Later Positive Behavior

Often people directly ask someone to provide help for themselves or for other people. Clearly the person making the request exerts social influence. Under what conditions and for what types of request will help be given? In this section the effects of prior help on later helping behavior and the consequences on later prosocial behavior of positive and negative feedback to a person who attempts to help (the effects of verbal reactions to help giving) are explored.

In a study by Langer and Abelson (1972) a female confederate asked subjects on the street to help her either because she had to catch a train or because she had to go shopping at Macy's. Not surprisingly, when the person had to catch a train she got more help. Clearly her need was greater. These writers categorized the request for help to catch the train as legitimate; the other request, as illegitimate. They hypothesized that making a legitimate request would result in more help if first the need were stated, and then the target person were focused on; making an illegitimate request, just the opposite would be true. Thus the confederate either said, "I'm really upset and distressed, would you please mail this package for me? I have to catch a train [go to Macy's]," or she started by saying, "Would you please do something for me?" The results supported the hypothesis. It may be that facing someone with a request or demand at the beginning of an interaction exerts greater social influence than a delayed request, and when the request is less legitimate, greater social influence is needed to gain compliance.

It is clear, of course, that most experimenters realize the potentially different effects of different wording of an appeal by a model or of a request by a person needing help. In fact, one of the problems with research on prosocial behavior (and in other domains) is that this important influence is usually a hidden one. The wording of communication to subjects—about general procedures, or about the central purpose of the study—may be one of the most important determinants of behavior, perhaps more important than the experimental treatments. Usually this is an unexplored influence.

Kriss, Indenbaum, and Tesch (1974) conducted a study using the "wrong-number technique"—a person is stranded on the highway with a broken-down car, and calls "Ralph's Garage" but gets the wrong number. The caller claims to have used his last dime and asks the subject to call the garage. Kriss *et al.* explored the influence of differences in how the request was made on helping behavior. Both a positive appeal and a simple request resulted in more helping than a negative request. People who made such a request in a slightly obnoxious manner ("Look, think how you would feel if you were in a similar position and you weren't helped. So please call my garage for me.") were more likely to be left stranded on the highway than those who made a straightforward request ("Would you please call my garage for me?"). A reactance explanation may be applicable, in that the negative request involved unnecessary arm-twisting. Alternatively, the somewhat obnoxious behavior may have led to dislike for the caller. The lack of a difference between a simple and a positive request is reminiscent of the lack of difference in the effects of neutral and positive models (Hornstein, 1970).

Several studies explored the effects of varied verbal reactions to a helpful act or lack of it on people's willingness to do something prosocial later. Kraut (1973) examined the effects of labeling people as charitable or uncharitable. A confederate collected money for a charity at the subjects' homes. Some people donated, others did not. Half the donors were told, "Thank you very much for doing this. You are a charitable person." The other half were told nothing. Half the nondonors were told that they were uncharitable, and the other half were told nothing. About 1–2 weeks later another confederate asked subjects to donate for another charity. Those donors who had been told that they were charitable donated significantly more. The nondonors who had been told that they were uncharitable donated somewhat less than the other nondonors. If the labels *charitable* and *uncharitable* functioned as positive reinforcement and punishment, respectively, nondonors should have donated more after being called uncharitable. Thus a reinforcement explanation cannot be applied to all the findings. An alternative form of reinforcement explanation may be, however, that labeling subjects as uncharitable made it aversive for them to have anything to do with people who collect for charities.

Bem's (1972) theory of self-perception offers a more comprehensive explanation. According to this theory people attribute characteristics to themselves on the basis of their own behavior. Thus, having acted charitably might lead people to think of themselves as charitable, this increasing the probability of later charitable behavior. When others label someone as charitable or uncharitable, that person may be more likely to make such self-attribution.

Changes in Self-Perception and Positive Behavior

Relevant to the self-perception explanation are research findings of studies using the "foot-in-the-door" technique (Freedman & Fraser, 1966). This is a technique in which a small request is made of people at one time, and then a larger request is made at a later time. People tend to comply with a small request, and subsequently cooperate with a second, larger request to a greater degree than control subjects who only receive the second request. Again, these findings may be interpreted in terms of self-attribution and self-perception. Having complied earlier, a person may think of himself as the kind of person who cooperates with requests. Since the first and second request are usually somewhat different in nature, and are made by different persons, explanations in terms of attitudes that develop toward the kind of favor that is asked or the person who asks them do not seem appropriate.

Several studies replicated the foot-in-the-door effect in varied contexts (Pliner *et al.*, 1974; Lepper, 1973; Snyder & Cunningham, 1975; Uranowitz, 1975). Snyder and Cunningham (1975) argued that if the self-perception interpretation were correct not only would people who complied with a small request later comply with a larger one, but people who refused a large request would define themselves as noncompliers and later refuse a smaller request. They asked people in one condition to respond to 8 questions in a telephone interview, a small request that usually led to compliance. In another condition they asked subjects to respond to 50 questions, a large request that usually led to noncompliance. At a later time subjects in both these groups, and in a third no-initial-request group, were asked to respond to 30 questions sponsored by a different public service organization. Subjects in the small-initial-request group showed a higher rate of compliance and those in the large-initial-request group showed a lower rate of compliance than those who received no initial request. Thus, the findings supported self-perception theory. The questions were not really asked, however; if the subjects agreed, they were told that at this time the interviewer was lining up people for the survey, which would take place at a later date. The large-initial-request subjects, since they tended to refuse the request, did not find out that no interview was to have taken place at the time of the request.

Cialdini and his associates (1975) reasoned that the refusal of a large request should enhance compliance when the same person makes a second, smaller request. They reasoned that mutual concessions are crucial for people to be able to continue working together toward common goals. They proposed that a principle or norm of "reciprocation of concessions" exists, which would lead a person to respond positively to the concession represented by the lessened demand. In their study, making a large request (for example, to counsel young juvenile delinquents for at least a 2-year period —which was always refused) resulted in greater compliance with a second, smaller request (to take a group of delinquents on a 2-hour trip to the zoo) than making only the smaller request. Although Snyder and Cunningham (1975) found that refusal of a large request decreased the likelihood of agreement with a smaller request, and Cialdini *et al.* found the opposite, these findings do not conflict. In the Cialdini *et al.* study the same person made both requests, one after the other. The "concession" he made by making a substantially reduced second request may have led to the compliance. To state this another way, one may reason that saying no to a direct request is difficult for most people. Having done so, saying no to another and in this case milder request is even more difficult. Refusal of a request is a self-assertive act. It may bring disapproval, dislike, even abuse.

Other studies also found that performing one helpful act increased the likelihood of another being performed (Harris, 1972; Uranowitz, 1975). Uranowitz reasoned that this would only happen if the conditions under which the first helpful act took place allowed self-attribution of the reasons for the behavior. When the external pressure that operates on a person is strong, so that the helping behavior is attributed to external factors, prior help will not increase later help. Uranowitz had a male confederate, who carried five grocery bags, approach a woman walking out of a shopping center department store and ask her to watch his bags. He either told her, in an agitated manner, that he wanted to retrieve his lost wallet, which had a "lot of money" in it (high justification), or he said calmly that he wanted to retrieve a lost dollar (low justification). Every person who was asked agreed to watch the bags. Later, further down the street, a female confederate carrying a large grocery bag and a "small, flat bag" dropped the latter. Subjects in the low-justification condition, which presumably allowed greater self-attribution of the reasons for the first helping act, helped this person significantly more than subjects in the high-justification condition or control subjects who had not been exposed to the first opportunity to help. The last two groups did not differ in their helping behavior. (An alternative explanation may be that treatments affected subjects' perceptions of the benefits that resulted from their behavior, and this affected their subsequent behavior.)

People who act prosocially once appear more likely to do so again. This was also shown by studies that I discussed earlier, which showed that children who were led to donate rewards one time were more likely to do so another time (White, 1972; White & Burnham, 1975). A broadly conceived self-perception explanation seems reasonable. However, the findings do not allow specification of the kind of cognitive and affective changes that result. Instead of perceiving themselves as more helpful or cooperative with requests, having helped someone may lead people to perceive helping as more valuable or the consequences of helping others as more beneficial. Because helping behavior is socially valued and most people appear to regard it as desirable, having helped another person may lead to feelings of satisfaction, enhanced self-esteem, and in turn to the anticipation of future satisfactions from helping people. In my view, these cognitive and emotional changes are interrelated, and some or all of them may follow a helpful act. In Volume 2, I discuss participation in prosocial behavior as an important method of the socialization of prosocial behavior, as a form of "natural socialization" where the experience of some activity itself results in certain kinds of learning or development. Consistent with cognitive-dissonance theory, the findings suggest that when less force is exerted on a person in inducing helping behavior, self-attribution and subsequent behavior change is more likely than when greater force is exerted.

Although changes in self-perception and in perception of the meaning and value of an activity or its outcome seem a reasonable explanation of how people change as a result of having behaved in a certain way, an apparent contradiction needs to be considered. Jones and Nisbett's (1971) proposition that actors regard the circumstances as the cause of their behavior whereas observers consider the actor's personal characteristics as the cause of the actor's behavior has received experimental support. If actors consider the situation as the cause of their behavior, changes in self-perception should be limited. However, the issue is complex. A person may think, "I acted generously because that poor person really needed what I had," seemingly a situational attribution. This attribution may, however, sensitize the actor to others' needs, increase the actor's later prosocial acts, and ultimately change the actor's self-perception. This sequence is more likely to occur, however, following repeated and/or more extensive engagement in prosocial behavior than what people engaged in for most of the experimental research I have described. The effects of more extensive participation in prosocial behavior are discussed in Volume 2.

There is evidence that both circumstances and personality affect self-attribution; the conditions under which change in self-perception and later behavior does or does not occur must be further specified. The findings of a study by Taylor (1975) indicate that people use information to change their preferences only under certain conditions. Women who rated the attractiveness of pictures of men overheard information about their physiological reactions to pictures. In some cases they were made to believe that their physiological reactions were consistent with their initial ratings of the pictures—for example, that their physiological reactions were strong in response to the picture of the man whom they rated as attractive. In other cases their reactions were said to be somewhat inconsistent—for example, strong in response to the picture of the man originally rated as moderately attractive. Inconsistent feedback enhanced the ratings of attractiveness of the moderately rated man, but only when no future meeting was expected with the man. When their attitudes had practical consequences, when the women could determine which men were to be invited to a future meeting, feedback about physiological reactions that was inconsistent with the original attitude did not affect subsequent ratings of attractiveness. In this condition, the women apparently engaged in more extensive consideration of their preferences and disregarded information communicated to them about their arousal. The extent to which people use their own behavior as a basis for self-perception or self-attribution is also a function of personality. Snyder and Tanke (1976) found that individuals who usually monitored their own behavior more considered the influence of a situation on their behavior to a greater degree and were less likely to accept behavior that was contrary to their true attitudes as representative of their attitudes. For such persons, there was no correlation between the degree of the "counterattitudinal" behavior induced in the experiment and their final attitude. For low-self-monitoring persons, this relationship was high and positive, suggesting that they used their behavior as a source of information about their attitudes. The circumstances that lead people to engage in some behavior, and personality, are likely to act jointly to determine self-attribution.

Additional evidence relevant to the influence of self-attribution has been provided by experiments that showed that children are affected by the characteristics attributed to them, that they behave consistently with the attributed characteristics. Jensen and Moore (1977) had pairs of 7- to 12-year-old boys who had learning and behavior problems work on a tower-building task. Previously each member of the pair was told either that he was a cooperative person or that he was a "winner" who could get things done and be the best at the things he did. Cooperative attributions led to substantially more cooperative behavior on the building task than competitive attributions. Unfortunately, without a control group, we do not know to what extent each of the two types of information affected the boys' behavior. Miller, Brickman, and Bolen (1975) found that telling fifth-grade children once a day for 8 days that they were neat and tidy people reduced their littering more, as measured both on the tenth day and 2 weeks later, then telling them that they should be neat and tidy and giving them reasons for it. Apparently the children accepted the information provided them by others about their characteristics, and they proceeded to act in ways consistent with this information.

Additional Studies of Reactions to Help Giving
and Positive Behavior

How do reactions to one's prior help affect later helping behavior? Moss and Page (1972) had a confederate ask for directions and then give either positive or negative feedback to the person who was giving him directions. In a control condition neutral feedback was given. Afterward another confederate dropped a bag in front of the subject and continued walking. Negative reaction to the prior attempt to help reduced helpfulness. The positive reaction did not increase help in comparison to the neutral condition. As the behavior of neutral helping models (Hornstein, 1970), a simple acknowledgment of a helping act may remind people of positive values and norms. Such acts may also be intrinsically reinforcing for most people and may lead to positive self-attribution.

However, we do not know how the behavior of people who did not have prior opportunity to help would have compared to the behavior of those who helped and received neutral or positive feedback. On the basis of varied findings reviewed in this chapter, participation in prosocial behavior can usually be expected to increase later prosocial behavior. I would sometimes expect, however, the opposite effect. When a prosocial act demands effort and is costly to the helper (which was not the case in Moss and Page's study), equity considerations may decrease the helper's willingness to help immediately afterward. People may consider own equity, and feel that they have already done their share and are not required to do more for others at that time. The degree of need associated with the second helping act, whether the recipients are the same or different, and other considerations may also enter into determining whether having helped before will increase or decrease helping immediately afterward.

Clark's (1975) subjects also provided help by giving directions, to a confederate, of course, and received positive or negative feedback (reward or punishment). Clark had no control group. Following this experience the subject passed by another confederate who was carrying a pile of books and dropped one without being aware of it. In a high-dependence condition the confederate was walking with the aid of crutches. Help was given significantly more frequently by those who had been reinforced, in comparison with those who had been punished. Without a control group, however, we do not know whether one increased helping, the other decreased helping, or both happened. High dependence resulted in significantly more help. People tended to help by picking up the book, except in the punishment, low-need condition where they were more likely to tell the confederate that he or she dropped the book. Those who were rebuked and thus embarrassed for their attempt to help may have wanted to limit their subsequent contact with other people. The help-reducing effect of prior negative reactions to one's attempts to help may best be accounted for by its effects on mood (see Chapter 6) and/or by concern about a repetition of the negative experience.

In another study that explored the effects of reward and punishment on prosocial behavior, Tipton and Browning (1972a) had a confederate drop groceries. People who helped were either thanked or rudely rebuked. Subjects in the control group were not exposed to the dropped groceries. Then the subject saw a person in a wheelchair who was unable to negotiate a curb. None of the subjects in the two experimental groups (all white females, 30 in each group) offered to aid the handicapped confederate; 36% of the subjects in the control group helped. Perhaps subjects who helped before and were reinforced felt that they had done their share; they had already spent whatever time they had available for helping others. This is a possibility, but the explanation seems incomplete. Subjects who were rebuked for attempting to help may have wanted to avoid the repetition of an aversive experience.

The research findings that have been reviewed so far have shown that small variations in the stimulus for help or in the surrounding conditions can substantially affect people's willingness to aid others. They also suggest that these variations may result in different perceptions and interpretations of the situation. In Tipton and Browning's study, special conditions may have operated that led to the extremely low frequency of helping the person in the wheelchair. Possibly people do not know how to relate to a handicapped person and therefore expect that the interaction would be awkward and aversive. Handicapped persons are stigmatized (Goffman, 1963) and perceived as different. This, combined with lack of experience with them, would make their reactions seem unpredictable.

An attempt to help may have also been judged inappropriate. An important reason for not offering help to the person in the wheelchair, and to people under other conditions of need, may be consideration for the feelings of the person in need. Subjects may have felt that the person in the wheelchair would want to feel self-sufficient. An offer of help would expose her condition of helplessness and might be unwelcome. This is particularly so in that a person in a wheelchair must have to face the problem of getting up on a curb many times. Having previously faced another person's need for help may increase sensitivity to people in need, thereby reducing the willingness to offer help that may be unneeded and unwelcome. Although these considerations are certain to apply in many helping situations, there is no independent evidence to show whether or not they apply to Tipton and Browning's study.

Unexpected findings—such as the low frequency of help and lack of reinforcement effect—make it imperative that investigators conduct additional research—to clarify the determinants of these findings. Otherwise, many pieces of puzzling data will accumulate. With our ingenuity as hypothesis-making organisms, we will fit them into patterns, but, all too likely, into empirically incorrect ones. With regard to the Tipton and Browning study it is even possible that the configuration of the person's characteristics and apparent need made no sense to the subjects—as in the Staub and Baer (1974) study described earlier—or that her apparent difficulty getting on the curb was not convincing. Either of these possibilities could be explored.

I have been discussing evidence that verbal communications exert social influence and often lead to positive behavior. But this does not always happen. The more direct a demand and the more forceful it is (given that the cost of refusal is not extremely high), the more likely people are to experience reactance and refuse to cooperate. Willis and Goethals (1973) conducted a study in which this seemed to happen. Male high-school seniors received a test to evaluate their degree of social responsibility. They were asked to bring a friend along because they might win a trip to California (from the East, where the study was conducted) for the two of them. The friend was asked to act as a confederate. In a second session, subjects were told that the test measured the true qualities of people and that their friend showed leadership abilities on the test but they themselves proved to be very submissive. They were told that it was good that the friend was along because if they were to go to California the other person would be able to direct them. Following this the subjects were exposed to several modeling conditions. There was a no-model control group. In an absent-model condition the friend–confederate was in another room, but the subject overheard him saying that if he won the trip he would be willing to give it up for the sake of poor children at an orphanage. In a model-present condition the friend also indicated that he would be willing to give up the trip. Finally, in a high-pressure-model condition the friend said to the subject: "I am willing to donate the trip, and you are going to do it too, right?" This last procedure significantly reduced subjects' willingness to sacrifice the trip. It seems reasonable to interpret this result in terms of psychological reactance. Certain conditions arouse the desire to assert one's freedom of action, and lead to resistance to pressure exerted by others.

Stimulus Influence

Degree of Dependence and Need

Many aspects of the stimulus situation surrounding some need for help may affect people's reactions to it. Sometimes these stimulus elements are not entirely separable from social-influence factors. How do variations in the *stimulus for help* affect helping?

Berkowitz and his associates proposed that there is a norm of social responsibility operating in our society that requires people to help those who are dependent for help upon them. In their view, the perception of dependence arouses feelings of responsibility for dependent others, and the outcome is a heightened instigation to help them achieve their goals (Berkowitz & Daniels, 1963, p. 630). Berkowitz (1972) contrasts this norm with the norm of reciprocity (Gouldner, 1960; Staub, 1972a). In his view the norm of social responsibility guides people to aid others without expectation of gain or reward, because it is the right thing to do. In contrast, the norm of reciprocity leads to helpfulness in expectation of self-gain, since benefits are expected to be reciprocated. It is questionable that the two norms are so sharply distinct. This issue is explored in Chapter 8.

Berkowitz and his associates conducted a number of experiments to explore how the degree of dependence for help affects behavior. The basic procedure of all these experiments was highly similar. Most of the subjects were introductory psychology students who participated in order to fulfill a course requirement. Subjects participated in pairs, and they were told that "the purpose of the experiment was to develop a test of supervisory ability based upon work samples." One member of the pair was the supervisor, whose task was to tell the other member (the worker) how to construct paper boxes. The two were to be in separate rooms, but the supervisor could communicate with the worker by means of notes. The experimenter pointed out that the written notes would provide a record of the supervisor's instructions that could later be scored (Berkowitz & Daniels, 1963). Actually, each member of the pair was assigned the role of the worker. The major and constant experimental treatment in the whole series of experiments was variation in the degree of the supervisor's dependence on the worker. The worker's task was to build paper boxes; all subjects were told that the supervisor would be evaluated on the basis of the notes sent to the worker. In the high-dependence condition, they were also told that the supervisor's evaluation depended on the worker's productivity, that is, the number of boxes made by the worker. In the low-dependence condition they were told that the supervisor's evaluation was not dependent on the worker's output, presumably because of great variation in the workers' ability. In some of these studies an additional variation was added; in the high-dependence condition the supervisor either did or did not have a chance to win a reward. This chance depended on the worker's productivity. The dependent measure was either the number of boxes that subjects made, or the difference between the number of boxes they made in a preexperimental practice period and the number they made after the experimental treatment was administered.

Several characteristics of the experimental situation are important to consider. First, a distinction should be made between *dependence* and *need*. The degree of dependence is the degree to which another person's help is necessary if someone is to achieve a goal, to bring about a desired outcome. The degree of dependence on a particular person is a function of how many people, in addition to this person, are in a position to provide help. Degree of need, in contrast, refers to the state of deficiency of the person who requires help, the greater the deficiency, the greater the need. A person might experience various degrees of deficiency in comparison to the normal or desirable condition of human beings. He might experience physical or psychological distress, or he might experience no need but is dependent on help to bring about personal gain, an improvement in his condition in comparison to some normal or usual state. Need and dependence frequently occur together, but they are not identical. In the studies by Berkowitz and his associates the degree of dependence of the supervisor is high in the high-dependence condition, because he needs the worker's help to bring about desirable outcomes and because the worker is the only person who can help him achieve those outcomes. However, the degree of need is low, since help would simply contribute to the personal gain of the supervisor, who experiences no deficiency.

Another aspect of these studies is that the cost of providing aid is low. The subject is present anyway; the only question is whether he will work a little faster or a little slower in making boxes.

These studies consistently showed that in high-dependence conditions the subjects worked harder and produced more boxes than in the low-dependence conditions (Berkowitz & Daniels, 1963; Daniels & Berkowitz, 1963; Berkowitz, 1972). Why? Did subjects feel an obligation to help someone who was dependent on them? Did they feel responsible? Or did they feel that it was expected of them to help, by the experimenter or by the supervisor, or by both? Did they act according to an internalized norm, or did they adhere to a social–situational norm for external reasons? Berkowitz and his associates believed that subjects were motivated by an internalized norm and not by concern about the social consequences of their behavior. They attempted to support this view by further experiments. In one study, when the subjects were told that the supervisor would find out about their productivity in the course of the experiment, they produced a greater number of boxes in the low-dependence condition than if they were told that the supervisor would find out about their productivity only a month or more later (low-awareness). However, variation in the supervisor's awareness of the worker's performance made no difference in their productivity with highly dependent supervisors (Berkowitz & Daniels, 1963, 1964).

The purpose of the awareness manipulation was to ascertain whether the subjects' behavior was due to the expectation of approval by their peer for having worked for him or to the fear of disapproval for not having helped when help was needed. Berkowitz (1972) concluded that concern about the supervisors' reactions was not the reason for subjects' greater productivity when the supervisor's dependence was great. To eliminate the possibility that the greater productivity in the high-dependence condition was due to the expectation of the experimenter's approval for doing what the subjects might have believed was the "right" thing, helping the person who was dependent on them, Berkowitz, Klanderman, and Harris (1964) conducted an experiment in which they varied how soon the experimenter would find out about the subject's performance. Subjects were told either that the experimenter would keep track of their performance during the session, or that they were to place the boxes they made in a closed carton that would not be opened until the end of the semester, a month later. Again, there was a highly significant effect of variation in dependence but not of the other experimental variables, which included sex of subjects and sex of experimenter. Although high dependence resulted in greater effort than low dependence, internal analyses suggested that when an experimenter of the same sex was immediately aware of the performance, productivity tended to be lower in the high-dependence condition in comparison to the other high-dependence group. Berkowitz (1972) suggested that subjects tended to resent the pressure imposed on them by the combination of "the dependency relation and the implied expectations of the same sex person who was, so to speak, looking over their shoulders [p. 10]." He suggested that psychological reactance may have operated, that the subjects resented pressures that decreased their psychological freedom. Here, again, this seems a reasonable explanation.

How convincingly do these findings support the conception that in the high-dependence condition the subjects' behavior was motivated by an internalized belief in responsibility to help dependent others rather than by concern about approval or disapproval by the supervisor or the experimenter? The communication about the high-dependence condition can be regarded as a strong social-influence procedure. Even for subjects who minimally valued helpfulness it was likely to invoke social norms that prescribe help for others. In conjunction with this, we need to consider that none of the subjects were told that neither the supervisor nor the experimenter would find out about their productivity right away. Therefore, subjects might have remained concerned that one of these individuals might know about and evaluate their behavior. It is reasonable to assume that in psychological experiments in general, and in these studies in particular, participants usually believe that their activities will be known to the experimenter and/or to the other participants. Thus, even if the subjects believed the low-awareness manipulations, a potential source of immediate disapproval or approval always remained. Moreover, even in the low-awareness conditions others would eventually find out about the subjects' behavior, although at a later time. Given the low cost of helping, if subjects are concerned about the evaluation of others, why should they not help?

That external rather than internal motivation was involved appears to receive support from further findings of Berkowitz and Daniels (1964). The scores of female college students on a questionnaire measure of social responsibility were positively related to their helping behavior, under both high and low dependence, only if they themselves received prior help. Otherwise the relationship between these scores, indicating a personal orientation toward social responsibility and helping behavior, was slightly negative under both low and high dependence. High dependence apparently did not activate the orientation toward social responsibility.

A further variable of interest to Daniels and Berkowitz (1963) was the worker's liking for the supervisor. They reasoned that in our society the concept of friendship implies an obligation to help a friend, and liked others may be reacted to as friends. They noted previous research findings showing that liking for others who are likely to gain by conformity to a norm tends to increase such conformity. This may also happen in the case of the social-responsibility norm. As expected, the authors found that a communication to the participants that they would probably like their partners because they were especially well-matched increased productivity of workers in a high-dependence condition, in comparison to the productivity of workers who were told that they might come to dislike their partners by the end of the experiment because they were very different from each other. These manipulations had little effect in the low-dependence condition. Semantic differential evaluation of the supervisor and responses on a questionnaire also indicated that the liking manipulation was successful. The manner in which the liking manipulation affected the subjects is unclear; it may have affected their sense of obligation, changed their concern about evaluation, varied their desire for friendship, or varied the degree to which they identified with the other person and adopted his goals. How the relationship between a potential helper and a recipient affects helping is discussed in detail in Chapter 7.

In one experiment by Berkowitz and Daniels (1963) a high-reward condition, in which the supervisor could win $5 if he received the highest rating as a supervisor, did not enhance productivity in comparison to a low-reward condition in which the supervisor with the highest rating would simply be informed of his rating. Should not the norm of social responsibility enhance attempts to help another student gain $5? Perhaps subjects thought that the chances of their supervisor gaining the highest rating was low, and they therefore did not try hard. More likely, an equity explanation applies; subjects were unwilling to work hard to produce what they might have regarded as an unearned benefit by the supervisor. The implications are important: Sometimes helping behavior might be lower when the benefit it would produce is greater. Support for this explanation is provided by responses to questionnaire items following the work period. In the high-dependence condition subjects tended to indicate that they missed having some personal incentive, such as a prize. In the low-partner-awareness subgroup subjects tended to express dissatisfaction with their supervisor. (They may have feared detection in the high-awareness subgroup.) Both responses indicate that subjects who worked for a highly dependent supervisor felt resentment

—with the experimental situation, the person they tried to help, or both. Nevertheless, they apparently attempted to help. Unfortunately, in the experiment that included variation in reward (Berkowitz & Daniels, 1963, Experiment 1) there were no relevant questionnaire data. If workers evaluated a $5 reward for the other person as a much greater gain than a good rating, their resentment may have been greater, inhibiting greater efforts.

The findings of Berkowitz and his associates clearly show that greater dependence leads to more helping, but their demonstration applies primarily to circumstances where the helper's behavior is actually or potentially public. The kind of need for help may be important. Enhancing a stranger's welfare when no need or deficiency exists may be resented. If so, the greater the benefit, and the more private the behavior, the less help may be forthcoming.

Sex Differences in Reactions to Dependence

Other investigators also explored how the degree of a person's dependence on help affects the willingness of others to help. Schopler and Bateson (1965) had a graduate student in psychology ask undergraduates to participate in his dissertation research. He was either desperate to finish, or he was not under time pressure. To the investigators' surprise, degree of dependence produced no significant difference in helping. However, a significant dependence by sex interaction was found; females helped more when the dependence was greater, but males responded to the request more when the dependence was small. (These and other authors often used the term *dependence* to refer to need; see the distinction suggested on pp. 226–227.)

In two other experiments Schopler and Bateson varied both the degree of dependence and the cost of helping, using a gamelike situation. The similarity between the way people behave in playing games and the way they behave in real-life settings can be small (see Chapter 9). A game might activate a variety of motives that are specific to game playing, such as the desire to play the game well, however that is defined by a participant, and the desire to make the game interesting. Depending on the characteristics of the game, a person may assume a helpful or competitive role, or some other role, which may only mildly correspond to the kind of role this person would assume in real life.

Schopler and Bateson found that when the cost of helping a partner was low, as in their first study, a dependence by sex interaction was found in the degree to which the partner was helped. This interaction was not found when the cost was high. According to Schopler and Bateson (1965), males are more concerned with maintaining a favorable outcome, in comparison to another person, than females, and that is the reason that males help less when another's dependence is greater. "Males will not conform to the social responsibility norm when such conformity threatens their status, in this instance, decreasing their chances of winning in order to help a partner win. Females, however, respond to the partner's dependence by conforming to the norm [p. 253]."

To explore the hypothesis that relative status advantage is more important for males and they are more likely to protect it than are females, Schopler (1967) conducted another experiment. Again, subjects participated in a gamelike task, in which they had the power to maximize their own monetary gain and the opportunity to sacrifice their gain in favor of their partner's. Following an initial period of playing the game, some received a note from the experimenter asking them to increase their partner's gain. Both males and females tended to yield to this request, a result that is not surprising. Others received a note from their partner ("I think you should give me more money"), which increased the helpfulness of females and reduced the helpfulness of males. Unfortunately, the male subjects who received the note from their partner were less helpful prior to receiving the note than subjects in the other experimental conditions, which raises the possibility that they differed in some personality characteristic. Moreover, we do not know to what extent these experimental treatments successfully varied status advantage.

Schopler again explained the findings as the result of the tendency of males to preserve status advantage. This explanation implies that when another's need or dependence is low, males do not see a status advantage, and since they have nothing to preserve they help more. This is a possible explanation, but not a well-substantiated one. By helping in a low-need condition, would not people create a status disadvantage for themselves? Does the need of another person by itself induce considerations of status? Maybe it would do so when another person, by receiving help, would gain undeserved rewards. In a relevant study McGuire and Thomas (1975) had children win rewards in a bowling game under circumstances that were made to seem competitive or not competitive. Children played the game in pairs. In the competition group, the child with the higher score always received a reward; one child had higher scores on some trials, the other had higher scores on other trials. In another group, children received rewards independently of their performance. Boys in the former condition shared substantially less of their rewards with a boy who performed much better on the game but did not get any rewards, in comparison to boys in other groups. Sharing with a boy who did as well as the subject or less well, sharing by boys who received a reward on each trial so that no competition and deserving was involved, and sharing by girls across all conditions were not significantly different. The authors suggest that doing less well than another boy under competitive conditions led boys to perceive a disadvantage, which diminished their sharing behavior.

In other studies Midlarsky and Midlarsky (1973, 1976) explored the influence of "achieved status," "ascribed status," and status inconsistency on males helping others by manipulating small objects for them and suffering the electric shocks that the other person would have received in the course of manipulating these objects. Both achieved status (information that the subjects were very good in dealing with electric shocks) and ascribed status (communications that praised their intelligence, astuteness, and capacities) increased subjects' help for the confederate. It is possible, in fact, that a sense of importance or status in relation to others increases the willingness to do good things for other people. Research directly relevant to this point is minimal, as yet. A great deal of research shows, however, that varied positive and negative experiences—which presumably affect mood, feelings about the self, and other internal conditions—affect subsequent prosocial behavior. The experimental treatments of Midlarsky and Midlarsky may have affected such internal states. Sometimes positive and negative experiences can lead to perceived differences in one's status relative to others, which then mediates the willingness to help. In Chapter 6, where this research is described, some of the differences between the self and others that result from positive and negative experiences are discussed in terms of their influence on the perception of relative well-being—"hedonic balancing," a very special form of status inequality.

The original findings of Schopler and his associates may be the result of greater sensitivity by males than females to limitations on their freedom, and of their greater concern with equity. A high degree of dependence, and particularly a direct request, would activate opposition in males. Males' greater concern with equity rather than equality, and their tendency to maximize their own equity in comparison to females, was shown in experiments that were reviewed in Chapter 4. In two of the Schopler and Bateson (1965) studies, the nature of the tasks may have led subjects to feel that their partner's greater dependence was due to less skill and/or ability which resulted in the partner's poorer performance. Thus, in the high-dependence condition they may have felt that it was more equitable to keep the "money" they had.

In another study Gruder and Cook (1971) varied the sex of the subject, the sex of the person who needed help, and the degree of dependence. When the participants appeared for a "class project" they found a note, instead of the experimenter. The note asked their help with collating and stapling a questionnaire; the material was needed immediately or a week later. The degree of dependence and the sex of the experimenter interacted in determining the subjects' reactions. Highly dependent females received more help than less dependent ones, and somewhat more help than highly dependent males. Males were helped more than females when dependence was low. A possible interpretation of these findings is that appearing highly dependent and requesting help is a culturally more appropriate role for females than for males. (At least this was so in the late 1960s, before the prime of the women's liberation movement.) In this study, males and females did not differ in the amount of help they gave to either highly dependent or less dependent experimenters. This suggests that only under some as yet unspecified conditions do sex differences exist in reaction to a partner's dependence. One condition may be when the other's need can be seen as the result of insufficient abilities that lead to poor performance. Alternatively, an explanation for many of the preceding findings may simply be that a highly dependent female is more likely to receive help, from subjects of either sex, than a highly dependent male. Since same-sex subject–recipient combinations were usually used, the result would be more help by females than by males for a highly dependent person.

Internal versus External Sources of Dependence

When another person needs help, the reason for his need may be an important determinant of willingness to help him. A person may need help because of circumstances beyond his control—accidents, other people's irresponsibility, and the like (externally caused need or dependence)—or because he acted unwisely, irresponsibly, or incompetently (internally caused need or dependence). In the latter instance, other people may diminish their feeling of responsibility to help or inhibit empathic reactions by various justifications. They may decide that since this person brought about his own need or dependence, he deserves the negative consequences that arise from it. They may even devalue this person, which makes it easier to forgo attempts to aid him. However, such help-inhibiting processes are likely to occur only with certain types of internal causation. In some instances, the fact that a problem was internally caused might even enhance the degree of perceived need and/or the concern about a person's welfare.

Schopler and Matthews (1965) attempted to vary the perception of a partner's dependence as either environmentally caused or the result of choice. Again in a gamelike situation, subjects who participated in "a study of partnerships" could provide their partners with letters of the alphabet. These were used in completing crossword puzzles that were rewarded with small amounts of money. When the locus of dependence was external, the partner could only complete his puzzles by requesting letters from the subject, who always had the role of the director. In the internal-locus-of-dependence condition the partners could get letters either by drawing them from a random pool or by requesting specific letters from the director. The partners chose to do the latter. In both conditions, out of 15 trials, 12 of the partners' requests were for letters that the subjects had used in completing their own crossword puzzles. Under these conditions the partners received more help (i.e., they were provided with more letters in response to their requests) when dependence was externally imposed on them.

The *degree* of dependence of the partner was not equal, however, in the two conditions. The externally dependent partner was completely dependent on the subject, whereas in the internal-locus condition the partner had another way of getting letters. As a result, subjects may have felt, when the dependence was internally caused, that their partner acted in a somewhat selfish manner, choosing to ask them to sacrifice their letters rather than taking his chances with the random pool.

In another study that found a difference in helping as a function of the reasons for a person's dependence, Berkowitz (1969) had subjects supervise two same-sex "workers." The supervisors were to write instructions for the workers and to supply any extra material they might need. They were also allowed to help with the workers' task (making paper pads), but the workers would not find out about their help. In one condition, one of the workers sent a note to the supervisor asking for help because the experimenter provided the wrong kind of paper and now, "I have fallen behind." In the other condition, a worker requested help because he took it easy during the first period and had fallen behind. In the former condition, where the source of dependence was presumably external, the supervisor provided more help than in the latter condition, where it was internal. The person who asked for help was liked less than the one who did not, and the internally dependent worker was liked less than the externally dependent one. Although women helped significantly more than men, they resented helping as much as men did. Berkowitz reasons that with an illegitimate demand it is easier to refuse a request that one does not really want to satisfy in the first place.

There was variation in the degree of the worker's dependence (low, moderate, high). When dependence was high there was a greater difference between the external and internal conditions; internally dependent workers received less help. It is possible that the reason for this was the supervisor's judgment of whether the internally dependent worker deserved to be helped and to have his chances of gaining a reward improved, relative to the other worker who did not ask for help. Someone who did not work hard may not deserve help to gain a reward. It would be unfair for such a person to win, in place of others.

Horowitz (1971) varied both whether subjects had a choice in giving help and the locus of dependence. Subjects either had to participate in a second experiment, in order to get credit, or could choose whether they would participate in the second experiment. A graduate student needed the subjects' help. When his dependence was externally caused, he was presented as someone who suddenly had to complete his dissertation because of a new development, his advisor leaving. He was described as a characteristically strong, independent person. In another condition, to make the dependence seem internally caused, this person was said to have planned poorly and underestimated the number of participants he needed. He was also presented as a dependent and weak person. The amount of time that subjects could volunteer to spend for his experiment (a sensory deprivation study) varied from none to 8 hours; this was the dependent measure. Subjects who had a choice helped more. A significant interaction was found between the effects of choice and the reason that help was needed. Contrary to expectations, when subjects could freely choose whether they would participate, they volunteered more help for the internally dependent person. When they had no choice, they volunteered more help for the externally dependent person. These findings do not support the assumption that when people's dependence or need is internally caused they will generally receive less help. Reactance may have operated. The significant effects of choice clearly suggest this. It also seems reasonable to assume that the need of the person who was a poor planner, dependent and weak, appeared greater than that of the highly capable person, who may be seen as someone who can overcome adverse circumstances. The greater need, based on the person's character and thus internally caused, led to more help when people were free to offer or to withhold help. When external constraints eliminated choice, the greater pressure exerted by such need may have increased reactance.

In a pilot study to explore reactions to a person's psychological distress, I varied the source of a female confederate's distress (Staub, 1969). The subject and the confederate were reading passages from short stories and attempting to evaluate the personality of characters described in the passages. The confederate, acting distraught, began to tell the subject about her car accident the day before. She was with a good friend, who had been injured and hospitalized. The confederate was the driver of the car, either responsible for the accident (having made a turn on a red light) or a victim of another driver who went through a red light and hit her. The confederate communicated a number of "units" of information. Interaction in the course of this communication and after it was determined by the subjects' responsiveness. There was no difference in subjects' responsiveness to the confederate, in the amount of verbal communication to her, as a function of her responsibility for the accident. In both distress conditions responsiveness was much greater than in a control condition in which the confederate started to talk about a movie that she had seen the day before. The damage that was created by the accident was identical in the two conditions. Presumably (although I have no data on this point), the confederate's perceived distress was also identical, since her distress focused on her girlfriend's injury. It is possible that when a person's distress, either psychological or physical, is relatively intense, people frequently disregard its source in responding to it. Could this be the case even when people are negatively evaluated because they brought about their misfortune by some unwise action? (See Stokols and Shopler, 1973; also Chapter 4, p. 160.)

In summary, contrary to conclusions by most writers on this issue (Krebs, 1970), internally caused need for help probably does not diminish helping under most circumstances. A distinction between internally caused need and internally caused dependence may be useful. In the latter a person intentionally creates circumstances under which another's help is needed to satisfy some need or reach a goal; also, the person may choose to rely on others' help when such help is not truly necessary. Such dependence can result in less help than dependence that is external in origin. When a person suffers distress or deprivation (i.e., experiences a genuine need), this is rarely seen as the result of choice. Therefore, the extent to which the need is internally or externally caused has less influence.

Additional Studies on How the Degree of Need and the Degree of Cost Influence Helping

On the whole, research findings indicate that the greater a person's need, the more likely others are to help. I noted earlier that when a person who was carrying a pile of books and dropped one was walking with crutches he received more help than one without crutches (Clark, 1975). In another study Bickman and Kamzan (1973) found that more female shoppers at a supermarket (58%) gave a dime to a female confederate who needed it to buy a carton of milk than to a confederate who wanted to buy a package of cookie dough (36%). Milk is a more important item.

Test and Bryan (1969) found that a person who had limited vision received more help on a task. Midlarsky (1971) found that males helped a man with a visual impairment to manipulate small objects, even though they received electric shocks when they touched these objects, to a greater degree than they helped a person who had no problem with his eyesight. However, greater cost, in the form of experiencing more intense electric shocks each time they touched an object, resulted in less help than smaller cost did.

Harris and Meyer (1973) had conservatively dressed males and females, in their late twenties, sit in a shopping mall with one of three signs. In the low-dependence condition, the sign simply asked for the signatures of passersby. In the medium-dependent condition, the sign requested signatures and noted that if 50 were collected the person would receive bonus points in a research methods course. In the high-dependence condition the sign announced that if the person collecting the signatures did not get 50 signatures he would fail a research methods course. In a low-threat condition people were asked to sign their name and write down their favorite color; in a high-threat condition they were asked to sign their name and provide their telephone number. More subjects signed their name in the high- than in the medium- or low-dependence condition, and the last two groups also differed. More signed in the low- than in the high-threat condition, but the difference was only significant for females. However, dependence and threat interacted so that in the high-dependence condition, high threat did not affect helping, but in the other two dependence conditions high threat was associated with less helping. The authors conceptualized threat as the possibility of future contact created by providing one's telephone number, a reasonable view. However, there is also an element of senselessness in the procedures, particularly in the low-dependence condition, where no reason at all was provided for collecting the signatures, and in the high-threat condition, where the reason for requesting the telephone number was not specified. The degree of responsiveness by passersby in the high-dependence, high-threat condition is somewhat surprising.

Harris and Meyer note that the increased help with increased dependence, particularly since it occurred under both low- and high-threat conditions, is not congruent with a reactance hypothesis, although the generally smaller frequency of help under high threat is congruent. The latter finding seems more relevant, however, to the effect of cost on helping. Many people would probably fear that providing their telephone number would lead to future, possibly unpleasant, contact. Moreover, the conditions employed in the study—no pressure was exerted and escape was relatively easy—may have minimized reactance. The absence of pressure allows other conditions, such as variation in need, to affect behavior. That it does so even under such unusual circumstances as these may show the power of the influence of need and dependence.

Findings that the age and sex of the person receiving help affect helping can sometimes be related to perceived variation in need. Tipton and Browning (1976) found that obese people received more help than thin people, and older people (50–60 years old) received more help than younger ones (20–30 years old), in picking up groceries they had dropped. Both differences may have been due to perceived need for help. In many situations females receive more help than males. This may be due to a variety of reasons, which have not yet been disentangled. Variation in perceived need may be one reason. For example, a female may be thought of as less capable of fixing a broken-down car than a male, and this may lead to more help for her (West *et al.*, 1975). It is probably a common stereotype that females are more helpless and fragile than males. Therefore, their need for help may be perceived as greater even under conditions where physical strength, skill, and competence are irrelevant. This may partly account for female hitchhikers being helped more than males (Morgan, 1973; Pomazal & Clore, 1973). Differences in threat to the driver and in male drivers' extrinsic motivation, such as their sexual interest, may also be involved.

In a study that examined the influences of modeling, degree of need for help, and cost of helping, the importance of how people perceive the nature and degree of another's need was shown (Wagner & Wheeler, 1969). Navy enlisted men engaged in a target-detection task. They were to transcribe signals communicated to them from an adjoining room through an intercom by another subject who was actually a confederate. The participants overheard someone entering the adjoining room and soliciting a donation from the confederate. Subsequently this person solicited donations from the subject. Surprisingly, the subjects did not donate more money to help the parents and two sisters of a dying Navy man fly to his bedside (high need) than to build up the reserve of the local servicemen's fund (low need). When the confederate in the adjoining room acted as a generous model, donating $20, the subjects themselves were more generous. When the confederate was selfish and donated nothing, the subjects were more selfish than those in a control group. Low cost, when donations were to be deducted from paychecks, $1 a month, led to more donations than high cost, when the donations were to be deducted all at once. There was a model by cost interaction, that is, substantial modeling effects under low cost, but no significant effects under high cost.

These investigators found the lack of any influence of need perplexing, and proceeded to a more detailed analysis of their data. They found a significant difference in the way the generous and selfish models were described by the subjects under high and low need. For example, the generous model was described on the postexperimental questionnaire as a "nice, generous guy" under high need, but as "very easily influenced" under low need. The authors proceeded to define certain descriptions as indicating that the need was perceived as valid, others as indicating that it was perceived as invalid. A chi-square analysis showed that the need was perceived as valid significantly more often in the high-need condition than in the low-need condition. The amount that was donated under valid need was significantly greater than the amount that was donated under invalid need. The authors concluded that "objective manipulation of need (Hi–Lo) was not predictive of helping behavior because it was imperfectly, although significantly, related to subjectively perceived need (Val–InVal) which was the more proximate determinant of helping [Wagner & Wheeler, 1969, p. 114]."

This kind of analysis and the conclusions suggested are of substantial importance. They point to individual differences in the perception of a situation and its resulting influence. However, the empirical findings are only tentatively suggestive of the conclusions. Presumably, "valid need" was related to generosity partly because people who donated would want to judge and present their behavior as reasonable; consequently they indicated on a questionnaire administered to them later that they donated in response to a valid need. That is, the subjects' behavior was likely to be an influence on subsequent evaluations.

Additional analyses showed a significant difference in the perception of need as valid or invalid as a function of exposure to generous and selfish models. The authors argue that this was not due to rationalization, since the relationship between variation in cost and perceived validity of the need was not strong, even though it could be expected if subjects rationalized their behavior. They conclude that "models may influence the helping behavior of prospective donors by increasing perceived need validity through generous behavior and by decreasing perceived need validity through selfish behavior [Wagner & Wheeler, 1969, p. 115]."

Overall, the findings show that people usually respond more to greater need and/or dependence, but there are surprising exceptions. Pomazal and Clore (1973) varied the apparent need of hitchhikers. In one condition the hitchhiker wore both a knee brace and an arm sling. Only 16 of 100 drivers offered a ride to the disabled hitchhiker, in contrast to 34 of 100 drivers offering help to the physically sound hitchhiker. This is somewhat reminiscent of the very low frequency of help for the person in the wheelchair (Tipton & Browning, 1972a), and for our healthy-looking confederate who appeared to have a heart problem (Staub & Baer, 1974). In each case, one can argue that some form of cost decreased helping behavior. It is an oversimplification, however, to consider the many and varied forms of cost as if they had the same meaning or even the same effects. Discrepancies between stimulus characteristics representing need and other stimulus elements may reduce helping (Staub & Baer, 1974). It is difficult to know, without data, whether such discrepancies were present in these studies. Another possibility is that, as Bar-Tel (1966) suggests, in the Pomazal and Clore study "drivers probably considered it too costly to take the physically disabled hitchhiker, who might cause some inconvenience [p. 73]." A cost effect with several components may have operated. Part of it would be the greater effort and inconvenience involved having a disabled person get in and out of the car. Drivers may also weigh the difficulty of dropping such a person off as his destination and their own destination diverge; his condition may create an obligation to give him a ride all the way. Another important aspect of cost may have been the discomfort people experience in interacting with a person who has an unusual condition, a stigma. Being in a wheelchair, wearing a knee brace, having a disfiguring birthmark on one's face (Piliavin *et al.*, 1975) are such conditions.

The recurring uncertainty about the proper interpretation of findings points to the need to explore cognitive and affective consequences as well as the behavioral consequences of stimulus conditions to which people are exposed.

In summary, it appears that, with an increase in need, helping behavior increases. Exceptions exist, however. Sometimes need does not enhance helping, seemingly when either the need appears very great or when the person in need has some unusual characteristics that make association with that person uncomfortable, or when a combination of these two factors operate (Wagner & Wheeler, 1969; Pomazal & Clore, 1973; Staub & Baer, 1974; Tipton & Browning, 1972a). One reason for great need sometimes not resulting in great help is the associated greater cost of helping, either actual cost or the expected difficulty in relating to or being with a very needy person. Greater dependence, as greater need, is also usually associated with more help, although a sex difference exists. Women, who appear more equalitarian, respond more to greater than to lesser dependence. Men, perhaps because of their needs for status or power, but possibly because they perceive someone who is more dependent as less deserving than they themselves and because greater dependence exerts greater pressure on them and activates reactance, respond less to greater than to lesser dependence. This was found, however, in the laboratory, often under gamelike conditions, when the degree of need—distress, deficiency, and so on—of the person dependent on help was not great.

The available research findings show that helping behavior is reduced as the costs of helping increase. The experiments of Schopler and Bateson (1965) and Wagner and Wheeler (1969), which were reviewed earlier, included variation in costs that affected helping. Midlarsky and Midlarsky (1973) showed that the greater the sacrifice demanded, the less willing people were to help. Male subjects who received more intense shocks when they helped another person manipulate small objects in a manual dexterity task helped less than those who received less intense shocks. People who were asked to come to the university to spend 20 minutes filling out a questionnaire agreed less frequently (49%) than people who could fill out the questionnaire at home and return it in a stamped, self-addressed envelope (81%). Aversive conditions were also found to reduce helpfulness. For example, a very loud lawnmower reduced help by passersby for a person who dropped some books from the top of two boxes of books he was carrying (Mathews & Canon, 1975). The authors argue that this was not a cost effect, since in their laboratory study subjects who were working in a room were less likely to help a person pick up papers and books when there were increased levels of noise in the room, even though subjects could not diminish their discomfort by leaving the scene. Both the possibility that noise reduced attention to peripheral cues, "that is, those not related to central ongoing activities and concerns [p. 575]," and the desire to escape from the unpleasant experience may have been at work in the field study, however, where the level of noise was substantial, much greater than in the laboratory. Another important aspect of this study was a need by noise level interaction. The nature of this was as follows: A confederate who wore a cast on one arm from wrist to shoulder was helped more than an unencumbered confederate; however, although normal conditions produced substantially more help for the confederate who wore the cast, the unpleasant noise led to low frequencies of help regardless of the confederate's condition. The incident took place when the subject was about 6 feet from the confederate and was moving in his direction. Loud noise and other stressors would not affect what people see, but might affect either the manner in which they process the stimulus or what they decide to do about it. The effects of negative experiences on helping are considered in Chapter 6.

Although costs reduce helping, the limits of their influence are not known. For example, will variation in relatively minor costs affect helping even if the need is great? What differences in personality lead to more or less sensitivity to costs? How much effort, energy, time, emotional burden, physical pain or danger, or material goods do people think is reasonable to expend for others? How much do they believe is expected of them, and how much do they expect of themselves? How does this amount vary as a function of others' needs, people's relationship to the person in need, their own state of well-being, their moods, as well as their values and beliefs? The influence of another type of cost, interference with the satisfaction of personal goals—such as achievement, a developing relationship, or the pursuit of other activities beneficial to the self—has rarely been explored. Attention to the satisfaction of their own goals, involvement in some pursuit, should reduce people's availability and helpfulness to others.

I believe it is important, however, to recognize that the "objective" and "subjective" costs of helping are often not identical. Helping other people can be highly rewarding. When a person is committed to helping another, what appears to an outsider as increase in cost may be perceived by the actor as an increased source of satisfaction. It can be extremely rewarding to make great sacrifices for people we love or for people we strongly identify with. We need to explore conditions and personality characteristics that turn costs into rewards. Prior association and other conditions that lead to identification with needy others (Chapters 7 and 9) would be involved.

The Meaning and Validity of Research

At least three serious issues can be raised with regard to many of the studies discussed in the preceding section. First is the issue of ecological validity, the degree to which events have a real-life character so that subjects experience them as real rather than as contrived and artificial. The fact that in many of the studies people have never before seen, and do not ever expect to see again, the person who is to be helped, even when this person is a partner in a game, raises questions about ecological validity. If circumstances and the need for help are perceived as unreal or as gamelike in character, people may behave according to the rules that they perceive to operate under the special conditions that exist, rather than according to how they would behave under natural circumstances. A related issue is the degree to which the specifications of the conditions of the experiment contain implicit, as well as explicit, rules about appropriate, expected, or reasonable behavior, which may then either be followed or rebelled against, without the researchers being able to determine which of these two happened and to what degree. A good example of what might happen is provided by findings of verbal-conditioning studies. Farber (1963) found that some conditioning occurred before the subjects realized that the experimenter gave positive reinforcement for certain types of verbalizations. At some point, subjects realized what the experimenter was doing, and then some of them apparently decided to cooperate, resulting in a sudden increase in their use of the reinforced verbalizations. Others decided not to cooperate, resulting in a sudden drop in the frequency of the reinforced verbal statements. A third issue is the legitimacy versus illegitimacy of need and/or dependence in some of the studies. Is there a real need? What determines whether another person or oneself is selected to gain some resources? What business does anyone have to ask another to volunteer for an experiment and then to expose that person to the need of a graduate student he has never seen or heard of before? A saving grace of the research is its extensiveness, in that the influence of certain kinds of variables has been demonstrated under varied conditions. Nonetheless, the limitations discussed need to be corrected in future research.

Decision Making, Personal Norms, and Helping Behavior

As I noted in describing the pioneering work of Latané and Darley (Chapter 3), they proposed a sequence of steps that people have to go through to help another person in need. These are presented as steps in a decision-making sequence. After they notice an event, people have to decide that what they see is an emergency; then they have to assume responsibility for providing help, decide what to do and how to help, and carry out the action they decided on. This analysis focused on helping in emergencies. Clearly, such a sequential decision-making model can also be applied to the manner in which people respond to any form of need, any stimulus that may potentially activate positive behavior. Other writers have proposed decision-making models and/or have extended the one proposed by Latané and Darley by considering how personality characteristics enter into the decisional process (Bar-Tel, 1976; Pomazal & Jaccard, 1976).

Schwartz's Decisional Model

Schwartz presented and progressively elaborated a model (Schwartz, 1968, 1970b, 1977) that concerns itself with internalized norms as the motivators of "altruistic" behavior. The activation of internalized norms generates feelings of obligation in people. Altruistic behavior is influenced by feelings of moral obligation and differences in the intensity of these feelings. Schwartz concerned himself with conditions that determine whether or not feelings of moral obligation are generated. These conditions include characteristics of the situation, basically those that were considered earlier as influences on prosocial behavior, such as degree of need. Individual differences in both personal norms and in the awareness of the potential consequences of one's behavior for other people (awareness of consequences, AC) enter into determining whether situations that have the potential to give rise to feelings of moral obligation will actually do so. Another personal characteristic that Schwartz proposed as important in determining prosocial behavior is the ascription of responsibility (AR) to the self or away from the self for other people's welfare. The activation of personal norms and a sense of obligation may be enhanced when people ascribe responsibility to themselves. However, Schwartz emphasized the significance of this characteristic in denying responsibility. He noted that the moral obligation that people experience "may be neutralized in advance of overt action by defenses against the relevance or appropriateness of the obligation [Schwartz, 1977]." The influence of these two personal characteristics (AC and AR) can be summarized in Schwartz's words:

> Having recognized that a moral decision may be in order by becoming aware of potential consequences for others of certain actions, a person must next decide if he himself is responsible for these actions and their consequences. . . . Whether or not one does accept some personal responsibility is a function of both the structure of the situation and of his own individual tendencies [1970b, p. 129].

In the latest formulation, Schwartz (1977) presents four steps in the sequential process that can lead to helping. Each of these steps can be analyzed in detail. First is the *activation step,* which involves the perception of need and responsibility. Second is the *obligation step,* which involves norm construction and generation of feelings of moral obligation. This refers to the conception, a highly reasonable one, that people have to construct a norm for each specific situation that they find themselves in. They do so on the basis of general norms and values. Third is the *defensive step,* which involves assessment, evaluation, and reassessment of potential responses. And fourth is *action or inaction responses,* which refer to the actions that people do or do not take.

In varied experiments Schwartz attempted to show the importance of personal norms, feeling of obligation, awareness of consequences, and ascription of responsibility to helping behavior. His research and relevant research by others have not addressed the sequential steps in the decision-making process and thus provide no evidence relevant to that aspect of the model. Since awareness of consequences and ascription of responsibility presumably determine whether a norm is activated and/or neutralized, Schwartz attempted to measure a personal norm and then to show that only people who ascribe to the norm and are also characterized by a high awareness of consequences and/or a tendency not to ascribe responsibility away from the self, act in a manner consistent with the norm in a specific situation. In most of the studies, the moral norm was measured by a single item, which used the word *obligation* as the "operative" term to define the norm [e.g., "Under circumstances X, would you feel a (moral) obligation to do Y?" "If a stranger to you needed a bone marrow transplant, and if you were a suitable donor, would you feel a moral obligation to donate bone marrow?" (Schwartz, 1973)]. In contrast, both awareness of consequences and ascription of responsibility have been measured in much more elaborate ways—the former by stories on a projective measure, the latter by a 35-item questionnaire.

In summary, this decision-making model suggests that when certain social norms apply to a situation people will or will not behave according to them as a function of whether existing conditions (internal and external) lead to these norms being psychologically activated or neutralized. In one study (Schwartz, 1970a) various elements of the model were situationally manipulated, externally imposed on subjects through verbal communications to them. The findings are clearly relevant to the previous discussion of verbal influence on helping. Experimenters approached individuals who had just donated blood, asked if they could talk to them, and told them about bone marrow donations and their importance for patients with leukemia and other types of medical problems. The experimenters then proceeded with one of several experimental manipulations. One was a "salience of consequences" manipulation in which they said (a) that a young woman needed a bone marrow donation, (b) that a young mother needed it, or (c) that a mother with several children needed it, emphasizing the potential consequences to the children's welfare. Another manipulation was a "salience of responsibility" manipulation. The interviewer told the subject either that the purpose was to test the blood of people who had already donated blood to see whether they would be appropriate for donation, or that the purpose was to look for potential donors in the general population. Presumably responsibility would be felt to a greater degree if the search for donors was restricted to a much smaller group of people that included the subject. Finally, Schwartz varied the odds of the subject's capacity to donate. The odds that any one person's blood would show that they could donate bone marrow was said to be either 1 in 1000 or 1 in 25. The subjects' agreement to several presumably hierarchically ordered requests determined their helping score. The first request was to have their blood tested, whereas the last request was to join a pool of bone marrow donors who could be called upon to donate.

Greater responsibility due to the restriction of the population of potential donors increased the willingness to help. Variation in the consequences also had a significant effect, with moderate consequences producing the greatest willingness to help. A significant interaction was also found between the consequences and odds manipulations. When the odds that any one person could donate bone marrow were very low, the more serious was the stated need (consequences) the greater was the willingness to help. When there was a substantially greater likelihood of being a compatible donor, and when the consequences were highly "salient," the willingness to help dropped significantly. In this condition the subjects were told about a young mother whose survival was unlikely if a matching donor was not found. The tragedy of her children losing their mother and the emotional consequences of growing up without here were also mentioned. Combined with a strong likelihood that the subject would be a compatible donor (1 out of 25 people), this situation exerted a very strong pressure on the person. Subjects may have resisted, reacted negatively, because too much force was exerted on them, producing reactance. In several other studies Schwartz (1977) found less help under high pressure on subjects; he provides explanations for this consistent with reactance conceptions.

This study demonstrates that different types of verbal communications affect verbal agreement to help (actually to be a potential helper) in meaningfully predictable ways. However, in interpreting the findings, an issue has to be considered that was already discussed in conjunction with research on the consequences of harmdoing: the meaning of a purely verbal commitment. Does verbal agreement mean that subjects will actually do what they agreed to do, or even that they intended to do it when they agreed? Or is it that under the pressure of the circumstances the easiest way to get away is to say, "Yes, I'll go along with it"? In one study, most people who verbally agreed to donate blood did not actually do so (Kazdin & Bryan, 1971), and they did not respond to attempts to get in touch with them. Moreover, in Schwartz's study when experimenters later encountered some subjects who again donated blood, they avoided the experimenter and did not want to talk to him.

Under different circumstances a verbal agreement represents different degrees of commitment to action. We can look at what transpired between the experimenters and the subjects from a subject's point of view. It is reasonable to assume that a person's perception of a situation is an important determinant of behavior. When the odds of being able to donate bone marrow were high but the need was not presented in a dramatic fashion, the subjects may have felt that even if they verbally agreed they could later opt not to actually donate. When, however, the need of a young mother and her children was presented in a dramatic fashion, subjects may have felt less free to withdraw once they agreed to participate, a verbal agreement representing a more serious commitment on their part. As a result, when the high odds made it appear substantially more likely that they could donate bone marrow, their unwillingness to do so resulted in an unwillingness to agree verbally to the experimenter's request. This interpretation—stressing the differences in the meaning to people of the verbal commitments they make —seems an alternative to a reactance interpretation of the consequences–odds interaction.

The generally high agreement to the verbal request for help (59% willing to join a donor pool) may have been due to several factors: the nature of subject group (blood donors), the force of a direct request that implies a moral obligation, the foot-in-the-door nature of the request (the subjects had just donated blood, then agreed to be interviewed), and, of course, the possibility of refusing cooperation at a later time. Although the terminology that Schwartz employs differs, his independent variables are those we have encountered before. Variation in consequences seems equivalent to variation in degree of need. Variation in responsibility may be considered as variation in the degree to which responsibility is focused on a person to help. Both the odds and responsibility manipulations may have been perceived as relating to one's chances of being an eligible donor. Although the findings of this study meaningfully contribute to the literature on verbal influences on helping and to the clarification of the processes through which they affect helping, since all the variables were "externally" manipulated, they do not test Schwartz's model.

Other studies do so to a greater degree. In his earliest study, Schwartz (1968, 1970b) administered paper-and-pencil measures of norms, salience of consequences, and salience of responsibility to 108 undergraduates who lived together in residential units prior to the study for at least 4 months. In addition he obtained peer ratings of behavior in a variety of everyday situations involving considerateness, reliability, and helpfulness toward peers. The total sample was subdivided into subsamples differentiated by awareness of consequences, ascription of responsibility to self, and their combination. Among those high on awareness of consequences, and among those high on ascription of responsibility to self, significant positive correlations were found between the individuals' moral norms and their behavior as measured by peer ratings. Most of the norms that participants endorsed were prosocial, favoring action in others' behalf. Among those high on both of these personality measures, the correlations between norms and behavior were substantial; the correlation between summary indices of personal norms and peer ratings of behavior was $r = .47$ ($p < .01$).

In another study, Schwartz (1973) mailed out a questionnaire about attitudes toward bone marrow donations to young female clerical workers. The questionnaire was presented as part of a national survey. One question asked whether the respondant would feel a moral obligation to donate to a stranger who needed bone marrow—in Schwartz's view, a measure of normative belief. People could respond to this question on a 5-point scale. The questionnaire also included the ascription of responsibility measure. Subsequently Schwartz sent an appeal to these people, and to some others who did not get the questionnaire, to become part of a pool of donors. Only 24% agreed to further contact. The difference from the previous study could be due to the greater social influence exerted by a verbal appeal in contrast to a questionnaire, or it could be due to the nature of the subject population. Subjects who tended to ascribe responsibility away from themselves (had low scores on the measure) showed no relationship between their response to the appeal and their expressed belief that it was their moral obligation to donate for a stranger. Given a strong tendency to ascribe responsibility to the self, the greater the degree to which people expressed the belief that it was their obligation to help a stranger, the more they were willing to cooperate. Schwartz again interpreted these findings as evidence that ascription of responsibility to the self is a condition that determines whether a norm will be activated.

In another study (Schwartz, 1974), female undergraduates had the awareness of consequences, ascription of responsibility, and Rotter's internal–external (I–E) control scale administered to them. Later—for most of the subjects after an interval of more than 10 months—they received a call about a bake sale to raise funds for Head Start. Head Start mothers would do the baking, but volunteers were needed to sell. In the subsequent appeal to the subjects to volunteer, the salience of the consequences of volunteering was varied. In one condition (high salience) subjects were told that if there were enough volunteers, the mothers could stay with their children during the day rather than having to be away from them. In the low-salience condition, the consequences of help on the mothers and children were not emphasized.

Scores on awareness of consequences ($r = .26$) and ascription of responsibility ($r = .48$) were significantly related to helping, as measured by the amount of time the subjects volunteered. In a covariance analysis, with the influence of ascription of responsibility eliminated, the high-salience treatment led to significantly more volunteering. However, there was a salience by awareness of consequences interaction, as follows. Subjects were divided into five levels of awareness. In the low-salience condition the amount of time volunteered increased as the level of awareness increased. Among those who were exposed to the high-salience treatment there was a progressive increase up to the third level of awareness, and a subsequent decrease, significant at the fifth level. Schwartz suggests that even though the high-salience appeal was not very strong, high-awareness subjects are so aware of interpersonal consequences that they found the appeal manipulative and experienced reactance.

Specific Norms versus General Orientations

What is the meaning of these findings—the theoretical significance of the relationship between norms as measured by statements of moral obligation, ascription of responsibility, awareness of consequences, and prosocial behavior? Schwartz (1977) considers individual differences in the "cognitive structure of values and norms" as primary, with ascription of responsibility and awareness of consequences as "personality tendencies which affect norm activation and defense." He focuses on the specificity of the mesh that is required between the person, the situation, and the type of help required —which is reasonable—but he also states that his own and others' research findings argue against the existence of a general propensity toward altruistic behavior. However, Schwartz's data make it appear that individual differences in awareness of consequences and ascription of responsibility are general characteristics that are directly relevant to prosocial behavior. Rather than being mediating characteristics that determine the manner in which situations and personal norms are connected to one another and to action, they seem to tap prosocial values, to be aspects of a prosocial orientation or a prosocial goal as conceptualized in Chapter 2.

Awareness of consequences was measured by responses to projective stories. In one example Schwartz (1970b) provided, a person is awakened early Sunday by the alarm clock. He does not feel like getting up, but friends are coming to pick him up. If he does not start moving he will keep them waiting. Subjects responded to the question, "What thoughts and feelings might be going through Bob's mind as he debates with himself about what to do?" Responses indicating awareness of consequences presumably refer to consideration by Bob of the negative consequences for his friends of his staying in bed.

Schwartz (1977) writes this about the awareness of consequences measure: "A score of 0 indicated no awareness of others' needs, a score of 4 indicated awareness of detailed needs, adopting the perspective of others, and reflecting on the consequences of actions from their viewpoint [p. 28]." Clearly, more seems involved than awareness. Taking others' perspectives, considering events from others' points of view are concepts akin to role taking, which may lead to an empathic perceptual orientation and thereby may enhance prosocial behavior. Since the "inner dialogue" of the characters in the projective stories that the subjects are asked to describe relates to these characters' consideration of others' welfare, the measure probably goes beyond role taking and tests concern about others' welfare.

Similar considerations apply to the measure of ascription of responsibility, which includes questions about the extent to which a person feels personally responsible for others' welfare, about judgment of the goodness of human beings, and so on. In part this may be a measure of internalized responsibility or obligation for others' welfare. As an example, consider the following items from the test: "Professional obligations can never justify neglecting the welfare of others" and "If a good friend of mine wanted to injure an enemy of his, it would be my duty to try to stop him." Does not the question about one's moral obligation to help a stranger by donating bone marrow (Schwartz, 1973) measure the same thing within a specific domain? Given a high AR, an expressed belief by a person in his obligation to donate bone marrow to a stranger indicates the applicability of his concern about other people's welfare and a sense of obligation to further others' welfare to this specific domain. A similar response about one's moral obligation to donate bone marrow without an indication of generalized concern about or responsibility for others' welfare certainly seems inconsistent, and may be motivated by a variety of nonaltruistic goals. One such goal is the social desirability of saying that one would feel obligated to donate bone marrow. This reasoning suggests that one would not expect a single statement of obligation to relate to subsequent behavior simply because such a single statement may be provided for quite varied reasons and may not reflect any genuine concern about others and the desire to benefit them. Schwartz (1976) noted, in fact, that more elaborate measures of the "normative structure," as well as consistency in an individual's normative structure, lead to better norm–behavior relationships. The varied motivation underlying specific statements of moral obligation and the instability of a limited measure may explain the lack of relationship between such measures of moral norms and either awareness of consequences or ascription of responsibility.

Varied studies found that indices of specific personal norms or of moral obligation in relation to some specific conduct are associated with the actual behavior they prescribe. Schwartz (1977) notes that in the few instances when this relationship was substantial the behavior index was composed of self-report, or the behavior was recurrent so that some instances occurred before the norm was assessed (Heberlein & Black, 1976; Pomazal, 1974). In other cases, the personal norm–behavior relationships were significant, but relatively small, between .24 and .26. Schwartz suggests that a small relationship can be expected until the manner in which these relationships are modified by "conditions conducive to norm activation and defense are considered."

However, many of Schwartz's studies reported significant and sometimes substantial relationships between the measure of awareness of consequences, or of ascription of responsibility, and some prosocial behavior. This has been found in Schwartz's first study, where peer ratings of the subjects' behaviors that were judged prosocial correlated $r = .22$ with AC, and also $r = .22$ with AR. The multiple correlation of the two measures with the combined index of prosocial behaviors was $r = .36$. All these relationships were significant. In the study of volunteering for the bake sale to help Head Start mothers, significant relationships were again found between scores on each of these measures and the degree of subjects' helpfulness ($r = .26$ for AC; $r = .48$ for AR). Schwartz assumes that the reason for such a positive relationship is that people ascribe to prosocial norms, the expression of which is then mediated by these two personality characteristics. Instead, these two characteristics seem to measure aspects of general personal orientations that increase the likelihood that people will behave prosocially under varied conditions.

Significant relationships between the ascription of responsibility to oneself for others' welfare and prosocial behavior have also been found in studies of people's reactions to emergencies (Schwartz & Clausen, 1970; Staub, Erkut, & Jaquette, as described in Staub, 1974a). These studies showed that variation in these characteristics modifies the influence of situations. In Schwartz and Clausen's study, AC did not affect helping, perhaps because of the measure's focus on people's awareness of how another person may feel, and on consideration of others' feelings. However, in the emergency, the victim's discomfort and need for help were relatively clear.

In several studies that my students and I conducted the AR test was included in a battery of tests that aimed to measure prosocial orientation (Staub *et al.,* in Staub, 1974a; Feinberg, 1977; Grodman, 1977). In three studies scores on this measure had high loading on a factor that appeared to be a prosocial orientation factor. In fact, the results of these factor analyses, particularly in Grodman's study, may provide some understanding of why AC and AR themselves are uncorrelated (Schwartz, 1977). In this study the AR scale had a high loading on a first factor, together with Berkowitz and Lutterman's scale of social responsibility and Christie's measure of a Machiavellian orientation (which had a negative loading). Hogan's (1969) measure of empathy, which is basically a test of interpersonal sensitivity, and some other measures (for example, Midlarz's trust scale—see Chapter 9) had high loading on a second factor. Interpersonal sensitivity (which includes taking the point of view of others and consideration of others' feelings and of the potential consequences of one's behavior on others—the kinds of things that AC appears to measure) is one characteristic that in some ways contributes to helping others. Belief in one's responsibility for others' welfare and/or in one's obligation to be helpful is another characteristic that can contribute to prosocial behavior. In some cases one or the other characteristic, in other cases both, may be important for helping to occur. A substantial body of research findings showed that external focusing of responsibility on people enhances their prosocial behavior (Chapter 3). The AR test appears to be an index of internal focusing of responsibility. People who score high on the test assume responsibility for others' welfare and under certain conditions proceed to act accordingly.

An Additional Decision-Making Model

In another decision-making approach, Pomazal and Jaccard (1976) emphasized the importance of information that is available to people for making decisions about action. The decisions people make, their behavioral intentions, determine whether or not they will help. Pomazal and Jaccard's study was guided by the theory of behavioral intention proposed by Fishbein (1967, 1972). According to this theory, a person's intention to perform a behavior is a function of two major factors: "(*a*) an individual's belief about the consequences of performing the behavior weighted by the value those consequences have for the individual and/or (*b*) an individual's beliefs about what important others think he should do weighted by his motivations to comply with those others [Pomazal & Jaccard, 1976, p. 318]." The first factor expresses personal motivation; the second one expresses concern about social considerations of a particular kind. In Fishbein's terms the two factors represent attitudinal and normative components. These researchers measured each of the two kinds of beliefs and the weights (the value or significance for the person) of these beliefs in relation to donating blood. They used a single questionnaire, which also measured related information (attitude toward the act, subjective norm of donating). For example, to measure beliefs about donating blood the questionnaire included 10 questions, such as: "donating blood at the upcoming blood drive would give me a feeling of satisfaction." A third factor, based on Schwartz's work, was also included. This was a statement of moral obligation to donate. The intention to donate blood was also measured. The questionnaire was administered to three groups of subjects—prior donors, people on campus, and people selected from the student directory—just before a blood drive. Responses on this questionnaire, information on who actually donated, and a post-blood-drive telephone interview provided the data for the study.

Of the subjects who intended to donate, 53 actually did but 102 did not. Only 2 of 99 who did not intend to donate did donate. This provided a correlation of .46 ($p < .01$) between intention and actual donation. Considering the subjects' ability to donate—self-reports by subjects that they were rejected because they could not pass a physical exam or that they were turned away because of overcrowding—this relationship increased to .59. Among people who did not intend to donate, some apparently had positive attitudes toward donating but knew that they could not, and this probably affected their stated intention. Clearly, ability is important in making a decision. It is also clear, however, that the stated intention to do something —even if it is based on the rather careful consideration that must have entered into filling out the questionnaire—is no guarantee of action.

A regression analysis specified the predictors of the intention to donate. The attitude toward the act of donating—which was related to but not identical with beliefs about donating weighted by the value of donating, the first factor in the model—had the highest regression coefficient ($r = .48$, $p < .01$), followed by moral obligation ($r = .29$, $p < .01$). The social or subjective norm component did not further predict intention. Among subjects "able" to donate, attitude toward the act related $r = .38$, whereas moral norm related $r = .43$ to actually donating blood.

In their questionnaire Pomazal and Jaccard measured other variables that "in the past have been shown to be related to helping. . . . donating experience, reciprocity, social responsibility, need" and so on. It is not indicated how these were measured; they may have been measured by single items, or by more elaborate procedures, as social responsibility has been measured in other studies. Presumably these variables were measured in a general form, not specifically in relation to donating blood. Pomazal and Jaccard concluded that these variables add little to either the prediction of behavioral intention or the prediction of actual behavior beyond the components of the model they used. However, several of these variables correlated very highly with behavioral intention. Social responsibility correlated .52, which contrasts to .59 for attitude toward the act. If social responsibility has been measured as a general orientation toward other people (and probably with only a few items), it is highly significant that it "predicts" behavioral intention just about as well as a set of ratings that are specifically relevant to the behavior in question. Unfortunately, the relationships between social responsibility and other variables "external" to the model (such as need) and actual donations were not reported.

A major aspect of the decisional models, in contrast to other approaches to predicting prosocial behavior, is the specificity of the predictors employed. Emphasis on situationally relevant predictors, whether a moral norm or attitudes, beliefs, and values specifically related to a particular action, may lead to better prediction of the specific behavior than information about general personality orientations. However, having collected such specific information about thoughts and feelings related to one behavior, one has to start from scratch to predict another prosocial behavior. To the extent that there are some general personality characteristics that are regarded as important in Schwartz's model, although they are not considered to have direct predictive value for prosocial behavior, strict specificity applies to that model to a lesser degree.

A more meaningful approach may be to consider general value orientations and other general characteristics that enable us to make predictions in a variety of circumstances. In addition, our prediction of a specific act in a specific situation would be improved by assessing the specific norms, beliefs, or attitudes that people hold with regard to that situation and action—the range of applicability of their more general values and norms to the situation in question.

To elucidate this further, how do decision-making models differ from the model described in Chapter 2? First, decision-making models imply that there is a rational, deliberate decision-making process that leads to some resolution, or to different resolutions in a sequence. Often, however, circumstances and personal characteristics can lead to interpretations of events, to choices and decisions, without conscious deliberation. Such decisions are still cognitively based, but values, beliefs, and plans derived from past experience can lead to decisions without deliberation. Moreover, affective reactions that are generated by values, beliefs, goals, and the availability of plans will affect both the way people reason and their "automatic" (nondeliberative) decision making. Second, decision-making models concentrate on a single circumstance or situation, elucidating the influences that operate in making decisions about action. They are molecular in their focus. Third, they emphasize personality characteristics that are relevant to the single action in question—a moral norm or attitude that specifically relates to the conduct being examined. My model considers broad motivational orientations, both promoting and inhibiting help, as well as some other characteristics of the person such as competence, in attempting to make predictions. The motivational characteristics are relevant to a broader range of situations. As I noted, the applicability of these characteristics to specific situations must be carefully considered: Specific moral norms may be indices of the range of applicability. In a sense, the two approaches are additive. One emphasizes the ability to predict to a broader range of situations from personality, recognizing that the specificity of situations and the nature of helping acts exert influence; the other focuses on the specific helping act required and considers values, beliefs, and norms relevant to specific acts.

Individual Characteristics and Helping Behavior

The examination of individual differences in relation to helping behavior is embedded, to a large extent, in various chapters in this book. Here I shall discuss relationships between personality and helping others in nonphysical need, including sharing with and donating to others. The relationship between age and helping is considered in Volume 2, since age is regarded as a developmental variable. The relationship between race and helping is discussed in Chapter 7, in conjunction with the discussion of the connection between the self and others. Much of the research that examined the relationship between prosocial acts and personality has been relatively atheoretical. Clearly, few researchers select personality measures for inclusion in their studies without considering their relevance, but frequently the relevance is tangential. A locus of control (or other) measure may be included in a study either because it is a widely used measure and to see how it functions in a particular context may be interesting, or because it is likely to be relevant to most types of activities. Careful specification of how certain personality measures would relate to behavior under the conditions of an experiment, on both theoretical and practical bases, has been rare.

Sex Differences and Helping Behavior

The relationship between sex and helping is examined in different places in this book. Here only a few issues are noted. First, the helping behavior of males and females is likely to be affected by how sex-appropriate particular kinds of behavior are regarded by the culture. Also influential are individual differences in the characteristics of males and females that are the result of socialization. Socialization inculcates different characteristics according to cultural beliefs and stereotypes as to what men and women are like and what they ought to be like. Some sex differences are likely to diminish if the culture continues toward accepting and valuing androgyny, the combination of feminine and masculine characteristics in members of both sexes. Some sex differences may, of course, be hereditary. Findings to date indicate that females help less than males in emergencies, but primarily as the number of bystanders increases (Darley & Latané, 1968; Schwartz &

Clausen, 1970). When a male is present, females sometimes defer to him. However, they do not help less than males under many other emergency conditions (Latané & Darley, 1970; Piliavin & Piliavin, 1972; Staub & Baer, 1974). When females are alone, and when the victim's visibility or great need focuses responsibility on them, females help as much as males. Females were found to approach motorists who apparently had car trouble less than males did (West *et al.*, 1975) and to respond less to telephone callers who reached the wrong number and needed help to get their call through (Gaertner & Bickman, 1971). Females appear to help less than males when helping may be dangerous, or when special skills that men rather than women are likely to have are needed. When certain kinds of social initiative are called for, particularly when danger or the aforementioned special skills enter into the situation, if a male is present females are likely to let him take charge.

Under certain circumstances females may be more helpful than males, because they are competent in a particular area, because being helpful is more socially appropriate for them, or because certain characteristics they acquired (or tend to possess by heredity) make them more likely to be helpful. As I noted earlier in this chapter, when another person's dependence is greater, females are likely to help more, and males are likely to help less, than when dependence is lower. Females also are likely to favor themselves less than males when they have the opportunity to distribute rewards they earned and thus deserve between themselves and others (see Chapter 4). O'Bryant and Brophy (1976) reported that fifth-grade girls helped a younger child with a task significantly more than fifth-grade boys did. Moreover, a significantly larger proportion of girls than boys helped. This finding is consistent with the report of Whiting and Pope (1973) that in varied societies girls tend to offer help and give support to others more frequently than boys. Moreover, offers of help and support increased with age in girls as comparisons between 3–6 year old and 7–11 year old girls showed, but did not change with age in boys, suggesting the influence of differential socialization. In several experiments that my associates and I conducted, fifth- and sixth-grade girls wrote substantially more letters to hospitalized children, made more toys for them, and donated more gift certificates for them than boys. However, under certain experimental conditions boys donated as much and extended as much effort in making toys as did the most helpful group of girls (Staub, 1975b, 1978b; Staub & Feinberg, 1977a; Volume 2). This suggests that the range of conditions that elicit helpfulness by girls may be greater. Hartshorne, May, and Maller (1929) also found that girls scored higher in helpfulness and service than boys. In another study teachers' ratings indicated that adolescent boys were less considerate and socially responsible than girls (Bronfenbrenner, 1961). These findings contrast with the conclusions of Maccoby and Jacklin (1974), who did not find girls to be more helpful than boys. However, Maccoby and Jacklin's conclusions were based largely on studies of generosity and on my research on helping behavior in response to sounds of distress. In such "rescue" studies, as in many of the adult emergency situations, no differences were found in boys' and girls' helping behavior. Perhaps girls' greater concern about others' welfare and boys' orientation toward instrumental competence and initiative (see next section) resulted in similar helping behavior.

In contrast to their sometimes greater helpfulness, studies indicate that girls are not more generous than boys. On the basis of lack of sex difference in most of the studies of donating behavior that I reviewed earlier, both Krebs (1970) and Maccoby and Jacklin (1974) concluded that boys and girls do not differ in their willingness to donate material rewards for other children. However, in one study in which pairs of fourth-grade children interacted with each other, boys who had candy shared more with their same-sex partner than did girls (Staub & Sherk, 1970). This study differs from most other research in that children did not donate for absent persons, but shared something of their own with a person who was listening to a tape-recorded story with them. Moreover, the pattern of the findings suggested that it was unclear, to the member of the pair who possessed the candy, to what extent sharing was appropriate. This child received the candy ostensibly to make listening to the tape-recorded story enjoyable. Then, unexpectedly, the other child was brought to the room to listen to the story with the first child. Children's uncertainty about appropriate behavior was indicated by a negative relationship between their need for approval, as previously measured by a paper-and-pencil test, and both the amount of candy they shared and the amount they themselves ate. Children whose need for approval was high may have tried to avoid disapproval by neither eating nor sharing the candy. Under these circumstances greater sharing by boys may be an indication of greater initiative. Initiative, however, is frequently necessary for prosocial behavior to take place.

Personality Differences in Boys and Girls. To increase the understanding of sex differences in behavior, we have to consider differences in those characteristics of boys and girls that may affect positive behavior. It has long been thought that girls are more empathic, understanding, sensitive, and considerate than boys, and that they are expected to be so in our culture. Is there any evidence for sex differences in personality and dispositions toward other people?

Sagi and Hoffman (1976) recently reported that in their studies with newborns, on the average 30 hours old, the babies cried more when they heard the tape-recorded cries of another infant than when they heard a "synthetic cry" of the same intensity, or some other control noise. Moreover, although the differences were not significant, both in their studies and in those of Simner (1971)—altogether in six studies—girls always responded more strongly than boys to another newborn's cry. Sagi and Hoffman raise the possibility that girls are more empathic than boys, perhaps by heredity, perhaps due to early conditioning (see Volume 2, Chapter 3). Unfortunately, the stimulus cry was always that of a girl, so that greater responsiveness by girls may have been due to the quality of the sound. Moreover, the newborn's crying may have been due to fear or anxiety elicited by another's cry, rather than to empathy. Nonetheless, it is an indication of responsiveness to another human being.

In other research, females responded with greater physiological arousal to other's distress than males (Craig & Lavery, 1969). As I earlier reported (Chapter 4), in dividing rewards between two other children, preschool girls, in contrast to boys, tended to give the first reward to the child who performed less well. These girls may have been motivated by consideration of this child's feeling and by empathic affect. Using a measure in which children are exposed to varied sets of pictures, each set depicting a series of events that lead to some affective experience by a child in the pictures, several authors found greater empathy in girls than in boys. Empathy was measured by the children's reports of feelings identical to those of the child in the pictures. The difference was marginal in two studies with 4-year-olds (Feshbach & Feshbach, 1969; Hoffman & Levine, 1976) and significant in 6- and 8-year-olds (Feshbach & Roe, 1968; Feshbach & Feshbach, 1969; Foy, 1970). It is of interest that although Hoffman and Levine's 4-year-old girls tended to give more empathic responses than the boys, boys tended to give significantly more active, coping, instrumental responses to the events taking place in the pictures ("I'd just follow his tracks," in response to a story about a lost pet). These findings, however tentative, suggest that girls start to give greater attention to others' feelings at an early age. Whether or not boys and girls differed in empathic affect cannot be determined, since there is no way of knowing whether the children actually experienced affect.

In a review article, Hoffman (1977b) notes that in 16 comparisons of females' and males' vicarious affective reactions to another's expressions of affect, although only a few of the differences were significant, in all cases the females obtained higher scores. Again, in most of these studies, the subjects' verbal responses, not their physiological arousal or other nonverbal indices of affect, were used as the measure of empathy. Although females appear more responsive to others' feelings, they are not more competent in affective and cognitive role taking, in understanding how another person feels and views events (Hoffman, 1977a). It must be noted, however, that most currently used measures of role taking do not provide an opportunity for taking the perspective of others in depth; they do not measure the extent to which people can enter another's inner world.

To what extent does the greater responsiveness to others' feelings by females than by males correspond to sex differences in values, in consideration for other people's welfare? More generally, do males and females differ in their morally relevant values, norms, and beliefs? Freud (1961) believed that males internalize moral values in the course of their resolution of the Oedipus complex, that they come to hold autonomous moral values. Females' superegos are less firmly developed, less independent of social influence and of others' moral views. Their moral decisions are guided more by "affections or enmities" than by principles. Aronfreed (1968) suggested similar differences and related them to an emphasis in our society on greater self-reliance and self-control by boys, greater responsiveness to others by girls. Hoffman (1975b) points out that findings about sex differences in guilt and fear of punishment following transgression have been minimal and inconsistent. Research on moral reasoning also found few sex differences. Using data from several of his studies that explored the relationships between socialization practices and internalized morality, Hoffman (1975b) examined differences in the internalized values of fifth- and seventh-grade middle-class boys and girls and their parents. The instruments used to measure internalization included projective story completions, reasoning about transgressions, and a scale of values that subjects were to rank-order. (See Volume 2, Chapter 2, for an extensive discussion of the measurement of internalization.) Of some interest is that, except for indices of internalization that were based on the same measure and conceptually related, the correlations among the different measures were low, in both the children's and the parents' data. These zero-order intercorrelations point to the relative specificity of the types of internal reactions that were measured.

Females were much more likely than males to report guilt following transgression, and the difference was greater among adult women and men than among their children. In contrast, moral transgressions were associated to a greater degree with fear of detection and punishment in males than in females. Hoffman suggests that this difference may be due to differences in child rearing practices with boys and girls: more affection and induction (pointing out the consequences of their behavior for others) with girls by mothers, more power assertion with boys. Hoffman found it puzzling that there were no significant sex differences in internal moral judgment, and attributed this to the task's producing a cognitive, problem-solving set rather than an affective set. In this study males and females did not differ in suggestions for instrumental actions (e.g., acts compensating victims of transgression), raising questions about the reliability of Hoffman and Levine's (1976) findings of such differences in preschool children.

The results with both children and adults suggest that consideration for others is a more salient and important value for females than for males. Females ascribed more to the values of "showing consideration for other people's feelings" and "going out of one's way to help other people" than males. I want to emphasize again the interrelatedness of cognitive processes and affective responses to the environment. It is our network of cognitions—thoughts, beliefs, and values—that guides, on the one hand, our perception of our environment and the manner in which we process those perceptions, and on the other hand, our affective responses. Consideration for others' feelings and welfare is likely to lead to empathic emotional responses. Finally, it is worth noting that in all adult and child samples achievement was a significantly more salient value for males than for females. They ranked items such as "to try your best in everything you do" and "to do well in your work" as important to them significantly more than did females. Jointly, these differences in consideration and achievement may indicate the arousal of greater concern for others' welfare and less conflict with achievement goals in females, and the opposite findings in males.

The findings under discussion are consistent with the results of relatively direct measures of the self-concepts of men and of women. Bennett and Cohen (1959) asked 1300 subjects to select descriptive adjectives that did or did not describe them. The adjectives were grouped in varied ways; 255 adjectives formed 15 sets of 15 adjectives each. Although in general men and women had similar self-concepts, women described themselves as "much richer" in the qualities of warmth and empathy. They perceived and/or represented themselves as more understanding, tender, sympathetic, affectionate, generous, and loving. They also felt that they were the weaker of the two sexes, and felt more helpless, timid, and fearful than males. The authors note that "such feelings seem in line with the cultural training of women toward dependency [Bennett & Cohen, 1959, p. 125]."

Morally Relevant Characteristics and Positive Behavior

Role Taking and Moral Judgment.   The tremendous current interest in how children's social cognitions develop, in their understanding of the world and of other people (Schantz, 1975), has been accompanied by a growing interest in how social cognitions in general and the capacity to view events from others' perspectives in particular relate to prosocial behavior. It is becoming increasingly clear that, contrary to earlier assumptions, perspective-taking ability is not unitary. Although varied kinds of perspective taking—the ability to consider another person's spatial perspective, what another person may think, how another person feels, and so on—all increase with age, the correlations among them are quite variable and often low (see Volume 2, Chapter 3). Certain kinds of perspective-taking capacities (e.g., affective role-taking) seem more relevant to prosocial behavior than do others. Furthermore, the capacity to view events from others' perspectives is no guarantee that a person will put himself into another's place and consider events from the other's point of view. Prosocial values and other characteristics that motivate perspective taking seem important for this to happen. However, the capacity to take the perspective of another may itself be correlated with prosocial values, since these would mutually support and reinforce one another, and thus contribute to mutual development. Depending on the extent of such a relationship, role taking would or would not motivate prosocial behavior.

Research on the relationship of role taking and prosocial behavior has centered on children; perhaps researchers tend to assume that role-taking capacity is fully developed by adulthood, so that no variations would exist. With regard to more complex types of perspective taking (the perception and understanding of other people's feelings, thoughts, and motives), this is unlikely to be true. People in general, and as a function of specific circumstances, are likely to vary not only in whether they take another's perspective, but also in the degree to which they do so, the extent to which they enter into another's thoughts, feelings, internal state. Perhaps as people more deeply enter the internal world of others, they experience the greater arousal of empathy. Research that showed the consequences of an "imagine him" observational set, reviewed in Chapter 4, suggests that this may be so. However, the research that is reviewed here has explored individual differences in role-taking *capacity*—which does not guarantee that on a specific occasion a person will actually take the perspective of another—using measures that are not sensitive enough to indicate differences in the extent that people can entertain and enter into the complex thoughts and feelings of others.

The relationship between moral judgment and positive behavior has also been explored. As I noted, moral judgment correlates with helping others in physical distress (Chapter 3), but in interaction with characteristics of the situation. I would expect the same interactive influence between moral judgment (and other personal characteristics) and situations when other forms of helping are explored. Since moral reasoning is an index of values, and may be considered an index of motivation, its relationship to prosocial behavior, although varying according to situational influences, may more frequently be positive than that of role taking.

In one study (Rubin & Schneider, 1973) the IQs and "communicative egocentrism" of 7-year-old children were measured. The children were to describe graphic designs to another child, to enable the other child to select the design they were describing from a set of designs. The more distinctive the features of the designs used in the descriptions, the less egocentric the children were considered to be. The less egocentric children were in their communications, the more boxes of candies they donated for poor children, and the more they helped a younger child in a second session to sort and arrange a pile of tickets. The younger child had about twice as many tickets to sort as the subject had. Following this second measure of prosocial behavior an adaptation of Kohlberg's measure was used to test moral reasoning. Kohlberg's (1969) measure presents children with stories describing moral conflict situations and examines children's reasonings about these conflicts. Advanced reasoning was significantly related to both the number of boxes of candy donated and the amount of helping given the younger child. However, the children's behavior may have affected their reasoning on the moral judgment test. An added finding in this study was that the correlations between egocentrism and prosocial behavior and between moral judgment and prosocial behavior increased when the children's IQs were partialled out (e.g., their influence eliminated by a statistical procedure). The authors suggest that situational cues may have led some of the children, as a function of their intelligence alone, to behave prosocially. Low egocentrism and moral judgment were significantly related in this study ($r = .59$). This finding is consistent with the reasoning that the capacity for role taking may be a necessary condition for the development of advanced moral reasoning (Volume 2, Chapter 3).

In contrast to the study just described, a study by Emler and Rushton (1974) found no relationship between two measures of role taking and a measure of generosity (children sharing rewards they won while playing a bowling game). A basic problem in trying to evaluate the relationship between role taking and generosity by considering the findings of varied studies is that substantial evidence shows that different measures of role taking are unrelated or minimally related (Volume 2, Chapter 3). The two role-taking measures (both adapted from Flavell et al., 1968) used in this study were different from that used by Rubin and Schneider (1973). One involved children trying to outwit an experimenter in playing a game; the children had to reason about how the experimenter would think. In another, frequently used measure, the children were first asked to make up a story on the basis of seven pictures. Then they were asked to describe the story that another person would make up after three of the pictures had been removed.

Emler and Rushton (1974) also measured moral judgment, using stories adapted from Piaget (1932) and questions that aimed to elicit children's conceptions of distributive justice. They found a significant relationship between moral judgment and generosity, as did Rubin and Schneider. Nonetheless, the issue of comparability of the meaning of performance on varied measures is highly relevant here. Recent research findings (Crockenberg & Nicolayev, 1977) show that not even those Kohlberg stories that were specifically prepared to parallel one another elicited equivalent reasoning from children. Moral reasoning on measures using different types of stories, different methods to elicit reasoning about the stories, and different scoring methods may be only slightly related to one another, and their relationship to behavior may also be variable. No theoretical conception of the relationship between measures and the relationship of these measures to behavior has been advanced by researchers concerned with moral judgment.

In a further study Rushton and Wiener (1975) found no relationship between 2 measures of role-taking capacity and 3 measures of altruism. Waxler, Yarrow, and Smith (1977) administered 10 perspective-taking tests and 6 measures of prosocial behavior to middle-class children ranging in age from 3 to 7. Correlations among the perspective-taking measures, computed separately for younger and older children, were predominantly nonsignificant. The researchers combined measures to form a "perceptual battery" and a "conceptual battery." For older children, the scores on the two batteries were significantly related to each other, pointing to the importance of more extensive measurement of role-taking skills. The correlations between perspective taking and prosocial behavior were not significant. With 3-year-olds alone, their scores on the total perspective-taking battery were marginally related to some forms of prosocial actions (sharing, comforting, and total prosocial scores). However, no relationships were found for older children.

Krebs and Sturrup (1974) used the same two measures of role taking used by Emler and Rushton (1974). They observed 23 children, 7 and 8 years of age, and coded their offers of help, offers of support, and suggestions to others for responsible behavior. No significant relationships were found between these measures of prosocial behavior and role taking, although the relationship between a composite prosocial score and the role-taking scores was significant. Performance on the role-taking tasks did correlate significantly with teachers' ratings of prosocial and cooperative behaviors. As Rushton (1976) notes, however, both IQ scores on formal tests and teachers' ratings of IQ correlated with all other measures. Thus, IQ may have entered into the relationships, and teachers' ratings may have been confounded by a halo effect (such as a tendency to evaluate more intelligent children positively).

Johnson (1975) measured children's perceptual and affective perspective-taking skills and related them to the extent of their cooperative behavior. Pairs of children engaged in several tasks together. To the extent that subjects attempted to maximize both their own and the other child's outcomes on these tasks they were considered to have a cooperative disposition; to the extent that they maximized their own outcomes but minimized the other's outcomes they were competitive. Unfortunately, the measures of perspective taking were administered in the same session, following these tasks. Behaving cooperatively or competitively on several interactive tasks could have affected the children's perspective taking, particularly on a measure that demanded attention to others' thoughts and feelings. (For evidence that a limited set of experiences can affect children's attentions to others' feelings, see Jarymowicz [1977], as described in Chapter 6.) Behaving competitively or cooperatively is likely to demand that children respectively minimize or maximize their attention to others' feelings. The perceptual perspective-taking task demanded that children accurately judge how blocks look to another person as a function of where that person sits. In the affective perspective-taking task the children listened to four tape recordings, each focusing on a certain emotion. They were asked to describe how the actor felt and why. Children were divided, on the basis of their total cooperation score, into high and low groups. The two groups did not differ on perceptual perspective-taking. However, high cooperators recognized others' feelings more accurately, understood motives or reasons for the feelings better, and also had higher total affective perspective-taking scores. Correlational analyses provided identical results, with the magnitude of the relationships quite substantial (total affective perspective-taking and cooperation $r = .57, p < .002$). The two types of perspective taking were unrelated.

Although the relationship may have been inflated because the affective perspective-taking task was administered shortly after the series of inter-actions between children that were used to measure cooperation, these find-ings are consistent with some others, suggesting that the capacity to under-stand or infer others' feelings and motives contributes to positive interaction with others. The measures of cooperation were different from most of the measures of prosocial behavior that were used in the studies I described earlier in that they measured positive interpersonal interaction rather than relatively impersonal acts of generosity or help. Several studies suggest that the capacity to understand and infer others' feelings, motives, and thoughts relates positively to popularity among peers, positive behavior by children, and positive behavior that is directed at children by peers. This research is reviewed in Volume 2, Chapter 7. One can conclude from such findings that the more children understand others' thoughts, feelings, and motives, the more they can effectively interact with others.

As I noted, two studies, using different measures of moral reasoning, found relationships to prosocial behavior (Rubin & Schneider, 1973; Emler & Rushton, 1974). Grant, Weiner, and Rushton (1976) used several measures of moral judgment: the Kohlberg-type measures employed by Rubin and Schneider, six pairs of stories to measure intentionality (Fay, 1970), and the measure of distributive justice employed by Emler and Rushton. Their 8-year-old female subjects, from North London, won tokens while playing a bowling game. They had the option of donating these tokens to a "little orphan child depicted on a charity poster." The children's distributive justice scores were positively but not significantly related to generosity ($r = .22$). The other relationships were insubstantial. Finally, Rushton (1975) found that moral judgment, as measured by children's conceptions of moral justice on Piaget-type stories, was significantly related to the number of tokens that the children donated, which they won playing the bowling game. Moral judgment and the behavior or verbal statements by models did not interact in affecting children's behavior. However, an interaction was found in children's evaluation of the model. Those with high-moral-judg-ment scores rejected the model who preached selfishness more than those with low-moral-judgment scores.

Anchor and Cross (1974) found that moral judgment, as measured on Kohlberg's test, was related to the frequency of noncooperative moves on a prisoner's dilemma game, by both hospitalized male psychiatric patients and male college students. Subjects played the game against a partner who co-operated 50% of the time but "defected," acted noncooperatively, so that his behavior harmed the subject the other 50% of the time. Among pa-tients, postconventional subjects (those with the two most advanced stages of moral judgment) cooperated more frequently than preconventional and conventional subjects, who did not differ. Among college students, the same pattern was evident. However, with the two groups combined, all three levels significantly differed. College students cooperated more than patients. People who differ in their moral judgments may also differ in their perception of how cooperative or uncooperative other people are (Kelley & Stahleski, 1970; Kuhlman & Wimberley, 1976) and in their preferred response to provocation. Accordingly, the unprovoked competitive behavior by another person in the Anchor and Cross study may have differentially activated retaliation and competitive behavior.

Other studies have specified some characteristics of antisocial children. Chandler *et al.* (1973) found that young (preadolescent) delinquent boys had substantially poorer role-taking capacities than normal controls. I have repeatedly noted that role taking and motivational characteristics are likely to combine in determining conduct. Delinquent children and adolescents apparently frequently attribute hostility to other people (Slavson, 1965; Staub, 1971c). Their poor perspective-taking presumably allows them to see hostility as the basis of behavior they do not understand. In turn, their own aggressive behavior can be motivated by anger, revenge, or the desire to defend themselves that is aroused by others' presumed aggression. Campagne and Harter (1975) compared the moral judgment of 21 "sociopathic" residents at a state-operated treatment center for sociopaths, with that of 23 normal children, using Kohlberg-type measures. To be selected for the study the sociopathic children had to have a history of at least six antisocial "behaviors" such as vandalism, impulsive behavior, or confinement in a correctional institution. Although matched on IQ, the sociopathic children clearly showed lower levels of moral reasoning than normal controls. The former thought at the preconventional level, and the latter were in transition between preconventional and conventional reasoning. A problem with this study is that the sociopathic children had spent an average of 18 months at the correctional institution, which may have substantially affected their moral reasoning. Reasoning that applies power, self-interest, and concern about punishment and reward to the resolution of moral conflicts—characteristic of preconventional thought—probably faithfully represents realities at a correctional institution.

Jointly, the varied findings suggest that role taking, particularly affective role taking, and moral reasoning can be related to helping, sharing, cooperative behavior, and socialized conduct. Most of the research is deficient in that perceptual–cognitive characteristics and motivational characteristics of individuals were not independently considered. Motivational characteristics may affect whether role taking capacity will be engaged and whether having taken another's perspective leads to the desire for prosocial action. The influence of competence-related characteristics which, in my view (Chapter 2), are likely to modify the relationship between perceptual–cognitive and motivational variables and behavior also remained unexplored. Moreover, in studies that explored the relationship between personality characteristics and a single behavior, neither the activating potential of the situation for role taking or moral judgment nor the activating potential of the situation for motivation to act positively has been carefully considered. One could argue, for example, that individual differences in the cognitive or perceptual capacity that is represented by a child's ability to construct a story from four pictures and thereby demonstrate understanding of what these pictures would mean to another person, after that child had previously constructed a different story from seven pictures, are irrelevant to what the child thinks when presented with posters of needy children and asked to donate, since the perspective of the needy child is presented to the child. More elaborate perspective-taking—differences in how children think about how a child who is deprived of some important things lives, feels, thinks—has not been measured.

Other Morally Relevant Characteristics, Situational Influence, and Behavior. Two studies that explored the relationships between morally relevant personal characteristics other than moral judgment and role taking and some forms of prosocial behavior were reported by Dlugokinski and Firestone (1973, 1974). In the first study these researchers found that children's understanding or judgment of kindness in various situations, their selection of other-centered in contrast to self-centered or neutral values on Rokeach's (1973) scale of values, the amount they donated to UNICEF from 50¢ they received, and peer ratings of their kindness and considerateness were all significantly related. The children were middle class fifth- and eighth-graders; they attended a parochial school. The magnitude of correlations was mostly around $r = .30$. Girls tended to be more other-centered than boys on several measures. Their ranking of other-centered values was substantially higher. The intercorrelations among measures were somewhat higher for fifth-graders and girls, but not significantly so. When three of the measures were used to predict the fourth, the correlations ranged from .42 to .51. For example, the combined relationship between children's values, their judgments of kindness, their donations, and their peers' judgments of their kindness and considerateness was $r = .51$.

One of the problems with many of the studies exploring personality and behavior relationships is that single indices of behavior may be influenced by many facets of the circumstances under which the behavior is measured. In fact, varied studies showed that composite indices of prosocial behavior relate to other prosocial acts to a greater degree than do single indices (see Mussen & Eisenberg-Berg, 1977; Staub, 1979; Volume 2, Chapter 1). A composite score may be a good index of prosocial motivation; a high score indicates that the person's prosocial goal is stronger than other goals in varied situations. Consequently, such a score is likely to be a good predictor of future prosocial behavior. Similarly, several different kinds of measures, each of which can be considered an index of prosocial motivation, may combine into a highly reliable index.

In a second study Dlugokinski and Firestone (1974) essentially replicated their previous findings, again with fifth- and eighth-grade subjects in a Catholic school. The intercorrelations among measures of other-centeredness were somewhat higher in this sample than in the previous one. This study had two additional aspects. First, the children's perceptions of their mothers' child-rearing styles were evaluated; the extent to which the mother used induction—pointing out the consequences of the child's behavior for others —and power assertion—exerting power directly to discipline or influence the child—was investigated. Second, in inducing children to make donations to UNICEF from 50¢ they received for their previous cooperation, either an inductive or a power-oriented appeal was used. The former emphasized consideration for others, and the latter stressed that the school principal and the teachers thought that the children should give to UNICEF.

Very high positive correlations were found between the degree to which children perceived their parents as inductive and the measures of other-centeredness (other-centered values, girls, $r = .68$, boys, $r = .46$; donations, girls, $r = .44$, boys, $r = .30$; peer perception, girls, $r = .46$, boys, $r = .51$; all correlations significant at $p < .01$). The relationship between perceived induction and perceived power assertion was negative. Between power assertion and other-centeredness the relationships were negative, mostly significant (except with peer ratings), but mainly in the .20 to .30 range.

Although children who perceived their mothers as inductive donated more, there was a highly significant interaction between the mother's perceived discipline style and the kind of appeal that children were exposed to, in affecting donations. The "inductive children" gave more when they heard an inductive appeal rather than a power-assertive one, whereas "power-assertive" children gave more when they heard a power-assertive rather than an inductive appeal. The children responded more to the appeal that was consistent with their experience or personalities. A grade by type of appeal interaction resulted from fifth-graders responding more to the power-assertive than to the inductive appeal, and eighth graders responding more to the inductive appeal. Finally, in one class children were exposed to a neutral appeal, which communicated little about either the source of the appeal or reasons for giving. Children in this class donated substantially less than those exposed to the other two appeals.

The findings of Dlugokinski and Firestone present substantial consistency in values, understanding of kindness, behavior in interaction with others as well as in a specific instance, and the children's perceptions of their parents' behavior toward them. Although a variety of experiments have reported consistency and stability of different kinds of prosocial behavior (see Mussen & Eisenberg-Berg, 1977; Rushton, 1976; Staub, 1971; Volume 2, Chapter 1), the degree of consistency reported by Dlugokinski and Firestone appears somewhat greater than the consistency found by others. This may simply be due to random variation in populations. In contrast, it may be due to the special characteristics of the subject population. These children attended a parochial school. They may have been exposed to influences both at home and in the school that emphasized consistency in the moral domain. If this is so, their behavior in school, where the study was conducted, may have shown even greater consistency than it would have in other environments.

The interaction between the children's past experience or their perception of it and the type of appeal for donations they heard supports the interaction view emphasized in this book. Children would perceive and respond to communication directed at them in accordance with their experience and characteristics.

The same, of course, can be expected of adults. Lazarowitz et al. (1976) divided female college students into three groups as a function of the level of their moral reasoning on a measure derived from Kohlberg's test. Each participant was told that the study concerned game-playing strategies, and that she would be making choices that determined how many points she and her partner would receive. Each point was worth money. Somewhat later, the subject was shown the first choice that the partner made, more generous than the subject's own first choice. The experimenter reported that the partner presumably made that choice (a) because she did not want to have the subject get mad at her, (b) because helping was nice and everybody should do it, or (c) because helping was an important ethical value and if everybody helped the world would be a better place to live in. The level of moral reasoning of participants and the partner's level of justification interacted in determining the number of points the subjects subsequently assigned to the partner. Subjects at the lowest level in reasoning were unaffected by the information about the verbal statements of the other person. Those at the middle and upper levels showed progressively greater generosity with increasing levels of justification; the linear trend was significant in both groups. The main effect of level of reasoning by participants was not significant, although the main effect for type of appeal was significant. Further studies on the interaction between a person's level of reasoning and the kind of appeals directed at them are reviewed in Volume 2 when socialization influences are discussed (Turiel & Rothman, 1972; Rothman, 1976).

In a complex study Penner et al. (1976) explored the relationship between personality characteristics that seem directly relevant to moral behavior and the extent to which college students returned a lost dollar. Three settings were used: a psychology laboratory setting, a quasi-laboratory setting (the office of a campus testing and placement service), and a field setting (a washroom on campus). Taking the lost dollar increased linearly, whereas returning the lost dollar decreased linearly, from the laboratory to the field setting. Presumably strong situational forces to return the dollar operated in the laboratory. This was also demonstrated by the lack of relationship between personality and behavior in the laboratory. The personalities of subjects whose behavior was tested in the washroom were not evaluated. Scores on a sociopathy scale, which presumably showed a "tendency to engage in antisocial behavior with little internalization of the rules and customs of society [Penner *et al.*, 1976, p. 289]," were linearly related to the behavior in the quasi-laboratory setting. People who returned the dollar scored lowest, those who ignored it scored in the middle, and those who took it scored highest on the scale. The subjects' ranking of six values, selected primarily because of their relationship to prosocial behavior in the study by Staub, Erkut, and Jaquette (Staub, 1974a), was evaluated. Penner *et al.* report that four of these values discriminated among returners, ignorers, and takers of the dollar in a manner that was "in perfect accord with Staub's findings [p. 289]." Returners considered equality most important and a comfortable life, ambition, and cleanliness least important. The opposite was true of takers. Rokeach (1973) found that low ranking of a comfortable life and high ranking of equality was significantly related to membership by whites in black civil rights' organizations. This combination of values was also related to a nonverbal index of positive interpersonal orientation to blacks (Penner, 1971). Placing importance on ambition, a self-oriented value, a comfortable life, an even broader self-oriented value, and cleanliness, which appears to be a traditional, conservative value (Staub, 1974a), may represent a combination of values that allows little concern for other people. Low value placed on these, combined with a high value placed on some moral, positive interpersonal orientation, such as equality, might provide an index of prosocial orientation. Surprisingly, valuing helpfulness was associated with taking the dollar in this study. Finally, value placed on honesty was associated with returning the dollar. Analyses that explored the joint influence of the personality characteristics of subjects were much more successful in differentiating between takers, ignorers, and returners, than were analyses of each personal characteristic.

Social Responsibility. Another morally relevant characteristic that has been studied is social responsibility. The term *responsibility* has several referents. First, it can imply responsibility for the welfare of other human beings, as measured by Schwartz's test of ascription of responsibility. As was shown earlier in this chapter, individual differences in this type of responsibility do relate to positive behavior. Second, the term implies a sense of responsibility for following moral rules and dictates; the rules and dictates can be either personal, or of society. Different people may, of course, feel the responsibility to follow somewhat different rules. Third, responsibility implies following up promises and agreements, punctuality, doing one's job. In this context, responsibility implies reliability. Usually *responsibility* has moral implications.

Performance on measures that emphasize seemingly different types of responsibility appears related. Staub, Erkut, and Jaquette (Staub, 1974a) found, for example, with 130 college males, a highly significant relationship between scores on Schwartz's AR measure and on the test that Berkowitz and Lutterman (1968) used to measure social responsibility, which seems to be a measure of some combination of the second and third types of responsibility described. Grodman (1977) found a similarly high relationship in her female college student sample. Items on these tests imply beliefs in certain values and norms, and a feeling of personal responsibility to act according to these beliefs. The relationship between these two components, belief and responsibility, probably varies in different individuals. Therefore, separate testing of values and norms on the one hand, and of feelings of responsibility on the other, would be desirable. Moreover, none of the tests seem "pure" measures of different types of responsibility orientations.

In a previously discussed study, Willis and Goethals (1973) found that subjects high in social responsibility as measured by the distribution of their values on the Allport–Vernon–Lindzey scale acted more prosocially than low-social-responsibility subjects. Social responsibility in this instance was measured by a combination of emphasis on social values and deemphasis on economic values, an unusual definition. Social values on this test are philanthropic, altruistic, and selfless attitudes. Positive behavior in this study took the form of sacrificing a trip that the subject could win, donating it to others. A high social and low economic value presumably minimized conflict between personal goals, since it combined a positive orientation toward people with unconcern about materialistic gain.

Harris (1957) developed a paper-and-pencil measure of social responsibility in children. For Harris, social responsibility meant attitudes that favor being reliable, being accountable for one's actions, being loyal, and doing an effective job. He used a large number of statements relating to these attitudes. He had children and teachers nominate the children who had these characteristics. Nominations for the different characteristics were correlated with one another. If children thought that another child was reliable, they also tended to think that this child was accountable, tended to do an effective job, and so on. Harris found varied evidence of the validity of the measure. For example, children who were members of 4-H groups tended to score higher on this measure than children who were not.

Berkowitz and Daniels (1964) used a variant of this measure with college students in one of their studies of reactions to varying degrees of dependence. They found that social responsibility was related to helping a supervisor in one experimental condition, when the female participants previously received help on a task and the supervisor was highly dependent on the subjects' help. Berkowitz and Daniels contend that the social responsibility norm, which demands help for dependent others, was most salient in this experimental group. However, in the low-need prior-help group, the relationship approached significance. Thus, regardless of the level of dependence, subjects who appeared more socially responsible in their questionnaire responses tended to help more if they had received prior help. Did these individuals feel obligated because they received prior help? The relationship between social-responsibility scores and helping was slightly negative when subjects did not receive prior help, regardless of the level of dependence. It seems possible that, given the nature of the dependence (discussed earlier in the chapter), social responsibility was not activated by high dependence. It was, rather, activated by a feeling of obligation created by another person's help. Wrightsman (1966) also used the test that Berkowitz and Daniels adapted from Harris (1957). He found that, of a group of people who were supposed to participate in a psychology experiment, those scoring high on this scale were most likely to actually come to the laboratory. Midlarsky and Bryan (1972) used Harris's social-responsibility scale with fourth- and fifth-grade children. Although the correlations were small, the scores on this measure were significantly related to children's donations of rewards they won on a bowling game, following their exposure to a model's behavior and verbalizations in an experimental setting, as well as to another measure of donations a week and a half later. Unfortunately, interactions between treatments and personality were not examined.

Stone (1965) administered Berkowitz and Daniels' measure of social responsibility, together with three measures of social desirability, to a group of newly admitted patients in a hospital. People who score high on social-desirability tests tend to agree with many positive statements as correctly descriptive of them. For example, they indicate that they always read the editorials in the newspapers, that they always use their utensils the right way even when alone, and so on. Such persons ascribe to so many positive statements that it appears more likely that they want to appear in a favorable positive light, presumably because they desire approval and fear disapproval, than that they describe themselves truthfully. There was a significant relationship between scores on the measure of social responsibility and scores on each measure of social desirability. Stone suggested that the social-responsibility scale may also be a measure of people's desire to be seen favorably. Because being a responsible person is regarded as a favorable characteristic, people tend to answer questions in a way that shows them responsible. Midlarsky and Bryan (1972) also found a significant positive relationship between social desirability and need approval among fourth- and fifth-grade children ($r = .26$). As I noted (Staub, 1972a), high social-responsibility scores may indicate (*a*) that a person believes that other people and society in general value socially responsible conduct and (*b*) that the person is concerned with gaining approval by behaving responsibly (perhaps in contrast to other ways). If people are guided by a desire to gain approval through acting responsibly, they may behave in a socially responsible manner in many situations. Moreover, internalization of values is a matter of degree, not an either–or matter, and high scores may indicate a certain degree of internalization. If high social responsibility scores only reflected concern about approval, presumably people with high scores would have been more helpful under high dependence in the Berkowitz and Daniels (1964) study. Finally, people may frequently hope to gain approval from others by doing what they themselves believe to be right.

Some additional research findings may be interpreted as support for the conception that socially responsible individuals identify with society's values rather than considering their values and beliefs as independent of society's. Berkowitz and Lutterman (1968) administered a brief version of the social-responsibility scale to a statewide sample of 766 adults in Wisconsin. These persons were interviewed about varied aspects of their values, beliefs, and activities. For purposes of analysis they were divided into those who identified themselves as middle class and those who identified themselves as working class. Each group was divided into low, medium, and high on the social-responsibility scale. Some of the many differences were the following: High scorers reported more involvement in the community, in terms of contributing money to educational or religious organizations, volunteering time for charitable, health, or civic organizations, and participating in civic groups. Political involvement in terms of interest, voting, and work for political candidates was greater among high scorers. On some measures middle-class subjects who scored in the middle range on the social-responsibility scale were in between low and high scorers; on other measures they were similar to low scorers. In the working-class sample, middle and low scorers were usually similar. With regard to beliefs about unemployment, government participation in social welfare, and other matters, middle-class, socially responsible individuals tended to be traditional and rather conservative; working-class individuals who were high scorers were less traditional and less conservative. Socially responsible individuals appear to accept and believe in the values of their social milieu. High scorers seem involved, traditional, inner-directed, and not alienated from their society. These self-report data show people scoring high on Berkowitz and Lutterman's social-responsibility scale to be concerned about duty and maintaining a reasonable social order, but not especially concerned about the welfare of individuals, social justice, and the like.

The Capacity for Control, Competence, Social Desirability, and Other Nonmoral Characteristics

As the analysis in Chapter 2 noted, competence-related characteristics are expected to enhance prosocial helping. When social conditions indicate the desirability of behaving prosocially, people who appear competent to do so would be expected by other people to help. Doctors, not plumbers, are expected to help a person with a physical injury. People who feel competent, who have a sense of instrumentality in accomplishing what needs to be done, would expect themselves to help more. Individuals whose moral values or empathic reactions provide a motivation to be helpful would be most likely to take action if they felt competent. Those who feel competent may also allow, to a greater degree, their motivation for help to be activated. It is possible, however, for competent people to be helpful for "irrelevant" reasons, because of motives unrelated to another's need. Satisfaction gained from the exercise of one's competence or from the desire to impress other people would be such a reason. High achievement motivation, the desire to excel or do one's best under all circumstances, would be another reason.

A number of studies have shown some relationship between prosocial action and individual differences in locus of control—in the degree to which people feel that they can influence events in their lives ("internals") in contrast to events being controlled by luck, chance, other people, and in general forces external to themselves ("externals"). Unfortunately, most studies examined the relationship between locus of control and some positive behavior without considering motivation.

In an early study Gore and Rotter (1963) found that black college students who engaged in social action were more likely to be internals than to be externals. In a follow-up study Strickland (1965) found that blacks who were active in the civil rights movement were more internal than subjects described by their professors as inactive. The groups did not differ in need for approval, but active persons were older and more educationally advanced.

Several experimental studies explored the relation between locus of control and some form of positive behavior. Midlarsky (1971) measured locus of control in a study where male subjects could help another male manipulate small objects, on what seemed like a motor-coordination task. This task was to be performed under stress, the subject receiving a shock each time he touched a small object. The subjects always completed the task first, and could help another person, the confederate, who was still working on his somewhat different task. There was a high correlation between locus of control scores and the amount that subjects helped ($r = .54$, $p < .001$). Unfortunately, the interaction between the influence of locus of control and the influence of the several experimental treatments was not reported. Such interaction may well have been found, since the treatment variations could have differentially activated a sense of competence in high-locus-of-control subjects. For example, feedback about the subjects' sensitivity to shocks and variation in the degree of dependence of the confederate may have differentially elicited feelings of control. That locus of control is related to helping in this situation was replicated by Midlarsky and Midlarsky (1973, 1976).

Locus of control in the studies just discussed was evaluated with Rotter's (1966) measure, or one derived from it, which has some limitations. First, it attempts to measure a generalized belief that one can influence events, across all domains of activity. However, an individual may believe that he can exercise little control in one domain of his life but a great deal in another domain. Mischel *et al.* (1974) developed two alternative tests for children, one to measure children's belief in their ability to influence the likelihood of positive outcomes, the other to measure their belief in their ability to exercise control over negative events, that by what they do they can avoid negative things happening to them. Children's scores on these two tests were unrelated. Another, related problem with Rotter's test is that many of the items focus on a particular domain of activity, the ability to exert influence in the political realm. Many people who feel limited ability to control events in this realm may have a strong sense of internal control in other realms. Complex and differentiated tests of competence are needed, not only of locus of control, but also of competence in the senses that I discussed (Chapter 2): the availability of plans of action, the capacity to generate plans, and competence in specific behaviors.

In another study (Staub, 1968), I measured fourth- and fifth-grade children's locus of control and the manner in which it interacted with success, failure, and intermediate performance on a bowling game in affecting children's donations of candy received as a reward for participating. There was a significant positive relationship between locus of control scores and sharing in the success group; a marginally significant negative relationship was found in the failure and intermediate groups. Subjects in the last two groups tended to behave similarly on all measures, suggesting that intermediate-performance subjects experienced failure. The difference between the correlation in the success group and in the failure and intermediate groups was significant. The more children felt that what happened to them was under their own control, the more they may have experienced satisfaction in their success on the game, which in turn enhanced their sharing. In contrast, when their sense of control was great the children may have experienced greater dissatisfaction following failure, and this may have decreased their willingness to share. These interpretations are consistent with the extensive findings about the influence of positive and negative experiences on helping (Chapter 6).

Some other evidence also suggests that people who feel competent to act will do so more. Midlarsky (1968) notes that in natural disasters, such as tornadoes, hurricanes, or floods, people who have had past experience with such disasters and/or have had training that makes them specially competent are more likely to take action to help the community. The reports about such events are primarily anecdotal. It is possible that persons with special training, such as firemen, and others with relevant experience feel special responsibility to act, sometimes even regard their behavior as part of their job responsibility. Thus competence, responsibility, and obligation may be confounded.

In a further study Lenrow (1965) differentiated children on the basis of their tendencies to overcome obstacles to the accomplishment of their goals in their everyday activities in nursery school. The children who were best at doing so were most likely to be helpful. The measure of help was of a special, and interesting kind: In the course of a puppet show the child could return an object, which fell off the stage, to one of the puppets.

Researchers have explored the influence of other characteristics not directly related to morality on positive behavior. For example, a child's need or desire for approval may suggest the extent to which the child would want to conform to socially desirable societal norms that prescribe positive behavior. Interestingly, need approval was found to be negatively related both to sharing and to children themselves eating candy in the course of their interaction with another child (Staub & Sherk, 1970). The children who possessed candy may have been uncertain about appropriate behavior. Their behavior may have reflected their uncertainty as to whether it was appropriate to share. One characteristic of people with a high need for approval may be that under ambiguous circumstances, when what is expected of them on the basis of social norms or other people's wishes is unclear, they may minimize the likelihood of disapproval by not taking any action. Thus, under conditions of ambiguity and uncertainty people with high need for approval may act less prosocially. In a further study (Staub, 1973) I found that children's need for approval interacted with other variables in predicting the amount of candy they left for other children. Third-grade children with a high need for approval who performed well on a bowling game shared less candy than children in other experimental groups. Presumably these children felt that they earned and deserved the candy, and since they had a right to it their behavior would not be disapproved of by others, even if it was known to them. Children with a high need for approval maximized their own gain when they believed that such behavior was socially appropriate.

Midlarsky and Bryan (1972) found generally negligible but positive relationships between social-desirability scores and children's donations. Only one correlation, boys' donations on a delayed posttest, was significant. In this instance, donating was clearly the appropriate behavior. In a further study Midlarsky and Midlarsky (1973) found that social desirability was unrelated to male students' helping behavior that demanded the suffering of electric shocks in order to save another person from shock. In neither of these studies was the interactive influence of individual differences in social desirability and of the experimental treatments analyzed.

What seems socially desirable to a person is likely to be a function of existing environmental conditions (including social influences that define what is good, desirable, and appropriate) and personal values and beliefs, which provide another source for defining what is good and desirable. To understand the relationship between individual differences in the need for social approval and prosocial behavior it is necessary to vary experimental conditions in terms of the social desirability or appropriateness of positive behavior, and to study need approval in conjunction with personality characteristics, which would indicate what people believe would be approved by others. A similar approach is necessary to study the influence of other personal characteristics.

Borden (1975) found, for example, that people's level of aggressiveness tended to match that of their opponents. When, however, they were made to believe that an observer of their behavior was a member of an organization with either aggressive or pacifist values, significant differences resulted in the intensity at which they set the shock levels to be administered to their opponents. Behavior was influenced by what other people valued. Would the influence of observers have been greater for people with high need for approval? The participants' own values regarding aggression, their need for approval, and experimental treatments may have interactively affected their behavior.

In one study McGovern (1976) explored the relationship between helping behavior and a personality characteristic seemingly similar to need approval: social anxiety. Social anxiety was measured by a test in which subjects were to indicate their choices between onerous and tedious activities, such as "cleaning out a cesspool," and embarrassing experiences, such as "having someone walk into a room while you are picking your nose." The extent to which a person chose the former over the latter was a measure of his social anxiety. Participants selected for this study were those in the top and bottom 15% of the distribution of scores. Subjects could push a button to prevent another person from receiving a shock. In a no-threat condition nothing was to stop them from doing so. In a physical-threat condition, if they pushed the button they would receive the shock themselves. In a social-threat condition, they were told to remain "as motionless as possible during the experiment," so that their physiological reactions could be accurately measured. This was essentially a prohibition condition, similar to conditions that were previously found to inhibit helping (Staub, 1971b, 1974a). Subjects high in social anxiety performed the helpful act, pushing the button, significantly less than those low in social anxiety. The difference was unaffected by treatments. People exposed to either social threat (31%) or physical threat (39%) helped substantially less frequently than those exposed to no threat (87%). McGovern explains the finding that high-social-anxiety subjects consistently helped less as due to the limited amount of time they had in which to make the decision about pushing the button (10 seconds) and to the fact that they were not told whether or not they should respond. The latter explanation seems more reasonable, particularly since there were several trials. Both ambiguity about what is appropriate and others' expectations may have strong impact on high-social-anxiety people.

Many other differences among people could be considered, and their relationships to positive behavior explored. For example, differences in educational level, socioeconomic class, and other demographic characteristics may be related to positive behavior. Differences in positive behavior are presumably mediated by personal characteristics associated with the demographic ones. For example, Almond and Verba (1963) reported that the values of generosity and considerateness were positively related to educational level. People with varied education are likely to differ, moreover, in their earning capacity, and therefore in wealth. This makes the sacrifice of material possessions less burdensome. What other values and beliefs are associated with social class and education? What behavioral differences exist? Research on these questions is extremely sparse. Although some studies found children and adults from upper-middle or middle classes to be more generous or more helpful than children or adults from lower classes (Doland & Adelberg, 1967; see Gergen *et al.*, 1972), lower-class housewives reported greater willingness to give to those who needed help, whereas middle-class housewives were more concerned with reciprocity (Muir & Weinstein, 1962). Moreover, in Turkey at least, the poorest children were most generous (Ugurel-Semin, 1952). On the whole, investigators have not focused, so far, on the relationship of these variables to helping.

The consequences of differences in religion, and in the extent that people are religious, on their positive behavior and related values are also relevant, but little known. The correlates of religion and religiosity are quite complex. Some of this may be due to differences in types of religious orientations. For some people, going to church and following some dictates of religion are part of properly filling a social role, as well as a source of social contacts. It may also provide comfort and security. The religiosity of others derives from deep-seated beliefs (Allport & Ross, 1967). Depending on the dictates of their religion, the latter, but not the former, might be expected to show greater consideration for others.

Issues for Future Research

Several issues ought to be noted with regard to the research that has been reviewed. The findings provide some knowledge about personality characteristics that relate to positive and, more generally, moral behavior. It is important to know that moral judgment, social responsibility, role taking, and other characteristics sometimes relate to positive behavior. If, however, we are to increase our understanding of prosocial behavior and morality, more elaborate studies, guided by both theoretical and methodological considerations, need to be conducted.

First, a particular personality characteristic, such as moral judgment, may affect behavior because of its perceptual influence. Second, it may affect behavior because differences in moral judgment lead to different types of reasoning about a situation and therefore to the application of different moral values, norms, and rules. Third, it may affect behavior because of differences in the affective reactions it leads to. Fourth, it may also affect behavior because of a sense of responsibility to act in promoting or reaching some goal that is implied by moral values and norms. Individual differences in instrumentality, in a sense of competence in dealing with a particular situation, are also important. In different people, perception, interpretation, the application of moral values and norms, feelings of personal responsibility, affective reactions, and instrumentality may be related in different ways. Thus, it seems important to attempt to measure each of these separately, and to study both the relationships among them and their individual and joint relationships to behavior. The interrelationships among varied characteristics are essential to consider. To some degree, this is being done. Role taking and moral judgment in particular are being considered in relation to each other. But, how do social responsibility of varied kinds and specific values relate to these characteristics? Do certain value orientations give rise to empathic reactions, as I suggested (Chapter 2)? A particular personality characteristic becomes meaningful primarily if its relationship to other characteristics and its independent and joint or cumulative relationship to both psychological processes and behavior are considered. The study of such interrelatedness of personality, psychological processes, and behavior will provide us with scientifically valid information that enhances not only understanding, but also our ability to predict.

We need theories that consider the influence of varied personal characteristics, circumstances, the psychological processes they generate, and behavior in relation to each other. I suggested, for example, that the activating potential of varied situations for varied personal goals needs to be specified (see the model described in Chapter 2); others may prefer different concepts. We need to address questions, however, such as the manner in which role taking capacities are necessary for helping and the relevance of certain moral values in contrast to others by analyzing role taking and moral judgment in relation to situations and the behavior required in them. Sometimes circumstances clearly specify the nature of the need and the feelings of the person who needs help. Values emphasizing the importance of the welfare of each human being may be relevant at one time, but more impersonal values, such as justice, may be most relevant at another time.

Finally, it is highly desirable to use meaningful measures of prosocial behavior, measures that reflect the demands that are placed on human beings by their social world in real life. We also need to use several, and varied, measures to gain a reasonable estimate of individual differences in behavior and of how different kinds of behaviors relate to one another (Staub, 1979; Volume 2, Chapter 1). In different research, or even in the same study, we may want to gain a broad estimate of behavioral tendencies and their relationship to other aspects of personality. We may also want to attempt to predict specific behavior on the basis of varied personal characteristics or prior behavior. Both are useful, and they complement each other.

Orientation to the Self and Others: The Effects of Positive and Negative Experiences, Thoughts, and Feelings

chapter 6

In the course of the preceding chapters the relationship between a person and others has been repeatedly considered. In the literature on prosocial behavior it is usually implied that a conflict exists between a person's own interests and those of other people; if so, to help others one has to sacrifice one's own interests.

Helping behavior represents a particular type of contact between the self and others. It involves three elements, each of which has varied components: the self, the other, and the connection between the two. The self has legitimate interests. When will such interests be sacrificed for others? External pressure as well as internal forces can lead to such sacrifice. However, the assumption of a conflict between the interests of the self and the interests of other people represents a limited view of helping behavior. Most likely, a person can see his goals as conflicting with, unrelated to, or identical with the goals of others. That is, the perceived connection between the self and others can be quite variable. Differences in orientation toward other people and in prosocial values provide a relatively enduring source of such variations. The degree of similarity to, familiarity with, or liking for particular other people and the degree of identification with their goals might also be important influences on how the connection between the self and others is perceived. Moreover, a person's orientation toward himself also affects helping behavior. Feeling good or bad, being more or less concerned about the self, liking oneself more or less, all are likely to affect the perception or experience of relationship between the three elements.

The Effects of Success and Failure, Moods, and Self-Concern on Positive Behavior

In a by now substantial group of studies, the participants, before they were provided with an opportunity to help someone, were exposed to experiences that presumably temporarily affected their psychological state: their feelings of competence, mood, self-esteem, self-concern, and the like. The findings strongly show that positive and negative experiences affect willingness to help others.

Competence

In one group of experiments researchers provided false feedback to subjects about their performance on tasks, to make them believe that they were either competent or incompetent in a specific activity. Observations of certain real-life events, for example, disasters such as tornadoes (Midlarsky, 1968), suggested that people who possess relevant skills or competence might be more helpful than others when such competence is demanded in helping others.

In one experiment Kazdin and Bryan (1971) had college students engage in one of two tasks. One task was related to physical capacities and health; the other task was related to creativity. The experimenters provided feedback, telling the subjects either that they were very good at the task, better than people their age usually were, or that their performances were about average. As subjects left the room they encountered a nurse in the corridor who asked them to donate blood as part of the ongoing blood drive at the university. Subjects who were made to feel competent were more likely to agree, regardless of the kind of task they had engaged in, whether they were made to feel physically healthy and strong or to feel creative.

In a second study Kazdin and Bryan attempted to evaluate whether people who volunteered would actually donate blood. They arranged for parental permission to donate before their subjects came to participate. The participants who agreed to donate were asked to do so immediately, in a room further down the corridor. With the first of the two experimenters who conducted this study, the competence manipulation had a significant effect. "Competent" subjects were more likely either to volunteer more or to volunteer and donate blood more, but competence had no effect on the act of donation alone. This was due to a large number of subjects who volunteered but later refused to donate. (Considering all subjects, guided by both experimenters, out of 24 who volunteered only 11 donated.) With the second experimenter, the competence manipulation had no effect. An experimenter difference is not particularly surprising; it has also been found in other studies (Staub, 1974a), and it would be found more frequently if in more studies several experimenters administered treatments and the differences in their influences were explored. Any kind of interpersonal interaction might be perceived differently and might create different feelings and experiences depending on the characteristics of the participants.

In another study Midlarsky (1971) had subjects ostensibly participate in a motor coordination task under stressful conditions. The male subject and male confederate were both manipulating small objects, receiving a shock each time they touched one of the objects. The confederate's task was always more difficult, because the objects he worked with were smaller, so that a fair amount of his task still had to be done at the time the subject completed his task. Subjects who were made to feel more competent in dealing with shocks and less sensitive to them were more helpful and manipulated a greater proportion of the objects that the confederate still had to work with after the subject's task was completed. However, in this study the competence manipulation was confounded. In order to establish differences in competence the "less competent" subjects received more intense shocks before the measure of help than did the more competent subjects. Differences in helping might have been due to differences in the expected cost and in sensitivity to the shocks that resulted from the prior experience.

In another study Midlarsky and Midlarsky (1973) eliminated this problem. The subjects received the same intensity shocks, but their apparent GSR reactions to the shock were varied, to indicate that they were more or less sensitive to (competent in dealing with) shocks. The researchers also varied the status of the subject relative to the confederate by communicating either to the subject or to the confederate, before the opportunity for help was provided, that the subject's or the confederate's opinions, as expressed on a preliminary questionnaire, were astute and that the experimenter would be interested in the subject (or confederate) as a potential research assistant. They also varied the cost of helping by varying the intensity of shocks in the course of manipulating the objects.

All three independent variables had significant effects. Variation in competence affected helping, but primarily in the low-status condition; that is, status and competence affected helping in an interactive manner. High-status subjects helped more in both competence conditions. The authors proposed that positive status discrepancy might lessen self-concern or result in a sense of noblesse oblige. Competence might lead to more help for the same reasons, or it might result in expectations that the cost of help would be lower when one was competent, higher when one was not.

The effects of both "status" difference and competence might be explained by the effects of these treatments on how the subjects felt about themselves. Status difference was created by the experimenter, who strongly praised and showed interest in either the confederate or the subject. Being praised in this manner would be likely to make a person feel good about himself; it would be likely to enhance self-esteem. When the subjects were praised they might also have felt superior to the confederate. Astuteness is probably more important a characteristic for college students than shock resistance. When participants were judged astute and obviously highly valued by a person in authority, information about their competence in dealing with shocks ceased to matter as an influence on their self-esteem. Consequently, high-status subjects helped more regardless of the competence treatment they received. When the confederate rather than the subject was praised, so that the latter had reason to evaluate himself poorly in relation to the former, the subjects who received information about their superior competence in receiving shocks might have been saved from a poor self-evaluation and the negative feelings associated with it, and this might have resulted in greater helping behavior.

The findings of both the Midlarsky and Midlarsky (1973) study and the Kazdin and Bryan (1971) study suggest that treatments affected some general state of the subjects, rather than their perception of special competence to provide help. Nonetheless, belief in some special competence may be important when helping requires such competence.

Kazdin and Bryan (1971) attempted to explore the effect of their treatments on the subjects' mood. Participants who were told that they were highly competent reported more happiness than less-competent subjects in both studies, but the two groups did not differ in reports of anger, anxiety, and fatigue. However, no correlations were found between reports of happiness and the participants' stated intentions to donate blood or their actual donations. It is possible, however, that self-esteem, preoccupation with the self, or a general sense of well-being, which were not measured, were affected by treatments. These in turn might have led to both higher ratings of happiness and the intention to be helpful.

In another study that varied competence (Harris & Huang, 1973) some subjects received high scores on a "visual creativity" test, and others received low scores. Verbal communications emphasized the excellent or the poor quality of the scores. Still other subjects received no information about their performance. The test consisted of block design and a picture sensitivity component. In the latter, the subjects recorded their impressions and interpretations of five abstract pictures. On their way out of the test room, each subject was asked to help the experimenter by writing creative color names on pieces of colored cardboard that were to be used in future tests of color sensitivity. The subjects in the high-competence group were divided into four groups. They either received no further communication, or they received one of the following communications: (a) that the task must have been easy for them because they were so creative; (b) that they must have enjoyed this kind of thing because they were so creative; or (c) that they had a responsibility to others to use their creativity. Analyses of duration of helping and of the number of items that subjects wrote showed nearly identical treatment effects.

Subjects who were made to feel competent but did not receive additional communications tended to help more than those who received no information and those who were made to believe that they were incompetent, but the differences were not significant. All three of the added communications given to "competent" persons significantly enhanced helping in comparison to the above three groups. Perhaps the relationship between feeling competent and helping became more salient, or the added statements increased demand characteristics; possibly they provided an elaboration of the competence procedure that was necessary to make it effective. Telling "competent" persons that the task must have been easy for them, which might have decreased how costly helping seemed, increased helping most. One likely aspect of cost is people's expectation of or concern about poor performance on a future task; the communication may have reduced such cost. Treatments had no effect on how happy, successful, responsible, or creative the subjects felt they were. However, subjects who helped differed from nonhelpers in that the former felt they were more creative and somewhat more successful. Perhaps the treatments affected those individuals who were predisposed to think of themselves as creative and successful.

One study in which experimental treatments attempted to communicate to subjects that they were either extremely sensitive or insensitive to various stimuli (olfactory, auditory, or tactile) found no subsequent difference in helping behavior (Rudestam *et al.*, 1971). Half the subjects in both the high- and low-sensitivity groups had their success or failure verbally emphasized by the experimenter. Upon leaving the experimental room the subjects encountered an attractive female who was going in the opposite direction, carrying a collection of large, seemingly heavy boxes. Males helped more than females, across all conditions. Possibly the experimental treatments had been unsuccessful in affecting feelings of competence, self-esteem, or mood. Participants may have been relatively unconcerned about their sensitivity to olfactory, auditory, or tactile stimuli.

To sum up, in several studies experimental treatments that attempted to vary feelings of competence enhanced helping. The effects may depend on the nature of the competence that researchers attempt to enhance or diminish, the nature of the subject population, how important that kind of competence is for them, and the characteristics of experimenters and how they relate to the subjects. In the studies discussed and other studies another source of variation in treatment effects may be the substantial differences in the nature of the dependent measures. In most of the studies control groups were not included, so it is difficult to say whether competence and the positive feeling that may have been generated by the treatments enhanced helping, or whether incompetence and associated negative feelings diminished helping.

Success and Failure

A series of experiments explored the effects of success or failure on a task on subsequent prosocial behavior. In what way are these experiments different from the competence studies that were just reviewed? From one point of view there is no difference: Subjects in the competence studies were made to believe that they did well on a task (and were competent) or that they did poorly (and were incompetent.) However, the competence studies originally attempted to explore the effect of treatments on the participants' willingness to help in an activity related to their competence or incompetence. The findings showed that competence in irrelevant domains—in other words, an experience of success or failure on a task irrelevant to the helpful activity—can have just as great an effect on helping behavior as success or failure in relevant domains. Thus, competence and success and failure manipulations might have the same psychological consequences.

In an early study Berkowitz and Connor (1966) provided subjects with the opportunity to earn $1 by completing a crossword puzzle within 2½ minutes. The subjects who were made to experience success helped more, subsequently, by making envelopes for a dependent supervisor, than subjects who were made to fail or those in a control group. Subjects who experienced failure helped somewhat less than control subjects, but not significantly so. Berkowitz and Connor reasoned that success generates a "glow of goodwill" that results in greater willingness to tolerate the costs associated with helping another person.

In another study Isen (1970) had male and female teachers work on a series of tasks that were presented as measures of perceptual–motor skills. The experiment was conducted in a school library. Subjects received, on completion of the task, $1 for participation. Then their performance was scored and they were told either that they did extremely well or that they did extremely poorly. While waiting to sign up for the second part of the experiment, someone placed in the room a collection box for donations for the air conditioning of the junior high school. Without any further solicitation and while alone, subjects who had succeeded donated significantly more ($.46) than those who had failed ($.07).

In a second study Isen (1970) used the same population of subjects, and the same experimental treatments, but different dependent measures. To evaluate helping behavior, a confederate carrying an armload of objects entered the subjects' room. Going through a series of prescribed actions, the confederate stopped at the desk to pick something up, coughed, approached the subject, stepped over some wires, and dropped a book she was carrying while passing the subject. Subjects who were told that they did very well helped (by offering help, picking up the book, or opening the door for the confederate) more than those who were told that they did poorly on their task. Subsequently, the subjects who succeeded remembered more of the actions of the confederate than the subjects who failed.

Isen (1970) conducted a third study, with college students as subjects. The procedures were nearly identical with those in the second study. A control group was added in which participants did not work on the perceptual–motor task but simply rated its difficulty. The subjects in the success condition were significantly more helpful than those in the failure and control groups. Although failure subjects helped slightly less than control subjects, the difference was not significant. In the success condition, males tended to be slightly ($p < .10$) more helpful than females.

On a written measure, failure subjects remembered significantly less of the confederate's actions than either success or control subjects, but success subjects remembered only slightly, not significantly, more than control subjects. In this study Isen included some additional tests of the effects of treatments, hoping that these would help explain the effect on prosocial behavior. Subjects in the failure group attempted to initiate conversation with the confederate significantly less frequently than those in the success group and marginally significantly less than those in the control group. Subjects in the success group expressed preference to work with others on the next task significantly more often than subjects in the control group, but failure subjects also preferred to work with others slightly more than controls, and did not differ from those in the success group.

Success and failure had multiple effects, but as with the effects of competence on moods and behavior the effects seem somewhat independent. For example, measures of attention and help did not relate to each other. As I earlier suggested, the experience of competence or incompetence, and also of success or failure, may affect general psychological states, which are expressed in a variety of ways. The nature and quality of such general states may vary depending on the exact nature of the experience. People who failed on a task may become concerned about how others evaluate them; they may feel negatively about themselves, perhaps somewhat ashamed and humiliated. Preoccupied with self-concern, their attention might turn inward, away from external events; their feeling of comfort in moving toward others and initiating interaction might decrease. The opposite might happen to subjects who had a successful experience. Under certain conditions either of these effects may in turn affect helping behavior. Under other conditions, when the amount of attention one has to pay to others in order to notice their need for help is minimal (e.g., probably most subjects noticed that the confederate dropped the book) and the degree of interaction that is required to help is also minimal, the subjects' prosocial behavior might be more directly affected by their underlying emotional state. The psychological consequences of positive and negative experiences are further discussed later in this chapter.

Warm Glow and Deserving. Will the "warm glow of success" (Isen, 1970) increase prosocial behavior at all ages, under all conditions? In a study that I conducted (Staub, 1968), fourth- and fifth-grade children played a bowling game. Some received very high scores; others, intermediate scores; and still others, poor scores. These scores were predetermined, electrically controlled. Then the children received a bowl of candy of their choice as a reward for participating. While they were alone, with the experimenter engaged in some activity behind a room divider, they could put their candy in a paper bag, and if they wished they could leave some candy in the bowl for another child, a classmate, who would not otherwise receive candy, since there was not enough left for all the children.

. Surprisingly, treatments affected children differently as a function of the relatively small age difference between fourth- and fifth-graders. Fourth-grade children shared less in the success group, and more in both the failure and intermediate-performance groups; the difference between success and failure was significant. For fifth-graders there was a reversal; children shared more in the success group than in the failure or intermediate groups. The interaction between age and treatments was significant.

On the one hand, children learn with increasing age that they ought to share their possessions with others. Sharing and donating are desirable actions, promoted by societal values and norms. Success in an activity might reduce the significance of material possessions to people. If success makes people feel good, they need material possessions less to make them feel good and they are more willing to sacrifice them and act in a socially valued manner. However, children are also likely to learn a norm or value contradictory to that of sharing—that if they work hard and perform well on a task they can earn rewards, praise, and other good things. Since they earn them, they deserve them, and have a special right to them. Children may come to believe that when their possessions are earned they have a greater right to them, and the values and norms that prescribe sharing are less applicable. Moreover, it is possible that working for and earning rewards adds to their value. Several studies have in fact shown that children who are made to believe that they earned and deserved their rewards share less of them than children whose rewards are unearned and/or less deserved (Long & Lerner, 1974; Staub, 1973; Staub & Noerenberg, 1978).

How do these two contradictory forces combine? Learning to share gradually increases with age, and sharing behavior is enhanced by success, except under conditions of deserving. The belief that under certain conditions one earns and thus deserves rewards is probably intensified after children enter school, since within most schools the notion of earning is stressed and has substantial influence for some time. Although the influence of "deserving" continues to exist throughout life, as the concept of equity and research supporting it show, its strength may decline with increasing age relative to norms and values that prescribe sharing. If the reversal reported earlier for the effects of success and failure is reliable, then for some reason the interval between fourth and fifth grade may be a turning point in the relative influence of these forces. If so, before fourth grade children would share less after success than after failure; after fifth grade, children would share more.

To explore this reasoning, in another study (Staub, 1973) I extended the age range of participants. This time, I used third- and sixth-grade subjects. There was again a significant treatment by age interaction. In third grade, as expected, children shared more in the failure and intermediate-performance groups than in the success group. Contrary to expectation, in sixth grade the treatments did not differentially affect sharing.

In these studies success and failure were viewed as experiences that affected children's feelings of deserving. In other research several investigators attempted to vary children's perceptions of having earned and deserved rewards more directly, and independently of variation in success and failure. In one study (Staub, 1973; Staub & Noerenberg, 1978) we had children play a bowling game and perform well, and then receive candy either as reward for their good performance, or for reasons unrelated to their playing the bowling game (so that they might enjoy themselves on the subsequent task). Children in both conditions listened, in the company of another child who did not have candy, to a tape-recorded story. The children who earned and presumably felt that they deserved the rewards shared less; the treatments also affected their own use of the candy. Variation in the potential recipients' beliefs about the other child's right to the candy—whether the latter earned the candy or received it for the two of them—strongly affected the recipients' behavior. When they believed that they, too, had a right to the candy they made requests and in other ways exerted influence to receive candy. This study demonstrated that a belief in deserving affects both a child's sharing behavior, and a potential recipient's behavior. What happens to the available resources is determined in a highly transactional manner, through interaction between potential donors and recipients.

In another study Long and Lerner (1974) had fourth-graders work on a task and receive a certain amount of money as compensation. They were made to believe either that the money was proper payment for children of their age or that it was proper payment for better qualified, older children. Since there were no older children available to do the task, the subjects were paid that amount anyway. Children who received proper payment presumably felt that they deserved the money. They subsequently shared less of their reward than children who had been told that they were overpaid and presumably felt less deserving of the reward.

Olejnik (1976) had kindergarten to third-grade children cut out either 20 shapes or 4 shapes from paper. Both groups received 19 candies as reward; this was the amount that other children had previously judged to be the proper payment for cutting out 20 shapes. A significant interaction between age and the effects of deserving was found. Kindergartners clearly shared less when they received the proper payment for their work, that is, when they presumably felt they deserved the rewards; they shared more when they were overpaid. However, there was a continuous increase by age in the amount of deserved reward children shared and a continuous decrease in the amount of undeserved reward they shared. By third grade, children shared more of the deserved reward and less of the undeserved reward.

In another study Miller and Smith (1977) used the procedure earlier employed by Long and Lerner (1974) to explore fifth-grade children's sharing with others. Some of their subjects received proper payment; others received overpayment. A third group of children were "underpaid"—they were told that they received the amount that less-qualified third-graders usually received. The children had the opportunity to share some of their earnings with others. These others either would not get money because there was not enough left for them (not responsible), or they had previously received money for their effort but lost it and would like it to be replaced (responsible). There was a significant effect of deserving and a significant deservingness by responsibility interaction, as follows. Children shared most when they were overpaid, less when they were properly paid, and still less when they were underpaid; all the differences were significant. In addition, the amount shared with responsible and not responsible others was not different when children were overpaid, but the subjects shared less with others who were responsible for their need when they were properly paid or underpaid.

Other research shows that variables that seem related to deserving rewards affect sharing behavior among children as young as 4 to 5 years of age. Masters (1971) varied social comparison; some children received less, others received more, and still others received an amount equal to what the child who was their partner in playing a game received. In two other groups, the children played the game alone. In one group they received less reward than what was deposited in a box for all the other nursery-school children. A second group was a no-comparison control group. Children who received an equal amount shared significantly more with their partners, after the partners left the room, than children in any other group. On a second measure of generosity, children who received less reward than the amount placed in the box (the social-comparison group) shared less with a friend in nursery school than those in the other groups. Perhaps this was due to the friend being one of the children in the nursery school who received the rewards placed in the box. Finally, children in both the low-reward and social-comparison groups rewarded themselves more than those in other groups. They took a larger share of goods than what they left the experimenter, in playing a game with her. Children in the equal-reward condition took less for themselves.

This study shows that what other people receive as rewards can serve as a standard for what a child feels he should receive. Social comparison is probably a frequent and important basis of belief about what one is entitled to. It is of interest, also, that children who received fewer rewards and those who received more rewards shared less with their absent partner than children who received an equal amount of the reward. Having received more may in itself have made children feel more deserving and may have led them to favor themselves. Having received less in comparison to the standard set by the reward that the partner received may have made them feel underpaid, receiving less than what they deserved; thus, they shared less. It should be noted that sharing behavior with a partner was not affected after children received more, less, or the same amount as the partner, if the partner remained in the room (Masters, 1968, 1969). The presence of the other child may have made it difficult for the subjects to act on the basis of social comparison and feelings of deserving.

Clearly, there is a substantial amount of consistency in these studies. Conditions that can be expected to result in feelings of having more or less deserved rewards affect subsequent donations for or sharing with others. Generally, children shared earned and deserved rewards less than undeserved rewards. Moreover, variation in one's own and in another person's deservingness seem to affect generosity jointly. However, there is also inconsistency in how deservingness was found to affect children's behavior at different ages. Partly, the effects of "deserving" at different ages may be a function of how clearly standards for what is deserved and what is under- or overpayment are built into the experimental situation, in contrast to children having to apply their own previously learned standards. Furthermore, different populations of children may have learned different standards about deserving and sharing at different ages. Whether the activities by which rewards are acquired are work, for which children receive payment, or performance on a game may also make a difference, since deserving may be more powerfully tied to the former in children's experience than to the latter. Another difference may be that following success and failure several psychological processes are active, in addition to deserving: feeling good as a result of the success, and a positive self-esteem; feeling bad following failure, and using the rewards either as self-therapy or to share and thereby repair one's image in others' eyes.

Feelings of success and failure associated with being a competent or incompetent person were probably produced in some of these studies but not in others, thus contributing to variations in treatment effects.

Success, Failure, and Maintaining a Positive Image.   The effects of success and failure on children's sharing behavior were explored in a series of studies by Isen, Horn, and Rosenhan (1973). These researchers showed, with fourth-grade subjects, that the experience of success in a bowling game resulted in greater charitableness than control experiences that involved playing a different game without feedback about performance, or observing an experimenter playing the game. Subjects who failed on the game were less charitable than those who succeeded, but they did not differ from control subjects. The measure of charitableness was the amount of money that children put into a collection box for the purpose of buying toys for poor children in Philadelphia. The box was brought into the room by a second experimenter. The children received the money that they shared for their help with the study *before* they played the game.

In a second experiment, with third-graders, the procedures were changed somewhat, mainly to associate the experimenter to a greater degree with the charity (she was the person collecting for the toy fund, and she mentioned the opportunity to donate even before children played the game). The failure and success treatments were more elaborate, to emphasize the experience more. Upon returning to the room the experimenter asked children how they performed. Under these conditions both the success and failure children contributed to charity more than control children, and more children from the success and failure groups than from the control group contributed. The greater sharing by children who failed was motivated, in the authors' view, by the desire for "image reparation." Children who failed, and did so relatively publicly, since the experimenter asked them how they performed on the game, attempted to improve their image (tarnished by the failure) by contributing to the charity for which the experimenter collected donations.

In a third experiment, again with fourth-grade subjects, Isen *et al.* attempted to differentiate between conditions under which failure would or would not result in attempts at image improvement. The researchers assumed that the experimenter's knowledge about the failure would be a crucial condition. Consequently, in one failure group the experimenter was present while children played the game; in another she was not, and she did not inquire later about the children's performance. In both groups, the experimenter related the charity to herself: She was the collector. Children whose failure was observed donated significantly more, subsequently, than controls or those in the other failure group. The last two groups did not differ. Isen *et al.* explain the findings of Staub (1968) of greater sharing following failure as the result of conditions that led to the desire by children to improve their image in the experimenter's eyes. (They did not consider, however, in offering this interpretation, that sharing was enhanced following failure in one age group but not in the other.)

In their series of studies Isen *et al.* attempted also to show that children's evaluations of rewards are affected by the success and failure experience, but they had minimal success. In one study girls who failed tended to overvalue the rewards (toys), and those who succeeded tended to undervalue them. These are the differences one would expect, but they were not found in the other studies, or with male subjects. It is possible, however, that although the judgment of the objective value of reward did not change, the importance of the reward to the child was affected by the treatments.

The experiments reviewed so far demonstrated that success usually increases willingness to sacrifice material possessions for others or to help others. None of the experiments found that failure significantly decreases helping or donations in comparison to control groups, although behavior following failure was consistently slightly less positive than it was following a control experience. Isen *et al.* identified one condition that, presumably by creating a desire in the children to improve their image, led to increased sharing by children after failure. In this condition, the adult experimenter knew about the failure. Another exception was suggested by the finding that young children donate *less* following success than following either failure or a feedback of intermediate performance on a bowling game, which might have also been perceived as a failure experience by some children (Staub, 1968, 1973).

The feeling that they earned and deserved rewards seems to decrease young children's willingness to give the rewards to others. The findings by Isen *et al.* are not directly relevant to the influence of deserving, because of an important procedural aspect of their studies. The children in their experiments received rewards for participation soon after they entered the experimental room, before they played the bowling game. It is unlikely, therefore, that the success and failure experiences differentially affected the children's feeling of deserving the rewards; even if they did affect it, it is unlikely that they did to the same degree as in our studies (Staub, 1968, 1973) in which children received the rewards immediately after they played the bowling game. It needs to be further demonstrated whether and under what conditions success might lead to a feeling of deserving and therefore reduce rather than increase sharing or donating. One possibility is that when potential recipients are not really in need, as in our studies in which other children in school would have received what children shared, a feeling of deserving will reduce sharing or donations to a greater degree. When another's need is great, deserving might inhibit sharing less.

Furthermore, if following public failure children donate in an attempt to improve their image, under some conditions children who succeed may feel that they have already created a positive image for themselves and do not need to share or donate in order to create or maintain such an image. Their success already proves their worth. Thus either under conditions that lead children to donate mainly to create a positive image, or with children whose personalities would lead them to donate in order to create a positive image, success may decrease donations. This hypothesis is not unrelated to the deserving hypothesis: If one earned and deserved rewards, one might not be negatively evaluated by others for not sharing, since others would also believe that a person who earned rewards for good performance has a right to keep those rewards.

This reasoning gains credence from some findings of the experiment in which third- and sixth-grade children experienced success, failure, or intermediate performance on a bowling game (Staub, 1973). The need for approval of the subjects in this study was measured several weeks before the experimental sessions. An analysis of variance in which subjects were divided into high- and low-need-for-approval groups showed that performance on the game, grade, and need for approval interacted significantly to affect the children's donations. It was the high-need-for-approval children whose sharing in third grade was reduced by success, both in comparison to low-need-for-approval children in the same group and to children in other groups. High-need-for-approval children are presumably greatly concerned about their evaluation by others. At least in the third grade, success diminished this concern and perhaps made the children think that they would not be negatively evaluated for keeping the candy, since they earned it by their success.

Finally, a study that extends the effects of success and failure to a different realm may be noted. Barnett and Bryan (1974) found that contributions made by second-graders to a charity were unaffected by children previously playing a game alone, or in competition with an absent other, and by either winning, losing, or having a tie in the competition. However, fifth-graders who lost the game donated less than children who did not compete; fifth-graders who tied in the competition donated even less. Not only did a failure in competition reduce generosity, but being pitted against another person itself reduced prosocial behavior. As Chapter 9 will show, cooperation, in contrast, increases positive reactions to others. Only when fifth-graders won the competition did they share as much as subjects who played the game alone, but they did not share more.

The Effects of Positive Experiences

Success and failure experiences are likely to have varied and complex effects; mood, self-esteem, preoccupation with one's image, deserving, and other psychological conditions might be affected, which in turn affect prosocial behavior. Isen and Levin (1972) explored the effect on people of experiences that may create positive moods but in no way imply personal success or achievement. In one study a confederate gave cookies to male college students who were studying in individual library cubicles. In the control condition, the confederate simply walked by the students. The first confederate was followed by a second, who asked the students to spend some time in an experiment "on creativity in students at examination times." Those who received the cookie volunteered more time than control subjects for this activity, but less time for another experiment, which consisted of distracting randomly selected students by making noise (for example, by dropping books beside them) so that their reactions could be evaluated. The positive experience did not indiscriminately increase the subjects' willingness to participate in all kinds of activities, to comply with requests, but had a differential effect. It led to more helping but decreased the willingness to disturb or annoy other people.

Evidence for a differential effect of positive and negative experiences on helping also comes from a study by Aderman (1972). He attempted to influence mood directly by asking male college students to read statements that gradually progressed from neutral in tone to either elated or depressed in tone. Those who read the positive statements (elation condition) were subsequently more willing to comply with the experimenter's request for a favor, as well as to volunteer for an experiment in which they would have to undergo an unpleasant experience (being in a hot room). Subjects who were in an elation–favor condition, where their help would constitute a favor, helped more (by writing down numbers) than those in a depression–favor condition. However, in an elation–requirement treatment, where participants had no choice about doing the favor, subjects helped the experimenter less than in the depression–requirement condition. The former subjects apparently resisted external pressure for a favor.

In a second study, with both male and female participants, Isen and Levin (1972) explored whether people who entered a phone booth and found a dime in the tray were subsequently more helpful than subjects who found no money. Only people who looked into the tray were included in the analysis. As the subject left the booth, a confederate, who had been standing at a shop window, started to walk alongside and slightly ahead of the subject. The confederate dropped a manila folder full of papers in the subject's path. People who found a dime, whether females or males, helped substantially more than those who did not. Thus, even when help was not solicited, a seemingly small positive experience affected helping behavior.

Levin and Isen (1975) again found, in Philadelphia, that people who found a dime in a telephone booth acted more helpfully (they were more likely to mail a lost letter). Weyant and Clark (1977) found a slight trend by females in this direction, in Tallahassee, in one study, but not in another study. Moreover, males were unaffected by this experience. Blevins and Murphy (1974) could not replicate the original findings of Isen and Levin (1972). Some of the variations in results may be due to regional differences in the meaning to people of finding a dime. The meaning to participants of the positive and negative experiences created in experimental studies ought to be explored. Although the effects of positive experiences in increasing prosocial behavior have been demonstrated in varied ways, clearly this phenomenon does not always occur.

In two important studies Isen, Clark, and Schwartz (1976) provided subjects with a positive experience, a free sample packet of stationery delivered to them, and then examined their helpfulness using the wrong-number technique. As noted before, this is a procedure in which a caller, who has apparently reached the wrong number, lets the person who answered the phone know that he is stranded on the highway with a broken-down car, and has just used his last dime. The subject can help by calling "Ralph's Garage" and delivering a message. These studies differed from previous ones in that Isen and her associates varied the length of time that elapsed between the "positive" experience and the opportunity for help. In one study they found that subjects who were called 1, 5, or 10 minutes after they received the gift were all more helpful than control subjects who received no gift, with subjects who were called 5 minutes after receiving the gift marginally more helpful than those who were called 10 minutes afterward. In the second study, helping behavior was tested over a 20-minute rather than a 10-minute interval following the delivery of the gift, and a control group was included in which the subjects were asked to indicate which of two kinds of stationery they preferred, but did not receive a gift. About 10% of the subjects helped in both the no-contact and "demonstration" control groups. Helping behavior, which was tested at 3-minute intervals, gradually declined from a peak at 4 minutes after the delivery of the gift. At 16 minutes subjects still helped significantly more than those in the control groups, but at 20 minutes they helped about the same amount.

Isen and her associates strongly believe that in these and other studies positive experiences induced good moods, which increased helping behavior. The effects "may be due to mood-based differences in what the person is actively thinking about, the categories for the processing of new information that are available or salient to him (or her), and his (or her) perception, on that basis, of costs and rewards for helping [Isen, Clark, & Schwartz, 1976, p. 390]." Their interpretations seem reasonable. It is unfortunate, however, that in most studies relevant to the effects of mood on prosocial behavior no attempts have been made to evaluate the subject's mood, current self-esteem, or other psychological states.

In ingenious research, Isen and associates (1978) showed that positive experience results in general optimism. These authors proposed that " a person in a good mood is more likely to retrieve positive than negative material from memory and that this improved access to positive material affects the decision-making process, with regard to behavior (especially behavior such as helping) [Isen *et al.*, 1978, p. 2]." In one study, they found that passersby on a suburban mall who received a small gift—a free advertising sample—subsequently rated the quality of their car and television set significantly more positively than people who had not received such gifts. In a second study, winning on a game led subjects to recall more words that they had previously learned. They particularly recalled more positive words, but not more negative ones. Thus, a positive bias in remembering existed, an improved recall for positive, although not for negative, material.

Apparently people can have both a more positive view of things and a selective recall for positive things when they have reason to feel good, small as that reason may be. According to Isen *et al.*, moods may affect the memory of past helping and what comes to mind about the advantages and disadvantages of helping.

In further studies investigating the effects of mood on prosocial behavior Rosenhan and his associates found that children's moods affect their willingness or ability to sacrifice material possessions for others. These researchers asked children to reminisce about experiences that had made them feel happy or sad (Moore, Underwood, & Rosenhan, 1973). The children earned rewards for their participation, and they were given the opportunity to donate their rewards to children who would not have the opportunity to participate. Children who reminisced about happy experiences contributed more than control subjects who were to simply count, whereas children who thought about sad experiences contributed less than controls. Positive moods may result not only in greater kindness to others, but also in greater kindness to oneself. Rosenhan, Underwood, and Moore (1974) found that children who reminisced about happy experiences both rewarded themselves more and shared more with others. Children who thought about sad experiences rewarded themselves but not others more than control subjects; in this study, their sharing did not significantly differ from sharing by control subjects. In these studies, the rewards were in no way contingent on children's performance; the rewards were given at the beginning of the session, and presumably children in different groups did not vary in their perception of how well they deserved the rewards.

One study that did not confirm the association between good mood (induced by asking children to think happy thoughts) and prosocial actions was conducted by Harris and Siebel (1975). They used the procedure that Moore *et al.* (1973) employed, and asked children to generate angry, sad, or happy thoughts, or simply to count very slowly to 30. At the very beginning of the experimental session the children received a bag of 25 balloons for helping with the research. Following the mood induction or control procedures, they were told that they could put some of their balloons into a box for other children who could not participate in the study and thus would not have a chance to earn balloons. The experimenter also told the children that they could play with some toys in the room. The children were left alone for a 2-minute period. The amount of aggressive action directed at one of the toys, a Popeye doll, during this time was scored, and subsequently the number of balloons the children shared was noted. No differences in sharing resulted from the experimental treatments. Boys in all three affect conditions were more aggressive than those in the control condition, whereas girls in all three affect conditions were less aggressive than girls in the control condition.

Two explanations of the lack of treatment effects on sharing may be considered. The first one is speculative but has general applicability. The effects of mood manipulations, particularly of the kind that were employed in the foregoing study, may be a function of the nature of the subject population. The characteristics of subjects—here, children—will determine whether the instructions lead children actually to think of positive or negative experiences, and in turn whether varied moods result. Differences may also exist with regard to the content of the children's thoughts and the nâture of positive or negative moods that result. That is, some children may think of receiving presents when they are asked to think of happy events; others may think of good interpersonal experiences; still others may think of doing well in school or of other experiences that would generate self-esteem. The kind of mood or feeling generated would thus differ, and so might, therefore, the behavior that followed. A child who thought of receiving presents and feels good as the result, so that the affect is contingent on having material possessions, may be less willing to share the balloons than the child who re-created experiences that enhanced his self-esteem. Unfortunately, none of the studies evaluated children's mood following treatments.

Second, in this study the children had an opportunity to engage in "aggressive" behavior—actually strenuous, self-expressive behavior—during the interval when sharing was to take place. This may have affected their moods and/or how the moods were expressed. Indeed, although Harris and Siebel do not report details, the relationship between balloons shared and aggression varied from — .53 to .59 in individual groups. Although no correlations were significant, because of the small number of subjects in treatment conditions, the correlations were large, and the variation is obviously substantial.

All the preceding studies included the opportunity for an alternative activity, playing with toys, during the time when children could donate. This may have altered the mood created by experimental treatments. In a further study (Underwood, Froming, & Moore, 1977) that again used the basic procedure of Moore *et al.* (1973), no alternative activity was provided. First- to fifth-grade children were the subjects. The measure of generosity (the number of pennies that were donated) showed a significant effect of the experimental treatments; there was a linear increase in donations as treatments to induce moods varied from sad to neutral to happy. This study also measured attention, to evaluate its potential role as a mediator of the effects of mood on behavior. No differences in the effects of mood on attention were found. However, the children's memory of some stimuli in the environment was the measure of attention. These stimuli had nothing to do with the need for sharing or with other aspects of donating.

In a further article Masters and Furman (1976) suggested that in everyday experience outcomes overlap in time with affects that they produce, so that a natural association exists between certain classes of outcomes and affects. As a result, "the induction of affective states induces generalized expectancies for outcomes that are commensurate with the affective state [Masters & Furman, 1976, p. 481]." That is, affective states lead to expectations of positive and negative outcomes. However, because people try to maintain positive affective states and terminate negative ones, the conditions for learning an association between positive affects and positive outcomes—but not between negative affects and negative outcomes—are ideal. Thus, a clear association would develop only between positive affect and the expectation of positive outcome. Masters and Furman did find, in fact, that subjects' expectancies for positive consequences that were unrelated to their own behavior were greater following procedures used to induce positive affect than following procedures used to induce neutral or negative affect. Expectancy scores in the negative condition were not reduced. Specific expectations of success on two tasks and locus of control scores on a paper-and-pencil task were unaffected.

These findings are consistent with those of the experiments reviewed earlier (that the induction of negative states has uncertain affects on behavior), as well as with research on delay of gratification, which showed that the induction of negative affect had no influence on children's delaying gratification (Mischel, Ebbesen, & Zeiss, 1971, 1973).

The Psychological Consequences That Mediate the Effects of Positive and Negative Experiences and States

Did the many treatment procedures that presumably affected the psychological states of participants influence subsequent prosocial behavior in the same manner, by creating variations in the same psychological states? The answer is not yet known. Probably there is communality in the manner in which the effects of varied positive and negative experiences are mediated, in the processes by which they influence prosocial behavior.

It should be noted that the effects of positive experiences in enhancing prosocial behavior are nearly uniform and usually greater than the effects of negative experiences in decreasing prosocial behavior. Except with young children, who shared more following success than failure (Staub, 1968, 1973), whenever a control group has been included in an experiment the experience of success was found to increase helping (Isen, 1970; Berkowitz & Connors, 1966) or donating (Isen *et al.*, 1973). Experiences that attempted to create positive moods usually increased helping (Isen & Levin, 1972; Isen *et al.*, 1976) and donating (Rosenhan *et al.*, 1974; Underwood *et al.*, 1973, 1977) in comparison to control groups. In contrast, failure experiences usually decreased helping or donating only numerically, to a slight degree, in comparison to control groups. However, Rosenhan and his associates, who induced children to think about negative as well as positive experiences, found that thinking about negative experiences had a significant effect in reducing children's donations. Moreover, Isen *et al.* showed that under conditions of surveillance, failure led to greater donations, presumably to repair an image tarnished by failure. On the whole, the effects of positive experiences in inducing prosocial action are more clearly established, and they are straightforward. Nonetheless, negative experiences or thoughts seem to have some effect in reducing generosity and perhaps helpfulness. How are the effects of positive and negative experiences accomplished?

In the preceding review of the literature a number of psychological consequences of different kinds of positive and negative experiences were proposed. These consequences in turn were thought to affect behavior. They included variation in mood, in temporary levels of self-esteem, in the recall and evaluation of events, in the expectation of positive and negative consequences of behavior, and in the value of reward objects. I shall now turn to a consideration of several relatively broad dimensions of special relevance to positive conduct, dimensions along which the psychological experience of individuals may vary as a result of positive and negative experiences.

I assume that variation in moods is an aspect of all these psychological experiences. Whether the mood variations are primary or just components of the experience is unclear. Certainly moods affect the content of what people say to themselves; they must also affect how people think about themselves and the world around them. My students, in a large class on personality, wrote term papers in which they analyzed their personal goals and conditions that inhibited the pursuit of these goals; quite a few specified experiences of failure and the mood that followed them as one such condition. Many wrote that a disappointing performance on an exam and sometimes disappointment in personal relations led to days of watching television or engaging in other activities that might be considered as "time out." It seemed as if a cybernetic system of some kind was operating, a self-correcting system that with the passage of time led to recuperation. The time out may function to remove people from activities that involve the application of self-evaluative standards, including human interaction in the course of which, of course, people apply very strong self-evaluative standards.

Even if variations in mood provide a "base," however, the psychological states within generally positive or negative moods can still vary substantially. Furthermore, general mood states such as happiness or unhappiness may, in fact, be unaffected sometimes by the kinds of positive–negative experiences that modify positive behavior or, even if affected, may not be the crucial mediators of behavior. Instead, specific moods that gain expression in or accompany some of the psychological states that will be described in the next section—such as feelings of positive affiliation with other people and of connectedness to others, or negative feelings about the self—may be important.

I will assume that positive and negative experiences affect what people attend to (e.g., themselves or other people) and how they evaluate things (including themselves and other people). The differences in evaluation can result both from differences in what people think about or even in what they remember, and from differences in how they evaluate the same objects, events, or experiences. The causal connections among moods, the content of thoughts and evaluations will probably be difficult to specify, since temporary feeling states (e.g., moods) are likely to affect thoughts and evaluations that in turn partly define, partly further influence feeling states. Thus, we are likely to deal with highly interrelated phenomena. People who feel sad think sad thoughts; we call them sad because they think sad thoughts (and express them verbally); sad thoughts are likely to make people feel sad. How this process starts, and how it stops, are highly important and interesting questions. It seems to me that variations in mood, thought, memory, and evaluation have a few primary dimensions that seem important to prosocial behavior. As a consequence of variations along these dimensions, the experience of the connection between the self and others is affected. It may become more or less likely that the interests of the self and others are regarded as identical rather than as conflicting, and the manner in which the interests of the self and of others are weighted may be affected.

Preoccupation with the Self and Self-Concern

Positive and negative experiences might reduce or induce self-concern. As a result of a negative experience, a person's attention may turn inward, away from external events, so that the person becomes self-preoccupied. Self-criticism, negative thoughts, and ruminations about one's image in others' eyes are some of the forms this turning inward may take. Negative experiences that have implications for one's value, goodness, or competence and thus affect self-esteem may lead to even greater preoccupation with the self. Other negative experiences may also lead to self-preoccupation but probably not to self-criticism and some of the other aspects of self-concern that I mentioned. In contrast, positive experiences or moods might diminish preoccupation with and concern about the self.

Such variation in self-concern and the direction of a person's attention might have several consequences. First, one's ability to perceive and process events in the environment might diminish or increase. Second, one's ability to be concerned with other people's needs and goals, to consider and respond to those needs, might be affected. Concern about one's own worth and status may diminish the capacity to be concerned about others' welfare; lessened self-concern may increase this capacity. People who are exposed to new places and experiences, to unfamiliar conditions (including laboratory experiments), probably have a fair degree of self-concern, which might then be reduced by positive experiences. People who were exposed to control experiences in some of the reported experiments may have been fairly self-concerned. Third, self-concern clearly implies concern about evaluation by other people. Following positive experiences people are less likely to worry about evaluation by others and may also be more able to tolerate negative evaluation.

A number of the findings that were reviewed can be interpreted as evidence for self-concern. Successful subjects remembered more of the confederate's actions than those who failed, in Isen's (1970) research. However, although remembering was diminished by failure, it was only slightly increased by success. (Sometimes diminished "remembering" can be a form of image reparation, a justification by some people for not having helped.) In contrast, success had a stronger effect on behavior than did failure. Children who failed were more generous when generosity would repair their image, which is also interpretable as an expression of self-concern. Less sharing by third-graders who had a high need for approval and succeeded on a task may be a sign of lessened self-concern. If so, this implies that diminished self-concern can also lead to less prosocial behavior. One can see young children who have had a good experience or are anticipating one—getting a toy as a present or knowing that they will go to an interesting place, for instance—brag to other children and put them down by pointing out to the others that they did not get such a toy, or will not go to that interesting place. Is this behavior limited by age? Does it take place only among younger children, who are less socialized? Do children later learn to act according to rules prescribing positive behavior, or are there conditions under which people in general, or some people with certain characteristics, will assert their superiority over others following good experiences? Are other, perhaps even more antisocial, behaviors brought about by good experiences, lack of self-concern, and high levels of temporary self-esteem? For example, will people who feel good sometimes avoid contact with others in distress because such contact may diminish their sense of well-being?

More direct evidence comes from a series of experiments by Berkowitz (1970) and his associates, showing that when people face evaluation that has some importance to them and thus presumably results in self-concern, their willingness to help another person decreases. In one study (Aderman, Jonson, & Berkowitz, reported in Berkowitz, 1970) males helped a high-status experimenter less with scoring data if they expected to later judge photographs as a test of social intelligence rather than simply as a test of preferences for facial expressions. A low-status experimenter was helped generally less than a high-status one; the subjects' behavior toward him was unaffected by treatments. Females were entirely unaffected by this impending evaluation.

In another study Johnson, Hildebrand, and Berkowitz (Berkowitz, 1970) found that females helped less if they expected to work on a task that was presented to them as a test of social sensitivity, a test that was apparently important for them. They were, however, unaffected by impending evaluation on a test of supervisory ability, in comparison to subjects who rated pictures simply to indicate their preferences. Males' helping behavior was reduced when they expected to work either on a test of social sensitivity or on a test of supervisory ability, in comparison to control subjects. Help in this study was measured by the amount of work that subjects completed in scoring data for an experimenter. Unfortunately, there is no information about the subjects' thoughts or feelings at the time they were asked for help. It is possible that an impending test of a personal quality that they regarded as important created anxiety, a quite specific negative state.

That variation in performance on a task can affect concern about evaluation by other people and about negative reactions from others was suggested by an experiment by Kiesler and Baral (1970). Male subjects were administered a test that presumably accurately measured intelligence and predicted later success in life. Some subjects were told they did well, others were told that they did poorly on the first part. During a break the experimenter took individual subjects to a cafeteria, where they joined a woman whom the experimenter knew. This person, who was a confederate, was made up to look either very attractive or moderately attractive. While the experimenter was absent under some pretense, the subjects who received positive feedback made more romantic overtures to the confederate when she was made up to look more attractive; those who received negative feedback made more overtures to her when she was made up to look less attractive. Presumably their experience on the task affected their sense of personal value and resulted in their matching themselves up differently with a person of the opposite sex.

I interpreted (in Chapter 3) the help-inhibiting influences of various conditions in emergency studies as due to the arousal of self-concern, to worry about potential criticism and negative evaluation. Isen's (1970) finding that failure reduced overtures to a confederate specifically indicated that initiative and the willingness for social exposure may be reduced by failure.

Sense of Potency

Positive and negative experiences may also affect a person's sense of potency. Self-preoccupation and self-concern would reduce a sense of potency, but lack of concern might not necessarily induce it. *Sense of potency* embraces several concepts that were previously discussed, for example, that success results in the expectation of future success, that it reduces the importance of material possessions to a person, and that it reduces the perceived costs of helping or sharing. A sense of potency is a feeling that one can do things, that things will turn out well. It may include a feeling of hope or optimism about the outcomes of one's activity, increased belief in one's ability to exercise control, and perhaps less attention to the costs of helping or sharing.

The findings of Kiesler and Baral (1970) imply variation in a sense of potency. The finding of Isen (1970) that success and failure subjects differed in the extent to which they initiated conversation with a confederate is also relevant. A sense of potency implies a greater willingness or ability to take the kind of initiative that is frequently required to help others. Following positive experiences a person's feelings might be expressed as "I am a valuable person" (high self-esteem) or "good things happen to me." Both feelings can in turn lead to the feeling expressed by the words "I can do things." Furthermore, material goods, often a source of good feelings and sometimes the means by which people improve their current mood, are not needed to generate or maintain good feelings. Belief in one's capacity to gain material goods may also be enhanced. Generosity may increase for both reasons—when feelings of deserving are not activated.

Benevolence to the Self, to Others: Strengthened or Weakened Bonds

Following positive experiences, people are kinder not only to others but also to themselves. When children are told that they can reward themselves with goods available to them, and no connection is implied between their performance on a task and the reward, children reward themselves to a greater degree following success than following participation in some control procedure. This has been found in a number of experiments (Mischel, Coates, & Raskoff, 1968; Masters, 1972; Masters & Peskey, 1972). In some of these studies children who experienced failure rewarded themselves less than control and success subjects, but in other studies they rewarded themselves following failure with substantial amounts. This has been interpreted as a form of self-therapy. Rosenhan, Underwood, and Moore (1974) found that children who were instructed to think positive thoughts both shared with others more and rewarded themselves more than control subjects, and the correlation between self and other gratification was highly positive ($n = .51$). In contrast, children who were to think negative thoughts took more reward for themselves than did control subjects, and although they did not share significantly less, the relationship between self and other gratification was strongly negative ($r = -.50$). These findings are consistent with some of the proposed explanations—for example, that negative experiences result in preoccupation with the self, partly manifested in concern about one's own well-being, and diminish one's capacity to get involved with others' needs.

Rosenhan, Moore, and Underwood (1974) suggest that "positive moods evoke a disposition to do unto others as one would have others do unto him [p. 251]." Positive experiences may create a generalized feeling of benevolence that embraces both the self and others. Such experiences may strengthen a sense of community with others, so that the experience of the connection between oneself and others becomes one of unity rather than of conflict. Similarly, negative experiences may have the opposite effect. An aspect of the greater benevolence evoked by positive mood might be the perception or evaluation of other people, and of human nature in general, in a more positive light. Carl Rogers has long proposed that an increase in self-acceptance is associated with increased acceptance of others. Analysis of changes in patients' statements about themselves and others—data not independent, of course, of the therapists' continuous influence—supports this argument.

Relevant to the issue of benevolence toward others are research findings with children that show that experiences of success and failure respectively increase and decrease liking for others. In one experiment with elementary-school children (Heber & Heber, 1957) groups constituted of either high-status or low-status children had success, failure, or neutral experiences. Regardless of the initial status of group members, shared neutral or success experiences resulted in more positive evaluation by group members of one another. A follow-up 2 weeks later revealed that the effects of experiences of success were more persistent. Group failure resulted in the members of the high-status group evaluating one another less positively, but group failure did not affect evaluation by members of low-status groups. Flanders and Havumaki (1960) found that reinforcement (praise) for children who sat in odd-numbered seats significantly enhanced the number of positive choices on sociometric tests for other children by the children who were praised. Praise directed at the whole group had no differential effect. Such diffuse praise might have less impact on individual children. Lott and Lott (1960) divided third- and fourth-graders into three-person groups to play a game together. Half the children received attractive rewards for successful performance; the other half did not. Afterward, on sociometric tests, rewarded subjects indicated a preference for a significantly larger proportion of play-group members than nonrewarded subjects. In all these studies positive experiences resulted in the expression of positive feelings for other children or of positive feelings for more children.

The preceding discussion implies that after positive experiences people will be less likely to derogate others in need, use justifications for inaction, or experience reactance as a result of the pressure exerted on them by others' need—all of which are psychological processes that can interfere with helping. Two important conditions are that the need appear genuine and help appear to have positive consequences. Compliance with pressure to do things that appear less important or justified seems to decline following positive experiences.

A theory proposed by Byrne (1971; 1974) suggests that an association between affective reactions and another person can affect the evaluation of that person, regardless of the source of the affect. Griffitt (1970) had undergraduates evaluate a stranger who was presented as either similar to or different from them, either under normal conditions or with the temperature in the room very hot and uncomfortable. Similarity increased attraction but the temperature also had a clear effect. The high temperature, which created negative feelings, resulted in significantly lower ratings of attraction. Griffitt and Veitch (1971) manipulated both temperature and population density, the number of subjects located per square foot. The experimenters assumed that overcrowding would lead to negative affect and dislike of other people. Subjects rated themselves more negatively, and disliked the room and the experiment more when population density was high. Both high temperature and overcrowding reduced ratings of attraction to a stranger. Environmental conditions that affect a person's state of well-being seem to affect feelings toward others and presumably the kind of bond that exists between people; these, in turn, are likely to affect prosocial behavior. The notion that a person's own affect influences attraction toward others and the related findings suggest that positive and negative experiences, which probably create positive and negative affects, affect feelings toward the people who need help.

Sense of Well-Being and Hedonic Balancing

Implied in much of the preceding discussion is the assumption that positive and negative experiences affect a person's mood, temporary self-esteem, and the positiveness or negativeness of his psychological state; they result in variation in a person's state of well-being. Variation in one's state of well-being may affect prosocial behavior in still another manner; to describe this other influence I have suggested the concept of *hedonic balancing* (Staub, 1973, 1975a, 1976a).

In previous chapters the importance of equity to people in deciding how they will conduct themselves in relation to others has been repeatedly suggested and demonstrated. Equity involves weighting one's own inputs and outcomes against those of others or against standards. Although equity has usually been discussed and researched with regard to how people apply it to specific experiences or events, people may have a more general sense of equity or inequity about their life circumstances compared to those of others. They may assess overall inputs and outcomes (e.g., "I put this much effort into something in my life and gained this much; you put that much in and gained that much"). This kind of weighting or balancing may influence how people perceive their relationship to others, the nature of the bond between self and others. Even this conception of equity might be deficient, however. It does not include the probably very important influence of a person's current state of well-being in weighting and "computing" what constitutes an equitable state of affairs. The perception of what constitutes equity is likely to be influenced both by one's current psychological state and by the perceived affective or psychological state of another person.

A general statement of hedonic balancing is that, faced with another person's need for help, a person considers both his own current state of well-being and how it relates to his accustomed level of well-being; the discrepancy between these two elements is then compared to the perceived discrepancy between the other person's current and usual states of well-being. A person might feel better off, the same, or worse off than what he considers normal, average, usual for himself, than his level of adaptation. Feeling better increases willingness to do things for others, because one has additional resources. (How those resources are acquired might make a difference. Some people might be unwilling to give away earned resources, whereas others might be willing to give away "extra" resources, earned or unearned.) An enhanced state of well-being, a positive hedonic state, may allow a certain amount of effort for the sake of others before the positive state wears off or an even balance is reached. Positive experiences in the course of benefiting others, externally or internally caused, may maintain the positive balance. In contrast, when people feel worse off than usual, their willingness to give of themselves or of what belongs to them may decrease. The greatest difference might be produced by small, just noticeable differences between usual and current states of well-being in either the positive or the negative direction.

Presumably, people compare their own current state of well-being with that of others. If people have reason to assume that another's well-being is greater than their own, serious self-sacrifice might be greatly diminished (although some help may still be forthcoming from a person who feels good). When people feel bad, their inclination to be helpful might decline, particularly toward people who feel better than they themselves do. However, they might still help a person who is much worse off than they are; the other's need might be so great that their own hedonic advantage will still be clear to them. The tendency for people to favor themselves in creating equity was apparent in research findings that were reviewed earlier. This suggests that people may weight more heavily their own negative states than those of others, so others might have to be clearly worse off than they are for helping to result.

Our current emotions and a comparison between our own and others' current states of well-being might be a large portion of the computation. But the notion that people compare discrepancies between their own current and usual states of well-being and those of others might enable us to make more precise predictions. When people meet strangers, they would have to judge their usual state of welfare in terms of some conception they have of the usual welfare of people, or what it ought to be. When they judge others who belong to particular, identifiable social groups, their reactions might be determined on the basis of some conception of the usual welfare of members of such groups. They might decide that "people like that" usually suffer, and their current negative state is not different from the usual (or that certain deprivations do not result in much suffering among such people)—clearly forms of justification, but they enter into the judgment of what is equitable, and into hedonic balancing. When a person in need is

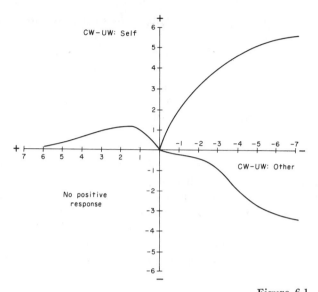

Figure 6.1

A rough conceptual representation of the consequences of hedonic balancing on voluntary prosocial conduct. CW, current welfare; UW, usual welfare. (The curve represents prosocial behavior as a function of the CW—UW_{self} and CW—UW_{other} relationship, its height above or below the baseline reflecting the magnitude of prosocial behavior.)

better known, particular beliefs or information about the person would enter into judgments about discrepancies in his current and usual states of well-being.

Figure 6.1 is a rough representation of my conception of how hedonic balancing affects behavior. Current welfare is designated by *CW,* usual welfare by *UW.* The curves represent prosocial behavior that results from the relationship between the CW − UW of the actor and the CW − UW of the other person. It embodies the following assumptions: (*a*) the greater a person's positive state, the more help he will provide for a person who feels negative; (*b*) the greater a person's positive state, the more help he will provide for a person who feels positive, but the overall degree of help will be much smaller; (*c*) a person's negative state will have an inhibiting effect on helping, but with greater need some degree of help will be forthcoming; and (*d*) a person who feels negative will not help someone in a positive state (except for extraneous reasons, such as expectations of benefit for the self, that are not considered in the figure). The figure represents the effects of hedonic balancing on prosocial behavior; it does not, however, incorporate other influences that would moderate this relationship.

A positive CW − UW represents a positive hedonic state; a negative CW − UW represents a negative hedonic state, a condition of deficiency or need. The outcome of hedonic balancing (as well as of each of the components that enter into hedonic balancing) may affect the momentary hierarchy of a person's goals and the likelihood of activation of prosocial goals. The combination of a highly positive hedonic state (a positive CW — UW) of one's own and a highly negative hedonic state of another person, a strong positive hedonic imbalance, represents a maximum activating potential for a prosocial goal. I have usually discussed activating potential as inherent in a situation, but of course activating potential for personal goals can also be inherent in a person's internal environment, his thoughts and feelings and interpretations of events. A highly negative hedonic state of one's own and a highly positive hedonic state of another represent a powerful negative hedonic imbalance that makes activation of a prosocial goal unlikely. A person's positive and negative hedonic states are also likely to affect the position of a prosocial goal relative to self-oriented, personal goals in a person's hierarchy of goals. Even if a prosocial goal is activated when a highly negative hedonic imbalance exists, no prosocial action is likely to be forthcoming, since that would increase the imbalance. Exceptions would result in circumstances in which the primary beneficiary of the prosocial action would be the *actor,* so that the negative hedonic imbalance and the negative hedonic state of the actor are diminished.

What evidence supports the concept of hedonic balancing, and what kind of evidence is still needed to provide support? Although many of the research findings discussed can be interpreted in terms of hedonic balancing, most of the research provides no directly relevant evidence. The conception of hedonic balancing specified four variables that enter into balancing. Most of the research has manipulated variables relevant to one of these four—the current state of welfare of a person—and has evaluated certain consequences produced by this variation. Research examining the degree of need of another person on helping is relevant to another one of the four variables, the current welfare of another person. To consider hedonic balancing properly, current states of welfare both of the subject and of another person should be varied, the usual or customary state of the subject should be evaluated, and either information should be provided about the usual state of welfare of the person in need, or the subject's perception and evaluation of the other's usual welfare should be obtained, ideally prior to the time that balancing and its effect on helping are evaluated. Some of the findings of Jarymowicz (1977), described later in this chapter, which show that people with high self-esteem are less affected by experimental treatments aimed at increasing self-esteem than are people with low self-esteem, can be interpreted as support for hedonic balancing; the discrepancy between current and usual states is smaller for such individuals.

The Effects of Negative Experiences and Moods, Revisited. Before closing the discussion of how positive and negative experiences exert their influences, I would like to note that under some circumstances negative experiences may increase helping. Experiences that result in guilt are a special kind; these I have already discussed in Chapter 4. However, negative experiences that do not involve any kind of wrongdoing or transgression may also increase later prosocial behavior. Negative experiences may also lead to self-concern and self-preoccupation; they may lessen a sense of potency and thereby lessen the capacity or desire to initiate action. They may have other consequences that interfere with helping. However, as the research findings that were reviewed clearly show, after negative experiences people may try to engage in self-therapy of some kind—for example, doing good things for or to oneself. One might, as a form of self-therapy, avoid realms of activity in which one has to apply standards to judge one's behavior. By doing this one would avoid both effort and the negative self-evaluation that may follow if the behavior falls short of one's standards. The implication is that prosocial behavior that fulfills an obligation rather than expresses a desire to help, or that would be elicited by ambiguous cues, may become less likely, except for the sake of image reparation. However, prosocial behavior can function as a form of self-therapy for some people under certain circumstances. Helping a person in certain kinds of need may be a safe form of approach to and affiliation with others. It may give a person a sense of superiority, and in other ways satisfy existing needs. It may improve a person's self-esteem, if such behavior is consistent with the person's self-image, and may result in positive moods. The conditions under which any of this happens, and the personal characteristics that make them more or less likely, should be explored in future research. For example, a personal tragedy, such as someone's illness, may increase prosocial behavior that leads to social contact because contact with other people is needed and especially satisfying at that time. Loneliness, which is regarded as a negative emotion, may have contradictory effects: It may diminish a sense of potency and thereby inhibit approach to others while increasing the desire for approach.

I am suggesting, in this discussion, that it is not only the kind of help needed that may affect whether people help others following negative experiences, but also the nature of the experience and the resulting psychological states. Some experiences result in self-concern and shame, and diminish the feeling of bond to other people, whereas other experiences may have psychological consequences that increase the desire for contact, or for the experience of a bond to other people.

Cialdini and Kendrick (1976) found that inducing students to generate sad experiences, to reminisce about them, resulted in substantially more donations of coupons to other students by tenth- to twelfth-graders than an experience aimed at minimizing affect (neutral mood). They found slightly more donations by fifth- to seventh-grade subjects in the sad-experience group than in the neutral group, and slightly less by first- to third-grade children in the sad-experience than in the neutral group. The last two differences were not significant.

Cialdini and Kendrick, following Cialdini et al. (1973), proposed that prosocial behavior would increase following both positive and negative moods in comparison to neutral affective states. As evidence they cite varied studies, focusing on the research on observing and causing harm to others that was reviewed in Chapter 4. They suggest that negative moods lead to increased altruism because altruistic behavior is reinforcing, and people will use the opportunity to improve their mood by engaging in a reinforcing activity. Cialdini and Kendrick went on to reason that the reinforcing quality of altruistic behavior is acquired in the course of socialization. Altruism is not reinforcing for young children, but it becomes progressively reinforcing with increasing age. Therefore, negative mood did not increase altruism in studies with young children (e.g., Moore *et al.*, 1973), but would be expected to do so with older people. These authors suggest that their data, which show progressive increase in donations to other students with increase in age, provide support for this theory.

It is certainly possible to provide alternative explanations for the findings of any one study that deviates from a body of other findings, as this study does to some degree. However, many aspects of the reasoning advanced by Cialdini *et al.* seem appropriate and also consistent with the reasoning I have thus far advanced. We differ, however, in that they suggest that negative affect beyond early childhood generally increases prosocial behavior, whereas I believe that the findings indicate that negative experiences of many kinds, or the threat of such experiences, and the resulting psychological states either have no effect on prosocial behavior or decrease it. We should specify differences that we would expect in the effects of varied negative and positive moods and states on positive behavior and test these hypotheses. I would expect that negative experiences that lead people to question their own value and effectiveness as well as those that lead to feelings of negative social affiliation (that result from bad experiences with other people) would diminish positive behavior, perhaps differentially depending on how the behavior and its outcome relate to the mood. In contrast, negative experiences that are impersonal in character—that is, that neither call one's own value or the goodness of human beings into question—can even result in a feeling of shared humanity with others and increase positive behavior. The experience, for impersonal reasons, of sadness may be a negative affective state that increases the bond to others. Feeling guilt or distress for having caused harm to someone may create a bond to the harmed person, although circumstances can often lead to devaluation and the desire to distance oneself.

That negative affective states can reduce helping by adults as well as by children has been shown. Underwood and associates (1977) found that people who had just seen sad movies were less willing to donate money for a charity than were people who had just seen movies that the authors judged neutral in affect. The frequency of donations was significantly smaller after the sad movie, whether people were directly asked to donate as they were leaving the theater or they passed by a person sitting at a table on which there were signs calling attention to the charity. Again, the quality of the experience must be considered. The word *negative* can refer to many different experiences and moods. Even considering sadness alone, different people may think sad thoughts quite different in quality and meaning. The movies that were judged sad by the experimenters may have varied greatly in the quality of affect they induced and in their effects on a feeling of connectedness to other people, or a desire for connectedness. Attempts by experimenters to determine the meaning of positive and negative experiences for participants in their research, to demonstrate that they affect moods and other internal states, and the quality of affect and thoughts about other people evoked by these experiences, would be important.

Individual Differences in Sense of Well-Being, Characteristic Moods, and Levels of Self-Esteem

The research findings and related theorizing presented in this chapter suggest that stable individual differences in a person's mood, self-esteem, and overall sense of well-being would be important determinants of prosocial behavior. That stable individual differences in self-esteem exist has long been a basic assumption of varied theories in psychology (Rogers, 1959; Epstein, 1973). Some evidence of the stability of self-esteem over a period of years also exists (Coopersmith, 1967). It is likely that individual differences in characteristic levels of self-esteem and mood exist, even though specific circumstances are likely to result in substantial variation in both (Gergen, 1976). Substantial individual differences in the variability of self-esteem and mood states are also likely.

People who tend to have positive moods, high self-esteem, and a positive sense of well-being may be less preoccupied with themselves, have a greater sense of potency or strength, and perhaps even feel more benevolence toward others than individuals characterized by more negative moods, low self-esteem, and a poor sense of well-being. Consequently, the former may tend to be more helpful, on the whole, than the latter. Moreover, people varying in characteristic mood, self-esteem, and well-being may be differently affected by experiences that might influence momentary moods, temporary self-esteem, and a sense of well-being. However, predictions are far from simple and straightforward. Individuals whose characteristic states are positive may be more resistant to the effects of negative experiences, their psychological states may be less affected by them. But this may only be true of their responses to certain kinds of experiences. Persons who have high self-esteem may be strongly affected by negative experiences that are directly related to their sources of self-esteem; they may even be more strongly affected than persons whose self-esteem is low. There is the interesting possibility, moreover, that some positive experiences affect the prosocial behavior of individuals with a characteristically highly positive sense of well-being less than they affect the prosocial behavior of individuals with a more negative characteristic state of well-being because the discrepancy between their current and usual states is smaller.

A Polish investigator, Reykowski, and his associates (Reykowski, 1974; Reykowski & Jarymowicz, 1976; Karylowski, 1976; Jarymowicz, 1977) collected data about the influence of self-esteem, and the relationship between a persistent level of self-esteem and experimentally enhanced self-esteem, on "prosocial sensitivity" and prosocial behavior. Their work is based on Reykowski's theory, which is consistent with reasoning presented earlier. The theory proposes that a prosocial motivation will be activated by the cognitive representation of the needs of a social object. It is the discrepancy between the perceived state of the social object and the normal or ideal state that gives rise to the motivation to help. Competing motivation decreases prosocial action. The major competing motive is tension related to the self. Reykowski and Jarymowicz (1976) state that this is a function of the position of the self-structure in the individual's system of values and the degree of self-concentration, both temporary (evoked by stress factors) and permanent (due to uncertainty as to the subject's self-value, self-competence, or identity). The last proposition, which is the central element of the theory, essentially states that self-concern, because of environmental conditions or a low self-esteem, diminishes attention to others and prosocial behavior. It is this proposition that was primarily explored by these investigators. In two experiments they found that children at a medium level of self-esteem, in contrast to those whose self-esteem was very high or low, tended to be more prosocial. In one of the studies this was demonstrated by the children's greater accuracy in perceiving the problems and emotions of a child portrayed in a film about 10- to 11-year-old schoolchildren. Although well-mannered, this child, a newcomer to school, was out of place, awkward, isolated, scared, and the object of aggression. The researchers found that the feelings and problems of an aggressor (the gang leader, a forceful, aggressive, antisocial child) were less well perceived by children with moderate self-esteem than were the victim's problems. Children with high self-esteem perceived the feelings and circumstances of the two children about equally well. Research on peer interaction presented in Volume 2 includes evidence that children with a medium level of self-esteem tend to be more prosocial than children whose self-esteem is high, apparently because they are more concerned about their relationship to and worth in the eyes of others.

In a study with 16- to 18-year-old high-school students, Jarymowicz (1977) divided subjects into three groups: those with low self-acceptance, those with medium or high self-evaluations whose expectations about other students' evaluations of them were inconsistent with their own self-evaluations (inconsistent), and those "without self-worth problems," whose self-evaluations were medium or high and consistent with their expected evaluations. The measures of self-evaluation were elaborate paper-and-pencil measures. Some of the subjects from each of the three groups had treatments administered to them that aimed at increasing their self-esteem. The treatments had three components: (a) information about positive ratings by their classmates on important dimensions; (b) praise by the experimenter regarding their abilities as demonstrated by stories they wrote in response to pictures of a projective test (TAT); and (c) comparison between their scores on an intellectual aptitudes test and norms based on much younger children, that is, an experimentally created success experience. In the experimental group, the subjects performed equally well on the measure of prosocial sensitivity described earlier (the perceptions of victim and aggressor in the film excerpt), regardless of level of self-esteem. Control subjects, who did not experience the treatments, showed as high prosocial sensitivity in the high-self-worth group as did experimental subjects, but progressively less in the inconsistent and low-self-acceptance groups. That is, treatments and level of self-worth interactively influenced subjects' perception of and judgment about the characters in the film they saw. On a measure of "motivational sensitivity"—a measure of the subjects' willingness to volunteer to help other students with their problems—there was again no difference between experimental and control subjects who were without self-worth problems, and neither was a difference found in the low-self-acceptance condition. In the inconsistent group, experimental children volunteered significantly more than did control children. It should be noted that although this was a measure of intention, subjects had to sign a statement that they would help, would help to a limited degree, or would not help.

In summary, higher and more consistent self-esteem was associated with greater skill and sensitivity in social perception. Both consistent self-worth and low self-acceptance were associated with greater volunteering, in comparison to inconsistent self-worth. Low self-worth resulted in greater volunteering—according to Jarymowicz, because of fear of rejection.

Both the findings and the explanation are consistent with the preceding discussion. The experimental treatment had no effect on those who had no self-worth problems and already showed a high level of prosocial sensitivity and volunteering, but, surprisingly, increased not only volunteering in the inconsistent group, but prosocial sensitivity in both the other groups. Seemingly, it is not competence that limits low-self-esteem subjects' ability to perceive others' feelings; rather, it is their psychological–motivational state. Moreover, the effects were found several hours after the completion of the experimental treatments. Thus, with relatively extensive treatment procedures (that provided information presumably affecting self-esteem rather than temporary mood) the treatment effects were much more enduring than those reported by Isen *et al.* (1976).

Additional evidence about the combined influence of persistent individual characteristics and specific experiences was provided by Wine (1973). She measured fourth-grade children's level of test anxiety, then divided the children into three groups (low, medium, and high) on the basis of their performance. A great deal of literature indicates that individuals with high test anxiety tend to have worries about their performance and "talk to themselves" (Meichenbaum, 1974) in an anxiety-producing and self-distracting manner, at least while they take tests Sarason, 1972). They would be expected to become more self-preoccupied when they face evaluation. Wine administered to the children the Peabody Picture Vocabulary test under either evaluative or nonevaluative conditions. Some children were told that the test showed how well they could do in school and that they should try hard to do well. The test was then administered by a stern experimenter, and no feedback was given afterward. Other children were told that the task was a game that the experimenter made up. Subsequently, a third-grade child was brought to the room, asked to sort out blue and yellow sheets that were all mixed up. The experimenter left without in any way implying that the older child should help. Level of test anxiety and treatment interacted in affecting helping behavior. The high-test-anxiety children helped significantly less in the evaluative condition than the middle- or low-test-anxiety children, or the high-test-anxiety children in the nonevaluative condition. The high-test-anxiety children in the nonevaluative condition helped significantly more than the middle-test-anxiety children in that condition. Middle- and low-test-anxiety children did not differ in either condition.

Thoughts about self and others, which are likely to affect attention to external conditions, the evaluation of external conditions, feelings, and in turn conduct, are seemingly affected by persistent personal characteristics and expectations about specific experiences. The manner in which the effects of mood, self-esteem, and a sense of well-being (derived from the combination of persistent and temporary influences) interact—not only with one another but with a person's personal goals and value orientations—in affecting behavior is an important subject for future research.

Self-Esteem and Prosocial Action in Everyday Interactions

The preceding research findings and discussion point to the influence of shifting self-conceptions and varied moods on prosocial behavior. In this context it is important to note that interpersonal interactions of many kinds affect a person's self-conception and self-esteem.

Gergen and Wishnow (1965) found that in interacting with an egotistical person people described themselves in more positive terms than before; when interacting with a humble person, they described themselves in more humble terms. The level of expressed self-esteem changed as a function of the characteristics of the other person. Generally subjects afterward felt that they were honest in their presentation of themselves. In another study (Gergen, 1965) an interviewer responded positively, with smiles, nods, minimal verbal reinforcement, to the subject's expressing positive feelings about herself, and slightly negatively to this person's expressing negative feelings about herself. In comparison to those in a control group, these subjects' showed greater self-esteem in their verbal statements during the interview and also on a test following the interview. Perhaps an even more impressive demonstration of shifts in self-esteem was provided by Morse and Gergen (1970). The self-esteem of undergraduates who were applying for a lucrative summer job—as measured by self-report on a paper-and-pencil test—was substantially increased by the appearance in the waiting room of another applicant who wore torn clothes, was unshaven, and generally looked sloppy (Mr. Dirty). In contrast, the appearance of a person who was immaculately dressed and carried an attaché case, a slide rule, and a copy of Aristotle (Mr. Clean) resulted in a substantial decline of the subjects' self-esteem. Self-esteem, among other things, is a function of social comparison.

There are other studies whose findings buttress the point (Gergen, 1976), but those provided are sufficient to demonstrate that the characteristics of another person and of the conditions under which interaction takes place affect feelings about the self. Although none of these studies explored the consequences on behavior toward people, other than self-presentation, it is reasonable to assume, on the basis of the material in this chapter, that prosocial behavior, such as initiating positive interactions, doing favors, being kind, and cooperating might all be affected by the feelings that a person has about himself that are due to other aspects of the interaction.

The Connection between Self and Others: Similarity, Attraction, and Common Group Membership

chapter 7

Can the bond between self and others be relatively directly affected to increase or decrease a person's adoption of or identification with others' goals? Can a person be moved to regard his interests as either conflicting or identical with those of others? There probably are persistent individual differences in orientation to other human beings, and these differences probably result in a tendency to identify with or distance oneself from others' needs and goals. In addition, differences in orientations to particular persons that derive from past experience with them, information about them, or specific circumstances, are likely to affect the bond with them.

A variety of theoretical positions suggest that certain conditions create bonds between specific individuals or groups, whereas other conditions create barriers, thus increasing or decreasing the likelihood of prosocial behavior. The theoretical positions vary in the conditions they stress as affecting the bond, and in the kinds of psychological experiences that they assume will result from these conditions.

Hornstein (1972, 1976), suggests that under some circumstances other people are included in the concept of "we," regarded as part of our in-group. Under other circumstances other people are thought of as "they." When we define people as "we," we are more likely to help them. Varied conditions may lead to defining others as part of one's in-group or as part of one's out-group.

Hornstein (1972, 1976) reasoned about the determinants of prosocial behavior from a Lewinian perspective. Lewin (1935) proposed that the

313

existence of psychological needs or intentions creates tension in individuals. Tension has direction, force, and point of application. Tension disrupts equilibrium, so organisms must strive to fulfill their needs, attain their goals, and thereby reduce tension. If in a person's "psychological environment goal regions exist which are relevant to the tension, psychological forces may lead to actual locomotion as well as thinking about goal-oriented activity [Hornstein, 1972, p. 192]." In other words, the existence of unfulfilled goals will give rise to tension that results in activity leading to the fulfillment of the goal and the reduction of the tension. Lewin identified three sources of tensions: one's own needs, such as the desire for a walk or sexual intercourse; induced needs, such as a mother forcing a child to wear a coat; and the need to satisfy impersonal demands, such as the rules of a situation or the legal code.

Hornstein proposed a fourth source: the empathic experiencing of another person's need or goal, someone else's desire to move toward or away from a goal. He called the tension arising from this source *promotive tension* and defined it as "tension systems coordinated to another's goal attainment [1972, p. 193]." He attempted to demonstrate that people experience such tension. He also tried to identify the circumstances under which people are aroused by another's goal attainment in a manner similar to being aroused by their own goals. Hornstein assumed that similarity between one's own opinions and attitudes and those of another person would give rise to liking and promotive tension, and that dissimilarity would decrease promotive tension and helpfulness. Lewin's conception of the strength of psychological forces provided the basis for another of Hornstein's assumptions, that more help would be forthcoming to attain the goal of a liked person if pursuit of that goal were interrupted near its attainment, rather than far from its attainment. There is an approach gradient when people work toward the fulfillment of their own goals; the nearer the goal, the more tension aroused. When promotive tension is created by similarity, there should be evidence for an approach gradient. With disliked others, since promotive tension should not be evoked, no approach gradient should be found. Hornstein assumed that the approach gradient should be found when the goal of a liked person is valued (*positively valenced*) by the subject. In contrast, when the goal of the liked person is disliked (*negatively valenced*) more help should be given when goal attainment is further away.

Hornstein's theory is essentially a theory of identification that specifies the psychological processes that result from identification with another person. This theory is in part an alternative, in part an elaboration, of a motivational theory of empathy. Certain conditions are expected to result in the arousal of empathy and to lead people to respond to another person's fate as if it were identical with their own. Hornstein substituted promotive tension for empathy, focused on some conditions that are expected to arouse promotive tension, and proposed novel properties of the motivational state that results (e.g., goal gradients). Other researchers, who were concerned with empathy, showed that similarity to another person makes the arousal of empathy more likely (Stotland, 1969; Krebs, 1975; Feshbach & Roe, 1968) and that empathy in turn can motivate prosocial action. This research has been reviewed in Chapter 4.

A difference between the motivational theories of empathy and the theory of promotive tension lies in the nature of affect a person is expected to experience. Empathy implies the simultaneous experience of real affect, in some sense similar to that of another person. The tension in Lewinian theory, however, appears to be a theoretical construct.

A still different conception of the nature of the bond between the self and specific others was proposed by Byrne (1971). Specific experiences and/ or certain kinds of information about other people affect the reward value of these people. The greater the other person's reward value, the more reinforcing it will be to help him (Kelley & Byrne, 1976). Similarity between another person's opinions, interest, and personality traits and one's own makes the other person attractive, that is, increases his reinforcing value (Byrne, 1971). This, in turn, will increase prosocial behavior. Receiving information about another person's opinions or attitudes that are different from one's own has a punishing effect, decreasing the other's attractiveness and presumably the likelihood of positive behavior toward the other. Direct positive or negative experiences with another person should have similar effects.

Conditions That Affect the Bond between the Self and Others

Similarity in Attitudes, Opinions, and Personalities

To test aspects of his model, Hornstein and his associates conducted a series of studies. In one, Hornstein *et al.* (1971) had 175 pedestrians in a heavily Jewish section of Brooklyn find two lost envelopes. One envelope contained a public opinion questionnaire. On an item of this questionnaire that pertained to the Middle East, the respondent indicated either pro- or anti-Israeli views. The second envelope contained a contribution to the Institute of Research in Medicine and information that the respondent was either near or far from completing his goal of 10 contributions. When the person who lost the envelopes had pro-Israeli views and was presumably liked by the finders, the closer he was to completing his goal the more likely people were to mail the envelope for him. With the disliked person, nearness to the goal made no difference. Although similar or liked others were helped more close to the goal than dissimilar or disliked others, there was no difference far from the goal. This seems somewhat contrary to the basic conception of promotive tension. Moreover, in a control group, when subjects did not receive the attitude information, they behaved nearly identically to those in the pro-Israeli condition. Hornstein (1972) speculates that such similarity in behavior would only happen when helping involved little sacrifice, and that only liked subjects would receive help when helping demanded substantial sacrifice. The findings in this study showed that when people had the opportunity to fulfill a goal of another person that they themselves probably also valued, they tended to be helpful. Possibly, people wanted to help the charity, rather than the contributor. Only disagreement with the contributor on an emotionally charged issue diminished helpfulness, and then only near the goal.

In another study, Hodgson, Hornstein, and Siegel (1972) varied the subjects' "cathexis of the goal region," their liking for the goal. Envelopes containing contributions to either the International Tuberculosis Foundation or the International Nudist Foundation were found by 475 people. The findings of this study were complicated and are difficult to evaluate because no control group was included. There was some support for the notion of an approach gradient for liked subjects, with valued goals, but it appeared only when the loser of the envelopes indicated a strong desire to make his contribution rather than a weak desire and then it was the result of a strange finding: Fewer subjects in the liked other, valued goal, far from the goal condition were helpful, at least numerically, than in any of the other conditions in which the subjects presumably valued the goal, including all the dislike conditions. Not surprisingly, the most substantial difference was found in the subjects' help in fulfilling a liked in contrast to a disliked goal. An interesting finding with regard to goal gradients was that liked subjects were helped more in fulfilling their disapproved goal far from its completion than near its completion.

In a later series of three studies (Sole, Marton, & Hornstein, 1975) subjects again found two lost envelopes. One held a $2 contribution to a charity and the other held information about the person's attitudes on four issues. The four issues were of uniformly high importance to the subjects in the first experiment, of uniformly low importance in the second experiment, and of mixed importance in the third experiment (two high, two low). In the first study, a single dissenting opinion substantially reduced rates of helping—as much, in fact, as complete dissimilarity on all four issues. In the second study, the effect of similarity of opinions was gradual; agreement on each additional item contributed to helping. However, with complete disagreement on all four unimportant items, the subjects in this study helped substantially less than the subjects in the first experiment, who experienced complete disagreement on all four important items. This contrasts with Hornstein's conclusions that agreement or disagreement on unimportant items has little influence on people's attraction toward others and on their prosocial behavior (Hornstein, 1976). It seems as if people said to themselves, "If we disagree on unimportant issues, we certainly must be different." However, when information about another person's views on unimportant matters is combined with information on their attitudes toward important matters, the context diminishes the influence of unimportant issues. The third study showed that when agreement on important issues exists, disagreement about unimportant issues does not affect the fulfillment of another's goal.

Several studies provide more evidence that variations in similarities between oneself and another person affect later prosocial behavior. For example, Karabenick, Lerner, and Beecher (1973) found that on Election Day, 1972, passersby were more likely to help a confederate pick up dropped Nixon or McGovern placards if they had the same political preference. The subjects' political views were ascertained by a second experimenter who interviewed them. Suedfeld *et al.* (1972) had a woman approach peace demonstrators in Washington in 1971 and ask them to help her male friend, who was ill. This friend was helped more by the antiwar demonstrators when he had a "dump Nixon" rather than a "support Nixon" sign on him. Research purporting to study empathy, which was reviewed earlier, also showed that information about similarity between oneself and another person, in personality, appearance, or interests, affected both empathic arousal, as measured by physiological reactions and people's descriptions of their feelings (Stotland, 1969; Krebs, 1975) and subsequent prosocial behavior toward this person (Krebs, 1975).

There is little question that similarity sometimes affects prosocial behavior. It is not clear to what *extent* similarity or agreement on issues increases and dissimilarity decreases prosocial behavior. The reasons for the effects of variation in similarity are also not clearly established. Empathic emotional reactions are apparently involved. Identification with others that may lead not to empathic arousal but to an adoption of others' goals is a possibility. The properties of promotive tension, which is presumably involved in identification, and the nature of its influence have not as yet been convincingly demonstrated. The degree to which the reward value of another person is affected by similarity and differences, as Byrne believes, and the degree to which this in turn affects prosocial behavior are also unclear. It is certainly possible that all these states are affected.

The preceding research and related theorizing were based on the assumption that similarity and dissimilarity have consequences in themselves, regardless of their nature or meaning. A study by Ajzen (1974) showed, however, that when similarity–dissimilarity in personality and positive and negative affective values of personality characteristics were independently varied, only affective value had a significant influence on attraction to other individuals. The findings were similar when these conditions were simulated in role playing, and when information about another person's opinions rather than personality was provided. Ajzen suggests that similarity is usually related to attraction because positive affective value is usually empirically associated with similarity. The "affective value" of other people may, therefore, be affected by their similarity to us.

Prior Experience with Another Person

The perceived attractiveness of another person has also been designated as the reason that various kinds of similarities between the self and others, and/or prior experiences with another, contribute to prosocial behavior. Kelley and Byrne (1976) provided some evidence that a positive or negative experience with another person affects attraction and subsequent prosocial behavior toward that person. They measured the changes in the speed of a response, over trials, that terminated the experience of electric shock by another person. Either this other person, the victim, or a bystander previously provided a positive or negative evaluation to the subject. This procedure allowed the experimenter to separate the effects on the subject's behavior of mood, which presumably was affected by the evaluation regardless of its source, and specific feelings of attraction toward the victim. A no-evaluation control group was included. Highly significant group differences were found. Subjects who received a positive evaluation from the victim showed the greatest increase in the speed of their response over seven blocks of two trials, whereas subjects who received the negative evaluation from the victim showed no change in speed from the first trial. Both groups differed significantly from the control group, in which the speed of response moderately increased. The treatments had a significant effect on attraction ratings also. Moreover, when subjects were evaluated by the victim, attraction ratings and mean response speed over all trials were highly significantly correlated ($r = .57$, $p < .001$). In the other conditions this relationship was insubstantial. In this study, the specific feelings about the person in need had, clearly, greater effect than some general mood state that might have been created by evaluation from a bystander, although the latter was not measured.

Baron (1971) conducted an experiment that varied both similarity to and prior experience with another person. Female subjects interacted with someone whose opinions on various issues were either exactly the same as theirs or totally different. Many experiments by Byrne and his associates (Byrne, 1971, 1974) showed that such similarity increases attractiveness, as measured by a paper-and-pencil test. In this study there was also an exchange of written comments in which the confederate evaluated the subjects positively in the similar condition and negatively in the dissimilar condition. The combined effect of similarity and evaluation on attraction toward the confederate was significant. When the experiment seemed to be over, the confederate made one of three requests of the subject. These requests varied in the amount of effort called for. Most subjects in both groups complied with the "easy" request (to return a notebook to a girl who lived in the subject's dormitory). However, significantly more subjects who were induced to like the confederate complied with the moderate and difficult requests (90% and 100% respectively) than subjects who were induced to dislike the confederate (30% and 50% respectively).

It is not only the way others behave toward us but our own behavior toward them that can affect our feelings about them. Schopler and Compere (1971) instructed subjects to be either kind or harsh in providing continuous verbal feedback to another person about his performance on a task. Subsequently, kind subjects evaluated the other person significantly more positively than harsh subjects. Unfortunately, there was no control group to help determine whether being harsh or being kind was responsible for the effect, or whether both had influence. Differences in the evaluation of the other person were not mediated by differences in the evaluation of his performance on the task, which in reality was equal in the two treatment groups, and was perceived as equal.

These findings indicate that people use their own behavior toward other people for inferring their attitudes toward others. Or, to go a step further, people's behavior toward others can create their attitudes toward them. This is consistent with the earlier research and discussion of justification processes. Cognitive activity tends to be in some rough correspondence with overt behavior; one supports the other. Negative behavior toward other persons may lead to devaluation, the experience of dislike. Under some conditions, it will lead to guilt, but guilt may lead to dislike if no compensatory behavior follows. Another's behavior toward us, not surprisingly, also generates feelings and cognitions that are consistent with its perceived consequences and with our judgment of the intention that guides the behavior. Evidence that helping others and being helped by them lead to a positive inclination toward them is also presented in Chapters 8 and 9.

Chapter 5 described research findings showing that people who helped once are more likely to do so again. I discussed self-perception explanations: A person comes to think of himself as a helper, which leads to behavior consistent with the self-image. Another possibility is, however, that helping others affects one's perception of other people; it may lead the helper to extend the boundaries of self to include other human beings to a greater degree, in part as a result of a more positive evaluation of others that leads to greater feelings of benevolence toward them.

Past experience with others clearly affects later behavior toward them, but the effects are complex. Here I would like to note some examples of this complexity. Children say that they would behave much more altruistically toward their best friend than toward their sixth best friend—at least Israeli children do (Sharabany, 1974). However, there is some evidence that children will give more of some possessions to a stranger than to a friend (Wright, 1942; Floyd, 1964). Presumably, the reason for this is their desire to develop friendship with another child, although it may also be greater competitiveness with a friend than with a stranger. However, they are less likely to retaliate for the selfishness of a friend than for the selfishness of a child who is not their friend (Staub & Sherk, 1970). Presumably, among friends, these things can be worked out over a longer period of time. Clearly, past relationships have a complex influence on behavior.

Common Group Membership: Race, Sex, Nationality, and Other Criteria

Cross-Racial Helping.   A number of experimenters examined the influence of the race of a potential helper and of a victim on helping behavior. Certainly, race is an important kind of similarity, at least in countries where racial lines are strongly drawn, and consequently a likely basis of regarding other people as "we" rather than "they," or of reacting empathically to them.

On the whole, the studies found slight and complex effects of race on helping behavior. In the Piliavin *et al.* (1969) study of helping behavior in the subway, whites and blacks helped equally when the victim's distress appeared to originate from a natural cause. When the victim appeared to be drunk, people helped those of their own race substantially more. Piliavin *et al.* explained this finding as the result of differential costs of helping; there is greater fear of helping a drunk who is of another race. It may be, however, that certain conditions activate prejudice, make justifications easier, and/or diminish identification to a greater degree; drunkenness might be one of these, and it may have led to greater devaluation of the victim who was the member of another race. Moreover, for members of many minorities, racial or other kinds, an important basis of identification with members of their group may be shared discrimination, suffering, and humiliation. Consequently, certain conditions, such as another's drunkenness, may elicit the sense of identification to a greater degree.

Gaertner and Bickman (1971) used the previously described wrong-number technique to create an opportunity for help. The race of the caller was manipulated by manner of speech, and the race of the subjects was determined by selecting people in the telephone book who lived in either black or white areas of Brooklyn. Previously, the perception of callers as black or white was established. Whites helped blacks significantly less than they helped other whites, and blacks helped whites somewhat more than they helped other blacks. The latter difference was mainly due to the behavior of black females, who helped whites marginally significantly more than blacks; black males did not differ in their help for blacks and whites. The differences that were noted were not substantial in terms of the percentages of people who were helped. Bryan and Test (1967) showed that black females, who were collecting for the Salvation Army and wore Salvation Army uniforms, received fewer donations from white shoppers than did white females.

Complex findings were reported by West *et al.* (1975). In their study, black and white drivers, males and females, had trouble with their cars. The first study took place in white or black residential areas, and the second study was conducted both in residential areas and near either a white or a black college. In both studies, the large majority of helpers were males, and females received help substantially faster than males. In the first study, blacks were helped faster in black neighborhoods, whites faster in white neighborhoods, and in both neighborhoods the drivers were mainly helped by members of their own race. In the second study, the findings were replicated for the noncollege areas, but in college areas black victims were helped faster near the white university, and white victims were helped faster near the black university. Of substantial interest is that whites helped mainly whites, but blacks tended to help both blacks and whites. Moreover, the high speed of help for blacks in the white college areas was due to fast responding by blacks, but the high speed of help for whites in the black college area was due to fast responding by both whites and blacks. The findings suggest a sense of identification by black college students with their fellow blacks, and perhaps the desire to rescue them in a white neighborhood. The findings again show racial discrimination by whites in responding to another person's need, and, on the whole, relatively indiscriminate responding by blacks. The variation in cross-racial helping by blacks in different locations may be partly the result of their unwillingness to help whites in neighborhoods that are predominantly white. Possibly they feel uncomfortable and restricted in such neighborhoods.

Several studies found no discrimination by people in helping others of the same or different race. Wispé and Freshley (1971), with their "broken bag caper," found that whites and blacks helped about equally white and black shoppers whose shopping bags tore in the parking lot of a supermarket, and whose groceries scattered on the pavement. Black males tended to help more than white males, and black females tended to help less than whites, but no overall race difference was evident. Thayer (1973) also found that blacks and whites helped black and white confederates to the same degree. "Deaf" confederates approached the subjects in Grand Central Station in New York City, handed them a dime, and asked them to make a phone call. Of those asked, 55% helped and many offered to wait with the confederate for the person whom they called. Bickman and Kamzan (1973) reasoned that when a person's need is high, other people may respond regardless of personal characteristics, but they will make racial discriminations when the need is low. They had black and white female confederates approach white female shoppers in a supermarket. The confederates had either a carton of milk (high need) or frozen cookie dough (low need) in their hands—items selected by pretesting. The confederates said that they were short of money and requested $.10 from the shopper. Although white confederates received somewhat more help than black confederates (52% versus 42%), this difference was not significant. Requesting help to buy the more basic food item resulted in significantly more help. Attitude surveys show greater prejudice than the actual behavior in research would indicate. Bickman and Kamzan suggest that the level of social involvement, a concept proposed by Linn (1965), may be useful in understanding situations in which prejudicial attitudes are inconsistent with behavior.

The level of social involvement comprises (*a*) the amount and degree of visibility of interaction with the attitude object; (*b*) the audience for the interaction; and (*c*) the potential consequences of the interaction. An aspect of social involvement is the degree to which one's behavior is actually or potentially under surveillance, and by whom. For example, Boyanowsky and Allen (1973) report a decrease in discriminatory behavior by highly prejudiced whites when their responses were not observed by in-group members. The effects of surveillance are a function of a person's beliefs about the attitudes of the in-group. The nature of the help needed is also important. Helping someone fix a car may lead to extensive interaction; some other forms of help may be more transient. Also, a direct request or a suddenly emerging need in one's immediate vicinity can exert a great deal of social influence on a person. On the other hand, circumstances that demand that a helper approach a victim allow more self-selection, and behavior may be guided by attitudes toward another person based on race, similarity of opinions and beliefs, and other sources of categorization.

Wegner and Crano (1975) argued that in many prior studies black subjects had been tested in black areas of a city and white subjects had been tested in white areas (Gaertner & Bickman, 1971; Wispé & Freshley, 1971), so that the effects of the race of the subjects were confounded with the effects of the physical location. Wegner and Crano had black and white confederates drop a large number of computer cards in front of black and white students in the hallways of a large midwestern university. Females in this study helped more than males. An interaction was found between the race of the subject and the race of the victim; white subjects helped white and black victims equally, whereas black subjects helped white victims less and black victims more than did white subjects. As the authors note, "It might be proposed that the altruistic activities of minority group members would more often be aimed at fellow members when the group comprised only a small fraction of the immediate population [Wegner & Crano, 1975, p. 904]."

Clearly, the degree to which members of a minority are surrounded by a large majority is likely to affect the degree of minority group members' identification with their group. The nature of the surrounding world, how alien or familiar, friendly or unfriendly it seems, is also important. In the study conducted by West *et al.* (1975), which took place in the South, black students may have felt more at home than those in the Midwest; they also comprised a larger percentage of the surrounding population. Unfortunately, Wegner and Crano provide no information about the percentage of blacks on the campus.

In a study guided by a different and more elaborate conception than most of the preceding studies, Katz, Cohen, and Glass (1975) assumed that white Americans' attitudes toward blacks are essentially ambivalent rather than clearly positive or negative. Such ambivalence creates a tendency toward behavioral instability, so that circumstances determine how a person will act (Katz *et al.*, 1973). They note that in a Canadian study (Dutton, 1973) whites helped blacks who actively sought help for a humanitarian cause more than they helped whites and they suggest that the discrepancy with the findings of American studies is due not to national differences, but to the nature of the circumstances under which helping behavior was studied. They suggest that under varied circumstances one would expect whites to help blacks more than other whites. Their altruism toward blacks might be promoted by several motives: because they want to reinforce positive conforming behavior of a potentially dangerous minority, because sympathy toward the underdog is activated, and because they want to promote or defend their positive self-esteem by acting in a positive way when they are confronted with behavior by minority-group members that challenges their stereotypes. Three studies were conducted, exploring the hypothesis that when blacks seek aid for a socially valued activity, even if it is to promote a valued personal goal, when it is done in a manner that is "acceptable" to whites, blacks will be helped more. This result was actually found in two experiments, in which white and black confederates asked whites, or members of both races, for an interview about some product, either on the telephone or at a subway station. The confederates either presented themselves as students who were conducting the interview as part of a part-time job, or indicated that the interview was being done in the course of their regular employment. When the subjects were simply asked for change of a quarter—presumably not a socially valued goal and therefore not activating any of the aforementioned motives—whites were helped more.

Once again, the complexity of cross-racial helping is indicated by the findings, particularly when compared to those of other experiments. This study, conducted in New York City, as a number of other studies were, suggests that when help is needed to promote a positive goal, to achieve self gain (but not of any substantial proportion) of a respectable variety in a respectable manner, whites will help blacks more than they will help other whites. Dutton's (1973) findings show this when blacks and whites work for a humanitarian cause. The data from the previous studies, and even from this one, are fairly consistent in showing, in contrast, that when some condition of deficiency or need exists, whites frequently help blacks less than they help other whites.

Gaertner and Dividio (1977) suggest a useful hypothesis to further explain why whites sometimes help blacks less, and other times more, than they help other whites. They propose that people are disinclined to engage in behavior that would lead to the attribution (including the self-attribution) of racist motives. Since in our society equalitarianism is highly valued and professed but socialization and the nature of society often foster prejudice, expression of prejudice would frequently be subtle. "This attitudinal framework suggests that whites are more likely to discriminate against blacks in situations where failure to respond favorably could be attributable to factors other than a person's race [p. 693]." Consistent with my views of justification processes (Chapter 4), when circumstances make justifications easier, the race of a victim will affect helping. When circumstances make justification of not helping and/or devaluation of the victim difficult, race will not have an effect. Because of the high cost of discriminating against blacks in the latter kinds of situations, blacks may receive help more frequently than other whites.

Gaertner and Dividio (1977) found that when they were alone, white female undergraduates responded slightly (not significantly) more to the plight of a black than of a white victim, who was in a different room. When, however, the subjects believed that there were other (also white) witnesses to the emergency, they helped the black victim less than the white victim. As I suggested in Chapter 3, when the subject's responsibility is less—in this case, diffused—conditions that may reduce helping are more likely to exert influence. In this study, subjects who on a questionnaire previously expressed more or less prejudice did not differ in their responses to the black and white victims. There was a strong relationship between subjects' physiological (heart rate) responses to the emergency and their helping. The greater the heart rate acceleration, even during the first 10 seconds of the emergency, the more the subjects helped. Heart rate deceleration, however, was negatively associated with helping.

In interpreting these findings, we must consider the possibility that, in the presence of other bystanders, subjects may have helped the black victim less than the white victim not because the diffusion of responsibility allowed an expression of their own prejudice or ambivalence toward blacks, but because of their assumptions about the prejudices of the other white bystanders and about the behavior they would regard as appropriate. As prior research findings suggested (Horowitz, 1971; Poulos & Liebert, 1971; see Chapters 3 and 5), depending on their perceptions of (or beliefs about) others' values and norms, surveillance by others may have different effects on people's behavior. This reasoning is also supported by the findings of a second study by Gaertner and Dividio (1977). Subjects who could attribute arousal created by the emergency to a placebo pill helped less in a mild emergency (the authors intended to vary ambiguity, but in my opinion the primary difference was apparent need), although not in a severe emergency. However, the possibility of misattributing the source of arousal led to only very slight and unclear differences in reactions to black and white victims.

The Influence of Other Group Memberships. Differences between same-sex and cross-sex helping behavior, which was to a limited extent examined in some of the research described, cannot be regarded as simply the result of common group membership. Sometimes when males help females more than they help other males a sexual motive is possible. For example, in Bryan and Test's (1967) study of helping a motorist with a flat tire, and in Wispé and Freshley's (1971) study of helping a shopper pick up groceries, males helped more than females; the person in need was always a female. The difference may be due to males' interest in sexual possibilities, their greater competence in the activity demanded for help (as in the West *et al.* study), or the greater appropriateness, in the sense of social custom, for males to help. When females have the opportunity to help a male, they may be inhibited by fear or concern about the inappropriateness of approaching a strange male or by fear due to the greater physical strength of males and fear of violence. Thus, differences in cross-sex helping may have complex meaning.

There is relatively little research on differences in people's responsiveness to compatriots and to foreigners, obviously another criterion for group membership. Feldman (1968) found that, given a variety of different opportunities to respond to compatriots and foreigners, Parisians and Bostonians helped compatriots more, and Athenians helped foreigners more. The opportunities for help included a request for directions and a request to mail a letter; the opportunity to cheat the other person was also provided. It may be, however, that Athenians also acted according to the principle of helping in-group members more. Feldman notes that Triandis Vasilou, and Nassiakou (1968) examined the definitions by Greeks of the concepts of in-group and out-group: The in-group includes family, friends, friends of friends, and tourists. Other Greeks are regarded as out-group members.

Hornstein (1976) suggests that the greater helping of whites by black subjects in some studies (e.g., Gaertner & Bickman, 1971) is the result of conditions in which "we" become "they," and "they" become "we." When people learn to disapprove of aspects of themselves, or even to hate them, "people with similar attributes are condemned as 'they,' and their plight is of no concern [p. 32]." This speculation is worth noting even though, reasonable as it seems, the findings previously discussed provide little support for it. It is possible, of course, that by the time most of the research was conducted black racial identification had become positive, but such a reversal in "we" and "they" would have been found earlier. In 1958 the

Clarks found that young black children preferred white dolls to black dolls, but indications that this preference has now reversed points to a shift in black identification. The variable findings about cross-racial helping— seemingly a decreased tendency by blacks to help whites more in the later research—may be due to such a shift taking place from the late 1960s to the early 1970s, a period of rapid social progress in civil rights, race relations, and black self-assertion.

A slight tendency toward greater helping by blacks of whites than of blacks in some of the early research may have been the result of fear of retaliation for not helping. The same factor may account for lack of discrimination by blacks in helping blacks and whites. Alternatively, when another person is in need, blacks may not consider color as a source of categorization but may respond to the need. Finally, both the occasionally greater help for whites, and blacks' indiscriminate helping, which was the most frequent finding, may be explained as blacks' reaction to the opportunity to assume a superior role in relation to a white person, that of helper, in contrast to the inferior role society has traditionally forced them to assume. Unfortunately, there are no data available with which to evaluate the relative influences of these factors.

Common Group Membership, Revisited. The research on cross-racial differences in helping behavior, on cross-sex helping, on people helping compatriots and foreigners, is important from both a social and a practical perspective. However, the complex determinants of such behavior limit its usefulness in establishing how group membership affects behavior toward people in the in-group and in the out-group. In addition to the fact of membership in a group, the meaning of the group to the person, attitudes toward membership in the group, and other conditions have to be measured and their influences considered. The practical importance of this issue is substantial, because humans tend to divide the world into various groupings; children learn to do so from an early age. I. F. Stone noted, at a talk he gave at Harvard University at the height of the Vietnamese war, that the world will not know peace as long as we divide ourselves into "we" and "they," "us" and "them," as we now do and teach our children to do.

A number of experiments show that grouping people on arbitrary and/ or rather trivial bases leads to discrimination by them in favor of their in group, at the expense of the out-group. In these experiments subjects were divided into groups for a "judgment task" that was to follow. The nature of the task was not specified. It was implied that the nature of the division did not really matter, and for convenience the basis of the division was to be the subjects' preferences, on an aesthetic preference task, previously administered, for Klee or Kandinski. In the first such experiment, Tajfel, Flammont, and Bundy (1971) found that people subsequently divided rewards to favor members of their in-group, the Klee group or the Kadinsky group, whichever it was, at the expense of the out-group. Later, Billig and Tajfel (1973) explored the possibility that the reason for the discrimination was that people assumed that members of their in-group had beliefs similar to their own, in line with the belief-similarity theory of discrimination of Rokeach and his associates (1960). The subjects in this study were told either that categorization into groups was random or that it was contingent on their preferences for paintings. Discrimination resulted regardless of the basis of assignment to groups, but it was somewhat greater when groups were created on the basis of aesthetic preference.

Allen and Wilder (1975) measured the subjects' attitudes on a variety of topics and then divided them into groups on the basis of their preference for Klee or Kandinski. The experimenters provided information about the beliefs of the in-group and out-group members to subjects, creating similar and dissimilar in-group and similar and dissimilar out-group conditions. In assigning rewards to members of in-groups and out-groups (with themselves excluded) the subjects again strongly favored the in-group, at the expense of the out-group. Allen and Wilder suggest that the findings support the explanation provided by Tajfel *et al.* that the categorization of people into in-groups and out-groups results in discrimination because of the existence of a social norm that people should favor in-group members. However, belief similarity with group members enhanced discrimination in favor of the in-group, whereas belief dissimilarity with in-group members diminished discrimination in their favor. Somewhat surprisingly, belief similarity or dissimilarity with out-group members had no effect on degree of discrimination against them. Allen and Wilder note that previous research supporting the belief-similarity hypothesis usually dealt with race and used questionnaire responses rather than allocation of rewards (the latter is presumably a more "real" behavior). In their study, group assignment preceded variation in belief similarity and may therefore have had a primary influence.

In these studies subjects were apparently presented with the task of allocating rewards to in-group and out-group members without a meaningful rationale, certainly without one that would have made them think that the task had a purpose other than that of testing them. The findings may be the result of rational deliberation of a problem-solving type rather than manifestations of an inclination to respond one way or another to members of in-groups and out-groups. However, that such rational deliberation would lead to discrimination is particularly interesting.

The possibility that division of people into in-groups and out-groups has important consequences on how people perceive and respond to one another is important. Is such division usually due to existing social norms, to socialization and cultural conditions that teach children to categorize people according to group membership, or possibly to a basic human tendency to seek identification with others—perhaps at the expense of a sense of separateness from or even adversity toward those who are regarded as outsiders? If the last is true, to what extent can socialization overcome this tendency?

Campbell (1965) proposed that the interests of groups frequently conflict. Historically, the conflict may have involved scarce resources and survival itself. Campbell, at that time arguing for the biological basis of altruism, also argued that the willingness for self-sacrifice for the group, even to the extent of sacrificing one's life, was essential for the survival of the group and its members. However, even if identification with the group has survival value, its source can still be the individual experience, rooted in biology. For a long time, children are helpless and dependent and need the protection of adults. Therefore children develop an extremely strong sense of identification with those immediately surrounding them, at least under minimally acceptable conditions to the child (minimal satisfaction of needs, minimal nurturance and responsiveness), and perhaps a continuing need for close identification with other individuals and groups will remain. Because of the nature of families—they are usually limited in members and function as in-groups that face the rest of the world, the out-group—children are likely to learn the differentiation between in-group and out-group well. The degree to which this distinction and the need to identify with an in-group develop and are maintained may be fostered or minimized by a culture as a function of both family organization and the type of connection that exists between families, the values, standards, and orientation of the culture in creating distinctions among its members and between its members and the outside world, and the extent and nature of contact with other groups.

These factors will affect both the extent to which the in-group and the out-group are perceived as similar or different, and on what dimensions. Knowledge about varied groups within one's culture and about groups outside one's culture may be important by itself, since large discrepancies between what one knows and expects and particular stimuli (such as "strange" customs and behavior) tend to give rise to negative emotions (Leventhal, 1974). It is conceivable for members of a culture to learn about the many differences between themselves and others without negative evaluation of these differences, and at the same time to emphasize fundamental similarities, a shared "humanness." Presumably such socialization and experience would diminish discrimination against outsiders and increase positive behavior toward them.

Shared Humanity and Orientation toward Other Human Beings

In earlier chapters I noted that important individual differences in people's orientations toward other human beings exist and affect the perception of others as good or bad, friendly or hostile. I noted that positive experiences may affect prosocial behavior because they create a greater sense of benevolence toward others.

In a series of experiments Hornstein *et al.* (1975) demonstrated that specific experiences may affect a person's orientation toward other human beings in general and prosocial behavior in interaction with a specific person in particular. In these studies subjects listened to music on the radio while waiting for an experiment to continue. In the two experimental groups the music was interrupted for one of two brief newscasts. One told about a person who performed a highly self-sacrificial act, donating his kidney to save a stranger's life. The other reported a vicious act, the murder of a kind old woman. Subsequently, subjects were to play a single-trial prisoner's dilemma type game, with a high reward at stake. A combined dependent measure was used for primary analysis: a cooperative choice, a cooperative choice expected from the other person, and a cooperative goal attributed to the other, in contrast to a competitive response on all three dimensions. Subjects who heard the positive news items responded significantly more cooperatively than those who heard either the negative news item or music only. The last two groups did not differ in the pattern of their responses.

In a second experiment, following the experimental treatments the subjects were asked to fill out a questionnaire that measured philosophies of human nature. Among males, significant differences resulted from the broadcast. While in behavior hearing the positive broadcast enhanced cooperation, on this measure there was little difference between control subjects and those hearing the prosocial broadcast. Hearing the antisocial broadcast resulted in more pessimistic evaluation of people. In a third study, listening to the broadcast had no effect on participants' moods, as measured by an adjective checklist, but in a fourth study, in which specific attention was called to the broadcast, listening to it affected moods. The experimenters suggest that the usual findings of the effects of experimental treatments on moods might represent demand characteristics. People know that certain experiences would be expected to create certain moods, so they might then report their own moods accordingly. However, the effects on moods are not at all uniform, less so than the effects on behavior. In other research, subjects who heard antisocial news (Kaplan, 1974) were intolerant of differences between themselves and another person, whereas those hearing prosocial news were quite tolerant. In the former case subjects sharply differentiated between a person who was similar to them and one who was dissimilar in evaluating performance on building boxes, in evaluating them as persons, and in distributing rewards between them. When they heard the prosocial news, subjects engaged in little discrimination. What is again impressive about these findings is the seemingly unimportant and irrelevant nature of the similarity or dissimilarity: the tendency to overestimate or underestimate the number of dots in a scatter plot.

As in research reviewed in the preceding chapter, the studies of Hornstein *et al.* showed discrepancies in the effects on behavioral and cognitive–affective measures of hearing newscasts about another human being acting in a highly positive or negative manner. As with competence, success and failure, and positive experiences, the good news increased prosocial behavior whereas the bad news did not significantly decrease positive or increase negative behavior in comparison to a control group. However, in the participants' evaluation of other human beings it was the bad news that led to negative judgments; the good news had no effect. Clearly, past research has had trouble with specifying and measuring the exact psychological conditions that result from positive and negative experiences and in turn affect prosocial behavior.

With regard to moods, as I noted (Chapter 6), relatively specific moods, such as feelings of positive affiliation or negative feelings about the self, rather than general moods, such as happiness, may be the primary mediators of positive social behavior. Such moods may result, or be expressed in, or can be aspects of psychological states such as self-concern and self-preoccupation, a person's state of well-being and feeling of potency, and feelings of benevolence toward self and others. These psychological states also have more specific aspects, such as variations in the importance of material goods and the expectation of success and failure in attempts to help. Different experiences may have different effects, and different persons may react to the same conditions in different modes. An experimental strategy that would specify the mediators of increased prosocial behavior following positive experiences and positive information about other people is needed. A strategy that simultaneously evaluates behavioral effects in some treatment groups, and thoughts and feelings in other, identical groups, in several domains, might be effective. Hornstein *et al.* followed such a strategy, to some degree, in successive experiments, but they examined the psychological consequences of hearing the news only in limited domains.

Personality and the Bond between Self and Other:

One may expect differences in people's orientations toward other human beings or toward themselves, and the interaction between these personality differences and specific conditions, to affect feelings about and behavior toward other people. As in other realms, the relevant evidence is sparse.

Mitchell and Byrne (1973) assessed the authoritarian tendency of subjects and later asked them to judge a person who was accused of stealing an examination. Subjects received information indicating that on five issues their attitudes were either similar to or at variance with those of the accused. Both in rating how positively or negatively they felt about the defendant, and in assessing his guilt or innocence, authoritarians favored the accused when he was presented as similar to them, and were negatively inclined toward him when he was dissimilar. On the other hand, the judgment of less authoritarian subjects did not vary as a function of similarity.

In a study conducted in New York, Gaertner (1973) found that, in responding to the need for help presented by the wrong-number technique, registered members of the Liberal party discriminated against blacks less than registered members of the Conservative party. Interestingly, members of the Liberal party hung up somewhat more frequently before the need for help could be communicated to them when the caller was black. It is possible that discrimination on their part took a different, more subtle form.

As I have noted in discussing a variety of experiments, similarity in attitudes, opinions, and beliefs increased ratings of attraction for other people. Similarity, including information about similarity in personality, also increased empathy and prosocial behavior directed at that person. Are there limiting conditions to these relationships? Ajzen (1974) found that the affective value of another's characteristics, not similarity itself, determines attraction. The similarity–attraction relations may be due to the assumption that those who are similar to us have positive characteristics. However, people whose self-esteem is low may not make such an assumption. Perhaps people who assign low affective value to themselves, in the sense of a low self-esteem, will show no preference for or attraction to those similar to themselves. People who have a low self-esteem may also show less kindness to others because they respond like people who have a temporarily negative self-esteem following a negative experience. Might they show less kindness particularly toward those similar to themselves? Would this happen because they treat themselves unkindly, and they so treat the similar other? Alternatively, they may extend benevolence to themselves, but they may dislike similar others and not respond positively to them.

In one study there was a slight indication that variation in self-esteem and similarity may interact in influencing attraction toward others, but no clear picture emerged (Hendrick & Page, 1970). Karylowski (1976) used elaborate measures of self-esteem and varied similarity between Polish high-school girls and the confederate who interacted with them. He found a strong positive relationship between similarity and liking among subjects with high self-esteem, but no relationship among subjects with low self-esteem. The subjects also engaged in an activity in the course of which they could win money, either for themselves or for the other person. This activity consisted of quickly and accurately pressing buttons in response to stimulus lights. The similarity manipulation took place during a break in this activity, and prosocial behavior was measured by the relative change in the number of the subjects' correct responses for themselves and for the other person. There was no interaction in the effects of self-esteem and similarity on prosocial behavior, as there was on attraction. However, similarity had a significant effect and led to better performance for the other person, replicating other findings. There was no correlation between self-esteem and prosocial action in either the high- or low-similarity group. Karylowski does not specifically report whether any differences in pro-social behavior were found that were due to differences in self-esteem alone. Some of the findings may have been affected by the reliance on *t* tests, without an analysis of variance to test interactions. Karylowski (1976) writes that the findings, including a lack of correlation between attraction and prosocial behavior, led him to believe "that the relationship between similarity and altruistic motivation is, at least in some part, independent (sui generis), and not entirely derived from the similarity–interpersonal attraction relationship [p. 73]."

The lack of influence of similarity on attraction among people whose self-esteem is low could be defensive in nature, instead of representing a transfer of low affective value from oneself to others. Persons with low self-esteem may not *admit* attraction to similar others because they fear dislike and rejection. Furthermore, similarity and/or common group membership might lead to identification with others and greater helping without attraction and liking. Hornstein *et al.* (1971) have also proposed that attraction was not the mediator of differences in helping people who varied in the similarity of their attitudes to those of subjects, but they made this proposal on the basis of very tentative findings. The findings point primarily to the need to explore the manner in which self-esteem, similarity, and attraction relate to one another in affecting prosocial behavior.

The moderating influence of self-esteem on the similarity–attraction relationship was further confirmed by a study conducted by Leonard (1975). Subjects interviewed confederates who posed as job applicants. Similarity to the subject was varied both by the confederate's behavior and by information provided about attitude similarity, using the paradigm employed by Byrne (1971). Subjects with favorable self-concepts showed greater attraction for similar than for dissimilar others, and those with unfavorable self-concepts did not differentiate between similar and dissimilar others. As Leonard notes, additional "boundary conditions" to the similarity–attraction relationship ought to be explored.

Variations in the Bond between the Self and Others

Theory and research findings have identified a variety of conditions that apparently affect a person's orientation and subsequent behavior toward others. These conditions include varied forms of similarity between the self and specific others, positive or negative past experiences in relation to others (how others behaved toward the person and how the person behaved toward them), and common or different group membership. Conditions that affect a person directly rather than the bond, positive and negative experiences, can in turn affect orientation toward others. These conditions may affect identification with others' needs and goals, the arousal of promotive tension and of empathy, the experience of attraction to another person or persons, the affective value placed on others, the expectation of rewarding future interaction, and perhaps other internal states. Some of these are overlapping psychological states; some are independent.

It is unlikely, for example, that an inebriated person of one's own race is perceived as highly attractive, but people nonetheless approach and help such a person although they seem disinclined to help a person of another race in such a condition. It is also unlikely that people experience empathy, in the sense of arousal of an identical emotion, for a person who lost a wallet containing a contribution to charity. Nonetheless, they help less when that person holds views different from beliefs of their own. As I noted, the broadest theoretical position appears to be that of Hornstein, dealing with the basic issue of identification with others. Sometimes, however, it is empathy, perhaps a more powerful form of identification than "promotive tension," and at other times it is the reward value of another person and attraction toward him that is the primary influence on behavior. Thus varied psychological states may strengthen or weaken the bond with others. They are probably created by different experiences and have somewhat different consequences.

I have repeatedly suggested that people vary in their orientations toward other people. This variation will often interact with specific experiences in affecting behavior toward others. In general, we have to consider the effects of the conditions that influence feelings about the self and the bond between self and others in conjunction with personality characteristics. Similarity and the creation of common group membership may exert influence by extending the range of applicability of prosocial orientation to other people. If so, when a person's prosocial values and empathic capacity are extremely low, similarity and common group membership would not affect prosocial behavior. Membership in a restricted group that has specific values and norms of its own would affect behavior as a function of what these values and norms are.

The findings again point to the perceptual–evaluative–cognitive determinants of behavior, to the processing and using of varied information about others as well as about the self. What is the nature of the self-guidance that determines whether people initiate and persist in some activity? Feelings about the self and about others create a flow of thought and consciousness that determines whether action is initiated in favor of others and whether it is maintained. It would be worthwhile to study this flow by having people attend to and describe their thoughts and feelings under varied conditions, and by varying the units of input that would guide and direct the flow and then examining the behavioral consequences. Limited attempts in the latter direction, at least with children, have been reported (Masters & Samrock, 1976; see Volume 2, Chapter 4).

Exchange and Reciprocity in Positive and Negative Behavior

chapter 8

In this chapter I shall discuss prosocial behavior that takes place in the course of interaction between people. The interaction, however minimal, establishes a relationship. Prosocial behavior is certainly most frequent in everyday life among people who are in a continuing relationship. Doing favors, going out of our way to help, responding to others in distress or in need, and trying to help others achieve their goals usually involve people we know. The research discussed in the preceding chapters dealt mostly with helping among individuals who had no prior familiarity with one another. Unfortunately, the research discussed in this chapter deals mostly with helping behavior in "minimal relationships." Usually the relationship is established when one person performs or withholds an act (whether helpful or harmful) and the second person has an opportunity to respond. It is useful to regard such interactions as representing minimal relationships because they are likely to be involved in establishing actual relationships, and some of the determinants of behavior in them seem similar to those in more extensive relationships. In Chapter 9, on the basis of both the limited available evidence and theoretical considerations, the determinants of positive social behavior within extended relationships and among intimates are considered.

Exchange, reciprocity, and cooperation are relevant to the very basis of the organization of social groups and societies. Without cooperation, positive exchange, and trust in others' goodwill and in their willingness to base social life on mutual cooperation and helpfulness, societies could not func-

335

tion very well and/or the material and psychological welfare of their members would be diminished. Such goodwill arises not only from persons themselves, but from the social organization, which exerts pressure on individuals (as well as on institutions) to act in a manner that will contribute to the common good. At best, the common good is the good of society as a whole with the inclusion rather than disregard of the good of each of its individual members. Although the discussion in this chapter focuses on the individual rather than on the abstract institutional or societal level, it clearly has implications for the latter.

The Nature of Social Exchange

A number of social psychologists have proposed that social behavior is guided by principles of exchange (Homans, 1961; Blau, 1964; Chadwick-Jones, 1976). Homans (1961), for example, viewed the probability of particular social behavior as a function of profits obtained. Profits were defined simply as rewards minus costs. Individuals attempt to maximize their benefits in interaction with others. However, since each person in an interaction attempts to maximize benefits, interactions between people stabilize when a maximum joint benefit is reached (Gergen, 1968a). Blau (1964) described social exchange as "voluntary actions of individuals that are motivated by returns they are expected to bring, and typically do, in fact, bring from others [p. 91]."

Many acts and assets in everyday life can be commodities of exchange: effort extended for another, enjoyment gained from or through another person, spiritual and other gains, approval and liking, prestige and status conferred by one person on another, as well as material objects. An important component of social exchange is expected reciprocation of benefits that are produced. This is clear from Blau's definition, cited previously. Boulding (1962) noted that an exchange system begins with promises of reciprocity. Without reciprocation of benefits the exchange situation is normally not maintained. As the relationship between two or more individuals continues, norms derived from their experience and negotiations with each other will develop. These norms concern what the contribution of each will be—what kind and amount of "commodity" each will contribute (Homans, 1961).

Norms probably develop in the relationship between two people (e.g., on the dyadic level) or in the interaction among members of groups or societies because they have important functional value. They protect individuals from exploitation by others, since the contribution of each person to the exchange relationship is specified by the norm. Societal norms also specify the obligations entailed by persons in particular roles or situations. More generally, norms regulate social interactions and thereby diminish confusion and the necessity for constant decision making. Without specification of social expectations embodied in norms, people would have to work out and decide on rules of interaction on every occasion. An interesting aspect of normative control is that although norms develop for functional reasons, they tend to acquire a moral character and the behavior they prescribe comes to be regarded as obligatory.

One commodity of exchange that social-exchange theorists emphasize is social approval, which provides a basic form of "payment." That social approval is an important reinforcer of behavior and can influence a wide variety of actions has been extensively demonstrated (Crowne & Marlowe, 1964; Nord, 1969) and is generally accepted. More important for exchange notions, it has also been shown that social approval can be used to repay a debt or to become a creditor. In a study by Chalmers, Horne, and Rosenbaum (1963), subjects, especially females, who were given social support by another tended to support the other when the situation called for it. In another study Slater (1955) found that people in a group who gave the most support tended to be best liked.

Social approval and support may also be used as "social investment." Jones (1964) describes "other enhancement" as a technique of ingratiation in which people give social approval to someone in order to make themselves attractive to that person. Findings by Rosenfeld (1966a, 1966b) support Jones's hypothesis; subjects who were instructed to seek approval from others were more active gesturally and vocally, used more smiles, exhibited fewer negative head nods and referred less to themselves, than subjects instructed to avoid approval. These actions tended to be reciprocated by others; positive social acts evoked similar positive responses. According to Lott and Lott (1965) there is "clear agreement among many contemporary theorists that attraction will follow if one individual either directly provides another with reward or need satisfaction, is perceived as potentially able to do so, or is otherwise associated with such a similar state of affairs [p. 287]."

Social approval may be subject to what economists call the *law of diminishing marginal utility*. As a function of increased use, the effects of social approval in producing attraction—or its exchange value in general—may decrease. Blau (1964) suggested that if a person gives social approval too freely, he depreciates its value. It it known that the reinforcement value of a reinforcer diminishes as the result of satiation, and this is also likely to happen with social approval as the reinforcer.

Many other behaviors, possessions, and individual characteristics can be commodities of exchange. In Western societies, a woman's attractiveness and a man's social status or wealth have often been commodities that were traded for each other. Elder (1969) found that high-school girls who were rated as better looking were more likely later to marry higher status men than were their less attractive classmates. Rubin (1973) notes that in the small towns of eastern Europe, wealthy Jewish merchants frequently tried to marry their daughters to poor boys from the local yeshiva who were respected for their scholarly abilities. In rating the values of different characteristics of other people, college students thought that on initial contact physical attractiveness was particularly important (Levinger & Snoek, 1972). However, at later stages of the relationship less visible characteristics, such as considerateness and the need to give and receive love, were judged substantially more important. With experience, most people are likely to learn their own exchange value in physical attractiveness, as well as in other domains. Although people may tend to initially overvalue themselves, with experience they learn that they have to accept other people whose value in a particular domain (e.g., physical attractiveness) reasonably matches their own, unless they can offer additional "commodities" of value. (Might considerateness and other such qualities be more likely to develop in physically less attractive persons because they need them more as commodities of exchange?)

Interaction among people is likely to be affected not only by the expected or actual benefits they provide each other, but also by the comparison of these benefits with an expected level. Thibaut and Kelley (1959) suggested that people operate as if they were comparing outcomes at a given moment with a standard, or a Comparison Level, thereby evaluating the relative satisfaction received from that outcome. Relationships with other people will be maintained according to the satisfaction experienced relative to the Comparison Level. The Comparison Level is determined by what people have experienced in the past and what they have seen others experience. Thibaut and Kelly (1959) also proposed a Comparison Level for Alternatives. This appears to explain why people maintain apparently unsatisfactory relationships, such as a bad marriage, work for an impossible boss. They may do so because their alternatives appear even worse.

The only conditions clearly specified by exchange theorists for satisfaction in the exchange situation are the profits gained in the interaction and the value of these profits in comparison to standards or Comparison Levels. Of course, outcomes that may seem minimal or even negative to outside observers may satisfy some particular need or goal and thus directly contribute to the maintenance of a relationship. A dependent person may enjoy a dominant, authoritarian partner; a masochist does need a sadist.

The terminology of exchange theory, with its economic and material terms, its emphasis on profits and losses, might not appeal to many people. However, such concepts can be humanized by the manner in which we conceive of commodities and profits. Even if we lose something in referring to affectionate responsiveness or sensitivity to other people's needs as commodities of exchange, a firm conceptualization of such social behavioral tendencies and how they enter into people's interactions with other people is useful. To remain consistent with existing terminology, I will occasionally continue to refer to commodities and profits, which represent very initial steps toward such a conceptualization. Furthermore, more important for our purposes are the concept of positive exchange and the principles that guide it, which include reciprocity, equity, and justice (as we shall see). These appear to be basic principles and processes that, jointly with other influences, guide cooperation and mutual aid. Exchange and reciprocity are not likely to be the primary principles that guide our reactions to strangers in need. However, the motivators of prosocial behavior that were discussed before, such as prosocial norms, personal responsibility, empathy, and identification, combined with rules of exchange, are likely to determine our reactions to others' goals, desires, needs, and despairs. Moreover, although frequently it may not be self-interest that leads to the initiation of positive interactions, some form of reciprocity of benefits is necessary to maintain them.

Sorokin (1971), emphasizing the importance of love, noted that "love begets love and hate begets hate." In a relatively casual, not highly controlled study with Harvard and Radcliffe students and patients at a hospital in Boston, he found that 65–80% of friendly and aggressive approaches were met by like responses. In another informal study, hostile relationships between pairs of students at Harvard and Radcliffe were turned into friendly ones over a period of 3 months by the "method of good deeds," that is, by inducing one member in each pair to render good deeds to the other. This is consistent with research that has been and will be reported, showing that both receiving and proffering kindness can lead to liking for another person. Kindness as a commodity of exchange can engender feelings that will lead to more kindness.

Sorokin's informal research is important from another perspective. Newcomb (1947) proposed what came to be known as the *autistic hostility hypothesis* to account for the perpetuation of antagonistic feelings between people. Once hostility between persons develops they tend to avoid or restrict mutual communication and common experience. Consequently, the antagonism will not be resolved or changed. Sorokin's approach suggests that mutual antagonism can be changed by inducing one person to initiate good deeds.

A limitation of exchange theory has been the lack of attention given to the kinds of commodities that can reasonably be exchanged. Will money buy love? Can information be exchanged for status? Recently Foa and his associates (Foa, 1971; Foa & Foa, 1974) in their studies on resource theory, distinguished between different basic resource classes (money, goods, information, services, status, and love) in terms of particularism and concreteness. They proposed hypotheses about the types of resources that can be meaningfully exchanged. In this system, "*Love* is defined as an expression of affectionate regard, warmth, comfort; *status* is an expression of evaluative judgment that conveys high or low prestige, regard, or esteem; . . . *goods* are tangible products, objects, or materials; and *services* involve ac-

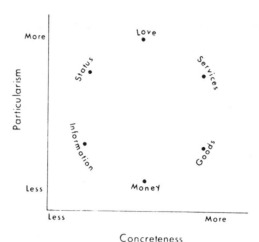

Figure 8.1.
A model showing the relative concreteness or particularity of various resource classes. (From Donnenworth and Foa, 1974.)

tivities on the body or belongings of an individual that often constitute labor for another [Donnenwerth & Foa, 1974, p. 786]." The *concreteness* dimension refers to resources or products that have a tangible quality. Services and goods are highly concrete. Status and information are minimally concrete since they are typically conveyed by verbal or symbolic means. Love and money are intermediate since they can be exchanged in both concrete and symbolic forms. On the *particularistic* dimension love has the highest position. Whether or not we value love depends on the person we receive it from; who offers love matters a great deal in determining "reinforcing effectiveness." Money is the least particularistic resource. It has similar value regardless of the relationship between giver and receiver. Services and status are regarded as less particularistic than love, but more particularistic than goods or information.

This conception (depicted in Figure 8.1) represents an initial step in considering the significance of the nature of resources in exchange relationships. However, the kinds of commodities that are appropriate and satisfying in exchanges are probably also a function of the characteristics of the individuals involved and of the norms and rules they developed in the course of their history of interactions.

Reciprocity and Equity in Social Exchange

Why should a person initiate a positive exchange relationship with another? Obviously, there can be several reasons. He might not, in fact, initiate any relationship; he might simply do something beneficial for another. The reciprocation of this kindness by the other person initiates the exchange relationship. Or a person might do something kind because he hopes to gain a specific benefit of some kind in the future, because he wants to be generally well treated by the other person, or because he wants to start an extended relationship. In the latter instances, the initiator expects his action to be reciprocated. Sometimes, when his act involves substantial sacrifice or provides the other person with the opportunity to harm him (as in giving important information about oneself that might be exploited), he demonstrates trust that he will get positive reciprocation.

Why should the recipient of benefits reciprocate? First, of course, there is the expectation of a beneficial exchange relationship which may provide the satisfaction of needs and the accrual of further benefits. That is, reciprocity may be due to self-interest. Second, a positive initiation by another person might lead to positive feelings toward the initiator, which make further interaction itself rewarding.

In addition, however, several writers have proposed that reciprocation of benefits may be due to cultural expectations that benefits will be returned. In the best-known formulation of this idea Gouldner (1960) proposed the existence of a universal principle or norm of reciprocity. According to Gouldner, this is an important moral norm that serves a variety of functions. For example, it tends to minimize exploitation by the powerful, since even they feel that benefits received ought to be reciprocated. This norm even bends egoism to the service of others; people may initiate behavior that will benefit another in the expectation that this person will reciprocate and his behavior will benefit them in return. According to Gouldner (1960), "We owe others certain things because of what they have previously done for us, because of the history of previous interaction we have had with them. It is this kind of obligation which is entailed by the generalized norm of reciprocity [p. 171]." Gouldner proposed that the norm of reciprocity, in its universal form, makes two interrelated, minimal demands: (*a*) that people should help those who have helped them and (*b*) that people should not injure those who have helped them. Obligations for repayment are contingent upon the imputed value of the benefit received. The value of the benefit (hence the debt) is in proportion to and varies with (*a*) the intensity of the recipient's need at the time the benefit is bestowed; (*b*) the resources of the donor ("he gave although he could ill afford it"—thus the obligations imposed by the norm of reciprocity may vary with the status of the participants within a society); (*c*) the motives imputed to the donor ("without thought of gain"); and (*d*) the nature of the constraints perceived to exist or to be absent (e.g., he acted out of his free will or he was coerced).

In addition to its positive form, the norm of reciprocity seems to have a negative form guiding retaliation for harm. Although people probably vary in their feelings as to whether or not they are "expected" to retaliate harm, as a function of socialization people do seem to feel justified in harming those who have harmed them. The ancient code of Hammurabi, "a tooth for a tooth and an eye for an eye," is a statement of negative reciprocity.

Although most of the research evidence deals with minimal relationships, exchange and reciprocity might strongly affect behavior in intense human relationships. Carson (1969), whose analysis of socially significant conduct and interaction among people is examined in Chapter 9, quotes Sullivan (1956):

> Let us say that a man (call him Mr. X) with a strong hysterical predisposition has married, perhaps for money, and that his wife, thanks to his rather dramatic and exaggerated way of doing and saying things, cannot long remain in doubt that there was a very practical consideration in this marriage and cannot completely blind herself to a certain lack of importance that she has in her husband's eyes. So she begins to get even. She may, for example, like someone I recently saw, develop a never-failing vaginismus, so that there is no more intercourse for him. And he will not ruminate on whether this vaginismus that is cutting off his satisfaction is directed against him, for the very simple reason that if you view interpersonal phenomena with that degree of objectivity you can't use an hysterical process to get rid of your own troubles. So he won't consider that, but he will suffer terribly from privation and will go to rather extravagant lengths to overcome the vaginismus that is depriving him of satisfaction, the lengths being characterized by a certain rather theatrical attention to detail rather than deep scrutiny of his wife. But he fails again and again. Then one night, when he is worn out, perhaps has had a precocious ejaculation in his newest adventure in practical psychotherapy, he has the idea, "My god, this is driving me crazy," and goes to sleep.
>
> Now the idea, "This thing is driving me crazy," is the happy idea that I say the hysteric has. He wakes up at some early hour in the morning, probably at the time when his wife is notoriously most soundly asleep, and he has a frightful attack of some kind. It could be literally almost anything, but it will be very impressive to anyone around. His wife will be awakened, very much frightened, and will call the doctor. But before the doctor gets there, the husband, with a fine sense of dramatic values, will let her know in some indirect way that he's terribly afraid he is losing his mind. She is reduced to a really agitated state by that. So when the doctor comes, the wife is in enough distress—in part because of whatever led to her vaginismus—to wonder if she might lose her own mind, and the husband is showing a good many odd symptoms. And the doctor probably doesn't know anything about losing minds anyway, and so he begins to wonder if he is going to lose *his* mind. But presently things quiet down [pp. 2–4; pp. 204–206 in Sullivan, 1976.)

Carson goes on to say,

> We see a mutually punitive interaction, in which Mrs. X retaliates with satisfaction–deprivation for her husband's exploitative indifference to her, and is herself victimized by her husband in counterretaliation. This

entire transaction takes place on a level of communication where it is unnecessary, and perhaps impossible, for the parties involved to acknowledge their participation [p. 4].

Clearly, the benefits or harm exchanged need not be of the same kind. Neither the return of kindness nor the infliction of harm need be achieved by the use of the same commodities. But there is a good chance that some form of reciprocation of kindness and generosity will take place; otherwise, it is likely that the relationship will be discontinued. And, perhaps, relationships can be maintained by the bond that is created through the mutual damage that people inflict on one another, at least for some period of time. This would suggest that a reciprocal relationship, even of a negative kind, has some value, or at least serves some function.

The concept of a reciprocity norm seems related to concepts of equity. In fact, equity notions have been strongly influenced by and derived in part from conceptions of exchange. According to Homans (1961), previous experience with exchange relationships and comparisons between one's own inputs and outcomes and those of others lead to a desire for distributive justice—wanting all people involved in a given social relationship to be equal in their ratio of rewards to investments. Definitions of equity (see Chapter 4) are nearly identical to Homans' definition of distributive justice.

Beliefs about and Preferences for Reciprocity

Several experiments show that people believe in the reciprocation of benefits and that reciprocity, a proper balance between what one receives and what one gives, is preferred to unilateral gain.

Durkin (1961) asked children how they would behave in several hypothetical situations, and why. Some children said that they would not share with a child who did not share with them, suggesting that reciprocity is also a retaliatory norm. Other children said they would share despite the other's selfishness, about half of them reasoning that their action would lead to eventual return of their generosity. Belief in reciprocity may thus underlie the initiation of positive acts. Muir and Weinstein (1962) employed intensive interviews with housewives to ascertain what they regarded as appropriate behavior in the course of exchanging small favors and how they usually behaved. Upper-middle-class women viewed favor-doing more in terms of reciprocity and exchange than did lower-class women, who seemed to believe more in giving without consideration of return. The former were harsh creditors and tended to avoid the role of debtor, but the latter tended to give when they were able to do so, viewing favor-doing in terms of mutual aid. Thus differences, at least in verbal reports, in how reciprocity guides behavior were found between socioeconomic groups. However, both groups of housewives thought that the magnitude of debt was related both to the original need and the original resources of the donor, thus providing support for Gouldner's (1960) view that these conditions affect reciprocity. Tesser, Gatewood, and Driver (1968) found that undergraduates believed that they would feel more gratitude if the benefit they received were intentional, if it were valuable, and if it cost the benefactor a great deal. This finding provides additional support for Gouldner's propositions about the conditions that affect reciprocity, assuming that gratitude leads to a feeling of obligation to reciprocate.

People both value reciprocity and seem to consider it an obligation. On the other hand, they consider generosity that is based on reciprocating a benefit less worthy than generosity that is simply a response to someone's need. Peterson, Hartman, and Gelfand (1977) found that kindergarten to third grade children saw substantially more merit in the actions of a child who gave to another, needy child—one without a toy—than in those of a child who gave to another child after having been the recipient of the other child's donation. This difference in judgments increased with age. Generosity based on reciprocity may be perceived as less voluntary, less guided by the desire to benefit the recipient.

There is evidence that people do not like to be in debt. According to Walster, Berscheid, and Walster (1973),

> On the basis of ethnographic (cross-cultural) data, Mauss (1954) concluded that three types of obligations are widely distributed in human societies in both time and space: (a) the obligation to give, (b) the obligation to receive, and (c) the obligation to repay. Mauss (1954) and Dillon (1968) agreed that when individuals are prevented from discharging their obligations, mutual distress is the result. They noted that while reciprocal exchanges breed cooperation and good feelings, gifts that cannot be reciprocated breed discomfort, distress, and dislike [p. 168].

These authors, along with Blau (1955) and Smith (1892) agreed that the ability to reciprocate is an important determinant of how nations respond to help from a neighboring country. In support of this point Gergen (1968a) found, in interviews conducted in several countries to ascertain how people felt about United States aid, that gifts that are accompanied by clearly stated obligations are preferred either to gifts that are not accompanied by obligations or to gifts that are accompanied by excessive obligations.

Indebtedness, Help Seeking, and Reactions to Receiving Help

In addition to interview data, other evidence exists that people prefer a condition of reciprocity, that they do not like to be indebted (even though repayment obviously involves costs), and that they are less likely to ask for help when the opportunity for reciprocation is remote or nonexistent. In a cross-cultural experiment, Gergen, Ellsworth, Maslach, and Seipel (1975) investigated feelings about reciprocal and nonreciprocal exchanges in the United States, Sweden, and Japan. Cultural differences in responses were slight. Subjects who received a favor from another person in the course of a laboratory gambling game (10 chips that enabled them to continue the game and eventually win it) tended to evaluate the donor more positively if he asked that the favor be returned in equal amount and to like him less when he indicated that the favor was a present that need *not* be returned or when he asked for more in return. The one cultural difference was found in Sweden, where the lender who asked for more chips in return was liked even slightly more (not significantly) than the one who asked for an equal return. The one who asked for less in return was liked significantly less, as in the other two cultures. In all three cultures reciprocity seemed to be a preferred condition.

In a second experiment (Gergen, Diebold, & Seipel, unpublished study) subjects in the same three countries played the same game. When they were low on chips, they again received a present of some chips from a partner, who asked that the subject return the same number of chips when the game was over. Some of the subjects subsequently won the game, and thus could return the chips they were loaned; others lost and could not repay the loan. Attractiveness scores that were derived from the subjects' ratings of the other person indicated that subjects who could repay the loan liked the donor more than subjects who could not repay it.

Several additional studies showed that people prefer conditions under which they can reciprocate a favor. Gross and Lubell (1970) found that subjects who had no opportunity to reciprocate a favor liked the helper substantially less than subjects who could reciprocate in various ways or those in a control group. When the opportunity to reciprocate existed, but the intention to reciprocate could not be carried out because the subjects were interrupted by the experimenter, they liked the helper as much as those people who could actually reciprocate. Gross and Latané (1974) found that a benefactor is liked more when the recipient of aid is allowed to reciprocate or to offer aid to a third person. The pattern of means in this study suggested also that the subjects felt more positive toward people who helped them and/or people whom they could help. Castro (1975) found that subjects felt most positive toward people who helped them if they could reciprocate, less positive if they could help a third person, and least positive if they had no opportunity to help anyone.

It might be important for people to maintain own equity, a proper ratio between their own inputs and their own outcomes, probably both in their own eyes and in the eyes of the world, not only in the sense that they get as much as they deserve, but also in the sense that they give as much as they receive. They react negatively to the people who are instrumental in depriving them of the opportunity to establish own equity. Equity may provide a standard by which one's status, role, and existing obligations toward others are evaluated. These findings also suggest that being placed in a dependent position without the opportunity to act in an independent and helpful way is an important source of the negative reactions associated with being a recipient of help.

Equity seems to be involved in other ways in the willingness to accept or request help. Gross and Somersan (1974) found that when the amount of prior input or effort of a potential helper was perceived as low, subjects requested more help than when it was high. Presumably, help provided by the other person would have contributed to other equity and was therefore more acceptable than help that would have pushed the helper's efforts beyond what was equitable. Under one set of conditions of this study, the subjects requested help sooner when the helper's previously received benefits appeared greater. Again, providing help would have been more equitable for this helper than for someone whose benefits were lower.

In two similar experiments, Greenberg (1968) and Greenberg and Shapiro (1971) attempted to show that willingness to ask for help is reduced when people do not expect to have an opportunity to provide help in return. Indebtedness, the felt obligation to repay a benefit, is thought of as an unpleasant psychological state that people will attempt to minimize. Greenberg and Shapiro (1971) ostensibly explored the effect of physical disability on performance. The subject was always assigned, apparently by chance, the role of a person who was motorically incapacitated (his arm was in a sling), whereas the confederate had the role of a visually handicapped person (he wore sunglasses). Both were to work on two tasks for which they could earn money. They tried out each task before beginning their work in earnest. On the first task the confederate was clearly superior. On the second task, the confederate was either equal to the subject (no opportunity to reciprocate) or inferior to the subject (opportunity to reciprocate). The two were told that they could ask each other's help while they worked on the two tasks. Would subjects working on the first task ask for help after the confederate finished his quota? When there was an opportunity to reciprocate, (e.g., when the subjects knew that on the second task they would be better than the confederate), subjects were much more likely to request help. They requested help sooner, and they let the other person help for a longer time.

There is a problem in interpreting these results, however. When there was an opportunity to reciprocate, both the subject and the confederate received praise for their performance on one task, and they received criticism and a request to try harder on the other task. When there was no opportunity to reciprocate the subject performed poorly overall in comparison to the confederate and received more criticism. The subjects might not have asked for help because negative feelings were aroused in them. Feeling incompetent, they might not have wanted to create further status inequality, or they might have feared rejection of their request to a greater degree. Morris and Rosen (1973) explored the possibility that when people do not feel incompetent, when they do not experience failure, they will ask for help even when they have no opportunity to reciprocate. Using Greenberg and Shapiro's basic procedure, they varied opportunity to reciprocate by letting subjects know either that there was plenty of time for the experiment, or that only a short time—presumably just enough to complete the first task—was available so that it would be impossible to reciprocate for help received on the first task.

Subjects were told either that they did very well or that they did very poorly in trying out the first task. Those who were told that they did very well were more likely to ask for help from the confederate; the opportunity to reciprocate had only a slight effect. Subjects who had an opportunity to reciprocate did not ask for more help, but asked for help somewhat faster. Failure might lead to self-concern; following failure people tend to help less and ask for help less. Failure is likely to reduce self-esteem, at least momentarily, increasing sensitivity to the possibility of rejection and decreasing the willingness to admit a need and thereby present the image of a weak, incompetent person. A related explanation is that public failure makes a person feel inadequate and less competent than other people, and seeking help would enhance this undesirable difference. Success is likely to have opposite effects.

A possible explanation of the somewhat divergent experimental findings of Greenberg and Shapiro and Morris and Rosen might also be that help seeking is reduced when reciprocation seems impossible because of one's own deficiencies, but it is less affected when external causes prohibit reciprocation. This explanation is supported by the findings of Calhoun, Pierce, Walters, and Dawes (1974). Respondents to a questionnaire perceived people who sought help for an internally caused problem as more likely to be rejected than people who sought help for an externally caused problem. Tessler and Schwartz (1972) found more requests for help when help seeking was defined as the norm of the situation, and when it was easy to attribute the need for help to difficult circumstances rather than to a personal inadequacy. This suggests that maintaining own equity, a balance between one's outcomes and varied inputs, might be particularly important for people when not doing so has implications for their competence, status, or importance, and less important when external circumstances inhibit or eliminate the possibility of making a contribution.

Not being able to reciprocate a favor, or receiving aid that is not part of an ongoing relationship in which there is mutual help and support may reduce self-esteem. The ability to make a contribution and keep inputs that benefit others equitable with outcomes received from others would maintain self-esteem. Fisher and Nadler (1974) found that even when help was offered without a request subjects felt that they had failed and experienced loss of self-esteem. This happened to a greater degree when the help was offered by a person who could be viewed as in some sense comparable to the subject, less when it was provided by a "non-social-comparison" person. In another study Fisher and Nadler (1976) found that receiving aid from a donor who had greater resources had a more negative effect on the self-concept than receiving aid from someone whose resources were smaller. On the one hand, when another person's resources are substantial in comparison to one's own, the differences in status or importance is already high, and accepting help further lowers one's status, enhancing this difference. On the other hand, help from a person with greater resources demands less sacrifice from him and contributes to other equity. In the domain of getting as well as in the domain of giving, people seem to attribute more importance to own equity than to other equity; they evaluate events more from the standpoint of own equity. In the domain of giving, this was clearly suggested by some of the findings of equity research reviewed in earlier chapters. When the need for help is clearly externally caused rather than internally caused, people might be more willing to ask for help from a person with greater resources.

In the Tessler and Schwartz (1972) study high-self-esteem women sought less help on an important task than on one of peripheral importance. Wallston (1972) replicated these findings with male subjects. The findings of these and of the already reviewed laboratory and interview studies on help seeking seem consistent with a phenomenon in everyday life and clinical practice: The stronger a person's need is, the more difficult it can be for the person to request help. Although no actual data exist, my impression is that when the need for love, affection, kindness from others, or for other central satisfactions is especially great, many people find it particularly difficult to request aid. The voluntary offering of unsolicited aid may be highly valued at such times. One reason for this phenomenon may be that when the need is great the possibility of rejection is particularly threatening. Another reason may be that at least some people perceive intense needs of the kinds mentioned as a personal inadequacy, certainly internal rather than external in origin. Their willingness to seek others' aid or positive response is thus reduced, for the reasons already discussed. Strong needs may also give rise to concern about inequity in the relationship, or to concern that one's partner will perceive it as inequitable, both with regard to efforts and sacrifice extended and with regard to underlying feelings of love and affection. Believing that the degree of one's love or need for another person is greater than the degree to which such feelings are returned may be particularly threatening, partly because it indicates a difference in power between partners in a relationship. Such difference in power can be a source of concern for good reason, since it can be and often is exploited by the more powerful partner.

An imbalance of this kind can be a serious problem at the beginning of a relationship and can inhibit its development. In clinical practice, I found that one of the skills many people have to learn, if they are to develop continuing relationships with others, is to inhibit strong expressions of need, liking, or affection early in the developing relationship. Unless such feeling is mutual, 'it tends to alienate the partner. A person with needs stronger than our own, and affection that we cannot match, may be devalued. The need may be perceived as indiscriminate, not as specifically related to us, leading us to suspect that it could be filled by just about anyone. Concern about the demands on us that might arise from another person's strong need or strong and as yet unreciprocated affection may also lead to psychological reactance, which can be reduced by leaving the field.

When existing needs are not satisfied in one's relationships with other people (or even with social agencies and organizations), those needs may intensify. Progressively, the degree to which a person regards the need as a result of a personal inadequacy may increase, and this may lower self-esteem. Nadler, Fisher, and Streufert (1974) suggested that when there is little possibility of repaying a helper or when the helper's motives are suspect, the helper will be resented and consequently derogated. When it is difficult to derogate the helper because of his status, importance (e.g., doctors), or relationship to us, we will tend to devalue ourselves. I am suggesting that such devaluation of self may be the result not only of receiving help and being unable to reciprocate, but also of not getting the help needed to satisfy one's needs, desires, and goals. Intense, chronic, unfulfilled needs are humiliating, and so is the lack of aid from those who have the power to aid.

It makes sense, in light of the previous discussion, that voluntary help, offered without being asked for, would be preferred to help that is contingent on a request. Gross and his associates found this to be the case in a number of experiments. These findings were contrary to their original hypothesis, which was based on reactance theory. They reasoned that "negative feelings toward assistance should be greatest when help is externally imposed and least when the recipient can choose when, where and how he is helped [Gross, Wallston, & Piliavin, 1978, p. 7]." People probably do resent *unneeded* help, or help that is needed but provided in a demeaning manner that reduces their dignity. Likewise, people probably do prefer to receive help that is genuinely needed without having to ask for it.

In one study (Berman, Piliavin, & Gross, 1971) undergraduate business majors participated in a difficult laboratory computer game. They had to make financial decisions; then, on the basis of standard feedback, they had to make further decisions. Contrary to the authors' expectations, the students who were visited by a consultant who offered help at regular intervals (helper-initiated condition) accepted more help than was requested by students who could signal that they required help (recipient-initiated condition). Before they received feedback from the first set of decisions the subjects who had to request help indicated significantly greater anxiety and more negative self-ratings on a self-concept test than did subjects in the helper-initiated condition. The anticipation of confessing their need seems to have been more threatening than the acceptance of regularly available aid. Additional studies by these researchers produced similar findings: "There were tendencies for more help to be obtained and for the helper to be better liked in helper-initiated conditions [Gross *et al.*, 1978, p. 14]." Broll, Gross, and Piliavin (1974) found, for example, that subjects working on extremely difficult logic problems that were "virtually impossible to complete" received 47% more help and liked the consultant better when they were periodically offered a consultant's help and were free to accept or reject that help, in contrast to subjects who had been allowed to request help whenever they wished. Greenberg and Saxe (1975) found that subjects, in evaluating a story in which a student needed assistance, expressed the view that this student would feel more obligated to the helper when he had to request help than when he received it without request.

The findings, considered along with others on indebtedness, suggest that when help is offered by a person whose role involves providing help, and there is freedom either to accept or to reject offers of help, the negative consequences arising from indebtedness or inability to reciprocate might be lessened or eliminated. Research comparing the psychological effects of help proffered by persons who either are or are not in the designated role of helpers with the effects of help requested from such individuals would further highlight the consequences of being a person in need.

Gross *et al.* (1978) suggest on the basis of their research findings that problems are created by federal policies of dealing with welfare recipients. These policies specify that financial aid is to be separated from other services. Welfare recipients are consequently not allowed to receive other types of services, such as counseling, from a financial caseworker with whom they are in continuing interaction. Clients have to request help, which is then provided by a different person (a nonfinancial counselor). This demands that the client acknowledge problems leading to the request, which may have the consequences already discussed. As a result, such aid may not be requested, and existing problems and needs may not be relieved.

Reciprocity in Behavior

The research reviewed so far has shown that people believe in and prefer conditions of reciprocity and dislike indebtedness and the people who are responsible for it, particularly when the need for help can be regarded as the consequence of personal inadequacy. Many experiments have demonstrated that people do in fact tend to behave reciprocally. The experiments show that prior helping or harmdoing affects subsequent helping or harmdoing by the recipient. However, many conditions affect whether there will be reciprocation, as well as its extent and nature. The amount of benefit originally produced, the degree of sacrifice it represented, and the intention attributed to a benefactor are some of the influences on subsequent reciprocation.

Berkowitz and Daniels (1964), using the supervisor–worker paradigm, varied the degree of a supervisor's dependence on the worker (the subject) for receiving high ratings as a supervisor and/or having an opportunity to get a monetary reward. They also varied whether the subject previously received help from the other person. The female subjects first worked on a letter-writing task with another person. They were told that whoever finished first might help the other. When the subjects received no prior help, greater dependence did not significantly enhance their helping behavior. This contrasted with findings of previous experiments in which the possibility of prior help did not exist. Prior help significantly enhanced helping the supervisor whose dependence was low. In the high-dependence, prior-help condition there was a significant correlation between scores on a social-responsibility scale and helping, but the relationship was small in the other conditions. Berkowitz and Daniels believe that the findings indicate an increase in the salience of responsibility to help a dependent other following the receipt of help. Possibly, however, the findings imply something about the meaning of the social-responsibility scale. People who score high on the scale might have a greater tendency to follow social rules (see Berkowitz & Lutterman, 1968), one of which dictates that one should reciprocate help.

In another study Pruitt (1968) employed a mixed-motive game (a version of the prisoner's dilemma game) to explore conditions of reciprocity. In mixed-motive games, partners can maximize joint outcomes. Each chooses one of two buttons to push, one representing a cooperative, another a competitive choice. However, if person A makes a "cooperative choice," he can be exploited by person B, who might choose the button representing the competitive choice; this would result in less reward for person A than if they both made the cooperative choice, and more reward for person B. When both partners push the competitive button they receive equal but small rewards. The motives for action might be maximizing joint outcome, which would lead to the cooperative choice, or minimizing the chances for exploitation by one's partner, or desiring to "exploit" one's partner, to enhance the difference between one's own and the other's outcome. The last two motives would lead to what is usually called the competitive choice. Clearly, cooperation and competition can also be the result of individual values and preferences. Some people may cooperate primarily because they believe that it is right to cooperate, regardless of the outcome. Pruitt, using a modified version of this game, found that undergraduates "gave" more to a partner during the game if they had previously received a lot rather than a little from him. They also gave more when they had received an amount that was a substantially larger percentage of the other's resources. The degree of sacrifice on the part of another person did affect reciprocation.

In another study of reciprocity Wilke and Lanzetta (1970) found that reciprocation was a monotonic increasing function of the amount of prior help that subjects received. The more help they received, the more they helped. Subjects both received and reciprocated help in the context of a game, however, without any particular costs involved in providing help. As the authors point out, the situation may have created strong demands for exact reciprocity; the subjects were highly dependent on one another, and the help that was received or provided was easily and exactly scalable. The correlation between perceived help and the help provided by the subjects in return was greater than that between actual help received and reciprocated. This finding suggests that under conditions that make the amount of help received difficult to scale, or where people are motivated to distort the perception of how much help they received, such exact reciprocity might not be found.

Several researchers explored the hypothesis that it might be attraction that mediates positive reciprocity. A variety of experiments found that when people do favors for others, they tend to develop a liking for the people they benefit (Berkowitz & Daniels, 1964; Schopler & Compare, 1971). If the beneficiary also shows increased liking for the benefactor, this may suggest that people respond positively to someone who aided them because the other person became more attractive, better liked as a result of his helpful act. As already suggested, there is evidence that being the recipient of another's kindness increases liking for the benefactor (Nemeth, 1970a; Greenberg & Frisch, 1972; Lott & Lott, 1969). The research findings on indebtedness and on receiving help without the opportunity to reciprocate suggest exceptions; under certain conditions, dislike for a helper may result. Nonetheless, the findings that both benefiting others and receiving benefits can increase liking for others has implications for how people might generate positive social interactions.

Stapleton, Nacci, and Tedeschi (1973) manipulated the attractiveness of a confederate. As in most other studies manipulating attractiveness, some subjects were made to believe that the confederate had attitudes and beliefs similar to their own. Other subjects were told that the confederate had different attitudes and beliefs. Such variation in information about similarity does seem to affect ratings of attraction and did so in this experiment. Next, the subject and confederate enacted the roles of "estimator" and "operator," then exchanged roles. The task involved estimating the number of points the estimator would receive from the operator on a series of trials. The points functioned as rewards; the larger the number of points, the greater the benefit received. The subject started out as the estimator, and the degree to which the confederate rewarded the subject was varied. When they exchanged roles the subject rewarded the confederate according to how much the confederate had rewarded him; prior attraction for the confederate did not influence the subject's behavior. Thus, attraction did not mediate reciprocity. However, ratings of attraction for the confederate changed after the task as a function of the degree of benefit provided by the confederate. In the high-attraction group, receiving more points did not increase attraction but receiving few points decreased attraction. In the low-attraction group, receiving few points did not affect attraction, but receiving more points increased attraction.

As Stapleton *et al.* suggest (1973), the degree to which another person's behavior affects liking for him is a function of the degree to which his behavior is consistent with or deviates from prior expectations. However, the degree of prior attraction did not affect reciprocity. Is this always the case? As later discussion will show, the existence and nature of a prior relationship have complex effects on reciprocity. In the instance just discussed, the amount of benefit that the confederate bestowed on the subject was extremely explicit and easily scalable. The benefit that the subject could return was exactly the same in kind. In addition, although the manipulation of similarity in behavior and attitudes affected attraction ratings, the degree of prior relationship between the subject and the confederate was minimal. Under such circumstances, but perhaps not under others, behavior toward another person would tend to be strictly reciprocal.

Another consideration is that judgment of character, personality, attractiveness might be based on what a person says about himself, on what others say about him, and on his actions. When these elements are clearly in conflict, actions may have a stronger influence than words on evaluation. This may be so particularly when there is no time for a verbally created first impression to take hold.

It may be the case that people categorize exchange situations. Some exchange situations may be regarded as strictly business arrangements, guided by mutual interest and the normative rules of strict reciprocity. Particularly when the commodities of exchange are of exactly the same kind, deviation from strict reciprocity in such arrangements may be psychologically difficult. Deviation might result from conditions that emphasize competition, from lack of trust in a partner, or from other interference. In other types of situations exchange and reciprocity may be viewed as in the service of developing, promoting, or maintaining interpersonal relationships. The degree of reciprocity might then be affected by interest, liking, and other personal emotions.

Some further evidence that in a minimal relationship liking does not affect reciprocity comes from a study by Regan (1971). In this study, the subject and a confederate rated paintings and each other in a study of aesthetic preference. To vary liking, the subject was made to overhear the confederate talk pleasantly or unpleasantly to someone on the telephone. The overheard conversation had only a slight effect on the subject's doing a favor for the confederate and on how the confederate was rated, but the intervening experiences may have minimized the effect of this treatment variation. If the confederate later bought the subject a soft drink, the subject was more likely to buy raffle tickets from the confederate and to buy a larger number of tickets. The favor of buying the soft drink significantly enhanced liking for the confederate, although there was no significant relationship between liking scores and the magnitude of compliance with the request for buying the tickets.

One experiment explored the influence of belief similarity and prior aggression by another person on both aggression toward him and how he was evaluated. Hendrick and Taylor (1971) told subjects that they were exploring the effects of competition on reaction time. They were told that reaction time might be affected by knowledge about the (nonexistent) person with whom they were competing. Subjects were given information showing that the other person was similar or dissimilar to them in a variety of beliefs. This was followed by reaction-time trials. Following each trial, the loser, the person who had the slower reaction time, was to receive a shock. Before each trial the subjects could set the level of shock to be administered to their opponents. The opponents always set either high shock levels or low shock levels. The subjects won on half of the 18 trials. Subjects who received stronger shocks retaliated by setting high shock levels; shock levels were unaffected by belief similarity. Some ratings of the other person were affected by the similarity manipulation (honesty and intelligence). Both belief similarity and aggressiveness affected the ratings of how likable the opponent was. Ratings of the opponent as thoughtless, cruel, unfair, or kind were affected only by the degree of the opponent's aggressive behavior. The other person's actions had a much stronger effect on both the behavior and the perceptions of subjects than the similarity of his beliefs to their own.

The findings in this section have shown that people show strong reciprocity in their behavior toward a stranger. A stranger's actions have stronger effects on a subject's evaluation of him than information about personality, beliefs, or attitudes that is provided by an experimenter. Reciprocity seems a basic principle of human interaction; even the amount of time young infants spend looking at each other is characterized by a high degree of reciprocity (Lewis, Young, Brooks, & Michalson, 1975). Interactions among children in groups—classrooms, nursery groups, summer camps—are also characterized by a substantial degree of reciprocity. Reciprocity under such relatively unstructured circumstances, and the long-term effects of positive and negative patterns of interaction with peers, are discussed in the context of peer socialization in Volume 2, Chapter 7.

In a study involving male and female high-school students Nemeth (1970b) found that receiving help affected liking for the helper, but did not affect subsequent willingness to help him. Whether help was voluntary or mandatory (in compliance with instructions by the experimenter) was varied. There was both a main effect of prior help on liking and an interaction between help and voluntariness. The subjects liked the person who helped them voluntarily more than the one who was instructed to help, and they liked the person who did not help because he was so instructed more than the person who voluntarily refused to help. The effect of treatments on subsequent help by the subjects was slight, and highly complex. Here and in some other experiments the findings might have been affected by the rather unnatural behavior of the confederate. In this study the same sex confederate, upon finishing the task, always asked the subject what the experimenter had told them he or she was supposed to do. In the no-help condition, when reminded that the experimenter said whoever finished first could help the other if he or she wanted to, the confederate said, "No, I don't want to." People do not usually explicitly state negative intentions in real-life interactions. Negotiations about helping and communications about not helping are mostly implicit, nonverbal, or at least milder in form. The explicit refusal to help as well as strong verbal expression of prosocial intentions might be unusual and might affect the perception of the communicator and of his intentions. This is discussed later in this chapter in greater detail.

Generalized Reciprocity

Many experiments have included conditions in which a subject received help from one person and then had the opportunity to provide help to another. If prior help by one person increases help for another, is this best explained by a concept of reciprocity, which refers to obligations existing between two people? Sometimes this has been referred to as *generalized reciprocity*. However, "It is possible that the dynamics of owing are not operative at all [Krebs, 1970, p. 296]."

The bulk of the evidence suggests that people are more likely to help third parties if they themselves were helped before (Berkowitz & Daniels, 1964; Goranson & Berkowitz, 1966), but the help they give the third party may not be as extensive as the help people give a person who helped them. I shall review most of the evidence in the course of discussing other issues. Other evidence indicates that if people do *not* receive needed help or are refused help they sometimes help third parties less. This evidence, however, is equivocal. For example, Greenglass (1969) found that subjects who had received aid helped a person who was dependent on them more than those who had not received prior aid, whether the dependent person was similar or dissimilar to the person who helped them. However, subjects who were hindered by another person helped a dependent other significantly less only when this person was similar to whoever hindered them; they helped more when the dependent person was dissimilar.

It is possible that receiving help constitutes a modeling effect, which calls subjects' attention to norms that prescribe help for people who need it. Test and Bryan (1969) found that both being helped with a task and observing a model help a third person enhanced a subject's subsequent help-fulness. Similarly, the increased helpfulness for a person who was dissimilar to someone who hindered them, demonstrated by Greenglass, might be due to the phenomenon that I discussed earlier: An obvious violation of a societal norm by another person increases the tendency to adhere to the norm.

To understand generalized reciprocity, we should consider that the norm of social responsibility (or, more generally, norms that prescribe help-ful conduct) and the norm or principle of reciprocity are related principles. They are probably related both in their origin and in their use. For ex-ample, reciprocity is more likely to take place if a person's prosocial act appears unselfish in origin, guided by the interest of the recipient; that is, it appears to originate from a desire to help rather than from a desire to gain reciprocation (see next section). Norms prescribing help for strangers may have originated from the extension of a reciprocal exchange network from families or small units to all members of a social group, so that each in-dividual was expected to help others in need and in turn could expect to be helped by others. Generalized reciprocity may represent an intermediate step between the two norms. Kelley (1971) suggested that if temporal and social dimensions of reciprocity are greatly extended, people may even help others in expectation of benefits returned by some supraindividual or even suprasocial system.

Several explanations of the phenomenon of increased helpfulness toward third parties may be valid; several psychological processes may be at work, perhaps jointly. The earlier discussion of indebtedness is relevant. When a person is helped by someone a feeling of obligation arises. This feeling can be discharged by helping anyone who needs help. As suggested earlier, a person who has received help can maintain own equity by making a contribution to others in proportion to the contribution he received. If receiving help also produces feelings of dependence, inadequacy, or lack of potency, all these feelings can be eliminated by providing help for another person. The lesser help given third parties may be understood if we con-sider that the individual's sense of owing something to the person who helped them and the social expectation of reciprocity are not active in help-ing a third party.

A mood explanation may also apply. People like those who help them, but not as much when receiving help results in indebtedness due to the lack of opportunity to reciprocate. People also like those they help. Receiv-ing help may bring about good feelings if one has the opportunity to dis-charge obligations and reassert one's potency, which can be accomplished by helping another person. The previously offered explanation and this one are related; this one suggests that helping third parties may involve the management of mood and self-esteem.

It would be important to know whether other (not prosocial) action can serve the same functions that generalized reciprocity serves. In the existing research the only available avenue for managing mood and demonstrating independence and potency was to help a third party. In real life, other avenues might also exist: a nonhelpful but self-assertive act, even aggression. Is generalized reciprocity of positive acts preferred over such behavior? Just as there are varied behavioral and cognitive processes people can use to deal with harm they have inflicted (instead of balancing it by helping someone), so there might be varied behavioral acts and cognitive processes they can use to respond to a benefit they have received (instead of reciprocating). Some of these processes have already been suggested—for example, derogating the benefactor. Certain forms of derogation are highlighted in the next section in the discussion of attribution of intent to a benefactor.

Perceived Intent of a Benefactor (or Harmdoer) and Its Effect on Reciprocity

It has been proposed by a number of writers that our behavior toward other people is not only a function of how they behave toward us, but also a function of what we perceive as the reasons for their behavior. Most of us much of the time consider and make inferences about the motives, intentions, and purposes of other people in their behavior toward us, as well as toward others. If somebody is kind to me, is it because this person genuinely wants to benefit me? Or does he want to do the "right" thing? Does he want to appear kind? Does he want to gain something for himself, perhaps by believing that I will feel obligated to reciprocate? Reciprocation of kindness, and more generally our behavior toward other people, will be affected by the motives we impute to them.

Knowing another person's intentions is important because it enables us to predict his later behavior toward us, to estimate whether positive or negative behavior can be expected in the future. Our sense of security, of predictability, and even of control over events depend on perceiving others' motives accurately, since motives are presumably a much better guide to a person's future conduct than his behavioral acts, which can serve a multiplicity of motives. A prosocial act, if it is based on self-serving motives, cannot be expected to recur under circumstances in which prosocial behavior would not serve the interests of the actor. Understanding others' motives also gives us grounds for judgment; we learn to judge people as morally good or bad on the basis of their intentions. As a result we react to perceived good and bad intentions. Probably this is partly due to childhood instruction. That we should receive such instruction is not surprising, since morality is often regarded as inherent in intentions, not in action. To repeat, any one act can be the result of a variety of motives, good and bad; any one outcome can be the accidental by-product of behavior serving other purposes, the result of varied motives.

Piaget (1932) describes young children as characterized by moral realism; older children come to view transgressions with moral relativity. Children first judge actions on the basis of their consequences. A child who breaks a larger number of cups accidentally is judged as having committed a more serious transgression than a child who breaks a smaller number of cups intentionally. At a later age the seriousness of transgressions is judged on the basis of the actor's intention. In Piaget's view this change is the result not of instruction but of cognitive change and development that derives from children's experience with the world around them, particularly interactions with peers. The cognitive structures of children (and adults) that determine how they view the world—how they interpret events—change as a result of experience. Children come to perceive reciprocity, for example, as the "logic" of interpersonal relationships, their basic rule. They also come to evaluate actions in terms of intentions rather than consequences. They move from a heteronomous to an autonomous moral stage. That people come to evaluate behavior according to underlying intentions is only true to a degree. To some extent they continue to judge responsibility for negative events on the basis of the severity of an act's consequences, as the literature on assigning responsibility for accidents has indicated. There is some similar evidence about behavior that has positive outcome. Such evidence indicates that the more positive the outcome the more likely it is that responsibility or the intention to do good is attributed to the actor. The perception of responsibility and the perception of intention are not identical but seem closely related; sometimes a person can be seen as responsible for an outcome he did not intend (e.g., negligence). Possibly when an act has extreme consequences it is difficult for people to judge it as unintended.

The perception of selfish intentions might also decrease prosocial behavior toward a person who helped us because it makes us feel that the other person expects reciprocation. This might lead to a feeling of reduction in freedom and consequently to reactance. It might make the recipient of help feel that he has no control over the kind of repayment that the other person wants. Rather than being free to reciprocate in any manner he pleases, he might have to reciprocate according to the benefactor's particular needs. This results in an unpleasant form of indebtedness that decreases the chance of reciprocity. It might even lead to a denial of debt.

This discussion suggests that certain circumstances, such as perceiving others' motives as selfish or bad, might legitimize the withholding or minimizing of the return of benefits we received. If so, it becomes possible to use a deliberate (or unconscious) strategy of attributing selfish motives to others to reduce the need for reciprocity. Individual differences in attributional tendencies might, in this manner, lead to reliable differences in the tendency to reciprocate favors—either decreasing or increasing reciprocation.

One type of research on the effects of perceived intention on subsequent behavior explored variation in whether the person who helped acted prosocially out of free choice or because he was forced to do so by the circumstances. Only free choice would allow the perception of prosocial intent. In one experiment, Goranson and Berkowitz (1966) found that undergraduate females did more work for supervisors after having received help from them when the help they received was voluntary, but not when the help was compulsory. This was true even though subjects did not expect to see the other person again. In another experiment Greenberg and Frisch (1972) assigned male undergraduates to one of four conditions. Paired subjects worked on a problem-solving task, and each subject was manipulated to believe that the other subject had (a) intentionally helped them succeed in completing the task; (b) intentionally helped them to partially complete the task; (c) accidentally helped them succeed in completing the task; or (d) accidentally helped them partially complete the task. Then subjects worked on a second task, which provided them with the opportunity to reciprocate. In this experiment, the more help subjects received, the more they returned. In addition, more help was reciprocated in the deliberate-help than in the accidental-help condition. An additional group of subjects was asked to act as judges and imagine themselves in the role of subjects in this experiment. Their ratings indicated that they perceived receiving deliberate help as leading to a greater feeling of indebtedness and stronger feelings of obligation to reciprocate than receiving help accidentally given.

In another group of experiments the apparent intention of the helper was varied. In one experiment, Kahn and Tice (1973) had subjects participate in tasks in a supervisor–worker relationship. A confederate, the supervisor, could benefit the subjects to a larger or smaller degree. His stated intention to benefit or not to benefit the subject was varied. In a third condition, no intention was stated. After role reversal, subjects could select a task for the other person, varying in difficulty, and subsequently could help him by rating the quality of his product generously and assigning more points to it. In the first experiment the magnitude of prior help affected subjects' helping behavior. More help led to a larger number of points assigned when the target of help was the previous helper rather than a stranger. The helper's intentions did not affect subjects' behavior. The intention manipulations had some strange effects, however. They affected subjects' ratings of how hard the confederate tried, how good a job he did, how enjoyable he found the task, and how much he tried to be helpful. These effects, together with the lack of behavior effect of intention, may have been due to the rather unnatural form in which intentions were communicated. In the no-intention-to-help condition, for example, the supervisor said that he had never been a supervisor before and did not like being one; no doubt the subject would not get many points from him. He added that he could give the other person a hint but did not feel like bothering. In real life, people do not usually explicitly and rudely communicate their intention not to help another person. Such behavior is likely to be perceived as strange and unusual. Paradoxically, when the confederate did not intend to help but actually helped, he probably seemed like a person who, despite frustration and discomfort, managed to help; the emphasis then appears not on his negative intention but on the magnitude of his sacrifice. This situation is different from one in which a helper is guided by selfish intentions.

Kahn and Tice (1973) conducted a second experiment in which they had the subjects believe that the other person did not know that his intentions were known to the subject. The subjects saw a form, presumably filled out by the supervisor, in which the supervisor either indicated that he himself would have a hard time and did not care how the subjects would do or expressed no intention. As in the first study, the two measures of reciprocity were uncorrelated. In the first measure, selecting a task for the supervisor, the helper's intention had a marginally significant effect. The second measure, rating the other person's product, was affected by actual help received but not by statements of intention. Thus, the milder statements of intention that were not directly communicated had some effects on reciprocity. Intention might have greater influence under more ambiguous, complex circumstances when a person does not help but appears to have good intentions, or does help and there are reasons to question his purpose in doing so. Again, reciprocity was greater when help was directed at the person who provided help rather than at another person.

Epstein, Shortell, and Taylor (1970) and Epstein and Taylor (1967) varied the intention of a "partner" to administer shock to the subjects and the actual amount of shock that the subjects received. Intentions of both partners and subjects were indicated by their setting of shock levels to be administered to the other if the other lost on competitive reaction time trials. Thus, intention in this situation was a rather direct indication of what would happen if the person who expressed the intention actually had an opportunity to act as he intended. However, when the subject's reaction time was faster, he did not receive shock. In both studies another's intention to harm increased subjects' aggression toward him independently of actual harm they experienced. In a further experiment, Mallick and McCandless (1966) studied reciprocity of aggression by children, as a function of a harmdoer's intentions. Third-grade children were frustrated by older children, who interfered with their completion of work on several tasks and thereby deprived them of winning money. The younger children were subsequently given the opportunity to slow down the frustrators' work by pushing buttons. Such aggression or retaliation was greatly reduced when the children were told that their frustrators, sixth-grade children, acted not from malice but from fatigue and clumsiness. In other research, the degree of arbitrariness of a frustrator's behavior was found to affect subsequent aggression toward him—with greater arbitrariness leading to greater aggression (Pastore, 1952; Fishman, 1965). Greater arbitrariness may result in victims' attributing more hostile intent to the actor or perceiving the actor as unprincipled and dangerous. A study by Sanford (1970) also showed that children's reactions to a frustrator—their subsequent retaliation—were affected by information about the other person's intentions. When the frustrator's intent was described as less malicious, retaliation was generally milder.

Retaliation or counteraggression probably has several functions. For instance, retaliation may serve to administer justice, to punish a harmdoer. Bad people deserve to be punished. A conservative political position in America, and probably a widespread belief, is that lawbreakers should be punished simply because through punishment justice will be established. Seemingly, rehabilitation is not considered as important as justice. Our beliefs about good and bad, what is moral and what is immoral, include beliefs that harm produced without malicious intent is not as bad as harm produced with malicious intent. Counteraggression may also avert further harm. Counteraggression presumably establishes that another person's aggressive behavior will not go unpunished, that aggression does not pay, and it might decrease subsequent aggressive acts. If a harmdoer did not intend to produce harm or was not malicious in intent, it is less necessary to retaliate to avert further harm. Counteraggression may also be self-protective in that it decreases devaluation of the victim. This is strongly argued by some proponents of an equity position (Walster *et al.*, 1970). In their view, counteraggression creates equity in the inequitable relationship that was created by the other person's aggression. Expressions of positive intent by the aggressor, which are likely to include indications of regret and guilt over having caused harm, might also reestablish equity in the relationship, thereby reducing the need for retaliation.

If the perception of another person's intent strongly affects reactions to his behavior, whether it be helpful or harmful, it becomes important to understand what shapes the perception of another's intent. What are the conditions that determine what kinds of intentions are attributed to others? The intention that is attributed to another person might, of course, be inaccurate. However, it is the perception itself, regardless of its accuracy, that will determine a person's reaction to the help that he receives.

Conditions That Affect the Attribution
of Prosocial Intention

Schopler (1970) suggested several conditions that are likely to affect whether a benefactor's intent is perceived as selfish or as generous. If the recipient of a favor is in a position to benefit the donor, it is more likely that a favor will be perceived as selfish, or donor-instigated. On the other hand, if the benefit that is provided and the recipient's need match, in other words, when a favor satisfies a real need, it is more likely that the act is perceived as motivated by the desire to benefit the recipient, or recipient-instigated. For example, consider the student home for vacation who is upset and unhappy and would like to talk to his father. His father gives him $50 to go out on the town and enjoy himself. The student might perceive the gift as instigated by the father's desire to get rid of him, because the benefit did not match his need. Another determinant of perceived intent, according to Schopler, is the appropriateness of the benefit, the extent to which it fits the nature of the relationship between the person doing the favor and the recipient. If the nature of the relationship makes the favor appropriate, it is more likely to be perceived as recipient-instigated. If it is out of context, inappropriate, it is more likely to be perceived as donor-instigated.

In addition to the factors suggested by Schopler, others may exist. Before I discuss them, however, it might be worthwhile to examine the last condition mentioned. Kelley (1967) proposed that unusual behavior is more likely to lead to the attribution that it expresses characteristics of the actor, that it is caused by him rather than by the situation or his role in that situation. Favors that are inappropriate in the sense that they are not a natural outcome of the ongoing relationship between the parties in the interaction might be perceived as recipient-instigated even more, perhaps, than appropriate favors, if they exactly match the need of the recipient and if the recipient has no power to benefit the donor. The manner in which the three elements that Schopler proposed covary and their relationship to other conditions may determine their influence on attributing selfish or generous intention to the helper.

Favors can be motivated by other than prosocial or selfish intentions. For instance, a "favor" may be performed as part of a job; a stewardess brings a cup of coffee to a passenger. This may or may not be perceived as a favor. If it is perceived as a favor it may simply be regarded as part of the stewardess' role, demanding only minimal reciprocation—a thank you—or none at all. A favor can also be seen the result of special circumstances, situationally induced, resulting in minimal attribution of prosocial intent and less reciprocation than a recipient-instigated favor. A positive act may be seen as the result of positive characteristics of the actor—of his tendency to be kind and helpful. Although selfish concerns are not involved, such an act is also an instance of donor-instigated rather than recipient-instigated help. It may result in less reciprocation than help that leads to certain other positive attributions. Although attribution of prosocial intent may generally increase reciprocation of positive behavior, perceiving others' kindness as specifically directed at oneself may increase reciprocation to an even greater degree. Others' kindness may be elicited by one's need, but they may respond as they would to anyone else's need. Alternatively, the positive behavior may be highly specific. The helper may be responding to the person in need as a unique individual, signaling a special bond (Worchel, Andreoli, & Archer, 1976). Generally, the more prosocial the perceived intention, and the more the behavior is seen as uniquely directed at a person, the more reciprocation I would expect. Unfortunately, there is as yet little information about the differential influence of such attributions. The nature of a positive act may affect both the attributions that are made and their influence. If a person is in great psychological distress, a sensitive and effective response to the distress is likely to be perceived as an expression of special interest; a response to an obvious and less intense need is less likely to be perceived this way. Even if help in the former instance is attributed to the character of the helper, reciprocation may be more likely for this behavior than for equally helpful behavior that is less sensitive and particularistic. One reason for the inadequacy of reciprocation with highly discrepant kinds of resources (e.g., money to reciprocate love) (Foa, 1971; Foa & Foa, 1974) may be the less prosocial and/or particularistic attributions made about the reciprocal act when it is made in resources substantially different from those originally provided.

Two more determinants of perceived intention might be the magnitude of the benefit produced and the verbal and stylistic self-presentation of the benefactor. With regard to magnitude of benefits, just as greater harm caused by a person tends to result in more assignment of responsibility to him, greater benefit might also result in attribution of responsibility and of the intention to produce good. Finally, the manner in which a person presents himself might be a strong determinant of how people perceive his intentions. People verbally or stylistically communicate whether they are kind or unkind individuals. Strong verbal statements of positive intentions or of positive self-descriptions are frequently suspect. However, subtle statements might be effective and might even make it difficult to attribute selfish intent to the person, even when other cues indicate selfishness. Following extensive and skillful positive self-presentation people might even discard the evidence of selfish behavior until such evidence becomes substantial. It is of interest to note that people also take their own self-presentations seriously. Presenting themselves positively or negatively affects their self-esteem, even if these self-presentations are produced as the result of instructions that they received (Gergen, 1968b).

It is apparently desirable for benefactors that their prosocial behavior appear genuine, arising out of concern for others' welfare. Since prosocial intentions have great social value, people are likely to try to hide selfish intentions and to attempt to convince other people that their prosocial acts are recipient-instigated and, more generally, that they are kind people. The degree of skill that a person has in doing this (e.g., stylistic variations in self-presentation) would partly determine his success. A recipient's attributions about other people are also likely to be colored by his own motivations and personality. For example, individual differences in trust and in other characteristics may affect attribution of prosocial or hostile intent. Some of these issues are discussed later in this chapter.

Several experiments explored how some of the proposed determinants of the attribution of intention affect reciprocity. Brehm and Cole (1966) found in one experiment that receiving a favor when the recipient had greater power to benefit the donor resulted in less reciprocation than when he had less power to benefit the donor. The investigators interpreted this finding as evidence for psychological reactance produced by the favor, but an interpretation in terms of attribution of differential intentions is certainly possible. In another experiment, Kiesler (1966) hypothesized that reactions to favor-doing are a function of the appropriateness of the favor. High-school males participated in the experiment. In their work on a task, either cooperation between them was stressed—although each of them could keep the money he won, their joint earnings was to determine whether they would win a large reward for joint performance—or competition was stressed, with the large reward a function of individual performance. The subjects won substantially less money—51¢ in contrast to their partner's $3.45, in both treatments. In one condition, the partner did not share. In another condition, the partner was told by the experimenter to share. In a third condition, the partner shared on his own initiative, saying in a note, "We are in this together." There was a greater increase in ratings of attraction for the confederate from before the task to after in both sharing conditions, when compared individually with the condition without sharing. There was a greater increase in the no-sharing condition when the subjects were competing rather than cooperating. This suggests that competition might have made the lack of sharing behavior by the other subjects seem appropriate, whereas cooperation made it inappropriate and therefore negatively evaluated. However, sharing enhanced ratings of attractiveness regardless of whether the subjects were in the cooperation or competition condition; thus there was no negative reaction to the "inappropriate" favor in the competition condition. As I suggested earlier, given supporting conditions an "inappropriate," out-of-role favor is likely to be perceived as the result of the good intentions of the favor-doer. It may therefore lead to even stronger liking and greater reciprocation.

Schopler and Thompson (1968) also explored reactions to a favor as a function of the interpersonal context. Female subjects participated individually in a brief interview with a representative of a company, and then they were asked to help try out a product, a new shirt, by washing the shirt repeatedly. They were asked how many times they were willing to do this. In the favor condition the experimenter picked up a flower during the interview and gave it to the subject. This reduced the subjects' willingness to wash the shirt. The subjects rated the communicator in the favor condition in more negative terms than the communicator in the no-favor condition. In a second experiment, Schopler and Thompson tried to vary the appropriateness of the favor. Half the subjects were told that the interview was formal; the other half were told that it was informal. Variation in the behavior of the interviewer was minimal. The major differences were the description of the interview as formal or informal and the use of a stop-watch to time the formal interview. In the favor condition the experimenter gave the subjects a single rose in a vase. Subjects were then asked how many times they would be willing to wash the shirt, in the course of a week; they were asked to do it anywhere from 1 to 50 times. Subjects who received the favor in the formal condition agreed to do fewer washings than those who did not receive a favor, whereas subjects who received a favor in the informal condition agreed to do a larger number of washings. The favor dramatically reduced the positiveness of ratings in the formal condition but did not augment them in the informal condition. Perhaps a difference was not possible because 90% of the subjects in the no-favor informal condition rated the communicator very highly. In this study, as in others that were previously reviewed, liking for the donor and reciprocation appeared to be independent. Correlations between liking and reciprocation were low in both studies, but they were higher in the informal condition.

I wonder about the meaning of these findings. The favor could at best be viewed as a gesture without providing any real benefit or serving an existing need. Occurring in the context of an artificially created formality (e.g., the use of the stopwatch), and preceding the experimenter's request for a rather large favor, it could be viewed as completely self-serving, as a form of bribery, affecting the attribution of intent and creating psychological reactance. The findings may show that positive gestures in the course of interacting with other people can have varied effects depending on their nature and on the context, but they tell us little about how an interpersonal context modifies the influence of genuine, meaningful prosocial acts.

Thompson, Stroebe, and Schopler (1971) conducted another study to evaluate some of Schopler's ideas about conditions that affect the intent attributed to a favor-doer. In this study male subjects read stories about a person who did not act helpfully toward either one or two of his peers, claiming lack of money or time as the reason for his inability to help. Then, however, this person helped a third party. This help, which demanded either money or time—the resource the person supposedly had little of—was provided either to a professor or to a janitor. The person who helped the janitor was evaluated more positively (as friendly, likable, and kind) than the person who helped the professor, and more positive attributions were made about him (generous rather than selfish, considerate rather than inconsiderate, and so on) than about the other person. Presumably the professor's power to bestow benefit made the helper's action appear selfish. The help provided to the professor was rated as substantially less appropriate than the help provided to the janitor. The recipient of help who had low power, the janitor, was judged to perceive the help as more selfless and more positive, as well as more appropriate, than the high-power recipient. All the ratings indicated that help provided to the more powerful person was evaluated as less appropriate than the help provided to the less powerful person. This is consistent with everyday observation; initiating positive interaction with a more powerful person is frequently regarded as out of line with social custom, as presumptuous.

Attribution and Reactance. I noted that Brehm and Cole (1966) proposed that reciprocity may be reduced if reactance is induced by a favor. They proposed and found a decrease in reciprocity when the recipient of the favor had the power to benefit the favor-doer. A confederate, pretending to be another subject, brought the subject a soft drink during the experimental session. I noted that this favor may have led to the subject's attributing selfish intent to the confederate because the subject was supposed to make presumably important evaluations of the confederate. This experiment raises the question of whether the influences of attribution of intention and the arousal of reactance can be separated.

I noted that when another's intentions appear to be selfish, the implication is that reciprocation is expected; this evokes reactance. When another's intentions do not appear selfish and benefits received are great and highly needed, they may be willingly reciprocated, since they induce both positive feelings toward the helper and gratitude. When benefits are less needed, the necessity to reciprocate is likely to evoke resentment. However, the less needed the benefit, the less prosocial the helper's intention may be judged. Thus, substantial benefits that are not perceived as recipient-instigated may be resented and may evoke reactance. At the opposite end of the spectrum, under certain conditions benefits that appear to indicate a special bond, that appear to be motivated by prosocial intention and directed specifically to the recipient, may also evoke reactance. Such a benefit may give rise to the desire to reciprocate, but it also imposes the obligation to do so. In general, when people have to compromise themselves or fulfill an obligation somehow imposed on them, or make a substantial sacrifice to reciprocate, they may experience a restriction of freedom and respond with opposition (Worchel *et al.*, 1976). Worchel *et al.* had a confederate share money that she won on a task with her female partner. The subjects were made to believe (*a*) that this generosity was due to the nature of the situation, most people acting in this situation in this manner; (*b*) that their own unique characteristics elicited it; (*c*) that the unique characteristics of the other person led her to share; or (*d*) that the combination of their own unique characteristics and those of the other person resulted in sharing (the special-bond condition). The subjects knew that they were to evaluate the confederate on various dimensions and that the accuracy of their evaluation was important (for themselves, because they could win money for accurate evaluation, and for the other person) or unimportant. An important aspect of this study was that subjects were led to believe that the confederate did not know, before she shared the money, that part of the task was to make evaluations, so that she could not have shared in order to gain favors.

Worchel *et al.* expected that when evaluations were important, subjects in the special-bond condition would be least positive because they would experience the most reactance. When evaluations were unimportant, these subjects were expected to be most positive toward the confederate. There was a significant overall difference between high-importance and low-importance conditions. High-importance subjects in the special-bond condition tended to help the confederate more with sorting sheets of paper (but the procedure involved the experimenters asking subjects to help) than did subjects in the other high-importance conditions. High-importance conditions produced less favorable evaluations than low-importance conditions. The special-bond condition led to the least favorable evaluations when evaluations were of high importance, and to the most favorable evaluations when they were of low importance.

Personality Differences in Making Attributions and in Reciprocity

Personality characteristics of the perceiver can also determine the intent that he attributes to others. Hostile individuals are characterized by the tendency to attribute negative intent to others. Murstein (1961) found, for example, that individuals who were judged to be hostile by their fraternity brothers tended to deviate from the rest of the group in their judgment of others' hostility. Murstein also found that less insightful individuals deviated from the rest of the group in their judgment of others' hostility. *Insight,* in his definition, is the ability to consider others' motives, intentions, and desires; the concept appears to be similar to that of role-taking capacity. Aggressive, antisocial individuals, such as juvenile delinquents, tend to be hostile and show little insight about the reasons for their own and others' behavior (Staub, 1971c). They may attribute hostile intent to others and this increases their aggression toward them. At the other end of the scale, there may be individuals who are less likely to perceive hostility in other people; some may learn to deny hostility. Nadler and Altrocchi (1969) speculated that there were rare individuals, such as Billy Budd or Desdemona, who "bearing malice toward none are incapable of sensing its presence in others." Billy Budd, the hero of Melville's famous novel of the same name, was incapable of seeing evil. He could not entertain the idea that the man who was persecuting him had malicious intent. Similarly, Desdemona, the wife of Othello in Shakespeare's *Othello,* could not see Iago's manipulations against her. Nadler and Altrocchi suggest also that, in view of the fact that Desdemona and Billy Budd perished, it would be wise to consider that recognizing hostile intent is a necessary and self-preserving facet of human functioning. If one does not perceive hostility in others, necessary action for self-preservation often cannot be taken. As I noted, reacting appropriately, at an early stage, to mild or indirect hostility or aggression may inhibit later violence. Not reacting on the other hand, may lead to the aggressor's devaluation of the object of violence and may increase the possibility of subsequent attack.

In addition to differences in attributional tendencies, other personal characteristics might also affect people's reactions to favors. Berkowitz and Freedman (1967) suggested that middle-class individuals who come from an entrepreneurial background, where competition is emphasized, would behave according to a reciprocity norm. Middle-class people who come from families of bureaucrats would be more influenced by a norm of social responsibility. In Berkowitz and Freedman's study, entrepreneurial middle-class boys acted according to reciprocity considerations. They worked hardest for a supervisor who helped them earlier and least when they received little prior help. Boys coming from either bureaucratic-middle-class or working-class families helped the same amount, produced the same number of paper boxes for the supervisor, after having received little or much prior help. In another experiment, however, working-class boys from England worked hardest for those who had previously helped them, especially when their helpers were also working-class boys (Berkowitz, 1966). Bureaucratic-middle-class boys helped about the same amount regardless of how much prior help they received. However, they worked less for working-class than for middle-class partners, regardless of their prior experience. There were no entrepreneurial-middle-class boys in this study. Whether and how a norm of reciprocity influences behavior seem to be functions of the characteristics of the actor and of the potential recipient or prior-favor doer. In contrast to previous studies (Stapleton *et al.*, 1973), similarity between partners affected reciprocity in this study.

Class differences in beliefs in reciprocity have already been reported: Muir and Weinstein (1962) found that reciprocity characterized the beliefs and also, according to their self-reports, the behavior of middle-class housewives but not lower-class housewives. Dreman and Greenbaum (1973) found that among Israeli kindergarten children middle-class boys shared more candy when reciprocity by the recipient was possible; neither lower-class boys nor girls of either middle- or lower-class origin were affected by reciprocity conditions. These findings supported the expectations of the authors that lower-class children would be less affected by consideration of reciprocity and that females would rely on the norms of social responsibility in their dealings with other people. The children received candy and were told about others in the school who would not get any candy unless other children shared with them. The variation in the opportunity for reciprocity was created by telling children either that the recipient would be told who the donor was, or that the recipient would not be told. The recipient's knowing the identity of the donor presumably created the opportunity for reciprocation.

Although the research findings are limited in quantity and not entirely consistent, they clearly suggest that the degree to which expectations of reciprocity increase positive behavior and the degree to which past favors lead to positive behavior are influenced by the characteristics of the actor and of the potential recipient or prior-favor-doer. Similarity between the actor and recipient, at least in social-class origin, has affected reciprocation, just as similarity of various kinds has been shown to affect helpfulness.

Reciprocity between Friends, and Transactions in Prosocial Behavior

Much of the research discussed so far has examined reciprocity between individuals who had no prior relationship. It is the helpful act of one person toward another that establishes a minimal relationship between them. What are the rules guiding exchange and to what extent does reciprocity affect interaction between people who have more extensive relationships? Existing relationships between pairs of individuals might include specific rules that determine reciprocation: how soon one reciprocates after receiving a favor, what one should contribute, and so on.

Research findings with children indicate that interaction between friends is guided less by reciprocity of an immediate kind. In a study by Floyd (1964) children tended to increase the number of trinkets they gave to nonfriends after receiving many trinkets from them. However, they tended to decrease the number of trinkets they gave to friends after receiving many. Furthermore, selfishness by friends resulted in an increase in the number of trinkets that children gave them. Exchange and reciprocity by friends take place in the context of an extended history of interaction that is likely to include many reciprocal exchanges. Friends can balance out benefits over a longer period of time. Knowing that they can do so may decrease their concern about immediately reciprocating benefits they received. Selfishness by a friend may, on the other hand, be perceived as a threat to the friendship and may result in greater sharing, perhaps to eliminate the threat. Among nonfriends, generosity by another person may be seen as the initiation of a relationship, and it may lead to the expectation of a closer relationship if it is reciprocated.

In Floyd's study (1964) the subjects did not actually interact with others. The subject was in one room, and another child, either a friend or not a friend, was supposedly in an adjoining room. The trinkets that were shared were "delivered" by the experimenter. In two experiments that we conducted, children were placed in a genuinely interactive situation. In one study (Staub & Sherk, 1970) with fourth-grade subjects, one child (the Giver) received a bowl of candy to eat, ostensibly so that he or she would enjoy himself or herself during the experimental task, which was to listen to a tape-recorded story and thereby help the experimenter find out how much children liked different stories. Then another child of the same sex was brought into the room (the Receiver) to listen to the tape-recorded story with the Giver. The second child was always someone the first child had selected as a favorite companion on a sociometric measure administered several weeks earlier. About half the Receivers also selected the Giver as a favorite companion (mutual friends), and the other half did not (nonmutual friends). While listening to the story the Giver could share candy with the Receiver. Subsequently, the experimenter asked the children to draw something that they heard in the story. She showed them a clock and told them that they had 5 minutes to make the drawing, then gave both drawing paper. Having "found" only one crayon, she gave it to the Receiver and left the room. Reciprocity characterized sharing between Givers and Receivers. The more candy Givers shared the more the Receivers shared the use of the crayon. Moreover, the larger the difference between the amount that Givers ate in the Receivers' presence and the amount they shared (sharing difference), the less time did boys ($r = .58$, $p < .01$), but not girls ($r = -.16$; not significant), share the crayon. That is, boys retaliated for the other child's selfishness. The lack of retaliation by girls is consistent with findings of other research that girls' sharing is less affected by expected reciprocity (Dreman & Greenbaum, 1973) and their behavior is less influenced by concern about equity (see Chapter 4). A small group of children who ate candy in the Receiver's presence but shared none received the crayon for very little time, if at all.

Mutuality of friendship also affected reciprocity. Receivers who selected the Givers they were paired with as favorite companions shared the crayon substantially more than those who did not. Moreover, although retaliation, the negative relationship between sharing difference and crayon sharing, was highly significant among nonmutual friends, it was insubstantial among mutual friends.

Other studies further suggest that sharing and reciprocity are means by which friendships are formed and/or maintained and that the relationship between children affects the degree of sharing and reciprocity (Staub, 1973; Wright, 1942). For example, in an early study Wright (1942) found that children would give more valued possessions to a stranger (who was not present) than to a friend, perhaps as a means of developing a relationship with the stranger, and with the hope of reciprocation from him. Staub and Noerenberg (1977), in a study similar in methodology to that of the Staub and Sherk (1970) study, explored a variety of influences on sharing and reciprocity. Givers in this study were made to believe either that they earned candy or that they received candy without having earned it; receivers were told either that the Giver earned the candy in his possession or that the candy was for both of them, so that they would enjoy themselves during their task, which was to listen to a tape-recorded story. Again, Givers and Receivers were either mutual friends or nonmutual friends, in the latter case the Giver showing a preference for the Receiver as a companion on a sociometric measure, without the Receiver showing a similar preference for the Giver. Following the opportunity for Givers to share their candy, the children were asked to make a drawing and were given drawing paper; a 5-minute time limit was set. Before leaving the room the experimenter gave the only drawing pencil to the Receiver. Under these circumstances the Giver's sharing of candy had only a limited influence on the Receiver's sharing of the use of the drawing pencil. The original experimental treatments had a much greater effect, complex in nature, but apparently meaningful. Considering all groups together, Receivers who liked their Givers offered the drawing pencil to the Givers after a substantially *longer* time than Receivers who were not mutual friends. However, there were substantial differences in treatment groups; the two types of experimental treatments (variation in deserving by Givers; variation in Receivers' perception of the right to the candy) and mutuality of friendship interacted in affecting the Receivers' sharing of the drawing pencil. Receivers who were mutual friends offered the drawing pencil to Givers after a longer period of their own use when the experimental treatments were such that there was no conflict between the Givers' and Receivers' perceptions of the situation— when both believed that the Giver earned the candy, or when neither believed that the Giver earned it. When no conflict existed in perception and in the resulting transactions that surrounded the exchange of candy (which included offers, requests, and refusals of candy), mutual friends, presumably because they felt secure in the existing relationship, acted according to their own interests. When, however, the perceptions created by the experimenter (and the resulting transactions) were divergent (for example, the Giver believing that he did not earn the candy and the Receiver thinking that the Giver did earn the candy, or vice versa), mutual-friend Receivers offered the drawing pencil after a substantially shorter time. Under these circumstances the interaction might have produced some conflict and disequilibrium in the relationship, leading the Receivers to share more, perhaps to maintain or reestablish positive contact. In contrast, Receivers who indicated no preference for their Givers offered them the drawing pencil after a shorter time when their perceptions of the situation were in agreement, presumably because under these circumstances the interaction offered the opportunity for the development of a relationship. They shared less when their perceptions were divergent. The strongest reciprocity was found between non-mutual friends when the Giver believed that he earned the candy and the Receiver thought that it was for both of them. In this condition nonmutual-friend Receivers retaliated against the Givers' selfishness, and a high positive relationship was found between sharing difference and the length of time before the Receivers offered the Givers the drawing pencils.

The transactional nature of a great deal of prosocial behavior is at least implicit in much of the theorizing and research presented. The potential recipient of a prosocial act can exert great influence on the actor, determining whether a particular kind of prosocial behavior will take place. In the study I just discussed, whether the pairs of children believed that the child who possessed the candy earned it, received it for both of them, or whether they had conflicting beliefs gained expression not only in what the child who possessed the candy did with it, his sharing or not, but very powerfully through the behavior of the would-be recipient. Requests, demands, various actions by this child were a powerful determinant of "sharing" by the one who possessed the candy. What happened with regard to the candy affected, in turn, the subsequent sharing behavior of the drawing pencil by the recipient.

Reciprocity in Everyday Life

To what extent do principles of reciprocity guide behavior in everyday life? I mentioned one situation where exact reciprocity certainly does not hold, and that is the case of friendship. Further evidence for this comes from research on self-disclosure. A high degree of reciprocity exists when people provide information about themselves to strangers, but among friends the intimacy level of disclosure by one person is unrelated to the intimacy level of the other's subsequent self-disclosure (Derlega, Wilson, & Chaikan 1976; see also Chapter 9). In intimate relationships reciprocity is probably far from exact. The participants do not keep an account of how much they give and how much they get. As long as the relationship is satisfying and there is reasonable reciprocity overall, partners can frequently act nonreciprocally. But if giving becomes one-sided, resentment is likely to build up and problems develop.

Under what conditions can people have a nonreciprocal relationship? When the recipient is not in a position to reciprocate, principles guiding prosocial behavior might enter—norms that prescribe positive behavior, empathy, and the like. In reacting to people in need who do not have the resources to reciprocate (old people, poor people, and the like), a person may engage in positive behavior without expecting reciprocation, and a relationship can be maintained. The other's inability to return the benefits received may make this acceptable. Frequently, however, benefactors may expect reciprocation in commodities other than what they provide; a thank you or some form of approval may serve as reciprocation for favors of substantial magnitude.

Many people in our society engage in acts of charity anonymously, so that the possibility of reciprocation does not exist. It is a cultural value to do this. The range of prosocial acts that people engage in without expecting reciprocation may vary greatly according to cultural, religious, and other traditions, and individual characteristics. Varied religions stress the importance of charity and/or the importance of maximizing the self-respect of the recipient of help, both by providing the kind of help that leads to self-sufficiency (e.g., some means of earning a livelihood) and by making help anonymous (Epstein, 1959). The ideal of generosity and kindness without expectation of return is expressed in many ways. The hero of the novel *The Magnificent Obsession* by Lloyd Douglas gains tremendous personal strength and power by seeking people in great need and anonymously helping them, frequently by the loan (or donation) of large sums of money. People probably differ both in the extent to which they can engage in prosocial behavior without considering any reciprocation, and in the realm of activities in which they can do so. Someone may be a great philanthropist, acting completely selflessly, yet may demand reciprocation of kindness and helpfulness in personal relationships.

Normally, at least in American middle-class society, an acquaintance or casual friend who is invited for dinner but does not reciprocate may be invited for a second time, but then unilateral benefits are likely to be discontinued. But, of course, such invitations serve the purpose of indicating liking and interest, and if not returned lack of reciprocation of interest and liking is indicated. If liking is indicated by other means, the relationship can continue. A professor might invite a student to his house for dinner and drinks, once, twice, three times, many times. He probably does not expect reciprocation in kind, because students are usually not in a position to spend much money and are not well set up to entertain at home. But some indication of liking or gratitude or friendship is likely to be expected.

Rubin (1973) suggests that pairs in close relationships might not expect reciprocation for some positive acts because they define the pair as a unit, and consider gain by the other person as a benefit for the two of them. Douvan (1972) suggests that some relationships go beyond exchange: the parent–child relationship, or the relationships between close friends and good neighbors.

Although up to a point this suggestion is reasonable, such relationships involve exchanging often highly unequal and varied benefits rather than complete unconcern with what is received. Parents can be very unhappy if a child, who is old enough to be responsive to them, shows no indication of special fondness for the parents. Among friends, good neighbors, and loved ones, reciprocal giving asserts that one values the other members in the relationship. Insistence on certain forms of reciprocity can have positive value; it protects a benefactor from being taken for granted, exploited, and then devalued, which would disrupt the relationship.

In continuing human relationships it is certainly possible that a person acts out of liking, loving, or kindness. The expectation of reciprocity might not be the motive for positive behavior. Nonetheless, return of benefits might be necessary to maintain the relationship. The motives of love and kindness and affection have to be acknowledged and responded to. How much each person has to put into the relationship, what has to serve as "repayment," might be defined by norms that develop between the two people and regulate the interaction. There is no fixed value for the actions of one person toward the other in close relationships; the more intimate a relationship is, the more what different partners value in each other may vary. In minimal relationships, or in purely economic exchanges, money, status, and the like might be generally valued commodities. Love, on the other hand, cannot be easily offered to a stranger because of the absence of appropriate context. Varied and esoteric manifestations of love, however, might have substantial value in intimate relationships.

Not so long ago women usually provided affection, nurturance, and care in exchange for material security and usually affection from their husbands. Obviously, what each partner can and should provide is being redefined. It is not enough, in the new contracts that develop, for a man to provide affection and economic security; he is also expected to recognize the individual needs of his partner and to do things that enable her to satisfy those needs. The desire for an independent career is often one of these needs. Exchange relationships can be redefined at the individual level and at the societal level.

As I discussed earlier, one difficulty in relating to other people is the danger in giving them too much; the more we give of something of value, including love and the sharing of our private world, the more these commodities may lose their value to them over time. It is also true, I believe, that when we give unconditionally without any returns, what we give loses value; hence the protective character of insisting on reciprocity. Aronson and Linder (1965) found some evidence for the diminishing value of constant approval. In a laboratory experiment in which participants were exposed to different sequences of evaluation by others, a person who first made negative comments about the subject but then came to like the subject was liked more than someone who consistently liked the subject from the beginning. These findings may or may not say much, however, about our depreciation of constant liking or affection. Participants in this study may have made different attributions about their evaluators. The person who continuously liked them may have been regarded as someone who liked everyone, so his liking was not perceived as truly personal. In contrast, someone who starts out disliking another but comes to like him over time seems to have feelings that are evoked by the other as a person.

Rubin (1973) writes that Aronson's students dubbed his principle that a compliment from a stranger is new and interesting but the same compliment from a husband is boring because it is so well known as the "principle of marital infidelity." Approval from new and unfamiliar sources is exciting.

Rubin (1973) suggests two principles that offset the difficulty that is created in intimate relationships when the value of approval or of other, originally powerful, reinforcers is lost. The first principle is that disapproval by friends and loved ones continues to be highly potent, and people are often motivated to reestablish the intense relationship between them because of the hurt they experience from the other's disapproval. Although the two domains are somewhat distant, this proposal does gain support from the existing research on sharing behavior among children. As I noted, children tend to share less with friends but make special efforts and share more following a display of selfishness by their friends. Any threat to a relationship might reactivate efforts to repair it, and might even reestablish the lost value of reinforcers in the relationship. Rubin's second principle is that the value of reinforcers depends on the person they come from; once an intimate, loving relationship has come about, even highly repetitious, constant approval (or affection or whatever) retains its value. To some extent Rubin is probably right, but I fear he is overly optimistic on this score. Discrimination in approval and the extent to which interactions retain novel components and thus remain interesting are among the conditions that probably affect the extent reinforcers retain their value.

Trust in Other People

An important determinant of a person's manner of relating to other people is trust. Trust has a variety of meanings, but all forms of trust are likely to contribute to a person's willingness to initiate positive behavior toward others and/or to respond positively to others' initiatives. To initiate a positive interaction one has to believe, minimally, that one's efforts will not be rudely rebuked, that one's positive intentions will not be viewed as hostile or manipulative, and that some form of positive reaction is likely to follow. Given that reciprocity is affected by the attribution of intent to others, in order to reciprocate positive actions a person has to trust that others' positive behavior and verbal and stylistic manifestations of positive intent represent genuine positive intentions. Moreover, would people behave prosocially if they believed that no one would offer them a helping hand when they had important needs of their own? Who would make sacrifices for others if they did not trust others' willingness to help them in need?

Rotter (1967), in developing a scale of interpersonal trust, focused on one type of trust, the trust in other people's communications: "an expectancy held by an individual or a group that the word, promise, or written statement of another individual or group can be relied on [Rotter, 1971, p. 444]." Other kinds of trust that are important include belief in the goodness of man; belief that other people will not abuse one's confidence and will not attempt to cause harm; trust in others' willingness to help in times of need; and trust in their competence to do so. Erikson (1963) proposed that the development of basic trust early in life—trust by infants and young children that their caretakers will satisfy their important needs, and trust in the benevolence of their environment—is necessary for normal development. He viewed basic trust as a crucial ingredient of the healthy personality. Hartmann (1932) wrote, "All the strength derived from cooperation consists in men's reliance upon one another. . . . It is preeminently a communal value: it is the most positive unifying force which welds together a variety of individual persons, with separate interests, into a collective unit. . . . Distrust breaks all bonds [p. 294]."

Deutsch (1962) suggested that a person is confronted with the choice to trust or not to trust the behavior of another person (*a*) when he is confronted with an "ambiguous path" that can lead to either a beneficial or a harmful event; (*b*) when the occurrence of one or the other outcome appears to be contingent on the behavior of another person; and (*c*) when he perceives the intensity or strength of the negative consequence to be greater than that of the positive one. If he then proceeds to take the ambiguous path he has made a trusting choice. His choice may be based on confidence, but it may also be based on despair, conformity, impulsivity, masochism, virtue, and so on. This choice will be based on trust if it is the result of confidence, that is, the belief that the desired rather than the feared event will follow. Trusting choices made on the basis of "virtue," which as I see it refers to the belief that one ought to behave toward others as if one trusted them, or to the belief that trusting behavior is good, indicate prosocial values or norms, but not genuine trust. A mother who leaves a child with a baby-sitter makes a trusting choice, presumably (although I am sure not always) based on confidence in the baby-sitter. This choice could lead to beneficial or harmful consequences, and the harmful consequences, such as injury to the child, clearly outweigh the beneficial consequence of the child being cared for for a few hours. A suspicious choice (Deutsch, 1962) contrasts with a trusting choice in that it aims at reducing the likelihood of the potential harmful consequences of another person's behavior rather than on taking a chance on the beneficial outcomes.

Rotter (1967), in validating his measure of interpersonal trust, found a high positive relationship between scores on his measure and sociometric ratings of both trust and trustworthiness by members of sororities and fraternities who lived together for a period of at least 6 months. Gullibility and dependence were negatively related to trust. People who trust others are apparently reasonable individuals who do not trust blindly. In one study the experimenter told subjects that a machine that the subject saw malfunction (a big blue spark leapt out of it) was now fixed. High trusters acted appropriately to the experiment by pulling a knob to make a correct choice (although doing this earlier resulted in the spark) to a greater degree than low trusters (Geller, 1966). When subjects found out, however, that earlier the experimenter had misled them, high trusters stopped relying on his words; the relationship between trusting behavior and trust scores disappeared. In contrast to low trusters, moreover, when they were misled by an experimenter, who then admitted that he was wrong and apologized, high trusters continued to rely on this person's word for a period of time, in a sense giving him another chance (Roberts, 1967). Further validation of the trust scale has been provided by Wright, Maggied, and Palmer (1975), who found a relationship between introductory psychology students' scores on the trust scale and how they reacted to a stranger calling them and asking them to participate in a psychology experiment. Low trusters asked more questions in general, as well as more questions expressing suspicion, than high trusters.

Differences in personal characteristics of high- and low-trusting individuals have been sparsely noted, so far. Garske (1975) found that high and low trusters (the upper and lower quartile of subjects on the interpersonal trust scale) differed in their cognitive complexity. Male and female subjects rated individuals they regarded positively (closest friend, an admired person) and those they regarded negatively (a person "you find hard to like" and a person "with whom you feel uncomfortable") on 10 bipolar adjectives. Low trusters made significantly more differentiated ratings for both positive and negative stimulus persons than did high trusters. Garske noted that greater complexity has been viewed as an asset in social-information processing and judgment; it has been considered more useful in behavior discrimination and prediction than low complexity. He suggests that the low trusters might possess a relatively more adaptive cognitive mode, contrary to the implications of previous findings and the conclusions based on them (Rotter, 1971).

That different kinds of trust exist and are not all highly interrelated is suggested by findings on the relationship between scores on Rotter's test and openness in communication with other people. Although Gilbert (1967) found that subjects' willingness to disclose uncomplimentary personal information about themselves was related to trust scores, willingness for self-disclosure as measured by Jourard's scale (MacDonald, Kessel, & Fuller, 1970) and ratings of subjects' openness in sensitivity-training groups (Aronson, 1970; Stein, 1970) were unrelated to trust scores. Trust in other people's acceptance of and positive reaction to revealing information about oneself seems different from trust in the truthfulness and reliability of other people's communications.

Rotter (1971) and his associates also found that scores on the trust scale were unrelated to trusting behavior in experimental games; for example, in a prisoner's dilemma type game (MacDonald, Kessel, & Fuller, 1970). In a competitive stock market game where communications were exchanged and the subject could both demonstrate his trust in others and choose between lying and telling the truth (Hamsher, 1968), trust scores were unrelated to trust in others' communications, but they were significantly negatively related to lying to one's partners.

One reason for the low relationship between trust scores and game behavior might have been the strong situational force exerted on subjects by the nature of these games. Clearly trust and distrust can be situationally induced (Deutsch, 1960a, 1962) and the resulting behavior determined by expectations about others under particular circumstances rather than by general beliefs. Often prisoner's dilemma games induce competitive orientations in subjects, which might lead to the belief that one's partner will attempt to maximize his gain rather than cooperate. As Rotter (1971) wrote, in another context, "If the results of these [game] studies were characteristic of everyday behavior, the normal adult is so competitive, uncooperative, and untrusting that he could hardly go through a normal day's activities [p. 444]." The high degree of competitiveness might be due to the constraint of and orientation toward others that is induced by the structure of the game. This issue and the nature of situational influences on game behavior are discussed in Chapter 9. As Namath (1970a) noted, small variations in instructions often produce substantially different behavior during games. This suggests the degree to which behavior is under external, situational, rather than internal control.

In addition, when there is no exchange of communication in such games about the players' intentions, subjects' behavior may be more strongly influenced by types of trust other than the kind measured in Rotter's test. Several studies showed that variations in personality contribute to trusting and trustworthy behavior in games. Deutsch (1960b) found subjects who scored high on the F scale, a measure of authoritarian tendency, to be less trusting (more likely to make a competitive choice when they made the first move) as well as less trustworthy (more likely to make a competitive choice that reduced the other person's gain following the other's cooperative choice) than subjects with low F scores. Trust and trustworthiness were highly correlated. Wrightsman (1966) found that subjects who had high scores on a Philosophies of Human Nature scale—showing that they held positive beliefs about human nature and viewed other people as trustworthy, altruistic, and independent—were both more trusting and more trustworthy on a prisoner's dilemma type game than those with low scores.

A study that was conducted in my laboratory explored helping behavior as a function of both situationally induced variation in trust and trust as a personality characteristic (Midlarz, 1973). Two different trust scales and a variety of personality scales were administered to male subjects several weeks before the experimental session. In addition to the Rotter (1967) trust scale, we developed a 33-item scale to measure a variety of different kinds of trust: trust as the feeling that others are competent (i.e., one can trust them; they will do a good job); trust that others will not harm one; trust in the goodness of man; trust as the willingness to confide in another person; and trust as the willingness to depend on someone to do something for one. Six or seven items were used in each subscale.

Several weeks later the subjects participated in what was presented as a taste habituation experiment. To induce variation in trust, a confederate, acting as a subject, (*a*) knocked over a folder and replaced it (control condition); (*b*) knocked over a folder, found some money in it, and replaced it (trustworthy); or (*c*) knocked over a folder, found money in it, and put the money in his wallet, but then discovered that the folder belonged to the experimenter and, expressing fear of discovery, replaced the money (untrustworthy). Subsequently, the confederate had to taste something highly unpleasant, and the subject had to taste something pleasant. This division of tasks was ostensibly determined by a draw, after which the subject and the confederate were separated, the latter being taken to another room. Upon discovering that the unpleasant taste was bitter, the confederate told the experimenter that he had a particular aversion to bitter taste, and he wondered whether the other person would be willing to switch with him. The experimenter said that it was up to the other subject. This conversation was overheard by the subject over an intercom. The subject's willingness to switch, and the degree to which this willingness was freely offered upon the experimenter's return to the room (rather than prompted by the experimenter's questions) provided the helping scores.

The experimental treatments had no effect on helping. However, subjects who had high scores on the Rotter scale helped slightly more ($p < .10$), whereas subjects with high scores on the trust scale that Midlarz and I developed helped substantially more ($p < .01$) than low-trusting subjects. A correlational examination of the relationship between trust scores and help produced the same result over the whole sample. Examination of this relationship within groups showed that our scale was significantly related to helping behavior only when the confederate appeared untrustworthy; in this group, trust was positively related to helping. There was no relationship between trust and helping for the control group, and a marginally significant relationship was found between Rotter scale scores and helping for the trustworthy group. These findings suggest that the nature of the two trust scales is somewhat different. Belief in the other person's communications might have led subjects scoring high on the Rotter scale to help more in the trustworthy condition, but subjects scoring high on our scale, having more general trust in people, might have extended special consideration to the untrustworthy confederate. An interesting although marginal positive relationship was found in the untrustworthy group between subjects spontaneously encouraging the confederate to return the money and/or reinforcing his doing so, and their later helpfulness. Perhaps subjects who had a sense that they contributed to his change of heart or mind came to feel more benevolent toward him. Other personality measures—of social responsibility, a Machiavellian orientation, and ranking of Rokeach's values—were on the whole unrelated to helpfulness. Subjects for whom freedom was an important value were less helpful, suggesting a resistance effect. A high value placed on being helpful was associated with less suspicion of the experiment or the confederate. Suspicion, in turn, was associated with less help.

So far, our knowledge of the importance of trust, or even of the meaning and nature of trust, is limited. Varied kinds of trust are likely to exert important influences on how interacting individuals perceive each others' behavior, on how they judge each others' motives and intentions, and on the extent to which they hold positive or negative expectations about future interactions. For these reasons, whether trust is situationally induced, derives from a history of past interactions, or is characteristic of persons, it is likely to exert strong influences on interactive behavior and on the kinds of relationships that develop between interactive individuals. The joint (interactive) influence of varied sources of trust and how other personality characteristics relate to trust should be explored. Trust in other people was regarded as a component of prosocial orientation in the conception presented in Chapter 2.

Cooperation and Intimate Relationships: Further Explorations in Human Transactions

chapter 9

Prosocial behavior and altruism on the one hand, and cooperation on the other hand, are frequently treated as separate areas of inquiry. However, when a person cooperates, his behavior leads to benefits for others, and also benefits him personally. Cooperative behavior may be the result of self-centered motives, but many other types of prosocial activity result from such motives, as we have seen. Even if the motive is self-gain, the social significance of cooperation can be great. It has important social value that a person tries to gain benefit for himself by benefiting others rather than by using other, possibly antisocial, means. Moreover, people might often cooperate for the sake of the positive social-emotional consequences that cooperation leads to, that is, because it contributes to the satisfaction that people gain from relating to one another. Finally, cooperation may come to be valued in its own right, so that behaving cooperatively is valued and rewarding in itself. Cooperation is an everpresent form of prosocial behavior in the course of everyday life.

The most common element in definitions of cooperation is that of shared goals. Deutsch (1962) regarded a cooperative social situation as one in which the goals of separate individuals are so linked together that there is a positive correlation between their goal attainments. In addition to shared rewards, shared effort to achieve the goal or to gain the rewards is crucial for cooperation (rather than helping) to take place. The goals to be reached by cooperating individuals are not necessarily the same for all, but they are at least complementary. Homans (1961) writes that "cooperation occurs when, by emitting activities to one another, or by emitting activities in concern to the environment, at least two men achieve a greater total reward than either could have achieved by working alone [p. 131]."

Margaret Mead (1967) draws a distinction between cooperation and helpfulness. In cooperation, in her view, the goal is shared, and it is this shared relationship to the goal that holds the cooperating individuals together. In helpfulness, however, the helpers have a relationship to the goal only through their relationship to the individual whose goal it is. In one case, a person's relationship is to the goal, in the other case, to the individual he helps but not to the goal itself.

Although this distinction is useful, sometimes it is difficult to maintain. A person may help another achieve some goal, and the other may accept or even seek help; however, the goal in question may not be particularly valued by the latter. Instead, the two participants are cooperating in the service of the mutual goal of developing or maintaining a relationship between them. Thus what appears to be helpfulness is a form of cooperation. Moreover, when one person helps another achieve a goal and the two share the understanding that the other in turn will help the first achieve a different goal, a positive exchange relationship that involves mutual help exists and can certainly be regarded as a case of cooperation.

It might be possible to talk about concurrent and alternating cooperation. In *concurrent* cooperation two or more people concurrently extend effort that results in the attainment of a shared goal. Two people building a house in which they both will live is an example of this. In *alternating* cooperation two or more people might expend effort to benefit one of them, with the understanding that later they will work together to benefit another person, and so on, until all are benefiting from the common effort. Alternating cooperation is probably the most common form. In marriage it is understood that the partners will do things for each other that are necessary to satisfy each others' needs, to attain shared goals external to the relationship, as well as to maintain a positive relationship. In relationships between married partners, lovers, and friends, much of the behavior engaged in to benefit the other person is cooperative in nature; it is not performed purely out of the desire to benefit the other but with the understanding that ultimately mutual gain will result. Clearly cooperation, positive exchange, and reciprocity are highly interrelated concepts. Many of their determinants are likely to be similar.

Related to the concept of cooperation, at least in most of the research literature, is the concept of competition. One reason for the relationship is that much of the research on cooperation used prisoner's dilemma games and other types of games, where the structure of the activity forces subjects to choose between cooperation and competition. In cooperation two or more people contribute effort to maximize the outcomes for all, but in competition two or more people maximize their own outcomes relative to those of the others. The most important determinant of perceived success in competition is not absolute profit or gain, but the difference between one's own benefits and those of others. Under many life circumstances cooperation and competition are not alternatives in the same situation, so that people either compete or cooperate. On the other hand, people who are cooperating on one level might be competing on another level. Two people cooperating in the building of a house might compete in who is going to do more; they may evaluate their performances by the degree of their contribution relative to the other. Thus they might compete for the prestige or power that accrues to the one who makes the greater contribution (or for the satisfaction they experience from "winning"). This example highlights the possibility that most activities can be turned into competitive ones.

Cooperation and competition cannot be assessed along dimensions of tangible gains only. They have to be considered along dimensions of power, importance, self-image, and so on. A father may be teaching his child to throw a baseball (potentially a prosocial activity in that its apparent purpose is to benefit the child, and cooperative in that one throws and the other catches). This activity can easily turn into a competitive activity in the course of which the father demonstrates both his greater skill and the child's incapacity relative to himself. The gains and losses have to be evaluated in terms of psychological states.

Although there is plenty of competition in life, even more predominant are competitive feelings; competitive action is often inhibited by various cultural and individual values. Children may evaluate how well they do in sports, how popular they are, or how well they can perform in school relative to other children. Adults may evaluate their professional success, their wealth, even their happiness in a competitive manner, wanting to have more than other people. An interesting element of this may be that the closer one's relationship to other people is, the greater the competitive feelings that may be generated. People usually compete with others or feel competitive toward others who are relevant comparison persons for them. Thus they may evaluate their professional success, their wealth, their happiness relative to those they know, and even more so relative to their friends and even lovers and mates. Feelings of envy may arise mainly out of competitive evaluations in comparison to others whom one identifies with. Very few of us might feel poor because we have less money than the Rockefellers, but many of us may feel poor in comparison to friends in the same profession who are "doing better."

The reference groups or reference persons that people choose, and the degree to which they competitively evaluate themselves, are likely to affect their self-evaluation. A student (or professor) who is reasonably successful in his professional activities may have a good friend who is relatively unsuccessful and may evaluate himself in comparison to this friend. The result is high self-esteem and positive feelings. The same person choosing the most successful individual in his field of study or scholarship as a comparison other might experience distress and develop a negative view of himself. As the research and discussion on the effects of mood and self-esteem indicated, these subjective psychological states are likely to affect the manner in which people relate to others, their degree of self-absorption versus other orientation.

The hypothesis that I proposed, that people might be more sensitive to the degree of balance between their own state of welfare and those of their friends, between gains of their own and gains of friends, than to imbalance between themselves and strangers, is perhaps surprising. This hypothesis about "comparison distress" may also explain, in part, why children would share more with strangers or nonfriends than with friends (except when they *respond* to non-sharing by friends), a finding discussed in Chapter 8 (Floyd, 1964; Staub, 1973; Staub & Sherk, 1970; Wright, 1942). This hypothesis also points to areas of conflict. Presumably, people are more concerned with the welfare of others close to them than with the welfare of strangers. Would they not, therefore, want to help friends, intimates, and loved ones more than strangers or acquaintances? Perhaps a differentiated hypothesis is needed. First, the hypothesis about comparison distress may apply more strongly to acquaintances, colleagues (relative to strangers) than to reference persons with whom we are in intimate relationships. Second, people will want to enhance the welfare of intimates when they are in need more than the welfare of strangers or acquaintances, and more when they identify themselves with the other's goals, but may not feel like helping them to satisfy or reach certain goals that they regard competitively. In the latter case, their feelings of obligation and concern about the consequences on their relationships may still exert strong influence toward helping intimates.

I am suggesting that people in close relationships—of which there are varied kinds (see Huston & Levinger, 1978, for a review of attempts at classification) with probably different feelings between members and different rules of interaction—are concerned with each others' welfare and, at least in certain types of close relationships, also feel competitive, probably mainly in certain domains. Both the close feelings and concern about competitiveness may be reflected in Morgan and Sawyer's (1978) findings that in an adaptation of the prisoner's dilemma game friends more than acquaintances preferred equal rewards and actually chose to allocate rewards equally. Even when their partners made seemingly self-serving moves, friends were less likely to attribute competitive intent to their partner. Morgan and Sawyer suggested that friends try to maintain status equality and solidarity. Aware of potential problems, friends may frequently guard against the development of competition between them.

However, under some conditions people may not act prosocially even if they would benefit by reciprocating. They may be less interested in benefits accruing to them than in the difference between their own and others' benefits. To maximize this difference they are willing to give up benefits they could otherwise gain.

Determinants of Cooperation

Most experimentally gained knowledge about cooperation derives from studies in which participants played some type of game. Adult studies used the prisoner's dilemma or some variant of it, but other games have also been used. Children's cooperative behavior has also been evaluated through games of different kinds.

Several basic issues need to be considered in assessing the meaning of these studies. First, as I already indicated, the nature of most of these games forces a choice of two alternatives on participants—to cooperate or to compete. Second, interaction can only take place in one dimension, as defined by the behavioral alternatives provided by the game. The possibility of co-operating on one level but competing on another does not exist. Third, as I argued earlier, the similarity between a person's behavior in such games and his behavior in other settings might be slight or nonexistent (Krebs & Staub, 1971). The motives that are activated by playing a game may not apply to real-life interactions. For example, participants might want to make the game interesting; they might be bored by continuous cooperation and therefore vary their behavior. Furthermore, in our culture we learn from childhood that winning, not being nice and getting along well, is the primary purpose of playing games, and perhaps we also learn that other people have no right to resent it when we win. Consequently, games might automatically activate a competitive motivation. For these reasons (and because the tremendous amount of research available using the prisoner's dilemma and other games makes an exhaustive treatment here impossible), only a few studies that help demonstrate principles of cooperation are mentioned here.

Despite their shortcomings, game studies do make certain contributions. Even though game behavior and life behavior might be unrelated for specific individuals, the processes that determine cooperative behavior (communication, trust, power) in games and in real life might be similar. Knowledge gained about determinants of the former may very well be applicable to the latter. Moreover, game behavior might serve as a measure of motivational orientation. People might give rein to certain motives more freely in games than they would in real-life settings, where such motives might be considered socially undesirable. However, to diagnose motives by game behavior one has to be able to separate motives that are isomorphic to real life from those that are related to the game.

Deutsch explored how situationally varied motivational orientations and the opportunity by players to communicate with one another before making choices influenced the players' behavior in prisoner's dilemma games (Deutsch, 1960a, 1962). When a subject was told that he was to be concerned with both his own welfare and the welfare of the other person and that the other person had the same instructions (cooperative motivation), substantially more cooperative behavior resulted than when the subject was told to do as well as he could, to try to defeat the other person, and that the other person had similar instructions (competitive motivation). An individualistic orientation, in which the subject was told (*a*) that he was to do as well for himself as he could without considering how well the other person did and (*b*) that the other person had the same instructions, resulted in fairly competitive behavior, but less than in the competitive condition. Cooperation was increased when subjects could communicate before they made their choices, by writing notes to each other (actually, subjects were receiving notes prepared by the experimenter). The opportunity to communicate increased cooperation to the greatest degree when subjects received an individualistic orientation. The more of the following elements the notes included, the greater the degree of cooperation was: an expression of the intention to cooperate; an expression of the expectation that the other would cooperate; a description of how violations of that expectation would be reacted to, and an expression of the means by which cooperation could be reestablished after a violation had occurred ("If you decide to cooperate and make a cooperative choice after first not doing so, then I will cooperate"). In other research Loomis (1959) also found that the opportunity for communication between partners increased cooperation. Deutsch (1962) concluded that "mutual trust can be established in people with individualistic orientations through communication [p. 312]." However, the findings that I have just reviewed represent a special form of "trust." Cooperation increased to some degree when an opponent expressed the intention to cooperate but it increased more, in a nearly linear fashion, as a function of the partner indicating that he would retaliate if the subject were not trustworthy, and as a function of information given by partners about the conditions that would lead them to cooperate again. Seemingly "trusting" behavior increased when the partner or opponent had the ability and expressed the willingness to use power.

Deutsch (1962) reasoned that in this and in many other situations in which an individual might enhance his own satisfaction to the disadvantage of another (buyer–seller, husband–wife transactions, a crowd in the theater when there is a fire) by deviating from social rules that govern behavior, "rational" behavior follows only if conditions for mutual trust exist. Rational behavior seems to be defined by Deutsch as behavior that attempts to maximize joint gain. Clearly, however, conditions that promote mutual trust include the possibility of retaliation for betrayal. Frequently, the structure of circumstances makes short-term gain (as in the prisoner's dilemma) or long-term gain (as in an extended relationship) contingent on positive behavior or cooperation that depends on mutual trust. At other times, unfortunately, selfish or exploitative behavior can maximize certain kinds of gain of each party.

Both power and the willingness to use it seemed important preconditions for communication to enhance cooperation in these experiments, and even then communication had little effect in the competitive-orientation condition. In real-life interactions explicitly communicating that one will have negative feelings or reactions if another person does not cooperate, and perhaps telling the person how these will be expressed, may give power to people who otherwise have none. As in any social negotiation, the manner in which such threats are communicated matters a great deal. Direct threats may arouse anger or opposition and may lead to the unwanted behavior.

Further research on power variations showed that unilateral power held by one party does not increase cooperation by the powerless person; instead, it is likely to inhibit it. Having the power to retaliate enhanced cooperation (Deutsch, 1962). Deutsch and Krauss (1960) found in a "trucking game" that having the power to inhibit another person's gain without the other having power to retaliate was detrimental to cooperation. In other research (see Nemeth, 1970b), when one party acquired an invulnerable weapon—again, unilateral power advantage—the incidence of aggressive actions increased. Greater strength by one of the opponents did not inhibit aggression by the other. In evaluating the significance of these findings we must consider that even in a simple interpersonal interaction the retaliatory power of another person may have greater significance than it would have in a gamelike laboratory situation. On the other hand, considering some real-life players, Russia and the United States, the history of the 1950s and early 1960s clearly indicates that even though the United States was believed to have a great power advantage, this power advantage did not stop Russia from making many uncooperative moves, from provocation in Berlin to the invasion of Hungary. In games and in real life such noncooperation may result from the implicit assumption and even mutual understanding that unilateral power of an extreme kind will not be used, except in response to extreme provocation.

An opponent's greater strength does not increase the cooperation of the weaker partner: An opponent's lesser strength, combined with cooperation by him can have variable effects. In a game devised to provide unequal power, a completely pacifist strategy on the part of the player in the weaker position did not result in similarly pacifist—that is, cooperative—behavior on the part of the stronger opponent. Nonviolence of the weak did not result in mercy of the strong in this game (Shure, Meeker, & Hansford, 1965). In using the prisoner's dilemma game in which power is equal for two participants, a 100% cooperative strategy on the part of one partner evoked varied reactions. About half the participants continuously took advantage of a co-operating confederate, whereas the other half came to a level of complete cooperation themselves (Rapoport & Chammah, 1965). It seems to be important to determine differences in the personality characteristics of individuals who respond differently to the complete cooperation of other persons. Some people might exploit the weakness of others; they might have contempt for the weak and tend to interpret noncontingent cooperation as weakness. Other people might seek and appreciate "signs" of good intentions from others and respond positively to them.

Another strategy that has been explored in prisoner's dilemma games is the matching strategy. Either a stooge or feedback provided by the experimenter matches the actual performance of the subject, cooperation for cooperation, noncooperative choice for noncooperative choice. The matching may be for the subjects' current move or the previous one. In the latter case a player who defected on one trial, that is, responded to a cooperative choice with a noncooperative one, would be faced with defection (which may be viewed as retaliation) on the subsequent trial. The level of cooperation by the stooge is entirely contingent upon the subject's performance. This type of contingency is conducive to cooperation (Komorita, 1965).

These findings, demonstrative rather than exhaustive, but representing generalizations that can be derived from this research, suggest the importance of both a sense of control and respect for one's partner if cooperation is to follow. When a person has too little power to have a sense of control in the interaction, he may challenge his opponent and behave uncooperatively rather than acting "reasonably." When he has too much control because his opponent lets him get away with anything that he does, he may abuse the power granted to him. When he has control but is also kept in line by the behavior of his opponent, he may cooperate. The same spirit emerges from research on the effects of communication between partners. When participants receive notes that communicate the reasonableness of their opponents, their willingness to cooperate but also their determination to respond negatively to noncooperation, cooperation increases substantially.

The findings showed that differences in some personality characteristics, which might be related to trust, are associated with differences in both trusting (cooperative) and trustworthy behavior by the participants of games (Deutsch, 1960b; Wrightsman, 1966). It is unclear, however, how people differing in authoritarianism or in their beliefs about human nature are oriented toward the game; what it is that makes them behave cooperatively is not known. As noted earlier, they might trust the other person's cooperativeness, or they might hold values that lead them to cooperate. Some writers (Kelley & Stahleski, 1970) suggested that noncooperators and cooperators differ in their assumptions about other people. Noncooperators perceive other people as competitive and consequently not trustworthy in the game. They then proceed to compete, because otherwise they would be exploited. Cooperators, on the other hand, perceive others as cooperative. They give others the benefit of the doubt, but respond to noncooperation and exploitation by acting noncooperatively. Noncooperators, as a consequence, enact a self-fulfilling prophecy, in that they bring about noncooperation by their own behavior, which in turn fortifies their original beliefs. Although this analysis is highly interesting, Grzlec (1974), who, similarly to Kelley and Stahlesky, asked participants in games to predict whether their opponents would cooperate or compete, found that about 70% predicted cooperation, and about the same percentage proceeded to make competitive choices themselves. Grzlec suggests, on this basis, that many people act noncooperatively not to head off exploitation by their partner, but for other reasons. These might include a genuine competitive motive, and a preference for winning in contrast to gaining some rewards, at least in a game setting.

Inducing Cooperation and Its Consequences

A number of procedures have been used to increase cooperation. A variety of experimental studies show that reinforcement for cooperative behavior, in the sense that each participating child is individually rewarded for cooperative actions, increases cooperation among children. The withdrawal of reward and punishment decreases cooperation (Azrin & Lindsley, 1956; Vogler, Masters, & Morrill, 1970, 1971). Other researchers found that reinforcement based on both individual and group performance increased the cooperation in triads of 5- to 10-year-old children (Mithaug, 1969; Mithaug & Burgess, 1968). It is, of course, not surprising that children's cooperation can be increased by reinforcement. In these studies only the immediate effects of reinforcement were examined. For this reason the resulting behavior has to be considered a social-influence effect. In most studies with children the cooperative task demands the coordination of the children's behavior in the simultaneous pushing of a button or performance of some action. Exploitation of another's cooperation either is not possible or takes quite a different form in studies of children than of adults. Exploitation is possible when one child cooperates with another to move some object to the latter's goal region, which provides the latter with a reward, but the second child does not subsequently cooperate to ensure the first child a reward.

When children or adults in a group are individually rewarded for their accomplishments they subsequently cooperate less than children or adults receiving a reward for some accomplishment by the whole group. So-called "group-administered rewards" are more effective in inducing cooperation among group members than individually administered rewards are (Deutsch, 1949; Nelson & Madsen, 1968; Richmond & Weiner, 1973; Shapira & Madsen, 1969).

One reason for this interesting but not surprising effect of group reward might be that it affects the participants' feelings toward one another; it induces a cooperative rather than competitive motivational set. It might induce a "we" orientation rather than a "they" orientation, resulting in the kind of consequences that are produced by perceiving others as similar to oneself, and in some degree of identification with them. This view is consistent with Kagan and Madsen's (1971) findings that instructional sets that induce subjects to think of themselves as separate individuals or as members of the group also produce such differences in cooperation. Although younger children were unaffected by such instructions (4- to 5-year-olds), older children (7- to 9-year-olds) cooperated more when the instructions oriented them to think of themselves as group members. Children who were induced to think of themselves as separate individuals were substantially less cooperative, even though noncooperation resulted in the loss of rewards.

Such differences in individual versus group rewards, or in thinking of oneself as part of or separate from a group, can have important consequences in real-life activities. Fraser, Kelem, Diener, and Beaman (1973) found that grades of undergraduates improved when they were assigned on the basis of group performance rather than individual achievement. Students shared ideas and materials related to their work to a greater degree when they were evaluated on a group basis.

That motivational orientations might be produced by group versus individual rewards is further suggested by a study of Shapira and Madsen (1969) with urban and kibbutz children in Israel. Urban children were strongly affected by variation in the basis of the rewards, as in the other experiments. However, kibbutz children were unaffected by this variation, demonstrating a high level of cooperation under both conditions. Kibbutz children who are raised with and have to share toys and other possessions with their peers from an early age presumably develop a strong cooperative orientation toward their peers; this was not disrupted by the individual-reward condition.

An important finding of research, using varied procedures and techniques, is that cooperation among members of groups has a variety of positive consequences on the relationships of group members and can even positively affect their relationships with outsiders (Crombag, 1966; Deutsch, 1974; Wilson & Miller, 1961); Deutsch (1949) reported a variety of beneficial consequences when a group of individuals were "promotively" oriented toward one another, including division of labor, satisfaction, positive relationships among members, and productivity. Dunn and Goldman (1966) raised the question of whether cohesion within a group is a function of the group being in competition with other groups or whether it occurs when there is cooperation within groups and no competition between them. Campbell (1965) suggested that an external threat of some kind to a group of individuals leads to greater cohesion, friendliness, and cooperation within the group. In one study military groups that competed with other groups in the course of their normal training activities showed improvement in squad morale in comparison to control groups (Julian, Bishop, & Fiedler, 1966) as measured by the satisfaction and personal adjustment of their members. These effects may have resulted from the formation of psychological ties within competing groups. Competition may be one way in which a feeling of unity, or the perception of a number of individuals as one's group, can be achieved but it is presumably not the only way.

People continually divide the world into in-groups and out-groups. Such divisions are everpresent, whether the groups are formed along national, social, sexual, or religious lines (see Chapter 7). Does this happen partly because it increases one's identification with members of one's in-group, with the resulting satisfaction that seems to be associated with such identification? Can an equivalent degree of identification be created by other means? I hope that it can, because such divisions frequently also lead to intergroup conflict, aggression, and war. Dunn and Goldman (1966) found that group competition, consisting of similar and shared rewards for members within groups that were discussing human relations problems in a series of weekly meetings, and "group merit," where members were rewarded together but the group was not in competition with other groups, had some similar effects, differing both from individual-competition and from individual-merit groups. Subjects in the group competition and group merit conditions expressed more positive feelings. In addition, group-merit subjects rated more people within their classes as desirable partners to participate with in later group sessions than subjects who experienced group competition. Apparently when there is within-group cooperation without intergroup competition people come to accept others more, even others who are not members of their group.

Several studies with children showed beneficial consequences of learning to cooperate in a laboratory setting. Altman (1971) trained 3- to 6½-year-old children in a day nursery to cooperate on a laboratory game. The use of either one of two strategies by the children (for example, the simultaneous push of levers that controlled a lamp) resulted in the experimenter rewarding them with candies. Of 10 pairs of children, 7 pairs reached the criterion of 10 successful trials. The effects of this treatment were evaluated by examining children's interactions with other children during free play after the experimental treatments, and comparing them with interactions before the treatments. The children who successfully learned the task showed an increase in their awareness of common goals and interests with other children, an increase in friendly approach to others, and a decrease in hostile responses, that is, in behavior that interfered with others' activities. The children who did not learn the cooperative task showed an increase in the first two categories of activities, but only in relation to their experimental partners, not toward other members of their class. Although the subjects were few (and appropriate controls were lacking), this study shows a surprising degree of generalized positive consequence of learning to perform a cooperative activity. In another study Gottheil (1955) found that eighth-grade children who participated in a cooperative task showed positive changes in their sociometric ratings of other children. In comparison to children who participated in either a competitive task or a control activity, they showed a significant increase in their acceptance of children both in their group and in their class.

Cooperation between groups can also have positive effects. Cooperation with a formerly hostile group can reduce hostility and lead to positive feelings toward one's former antagonists. Sherif, Harvey, White, Hood, and Sherif (1961) conducted a classic "life experiment." They organized 22 white, middle-class boys, 11 years old, into two groups during their stay at a summer camp. The two groups initially did not meet each other; then they met for competitive activities. In the course of a series of such activities one of the two groups continuously lost, with unfortunate consequences. First, rather than increased cohesion within this group, the losers developed antagonism and hostility within the group. Some of the members, particularly some of the leaders, defected and tried to fraternize with members of the other group. In addition, intense hostility developed between groups, and destructive acts resulted. This experimental study suggests the negative consequences that can follow from unsuccessful intergroup competition. Perhaps cohesion, friendliness, and cooperation result only when a group is reasonably successful in facing threat from or engaging in competition with other groups.

After the antagonism between (and within) groups developed, the two groups were pushed by circumstances (some created by the researchers) to cooperate in several activities: pushing a stalled truck; fixing a broken water pipe that, had it remained broken, would have necessitated leaving the camp; and others. In the course of these cooperative activities, friendly relationships were established among the children from the two groups; positive interpersonal interactions and perceptions developed. Sherif *et al.* (1961) suggest that to reduce hostility between groups one needs to establish superordinate goals that necessitate joint, unified action.

Observation and other lines of evidence further suggest that facing a common threat, cooperation in the attainment of shared goals, as well as shared experiences or even their anticipation can lead to positive feelings toward other people. During a widespread blackout in the Northeast in 1965 a tremendous amount of cooperation, friendliness, and expression of positive sentiments and liking for other people was in evidence. In Cambridge, Massachusetts, strangers in coffee shops, sitting by candlelight, became fast friends; college students were directing traffic in Harvard Square. During the uprising in Hungary in 1956, it was common for strangers to strike up friendly conversations. Truck drivers picked up passengers everywhere, carrying truckloads of people, replacing the inactive public transportation system. (When one truck driver tried to charge his passengers, their indignation overwhelmed him.) Important shared experiences do bring people together—probably mostly when the experiences are not so threatening or frustrating that they lead to withdrawal, competition, and mutual suspicion. The general feeling of friendliness and cooperation in Hungary in 1956 was in evidence during a period of time when it seemed that the uprising had been successful.

In one study the anticipation of shared experience itself led to liking of strangers (Darley & Berscheid, 1967), who were evaluated on the basis of minimal written information about them. Although this finding is consistent with others (see Chapter 4) that showed that devaluation of strangers is less likely if future contact is anticipated, it is important to consider under what conditions such *anticipated liking* leads to genuine liking based on knowledge of the other person. Such issues will be considered in the next section. Certainly, as studies on the relationship between reciprocity and attraction have shown, negative behavior by another person leads to a decrease in the initial attraction for him that was based on written or verbally presented information.

The research that exists on the beneficial effects of cooperation indicates that participation in cooperative activities induces positive relationships and feelings among cooperators and toward other people. One explanation for these findings is provided by some of Heider's (1958) notions. He suggested that common fate and similarity lead to a "unit relationship," to perceiving oneself as belonging to the same larger unit with others. He also suggested that the tendency for balance and consistency leads to a "sentiment relationship," positive feelings, liking, and affection for others. However, positive feelings toward outsiders need further explanation. The experience of cooperation might lead to a view of people outside the cooperating unit as at least potentially cooperative. It might affect beliefs about other human beings, or humanity in general, enhancing positive orientation toward people.

The research findings on the consequences of cooperation partly support and partly help explain the findings reported in Chapter 5 that show that having been induced to engage in a prosocial act increases the probability of people's subsequent prosocial behavior. Positive behavior toward others, such as a helpful act or cooperation, may affect varied feelings and evaluations, at least temporarily—feelings toward people one helped or cooperated with, toward other people in general, feelings toward helpful acts, and a person's perception of himself as a helpful or cooperative person. Further research should attempt to specify the cognitive and affective consequences of cooperation.

A different but related positive consequence of cooperation is implied by another study. Johnson (1975) tested 9- to 11-year-old children's cooperativeness on several tasks. The summed scores were used as the indicators of children's cooperative versus competitive disposition. Subsequently Johnson measured the children's perceptual and affective role-taking skills. To determine the latter, children listened to tape-recorded stories, each focusing on certain emotions, and were asked to describe how the author of the stories felt, and why. Children with high cooperation scores were more skilled in recognizing others' feelings, and they were better able to describe others' reasons for their feelings than those with low cooperation scores. Johnson interpreted these findings as showing that role taking as a personality characteristic is associated with cooperation (see Chapter 5 for further discussion of this relationship). Instead, however, the repeated experience of cooperation may have led children to an empathic perceptual set. The research by Jarymowitcz (1977) on children's perception of others showed that specific experiences can have such effects (see Chapter 6).

The Development and Maintenance of Intimate Relationships

The study of positive social behavior must concern itself with positive behavior in close relationships. Levinger and Snoek (1972) proposed that there are three primary levels of relatedness among persons: awareness of another without contact, surface interaction, and deeper relationships. Huston and Levinger (1978) suggest that "evaluation of outcomes evolves from individualistic to joint criteria as the relationship moves toward deeper involvement [p. 133]." Presumably, different principles guide interaction between people as a function of their level of relatedness.

How do relationships between people develop? What determines whether they will be positive in nature and what degree of intimacy will be established? How do people become friends, lovers, intimates, mates? What determines the degree of satisfaction that people experience in such relationships? When such relationships are basically positive—and therefore their existence satisfies important goals of the participants by satisfying their desire or need for love, affection, sex, security, mutual support—their very existence can be regarded as prosocial. Intimate relationships provide mutual benefit for the participants. They are prosocial in the sense that any behavior that we discussed before is prosocial, but probably to a greater degree than many of them because the satisfaction arising from them is greater, or at least is potentially so. What principles determine and/or explain the nature of interaction among people in such relationships (whether dyadic or with more participants) and the nature and degree of positive behavior between them? To what extent are determinants of positive behavior similar or different among strangers, in minimal relationships, and in close relationships? We have as yet limited knowledge concerning these issues. To the extent that intimate relationships are satisfying and contribute to greater happiness, self-esteem, and positive moods and consequently lead people to behave in a more kindly, positive manner toward others outside the relationship (a theoretically reasonable although as yet empirically not established possibility), they are also important for the understanding of positive social behavior toward people outside the relationships.

Relationships: Their Formation and Nature

A variety of principles are relevant to the formation of relationships. Rubin (1973) extensively discussed the importance of first impressions, suggesting that first impressions activate implicit personality theories and tend to be relatively persistent determinants of how one person perceives another. Certainly positive first impressions might lead to continuing interaction, thereby allowing the growth of a relationship. Another principle that is called into play at the initial stages of the formation of relationships is the principle of "mere exposure." Exposure to (and the resulting familiarity with) another person leads to greater liking for them (Saegert, Swap, & Zajonc, 1973), as it does for nonsense syllables, music, paintings, and other objects and experiences (Zajonc, 1968). However, exposure might have such consequences only if first impressions are positive, and if no perceptual–cognitive tendencies exist that would inhibit the positive effect of exposure. Some research findings suggest that repeated exposure to something that is disliked, in this case paintings, can lead to increased dislike, although repeated exposure to liked paintings increases liking for them (Brickman *et al.*, 1972).

One may question the strict applicability of the mere exposure phenomenon to human beings. "Mere exposure" implies that nothing other than exposure takes place. This condition may almost never be fulfilled, however, in human social experience. Human beings process and create meaning out of their interactions with each other. Passing a stranger on the corridor at 9 o'clock every morning on the way to one's office, a person is likely to develop one kind of feeling about this stranger if over time the other shows recognition and thus a friendly exchange of good mornings can develop. "Mere exposure," in the sense of no indication of recognition, no apparent inclination to greet, is likely to have a negative meaning, to give rise to negative feelings.

Integration of blacks and whites within a housing project can substantially eradicate stereotypes and lead to much greater liking for members of the other race (Deutsch & Collins, 1951). The opportunity to interact, partly through exposure and partly by providing knowledge of what members of another race are really like, and perhaps the discovery of similarity in values, can have such salutary effects. On the other hand, already existing negative evaluations, perceptions, and beliefs about other people can persist or even increase in negativity as a result of exposure, partly because any one action or even pattern of behavior on the part of others can be interpreted in many different ways. Rubin (1973) quotes from Merton (1957):

> The very same behavior undergoes a complete change of evaluation in its transition from the in-group Abe Lincoln to the out-group Abe Cohen or Abe Kurakawa. . . . Did Lincoln work far into the night? This testifies that he was industrious, resolute, perseverant, and eager to realize his capacities to the full. Do the out-group Jews or Japanese keep these same hours? This only bears witness to their sweatshop mentality, their ruthless undercutting of American standards, their unfair competitive practices. Is the in-group hero frugal, thrifty, and sparing? Then the out-group victim is stingy, miserly, and penny-pinching [Merton, 1957, p. 428].

Whites living on the expanding border of a black neighborhood have been found to express more negative sentiments about blacks spontaneously to an interviewer than other whites do (Kramer, 1950). Given existing prejudices and stereotypes, physical proximity and exposure may even intensify negative feelings. Shared experiences and goals may then be necessary to overcome such barriers.

Another relatively ubiquitous principle is that proximity substantially contributes to the development of personal relationships. People living in the same housing unit are likely to develop friendships with others in nearby apartments on the same block (Festinger, 1951); students in dormitories are more likely to come to like people whose rooms are close to their own (Priest & Sawyer, 1967); people participating in activities that physically bring them together, even if they imply minimal shared interest or values such as working in the same office, often come to like one another and develop relationships. Newcomb (1961) rented a boardinghouse so that he could study the "acquaintance process." He found that roommates who were assigned on the basis of minimal compatibility, those who had discrepant attitudes on a variety of topics, developed a strong attraction to each other, just as those whose initial compatibility was high did. (However, as some research that is discussed later in greater detail shows [Taylor, 1968], over time people who live together may also come to like each other less.) The same principles apply to mate selection, in that people who get married are likely to live relatively near each other (Rubin, 1973). All this is not particularly surprising. Proximity, of a physical and functional kind, provides the opportunity for people to come to know each other. As Rubin points out, proximity in a dormitory and in living arrangements might be important because it allows people to have initial contacts without having to have a special excuse or reason for them. It is most natural to borrow salt from a next-door neighbor rather than from someone on the other end of the street.

Similarity of many kinds between people also contributes to liking. Friends have been found to come from the same religious, cultural, and social groups and to share similar values and beliefs (Laumann, 1969). Even similarity in height enhances liking for other people or for political candidates (Berkowitz, 1969). Presumably, similarity, real or perceived, enables people to enter into interactions with positive expectations, making positive initial interactions more likely. Once a relationship has begun, similarity is likely to develop further, by the mutual exchange of ideas and thoughts and the sharing of values and beliefs. Certain kinds of increase in similarity may be relationship-specific. In interacting with one friend many people might come to act in particular ways that are congenial for the relationship (with regard to both similarity in values and interests and, as I will discuss later, complementarity of needs), but they might talk and act in quite different ways with other friends or with strangers.

Some research findings show that the crucial type of similarity is that of values and beliefs; similarity in other personality characteristics is less important (Curry & Emerson, 1970). Other kinds of similarities—for instance, in social class or even in physical characteristics—might be important because of expectations that they create about shared values and interests. On the one hand similarity might decrease fear of the unknown and increase confidence in one's ability to control interactions with other people; on the other hand it is likely to contribute to the expectation of rewards and satisfactions that interactions might lead to.

Let us return to Newcomb's findings. Given physical proximity, as I noted, students both compatible and incompatible in their attitudes came to like one another. It should be noted that the subjects were new at the university, and they had no "compatible" individual living with them. When circumstances limited the opportunity for choice, "different" individuals came to like one another. Newcomb also studied the values of students in the house and their perceptions of the values of others in the house; these values were repeatedly evaluated. From the beginning, students *perceived* the values of those whom they liked as similar, and the values of those whom they disliked as dissimilar to their own values (frequently incorrectly). Progressively, there was an increase in actual similarity, but mainly as a result of changes in preferences for others. It seemed that actual value similarity had greater continuing influence, and not that liking resulted in value change.

A study by Nahemow and Lawton (1975) was conducted among people living in a housing project in Manhattan. The housing project consisted of seven 14-story buildings. Friendships within the project were formed on the basis of both proximity and similarity. Proximity had a substantial influence. People tended to choose as friends those who lived close to them, usually in their own building or on their own floor. Friends were also similar in age, race, even sex. These findings applied equally to younger and to older people. When people chose as friends those dissimilar to themselves, the influence of proximity was even more pronounced. Friends who lived at a distance were always similar in age and race; such similarity was not as frequent among those who lived near one another.

There is some indication that racial similarities might affect attitudes toward members of the same and different races because they lead to assumptions about values and beliefs. Within limits, information showing that a person's values are similar to one's own results in liking and acceptance even if that person is of a different race, whereas differences in values between oneself and a person of the same race decrease liking (Stern, Piliavin, & Smith, 1965). Cultural taboos that prohibit certain types of interactions with members of a different race (e.g., marriage) place limits on the extent to which value similarity leads to acceptance. (However, people may need excuses—justifications—to tell social psychologists about their prejudices. When their own values and the values of members of another race are presented as similar, justification for expressing less liking and acceptance is minimized.)

Although value similarity is important, complementarity in needs also contributes to positive relationships (Kerckhoff & Davis, 1962). A person who is insecure and needs reassurance might get along best with someone who is nurturant and self-assured, so that one person's need for assurance and the other person's need to provide nurturance are both satisfied.

Perhaps in the initial stages of the development of relationships physical proximity, exposure, and similarity in values and beliefs and in characteristics that imply such similarities are important. All these increase the likelihood of association in activities that lead to increased knowledge and appreciation. Complementarity in some important needs and goals might be crucial in determining whether a relationship will be continued. However, both similarities and differences of certain kinds can interfere with relationships. Two highly aggressive and competitive individuals or two people who need nurturance but have difficulty giving it might have a poor chance of developing a strong, continuing relationship. A person with low self-esteem might be threatened by someone who is self-confident and outgoing, and association between the two may become distressing. Thus the manner in which similarity and complementarity combine is important, but it is as yet an unexplored determinant of relationships.

There are questions and issues that arise about similarity and complementarity. Many people, particularly when they are reasonably secure and self-confident, appreciate novelty and complexity; they enjoy exploration. Even animals, children, and adults who have not lost the capacity tend to value and seek various forms of novelty (Deci, 1975). This suggests that, given certain similarities, we value novelty in people and might select them as friends because they are different from us. Rubin (1973) referred to the "lure of diversity." We do not yet know what kinds of people might prefer what kinds of novelty. Walster and Walster (1963) found that undergraduates about to join a discussion group strongly opted to join one composed of people different from themselves, such as night students and factory workers, rather than one composed of fellow undergraduates, unless they were prewarned to consider how other members of the group would react to them and urged to join a group in which people would be friendly to them. Students who were so prewarned were sensitized to threat; people whose personalities make them more easily threatened are self-sensitized and prefer to associate with others similar to themselves (Goldstein & Rosenfeld, 1969).

With regard to complementarity, in order to satisfy certain important needs of each other it may be necessary for people to have complementary needs or characteristics. We do not as yet know what dimensions of complementarity might be important in general, or for different people. If one person has strong dependence needs, the other cannot have the same needs; he has to enjoy being protective and caretaking if mutual satisfaction is to follow. On the other hand, both people in a relationship can have strong love needs, if they are both able to be loving. Complementarity will be further discussed later in this chapter.

An extremely important avenue by which relationships may develop, given a positive context (e.g., proximity, similarity, and positive first impression), is the sharing of thoughts, feelings, and information about the self (*self-disclosure*). Rubin (1973) stresses the importance of the development of commitment by people to one another; one avenue for that might be self-disclosure. The exchange of private information is also likely to be an important source of satisfaction in already existing relationships.

Self-Disclosure

The disclosure by people of information about themselves to others, particularly significant, intimate information, may be important in both developing and maintaining friendships and close relationships. Disclosing information about oneself, "showing" oneself to others, may itself be rewarding, if the recipient responds in an accepting and affirming manner. Intimate information provided by another person is likely to indicate trust and perhaps the desire to develop a relationship. It is understandable, in this light, that self-disclosure has been viewed as an important means of developing friendship (Jourard, 1964), and an important contributor to the growth of interpersonal relationships (Taylor, Altman, & Sorrentino, 1969). As Simmel (1964) wrote, "Obviously, all relations which people have to one another are based on their knowing something about one another [p. 307]." Nontrivial information about the self may also be regarded as a valued personal resource, the more intimate or private the information the greater its value, and as a consequence a valuable commodity of exchange.

It is interesting to contemplate that revealing thoughts and feelings and talking about significant personal experiences in an appropriate fashion, as well as listening to others who do this and responding sensitively and appropriately to them, are prosocial behaviors that importantly enter into positive social interactions. Toddlers bring toys and other objects and offer them to adults (Rheingold *et al.,* 1976). Later, in other ways, we want to share our perspective, our past, our inner life, and our experiences—what is important about ourselves, our private treasures. This seems to be both an important human need and an important opportunity for prosocial behavior.

On the whole, research findings indicate a high degree of reciprocity in either the amount or the degree of intimacy of information that a person receives from another person and discloses to this person (Cozby, 1973). In most studies, subjects and confederates exchanged written information about themselves, rated themselves on various self-descriptive measures, and/or indicated the kind of information they would be willing to communicate.

In many studies the amount of information or level of intimacy in the self-disclosure that was directed at a subject was prepared by the experimenter. The reciprocation of highly intimate information was found, contrary to the researchers' expectations, in several experiments (Levin & Gergen, 1969; Argyle & Kendon, 1967; Savicki, 1972). However, at high levels of intimacy the information that subjects provide is less intimate than the intimacy of the information that was communicated to them. Levin and Gergen, for example, had subjects receive a 40-item self-rating form from a partner on which 4, 6, or 32 items were checked. The average amount of information that subjects provided about themselves in turn by checking items was 10.5, 17.2, and 22, respectively. Argyle and Kendon (1967) found similar differences in response to variation in the degree of intimacy of self-disclosure that subjects were exposed to.

Worthy, Gary, and Kahn (1969) had groups of four female subjects spend 10 minutes getting acquainted with one another. Then they continued the "acquaintance process" by selecting and answering questions on 10 trials with identical sets of questions, and sending them to one of the other group members. There was a high degree of reciprocity between pairs of subjects in the level of intimacy of the questions they selected to answer for each other. Another index of reciprocity was a high degree of correlation ($r = .77$) between the average intimacy of all self-disclosures that the subjects received and made.

In most studies, people received information from a stranger who was in a separate room and whom they never expected to meet. Under these circumstances the "relationship" is limited. The findings may represent a form of the "stranger on the train" phenomenon, the tendency of people to be free and open in talking about intimate aspects of their lives with someone they never expect to see again. People may use strangers to unburden themselves, to discuss problems that are difficult to admit to people who are continuing parts of their lives. Providing intimate information to a stranger may be less threatening than providing such information to someone at the beginning of a potentially continuing relationship. The threat or anxiety that is associated with self-disclosure in beginning relationships, the fear that intimate information may be abused or result in negative evaluation, might be minimized when no further contact is expected, but some of the rewarding aspects of self-disclosure remain. Furthermore, self-disclosure by a stranger may elicit positive feelings, as mentioned before, leading to greater self-disclosure toward him. Reciprocity in self-disclosure might also represent adherence to norms, the result of a feeling of obligation to reciprocate, an expression of strongly held social and/or personal beliefs that one ought to reciprocate other people's confidence and create a balance. People may want to make a stranger feel that he gets as much as he offers and that they themselves are trustworthy, that no exploitation will take place. Finally, in an experimental situation the instructions to subjects, the task at hand (which is self-disclosure), and the self-disclosure by the other person may combine to define the appropriate level of self-disclosure by the subjects. Sometime these factors may make high levels of self-disclosure appear to be the situational rule.

The findings that were reviewed contradicted a hypothesis strongly held by most researchers, that high levels of self-disclosure by a stranger will be threatening and will not be reciprocated. Research findings by Rubin (1973) provide some information about the conditions under which high levels of self-disclosure will or will not be reciprocated. He had students approach people at the Boston airport and ask them to write something on a piece of paper for a class project on handwriting analysis. Since part of the project was to compare the handwriting of class members with that of other people the experimenter first wrote something on the sheet, and then handed it to the subject. What he wrote was either not very intimate, moderately intimate, or highly intimate. He either copied this material from a piece of paper so the message would not appear to be directed at the subject, or appeared to create the message on the spot. In the latter case high intimacy may have seemed to be evoked by the subject. Rubin expected that when the self-disclosure was impersonal and prepared beforehand, subjects would model the behavior of the confederate and respond with self-disclosure at a similar level of intimacy. He also expected that when the confederate's self-disclosure appeared to have been personally evoked by the subject, a high degree of self-disclosure would lead to suspicion rather than trust, inhibiting rather than facilitating reciprocal self-disclosure. With regard to length of subjects' statements—unfortunately, the only data Rubin (1973) reports—these expectations have been confirmed. Length increased in proportion to the intimacy of the experimenter's self-disclosure in the "copy" condition. However, after a similar increase from low to medium self-disclosure in the "create" condition, length fell off sharply in the high-intimacy condition. When another person, without any appropriate reason or justification, communicated highly intimate information about himself, reciprocal self-disclosure did not follow. Suspicion, negative evaluation of the other, even doubts about the other's sanity, may have been produced.

Derlega, Wilson, and Chaikin (1976) noted that in past laboratory studies self-disclosure occurred among strangers, and the results were generalized to intimate friends. They agree with Altman (1973) that among strangers "immediate reciprocity may be necessary to prove one's trustworthiness and to propel the relationship into more intimate stages. Between close friends, however, mutual respect and trust have been established over a long time period [p. 578]." Thus, friends may respond in varied ways to self-disclosure, depending on what is appropriate at the moment; they may listen sympathetically, ask questions, disclose intimate information in return, and so on. This view is consistent with the research findings that were reviewed earlier, noting minimal immediate reciprocity in friends' interactions, and with related discussion as to why this is so.

Derlega *et al.* (1976) had female undergraduates bring a close friend to the laboratory. Either these friends, who agreed to act as confederates, or strangers (also confederates, of course) sent notes to the subjects, disclosing information low in intimacy or high in intimacy. The friend-confederates wrote these notes on the basis of instructions they received, and the same note was used with one of the subjects in the stranger condition, a yoked control procedure. Friends were unaffected by the variation in intimacy, disclosing information about themselves in return at about the same level of intimacy as subjects who received a low-intimacy note from a stranger. Subjects who received a highly intimate note from a stranger disclosed significantly more intimate information than subjects in the other three groups. Correlating the amount of intimacy in the subjects' notes and in notes they received showed a high degree of positive reciprocity among strangers, but not among friends.

Rubin and Shenker (1978) examined self-disclosure in Harvard and Radcliffe dormitories between roommates and best-known hallmates. Participants rated their own and the other person's self-disclosures in increasingly intimate areas: taste, attitudes, interpersonal relations, and sex. Perceived reciprocity in self-disclosures (the relationship between subjects' reports of how much they disclosed and how much was disclosed to them) was much higher than actual reciprocity (the relationship between reports of self-disclosure by each member of the dyads), which was also substantial. Apparently, people have a strong tendency—presumably arising out of a strong need—to view their social relationships as reciprocal. Roommates reported greater disclosure than hallmates, and close friends reported much greater disclosure than not-close friend dyads. Friendship was most highly related to self-disclosure in intimate areas, but this was more true of women than of men. Greater proximity (roommate versus hallmate) was associated with greater self-disclosure in superficial areas. Friends, particularly women friends, report that they talk to each other intimately. The causal role of self-disclosure in the development of friendship and in the quality of relationships could not be established in this study.

Morton (1978) had young married people interact with their spouses or with strangers. They were to take turns choosing for conversation items that varied in intimacy and then to proceed to converse about them. Females communicated more intimately, particularly on an evaluative dimension, expressing personal feelings and judgments (in contrast to descriptive communication that referred to private facts). There was more descriptive intimacy in conversations between spouses than in that between strangers, but not more evaluative intimacy. Apart from the initial period, there was less reciprocity between spouses. The authors suggest that females' greater intimacy of communication may contribute both to the development and to the maintenance of intimate relationships between the sexes.

It is not surprising that people who know each other well and/or feel close to each other will communicate more intimately. For reasons described above, it is also not surprising that there is less immediate reciprocity between them. Nonetheless, Rubin and Shenker's (1978) findings clearly indicate that the existence of reciprocity is very important for people who have a continued and presumably generally positive relationship. People in close relationships probably need to believe that, overall, such reciprocity exists between them; otherwise, the relationship is threatened. Among strangers, immediate reciprocity is necessary even to continue with a smooth interaction and even more to "develop" the interaction or the relationship. Thus, in the course of getting to know each other people can be expected to try hard to maintain reciprocity in self-disclosure, as well as in giving to and receiving from each other in other ways.

Altman and his associates (Altman & Taylor, 1973) suggest, in their social-penetration theory, that self-disclosure usually follows a time course, with progressive increase in the amount of information that people are willing to expose to each other as a function of past rewards and costs associated with exchange and of expected future rewards and costs. Presumably, such a time course is important for the development of relationships; as I argue later in this chapter, high levels of early intimacy may interfere with such a development. This suggests that more information may be communicated to a stranger with whom one expects no continued interaction. Cozby (1973) describes a study by Murdock, Chenowith, and Rissman that varied the possibility of future interaction with a confederate. As expected, participants disclosed more to their partners when they did not expect future interaction to take place.

An important question that Davis and Skinner (1974) explored was the degree to which participants' response to self-disclosure by another person is a manifestation of reciprocity or of imitation, in the latter case the other person functioning as a model. In several interview studies self-disclosure by a model (Spiritas & Holmes, 1971; Marlatt, 1970, 1971) increased subsequent self-disclosure by interviewees. The latter's behavior may then be a form of disinhibition or it may represent adherence to some rule of the situation that is communicated to them by the model's actions. Davis and Skinner (1974) asked subjects to provide information about themselves on 10 topics that in previous research (Jourard & Jaffe, 1970) had received high intimacy ratings. Before responding, either the interviewers "made a full and frank self-disclosure on each topic" or subjects were exposed to a video-taped model who did so. In a control group subjects simply proceeded with their self-disclosure. The intimacy of self-disclosure by subjects following the interviewer's self-disclosure was significantly greater than in the other two groups; in the model condition it was marginally greater than in the control group. The findings also indicated that "deep" self-exposure by the subjects was original in content in the interviewer condition, whereas it tended to be an imitation of the model's disclosures in the modeling condition. The more the subjects imitated the model, the more they reported on a postexperimental questionnaire that they withheld information about themselves. This may have been the case, as the findings suggest, but it is also possible that the participants were concerned about having said too much to an interviewer when self-disclosures were not reciprocal; they may have been attempting to say that much of importance was still held in reserve. Ehrlich and Graeven (1971) also found that intimate self-disclosure by a partner was reciprocated in degree, but not in topical category. Worthy, Gary, and Kahn (1969) found that members of a group disclosed more to the specific persons from whom they received the greatest disclosure. All these findings together suggest that though modeling increases self-disclosure under certain circumstances, it does so to a lesser degree, and the information that it leads to is less genuine than when self-disclosure is reciprocal in nature.

To what degree does self-disclosure lead to liking, friendship, and positive relationships among people? Both Ehrlich and Graeven (1971) and Davis and Skinner (1974) found no greater preference by participants in their research for a high-disclosing confederate than for a low-disclosing one, even though they disclosed more information about themselves to the former than to the latter. "Reciprocity, it appears, is normative but not necessarily pleasurable [p. 783]," wrote Davis and Skinner (1974). In contrast, however, Worthy *et al.* (1969) found that female subjects expressed greatest liking for those who disclosed the most information to them. Clearly, this is not a simple issue. The findings may have been affected by the nature of the experimental circumstances, and by the time span in the course of which reciprocal exchange of information took place. If people feel forced to expose intimate information about themselves by the conditions of the experiment, by the behavior of another person, and by the social norm of reciprocity, one would expect little positive feeling to be generated by the experience. In the Worthy *et al.* study the subjects were females, in contrast to other studies, and Cozby (1973) suggests that females may feel more comfortable with high levels of early self-disclosure than males. Perhaps just as important is the fact that in Worthy *et al.*'s study a number of exchanges took place, so subjects could receive affirmation and acceptance of their self-disclosures through the continued disclosure by others to them.

Given the repeated opportunities for self-disclosure and a time-span greater than that employed in most studies, the Worthy *et al.* study also allowed more of a time course in which progressive self-disclosure could occur. Wortman, Adesman, Herman, and Greenberg (1976) explored the relationship between the timing of the disclosure of intimate information and liking for the discloser. In their study a male undergraduate and a confederate engaged in a 10-minute conversation. They were assured that the conversation would be private, and in fact the self-disclosure by the subject was not recorded. Either at the beginning of the conversation or near the end the confederate revealed "something quite personal—that his girlfriend was pregnant." The timing of this disclosure had a substantial effect. If it occurred early the person communicating this information was subsequently evaluated as "more immature and maladjusted and tended to be viewed as more phony and insecure than the late discloser [p. 189]." Late disclosers were perceived as more open and the subjects were more interested in getting to know them.

Wortman *et al.* interpret the differences in evaluation as the result of different attributions about the reasons for disclosure. In their view, the remarks of the late discloser were regarded as an indication of his interest in continuing and extending the relationship. Late disclosers were, in fact, described by subjects as having a significantly greater interest in getting to know them than early disclosers. If a highly intimate disclosure occurs early in an interaction between strangers, its cause may be viewed either as some need of the person to disclose this information, or the person's openness to strangers in general—not as an interest in the subject.

Obviously, the emerging picture indicates that varied conditions jointly affect self-disclosure and liking for one's partner in disclosure. Cozby (1973) found that subjects expressed the most liking for individuals who wanted to discuss issues of moderate intimacy, rather than very low or very high levels of intimacy. Thus, a curvilinear relationship may exist between intimacy in another person's disclosures and liking for that person. Daher and Banikiotes (1976) found that attraction was affected not only by the level of disclosure by another person, but by similarity in the content of disclosures. In this study the male undergraduates provided information about themselves first, and they received information about another person in a later session. Similarity in content resulted in more liking for the other person, and a higher level of disclosure was also associated with more liking. There was an interaction effect, so that the more intimate information that subjects received elicited significantly greater ratings of attraction only when it was similar in content to the subjects' own self-disclosures. The subjects may have responded not only to similarity in content itself but also to the responsiveness of the other person implied by the similarity. Finally, the subjects' own levels of disclosure interacted with the levels of disclosure they received in affecting attraction. Those who disclosed at a high level rated the person who disclosed to them at a high level more attractive, whereas subjects who disclosed at a low level did not show a differential response.

Hick, Mitchell, Bell, and Carter (1975) further explicated some of the determinants of self-disclosure. They showed that people provide more personal and less impersonal information about themselves when they hear a tape and talk into a microphone in contrast to receiving and sending written messages. Hearing another person's voice and being able to talk to him are more personal experiences than written exchanges; they are conducive to more intimacy. Although the self-disclosure that subjects received dealt with the same themes, in one condition adjectives referred to the monetary value of things and people; in another condition the references were to liking and caring. These differences in content affected the content of subjects' self-disclosure, resulting in significantly more references to money than to love in the former condition, and significantly more references to love than to money in the latter condition. These findings provide some support for reciprocity in content as suggested by Foa and Foa (1974) in their theory of interpersonal exchange, described earlier.

A person who wants to develop a relationship with someone has to be sensitive to the characteristics of the other person, in terms of both how much he discloses and the content of his disclosures. This is not news for most of us, but research on self-disclosure is just beginning to demonstrate the varied influences that determine the consequences of different kinds of self-disclosure. The surrounding circumstances must also be important in determining what kinds of information about the self, and at what point in time, are appropriate to communicate.

Does self-disclosure, as Altman and Taylor (1973) suggested, usually follow a time course? Does the degree of intimacy of information that people confide to one another progressively increase? Taylor *et al.* (1969) found that when a confederate and a subject talked to each other in four 45-minute interaction periods, the greatest intimacy occurred during the first period, although there was an additional, gradual increase in intimacy during the rest of the sessions. In different treatment groups the confederate responded in different ways to the subject's self-disclosures, but this time course was found regardless of the nature of the response: continuous positive, early negative later positive, early positive later negative, and continuous negative. The apparent task of the participants to disclose information about themselves might have resulted in more intimate early disclosures. Perhaps this itself interfered with later intimacy. Moreover, the laboratory setting and the necessarily limited interest by the confederate to form a genuine relationship would have constraining effects.

What can one reasonably expect to happen to potential relationships among people after early intimacy? An early, high degree of self-disclosure by a person might be expected to lead to some anxiety on his part, to worry about the exploitation of the information by others and about negative evaluation by them. Mutual trust in one another's benevolence and belief in one's acceptance by another person might have to be built up over some period of time. Our culture has strongly moved in the last decade in the direction of speedy intimacy, instantaneous high levels of self-disclosure. I wonder how frequently participants in sensitivity-training groups and other group experiences that lead to high degrees of self-disclosure follow up the group experience by continued relationships. My observations and experience suggest that among strangers very high levels of instantaneous intimacy are possible, arising out of openness and willingness to communicate following some exchange of cues that it is acceptable and desirable to do so. However, the probability of continuing a relationship is low. Rubin (1973) suggests that intimate disclosures generated under circumstances that have an inherent rule for high levels of self-disclosure, such as sensitivity-training groups, might not lead to later relationships because self-disclosure under such circumstances involves less risk, represents less investment in the relationship with other people, and may be attributed to conformity rather than trust and affection.

Feelings of intimacy might later be followed by regret and concern. In other cases they may be remembered as good experiences, but they may not be followed up because the level of intimacy that was reached was not based on a solid foundation of familiarity, making it difficult for the participants to know where to resume. In still other cases, despite the intimacy reached, which was made possible by new cultural values and personal skills, important differences between people interfere with the development of the relationship. In other words, in our current culture a high level of self-disclosure might come about over a short time span, but it will not necessarily lead to a continued relationship. Gradual increase in intimate self-disclosure may be more likely to lead to feelings of trust, mutual acceptance, and liking, feelings necessary for the formation of long-term relationships. However, much of this is speculative; given the same opportunities for further contact, a high degree of early self-exposure that is *reciprocal* in nature may be more likely to lead to a continued relationship than low degrees of early self-exposure. The reciprocal nature of voluntary self-disclosure, even if it happens fast, may decrease the anxiety created by revealing oneself to a relative stranger; after all, the participants took the same risks. This may be even more likely if people find, through the content of what they reveal, that they are similar to each other. Still, expectations created by very early intimate self-disclosure may be difficult to fulfill.

Part of the reason for this may lie in the imbalance created by intimate knowledge in some realms, and vast areas of ignorance in others. There are certain needs and desires that people cannot communicate in early intimate self-disclosure. A man probably cannot tell a woman that she is exactly his type, that she may be the kind of person he has long been looking for, that he would like to make love to her, and that doing so would ease his great loneliness. If he tells her this soon after meeting her, the chances of a long-term relationship seem limited. We all know that in early communications among people many things are unexpressed. Gradual intimacy and openness in self-disclosures may be more conducive for people to make positive attributions about each other's motives and intentions.

Gradual increase in intimate self-disclosure seems no guarantee of mutual liking. Taylor (1968) administered self-disclosure questionnaires to freshmen roommates after they had known each other for 1, 3, 6, 9, and 13 weeks. In about half the roommate pairs, both were high revealers; in the other half, both were low revealers. As one would expect, there was fast communication about nonintimate information, and a slow gradual increase in disclosure of intimate information for both types of pairs. There was no difference in liking by members for each other between the two types. Surprisingly, however, pairs in both groups showed a significant *decrease* in liking for each other over time; this happened to a more pronounced degree between high revealers. Cosby (1973) suggests that perhaps this happened not because familiarity breeds contempt, but because randomly chosen dyads might not be comfortable enough with each other to be able to tolerate a high degree of prolonged self-disclosure. However, as noted before, Newcomb's attitudinally "incompatible" pairs of students who were assigned to live together developed liking for each other. Perhaps the freshmen who lived in dormitories had more alternative relationships available to them than Newcomb's transfer students in the rooming house did.

If two people live together for a fairly long time, it seems almost inevitable that they will communicate to each other intimate information about themselves. Their actions say much about their personality, and they might often want to put their actions into perspective by verbally providing information about themselves. Moreover, the ups and downs of mood, joys and sorrows, often seek expression, and at least some of the time a roommate is a convenient although not always preferred outlet for them. What kinds of self-disclosure, communicated in what manner by what kinds of individuals, will lead to positive relationships, to the development of friendship? What other parameters of self-disclosure and interactive style are involved in the development and maintenance of relationships? In an attempt to achieve control over treatment variables, most studies provided single opportunities for subjects to exchange information with invisible strangers, so these studies provide no information that would help to answer such questions.

Moreover, considering self-disclosure without the characteristics of self-disclosing individuals necessarily puts limitations on the knowledge that will be gained. Similarities between people, complementarities, and certain types of diversities might be important determinants of the willingness for intimate self-disclosure and of its consequences. Finally, when we are dealing with long-term extensive relationships, such as roommates have, the ability to resolve conflicts, responsiveness to another's need, and many other conditions enter into determining the meaning and consequences of self-disclosure and into developing mutual liking. The findings that have been reviewed provide only minimal knowledge about the role of self-disclosure in the development or maintenance of friendly, positive, affectionate relationships.

Self-disclosure is not even related in any simple fashion to the satisfaction of people in marriage. Although greater satisfaction in marriage is reported by males as a function of their ability to disclose worries and anxieties to their partners, females reported no relationship between satisfaction and self-disclosure (Katz *et al.*, 1973). Levinger and Senn (1967) found that greater reported self-disclosure by marriage partners was related to greater satisfaction, but the relationship was high only for the expression of positive feelings and satisfaction. It should not be too surprising that people might have trouble tolerating the frequent expression of negative feelings. In a study by Shapiro and Swenson (1969), no relationship was found between satisfaction and self-disclosure.

The research and its review here have been guided by assumptions about the positive effects of self-disclosure. However, too much self-disclosure, as well as the expression of certain feelings, including negative or conflict-filled feelings about the relationship with the recipient of the self-disclosure, might lead to difficulties. As some of the earlier discussion suggested, the same might be true of the early expression of positive feelings, or of any feelings of great intimacy that are not immediately reciprocated, because they may create a feeling of indebtedness in the recipient. Cozby (1973) quotes Simmel (1964) as saying that retaining certain kinds of information may be important because privacy contributes to a sense of individuality, the loss of which might be detrimental to the self and as a consequence detrimental to the relationship in which individuality has been lost. Simmel also suggests that marital difficulties may result from too much self-disclosure, leading partners to take each other for granted in a matter-of-fact way, creating boredom.

Principles of Interaction
in Extended Relationships

What are the principles that guide interaction in long-term relationships? Empirical information is minimal. We know that similarity, liking, attraction, and prior helpfulness by another person all increase positive behavior, but this generalization is known to apply mainly to people who do not as yet have a relationship, to those who do not know or are just beginning to know each other. Reciprocity is a powerful principle of human interaction, but it guides the behavior of friends and of people characterized by a positive relationship in a different, at least less immediate, manner than of strangers or those characterized by a less positive relationship. Much of what we can say about determinants of interaction in long-term relationships, whether positive or negative, is based on research of tangential relevance, or is primarily theoretical in nature.

Studies already reviewed in this chapter showed more intimacy in close friends' reports of communications with each other (Rubin & Shenker, 1978) and in spouses' actual communications with each other in a laboratory setting (Morton, 1978) than between less close friends or strangers. Friends were found to equalize rewards and to attribute less competitive intent to each other (Morgan & Sawyer, 1978). These studies indicate more trust and sharing in close relationships—without which close relationships could not be called close—as well as more positive behavior.

The examination of how interaction is affected by the characteristics of individuals in relationships is just beginning. Peplau (1976) found that women who were identified as traditional in their sex-role attitudes performed less well in competing against their boyfriends than when they worked with them: The reverse was true of nontraditional women. Pleck (1976) found that men who indicated on a paper and pencil measure that they were threatened by competence in women performed better when competing against their dates, apparently trying harder to win, whereas men who did not report feeling threatened performed equally well whether they were competing with them or not. Varied characteristics of a person, the type of relationship, the specific rules of the relationship within a dyad, and the characteristics of the other person can all be expected to strongly affect both interactive behavior and the feelings and experiences of people in extended relationships.

Birchler, Weiss, and Vincent (1975) had married couples and strangers interact in the laboratory. Some couples had a difficult, distressed relationship. Distressed couples reinforced each other less positively, and more negatively, than nondistressed couples. However, both groups less frequently reinforced their spouses positively and more frequently reinforced them negatively than they reinforced strangers. This difference was not quite as large for distressed as it was for nondistressed couples. The nature of the interaction was partly free conversation, partly problem solving. The task was to resolve disagreement about who was responsible, a husband or a wife, for conflicts described in vignettes of typical marital situations. Participants were also asked to record aspects of their daily interactions. Distressed couples reported more exchanges that were displeasing and fewer that were pleasing than nondistressed ones, and engaged in fewer activities together.

Of special interest here is the lesser positivity of interaction between married couples, regardless of type, than between members of these couples and strangers. The authors noted that the responses to strangers were trait-like, that strangers were treated similarly. Behavior toward the spouse did not predict behavior toward strangers. "[Because] familiarity with another person may entail less of a demand to emit positive instrumental behavior (i.e., ingratiating or acquaintanceship behaviors), we are left with the problem of how to account for the increased nonfacilitative behaviors exchanged between spouses relative to strangers [Birchler *et al.,* 1975, p. 358]." These findings raise the question of whether there are progressive deteriorative processes associated with long-term, intimate, two-person relationships.

Gottman, Notarius, Markman, Bank, and Yoppi (1976) had distressed and nondistressed couples talk to each other on a "talk table." Only one person could talk at a time. Each person noted, when he or she finished, the intended impact of what had been said. The other person noted, before he or she started to talk, the perceived impact of what the other said. Distressed and nondistressed couples did not differ in the positivity or negativity of what they intended to communicate. For nondistressed couples, what they said was perceived as they intended; for distressed couples it was perceived more negatively. The authors interpreted this as support for a communication deficit explanation of marital distress.

The authors reason that in many research projects reciprocity in interactions is inadequately evaluated. The overall behavior of one kind or another by one person is related to behavior directed at that person. However, a strong relationship may not demonstrate a contingency in the actions of the interacting persons; it may only demonstrate that different pairs of individuals are characterized by higher or lower base rates of a certain activity. Although the authors are right, both types of relationships are important. Using a contingency analysis, Gottman *et al.* found little reciprocity in the behavior of either distressed or nondistressed couples. They propose that the data suggest a "bank account" rather than a reciprocity model of interaction in nondistressed marriages. In contrast to distressed marriages, there are more positive "deposits" than negative "withdrawals" in nondistressed marriages. Behavior is not contingent on the immediately preceding behavior of the spouse. They suggest that it may be precisely the lack of reciprocity in the context of high positive exchange that characterizes stable positive relationships. Certainly under such conditions retaliation and the possibility of a resulting cycle of negative emotions and actions are less likely to occur. As I noted, however, the perception of overall reciprocity, and thus equity, in the relationship is probably important.

The deterioration of long-term relationships has been suggested by the findings of both Taylor (1968) that freshman roommates came to like each other less over time and Birchler *et al.* (1975). In the former case the decline in mutual liking may be explained by the lack of selection by roommates of each other, by their youth and the insufficient skills in conflict resolution attendant upon youth. Certain kinds of deterioration in the relationship between marriage partners may be explained on an attributional basis. Rubin (1973) quotes Marie, Countess of Champagne: "Love cannot exert its powers between two people who are married to each other. For lovers give each other everything freely, under no compulsion of necessity, but married people are in duty bound to give in to each other's desires and deny to each other nothing [p. 188]." If these lines correctly characterize the kind of negative attributions, in terms of compulsion rather than positive intention, that married people make about each other's positive acts, the earlier discussion about perceived intent would support a deterioration in the relationship.

People in close relationships may frequently engage in less positive behavior, at least of a superficial kind, than acquaintances or strangers. As long as everything goes well in a relationship, partners may live by the rules of interactions, by the system they developed to guide the relationship, probably in an automatic fashion. They may also drift from the rules of the system. They may focus their attention outside the relationship, seeking satisfaction from novel and interesting relationships and activities, sometimes neglecting each others' needs. When, however, something calls attention to problems and issues in the relationship—a partner not sharing (e.g., the research findings with children), or expressing hurt and anger—in a basically positive relationship the other may then attempt to reestablish the positive exchange relationship that the rules probably prescribe.

Do certain types of long-term relationships usually deteriorate? Perhaps the promise of such relationships is greater than the fulfillment they actually bring. What conditions might lead to the kind of long-term relationships that fulfill our hopes? Do many long-term relationships deteriorate in certain aspects but continue to satisfy important needs and to provide important satisfactions?

A Model of Interpersonal Relationships

An extensive model of interpersonal interaction has been proposed by Carson (1969). This model is consistent with varied views that I expressed. It primarily relies on exchange conceptions. Brown (1965) derived, from a review of varied literature, two basic dimensions of human interaction: status and sociability. Carson extended Brown's analysis by considering factorial studies of interrelationships among social behaviors, and proposed that interpersonal behavior lends itself to characterization in terms of dominance versus submission (corresponding to status) and love versus hate (corresponding to sociability). Carson suggests that, taking these two dimensions as axes, a taxonomy of human behavior can be provided in the form of a circumplex model. In such a model dimensions of behavior are arranged in a circle. The most similar categories are next to each other, and the least similar are furthest away from each other, at the opposite points of the circle. Carson suggests that certain circumplex arrangements provide an empirically accurate taxonomy and accurate representation of the relatedness of interactive behavior. He expresses a preference for the circumplex model proposed by Leary (1957). This model uses the same two dimensions advocated by Carson and describes 16 distinctive, behaviorally defined segments: managerial–autocratic behavior; responsible–hypernormal behavior; cooperative–over-conventional behavior; docile–dependent behavior; self-effacing–masochistic behavior; rebellious–distrustful behavior; aggressive–sadistic behavior; competitive–narcissistic behavior.

A basic assumption of the model is that, independently of the costs and rewards of an interaction, complementarity in behavior along the basic dimensions is rewarding. Certain types of behaviors are hoped for and expected by actors to elicit certain types of complementary responses. Complementarity is rewarding partly because it protects people and provides feelings of security and partly because it helps the execution of plans and satisfies needs. Noncomplementarity results in the disruption of plans and produces anxiety and discomfort. Carson's conception of complementarity is different from mine as used in this book. "Generally speaking, complementarity occurs on the basis of reciprocity in respect to the dominance–submission axis (dominance tends to induce submission, and vice versa), and on the basis of correspondence in respect to the hate–love axis (hate induces hate, and love induces love) [Carson, 1969, p. 112]." If Carson's statement is translated into my terminology, dominance–submission is complementary, and love–hate is reciprocal. Moreover, it seems likely that dominance, aggression, and hostility can be intended to produce expressions of love and acceptance, that sometimes people hope to bring about such reactions, presumably mostly without success.

Carson's theorizing suggests that similar principles of interaction apply both in the initial and in the later stages of relationships. As people enter interpersonal interactions they examine the opportunities that are available to satisfy current needs. Then they engage in goal-directed behavior to satisfy certain needs, their actions leading to consummatory behavior, the enjoyment of the goal. People use plans that guide them in sampling the available outcomes from the standpoint of their currently salient motivation, and they execute plans to bring about selected outcomes. Good judgment seems important in selecting needs to be satisfied, since what is selected affects the chances that the other person's needs will also be satisfied. Clearly this analysis, although it does not employ the concepts of personal goals, activation of goals, competence, and so on, is consistent with the analysis of the determinants of prosocial behavior that I have presented (Chapter 2).

As people enter into interpersonal interactions they may want to maximize their own outcomes. This, however, entails the chance of negative outcomes if the other person does not cooperate. People are motivated to maximize their positive outcomes but also to avoid negative ones. In order to avoid maximum losses that may result from noncooperation, people will usually attempt not to maximize their own outcomes but to reach a maximum joint outcome. The outcomes of interacting individuals will then be relatively correspondent, not discrepant. Carson's model does not focus on relationships in which people so strongly identify with each other that they experience their needs, desires, and goals as identical—which may be rare and perhaps most frequently found as a temporary state of affairs, when, for example, people are in love, or circumstances temporarily create intense identification.

This model suggests that people will act on the basis of enlightened self-interest, in the spirit of one of the philosophical positions discussed in Chapter 1, and represented in some aspects of exchange theory. If the findings of research on cooperation in games are in any way indicative of other forms of human interactions, people may frequently have to insist that they get their share, that their partner consider their needs and provide them with satisfaction, if they are not to be exploited. Presumably, exploitation by one person of another at an early point in time will make it probable that the other person discontinues the relationship. Once a continuing relationship has developed and provides certain satisfactions for both partners, exploitation may have to be prevented by communication, threat of retaliation, and occasional retaliation in action.

An interesting aspect of Carson's model is that if a person's need for submission is to be satisfied, that person has to interact with someone who is willing to be dominant, preferably with someone who finds dominance satisfying. In particular interactions, whether temporary or lasting, hostile behavior by one partner may be satisfying to the other partner because it is complementary to the latter's interactive style. Friendly, positive behavior may be aversive and may lead to the discontinuing of the interaction or the relationship. Certain seemingly undesirable interactions can be satisfying, but Carson implies that a continued history of such interactive patterns can often lead to serious problems and disordered relationships.

A crucial aspect of Carson's model is his concept of complementarity. A great deal of the research that has been reviewed in Chapters 8 and 9 provides evidence of reciprocity, which is Carson's conception of complementarity along the love–hate dimension. However, very little evidence of what I consider as complementarity (along the submission–dominance dimension) exists. Moreover, even if people do behave in a complementary manner in that realm, are submissive reactions to dominant partners necessarily satisfying, or do people often submit in order to avoid serious conflict?

Carson suggests that the most basic personality characteristic of people is their favored interpersonal style, their tendency to engage in certain types of interpersonal behavior. Complementarity to one's interpersonal style is important for a person's sense of security. Interpersonal security is viewed in terms of the cue properties of the other person's behavior, "the maintenance of uninterrupted sequences of planned behavior; and the maintenance of congruent relations among one's self-concept, one's own behavior (as perceived) and the behavior of the other person (again, as perceived) [Carson, 1969, p. 144]." Some people may enter into interactions with others with a hostile-dominant interpersonal style (one of the subcategories that results from a circumplex model of interpersonal behavior that is derived from the two basic dimensions). They would then prefer a different kind of reaction, given preference for complementarity, than someone who enters with a friendly-dominant stance. One may begin to understand the great complexity of human interactions given the varied behavioral styles that are implied by the circumplex model, complementarity, and the fact that human interactions have the character of mixed-motive games. Any move may lead to cooperation, and thus to personal gain. Alternatively, noncomplementary reactions may follow (that is, competition) with a resulting loss for the actor. Consequently, people continuously monitor each other's reactions to determine the likelihood that some action that may lead to the satisfaction of one of their salient motives will result in a cooperative and thus gainful response, or in a competitive one with the attendant loss.

Carson's is a complex, carefully developed model of the principles and regularities of human interaction. Unfortunately, it is mainly a speculative model, derived from some research data and from Carson's clinical experience. The model implies that interpersonal behavior that is prosocial in the sense that it satisfies other people's needs, goals, and desires, may have to vary substantially from interaction to interaction. A prosocial person would have to be sensitive to the needs of the other person, capable of taking their role and accurately assessing their interpersonal style and current needs, and able to select needs of his own for satisfaction that would also contribute to the maximum possible satisfaction of the other's needs. A prosocial person would show interpersonal acuity; such a person would be cooperative, willing to engage in some self-sacrifice in that the personal need selected for satisfaction might not be the most salient or important one. Sometimes in order to behave prosocially complete self-sacrifice is necessary; only by interacting in some manner that is aversive for a person could another gain satisfaction. Presumably, people would prefer to avoid extended relationships with others who have such a basically noncomplementary interpersonal style that no joint satisfaction is possible.

Summary and Conclusions:
The Determinants of Positive Behavior

chapter 10

Limitations of Our Knowledge: Future Goals

Substantial knowledge about positive social behavior and positive morality has accumulated during the last decade. Nonetheless, our knowledge is as yet limited, and important tasks in theory and research lie ahead.

Many stimulus conditions that affect positive behavior have been identified, but the interrelationship among their influences is relatively unexplored. For example, in my view the research findings strongly suggest that conditions that focus responsibility on a person for another person's welfare, whether they are external or internal (personal values), enhance positive behavior. Greater costs of helping, in contrast, usually decrease positive behavior. But will greater costs decrease helping even when conditions focus the responsibility to help on a particular person? Although some limited evidence suggests that they will not (Morgan, 1978), we really do not know. Similarly, although we have reason to believe we know how some specific stimulus conditions affect psychological processes important to helping (feelings, thoughts, and subjective experiences, such as a feeling of responsibility for someone's welfare or devaluation of another person), we know little about how combinations of stimulus conditions affect them.

There are many indications of how we have not yet put our pieces of knowledge together. On the whole, we have *not attempted* to do so. The problem is partly definitional: Social psychologists think about situations, including the social influences exerted in them; personality psychologists

417

think about persons. Some people focus on helping among strangers; others study social exchange or intimacy but do not consider the principles guiding prosocial behavior among intimates as a relevant issue for them. Partly due to differentiation among domains, we do not know how the stimulus conditions and personality characteristics that have been found to relate to prosocial behaviors among strangers and the psychological processes that they give rise to are involved in exchange, cooperation, and other interactions among friends and other intimates. Do costs of helping have the same effects? Is it necessary for external conditions to focus responsibility on a person in order for him to help a friend, or is responsibility and even obligation inherent in the relationship? Whereas responsibility appears to be inherent in friendship, it certainly is not continuously experienced: What conditions make responsibility salient? Are they similar to or different from the conditions that give rise to a feeling of responsibility for a stranger's welfare?

Considering further what we do not know, the examination of most research shows both lack of knowledge and lack of conceptualization of how personality characteristics and stimulus conditions join together in guiding social behavior. Only the barest conceptualization of persons in situations can be found in research on positive behavior. Many psychologists frequently had as their primary goal the specification of universal principles of human functioning, but to omit the consideration of individual differences from our understanding of the principles of social behavior is to replace the psychology of the "empty" organism with a psychology of the nonexistent universal human being. Particularly in a culture as heterogeneous as ours, the same set of environmental conditions will usually give rise to different psychological experiences in different persons and lead to different behavior—or sometimes to the same behavior for different reasons.

The disregard of persons in the study of prosocial behavior has been made easier by another grave deficiency: the lack of measurement of psychological processes that presumably result from specifiable environmental conditions (and personal characteristics). The many psychological processes that were discussed in this book—including interpretations of events, the experience of responsibility, empathy, identification with another person, guilt, and the expectation of reciprocity—have been regarded as the most direct influences on people's behavior. Although we clearly recognize, then, the importance of internal cognitive and affective experiences, we usually make no attempts (or at best cursory attempts) to measure them. They remain hypothetical constructs seemingly universally applicable to everybody who is exposed to certain environmental conditions. We have to make serious attempts, using direct measurement, to verify our hypotheses about private, subjective experiences or psychological processes that presumably guide behavior. In the course of doing so, the significance of individual differences—as we realize that identical environmental conditions give rise to different cognitions and affects—will come to be highlighted. I have repeatedly suggested procedures for such measurement, essentially consisting of the replication of experimental designs with reports of varied thoughts and feelings, not behavior, as the dependent variables.

Another aspect of our task of pulling together the pieces of knowledge we have acquired into larger (and hopefully more accurate) wholes is to consider the joint influence of varied psychological processes. Many theoretical efforts in the domain of prosocial behavior and related areas implied the special significance of one concept, and the psychological process represented by that concept, as the basis of prosocial behavior. For example, equity has been presented as the determinant of many different types of social behavior, including prosocial behavior (Berkowitz & Walster, 1976; Walster *et al.*, 1970, 1973, 1978; Walster & Piliavin, 1972; Walster & Walster, 1975). Equity seems to be an important social norm and, for many people, an important personal norm as well. However, substantial individual differences certainly exist in the extent to which maintaining or restoring equity for other people as well as the self is an important value. Moreover, equity is only one of many norms, values, and beliefs that potentially exert influence. The extent to which equity is important for a person and the domain in which it is important, the relationship between equity and other personal values and norms, the relevance of equity in a person's relationship with a potential object of positive behavior, and the specific conditions in the environment that make equity considerations active influences on behavior are all important to consider.

The same considerations apply to the understanding of empathy, reciprocity, belief in a just world, and other concepts and psychological processes regarded as determinants of prosocial behavior. Who are more or less concerned with the world as a just place? In what relationship to other characteristics of individuals that potentially exert influence on prosocial (and/or other social) behavior does this concern stand? What conditions in the environment activate concerns for a just world, and how does the interrelationship among various potential influences on prosocial behavior change under varied external (and internal) conditions? Theories focusing on single processes have been useful; however, we must begin to build broader theories that specify the interrelationship among varied personality characteristics and environmental influences, the psychological processes that they lead to, and the consequences on behavior.

Prosocial behavior is multidetermined, and the determinants stand in dynamic, flexible relationship to each other. No major discoveries are likely to suddenly enhance our understanding of positive social behavior; instead, integration is now an essential task; it is a source of increased knowledge, and theoretical conceptions that are integrative and will guide new research are necessary.

In Chapter 2 I suggested a theoretical model that specifies personal characteristics that may promote prosocial behavior as well as how they affect behavior as a function of environmental conditions, in conjunction with other personal characteristics (such as personal goals unrelated to positive behavior, which may frequently conflict with a prosocial motivation and may sometimes support a prosocial motivation). Although I have not elaborated on the psychological processes that arise when prosocial goals are activated, I suggested that, depending on the nature of the cognitive network that characterized a person's prosocial goal, a person either *desires* to help and/or benefit another and experiences empathy, or a feeling of *obligation* without specific concern for another person's welfare may be active (see also Staub, 1979). I specified varied personal characteristics, such as competencies and perceptual orientations, that are also important in influencing prosocial conduct. I suggested that the important organizers of the interrelationships among the potential influences on prosocial behavior are the person's motives, his or her personal goals.

Either in Chapter 2 or in later chapters the relationships to the model of temporary states, of the use of justifications, and of other external conditions or psychological states that appear to affect positive conduct have been at least briefly discussed. All these influences can be embodied in the model: either as aspects of cognitive networks defining personal goals, or as values and norms that specify the range of applicability of a particular goal; and either as activators of prosocial or other self-related goals, or as conditions that may indirectly affect the likelihood that different goals would be activated (like certain temporary states). I believe that hedonic balancing is a potentially important concept because it focuses on the affective and subjective rather than on the rational and objective evaluation of inputs and outcomes in considering the self–other relationship, as well as on global considerations based on well-being rather than on the input and outcome values of specific acts at specific times, which are often irrelevant. Hedonic balancing is also important in that it can both affect the likelihood that prosocial or self-related goals are activated and, when a prosocial goal is activated, may affect the amount of help or the magnitude of sacrifice for another person. Other influences enter into the model, such as levels of competence or temporary feelings of competence. Finally, varied influences that have been identified affect perceptual orientation at a particular time, which is important since perception of an event, speed of judgment of its meaning, and how it is interpreted exert strong influences on how other personal characteristics get involved and how their situational activators are processed.

I strongly believe that we need a model of social behavior that is descriptive and also dynamic in that it considers the changing relationships among components. The notion that interrelationships change among components of a theoretical model that describes people reflects reality but creates problems. If at least a partially hierarchical organization among the components can be specified, such changes become more comprehensible and manageable. In the model I described, personal goals are organizers of the interrelationship among other personal characteristics in that they affect perceptual tendencies, are likely to lead to the development of some competencies related to their execution, and so on. In order for a theory of social behavior to be manageable, it should have, at least at the start, only a limited number of components. Such components or theoretical terms will ideally be abstract enough so that they have universal applicability over time and across cultures (Triandis, 1978) but concrete enough so that we can measure them and make predictions from them. I believe that personal goals and the other theoretical components of the model do have sufficient universality: The goals that people tend to possess may vary tremendously across cultures and over historical periods, and the degree of similarity between different persons' goals may vary across cultures, but it seems impossible to imagine a normally functioning human being (and probably even a psychologically malfunctioning one) without goals. At the same time, these concepts have sufficient concreteness so that they can be measured and predictions can be made from them.

Many research questions can be stated. Are most people characterized by general value orientations? Are there a few basic, specifiable value orientations in our culture (see Volume 2)? What is the relationship between such value orientations and personal goals: Do the former specify the latter? What is the relationship between general prosocial value orientations and specific values and beliefs such as equity, the just world, and others? Can the latter provide one type of index of the range of applicability of general motivational orientations? For example, valuing equity may lead people who have a strong prosocial orientation to be particularly sensitive to inequity that another person suffered but at the same time less concerned with suffering that a person "deserved" (i.e., brought upon himself or herself). Another person who values equity but has less prosocial orientation may be primarily concerned with inequity to the self.

Can the model I presented contribute to our understanding of social behavior? More importantly, can we measure general motivational dispositions and make predictions from these about behavior? Will our predictions improve if we consider varied personal goals and the activating potential of a situation for these goals? If we classify individuals on the basis of both the strength of their prosocial motive and a specific value or norm and expose them to situations that vary in their activating potential for both, will the accuracy of our prediction of behavior improve? Will it further improve if we consider relevant competencies? I believe the answers to these questions are in the affirmative.

At least two (usually more) major problems plagued past theories that attempted to describe the functioning of individuals in some detail. First, some theories become idiographic in nature because they attempted to specify so many relevant personal characteristics of individuals that each person, when appropriately described by the elements of the theory, was unique.

Surely every person has a unique combination of characteristics, but it should be possible to test a theory by focusing on a subset of seemingly important variables that are derived from a limited number of theoretical concepts. Doing so makes it possible to develop measuring instruments and to attempt behavioral predictions. To test the theoretical model I presented in Chapter 2 with greater specificity than was done in the studies I described there, I have been developing measures of three personal goals, prosocial, achievement, and approval, as well as measures of the activating potential of situations for these personal goals. A second problem with many theories that attempted to specify interrelationships among varied influences has been the lack of a concentrated effort to test them. The difficulties of testing —the demands for testable conceptualizations and hypotheses, the need for measurement devices, the extent of effort necessary—have to be overcome.

How Does Positive Behavior (Or Its Absence) Come About?

Varied personal characteristics and environmental conditions give rise to a flow of cognitions that determine a person's continued perception and appraisal of events, the emotional reactions that arise, and the sequence of actions that a person will engage in. Situations and personality exert continued influence from the moment a stimulus for help appears until it is dealt with in some manner. I will briefly review and summarize research findings and the accompanying analysis in this book by examining the nature of this influence and the resulting flow of cognitions.

A stimulus for help might be external and can be summarily dealt with by denial and by other perceptual and cognitive processes that make a person not even notice the stimulus or deny its significance as a stimulus. An internal stimulus—a thought, an image, an internal representation of someone's need or of some injustice—can also be dealt with in this manner, although there must be some prosocial motivation already present for the occurrence of such an internally produced stimulus. Thus, to deny its existence may be difficult, and to deny its significance may require more psychological "work."

Such a stimulus, whether external or internal, if noticed, must be processed. If any significance is attributed to it, then its meaning has to be further assessed. Varied personality and situational factors will affect even this initial step of noticing a stimulus for help and making a decision that it has significance, of whatever kind. The next step is to decide that there is some need or deficiency that exists on someone's part and that, because of that or for some other reasons, action is required to enhance others' welfare. One can proceed and elaborate the further steps of decision making that Latané and Darley (1970) and Schwartz (1977) as well as others have posited: a person deciding that a need for help exists, assuming (or denying) a responsibility to act, deciding to take action, and then actually proceeding to do so. The decision steps can be primarily cognitive or primarily emotional; usually they are both. It is the emotional quality of the experience, at each step in the decision making, that is likely to be primarily influential in determining what judgments or decisions are arrived at subsequently.

Decision making can be spontaneous: A "decision" can be made seemingly automatically, without decisional work. This is likely to happen when no conflict exists at particular points in decision making. Furthermore, the sequence of a person's perception of events, the interpretation of them, and the motivational push that may develop can form an uninterrupted flow of thoughts and feelings, together with the action that results. Separating this flow into units (e.g., perception, interpretation, assumption of responsibility, decision to take action, and taking action) is useful to enhance our understanding, but this division is not necessarily inherent in the phenomenon itself. Moreover, when the decisional work is short-circuited, a person may move directly from perception to action. This is likely to happen with professional helpers, such as firemen, whose job prescription and past experience may lead to the short-circuiting of intervening steps, but this is also likely to occur to persons in certain life situations that lead to spontaneous helping (see Chapter 3).

I am using the word "decision" in an unconventional way. There may be no deliberate cognitive activity involved in making a particular "decision" or in reaching one of the decision points identified in the sequence. Nonetheless, discussing the flow of cognition and the self-regulation that this flow provides in the form of a decisional sequence is a convenient device. I shall attempt to give an informal picture of how variations along particular dimensions in stimulus situations and variations in personality give rise to the flow of thoughts and feelings that move a person along this decisional sequence toward or away from positive behavior.

First, I would like to remind the reader of some of the "conceptual" dimensions that seemed important when considering situations (Chapter 3, as well as other places). These dimensions can be regarded as examples of a "relational classification" of situations. This designation reflects the fact that the dimensions are important because they stand in a certain relationship to characteristics of individuals, so that the combination of the situation and the person will give rise to psychological processes that move persons toward or away from positive behavior. For example, some situations activate prosocial goals, others affect a feeling of competence.

The dimensions that seem important include variation in ambiguity of the need for help, the ease or difficulty of escape from a situation, the degree of someone's need and the degree of benefit that another person may gain from being helped, the extent to which circumstances focus responsibility for help on a particular person, the cost of helping, and the activating potential of the circumstances for other than prosocial personal goals. Social influence is important in relation to several of these dimensions: It can define the meaning of a situation, focus responsibility on a person, and so on. One aspect of the relational nature of these and other dimensions of situations can be noted if we recognize that whereas a particular event can be located on these dimensions in a relatively objective manner and its intensity defined in an objective way, the subjective location of the event on these dimensions will, to an important degree, be a function of the characteristics of the person involved. For example, a person with a strong prosocial goal may, under identical circumstances, perceive the degree of another's need as greater or may feel greater responsibility for help than a person with a weaker prosocial goal.

Two other variables that cannot be firmly regarded as either aspects of the person or of the situation appeared to have special significance: the temporary states of a potential helper and the relationship between the potential helper and the potential recipient(s) of positive behavior. Temporary states may modify the usual relationship between situations and personality in the activation of positive behavior: The customary activating power of situations is altered by them. Although I discussed in detail the reasons why moods, self-esteem, and self-concern affect prosocial behavior, important questions are as yet unanswered. For example, do varied moods have the same effects on people with strong and weak prosocial goals or on people whose characteristic mood or self-esteem is more or less positive? The hedonic-balancing hypothesis implied that a person's usual or characteristic mood or self-esteem is important. Furthermore, one could argue that a strong prosocial orientation makes people more impervious to the effects of mood. Or, on the contrary, people who are usually concerned about others' welfare may be highly sensitive to their own temporary states, particularly to those that affect the perceived relationship between the self and others. Thus, variations in feelings about the self (in relation to others) and in other-related moods such as social affinity or guilt that results from prior interactions with other people may have their strongest effect on people with a strong prosocial motivation.

Prior relationship between oneself and others can affect positive behavior for varied reasons. For one thing, perception of similarity, of likeness, and a resulting sense of identification are likely to activate prosocial goals. Second, many other personal goals may be involved in acting positively (or negatively) toward others as a function of one's relationship to them, including the desire for approval or for other types of self-gain. Finally, in relationships special norms develop that guide interactions.

Moving from Perception to Action

Let us consider the decisional process. The first step may be partly a function of accidental circumstances. Curiosity, the extent to which a person tends to scan the environment, or fear of novelty, in themselves unrelated to any tendencies toward or away from helping, probably affect the likelihood of noticing events. A person's current state of well-being and whether or not he or she is preoccupied with activities related to the satisfaction of some already activated goal seem important even at this initial step in the sequence. Frequently, however, the need for help or the opportunity for positive conduct present themselves in barely perceptible form. Sensitivity to others and an openness to others' experiences must be present in order to notice others' unexpressed hopes and desires or the distress and unhappiness that they do not directly express. We must realize, however, that such "openness" may arise out of an awareness that one can best get along in the world if one knows how others feel, what they want, and that others' needs and desires can be exploited. In contrast, some people may eagerly look for opportunities to help, either out of a desire to benefit others or as a way of approaching them, and may even imagine such opportunities when none exist. Finally, some strong stimuli may so impose themselves that noticing is unavoidable.

What takes place between noticing an event and becoming aware of another person's need? A person may try to escape from a situation without an attempt to accurately interpret its meaning, in fact in order to avoid the necessity of such interpretation and the involvement that it can lead to. Whether such escape is possible or not depends on many factors. Perceptual–interpretive tendencies are relevant as to whether a person tends to suspend judgment about the meaning of events or to make fast though possibly inaccurate judgments. A person's current mood and feelings may affect not only attention to the outside world but also the willingness to get involved. Some people may be motivated to avoid certain types of involvement; involvement can be a negative goal, freedom from involvement and from demands and obligations a positive goal. Personality characteristics can lead people either to efforts to find out more about an event that has been as yet minimally processed but may involve others' needs or to efforts to avoid further processing of information. I am implying that the definition of the meaning of an event is not an either/or matter but instead represents a continuum. The relevance of personal characteristics is a function of the nature of the situation. Sometimes even a split-second exposure can lead to a reasonably clear perception of another's need; other times, it does not. Sometimes a person may easily escape from a situation: Physically, escape is possible. However, some people are not able to rid themselves of another's need in that way: They continue to be preoccupied with it in thought and imagination. Thus, escape may be psychologically difficult. But other people can deny the reality of need or distress or the relevance of these to themselves. The existence of an ongoing relationship would also make it difficult to disengage and leave when another person appears distraught.

The interpretation of an event is further guided by a variety of influences. First, the nature of the stimulus and the surrounding conditions may make interpretations simple and straightforward or may demand the resolution of ambiguities. Social influence, important at every step in the decisional sequence, is particularly important here. Other people may offer or provide interpretations on all occasions, whether one witnesses an emergency or sits in front of the television and watches the evening news that brings the suffering of the victims of some natural disaster. Interpretations by others are frequently accepted. Sometimes, when these are blatantly in contrast with some perception (or underlying motive) of our own, they can lead to opposite interpretations by us.

The clarity and extensiveness of information provided by a situation, temporary moods, and prior familiarity with a person who needs help, together with role-taking capacity and current and characteristic motivation, are likely to affect both the content and the depth (e.g., empathic quality) of the interpretation. A person may take an external perspective, what was described as a "watch him" orientation, and note another's need without entering into it. One can superficially see that a friend is in need, a stranger injured. In contrast, the meaning of the event for the other and his or her resulting feelings may be considered and vicariously experienced. Clearly, interpretations can vary not only in how the meaning of events is assessed, but also in depth or quality. A person who is concerned about others' welfare and is free of self-concern and experiences a state of well-being is more likely to consider others' circumstances and feelings in depth.

Motivation is likely to be involved in interpretation at varied levels. A set of circumstances that require or provide the opportunity for positive behavior can be seen as an opportunity to benefit someone, as presenting a duty or obligation, as an opportunity to exercise virtue, as a social demand, as a pleasing opportunity to further a relationship, as an interference with one's ongoing affairs and thus a nuisance, as the opportunity to exercise and demonstrate one's competence and superiority, as an unpleasant demand that reduces one's freedom, as well as a combination of these and other perceptions. Motivation can also enter into the assessment of what an event actually is at an earlier point, before its personal meaning is considered.

What determines whether a person has a desire to benefit another or feels for another in need or feels a moral obligation to help? Clearly, such feelings or beliefs do not arise in a vacuum; the previous "decision making" steps, the prior flow of cognition and affect, exert guidance. Interpretation, both its content and depth, exerts a strong influence on the next decision-making step, whether a person feels that he or she ought to do, is responsible for doing, wants to do, or will do something.

Circumstances may allow for the diffusion of responsibility, but less so for people with a strong prosocial motivation. Circumstances may also focus responsibility on a person. Again, most of the previously noted dimensions of situations and personality enter. Some, such as the ambiguity of an event, may be less important, but not irrelevant, at this point. If an event has been ambiguous, a person may proceed along the decision-making sequence, but a high cost of helping or other barriers may make it more likely that the event is redefined at a later point and that a person develops justifications that minimize need or responsibility. Belief in one's capacity to influence events may be important here, since its absence would motivate people to minimize their involvement, their desire to help, and their feelings of responsibility. Temporary states, other motives, would enter as before.

In deciding whether or not one will take action and in actually taking action, some special elements may be noted. First, the temporary states of the potential helper will enter into hedonic balancing, into a decision as to the relative claims of the self and of the other person and as to whether, given one's own state, it is justified or demanded that one expend effort for another. As I noted, this balancing is not a purely rational calculation but has varied and important affective components. Slight positive and negative states of a potential helper may exert particularly strong influence.

The relationship, potential or actual, between the self and another is particularly important here. Perceiving another person positively makes association with that person desirable and probably also activates empathy and prosocial motives. Similarity of group membership and of opinions and beliefs may lead to positive perception and, even without that, to a sense of identity. When a prior relationship existed, its nature is important. If the contract (implicit or explicit) that evolved in the relationship demands the satisfaction of each other's needs both in order to maintain the relationship and in order to receive the same benefits and thus to maintain reciprocity, a person may be motivated to help another to reduce suffering, to satisfy hopes, desires, and aspirations, and to gain satisfactions. However, temporary feelings toward the other person in the relationship may be also important: Anger may be acted out in withholding help or inflicting harm (except, perhaps, when a desirable relationship already seems endangered).

The greater the cost of helping—the amount of sacrifice, the social courage required—the less likely may be a decision to help or actual helping. This is generally assumed to be true and is supported by the existing data. However, to satisfactorily consider the significance of costs the nature and type of connection that exists between the self and others, the degree of interrelatedness that people perceive to exist between another person or persons and themselves, must be considered. People may identify with others to such an extent that their own interests and those of the other person are considered identical. Under such (presumably rare) circumstances, will people still help less if the costs of helping are greater? More frequently, the interests of the self and of others are interrelated but not identical. Many people who sacrifice their self-interest for social justice may feel that they themselves will also benefit. In cooperative activities, the interests of the self and of others are intertwined. Thus, when people engage in important positive acts, costs frequently cannot be computed without an understanding of the perceived relationship between self and others and between costs and benefits for the self.

Material sacrifice, time, effort, emotional demands and involvement, and the sacrifice of gains that would have resulted if a person had continued with or engaged in other activities in place of prosocial acts may have different effects on behavior. With regard to the latter, by understanding what motives are in an activated state and the importance of these motives for particular individuals, we could make differential predictions about the influence of costs.

This relatively brief step-by-step discussion of the flow of thought and affect that moves people through somewhat arbitrarily delineated decision-making steps focused on a single act of helping. As I implied, a similar process is probably involved in further helping acts, even in an extensive, continuous relationship, but, as with a first act, the decision-making flow may be short-circuited when additional influences enter. The analysis just given aims to highlight my belief that many of the same influences are active at different points in this flow from having noticed to taking (or not taking) action, but in somewhat different ways. It also aims to highlight the need to understand not only the stimulus and the personality influences, which have been considered in this book in great detail, but also how they enter into self-guidance. An increasing amount of current research shows how attentional strategies (Mischel, 1976) and the manner in which people talk to themselves—the kind of verbal or imaginal and related affective self-guidance they exert (Masters & Santrock, 1976; Meichenbaum, 1974)—as well as the self-reinforcement with which they provide themselves (Bandura, 1977; Masters & Mokros, 1974) are important means of self-regulation. Since much of this research was developmentally oriented, it will be examined in Volume 2.

Many research possibilities are implied by the preceding analysis. As I already suggested, people can be exposed to varied stimuli and their reactions predicted on the basis of the location of the stimuli on varied dimensions (that specify their activating potential for goals and their influence in relation to other personality characteristics), the measurement of relevant personal goals, the creation of varied affective states, and so on. One can both measure personal goals and create varied motivational states by instructions —as Deutsch did (1962) in exploring cooperation following individualistic, competitive, and cooperative motivational orientations created by instructions.

Instead of simply starting with the presentation of a stimulus, participants can be moved to different points along the decisional sequence by both the manner in which the stimulus is presented and by communications to them about it by experimenters or other "bystanders." Their further progress along the decisional sequence and in behavior could be explored as a function of their personal goals, competencies, temporary states, and other influences.

The Influence of Cultures

Cultural influences have been discussed only to a limited extent in this book, mainly because of our limited knowledge in this domain. Obviously, however, variations in the nature and characteristics of cultures, in the broader context that surrounds people, exert extremely important influences on behavior and development.

We know that cultures vary in their emphasis on cooperation versus competition, in generosity among members, and in the degree of aggression that is exhibited among members (see Chapter 1 and Volume 2). Most of this knowledge is based on informal observation, not on systematic data that would specify the frequency of positive behavior in different domains and the origins of these differences among cultures. However, certain cultures may have strong prescriptive norms for positive conduct or may foster empathy or a positive orientation towards others in the culture. As a result, greater uniformity may exist in the behavior of people who live in that culture, and different psychological processes may be important in motivating positive behavior.

In varied cultures, different aspects of the environment that are relevant to positive behavior may be dominant; we can speak of a "dominance classification," in contrast to the relational classification discussed earlier. When an aspect of a culture is dominant, relatively uniform motives, values, or behavior may characterize members of the culture in relevant domains, at least in comparison to people in other cultures. The cross-cultural studies of cooperation and competition among children suggest that competition is a more dominant aspect of U.S. culture than of Mexican culture. However, this has been shown primarily in terms of more competitive behavior among U.S. than among Mexican children in game-like activities, and the aspects of these cultures that emphasize competition versus cooperation have not been explored. Nazi Germany propagated values and norms that dehumanized Jews (as well as other groups) and made their suffering not only acceptable, but even desirable. This became a dominant aspect of the culture, and not only did it result in mistreatment but, over time, one would also expect progressive decrease in the likelihood of empathic feelings toward Jews in such a culture.

Cultures may vary in the extent to which they emphasize common humanity with members of out-groups or even among individuals in the same culture. They may also vary in the extent to which they emphasize interrelatedness and mutuality among human beings and thereby foster concern for others, in contrast to presenting human relationships in terms of a morality of duty and obligations. In the former cultures empathy and in the latter cultures anticipation of guilt and concern about one's worth as a human being may be, respectively, dominant influences on positive behavior. At the other extreme, cultures may emphasize individuality, conflict, and antagonism. Classification of cultures in terms of dimensions that identify dominant characteristics relevant to positive behavior would be useful not only for understanding the manner in which prosocial behavior is determined in specific cultures but also for understanding the development of relevant individual characteristics.

It is currently fashionable to argue that cultures and historical periods create the psychological processes that characterize people. One implication of this view is that our understanding of psychological functioning is necessarily limited to a particular culture and historical period. As I implied earlier in this chapter in the discussion of the universality of personal goals, I believe that human beings have certain basic commonalities. For example, they have active nervous systems, self-concepts (that may vary in content and in the extent to which they are consciously held), and motives (the nature of which may vary). The development, learning, and growth of people takes place in terms of a limited number of principles, such as conditioning, modeling, identification, learning through the resolution of cognitive discrepancies, and others (these will be discussed in Volume 2). In particular cultures learning and the development of children may take place more by certain principles than by others as a result of influences on children that affect *how* they learn (not just what they learn). Constant surveillance and feedback may enhance, for example, the role of conditioning.

We need to bring about greater integration of developmental, social, and personality psychology. The theory of social behavior that I sketched attempts an integration of personality and social-situational influences. It provides both descriptive terms for persons and situations and an initial identification of principles by which the interrelationship among components change (see Chapter 2). Whether this or another one, we need a testable theory, both descriptive and dynamic, that specifies what people are like and how they function, the interrelationship of personality, environment, and behavior. We also need to develop a conception of personality and social development that ties in with such a theory, a conception that enables us to understand how persons become as they are, how situations develop their meaning. We need to identify how varied influences contribute to children's development and the principles by which learning and development take place in general and as a function of specific influences. The development of personality and social behavior, with emphasis on positive social behavior and morality, is examined in Volume 2.

Cultures may emphasize the importance of positive behavior (or the inhibition of negative behavior) in different realms and to different degrees and may create environments and contexts in which different potential motivators of prosocial behavior will be important. I believe that there are a limited set of identifiable influences that promote positive conduct. As our knowledge expands, the characteristic differences in personality, in related psychological processes, and in behavior that are produced by cultures or in different historical periods will be identifiable and, when a culture or period is sufficiently known, even predictable.

References

Adams, J. S. Inequity in social exchange. In L. Berkowitz (Ed.), *Advances in experimental social psychology*, Vol. 2. New York: Academic Press, 1965.

Aderman, D. Elation, depression and helping behavior. *Journal of Personality & Social Psychology*, 1972, *24*, 91.

Aderman, D., & Berkowitz, L. Observational set, empathy and helping. *Journal of Personality & Social Psychology*, 1970, *14*, 141–148.

Aderman, D., Brehm, S. S., & Katz, L. B. Empathic observation of an innocent victim: The just world revisited. *Journal of Personality & Social Psychology*, 1974, *29*, 342.

Ajzen, I. Effects of information on interpersonal attraction: Similarity versus affective value. *Journal of Personality & Social Psychology*, 1974, *29*, 374–380.

Allen, V. L., & Levine, J. M. Social support, dissent, and conformity. *Sociometry*, 1968, *31*, 138–149.

Allen, V. L., & Wilder, D. A. Categorization, belief similarity and intergroup discrimination. *Journal of Personality & Social Psychology*, 1975, *32*, 971–977.

Allport, G. W. *Pattern and growth in personality*. New York: Holt, 1961.

Allport, G. W., & Ross, J. M. Personal religious orientation and prejudice. *Journal of Personality & Social Psychology*, 1967, *5*, 432–443.

Almond, G., & Verba, S. *The civic culture*. Princeton: Princeton University Press, 1963.

Altman, I. Effects of cooperative response acquisition on social behavior during free-play. *Journal of Experimental Child Psychology*, 1971, *12*, 387–395.

Altman, I. Some perspectives on the study of man–environment phenomena. *Representative Research in Social Psychology*, 1973, *4*, 109–126.

Altman, I., & Taylor, D. A. *Social penetration: The development of interpersonal relationships*. New York: Holt, 1973.

Anchor, K., & Cross, H. Maladaptive aggression, moral perspective, and the socialization process. *Journal of Personality & Social Psychology*, 1974, *30*, 163–168.

Ardrey, R. *African genesis*. New York: Antheum, 1961.

Argyle, M., & Kendon, A. The experimental analysis of social performance. In L. Berkowitz (Ed.), *Advances in experimental social psychology,* Vol. 3. New York: Academic Press, 1967.

Arnold, M. *Emotion and personality.* New York: Columbia University Press, 1960.

Aronfreed, J. Moral behavior and sex identity. In D. R. Miller & G. E. Swanson *et al.* (Eds.), *Inner conflict and defense.* New York: Holt, 1960.

Aronfreed, J. *Conduct and conscience.* New York. Academic Press, 1968.

Aronfreed, J. Moral development from the standpoint of a general psychological theory. In T. Lickona (Ed.), *Moral development and behavior.* New York: Holt, 1976.

Aronson, E., & Linder, D. Gain and loss of esteem as determinants of interpersonal attractiveness. *Journal of Experimental & Social Psychology,* 1965, *1,* 156–171.

Aronson, S. R. A comparison of cognitive vs. focused-activities techniques in sensitivity group training. Unpublished doctoral dissertation, University of Connecticut, 1970.

Asch, S. E. Effects of group pressure upon the modification and distortion of judgments. In H. Guetzkow (Ed.), *Groups, leadership and men.* Pittsburgh: Carnegie Press, 1951.

Asch, S. E. *Social psychology.* Englewood Cliffs, New Jersey: Prentice-Hall, 1952.

Ashton, N. L., & Severy, L. J. Arousal and costs in bystander intervention. *Personality and Social Psychological Bulletin,* 1976, *2,* 268–272.

Averill, J. Unpublished data. University of Massachusetts, 1977.

Averill, J. Emotion, mood and personality. In E. Staub (Ed.), *Personality: Basic issues and current research.* Englewood Cliffs, New Jersey: Prentice-Hall, 1979. (In press)

Azrin, N., & Lindsley, O. The reinforcement of cooperation between children. *Journal of Abnormal Social Psychology,* 1956, *52,* 100–102.

Bandura, A. *Principles of behavior modification.* New York: Holt, 1969.

Bandura, A. *Social learning theory.* New York: General Learning Press, 1971.

Bandura, A. *Aggression: A social learning analysis.* Englewood Cliffs, New Jersey: Prentice-Hall, 1973.

Bandura, A. *Social learning theory.* Englewood Cliffs, New Jersey: Prentice-Hall, 1977.

Bandura, A. & Rosenthal, T. L. Vicarious classical conditioning as a function of arousal level. *Journal of Personality & Social Psychology,* 1966, *3,* 54–62.

Bandura, A., Underwood, B., & Fromson, M. E. Disinhibition of aggression through diffusion of responsibility and dehumanization of victims. *Journal of Research in Personality,* 1975, *9,* 253–269.

Bandura, A., & Walters, R. *Social learning and personality development.* New York: Holt, 1963.

Barnett, M. H., & Bryan, J. H. The effects of competition with outcome feedback on children's helping behavior. *Developmental Psychology,* 1974, *10,* 838–842.

Baron, R. A. Behavioral effects of interpersonal attraction: Compliance with requests from liked and disliked others. *Psychonomic Science,* 1971, *25,* 325–26

Baron, R. A., & Byrne, D. Prosocial behavior: Altruism and helping. Unpublished manuscript, Purdue University, 1976.

Baron, R. A., & Byrne, D. *Social psychology,* 2nd edition. Boston, Massachusetts: Allyn and Bacon, 1977.

Bar-Tel, D. *Prosocial behavior: Theory and research.* Washington, D.C.: Hemisphere Publishing Co., 1976.

Beaman, A. L., Fraser, S. C., Diener, E., Kelem, R. T., & Westford, K. The effects of evaluation apprehension and social comparison on emergency helping behavior. Unpublished manuscript, University of Montana, 1974.

Bem, D. J. Self-perception theory. In L. Berkowitz (Ed.), *Advances in experimental social psychology,* Vol. 6. New York: Academic Press, 1972.

Bem, D. J., & Allen, A. On predicting some of the people some of the time. The search for cross-situational consistencies in behavior. *Psychological Review,* 1974, *81,* 506–520.

Benedict, R. Anthropology and the abnormal. *Journal of General Psychology,* 1934, 59–82.

Bennett, E. M., & Cohen, L. R. Men and women: Personality patterns and contrasts. *Genetics Psychology Monographs,* 1959, *59,* 101–155.

Berger, S. M. Conditioning through vicarious instigation. *Psychological Review,* 1962, *69,* 450–466.

Berkowitz, L. *Aggression: A social psychological analysis.* New York: McGraw-Hill, 1962.

Berkowitz, L. A laboratory investigation of social class and national differences in helping behavior. *International Journal of Psychology,* 1966, *1,* 231–240.

Berkowitz, L. Reactance to improper dependency relationships. *Journal of Experimental Psychology,* 1969, *5,* 283–294.

Berkowitz, L. The self, selfishness, and altruism. In J. Macaulay & L. Berkowitz (Eds.), *Altruism and helping behavior.* New York: Academic Press, 1970.

Berkowitz, L. Social norms, feelings, and other factors affecting helping behavior and altruism. In L. Berkowitz (Ed.), *Advances in experimental social psychology,* Vol. 6. New York: Academic Press, 1972.

Berkowitz, L., & Connor, W. H. Success, failure, and social responsibility. *Journal of Personality & Social Psychology,* 1966, *4,* 664–669.

Berkowitz, L., & Daniels, L. R. Responsibility and dependency. *Journal of Abnormal & Social Psychology,* 1963, *66,* 429–436.

Berkowitz, L., & Daniels, L. R. Affecting the salience of the social responsibility norm. *Journal of Abnormal & Social Psychology,* 1964, *68,* 302–306.

Berkowitz, L., & Friedman, P. Some social class differences in helping behavior. *Journal of Personality & Social Psychology,* 1967, *5,* 217–225.

Berkowitz, L., Klanderman, S. B., & Harris, R. Effects of experimenter awareness and sex of subject and experimenter on reactions to dependency relationship. *Sociometry,* 1964, *27,* 327–337.

Berkowitz, L., & Lutterman, K. G. The traditional socially responsible personality. *The Public Opinion Quarterly,* 1968, *32,* 169–185.

Berkowitz, L., & Walster, E. (Eds.). Equity theory: Toward a general theory of social interaction. In *Advances in experimental social psychology,* Vol. 9. New York: Academic Press, 1976.

Berman, A., Piliavin, I. M., & Gross, A. E. Some effects of imposed versus requested help. Unpublished senior honors thesis, University of Wisconsin, 1971.

Bernstein, M. R. Helping in children: The effects of recipient-centered verbalizations, the role of empathy. Unpublished masters thesis, University of Massachusetts, Amherst, 1975.

Berscheid, E., Boye, D., & Walster, E. Retaliation as a means of restoring equity. *Journal of Personality & Social Psychology,* 1968, *10,* 370–376.

Berscheid, E., & Walster, E. When does a harmdoer compensate a victim? *Journal of Personality & Social Psychology,* 1967, *6,* 435–441.

Berscheid, E., Walster, E., & Barclay, A. Effect of time on tendency to compensate a victim. *Psychological Reports,* 1969, *25,* 431–436.

Bickman, L. The effect of another bystander's ability to help on bystander intervention in an emergency. *Journal of Experimental Social Psychology,* 1971, *7,* 367–380.

Bickman, L. Social influence and diffusion of responsibility in an emergency. *Journal of Experimental & Social Psychology,* 1972, *8,* 438–445.

Bickman, L., & Kamzan, L. The effect of race and need on helping behavior. *Journal of Social Psychology,* 1973, *89,* 73–77.

Bickman, L., & Rosenbaum, D. P. Crime reporting as a function of bystander encouragement, surveillance, and credibility. *Journal of Personality & Social Psychology,* 1977, *35,* 577–586.

Billig, M., & Tajfel, H. Social categorization and similarity of intergroup behavior. *European Journal of Social Psychology,* 1973, *3,* 27–52.

Birchler, G. R., Weiss, R. L., & Vincent, J. P. Multimethod analysis of social reinforcement exchange between maritally distressed and nondistressed spouse and stranger dyads. *Journal of Personality & Social Psychology*, 1975, *31*, 349–360.

Blake, R., Rosenbaum, M., & Duryea, R. Giftgiving as a function of group standards. *Human Relations*, 1955, *8*, 61–73.

Blake, R. R., Berkowitz, H., Bellamy, R., & Mouton, J. S. Volunteering as an avoidance act. *Journal of Abnormal & Social Psychology*, 1956, *53*, 154–156.

Blaney, P. H. Genetic basis of behavior. *American Psychologist*, 1976, *31*, 358.

Blau, P. M. *The dynamics of bureaucracy: A study of interpersonal relations in two government agencies.* (Rev. ed.) Chicago: University of Chicago Press, 1955.

Blau, P. M. *Exchange and power in social life.* New York: John Wiley, 1964.

Blevins, G. A., & Murphy, T. Feeling good and helping: Further phonebooth findings. *Psychological Reports*, 1974, *34*, 326.

Block, J. Advancing the psychology of personality: Paradigmatic shift or improving the quality of research. In D. Magnusson & N. S. Endler (Eds.), *Personality at the crossroads: Current issues in interactional psychology.* Hillsdale, New Jersey: Lawrence Erlbaum Associates, 1977.

Boehm, C. Biological versus social evolution. *American Psychologist*, 1976, *31*, 348–351.

Borden, R. J. Witnessed aggression: Influence of an observer's sex and values on aggressive responding. *Journal of Personality & Social Psychology*, 1975, *31*, 567–573.

Bossard, J., Boll, E. S., & Boll, H. S. Child behavior and the empathic complex. *Child Development*, 1957, *28*, 37–43.

Boulding, K. E. *Conflict and defense: A general theory.* New York: Harper, 1962.

Bovard, E. W. The effects of social stimuli on the response to stress. *Psychological Review*, 1959, *66*, 267–277.

Bowers, K. S. Situationism in psychology. An analysis and a critique. *Psychological Review*, 1973, *80*, 307–336.

Bowlby, J. *Attachment and loss*, Vol. I: *Attachment.* New York: Basic Books, 1969.

Boyanowsky, E. O., & Allen, V. L. Ingroup norms and self identity as determinants of discriminatory behavior. *Journal of Personality & Social Psychology*, 1973, *25*, 408–418.

Bramel, D. Taub, B., & Blum, B. An observer's reaction to the suffering of his enemy. *Journal of Personality and Social Psychology*, 1968, *8*, 384.

Brehm, J. W. *A theory of psychological reactance.* New York: Academic Press, 1966.

Brehm, J. W., & Cole, H. Effect of a favor which reduces freedom. *Journal of Personality & Social Psychology*, 1966, *3*, 420–426.

Brickman, R., Redfield, J., Harrison, A. A., & Crandall, R. Drive and predisposition as factors in the attitudinal effects of mere exposure. *Journal of Experimental Social Psychology*, 1972, *8*, 31–44.

Brock, T. C. On interpreting the effects of transgression upon compliance. *Psychological Bulletin*, 1969, *72*, 138–145.

Brock, T. C., & Becker, L. A. "Debriefing" and susceptibility to subsequent experimental manipulations. *Journal of Experimental Social Psychology*, 1966, *2*, 314–323.

Brock, T. C., & Buss, A. H. Dissonance, aggression and evaluation of pain. *Journal of Personality & Social Psychology*, 1962, *65*, 197–202.

Brock, T. C., & Buss, A. H. Effect of justification for aggression in communication with the victim on post-aggression dissonance. *Journal of Abnormal & Social Psychology*, 1964, *68*, 403–412.

Broll, L., Gross, A. E., & Piliavin, I. M. Effects of offered and requested help on help seeking and reactions to being helped. *Journal of Applied Social Psychology*, 1974, *4*, 244–258.

Bronfenbrenner, U. Some familial antecedents of responsibility and leadership in adolescents. In L. Petrulo & B. L. Bass (Eds.), *Leadership and interpersonal behavior.* New York: Holt, 1961.

Brown, R. W. *Social psychology.* New York: The Free Press, 1965.

Bryan, J. H. Model affect and children's imitative behavior. *Child Development*, 1971, *42*, 2061–2065.

Bryan, J. H. Why children help: A review. *Journal of Social Issues*, 1972, *28*, 87–104.

Bryan, J. H. Children's cooperation and helping behaviors. In E. M. Hetherington (Ed.), *Review of child development research*, Vol. 5. Chicago: University of Chicago Press, 1975.

Bryan, J. H., & London, P. Altruistic behavior by children. *Psychological Bulletin*, 1970, *73*, 200–211.

Bryan, J. H., & Test, Mary A. Models and helping. *Journal of Personality & Social Psychology*, 1967, *6*, 400–407.

Bryan, J. H., & Walbeck, N. Preaching and practicing generosity: Children's actions and reaction. *Child Development*, 1970, *41*, 329–354. (a)

Bryan, J. H., & Walbeck, N. The impact of words and deeds concerning altruism upon children. *Child Development*, 1970, *41*, 747–757. (b)

Buck, R. W. Nonverbal communication of affect in children. *Journal of Personality & Social Psychology*, 1975, *31*, 644–653.

Buck, R., Miller, R. E., & Caul, W. J. Sex, personality, and physiological variables in the communication of affect via facial expression. *Journal of Personality & Social Psychology*, 1974, *30*, 587–596.

Byrne, D. *The attraction paradigm.* New York: Academic Press, 1971.

Byrne, D. *An introduction to personality.* Englewood Cliffs, New Jersey: Prentice-Hall, 1974.

Calhoun, L. G., Pierce, J. R., Walters, S., & Dawes, A. S. Determinants of social rejection for help-seeking: Locus of causal attribution, help source, and the "mental illness" label. *Journal of Consulting & Clinical Psychology*, 1974, *42*, 618.

Campagne, A. F., & Harter, S. Moral judgment in sociopathic and normal children. *Journal of Personality and Social Psychology*, 1975, *31*, 199–205.

Campbell, D. T. Ethnocentric and other altruistic motives. In D. Levine (Ed.), *Nebraska symposium on motivation.* Lincoln: University of Nebraska Press, 1965.

Campbell, D. T. On the genetics of altruism and the counter-hedonic components in human culture. *Journal of Social Issues*, 1972, *28*, 21–38.

Campbell, D. T. On the conflicts between biological and social evolution and between psychology and moral tradition. *American Psychologist*, 1975, *30*, 1103–1126.

Cannon, W. B. *The wisdom of the body.* New York: Norton, 1932.

Cantor, J. H. Individual needs and salient constructs in interpersonal perception. *Journal of Personality & Social Psychology*, 1976, *34*, 519–525.

Carlsmith, J. M., & Gross, A. E. Some effects of guilt on compliance. *Journal of Personality & Social Psychology*, 1969, *11*, 232–239.

Carpenter, C. R. *Naturalistic behavior of nonhuman primates.* University Park, Pennsylvania: The Pennsylvania State University Press, 1964.

Garson, R. G. *Interaction concepts of personality.* Chicago: Aldine, 1969.

Castro, M. A. Reactions to receiving aid as a function of cost to donor and opportunity to aid. *Dissertation Abstracts International*, 1975, *35*, 3644–3645.

Chadwick-Jones, J. K. *Social exchange theory: Its structure and influence in social psychology.* New York: Academic Press, 1976.

Chaikin, A. L., & Darley, J. M. Victim or perpetrator? Defensive attribution of responsibility and the need for order and justice. *Journal of Personality & Social Psychology*, 1973, *25*, 268–275.

Chalmers, D. K., Horne, W. C., & Rosenbaum, M. E. Social agreement and the learning of matching behavior. *Journal of Abnormal & Social Psychology*, 1963, *66*, 556–561.

Chandler, M., Greenspan, S., & Barenboim, C. Judgments of intentionality in response to videotape and verbally presented moral dilemmas: The medium is the message. *Child Development*, 1973, *44*, 315–320.

Christie, R., & Geis, F. (Eds.). *Studies in Machiavellianism.* New York: Academic Press, 1968.

Church, R. M. Emotional reactions of rats to the pain of others. *Journal of Comparative & Physiological Psychology,* 1959, *52,* 132–134.

Cialdini, R. B., Darby, B. L., & Vincent, J. E. Transgression and altruism: A case for hedonism. *Journal of Experimental Social Psychology,* 1973, *9,* 502–516.

Cialdini, R. B., & Kenrick, D. T. Altruism as hedonism: A social development perspective on the relationship of negative mood state and helping. *Journal of Personality and Social Psychology,* 1976, *34,* 907–914.

Cialdini, R. B., Vincent, J. E., Lewis, S. K., Catalan, J., Wheeler, D., & Darby, B. L. Reciprocal concessions procedure for inducing compliance: The door-in-the-face technique. *Journal of Personality & Social Psychology,* 1975, *31,* 206–215.

Clark, K. E., & Clark, M. P. Racial identification and preference in Negro children. In E. E. Maccoby, T. M. Newcomb, & E. L. Hartley (Eds.), *Readings in social psychology.* (Third ed.) New York: Holt, 1958.

Clark, R. D. The effects of reinforcement, punishment and dependency on helping behavior. *Personality & Social Psychology Bulletin,* 1975, *1,* 596–599.

Clark, R. D., & Word, L. E. Why don't bystanders help? Because of ambiguity? *Journal of Personality & Social Psychology,* 1972, *24,* 392–401.

Clark, R. D., & Word, L. E. Where is the apathetic bystander? Situational characteristics of the emergency. *Journal of Personality & Social Psychology,* 1974, *29,* 279–288.

Cohen, R. Altruism: Human, cultural or what? *Journal of Social Issues,* 1972, *28,* 39–57.

Comte, A. *System of positive polity.* New York: Burt Franklin, 1967. (Originally published London, 1875).

Coopersmith, S. *Antecedents of self esteem.* San Francisco: Fremont & Co., 1967.

Cozby, P. C. Self-disclosure: A literature review. *Psychological Bulletin,* 1973, *79,* 73–91.

Craig, K. D. Physiological arousal as a function of imagined, vicarious, and direct stress experience. *Journal of Abnormal Psychology,* 1968, *73,* 513–520.

Craig, K. D., & Lavery, H. J. Heart rate components of conditioned vicarious autonomic responses. *Journal of Personality & Social Psychology,* 1969, *11,* 381–387.

Crockenberg, S., & Nicolayev, J. Stage transition in moral reasoning as related to conflict experienced in naturalistic settings. Unpublished manuscript, University of California, Davis, 1977.

Crombag, H. F. (Eindhoven Institute of Technology, Netherlands). Cooperation and competition in means-interdependent triads: A replication. *Journal of Personality & Social Psychology,* 1966, *4,* 692–695.

Cronbach, L. J. Processes affecting scores on "understanding others" and "assumed similarity." *Psychological Bulletin,* 1955, *52,* 177–193.

Crowne, D. P., & Marlowe, D. *The approval motive: Studies in evaluative dependence.* New York: Wiley, 1964.

Curry, T., & Emerson, R. M. Balance theory: A theory of interpersonal attraction? *Sociometry,* 1970, *33,* 216–238.

Daher, D. M., & Banikotes, P. G. Interpersonal attraction and rewarding aspects of disclosure content and level. *Journal of Personality & Social Psychology,* 1976, *33,* 492–496.

Daniels, L. R., & Berkowitz, L. Liking and response to dependency relationships. *Human Relations,* 1963, *16,* 141–148.

Darley, J., & Batson, C. From Jerusalem to Jericho: A study of situational & dispositional variables in helping behavior. *Journal of Personality & Social Psychology,* 1973, *27,* 100–108.

Darley, J. M., & Berscheid, E. Increased liking as a result of the anticipation of personal contact. *Human Relations,* 1967, *20,* 29–40.

Darley, J. M., & Latané, B. Bystander intervention in emergencies: Diffusion of responsibility. *Journal of Personality & Social Psychology*, 1968, *10*, 202–214.

Darley, J. M., & Latané, B. Norms and normative behavior: Field studies of social interdependence. In J. Macaulay & L. Berkowitz (Eds.), *Altruism and helping behavior.* New York: Academic Press, 1970.

Darley, J., Teger, A., & Lewis, L. Do groups always inhibit individuals' responses to potential emergencies? *Journal of Personality & Social Psychology*, 1973, *26*, 395–399.

Darlington, R. B., & Macker, C. E. Displacement of guilt-produced altruistic behavior. *Journal of Personality and Social Psychology*, 1966, *4*, 442–443.

Darwin, C. *The descent of man and selection in relation to sex.* London: J. Murray, 1871.

Davidson, J. Cognitive familiarity and dissonance reduction. In L. Festinger (Ed.), *Conflict, decision and dissonance.* Stanford, California: Stanford University Press, 1964.

Davis, J. D., & Skinner, A. E. Reciprocity of self-disclosure in interviews: Modeling or social change? *Journal of Personality and Social Psychology*, 1974, *29*, 779–784.

Davis, K. E., & Jones, E. E. Changes in interpersonal perception as a means of reducing cognitive dissonance. *Journal of Abnormal & Social Psychology*, 1960, *61*, 402–410.

Deci, E. *Intrinsic motivation.* New York: Plenum, 1975.

Deci, E. Intrinsic motivation and personality. In E. Staub (Ed.), *Personality: Basic issues and current research.* Englewood Cliffs, New Jersey: Prentice-Hall, 1979. (In press)

Denner, B. Did a crime occur? Should I inform anyone? A study of deception. *Journal of Personality*, 1968, *36*, 454–466.

Derlega, V. J., Wilson, M., & Chaikin, A. L. Friendship and disclosure reciprocity. *Journal of Personality & Social Psychology*, 1976, *34*, 578–582.

Deutsch, J. Observational and sociometric measures of peer popularity and their relationship to egocentric communication in female preschoolers. *Developmental Psychology*, 1974, *10*, 745–747.

Deutsch, M. A theory of cooperation and competition. *Human Relations*, 1949, *2*, 129–152.

Deutsch, M. Trust, trustworthiness, and the F scale. *Journal of Abnormal & Social Psychology*, 1960, *61*, 138–140. (a)

Deutsch, M. The effect of motivational orientation upon trust and suspicion. *Human Relations*, 1960, *13*, 123–139. (b)

Deutsch, M. Cooperation and trust: Some theoretical notes. In M. R. Jones (Ed.), *Nebraska symposium on motivation.* Lincoln: University of Nebraska Press, 1962.

Deutsch, M. Field theory in social psychology. In G. Lindsey, & E. Aronson (Eds.), *Handbook of social psychology*, Vol. I. Addison-Wesley, 1968.

Deutsch, M. Equity, equality, and need: What determines which value will be used as the basis of distributive justice? *The Journal of Social Issues*, 1975, *31*, 137–150.

Deutsch, M., & Collins, M. E. *Interracial housing: A psychological evaluation of a social experiment.* Minneapolis: University of Minnesota Press, 1951.

Deutsch, M., & Krauss, R. M. The effect of threat upon interpersonal bargaining. *Journal of Abnormal & Social Psychology*, 1960, *61*, 181–189.

Diener, E., Dineen, J., & Endresen, K. Effects of altered responsibility, cognitive set, and modeling on physical aggression and deindividuation. *Journal of Personality & Social Psychology*, 1975, *31*, 328–337.

Dillon, W. S. *Gifts and nations.* The Hague: Mouton, 1968.

Dlugokinski, E., & Firestone, I. J. Congruence among four methods of measuring other-centeredness. *Child Development*, 1973, *44*, 304–308.

Dlugokinski, E. L., & Firestone, I. J. Other-centeredness and susceptibility to charitable appeals: Effects of perceived discipline. *Developmental Psychology*, 1974, *10*, 21–28.

Doland, D. J., & Adelberg, K. The learning of sharing behavior. *Child Development*, 1967, *38*, 695–700.

Dollard, J., & Miller, N. E. *Personality and psychotherapy.* New York: McGraw-Hill, 1950.

440   References

Donnenwerth, G. V., & Foa, U. G. Effect of resource class on retaliation to injustice in interpersonal exchange. *Journal of Personality & Social Psychology*, 1974, *29*, 785–793.

Douvan, E. Changing sex roles: Some implications and constraints. Paper presented at a symposium on "Women: Resources in a changing world." The Radcliffe Institute, 1972.

Dovidio, J. F., & Morris, W. N. Effects of stress and commonality of fate on helping behavior. *Journal of Personality & Social Psychology*, 1975, *31*, 145–149.

Dreman, S. B., & Greenbaum, C. W. Altruism or reciprocity: Sharing behavior in Israeli kindergarten children. *Child Development*, 1973, *44*, 61–68.

Dunn, R. E., & Goldman, M. Competition and noncompetition in relation to satisfaction and feelings toward own-group and nongroup members. *Journal of Social Psychology*, 1966, *68*, 299–311.

Durkheim, E. *Moral education.* New York: The Free Press, 1961.

Durkin, D. The specificity of children's moral judgments. *Journal of Genetic Psychology*, 1961, *98*, 3–13.

Duster, T. Conditions for guilt-free massacre. In N. Sanford & C. Comstock (Eds.), *Sanctions for evil.* San Francisco, California: Jossey-Bass, Inc., 1971.

Dutton, D. G. Reverse discrimination: The relationship of amount of perceived discrimination toward a minority group on the behavior of majority group members. *Canadian Journal of Behavioural Science*, 1973, *5*, 34–45.

Ehrlich, H. T., & Graeven, D. B. Reciprocal self-disclosure in a dyad. *Journal of Experimental Social Psychology*, 1971, *7*, 389–400.

Ekehammer, B. Interactionism in personality from a historical perspective. *Psychological Bulletin*, 1974, *81*, 1026–1048.

Elder, G. Appearance and education in marriage mobility. *American Sociological Review*, 1969, *34*, 519–533.

Elliot, R., & Vasta, R. The modeling of sharing: Effects associated with vicarious reinforcement, symbolization, age, and generalization. *Journal of Experimental Child Psychology*, 1970, *10*, 8–15.

Emler, N. P., & Rushton, J. P. Cognitive-developmental factors in children's generosity. *British Journal of Social & Clinical Psychology*, 1974, *13*, 277–281.

Epstein, I. *Judaism.* London: Pergamon Press, 1959.

Epstein, S. The self-concept revisited. Or a theory of a theory. *American Psychologist*, 1973, *28*, 404–416.

Epstein, S., & Rakosky, J. The effect of witnessing an admirable versus an unadmirable aggressor upon subsequent aggression. *Journal of Personality*, 1976, *44*, 560–576.

Epstein, S., & Taylor, S. Instigation to aggression as a function of degree of defeat and perceived aggressive intent of the opponent. *Journal of Personality*, 1967, *35*, 265–289.

Epstein, S., & Taylor, S. Instigation to aggression as a function of degree of defeat and the capacity for massive retaliation. *Journal of Personality*, 1970, *16*, 20–28.

Erikson, E. H. *Childhood and society.* (Second ed.) New York: W. W. Norton & Co., 1963.

Farber, I. E. The things people say to themselves. *American Psychologist*, 1963, *18*, 185–197.

Fay, B. The relationships of cognitive moral judgment, generosity, and empathic behavior in 6- and 8-year old children. Unpublished doctoral dissertation, University of California, Los Angeles, 1970.

Feinberg, H. K. *Anatomy of a helping situation: Some personality and situational determinants of helping in a conflict situation involving another's psychological distress.* Unpublished doctoral dissertation, University of Massachusetts, Amherst, 1977.

Feinberg, H., & Staub, E. Learning to be prosocial: The effects of reasoning and participation in prosocial action on children's prosocial behavior. Paper presented at the meetings of the Eastern Psychological Association, New York City, April, 1975.

Feldman, R. E. Response to compatriot and foreigner who seek assistance. *Journal of Personality & Social Psychology*, 1968, *10*, 202–214.

Feshbach, N. D., & Feshbach, S. The relationship between empathy and aggression in two age groups. *Developmental Psychology*, 1969, *1*, 102–107.

Feshbach, N. D., & Roe, K. Empathy in six and seven year olds. *Child Development*, 1968, *39*, 135–147.

Festinger, L. Architecture and group membership. *Journal of Social Issues*, 1951, *1*, 152–163.

Festinger, L. A theory of social comparison processes. *Human Relations*, 1954, *7*, 117–140.

Firestone, I. J., Lichtman, C. M., & Colamosca, J. V. Leader effectiveness and leadership conferral as determinants of helping in a medical emergency. *Journal of Personality & Social Psychology*, 1975, *31*, 343–348.

Fishbein, M. Attitude & prediction of behavior. In M. Fishbein (Ed.), *Readings in attitude theory and measurement*. New York: Wiley, 1967.

Fishbein, M. Toward an understanding of family planning behavior. *Journal of Applied Social Psychology*, 1972, *2*, 214–227.

Fisher, J. D., & Nadler, A. The effects of similarity between donor and recipient on recipient's reactions to aid. *Journal of Applied Social Psychology*, 1974, *4*, 230–243.

Fisher, J. D., & Nadler, A. Effect of donor resources on recipient self-esteem and self-help. *Journal of Experimental Social Psychology*, 1976, *12*, 139–150.

Fishman, C. Need for approval and the expression of aggression under varying conditions of frustration. *Journal of Personality & Social Psychology*, 1965, *2*, 133–139.

Fiske, D. W., & Maddi, S. R. *Functions of varied experience*. Homewood, Illinois: The Dorsey Press, 1961.

Flanders, N. A., & Havumaki, S. Group compliance to dominative teacher influence. *Human Relations*, 1960, *13*, 67–82.

Flavell, J. H., Botkin, P., Fry, C., Wright, J., & Jarvis, P. *The development of role-taking and communication skills in children*. New York: Wiley, 1968.

Floyd, J. Effects of amount of reward and friendship status of the other on the frequency of sharing in children. Unpublished doctoral dissertation, University of Minnesota. 1964.

Foa, U. G. Interpersonal and economic resources. *Science*, 1971, *171*, 345–451.

Foa, U. G., & Foa, E. B. *Societal structures of the mind*. Springfield, Illinois: Charles G. Thomas, 1974.

Fouts, G. T. Charity in children: The influence of "charity" stimuli and an audience. *Journal of Experimental Child Psychology*, 1972, *13*, 303–309.

Frankena, W. K. *Ethics*. Englewood Cliffs, New Jersey: Prentice-Hall, 1963.

Fraser, S. C., Kelem, R. T., Diener, E., & Beaman, A. L. Two, three or four heads are better than one: Modification of college performance by peer monitoring. Unpublished manuscript, University of Southern California, 1973.

Frederiksen, N. Toward a taxonomy of situations. *American Psychologist*, 1972, *27*, 114–124.

Freedman, D. G. Hereditary control of early social behavior. In B. M. Foss (Ed.), *Determinants of infant behavior: III*. New York: Wiley, 1965.

Freedman, J. L. Transgression, compliance and guilt. In J. Macaulay & L. Berkowitz (Eds.), *Altruism and helping behavior*. New York: Academic Press, 1970.

Freedman, J. L., & Fraser, S. C. Compliance without pressure: The foot-in-the-door technique. *Journal of Personality & Social Psychology*, 1966, *4*, 195–202.

Freedman, J. L., Wallington, S. A., & Bless, E. Compliance without pressure: The effect of guilt. *Journal of Personality & Social Psychology*, 1967, *7*, 117–124.

Freud, A. The infantile instinct life. In H. Herma & G. M. Karth (Eds.), *A handbook of psychoanalysis*. New York: World Publishing Co., 1963.

Freud, S. *Civilization and its discontents.* London: Hogarth, 1930.

Freud, S. Some physical consequences of the anatomical distinction between the sexes. In J. Strachey (Ed. and trans.), *Standard edition of the complete psychological works of Sigmund Freud,* Vol. 19. London: Hogarth Press, 1961. (Originally published 1925)

Fromm, E. *Escape from freedom.* New York: Holt, 1941.

Fromm, E. *The anatomy of human destructiveness.* New York: Holt, 1973.

Gaertner, S. L. Helping behavior and racial discrimination among liberals and conservatives. *Journal of Personality & Social Psychology,* 1973, *25,* 335–341.

Gaertner, S., & Bickman, L. Effects of race on the elicitation of helping behavior: The wrong number technique. *Journal of Personality & Social Psychology,* 1971, *20,* 218–222.

Gaertner, S. L., & Dovidio, J. F. The subtlety of white racism, arousal, and helping behavior. *Journal of Personality & Social Psychology,* 1977, *35,* 691–708.

Garske, J. P. Interpersonal trust and construct complexity for positively and negatively evaluated persons. *Personality & Social Psychology Bulletin,* 1975, *1,* 616–619.

Geer, J. H., & Jarmecky, L. The effect of being responsible for reducing another's pain on subjects' response and arousal. *Journal of Personality & Social Psychology,* 1973, *26,* 232.

Geller, J. D. Some personal and situational determinants of interpersonal trust. Unpublished doctoral dissertation, University of Connecticut, 1966.

Gergen, K. J. Effects of interaction goals & personality feedback on the presentation of self. *Journal of Personality & Social Psychology,* 1965, *1,* 413–424.

Gergen, K. J. *The psychology of behavior exchange.* Reading, Massachusetts: Addison-Wesley, 1968. (a)

Gergen, K. J. Personality consistency and the presentation of self. In C. Gordon & K. J. Gergen (Eds.), *The self in social interaction,* Vol. I. New York: John Wiley & Sons, 1968. (b)

Gergen, K. J. The decline of character: Socialization and self-consistency. In G. DiRenzo (Ed.), *Social change and social character.* Westport, Connecticut: Greenwood Press, 1976.

Gergen, K. J., Diebold, P., & Seipel, M. Intentionality and ability to reciprocate as determinants of reactions to aid. Unpublished manuscript, Swarthmore College, 1973.

Gergen, K., Ellsworth, P., Maslach, C., & Seipel, M. Obligation, donor resources, and reactions to aid in 3 cultures. *Journal of Personality & Social Psychology,* 1975, *31,* 390–400.

Gergen, K. J., Gergen, M. M., & Meter, K. Individual orientations to prosocial behavior. *Journal of Social Issues,* 1972, *8,* 105–130.

Gergen, K., & Wishnov, B. Others' self-evaluations and interaction anticipation as determinants of self-presentation. *Journal of Personality & Social Psychology,* 1965, *2,* 348–358.

Ghiselin, M. T. Genetic basis of behavior—especially altruism. *American Psychologist,* 1976, *31,* 358–359.

Gilbert, J. Interpersonal trust: Implications for psycho-therapeutic technique. Unpublished masters thesis, University of Connecticut, 1967.

Glass, D. C. Changes in liking as a means of reducing cognitive discrepancies between self-esteem and aggression. *Journal of Personality,* 1964, *32,* 531–549.

Glass, D. C., & Singer, J. E. *Urban stress. Experiments on noise and social stressors.* New York: Academic Press, 1972.

Godfrey, B. W., & Lowe, C. A. Devaluation of innocent victims: An attribution analysis within the just world paradigm. *Journal of Personality & Social Psychology,* 1975, *31,* 944–951.

Goffman, E. *Stigma: Notes on the management of the spoiled identity.* Englewood Cliffs, New Jersey: Prentice-Hall, 1963.

Goldschmidt, W. *Culture and behavior of the Sekei.* Berkeley and Los Angeles: University of California Press, 1976.

Goldstein, J. W., & Rosenfeld, H. M. Insecurity and preference for persons similar to oneself. *Journal of Personality,* 1969, *37,* 253–266.

Goranson, R. E., & Berkowitz, L. Reciprocity and responsibility reactions to prior help. *Journal of Personality & Social Psychology,* 1966, *3,* 227–232.

Gore, P. M., & Rotter, J. B. A personality correlate of social action. *Journal of Personality,* 1963, *31,* 58–64.

Gottheil, E. Changes in social perceptions contingent upon competing or cooperating. *Sociometry,* 1955, *18,* 132–137.

Gottman, J., Notarius, C., Markman, H., Bank, S., & Yoppi, B. Behavior exchange theory and marital decision making. *Journal of Personality & Social Psychology,* 1976, *34,* 14–23.

Gouldner, A. W. The norm of reciprocity: A preliminary statement. *American Sociological Review,* 1960, *25,* 161–179.

Grant, J. E., Weiner, A., & Rushton, J. P. Moral judgment and generosity in children. *Psychological Reports,* 1976, *39,* 451–454.

Greenberg, M. S. A preliminary statement on a theory of indebtedness. Paper presented at the meeting of the Western Psychological Association, San Diego, March, 1968.

Greenberg, M. S., & Frisch, D. M. Effect of intentionality on willingness to reciprocate a favor. *Journal of Experimental Social Psychology,* 1972, *8,* 99–111.

Greenberg, M. S., & Saxe, L. Importance of locus of help initiation and type of outcome as determinants of reactions to another's help attempt. *Social Behavior & Personality,* 1975, *3,* 101–110.

Greenberg, M. S. & Shapiro, S. P. Indebtedness: An adverse aspect of asking for and receiving help. *Sociometry,* 1971, *34,* 290–301.

Greene, P. J., & Barash, D. P. Section 2: Genetic basis of behavior—especially of altruism. *American Psychologist,* 1976, *31,* 359–361.

Greene, W. Triage. *New York Times Magazine,* January 5, 1975.

Greenglass, E. R. Effects of prior help and hindrance on willingness to help another: Reciprocity or social responsibility. *Journal of Personality & Social Psychology,* 1969, *11,* 224–231.

Greenwald, A. Does the Good Samaritan parable increase helping? A comment on Darley and Batson's no effect conclusion. *Journal of Personality & Social Psychology,* 1975, *32,* 578–583.

Griffitt, W. Environmental effects on interpersonal affective behavior: Ambient effective temperature and attraction. *Journal of Personality & Social Psychology,* 1970, *15,* 240–244.

Griffitt, W., & Veitch, R. Hot and crowded: Influence of population density and temperature on interpersonal affective behavior. *Journal of Personality & Social Psychology,* 1971, *17,* 92–98.

Grodman, S. M. The role of personality and situational variables in responding to and helping an individual in psychological distress. Unpublished doctoral dissertation, University of Massachusetts, 1978. (In preparation)

Gross, A. E., & Latané, J. G. Receiving help, reciprocation, and interpersonal attraction. *Journal of Applied Social Psychology,* 1974, *4,* 210–223.

Gross, A. E., & Lubell, B. B. Reciprocity and liking for the helper. Unpublished data, University of Wisconsin, 1970.

Gross, A. E., & Somersan, S. Helper effort as an inhibitor of help-seeking. Paper presented at the Psychonomic Society annual meeting, 1974.

Gross, A. E., Wallston, B. S., & Piliavin, I. M. The help recipient: A social psychological perspective. In D. H. Smith & J. Macaulay (Eds.), *Informal social participation: The determinants of socio-political action, leisure activity, and altruistic behavior.* San Francisco: Jossey-Bass, 1978. (In press)

Gruder, C. L., & Cook, T. D. Sex, dependency and helping. *Journal of Personality & Social Psychology*, 1971, *19*, 290–294.

Grusec, J. E. Demand characteristics of the modeling experiment: Altruism as a function of age and aggression. *Journal of Personality & Social Psychology*, 1972, *22*, 139–148.

Grusec, J. E., & Skubicki, L. Model nurturance, demand characteristics of the modeling experiment and altruism. *Journal of Personality & Social Psychology*, 1970, *14*, 352–359.

Grzlec, J. Paper presented at the Conference on Mechanisms of Prosocial Behavior, Poland, October, 1974.

Haan, N. Hypothetical and actual monal reasoning in a situation of civil disobedience. *Journal of Personality & Social Psychology*, 1975, *32*, 255–270.

Haldane, J. B. S. *The causes of evolution.* London: Longmans, 1932.

Hamilton, M. L. Imitative behavior and expression of emotion. *Developmental Psychology*, 1973, *8*, 138.

Hamilton, W. D. The genetical evolution of social behavior: I and II. *Journal of Theoretical Biology*, 1964, *7*, 1–52.

Hamsher, J. H. Jr. Validity of personality inventories as a function of disguise of purpose. Unpublished doctoral dissertation. University of Connecticut, 1968.

Handlon, B. J., & Gross, P. The development of sharing behavior. *Journal of Abnormal & Social Psychology*, 1959, *59*, 425–428.

Harris, D. G. The scale for measuring attitudes of social responsibility in children. *Journal of Abnormal & Social Psychology*, 1957, *55*, 322–326.

Harris,M. B. Some determinants of sharing in children. Unpublished dissertation. Stanford University, 1968.

Harris, M. B. Reciprocity and generosity: Some determinants of sharing in children. *Child Development*, 1970, *41*, 313–328.

Harris, M. B. Models, norms and helping. *Psychological Reports*, 1971, *29*, 147–153.

Harris, M. B. The effects of performing one altruistic act on the likelihood of performing another. *Journal of Social Psychology*, 1972, *88*, 65–73.

Harris, M. B., & Huang, L. C. Competence and helping. *Journal of Social Psychology*, 1973, *89*, 203–210.

Harris, M. B., & Meyer, F. W. Dependency, threat, and helping. *Journal of Social Psychology*, 1973, *90*, 239–242.

Harris, M. B., & Siebel, C. C. Affect, aggression, and altruism. *Developmental Psychology*, 1975, *11*, 623–627.

Hartman, D. P. Influence of symbolically modeled instrumental aggression and pain cues on aggressive behavior. *Journal of Personality & Social Psychology*, 1969, *11*, 280–288.

Hartmann, N. *Ethics,* Vol. 2: *Moral values.* New York: Macmillan, 1932.

Hartshorne, H., & May, M. A. *Studies in the nature of character,* Vol. I: *Studies in deceit.* New York: Macmillan, 1928.

Hartshorne, H., May, M. A., & Maller, J. B. *Studies in the nature of character,* Vol. II: *Studies in service and self-control.* New York: Macmillan, 1929.

Hebb, D. O. Drives and the C.N.S. (conceptual nervous system). *Psychological Review*, 1955, *62*, 243–254.

Hebb, D. O. Comment on altruism: The comparative evidence. *Psychological Bulletin*, 1971, *76*, 409.

Hebb, D. O., & Thompson, W. R. The social significance of animal studies. In G. Lindzey (Ed.), *Handbook of social psychology,* Volume I: *Theory and method.* Cambridge, Massachusetts: Addison-Wesley, 1954.

Heber, R. F., & Heber, M. E. The effect of group failure & success on social status. *Journal of Educational Psychology*, 1957, *48*, 129–134.

Heberlein, T. A., & Black, J. S. Attitudinal specificity and the prediction of behavior in a field setting. *Journal of Personality & Social Psychology*, 1976, *33*, 474–479.

Heider, F. *The psychology of interpersonal relations.* New York: Wiley, 1958.

Heilman, M. E., Hodgson, S. A., & Hornstein, H. A. Effects of magnitude and rectifiability of harm and information value on the reporting of accidental harm-doing. *Journal of Personality & Social Psychology*, 1972, *23*, 211–218.

Hendrick, C., & Page, H. A. Self-esteem, attitude similarity, and attraction. *Journal of Personality*, 1970, *38*, 588–601.

Hendrick, C., & Taylor, S. P. Effects of belief similarity and aggression on attraction and counteraggression. *Journal of Personality & Social Psychology*, 1971, *17*, 342–349.

Hick, K. W., Mitchell, T. R., Bell, G. H., & Carter, W. B. Determinants of interpersonal disclosure: Some competitive tests. *Personality & Social Psychology Bulletin*, 1975, *1*, 620–624.

Hobbes, T. Human nature: Or the fundamental elements of policy (1650). In W. Molesworth (Ed.), *The English works of Thomas Hobbes* (11 Vols.). Aalen: Scientia, 1962.

Hodgson, S. A., Hornstein, H. A., & Siegel, E. Socially mediated Zeigarnik effects as a function of sentiment, valence, and desire for goal attainment. *Journal of Experimental Social Psychology*, 1972, *8*, 446–456.

Hoffman, M. L. Parent discipline and the child's consideration for others. *Child Development*, 1963, *34*, 573–588.

Hoffman, M. L. Moral development. In P. H. Mussen (Ed.), *Carmichael's manual of child development.* New York: Wiley, 1970. (a)

Hoffman, M. L. Conscience, personality, and socialization technique. *Human Development*, 1970, *13*, 90–126. (b)

Hoffman, M. L. Developmental synthesis of affect and cognition and its implications for altruistic motivation. *Developmental Psychology*, 1975, *11*, 607–622. (a)

Hoffman, M. L. Sex differences in moral internalization and values. *Journal of Personality & Social Psychology*, 1975, *32*, 720–729. (b)

Hoffman, M. L. Altruistic behavior and the parent–child relationship. *Journal of Personality & Social Psychology*, 1975, *31*, 937–943. (c)

Hoffman, M. L. Empathy, roletaking, guilt, and development of altruistic motives. In T. Lickona (Ed.), *Moral development and behavior.* New York: Holt, 1976.

Hoffman, M. L. Personality and social development. In M. R. Rosenzweig & L. W. Porter (Eds.), *Annual Review of Psychology*, 1977, *28*, 295–321. (a)

Hoffman, M. L. Sex differences in empathy & related behaviors. *Psychological Bulletin*, 1977, *84*, 712–720. (b)

Hoffman, M. L., & Levine, L. E. Early sex differences in empathy. *Developmental Psychology*, 1976, *12*, 557–558.

Hoffman, M. L., & Saltzstein, H. D. Parent discipline and the child's moral development. *Journal of Personality & Social Psychology*, 1967, *5*, 45–57.

Hogan, R. Development of an empathy scale. *Journal of Consulting & Clinical Psychology*, 1969, *33*, 307–316.

Hogan, R. Genetic basis of behavior. *American Psychologist*, 1976, *31*, 363–366.

Holmes, S. J. The reproductive beginnings of altruism. *Psychological Review*, 1945, *52*, 109–112.

Homans, G. C. *Social behavior: Its elementary forms.* New York: Harcourt, 1961.

Hornstein, H. A. The influence of social models on helping. In J. Macaulay & L. Berkowitz (Eds.), *Altruism and helping behavior.* New York: Academic Press, 1970.

Hornstein, H. A. Promotive tension: The basis of prosocial behavior from a Lewinian perspective. *Journal of Social Issues*, 1972, *28*, 191–218.

Hornstein, H. A. *Cruelty and kindness. A new look at aggression and altruism.* Englewood Cliffs, New Jersey: Prentice-Hall, 1976.

Hornstein, H. A., LaKind, E., Frankel, G., & Manne, S. Effects of knowledge about remote social events on prosocial behavior, social conception, and mood. *Journal of Personality & Social Psychology*, 1975, *32*, 1038–1046.

Hornstein, H. A., Mason, H. N., Sole, K., & Heilman, M. Effects of sentiment and completion of a helping act on observer helping: A case for socially mediated Zeigarnik effects. *Journal of Personality & Social Psychology*, 1971, *17*, 107–112.

Horowitz, I. The effect of group norms on bystander intervention. *Journal of Social Psychology*, 1971, *83*, 265–273.

House, T. H., & Milligan, W. L. Autonomic responses to modeled distress in prison psychopaths. *Journal of Personality & Social Psychology*, 1976, *34*, 556–560.

Hovland, C. L., & Janis, I. J. *Personality and persuasability*. New Haven: Yale University Press, 1959.

Hunt, J. McV. Intrinsic motivation and its role in psychological development. In D. Levine (Ed.), *Nebraska symposium on motivation*. Lincoln: University of Nebraska Press, 1965.

Huston, T. L., & Korte, C. The responsive bystander: Why he helps. In T. Lickona (Ed.), *Moral development and behavior*. New York: Holt, 1976.

Huston, T. L., & Levinger, G. Interpersonal attraction and relationships. In M. R. Rosenzweig & L. W. Porter (Eds.), *Annual review of psychology*. Palo Alto, California: Annual Reviews, Inc., 1978.

Isen, A. M. Success, failure, attention and reaction to others: The warm glow of success. *Journal of Personality & Social Psychology*, 1970, *15*, 294–301.

Isen, A., Clark, M., & Schwartz, M. Duration of the effect of good mood on helping: "Footprints in the sands of time." *Journal of Personality & Social Psychology*, 1976, *34*, 385–393.

Isen, A. M., Horn, N., & Rosenhan, D. L. Effects of success and failure on children's generosity. *Journal of Personality & Social Psychology*, 1973, *27*, 239–248.

Isen, A. M., & Levin, P. F. Effect of feeling good on helping: Cookies and kindness. *Journal of Personality & Social Psychology*, 1972, *21*, 384–388.

Isen, A. M., Shalker, T. E., Clark, M., & Karp, L. Affect, accessibility of material in memory, and behavior: A cognitive loop? *Journal of Personality & Social Psychology*, 1978, *36*, 1–13.

James, W. *The principles of psychology*, Vols. I and II. New York: Henry Holt, 1890.

Jarymowicz, M. Modification of self-worth and increment of prosocial sensitivity. *Polish Psychological Bulletin*, 1977, *8*, 45–53.

Jensen, R. E., & Moore, S. G. The effect of attribute statements on cooperativeness and competitiveness in school-age boys. *Child Development*, 1977, *48*, 305–307.

Johnson, D. W. Cooperativeness and social perspective taking. *Journal of Personality & Social Psychology*, 1975, *31*, 241–244.

Jones, E. E. *Ingratiation: A social psychological analysis*. New York: Appleton, 1964.

Jones, E. E., & Nisbett, R. E. *The actor and the observer: Divergent perceptions of the causes of behavior*. New York: General Learning Press, 1971.

Jones, H. E. The longitudinal method in the study of personality. In I. Iscoe & H. W. Stevenson (Eds.), *Personality development in children*. Chicago, Illinois: University of Chicago Press, 1960

Jones, R. A. Volunteering to help: The effects of choice, dependence and anticipated dependence. *Journal of Personality & Social Psychology*, 1970, *14*, 121–129.

Jourard, S. M. *The transparent self*. Princeton, New Jersey: Van Nostrand, 1964.

Jourard, S. M., & Jaffee, P. E. Influence of an interviewer's disclosure on the self-disclosing behavior of interviewees. *Journal of Counseling Psychology*, 1970, *17*, 252–257.

Julian, J. W., Bishop, D. W., & Fiedler, F. E. Quasi-therapeutic effects of intergroup competition. *Journal of Personality & Social Psychology*, 1966, *3*, 321–327.

Jung, C. G. The psychology of the unconscious. In H. Read, M. Fordham, & G. Adler (Eds.), *Collected works*. New York: Pantheon Books, 1966.

Kagan, S., & Madsen, M. C. Cooperation and competition of Mexican, Mexican-American and Anglo-American children of two ages under four instructional sets. *Developmental Psychology*, 1971, *5*, 32–39.

Kahn, A., & Tice, T. E. Returning a favor & retaliating harm: The effects of stated intentions and actual behavior. *Journal of Experimental Social Psychology*, 1973, *9*, 43–56.

Kaplan, S. The effects of news broadcasts on discriminatory behavior toward similar and dissimilar others. Unpublished doctoral dissertation, Teacher's College, Columbia University, 1974.

Karabenick, S. A., Lerner, R. M., & Beecher, M. D. Relation of political affiliation to helping behavior on Election Day, November 7, 1972. *Journal of Social Psychology*, 1973, *91*, 223–227.

Karylowski, J. Self-esteem, similarity, liking and helping. *Personality & Social Psychology Bulletin*, 1976, *2*, 71–74.

Katz, I., Cohen, S., & Glass, D. Some determinants of cross-racial helping. *Journal of Personality & Social Psychology*, 1975, *32*, 964–970.

Katz, I., Glass, D. C., & Cohen, S. Ambivalence, guilt and the scapegoating of minority group victims. *Journal of Experimental Social Psychology*, 1973, *9*, 423–436.

Katz, I., Goldston, J., Cohen, M., & Stucker, S. Need satisfaction, perception, and cooperative interaction in married couples. *Marriage & Family Living*, 1963, *25*, 209–214.

Kaufman, H. The unconcerned bystander. *Proceedings of the 76th Annual Convention of the American Psychological Association*, 1968, *3*, 387–388.

Kazdin, A. E., & Bryan, J. H. Competence and volunteering. *Journal of Experimental Social Psychology*, 1971, *7*, 87–97.

Keating, J. P., & Brock T. C. The effects of prior reward and punishment on subsequent reward and punishment: Guilt versus consistency. *Journal of Personality & Social Psychology*, 1976, *34*, 327–333.

Kelley, H. H. Attribution theory in social psychology. In the *Nebraska symposium on motivation*. Lincoln: University of Nebraska Press, 1967.

Kelley, H. H. Moral evaluation. *American Psychologist*, 1971, *26*, 293–301.

Kelley, H. H., & Stahleski, A. J. Social interaction basis of cooperators' and competitors' beliefs about others. *Journal of Personality & Social Psychology*, 1970, *16*, 66–91.

Kelley K., & Byrne, D. Attraction and altruism: With a little help from my friends. *Journal of Research in Personality*, 1976, *10*, 59–68.

Kenrick, D. T., Reich, J. W., & Cialdini, R. B. Justification and compensation: Rosier skies for the devalued victim. *Journal of Personality & Social Psychology*, 1976, *34*, 654–657.

Kerckhoff, A. C., & Davis, K. E. Value consensus and need complementarity in mate selection. *American Sociological Review*, 1962, *27*, 295–303.

Kiesler, S. B. The effect of perceived role requirements on reactions to favor-doing. *Journal of Experimental Social Psychology*, 1966, *2*, 198–210.

Kiesler, S. B., & Baral, R. L. The search for a romantic partner: The effects of self-esteem and physical attractiveness on romantic behavior. In K. J. Gergen & D. Marlowe (Eds.), *Personality and social behavior*. Reading, Massachusetts: Addison-Wesley, 1970.

Kohlberg, L. Stage and sequence: The cognitive-developmental approach to socialization. In D. Goslin (Ed.), *Handbook of socialization theory and research*. Chicago: Rand McNally, 1969.

Kohlberg, L. Moral stages and moralization: The cognitive-developmental approach. In T. Lickona (Ed.), *Moral development and behavior*. New York: Holt, 1976.

Komorita, S. S. Cooperative choice in a prisoner's dilemma game. *Journal of Personality & Social Psychology*, 1965, *2*, 741–745.

Konecni, V. J. Some effects of guilt on compliance: A field replication. *Journal of Personality & Social Psychology*, 1972, *23*, 30–32.

Korte, C. Group effects on help-giving in an emergency. *Proceedings of the 77th Annual Convention of the American Psychological Association,* 1969, *4,* 383–384.

Korte, C., & Kern, N. Response to altruistic opportunities in urban and nonurban settings. *Journal of Social Psychology,* 1975, *95,* 183–184.

Kramer, B. M. Residential contact as a determinant of attitudes toward Negroes. Unpublished doctoral dissertation, Harvard University, 1950.

Kraut, R. E. Effects of social labeling on giving to charity. *Journal of Experimental & Social Psychology,* 1973, *9,* 556–562.

Krebs, D. L. Altruism—An examination of the concept and a review of the literature. *Psychological Bulletin,* 1970, *73,* 258–303.

Krebs, D. L. Empathy and altruism. *Journal of Personality and Social Psychology,* 1975, *32,* 1134–1146.

Krebs, D. L., & Staub, E. Personality and varied forms of helping. Unpublished research, Harvard University, 1971.

Krebs, D. L., & Stirrup, B. Role-taking ability and altruistic behavior in elementary school children. Paper presented at the annual meeting of the American Psychological Association, New Orleans, August, 1974.

Krebs, D. L., & Wispé, L. G. On defining altruism: A rejoinder to L. J. Severy. *Journal of Social Issues,* 1974, *30,* 194–199.

Kriss, M., Indenbaum, E., & Tesch, F. Message type and status of interactants as determinants of telephone helping behavior. *Journal of Personality & Social Psychology,* 1974, *6,* 856–859.

Krupat, E., & Coury, M. The lost letter technique and helping: An urban–nonurban comparison. Paper presented at the 83rd Annual Convention of the American Psychological Association, Chicago, September, 1975.

Kuhlman, D. M., & Wimberley, D. L. Expectations of choice behavior held by cooperators, competitors, and individuals across four classes of experimental games. *Journal of Personality & Social Psychology,* 1976, *34,* 69–81.

Lane, I. M., & Coon, R. C. Reward allocation in preschool children. *Child Development,* 1971, *43,* 1382–1389.

Lane, I. M., & Messé, L. A. Equity and the distribution of rewards. *Journal of Personality & Social Psychology,* 1971, *20,* 1–17.

Lane, I. M., & Messe, I. A. Distribution of insufficient, sufficient and oversufficient rewards: A clarification of equity theory. *Journal of Personality & Social Psychology,* 1972, *21,* 228–233.

Langer, E. J., & Abelson, R. P. The semantics of asking a favor: How to succeed in getting help without really dying. *Journal of Personality & Social Psychology,* 1972, *24,* 26–32.

Latané, B. *Theory of social impact.* Paper presented at the International Congress of Psychology, Paris, 1976.

Latané, B., & Darley, J. M. Group inhibition of bystander intervention. *Journal of Personality & Social Psychology,* 1968, *10,* 215–221.

Latané, B., & Darley, J. M. *The unresponsive bystander: Why doesn't he help?* New York: Appleton-Crofts, 1970.

Latané, B., & Rodin, J. A lady in distress: Inhibiting effects of friends and strangers on bystander intervention. *Journal of Experimental Social Psychology,* 1969, *5,* 189–202.

Laumann, E. O. Friends of urban men: An assessment of accuracy in reporting. *Sociometry,* 1969, *32,* 54–69.

Lavery, J. J., & Foley, P. J. Altruism or arousal in the rat? *Science,* 1963, *140,* 172–173.

Lazarowitz, R., Stephan, W. G., & Friedman, T. Effects of moral justifications and moral reasoning on altruism. *Developmental Psychology,* 1976, *12,* 353–354.

Lazarus, R. S. *Psychological stress and the coping process.* New York: McGraw-Hill, 1966.

Lazarus, R. S., & Alfert, E. The short-circuiting of threat by experimentally altering cognitive appraisal. *Journal of Abnormal & Social Psychology,* 1964, *69,* 195–205.

Lazarus, R., Longo, N., Mordkoff, A. M., & Davidson, L. A. A laboratory study of psychological stress produced by a motion picture film. *Psychological Monographs,* 1962, *76,* 34.

Lazarus, R., Opton, E. M., Nomikos, M. S., & Rankin, N. O. The principle of short-circuiting of threat: Further evidence. *Journal of Personality,* 1965, *33,* 622–635.

Leary, T. *Interpersonal diagnosis of personality; A functional theory and methodology for personality evaluation.* New York: Ronald Press, 1957.

Leeds, R. Altruism and the norm of giving. *Merrill-Palmer Quarterly,* 1963, *9,* 229–240.

Lefcourt, H. The functions of the illusion of freedom and control. *American Psychologist,* 1973, *28,* 117–125.

Lefcourt, H. Locus of control and coping with life's events. In E. Staub (Ed.), *Personality: Basic issues and current research.* Englewood Cliffs, New Jersey: Prentice-Hall, 1979. (In press)

Lenrow, P. B. Studies of sympathy. In S. S. Tomkins & C. E. Izard (Eds.), *Affect, cognition, and personality.* N.Y.: Springer, 1965.

Leonard, R. L. Self-concept and attraction for similar and dissimilar others. *Journal of Personality & Social Psychology,* 1975, *31,* 926–929.

Lepper, M. R. Dissonance, self-perception, and honesty in children. *Journal of Personality & Social Psychology,* 1973, *25,* 65–74.

Lerner, M. J. Observer's evaluation of a victim: Justice, guilt and veridical perception. *Journal of Personality & Social Psychology,* 1971, *20,* 127–135.

Lerner, M. J. Social psychology of justice and interpersonal attraction. In T. Huston (Ed.), *Foundations of interpersonal attraction.* New York: Academic Press, 1974.

Lerner, M. J. The justice motive in social behavior: Introduction. *The Journal of Social Issues,* 1975, *31,* 1–20.

Lerner, M. J. The justice motive: Some hypotheses as to its origins and forms. *Journal of Personality,* 1977, *45,* 1–53.

Lerner, M. J., & Matthews, G. Reactions to suffering of others under conditions of indirect responsibility. *Journal of Personality & Social Psychology,* 1967, *5,* 319–325.

Lerner, M. J., & Simmons, C. H. Observer's reaction to the "innocent victim": Compassion or rejection? *Journal of Personality & Social Psychology,* 1966, *4,* 203–210.

Lesk, S., & Zippel, B. Dependency, threat, and helping in a large city. *Journal of Social Psychology,* 1975, *95,* 185–186.

Leventhal, G. S., & Anderson, D. Self interest and the maintenance of equity. *Journal of Personality & Social Psychology,* 1970, *15,* 57–62.

Leventhal, G. S., Popp, A. L., & Sawyer, L. Equity or equality in children's allocation of reward to other persons. *Child Development,* 1973, *44,* 753–763.

Leventhal, H. Emotions: A basic problem for social psychology. In C. Nemeth (Ed.), *Social psychology: Classic and contemporary integrations.* Chicago: Rand McNally College Publishing Co., 1974.

Levin, F. M., & Gergen, K. Revealingness, ingratiation and the disclosure of self. *Proceedings of the 77th Annual Convention of the American Psychological Association,* 1969, *4,* 447–448.

Levin, P. F., & Isen, A. M. Further studies on the effect of feeling good on helping. *Sociometry,* 1975, *38,* 141–147.

Levine, C. Role-taking standpoint and adolescent usage of Kohlberg's conventional stages of moral reasoning. *Journal of Personality & Social Psychology,* 1976, *34,* 41–47.

Levinger, G., & Senn, D. J. Disclosure of feelings in marriage. *Merrill-Palmer Quarterly,* 1967, *13,* 237–249.

Levinger, G., & Snoek, J. D. *Attraction in relationship: A new look at interpersonal attraction.* Morristown, New Jersey: General Learning Press, 1972.

Lewin, K. *A dynamic theory of personality.* New York: McGraw-Hill, 1935.

Lewin, K. The conceptual representation and measurement of psychological forces. *Contributions to Psychological Theory,* 1938, *1,* 247.

Lewin, K. *Resolving social conflicts.* New York: Harper, 1948.

Lewis, M., Young, G., Brooks, J., & Michalson, L. The beginning of friendship. In M. Lewis & L. A. Rosenblum (Eds.), *Friendship and peer relations.* New York: Wiley, 1975.

Liebert, R. M., & Fernandez, L. E. Effects of single and multiple modeling cues on establishing norms for sharing. Paper presented at the meeting of the American Psychological Association, Miami Beach, 1970.

Liebert, R. M., & Poulos, R. W. Eliciting the "norm of giving": Effects of modeling and presence of witness on children's sharing behavior. *Proceedings of the 79th Annual Convention of the American Psychological Association,* 1971.

Liebhart, E. Empathy and emergency helping: The effects of personality, self-concern, and acquaintance. *Journal of Experimental Social Psychology,* 1972, *8,* 404–411.

Linn, L. S. Verbal attitudes and overt behavior: A study of racial discrimination. *Social Forces,* 1965, *43,* 353–364.

Locke, J. An essay concerning human understanding. In E. A. Burtt (Ed.), *The English philosophers from Bacon to Mill.* New York: Random House, 1939.

Loew, C. A. Acquisition of a hostile attitude and its relationship to aggressive behavior. *Journal of Personality & Social Psychology,* 1967, *5,* 335–341.

London, P. The rescuers: Motivational hypotheses about Christians who saved Jews from the Nazis. In J. Macaulay & L. Berkowitz (Eds.), *Altruism and helping behavior.* New York: Academic Press, 1970.

Long, G. T., & Lerner, M. J. Deserving, the "personal contract," and altruistic behavior by children. *Journal of Personality & Social Psychology,* 1974, *29,* 551–556.

Loomis, J. L. Communication, the development of trust and cooperative behavior. *Human Relations,* 1959, *12,* 305–315.

Lorenz, K. *On aggression.* New York: Bantam Books, 1967.

Lott, A. J., & Lott, B. E. Group cohesiveness as interpersonal attraction: A review of relationships with antecedent and consequent variables. *Psychological Bulletin,* 1965, *64,* 259–309.

Lott, A. J., & Lott, B. E. Liked and disliked persons as reinforcing stimuli. *Journal of Personality & Social Psychology,* 1969, *11,* 129–137.

Lott, B. E., & Lott, A. J. The formation of positive attitudes toward group members. *Journal of Abnormal Social Psychology,* 1960, *61,* 297–300.

Macaulay, J. A shill for charity. In J. Macaulay & L. Berkowitz (Eds.), *Altruism and helping behavior.* New York: Academic Press, 1970.

Maccoby, E. E., & Jacklin, C. N. *The psychology of sex differences.* Stanford, California: Stanford University Press, 1974

MacDonald, A. P., Kessel, V. S., & Fuller, J. B. Self-disclosure and two kinds of trust. Unpublished manuscript, Rehabilitation Research and Training Center, West Virginia University, 1970.

Maher, B. A. *Principles of psychopathology: An experimental approach.* New York: McGraw-Hill, 1966.

Mallick, S. K., & McCandless, B. R. A study of catharsis of aggression. *Journal of Personality & Social Psychology,* 1966, *4,* 591–596.

Markowitz, J. *A walk on the crust of hell.* Brattleboro, Vermont: The Stephen Greene Press, 1973.

Marlatt, G. A. A comparison of vicarious and direct reinforcement control of verbal behavior in an interview setting. *Journal of Personality & Social Psychology,* 1970, *16,* 695–703.

Marlatt, G. A. Exposure to a model and task ambiguity as determinants of verbal behavior in an interview. *Journal of Consulting & Clinical Psychology,* 1971, *36,* 258–276.

Maslow, A. H. Some basic propositions of a growth and self-actualization psychology.

In G. Lindzey & C. S. Hall (Eds.), *Theories of personality: Primary sources and research*. New York: John Wiley & Sons, 1965.

Masserman, J. H., Wechkin, S., & Terris, W. "Altruistic" behavior in rhesus monkeys. *American Journal of Psychiatry*, 1964, *121*, 584–585.

Masters, J. C. Effects of social comparison upon subsequent self-reinforcement behavior in children. *Journal of Personality & Social Psychology*, 1968, *10*, 391–401.

Masters, J. C. Social comparison, self-reinforcement, and the value of a reinforcer. *Child Development*, 1969, *40*, 1027–1038.

Masters, J. C. Effects of social comparison upon children's self-reinforcement and altruism toward competitors and friends. *Developmental Psychology*, 1971, *5*, 64–72.

Masters, J. C. Social comparison by young children. In W. W. Hartup (Ed.), *The young child*, Vol. 2. Washington, D.C.: 1972.

Masters, J. C., & Furman, W. Effects of affective states on non-contingent outcome expectancies and beliefs in internal or external control. *Developmental Psychology*, 1976, *12*, 481–482.

Masters, J. C., & Mokros, J. R. Self-reinforcement processes in children. In *Advances in child development and behavior*, Vol. 9. New York: Academic Press, 1974.

Masters, J. C., & Peskay, J. Effects of race, socioeconomic status, and success or failure upon contingent and noncontingent self-reinforcement in children. *Developmental Psychology*, 1972, *7*, 139–145.

Masters, J. C., & Santrock, J. W. Studies in the self-regulation of behavior: Effects of verbal and cognitive self-reinforcement. *Developmental Psychology*, 1976, *12*, 334–348.

Mathews, K. E., & Canon, L. K. Environmental noise level as a determinant of helping behavior. *Journal of Personality & Social Psychology*, 1975, *32*, 571–577.

Mauss, M. *The gift: Forms and functions of exchange in archaic societies*. Glencoe, Illinois: Free Press, 1954.

McGovern, L. P. Dispositional social anxiety and helping behavior under three conditions of threat. *Journal of Personality*, 1976, *44*, 84–97.

McGuire, J. M., & Thomas, M. H. Effects of sex, competence, and competition on sharing behavior in children. *Journal of Personality & Social Psychology*, 1975, *32*, 490–494.

McMillan, D. L. Transgression, self-image and compliant behavior. *Journal of Personality & Social Psychology*, 1971, *20*, 176–179.

McNamee, S. M. Moral behavior, moral development and needs in students and political activists, with reference to the law and order stage of development. *Dissertation Abstracts International*, 1972, *33*, 1800–1801.

Mead, M. *Cooporation and competition among primitive peoples*. New York: McGraw-Hill, 1937.

Mead, M. *Culture and commitment: A study of the generation gap*. Garden City, New York: Natural History Press/Doubleday & Co., Inc., 1970.

Meichenbaum, D. *Cognitive behavior modification*. Morristown, New Jersey: General Learning Press, 1974.

Merrens, M. R. Nonemergency helping behavior in various sized communities. *Journal of Social Psychology*, 1973, *90*, 327.

Merton, R. K. *Social theory and social structure*. (Rev. ed.) New York: Free Press, 1957.

Messick, D. M. Genetic basis of behavior. *American Psychologist*, 1976, *31*, 366–369.

Midlarsky, E. Some antecedents of aiding under stress. *Proceedings of the 76th Annual Convention of the American Psychological Association*, 1968.

Midlarsky, E. Aiding under stress: The effects of competence, dependency, visibility, and fatalism. *Journal of Personality*, 1971, *39*, 132–149.

Midlarsky, E., & Bryan, J. H. Training charity in children. *Journal of Personality & Social Psychology*, 1967, *5*, 408–415.

Midlarsky, E., & Bryan, J. H. Affect expressions and children's imitative altruism. *Journal of Experimental Research in Personality,* 1972, *6,* 195–203.

Midlarsky, E., Bryan, J. H., & Brickman, P. Aversive approval: Interactive effects of modeling and reinforcement on altruistic behavior. *Child Development,* 1973, *44,* 321–328.

Midlarsky, E., & Midlarsky, M. Some determinants of aiding under experimentally induced stress. *Journal of Personality,* 1973, *41,* 305–327.

Midlarsky, M., & Midlarsky, E. Status inconsistency, aggressive attitude, and helping behavior. *Journal of Personality,* 1976, *44,* 371–391.

Midlarz, S. The role of trust in helping behavior. Unpublished masters thesis, University of Massachusetts, Amherst, 1973.

Milgram, S. The behavioral study of obedience. *Journal of Abnormal & Social Psychology,* 1963, *67,* 371–378.

Milgram, S. Liberating effects of group pressure. *Journal of Personality & Social Psychology,* 1965, *1,* 127–134. (a)

Milgram, S. Some conditions of obedience and disobedience to authority. *Human Relations,* 1965, *18,* 57–76. (b)

Milgram, S. The experience of living in cities. *Science,* 1970, *167,* 1461–1468.

Milgram, S. *Obedience to authority. An experimental view.* New York: Harper, 1974.

Miller, D. T., & Smith, J. The effect of own deservingness and deservingness of others on children's helping behavior. *Child Development,* 1977, *48,* 617–620.

Miller, R. E., Banks, J. H., & Ogawa, N. Role of facial expression in "cooperative-avoidance conditioning" in monkeys. *Journal of Abnormal & Social Psychology,* 1963, *67,* 24–30.

Miller, R. E., Caul, W. F., & Mirsky, I. F. Communication of affects between feral and socially isolated monkeys. *Journal of Personality & Social Psychology,* 1967, *7,* 231–239.

Miller, R. L., Brickman, P., & Bolen, D. Attribution versus persuasion as a means of modifying behavior. *Journal of Personality & Social Psychology,* 1975, *31,* 430–441.

Mills, J., & Egger, R. Effect on derogation of a victim of choosing to reduce his distress. *Journal of Personality & Social Psychology,* 1972, *23,* 405–408.

Mischel, W. Theory and research on the antecedents of self-imposed delay of reward. In B. A. Maher (Ed.), *Progress in experimental personality research,* Vol. 3. New York: Academic Press, 1966.

Mischel, W. *Personality and assessment.* New York: Wiley, 1968.

Mischel, W. Continuity and change in personality. *American Psychologist,* 1969, *24,* 1012–1018.

Mischel, W. Towards a cognitive social learning reconceptualization of personality. *Psychological Review,* 1973, *80,* 252–283.

Mischel, W. *Introduction to personality.* (Second ed.) New York: Holt, 1976.

Mischel, W., Coates, D. B., & Raskoff, A. Effects of success and failure on self-gratification. *Journal of Personality & Social Psychology,* 1968, *10,* 381–390.

Mischel, W., Ebbesen, E., & Zeiss, A. Cognitive and attentional mechanisms in delay of gratification. *Journal of Personality & Social Psychology,* 1971, *21,* 204–218.

Mischel, W., Ebbesen, E., & Zeiss, A. Selective attention to the self: Situational and dispositional determinants. *Journal of Personality & Social Psychology,* 1973, *27,* 129–142.

Mischel, W., & Mischel, H. N. A cognitive social-learning approach to morality and self-regulation. In T. Lickona (Ed.), *Moral development and behavior.* New York: Holt, 1976.

Mischel, W., Zeiss, R., & Zeiss, A. R. Internal–external control and persistence: Validation and implications of the Stanford Preschool Internal–External Scale. *Journal of Personality & Social Psychology,* 1974, *29,* 265–278.

Mitchell, H. E., & Byrne, D. The defendant's dilemma: Effects of jurors' attitudes and authoritarianism on judicial decisions. *Journal of Personality & Social Psychology*, 1973, *25*, 123–129.

Mithaug, E. D. The development of cooperation in alternative task situations. *Journal of Experimental Child Psychology*, 1969, *8*, 443–460.

Mithaug, E. D., & Burgess, R. L. The effects of different reinforcement contingencies in the development of social cooperation. *Journal of Experimental Child Psychology*, 1968, *6*, 402–426.

Moore, B., Underwood, B., & Rosenhan, D. L. Affect and altruism. *Developmental Psychology*, 1973, *8*, 99–104.

Morgan, C. J. Bystander intervention: Experimental test of a formal model. *Journal of Personality & Social Psychology*, 1978, *36*, 43–56.

Morgan, W. G. Situational specificity in altruistic behavior. *Representative Research in Social Psychology*, 1973, *4*, 56–66.

Morgan, W. R., & Sawyer, J. Bargaining, expectations, and the preference for equality over equity. *Journal of Personality & Social Psychology*, 1967, *6*, 139–149.

Morgan, W. R., & Sawyer, J. *Equality, equity, and procedural justice in social exchange.* Unpublished manuscript, University of Indiana, 1978.

Moriarty, T. Crime, commitment, and the responsive bystander: Two field experiments. *Journal of Personality & Social Psychology*, 1975, *31*, 370–376.

Morris, S., & Rosen, S. Effects of felt adequacy and opportunity to reciprocate on help-seeking. *Journal of Experimental Social Psychology*, 1973, *9*, 265–276.

Morse, S., & Gergen, J. Social comparison, self-consistency, and the concept of self. *Journal of Personality & Social Psychology*, 1970, *16*, 148–156.

Moss, M. K., & Page, R. A. Reinforcement and helping behavior. *Journal of Applied Psychology*, 1972, *2*, 360–371.

Muir, D. E., & Weinstein, E. A. The social debt: An investigation of lower-class and middle-class norms of social obligation. *American Sociological Review*, 1962, *27*, 532–539.

Murphy, L. B. *Social behavior and child personality: An exploratory study of some roots of sympathy.* New York: Columbia University Press, 1937.

Murray, H. A. *Explorations in personality.* New York: Oxford University Press, 1938.

Mussen, P., & Eisenberg-Berg, N. *Roots of caring, sharing and helping.* San Francisco: W. H. Freeman, 1977.

Nadel, B. S., & Altrocchi, J. Attribution of hostile intent in literature. *Psychological Reports*, 1969, *25*, 747–763.

Nader, L. Forums of justice: A cross-cultural perspective. *The Journal of Social Issues*, 1975, *31*, 151–170.

Nadler, A., Fisher, J. D., & Streufert, S. The donor's dilemma: Recipient's reactions to aid from friend or foe. *Journal of Applied Social Psychology*, 1974, *4*, 275–285.

Nahemow, L., & Lawton, M. P. Similarity and propinquity in friendship formation. *Journal of Personality & Social Psychology*, 1975, *32*, 205–213.

Nelson, L., & Madsen, M. C. Cooperation and competition in four-year-olds as a function of reward contingency and subculture. *Developmental Psychology*, 1968, *1*, 340–344.

Nemeth, C. Bargaining and reciprocity. *Psychological Bulletin*, 1970, *74*, 297–308. (a)

Nemeth, C. Effects of free versus constrained behavior in attraction between people. *Journal of Personality & Social Psychology*, 1970, *15*, 302–311. (b)

Newcomb, T. M. Autistic hostility and social reality. *Human Relations*, 1947, *1*, 69–86.

Newcomb, T. M. *The acquaintance process.* New York: Holt, 1961.

Nisbett, R. E., & Valins, J. *Perceiving the causes of one's own behavior.* Morristown, New Jersey: General Learning Press, 1971.

Nissen, H. W., & Crawford, M. P. A preliminary study of foodsharing behavior in young chimpanzees. *Journal of Comparative & Physiological Psychology*, 1936, *22*, 383–419.

Nord, W. R. Social exchange theory: An integrative approach to social conformity. *Psychological Bulletin*, 1969, *71*, 174–208.

O'Bryant, S. L., & Brophy, J. E. Sex differences in altruistic behavior. *Developmental Psychology*, 1976, *12*, 554–555.

Ogston, K. M., & Davidson, P. O. The effects of cognitive expectancies on vicarious conditioning. *British Journal of Social & Clinical Psychology*, 1972, *11*, 126–134.

Olejnik, A. B. The effects of reward-deservedness on children's sharing. *Child Development*, 1976, *47*, 380–385.

Pastore, N. The role of arbitrariness in the frustration-aggression hypothesis. *Journal of Abnormal & Social Psychology*, 1952, *47*, 728–731.

Penner, L. A. Interpersonal attraction toward a black person as a function of value importance. *Personality: An International Journal*, 1971, *2*, 175–187.

Penner, L. A., Summers, L. S., Brookmire, D. A., & Dertke, M. C. The lost dollar: Situational and personality determinants of a pro- and antisocial behavior. *Journal of Personality*, 1976, *44*, 274–293.

Peplau, L. A. Impact of fear of success and sex-role attitudes on womens' competitive achievement. *Journal of Personality & Social Psychology*, 1976, *34*, 561–68.

Peterson, L., Hartmann, D. P., & Gelfand, D. M. Developmental changes in the effects of dependency and reciprocity cues on children's moral judgments and donation rates. *Child Development*, 1977, *48*, 1331–1339.

Piaget, J. The moral judgment of the child. London: Kegan Paul, Trench, & Trubner, 1932.

Pieper, J. *The four cardinal virtues*. Notre Dame, Indiana: University of Notre Dame Press, 1966.

Piliavin, I. M., Piliavin, J. A., & Rodin, J. Costs, diffusion and the stigmatized victim. *Journal of Personality & Social Psychology*, 1975, *3*, 429–438.

Piliavin, I. M., Rodin, J., & Piliavin, J. A. Good Samaritanism: An underground phenomenon. *Journal of Personality & Social Psychology*, 1969, *13*, 289–299.

Piliavin, J. A. Impulsive helping, arousal, and diffusion of responsibility. Paper presented at the XXI International Congress of Psychology, Paris, 1976.

Piliavin, J. A., & Piliavin, I. M. Effect of blood on reactions to a victim. *Journal of Personality & Social Psychology*, 1972, *23*, 353–362.

Pleck, J. H. Male threat from female competence. *Journal of Consulting Clinical Psychology*, 1976, *44*, 608–613.

Pliner, P., Hart, H., Kohl, J., and Saari, D. Compliance without pressure: Some further data on the foot-in-the-door technique. *Journal of Experimental Social Psychology*, 1974, *10*, 17–22.

Pomazal, R. J. Attitudes, normative beliefs, and altruism: Helping for helping behavior. Unpublished doctoral dissertation, University of Illinois, 1974.

Pomazal, R. J., & Clore, G. L. Helping on the highway: The effects of dependency and sex. *Journal of Applied Social Psychology*, 1973, *3*, 150–164.

Pomazal, R. J., & Jaccard, J. J. An informational approach to altruistic behavior. *Journal of Personality & Social Psychology*, 1976, *33*, 317–327.

Poulos, R. W., & Liebert, R. M. Influence of modeling, exhortative verbalization and surveillance on children's sharing. *Developmental Psychology*, 1972, *6*, 402–408.

Presbie, R. J., & Coiteux, P. F. Learning to be generous or stingy: Imitation of sharing behavior as a function of model generosity and vicarious reinforcement. *Child Development*, 1971, *42*, 1033–1038.

Priest, R. F., & Sawyer, J. Proximity and peership: Bases of balance in interpersonal attraction. *American Journal of Sociology*, 1967, *72*, 633–649.

Pruitt, D. G. Reciprocity and credit building in a laboratory dyad. *Journal of Personality & Social Psychology*, 1968, *8*, 143–147.

Rapoport, A., & Chammah, A. M. *Prisoner's dilemma: A study in conflict and cooperation*. Ann Arbor: University of Michigan Press, 1965.

Rawlings, E. I. Witnessing harm to others: A reassessment of the role of guilt in altruistic behavior. *Journal of Personality & Social Psychology*, 1968, *10*, 337–380.

Regan, D. T. Effects of a favor and liking on compliance. *Journal of Personality & Social Psychology*, 1971, *7*, 627–639.

Regan, D., & Totten, J. Empathy and attribution: Turning observers into actors. *Journal of Personality & Social Psychology*, 1975, *32*, 850–856.

Regan, D., Williams, M., & Sparling, S. Voluntary expiation of guilt: A field replication. *Journal of Personality & Social Psychology*, 1972, *24*, 42.

Regan, J. Guilt, perceived injustice and altruistic behavior. *Journal of Personality & Social Psychology*, 1971, *18*, 124–132.

Reykowski, J. Position of self structure in the cognitive system and prosocial orientation. Paper presented at the Conference on Mechanisms of Prosocial Behavior, Nieberów, Poland, 1974.

Reykowski, J. Introduction. In J. Reykowski (Ed.), *Studies in the mechanisms of prosocial behavior*. Warszawskiego: Wydaevnictiva Universytetu, 1975.

Reykowski, J., & Jarymowicz, M. Elicitation of the prosocial orientation. Unpublished manuscript, University of Warsaw, 1976.

Rheingold, H. L., Hay, D. F., & West, M. J. Sharing in the second year of life. *Child Development*, 1976, *47*, 1148–1158.

Rice, G. E., & Gainer, P. Altruism in the albino rat. *Journal of Comparative & Physiological Psychology*, 1962, *55*, 123–125.

Rice, M. E., & Grusec, J. E. Saying and doing: Effects on observer's performance. *Journal of Personality & Social Psychology*, 1975, *32*, 584–593.

Richmond, B. O., & Weiner, G. P. Cooperation and competition among young children as a function of ethnic grouping, grade, sex, and reward condition. *Journal of Educational Psychology*, 1973, *64*, 329–334.

Ridington, R. The medicine fight: An instrument of political process among the Beaver Indians. *American Anthropologist*, 1968, *70*, 1152–1160.

Riesman, D. *The lonely crowd*. New Haven: Yale University Press, 1950.

Roberts, M. D. The persistence of interpersonal trust. Unpublished masters thesis, University of Connecticut, 1967.

Rogers, C. R. A theory of therapy, personality, and interpersonal relationships, as developed in the client-centered framework. In S. Koch (Ed.), *Psychology: A study of a science*, Vol. 3. New York: McGraw-Hill, 1959.

Rokeach, M. *The nature of human values*. New York: Macmillan, 1973.

Rokeach, M., Smith, P. W., & Evans, R. I. Two kinds of prejudice or one? In M. Rokeach (Ed.), *The open and closed mind*. New York: Basic Books, 1960.

Rosenfeld, H. M. Approval-seeking and approval-inducing functions of verbal and nonverbal responses in the dyad. *Journal of Personality & Social Psychology*, 1966, *4*, 597–605. (a)

Rosenfeld, H. M. Instrumental affiliative functions of racial and gestural expressions. *Journal of Personality & Social Psychology*, 1966, *4*, 65–69. (b)

Rosenhan, D. Some origins of concern for others. In P. Mussen (Ed.), *New directions in developmental psychology*. New York: Holt, 1969.

Rosenhan, D. The natural socialization of altruistic autonomy. In J. Macaulay & L. Berkowitz (Eds.), *Altruism and helping*. New York: Academic Press, 1970.

Rosenhan, D. L., Moore, B. S., & Underwood, B. The social psychology of moral behavior. In T. Lickona (Ed.), *Moral development and behavior*. New York: Holt, 1976.

Rosenhan, D. L., Underwood, B., & Moore, B. Affect moderates self-gratification and altruism. *Journal of Personality & Social Psychology*, 1974, *30*, 546–552.

Rosenhan, D., & White, G. Observation and rehearsal as determinants of prosocial behavior. *Journal of Personality & Social Psychology*, 1967, *5*, 424–431.

Ross, A. S. *Modes of guilt reaction*. Unpublished doctoral dissertation, University of Minnesota, 1965.

Ross, A. S. The effect of increased responsibility on bystander intervention: The presence of children. *Journal of Personality & Social Psychology*, 1971, *19*, 306–310.

Ross, A. S., & Brabend, J. Effect of increased responsibility on bystander intervention II: The cue value of a blind person. *Journal of Personality & Social Psychology*, 1973, *25*, 254–258.

Rothman, G. R. The influence of moral reasoning on behavioral choices. *Child Development*, 1976, *47*, 399–406.

Rotter, J. B. *Social learning and clinical psychology*. Englewood Cliffs, New Jersey: Prentice-Hall, 1954.

Rotter, J. B. Generalized expectancies for internal versus external control of reinforcement. *Psychological Monographs*, 1966, *80*, 1–28.

Rotter, J. B. A new scale for measurement of interpersonal trust. *Journal of Personality*, 1967, *35*, 651–665.

Rotter, J. B. Generalized expectancies for interpersonal trust. *American Psychologist*, 1971, *26*, 443–452.

Rubin, K. H., & Schneider, F. W. The relationship between moral judgment, egocentrism, and altruistic behavior. *Child Development*, 1973, *44*, 661–665.

Rubin, Z. *Liking and loving: An invitation to social psychology*. New York: Holt, 1973.

Rubin, Z., & Peplau, L. A. Belief in a just world and reactions to another's lot: A study of participants in the national draft lottery. *Journal of Social Issues*, 1973, *29*, 73–93.

Rubin, Z., & Peplau, L. A. Who believes in a just world? *Journal of Social Issues*, 1975, *31*, 65–89.

Rubin, Z., & Shenker, S. Friendship, proximity, and self-disclosure. *Journal of Personality*, 1978, *46*, 1–23.

Rudestam, K. E., Richards, D. L., & Garrison, P. Effect of self-esteem on an unobtrusive measure of altruism. *Psychological Reports*, 1971, *29*, 847–851.

Rushton, J. P. Generosity in children: Immediate and long-term effects of modeling, preaching, and moral judgment. *Journal of Personality & Social Psychology*, 1975, *31*, 459–466.

Rushton, J. P. Socialization and the altruistic behavior of children. *Psychological Bulletin*, 1976, *83*, 898–913.

Rushton, J. P., & Wiener, J. Altruism and cognitive development in children. *British Journal of Social & Clinical Psychology*, 1975, *14*, 341–349.

Saegert, S., Swap, S., & Zajonc, R. B. Exposure, context and interpersonal attraction. *Journal of Personality & Social Psychology*, 1973, *25*, 234–242.

Sagi, A., & Hoffman, M. L. Empathic distress in the newborn. *Developmental Psychology*, 1976, *12*, 175–176.

Sampson, E. E. On justice as equality. *Journal of Social Issues*, 1975, *31*, 21–43.

Sanford, N., & Comstock, C. and associates. *Sanctions for evil*. San Francisco, California: Jossey-Bass, 1971.

Sanford, S. A. The effect of attribution of intention: Delinquents' and nondelinquents' responses to frustration. Unpublished doctoral dissertation, Harvard University, 1970.

Sarason, I. Experimental approaches to test anxiety: Attention and the uses of information. In C. Spielberger (Ed.), *Anxiety: Current trends in theory and research*, Vol. II. New York: Academic Press, 1972.

Savicki, V. Outcomes of non-reciprocal self-disclosure strategies. *Journal of Personality & Social Psychology*, 1972, *23*, 271–276.

Schachter, S., & Latané, B. Crime, cognition and the autonomic nervous system. In the *Nebraska symposium on motivation*. Lincoln: University of Nebraska Press, 1964.

Schachter, S., & Singer, J. E. Cognitive, social, and psychological determinants of emotional state. *Psychological Review*, 1962, *69*, 379–399.

Schneider, D. J. Implicit personality theory: A review. *Psychological Bulletin*, 1973, *79*, 294–309.

Schneider, F. W. When will a stranger lend a helping hand? *Journal of Social Psychology*, 1973, *90*, 335.

Schneider, F. W., & Mockus, Z. Failure to find a rural–urban difference in incidence of altruistic behavior. *Psychological Reports*, 1974, *35*, 294.

Schopler, J. An investigation of sex differences on the influence of dependence. *Sociometry*, 1967, *30*, 50–63.

Schopler, J. An attribution analysis of some determinants of reciprocating a benefit. In J. Macaulay & L. Berkowitz (Eds.), *Altruism and helping behavior*. New York: Academic Press, 1970.

Schopler, J., & Bateson, N. The power of dependence. *Journal of Personality & Social Psychology*, 1965, *2*, 247–254.

Schopler, J., & Compere, J. S. Effect of being kind or harsh to another on liking. *Journal of Personality & Social Psychology*, 1971, *20*, 155–159.

Schopler, J., & Matthews. The influence of the perceived causal locus of partner's dependence on the use of interpersonal power. *Journal of Personality & Social Psychology*, 1965, *2*, 609–612.

Schopler, J., & Thompson, V. Role of attribution processes in mediating amount of reciprocity for a favor. *Journal of Personality & Social Psychology*, 1968, *10*, 243–250.

Schwartz, S. H. Words, deeds, and the perception of consequences and responsibility in action situations. *Journal of Personality & Social Psychology*, 1968, *10*, 232–242.

Schwartz, S. H. Elicitation of moral obligation and self-sacrificing behavior: An experimental study of volunteering to be a bone marrow donor. *Journal of Personality & Social Psychology*, 1970, *15*, 283–293. (a)

Schwartz, S. H. Moral decision making and behavior. In J. Macaulay & L. Berkowitz (Eds.), *Altruism and helping behavior*. New York: Academic Press, 1970. (b)

Schwartz, S. H. Normative explanations of helping behavior: A critique, proposal, and empirical test. *Journal of Experimental Social Psychology*, 1973, *9*, 349–364.

Schwartz, S. H. Awareness of interpersonal consequences, responsibility denial, and volunteering. *Journal of Personality & Social Psychology*, 1974, *30*, 57–63.

Schwartz, S. H. Paper presented at the 23rd International Congress of Psychology, Paris, 1976.

Schwartz, S. H. Normative influences on altruism. In L. Berkowitz (Ed.), *Advances in experimental social psychology*, Vol. 10. New York: Academic Press, 1977.

Schwartz, S. H., & Clausen, G. T. Responsibility, norms and helping in an emergency. *Journal of Personality & Social Psychology*, 1970, *16*, 299–310.

Schwartz, S. H., Feldman, K. A., Brown, M. E., & Heingarter, A. Some personality correlates of conduct in two situations of moral conflict. *Journal of Personality*, 1969, *37*, 41–57.

Seligman, M. E. P. *Helplessness: On depression, development, and death*. San Francisco, California: W. H. Freeman, 1975.

Severy, L. J. Comments and rejoinders. *Journal of Social Issues*, 1974, *30*, 189–198.

Shantz, C. U. The development of social cognition. In E. M. Hetherington (Ed.), *Review of child development research*, Vol. 5. Chicago: University of Chicago Press, 1975.

Shapiro, A., & Madsen, M. C. Cooperative and competitive behavior of kibbutz and urban children in Israel. *Child Development*, 1969, *40*, 609–617.

Shapiro, A., & Swenson, C. Patterns of self-disclosure among married couples. *Journal of Counseling Psychology*, 1969, *16*, 179–180.

Shapiro, B. Genetic origins of altruism. Paper prepared for a course in personality and prosocial behavior, Stanford University, 1974.

Sharabany, R. Intimate friendship among kibbutz and city children and its measurement. Unpublished doctoral dissertation, Cornell University, 1974 (University Microfilms, #74–17, 682).

Sherif, M., Harvey, O. J., White, B. J., Hood, W. P., & Sherif, C. W. *Intergroup conflict and cooperation: The robbers cave experiment.* Norman: Institute of Group Relations, University of Oklahoma, 1961.

Sherrod, D. R., & Downs, R. Environmental determinants of altruism: The effects of stimulus overload and perceived control on helping. *Journal of Experimental Social Psychology,* 1974, *10,* 468–479.

Shure, Y. H., Meeker, R. D., & Hansford, E. A. The effectiveness of pacifist strategies in bargaining games. *Journal of Conflict Resolution,* 1965, *9,* 106–117.

Simmel, G. The secret and the secret society. In R. Wolff (Ed.), *The sociology of Georg Simmel.* New York: Free Press, 1964.

Simner, M. L. Newborn's response to the cry of another infant. *Developmental Psychology,* 1971, *5,* 136–150.

Simons, C. W., & Piliavin, J. A. Effect of deception on reactions to a victim. *Journal of Personality & Social Psychology,* 1972, *21,* 56–60.

Singer, J. L., & Singer, D. Personality. In P. T. Mussen & M. K. Rosenzweig (Eds.), *Annual review of psychology.* Palo Alto: Annual Reviews, Inc., 1972.

Slater, P. E. Role differentiation in small groups. *American Sociological Review,* 1955, *20,* 300–310.

Slavson, S. R. *Reclaiming the delinquent.* New York: The Free Press, 1965.

Smith, A. *The theory of moral sentiments.* London: Bell, 1892.

Smith, R., Smythe, L., & Lien, D. Inhibition of helping behavior by a similar or dissimilar nonreactive bystander. *Journal of Personality & Social Psychology,* 1972, *23,* 414–419.

Snyder, M., & Cunningham, M. R. To comply or not comply: Testing the self-perception explanation of the "foot-in-the-door" phenomenon. *Journal of Personality & Social Psychology,* 1975, *31,* 64–67.

Snyder, M., & Tanke, E. D. Behavior and attitude: Some people are more consistent than others. *Journal of Personality,* 1976, *44,* 501–517.

Sole, K., Marton, J., & Hornstein, H. A. Opinion similarity and helping: Three field experiments investigating the bases of promotive tension. *Journal of Experimental Social Psychology,* 1975, *11,* 1–13.

Solomon, L. Z., & Grota, P. Imitation of a helpful model: The effect of level of emergency. *Journal of Social Psychology,* 1976, *99,* 29–35.

Sorokin, P. A. The powers of creative unselfish love. In A. H. Maslow (Ed.), *New knowledge in human values.* Chicago: Henry Regnery Co., 1971.

Sorrentino, R. M., & Boutilier, R. G. Evaluation of a victim as a function of fate similarity dissimilarity. *Journal of Experimental Social Psychology,* 1974, *10,* 83–92.

Speisman, J. C., Lazarus, R. S., Mordkoff, A. M., & Davidson, L. A. The experimental reduction of stress based on ego-defense theory. *Journal of Abnormal Social Psychology,* 1964, *68,* 367–380.

Spiritas, A. A., & Holmes, D. S. Effects of models on interview responses. *Journal of Counseling Psychology,* 1971, *18,* 217–220.

Stapleton, R. E., Nacci, P., & Tedeschi, J. T. Interpersonal attraction and the reciprocity of benefits. *Journal of Personality & Social Psychology,* 1973, *28,* 199–205.

Staub, E. The effects of success and failure on sharing behavior of children. Paper presented at the meetings of the Eastern Psychological Association, Washington, D.C., April, 1968.

Staub, E. Reactions to psychological distress. Unpublished research, Harvard University, 1969.

Staub, E. A child in distress: The effects of focusing responsibility on children on their attempts to help. *Developmental Psychology,* 1970, *2,* 152–154. (a)

Staub, E. A child in distress: The influence of age and number of witnesses on children's attempts to help. *Journal of Personality & Social Psychology,* 1970, *14,* 130–140. (b)

Staub, E. A child in distress: The influence of modeling and nurturance on children's attempts to help. *Developmental Psychology*, 1971, *5*, 124–133. (a)

Staub, E. Helping a person in distress: The influence of implicit and explicit "rules" of conduct on children and adults. *Journal of Personality & Social Psychology*, 1971, *17*, 137–145. (b)

Staub, E. The learning and unlearning of aggression: The role of anxiety, empathy, efficacy and prosocial values. In J. Singer (Ed.), *The Control of aggression and violence: Cognitive and physiological factors*. New York: Academic Press, 1971. (c)

Staub, E. The use of role playing and induction in children's learning of helping and sharing behavior. *Child Development*, 1971, *42*, 805–817. (d)

Staub, E. The effects of persuasion and modeling on delay of gratification. *Developmental Psychology*, 1972, *6*, 168–177. (a)

Staub, E. Instigation to goodness: The role of social norms and interpersonal influence. *Journal of Social Issues*, 1972, *28*, 131–151. (b)

Staub, E. Children's sharing behavior: Success and failure, the "norm of deserving," and reciprocity in sharing. Paper presented at the symposium entitled "Helping and Sharing: Concepts of Altruism and Cooperation," at the meeting of the Society of Research in Child Development, Philadelphia, March, 1973.

Staub, E. Helping a distressed person: Social, personality, and stimulus determinants. In L. Berkowitz (Ed.), *Advances in experimental social psychology*, Vol. 7. New York: Academic Press, 1974. (a)

Staub, E. Varieties of self control. Position paper prepared for NIMH workshop on "Locus of Control and Related Variables." Washington, D.C., October, 1974. (b)

Staub, E. *The development of prosocial behavior in children*. Morristown, New Jersey: General Learning Press, 1975. (a)

Staub, E. To rear a prosocial child: Reasoning, learning by doing, and learning by teaching others. In D. DePalma & J. Folley (Eds.), *Moral development: Current theory and research*. Hillsdale, New Jersey: Lawrence Erlbaum Associates, 1975 (b)

Staub, E. The development of prosocial behavior: Directions for future research and applications to education. Paper presented at the Moral Citizenship/Education Conference, Philadelphia, June, 1976. (a)

Staub, E. Predicting prosocial behavior: How do personality characteristics and situations determine conduct? Paper presented at the International Congress of Psychology, Paris, July, 1976. (b)

Staub, E. *The development of positive social behavior and morality*. New York: Academic Press, 1978. (a)

Staub, E. Predicting prosocial behavior: A model for specifying the nature of personality–situation interaction. In L. Pervin & M. Lewis (Eds.), *Internal and external determinants of behavior*. Plenum, 1978. (In press) (b)

Staub, E. Understanding and predicting social behavior—With emphasis on prosocial behavior. In E. Staub (Ed.), *Personality: Basic issues and current research*. Englewood Cliffs, New Jersey: Prentice-Hall, 1979. (In press)

Staub, E., & Baer, R. S. Jr. Stimulus characteristics of a sufferer and difficulty of escape as determinants of helping. *Journal of Personality & Social Psychology*, 1974, *30*, 279–285.

Staub, E., & Conn, L. K. Aggression. In C. G. Costello (Ed.), *Symptoms of psychopathology*. Wiley, 1970.

Staub, E., & Feinberg, H. Experiential learning and induction as means of developing prosocial conduct. Unpublished manuscript, University of Massachusetts, Amherst, 1977. (a)

Staub, E., & Feinberg, H. Positive and negative peer interaction and some of their personality correlates. Unpublished manuscript, University of Massachusetts, Amherst, 1977. (b)

Staub, E., & Feinberg, H. Personality, socialization, and the development of prosocial behavior in children. In D. H. Smith & J. Macaulay (Eds.), *Informal social participation: The determinants of socio-political action, leisure activity, and altruistic behavior.* San Francisco, California: Jossey-Bass, Inc., 1978. (In press)

Staub, E., & Fotta, M. Participation in prosocial behavior and positive induction as means of children learning to be helpful. Unpublished manuscript, University of Massachusetts, Amherst, 1978.

Staub, E., & Kellett, D. S. Increasing pain tolerance by information about aversive stimuli. *Journal of Personality & Social Psychology,* 1972, *21,* 198–203.

Staub, E., & Noerenberg, H. Deserving, reciprocity and transactions in children's sharing behavior. Unpublished manuscript, University of Massachusetts, Amherst, 1978.

Staub, E., & Sherk, L. Need approval, children's sharing behavior, and reciprocity in sharing. *Child Development,* 1970, *41,* 243–253.

Staub, E., Tursky, B., & Schwartz, G. Self-control and predictability: Their effects on reactions to aversive stimulation. *Journal of Personality & Social Psychology,* 1971, *18,* 157–163.

Stein, A. The socialization of achievement orientation in females. *Psychological Bulletin,* 1973, *80,* 345–366.

Stein, D. A., Piliavin, J. A., & Smith, M. B. Race and belief: An open and shut case. *Journal of Personality & Social Psychology,* 1965, *1,* 281–289.

Stein, D. K. Expectation and modeling in groups. Unpublished doctoral dissertation, University of Connecticut, 1970.

Stein, G. M. Children's reactions to innocent victims. *Child Development,* 1973, *44,* 805–810.

Stern, W. *Psychology of early childhood: Up to the sixth year of age.* New York: Holt, 1924.

Stokols, D., & Schopler, J. Reactions to victims under conditions of situational detachment: The effect of responsibility, severity, and expected future interaction. *Journal of Personality & Social Psychology,* 1973, *25,* 199–209.

Stone, L. A. Rejoinder to Berkowitz: Social desirability or social responsibility. *Journal of Personality & Social Psychology,* 1965, *2,* 758.

Stotland, E. Exploratory studies of empathy. In L. Berkowitz (Ed.), *Advances in experimental social psychology,* Vol. 4. New York: Academic Press, 1969.

Strickland, B. R. The prediction of social action from a dimension of internal–external control. *Journal of Social Psychology,* 1965, *66,* 353–358.

Suedfeld, P., Bochner, S., & Wneck., D. Helper–sufferer similarity and a specific request for help: Bystander intervention during a peace demonstration. *Journal of Applied Social Psychology,* 1972, *2,* 17–23.

Sullivan, H. S. *Clinical studies in psychiatry.* New York: W. W. Norton, 1956.

Sykes, G. M., & Matza, D. Techniques of neutralization: A theory of delinquency. *American Sociological Review,* 1957, *22,* 664–670.

Tajfel, H., Flamant, C., Billig, M. Y., & Bundy, R. P. Societal categorization and intergroup behavior. *European Journal of Social Psychology,* 1971, *1,* 149–178.

Taylor, D. A. The development of interpersonal relationships: Social penetration processes. *Journal of Social Psychology,* 1968, *75,* 79–90.

Taylor, D. A., Altman, I., & Senentino, R. Interpersonal exchange as a function of rewards and costs and situational factors: Expectancy confirmation–disconfirmation. *Journal of Experimental Social Psychology,* 1969, *5,* 324–339.

Taylor, S. H. On inferring one's attitudes from one's behavior: Some delimiting conditions. *Journal of Personality & Social Psychology,* 1975, *31,* 126–132.

Tchudnowski, P. Paper delivered at the Conference on Mechanisms of Prosocial Behavior, sponsored by the Committee of Psychological Sciences of the Polish Academy of Sciences, Poland, October, 1974.

Tesser, A., Gatewood, R., & Driver, M. Some determinants of gratitude. *Journal of Personality & Social Psychology*, 1968, *9*, 233–236.

Tessler, R. C., & Schwartz, S. H. Help seeking, self-esteem, and achievement motivation: An attributional analysis. *Journal of Personality & Social Psychology*, 1972, *21*, 318–326.

Test, M. A., & Bryan, J. H. The effects of dependency, models, and reciprocity upon subsequent helping behavior. *Journal of Social Psychology*, 1969, *78*, 205–212.

Thayer, S. Lend me your ears: Racial and sexual factors in helping the deaf. *Journal of Personality & Social Psychology*, 1973, *28*, 8–11.

Theroux, S. S. The effects of modeling on cooperation in young children. Unpublished doctoral dissertation, University of Massachusetts, 1975.

Thibaut, J. W., & Kelley, H. H. *The social psychology of groups.* New York: Wiley, 1959.

Thompson, V. D., Stroebe, W., & Schopler, J. Some situational determinants of the motives attributed to the person who performs a helping act. *Journal of Personality*, 1971, *39*, 460–472.

Tilker, H. A. Socially responsive behavior as a function of observer responsibility and victim feedback. *Journal of Personality & Social Psychology*, 1970, *14*, 95–100.

Tipton, R. M., & Browning, S. Altruism: Reward or punishment? *Journal of Psychology*, 1972, *80*, 319–322. (a)

Tipton, R. M., & Browning, S. The influence of age and obesity on helping behavior. *British Journal of Social & Clinical Psychology*, 1972, *11*, 404–406. (b)

Tomkins, S. S. The constructive role of violence and suffering for the individual and for his society. In S. S. Tomkins & C. E. Izard (Eds.), *Affect, cognition, and personality.* New York: Springer, 1965.

Triandis, H. C. Some universals of social behavior. *Personality & Social Psychology Bulletin*, 1978, *4*, 1–16.

Triandis, H. C., Vassilou, V., & Nassiakou, M. Three cross-cultural studies of subjective culture. *Journal of Personality & Social Psychology, Monograph Supplement*, 1968, *8* (2).

Trivers, R. L. The evolution of reciprocal altruism. *Quarterly Review of Biology*, 1971, *46*, 35–37.

Trivers, R. L. Parent–offspring conflict. *American Zoologist*, 1974, *14*, 249–264.

Turiel, E. Developmental processes in the child's moral thinking. In P. Mussen, J. Langer, & M. Covington (Eds.), *Trends and issues in developmental psychology.* New York: Holt, 1969.

Turiel, E., & Rothman, G. R. The influence of reasoning on behavioral choices at different stages of moral development. *Child Development*, 1972, *43*, 741–756.

Turnbull, C. M. *The mountain people.* Simon and Schuster, 1972.

Ugurel-Semin, R. Moral behavior and moral judgment of children. *Journal of Abnormal & Social Psychology*, 1952, *47*, 463–474.

Underwood, B., Berenson, J. F., Berenson, R. J., Cheng, K. K., Wilson, D., Kulik, J., Moore, B. S., & Wenzel, G. Attention, negative affect, and altruism: An ecological validation. *Personality & Social Psychology Bulletin*, 1977, *3*, 54–58.

Underwood, B., Froming, W. J., & Moore, B. S. Mood, attention, and altruism: A search for mediating variables. *Developmental Psychology*, 1977, *13*, 541–542.

Underwood, B., Moore, B., & Rosenhan, D. L. Affect and self-gratification. *Developmental Psychology*, 1973, *8*, 209–214.

Uranowitz, S. W. Helping and self-attribution: A field experiment. *Journal of Personality & Social Psychology*, 1975, *31*, 852–854.

Urbach, N. M., & Rogolsky, S. Moral judgment in altruism and honesty situations. Unpublished manuscript, Institute for Child Study, University of Maryland, 1976.

Vinacke, W. E. Variables in experimental games: Toward a field theory. *Psychological Bulletin*, 1969, *71*, 293–318.

Vogler, R. E., Masters, W. M., & Morrill, G. S. Shaping cooperative behavior in young children. *Journal of Psychology*, 1970, *74*, 181–186.

Vogler, R. E., Masters, W. M., & Morrill, G. S. Extinction of cooperative behavior as a function of acquisition by shaping or instruction. *Journal of Genetic Psychology*, 1971, *119*, 233–240.

Wagner, C., & Wheeler, L. Model, need and cost effects in helping behavior. *Journal of Personality & Social Psychology*, 1969, *12*, 111–116.

Wallace, L., & Sadalla, E. Behavioral consequences of transgression, I: The effects of social recognition. *Journal of Experimental Research in Personality*, 1966, *1*, 187–194.

Wallington, S. A. Consequences of transgression: Self-punishment and depression. *Journal of Personality & Social Psychology*, 1973, *28*, 1–7.

Wallston, B. S. The effects of sex-role, self-esteem, and expected future integration with an audience on help seeking. *Dissertation Abstracts International*, 1972, *33*, 1838.

Walster, E. Assignment of responsibility for an accident. *Journal of Personality & Social Psychology*, 1966, *3*, 73–79.

Walster, E., Berscheid, E., & Walster, G. W. The exploited: Justice or justification? In J. Macaulay & L. Berkowitz (Eds.), *Altruism and helping behavior*. New York: Academic Press, 1970.

Walster, E., Berscheid, E., & Walster, G. W. New directions in equity research. *Journal of Personality & Social Psychology*, 1973, *25*, 151–176.

Walster, E., & Piliavin, J. A. Equity and the innocent bystander. *Journal of Social Issues*, 1972, *28*, 165–189.

Walster, E., & Prestholdt, P. The effect of misjudging another: Over-compensation, or dissonance reduction? *Journal of Experimental Social Psychology*, 1966, *2*, 85–97.

Walster, E., & Walster, B. Effects of expecting to be liked on choice of associates. *Journal of Abnormal & Social Psychology*, 1963, *67*, 402–404.

Walster, E., & Walster, G. W. Equity and social justice. *Journal of Social Issues*, 1975, *31*, 21–43.

Walster, E., Walster, G. W., & Berscheid, E. *Equity: Theory and research*. Boston: Allyn and Bacon, 1978.

Waxler, C. Z., Yarrow, M. R., & Smith, J. B. Perspective-taking and prosocial behavior. *Developmental Psychology*, 1977, *13*, 87–88.

Wegner, D. M., & Crano, W. D. Racial factors in helping behavior: An unobtrusive field experiment. *Journal of Personality & Social Psychology*, 1975, *32*, 901–905.

Weick, K. E., & Nesset, B. Preferences among forms of equity. *Organizational Behavior & Human Performance*, 1968, *3*, 400–416.

Weiner, F. H. Altruism, ambiance, and action: The effects of rural and urban rearing on helping behavior. *Journal of Personality & Social Psychology*, 1976, *34*, 112–124.

Weiss, R. F., Boyer, J. L., Lombardo, J. P., & Stick, M. H. Altruistic drive and altruistic reinforcement. *Journal of Personality & Social Psychology*, 1973, *25*, 390–400.

Weiss, R. F., Buchanan, W., Altstatt, L., & Lombardo, J. P. Altruism is rewarding. *Science*, 1971, *171*, 1262–1263.

Weissbrod, C. Noncontingent warmth induction, cognitive style, and children's imitative donation and rescue effort behaviors. *Journal of Personality & Social Psychology*, 1976, *34*, 274–281.

West, S. G., Whitney, G., & Schnedler, R. Helping a motorist in distress. The effects of sex, race, and neighborhood. *Journal of Personality & Social Psychology*, 1975, *31*, 691–698.

Weyant, J., & Clark, R. D. III. Dimes and helping: The other side of the coin. *Personality & Social Psychology Bulletin*, 1977, *3*, 107–110.

Wheeler, L. Toward a theory of behavioral contagion. *Psychological Review*, 1966, *73*, 179–192.

White, G. M. Immediate and deferred effects of model observation and guided and unguided rehearsal on donating and stealing. *Journal of Personality & Social Psychology*, 1972, *21*, 139–148.

White, G. M., & Burnam, M. A. Socially cued altruism: Effects of modeling, instructions, and age on public and private donations. *Child Development*, 1975, *46*, 559–563.

Whiting, B., & Edwards, C. P. A cross-cultural analysis of sex differences in the behavior of children aged 3 through 11. *Journal of Social Psychology*, 1973, *91*, 171–188.

Whiting, B. B., & Whiting, J. W. M. *Children of six cultures: A psychocultural analysis.* Cambridge, Massachusetts: Harvard University Press, 1975.

Wiggins, J. S., Renner, K. E., Clore, G. L., & Rose, R. J. *Principles of personality.* Reading, Massachusetts: Addison-Wesley, 1976.

Wilke, H., & Lanzetta, J. T. The obligation to help: The effects of amount of prior help on subsequent helping behavior. *Journal of Experimental Social Psychology*, 1970, *6*, 483–493.

Williams, G. C. *Group selection.* Chicago: Aldine-Atherton, 1971.

Willis, J. A., & Goethals, G. R. Social responsibility and threat to behavioral freedom as determinants of altruistic behavior. *Journal of Personality*, 1973, *41*, 376–384.

Wilson, D. S. A theory of group selection. *Proceedings of the National Academy of Science (U.S.A.)*, 1975, *72*, 143–146.

Wilson, E. O. *Sociobiology: The new synthesis.* Cambridge, Massachusetts: Belkap Press of Harvard University Press, 1975.

Wilson, E. O. Genetic basis of behavior—Especially altruism. *American Psychologist*, 1976, *31*, 370–371.

Wilson, J. P. Motivation, modeling and altruism: A Person × Situation analysis. *Journal of Personality & Social Psychology*, 1976, *34*, 1078–1086.

Wilson, W., & Miller, N. Shifts in evaluation of participants following intergroup competition. *Journal of Abnormal & Social Psychology*, 1961, *63*, 428–432.

Wine, J. Effects of test anxiety and evaluation on children's helping behavior. Unpublished manuscript, Renisen College, University of Waterloo, 1973.

Wispé, L., & Freshley, H. Race, sex, and sympathetic helping behavior: The broken bag caper. *Journal of Personality & Social Psychology*, 1971, *17*, 59–65.

Worchel, S., Andreoli, V., & Archer, L. When is a favor a threat to freedom: The effects of attribution and importance of freedom on reciprocity. *Journal of Personality*, 1976, *44*, 294–310

Worthy, M., Gary, A., & Kahn, G. M. Self-disclosure as an exchange process. *Journal of Personality & Social Psychology*, 1969, *13*, 59–63.

Wortman, C. B., Adesman, P., Herman, E., & Greenberg, R. Self-disclosure: An attributional perspective. *Journal of Personality & Social Psychology*, 1976, *33*, 184–191.

Wright, B. A. Altruism in children and the perceived conduct of others. *Journal of Abnormal & Social Psychology*, 1942, *37*, 218–233.

Wright, T. L., Maggied, P., & Palmer, M. L. An unobtrusive study of interpersonal trust. *Journal of Personality & Social Psychology*, 1975, *32*, 446–448.

Wrightsman, L. S. Personality and attitudinal correlates of trusting and trustworthy behaviors in a two-person game. *Journal of Personality & Social Psychology*, 1966, *4*, 328–332.

Wynne-Edwards, V. C. *Animal dispersion in relation to social behavior.* New York: Harner, 1962.

Yakimovich, D., & Saltz, E. Helping behavior: The cry for help. *Psychonomic Science*, 1971, *23*, 427–428.

Yerkes, R. M., & Dodson, J. D. The relation of strength of stimulus to rapidity of habit formation. *Journal of Comparative Neurology & Psychiatry*, 1908, *18*, 459–482.

Yerkes, R. M., & Yerkes, A. W. Social behavior of infrahuman primates. In C. Murcheson (Ed.), *A handbook of social psychology.* Worcester, Massachusetts: Clark University Press, 1935.

Zajonic, R. B. Attitudinal effects of mere exposure. *Journal of Personality & Social Psychology, Monograph Supplement 1*, 1968, *9* (2).

Zeigarnick, B. Über das Behalten von erledigten und unerledigten Handlungen. *Psychologische Forschungen*, 1927, *9*, 1–85.

Zimbardo, P. G. The human choice: Individuation, reason, and order versus deindividuation, impulse, and chaos. In *Nebraska symposium on motivation*. Lincoln: University of Nebraska Press, 1969.

Zuckerman, M. Belief in a just world and altruistic behavior. *Journal of Personality & Social Psychology*, 1975, *31*, 972–976.

Subject Index

A

Ability-induced responsibility, 96
Acceptance of status quo, 167
Accidental circumstances, function of, 424–425
"Achieved status," 231–232
Achievement orientation, 62–65
  in females, 65
  and goals, 48, 53, 61, 65, 226, 258, 335, 382
  high and low groups, 63–68
  individual, 390
  measures of, 48, 241, 422
  motivation for, 20, 62, 271
  need for, 48, 58
  and opportunity, 53, 301, 310
Acquaintance process, 396, 400, 412
Actions and activities
  children's, 147
  commitment to, 245
  consequences of, 248
  freedom of, 214, 216, 225
  mobilization for, 104–105
  probability of, 56, 71
  real-life, 390
  responses to, 243, 424–429
  sequences of, 422

  sex-typed, 65
  "sinful," 14
Activation and activating potentials
  goals and personality influence on, 47, 51–58
  and personal values and altruistic motives, 6–10, 113, 140, 243
Adaptation, levels of, 303
Adventurousness, factor of, 56, 92, 133
Affection
  as elicitor of altruism, 31
  and enmities, 257
  need for, 348–349, 394
  positive, 132
  providing for, 373
  responsiveness to, 135, 338
Affiliation
  interpersonal, 61
  motivation for, 20
  need for, 59
Age
  difference in, 3, 101, 284
  effects on helpfulness, 101, 253
  effects on reactions to deserving, 284–287
  empathy changes with, 150
  relationships between those of similar, 133, 179, 237

Age, *(cont.)*
  rewards divided equitably because
    of, 179
Aggression and aggressiveness
  animal, 38
  in antisocial individuals, 150, 199, 367
  behavior impulse models, 19, 149, 206,
    263, 357
  in children, 146, 150, 199, 360
  and "cognitive set," 155
  deindividuating conditions enhance, 155
  disinhibited, 199
  empathy inhibits, 149–150
  forms and levels of, 196, 274, 293, 387,
    429
  genetic, instinctual, and hereditary types
    of, 1, 19, 26
  harmful and undesirable traits, 195
  human manifestations of, 1, 19, 26
  inhibiting factors of, 138, 149–150, 387
  innocent people victims of, 162
  and the Just World concept, 151–170
  justification for, 155
  objects of, 162, 309
  prior, 354
  retaliation against, 195, 360–361
  sadistic behavior in, 413
  self-protective measures against, 361
  studies of, 18, 164
  sympathy correlation between, 149
Agreement
  similarity of on issues, 315–317
  verbal, 173, 245
Aid
  recipient of, 345, 348
  refusal of a request for, 216
  voluntary, 348
  willingness to, 224
Alienation, 122
Allport–Vernon–Lindzey scale of values,
    148, 268
Alternatives
  behavioral, 192, 200–201, 385
  Comparison level of, 338
  conflicting, 200
  cooperation opportunities, 382
  reinforcement explanations, 190, 219
Altruism
  in animals, 26, 37
  decisions on, 148
  definition of, 7

  and egoism, 7
  emotionalism and, 31
  evolutionary development of, 26, 29
  following harmdoing, 177
  genetic origins of, 25–38, 328
  toward kinfolk, 27–31
  in male and female, contrasts, 31
  of minority group members, 322–323
  motivation for, 6–10, 242, 332
  among older people, 31
  patterns and measures of, 26, 30–32, 35
  prosocial basis of helpfulness and help-
    ing, 111, 135, 247, 260, 268, 307, 378,
    381
  reciprocal development and interaction,
    27–30
  and reinforcement group, 139
  and self-punishment, 182
  and self-sacrifice, 27–29, 117
  has survival value, 27
  therapy increases, 15
Ambiguity
  and interpretation of events, 86–88
  of need for help, 104, 106, 423
  resolutions and conditions of, 99, 105,
    273–274, 306, 426
  variations in stimulus, 99, 104–105, 325
Ambition, value of, 60, 130, 267
Ambivalence toward blacks, 324
Amoral self-seeking character of man, 18
Anger
  in couples, 412
  experiences provoking, 143, 195, 263, 293
  over injustice, 202, 280
Animals
  aggressive behavior in, 38
  altruism in, 26, 37
  prosocial behavior of, 26, 29, 34–38, 120
  self-sacrificial traits of, 38
  sharing by, 35, 100
Antagonism, group, 392, 430
Anticonformity, 56
Antisocial characteristics, 329, 381
  of children, 263
  and individual aggressiveness, 150, 199,
    367
Anxiety
  of children, 311
  and distress-producing stimulus, 6, 100
  reports of, 280
  self-disclosure associated with, 400–401

social measurements of, 274
sources of, 100, 106, 299
test levels of, 311
Appeals
and humanitarian reactions, 214
positive, 218
power-oriented, 265
responses to and types of, 218, 246, 265–266
Applicability, range of, 47, 52, 253
Approach tendencies, 50
Appropriate social behavior, 202, 255, 273, 362
Approval
desire and motivation for, 20, 57
discrimination in, 374
need for, 123, 132, 271–274, 290, 298
by peers, 227
and social gain, 7, 122, 337
value of, 374, 422
Aptitude test, 31C
Arousal
bystander, 109
emotional, 110, 333
empathic, 138, 147, 149, 259, 314–317
levels of, 20, 39, 106, 110, 137
and performance, 112
physiological, 71, 136–138, 141, 144, 256
of promotive tension, 47, 333
of reactance, 214, 366
self-concern is, 122, 299
sources of, 137, 140, 325
Artificial selection and Darwin, 31
"Ascribed status," 231–232
Ascription of Responsibility (AR), 129, 131, 243, 246–250, 267–268
Assurance, need for, 398
Attention, measure of, 283, 294
Attitude(s)
of helpfulness, 120
opinions on, 251–252, 314–317, 354
toward other people, 319, 326
positive, 68, 291
practical consequences of, 222
prejudicial, 322–323
questionnaire on, 246
selfless, 268
and sex role, 410
similarity in, 315, 318, 332, 352
and social responsibilities, 268
Attraction and attractiveness

evaluation on, 318
and feelings toward victim, 352–353, 393, 405, 409
physical, 338
ratings of, 301–302, 318, 331, 352, 364, 405
and similarity relations, 331–332
Attribution
cooperative, 222
competitive, 222
and conditions affecting prosocial intention, 361–366
defensive, 159
as determinant of imitation, 204–208
hostility, 263
of intention and effect on reciprocity, 357–361
and personality differences, 367–369
and reactance, 366–367
of responsibility, 363
Authority and authoritarianism, 122, 166, 388
awe of, 21
ethics of, 15, 21
external, 15, 18, 23
legitimate, 84
measures of, 15, 330–331, 377
obedience to, 22, 80–83
in society, 15
Autocracy, changes in, 34, 413
Autonomy
concept of, 22
Durkheim's view of, 22–23
and morality, 10–11, 17, 22, 25, 257, 358
question of, 25
standards, 13
Aversive-conditioning studies, 137, 171, 224, 240
Avoidance tendencies, 50
Awareness
of common goals, 391
of consequences, 242–243, 246–249
levels ˜f, 227–229, 247, 394
of other people's needs, 248

B

Bad luck and badness, concepts about, 5, 150, 361
Baron's Complexity Scale, 119

Battery, perspective-taking, 260–261
Behavior
  by-products of, 9, 357
  consistency in, 40–41
  conventional forms of, 84
  impulsive, 263
  instability of, 323
  overt, 319
  patterns of, 19, 48, 98
  positive social, defined, 2, 7, 172, 178, 217, 223, 225, 422–429
  predictability of, 51, 71, 116, 170, 200
  prosocial, relation to morality, 2–10
  rational, 386
  reciprocity in, 350–355
  responsible, 261
Belief(s), 5, 270, 354, 419
  class differences in, 45, 368
  in essential goodness, 361
  inferences, 161
  kinds of, 250–253, 256–257
  personal moral and immoral, 273, 361
  in reciprocity, 45, 343–344, 368
  in responsibility, 228
  sharing of, 397
  and the similarity hypothesis, 327, 396–398
  in transcendant gods, 32
  and value system, 152, 165
Bem theory of self-perception, 219
Benefactors, perceived intent of, 357–361
Beneficial consequences of cooperation, 2, 391
Benefits
  degree of, 350, 352, 428
  exchange of, 24
  expectations of, 304
  magnitude of, 336, 363
  receiving of, 352, 372
  reciprocation of, 336, 341, 343, 369
  return of, 372–373
  unilateral, 372
Benevolence
  and environment, 375
  feelings of, 308, 319, 329, 330, 407
  issue of, 300–301
  morality lies in, 12
  and mutual trust, 8
  to self and to others, 300–302, 331
Biology and biologists, 14, 16, 26, 28, 32
Biosocial optimum, level of, 32

Blacks
  ambivalence toward, 324
  and civil rights organizations, 267
  college students, 271, 321
  cross-racial helping by, 321
  and discrimination, 324, 326, 331
  identification shift with, 321, 325–326
  integration of, 395
  self-assertion of, 326
  and white cooperation, 321–326
Blame, diffusion of, 88
Bodily reactions, 136, 146–147
Bond between self and others, 315–323, 332–334, 367
"Boundaries" of self, 319
Boys
  delinquent, 263
  personality differences with girls, 255–258
  self-control by, 257
Bystanders
  interviews with, 116
  nonreactive, 73–77
  personalities and helpfulness of, 101, 131–132
  presence of, 108, 203, 253, 318, 324, 428
  reactions of, 77, 97–99, 132

C

Carnegie Hero Commission, 4, 91, 95
Categorical Imperative thesis of Kant, 12
Causes
  passion for, 23–24
  promotion of, 4
  social, 166
Character, judgment of, 353
Characteristics, *see also* Personality characteristics
  competence-related, 270
  human, 12, 253
  measuring of, 60
  moods and individual differences in, 308–312
  of morally relevant and positive behavior, 258
  motivational, 263
Charity and charitableness
  anonymous, 22, 372
  and contributions, 3, 197, 288, 333

labeling people by, 218, 290
measure of, 287–288
religions stress, 372
Cheating and lying, prohibited, 172
Chemical–hormonal state of man, 20
Childhood
dependence in, 34
peers in, 41, 150
Children
actions and activities of, 146–147, 168
ages of and reactions to distress, 101
aggressiveness in, 146, 156, 198–199, 360
antisocial, 263
anxiety in, 311
approval needs of, 290
beliefs and values of, 204, 213, 284
bossiness of, 146
communications with, 207
competition among, 429
cooperative behavior of, 385
and cultural values, 187
deserving norm of, 152
distress sounds' effect on, 110, 132
donations made by, 207–210, 289
empathy and teacher ratings, 149–150
guilt feelings, 175, 177
helpfulness traits of, 90
identification, sense of, 328
interaction among and with peers, 150,
152, 354
I.Q.'s of, 260
Kibbutz, 390
moral realism of, 358
performance and moods, 146, 288, 293
reciprocity, perception of, 358
responsibility judgments, 159
responsibility to donate, 209
and rewards received, 179, 210, 221, 260,
287, 300
selfishness of, 390
sharing behavior of, 260, 286–287
sociability of, 100, 102, 146, 207
sociopathic, 263
urban, 390
willingness to sacrifice possessions, 210,
213
Chimpanzees, studies of, 35, 38
Choice(s)
competitive, 389
cooperative and noncooperative, 329, 351,
388

of cultural actions, 33
effects of, 233, 235, 252
freedom of, 206, 214–215, 359
to trust, 375
Christie's test of Machiavellian orientation,
52, 66
Chromosomes, effects on specific behaviors,
26–27
Church, the
attendance at, 166
as a higher authority, 15
Circumstances beyond man's control, 14,
233, 252
Civil disobedience, situation of, 126–127
Civil rights movement, effects of, 267, 271,
326
Clan togetherness and altruism, 31
Class
differences in reciprocity beliefs, 45, 368
social, 369, 397
socioeconomic, 275
working, 270, 368
Classical virtue, 12, 14
Cleanliness as an important value, 129–130,
267
Cognitive-developmental theory of moral
development, 17, 188
Cognitive-dissonance theory, 221
Cognitive–emotional consequences, 52, 221
Cognitive functioning, measure of, 40, 51,
135, 194
Cognitive network, 49
College students, 263, 268, 271, 278, 280,
283, 321
Commitment
concept of, 93, 95
induced responsibility, 92, 96
verbal, 245
on welfare, 4
Common group membership, 320, 325–328,
332–333
Communication(s)
descriptive, 403
lines of, 33, 98, 281, 385
nonverbal, 208, 355
opportunity for, 386
between partners, 388
verbal, 62–63, 95, 197, 201–205, 208–211,
214, 217, 225, 235, 244–245, 280
wording of, 218
"Communicative egocentrism," 259

Community with others, sense of, 300
Comparison Level of Alternatives, 338
Comparison processes, social, 79–80, 84, 286–287, 312, 348, 384
Compassion, capacity for, 152, 166
Compensation, amount of, 170, 182–183, 194, 319
Competence
  areas of, 124, 255
  characteristics related to, 263, 270
  differences in, 278–282
  expression of, 132, 297
  feeling of, 106, 132, 278, 280–281
  and helpfulness, 279, 330
  index of, 129
  intellectual, 43
  manipulation, 237, 278–279
  role of, 55–58
  sense of, 276, 429
  special, 280
  status differences and, 279
  studies of, 272, 282
  trust in, 375
  in women, 410
Competition and competitiveness
  attributions, 222, 320
  behavior, 40–41, 261, 263, 413
  concept of, 382
  and cooperation, 351, 382–383
  degrees of, 377
  emphasized, 364, 368
  failure in affects generosity, 290
  group and individual, 28, 391
  motivation for, 386, 390
  orientation, 377, 387
  and reaction time, 360
  rewards and successes, 231, 383
  tasks involved, 392
Complementarity, conception of, 413–414
Compliance
  findings on, 202
  interpretation of, 81–83
  motivator of, 175
  positive experience reduces, 190–191
  rate of, 219
  unreasonable, 80–81
"Conceptual battery," 260
Concessions, reciprocation of, 220
Concreteness dimension defined, 339–340
Conditions and conditioning, 45, 60, 99–101, 118, 184, 256, 367
Conduct, standards of, 200, 206
Confession reduces guilt, 185

Conflict
  when alternatives eliminated, 200
  and disequilibrium, 370–371
  goal, 49–53, 58, 71, 193
  group, 28, 391
  moral situations, 259, 263
  motivational, 117
  resolutions, 24, 49–51, 115, 409
  between self-interest and the interests of others, 7
  studies of, 49, 162, 430
Confrontation, fear of, 83
Conscience and conscientiousness, meanings of, 22, 48
Consciousness, unusual, 60
Consequences
  awareness of, 56, 242–243
  beneficial, 2, 391
  cognitive and affective, 239, 244
  cognitive–emotional, 52, 221
  of cooperation, 2, 391
  of harmdoing, 245
  negative, 233
  practical attitudes on, 222
  of prosocial acts, 2, 248
  psychological, 295–296, 306
  salience of, 246–247
  severity of, 159
  social, 171, 227
Considerateness, value of, 231, 246, 264, 275, 338
Consistency
  amount of, 265–266, 287
  in behavior, 39–40
  self-reports of, 48
  and stability, 41
  tendency for, 393
Consistent self-worth, 310
Constraints, external, 209, 235
Control
  conditions, 66, 157, 190, 290
  groups, 98, 104, 130, 173, 175, 184, 186, 208, 217, 222, 224, 238, 282–283, 292, 295, 312, 316, 318, 330, 345, 378, 391, 404
  internal–external, 129
  lack of, 56
  locus of scale, 166, 271–272, 295
  measures, 130, 147, 201 270
  no-model group, 225, 316, 319
  over events, 166
  subjects, 174, 190, 288, 292, 310, 329
Conventional social norms, 14, 84

Cooperation and cooperativeness, 40, 147, 290
  alternating, 382
  attributions, 222
  behavior results, 30, 261, 381, 389, 413
  choices, 329, 351, 388
  and competition, 351, 382–383, 429
  concept of, 382, 385–389
  exploitation of, 389
  favorable consequences of, 2, 391, 393
  goals of, 329, 381
  inducing helpfulness, 382, 389–394
  measures of, 262–263, 418
  motivational, 381, 386, 390, 428
  punishment decreases with, 389
  refusal of, 225
  reinforcement for, 389
  social groups based on, 3, 335, 381
Correspondence, rules of, 54, 66
Costs
  forms of, 239
  of helping, 228, 230, 236–241, 299, 320, 417–418, 427
  influence of, 428
  inputs and interaction, 66–69, 178
  material and physical, 109
  personal, 107
  rational calculation of, 115
  and rewards, 292, 336
  sensitivity to, 240
  of sharing, 299
Counter-aggression and retaliation, 195, 360–361
Courage
  defined, 56
  social, 427
  therapy increases, 15
Creativity
  need for, 15, 278
  student, 290
  therapy increases, 15
  visual testing of, 280
Criticism, potential, 299
Cross-cultural studies and data, 97, 344–345, 429
Cross-racial helping, complexity of, 320–326
Cross-sex helping behavior, 325
Cruelty, trait of, 151, 162
Culture and cultural factors
  and action choices, 33
  adequacy of, 33
  and beliefs, 253
  in children, 187
  classification of, 430
  and crises, 25
  differences and condititions of, 32–33, 327, 344–345
  equilibrium, existence in, 33
  evolution of, 33–34
  goals and expectations, 341, 421
  groups within and outside, 328, 396
  heterogeneous, 418
  standards determined by, 25
  taboos, 398
  values, 187, 372, 383, 407
  variations in, 17, 30, 188
Customs
  changes in, 34
  social, 325
  strange, 328

D

Danger, physical, 73, 240
Debt, magnitude of, 343
Decision making
  groups, 153–154
  models, 75–76, 244, 250–253
  personal norms and helping behavior, 242–253
  processes of, 115, 252, 292
  sequential steps in, 242, 247–248
  speed of, 121
  spontaneous, 423
  style perceptions in, 87, 336
  tendencies, 76, 123, 426
Decisions
  altruistic, 148
  freedom of, 216
  moral, 257
  rational, 109, 177
  Schwartz's model, 242–247
Deductive thinking processes, 60
Deeds and words, exposure to, 198–201, 205
Defensive strategies, 144–145, 243
Deficiency, degrees of, 227, 240, 304
Dehumanized conditions, 153–155
Deindividuating conditions enhance aggression, 77, 155
Delinquent boys, 263
Demands
  emotional, 428
  impersonal, 314
  resistance to, 174
  and self-sacrifice, 6
  verbal, 175

Democracy, changes in, 34
Demography, factor of, 275
Denial of responsibility, 144, 182, 186
Dependence
    childhood, 34
    concept of, 107, 413
    degrees of, 225–230, 268–271
    feelings of, 356
    high degree of, 223, 226–229, 232, 236–237, 351
    internal versus external sources of, 233–236
    locus of, 233–235
    low degree of, 216, 226–229, 236–237
    measures of, 282, 351
    medium degree of, 236
    need of, 225–230
    reasons for, 88, 226, 234–236
    sex differences in, 230–233
    variations in, 228
    of workers, 233–235, 351
Depression
    condition of guilt, 177, 291
    people less efficient, 177
Deprivation study, sensory, 234–235
Derogation
    consequences of, 153, 349
    establishes equity, 169, 182
    of others in need, 301
    of victim's suffering, 169, 183, 186, 192
Deserving
    and age-factor effects, 284–287
    norm of, for children, 152, 284
    and rewards, 286, 289
    warm-glow feeling and belief in, 284–289
Desire(s)
    approval and motivation for, 20, 57
    for connectedness, 308
    experience of, 414
    for friendship, 229
    to do good, 12, 306, 356
    satisfaction of, 415
    sexual, 20
    understanding of, 2
Detachment, situational, 160
Devaluation
    conditions affecting, 159–163
    consequences of, 153, 189
    and helping others, 168–170
    inhibits prosocial motivation, 151, 162–163
    justification aspect of, 162

    measures of, 156, 158
    need for, 169
    opportunity for, 161
    role-taking orientation lessens, 151, 163
    unwanted suffering and, 161, 170
    of victims, 152, 159–160, 164–165
Deviation from internal standards leads to distress, 24, 181
Dilemma games of prisoners, 262, 384–388
Disapproval
    fear of, 83, 227
    social, 7, 75, 113
Disasters
    natural, 91, 272
    social, 178
Discipline involves duty, 22–23, 265
Discomfort from being helped, 208, 249
Discrimination
    behavior, 213, 322, 329, 374, 476
    against blacks, 324, 326, 331
    cost of, 324
    decrease in, 322
    of outsiders, 150, 328
    racial, 321–322
    reasons for, 326–327
    sex, 166
    shared, 320
    tasks, 185
Disinhibition, demonstration of, 199
Disobedience
    civil, 126–127
    and the concept of sin, 15
Distress
    and anxiety-producing stimulus, 6, 100
    comparison, 384
    of couples, 410–411
    deviation from internal standards leads to, 24, 181
    empathy toward those in, 111, 135, 186
    equity, 179, 192
    experience of, 192–193, 384
    feelings of, 66–67, 177, 189, 240, 425
    female, 103, 235
    and guilt feelings, 186, 192–194
    and helpfulness, 4, 74, 76, 111, 116, 121, 124, 127, 135, 186, 197
    nonphysical, 108
    physical, 1, 4, 54, 70, 73, 76, 99, 116, 118, 121, 124, 127, 132, 150, 197–198, 200, 227, 259
    psychological, 4, 48, 67–70, 150, 170, 215, 227, 235
    reaction to cues, 84, 103, 105, 112–113

responsiveness to, 64, 128, 136, 235, 335
retaliation a possibility in connection with, 181
self-concept, 181
social consequences, 181
sounds of, 56, 59, 78–82, 85, 99, 102–104, 106, 110, 128, 130, 132
vicarious, 111, 161
visibility of persons in, 105–107
Distribution of rewards, 180, 329
Diversity, lure of, 398
Dominance versus submission, 412, 414, 429
Donations and donating
of blood, 244–245, 251, 278
by children, 207–210, 216, 221, 289
increase in, 294, 307
motives imputed to, 341
norm of, 251–255, 264–265
opportunity for, 205–207, 209
public, 205–209
of rewards, 204–208
and sharing, 284
studies of, 201, 210, 237–238
Drive, motivational, 20, 45
Drug-produced distress, 125
Duty
involves discipline, 22–23, 265
fulfillment of, 24
morality of, 430
and obligations, 426
and value orientation, 52, 167

E

Earning, notion of, 284–285
Ecology, harmdoing to the, 33–34, 194, 241
Economy, factor of, 268, 373
Education, different levels of, 274–275
Edwards Personal Preference Schedule, 53
Efficiency lessened in depressed people, 177
Egoism and egocentrism and factor of altruism, 7, 28, 76, 259–260, 311
Electric shocks
administering of, 156–164, 181, 195
continuous, 139
intensity of, 137–138, 279
painful, 169, 175, 183
punitive, 163
random, 185–186
reactions to, 141, 145, 147, 153, 188, 232, 273, 318, 336
self-administered, 177
Embarrassment, feeling of, 208

Emergencies
conditions and situations, 99, 162, 249, 254–255
help and responses to, 73–79, 90, 214, 242, 324
high and low levels of, 202–203
indifference to, 82, 117
inhibiting effects of, 202
interpretations of, 78, 81, 90
mild, 324–325
staged, 113
studies of, 54, 164, 214, 299
Emotion(s)
affection processes, 31, 160, 240, 283, 303, 309
cognitive consequences of, 45–46, 52, 221, 244, 381
demands and experiences of, 55, 110, 136, 142, 149, 333, 428
identical, 110, 333
inhibition of, 147
nature of, 31, 45, 149, 151
negative, 43, 306, 328
personal well-being and, 33, 353
primitive, 31, 45, 147, 258, 317
and reactions of observers, 45, 137–138, 142, 144, 146, 148, 194, 422
sharing responses of, 142, 146
stimuli, 110, 147, 333
Empathy, 4–5, 71, 100, 120, 338, 418
activation of, 151, 427
age factor in, 150
arousal results, 71, 138, 147, 149, 259, 314–317
capacity for, 32–33, 55, 166, 333
children's, 149–150
emotional, 31, 45, 147–149, 258, 317
experiencing of, 44, 146, 148, 420
false, 136
feelings and measures of, 147, 191, 250, 256, 429
and help and distress, 135, 140–146
identification with other people's, 44–45
influence on prosocial behavior, 135–150
inhibiting, 141, 145, 150, 187
lack of, 150, 162
motivational theory of, 136, 146, 314–315
of observers, 11, 140–142, 186
and perceptual orientation, 142, 248
physiological measures of, 256
predictive qualities of, 136, 426
reactions to, 45, 57, 110, 187, 189, 192, 233, 271, 276

Empathy, (*cont.*)
  reinforcement, 140
  issues related to, 148–150
  research and studies on, 45, 163, 317
  responses to, 37–38, 145, 147, 256–258
  with the sufferer, 107–108, 170, 189
Empirical evidence and man's nature, 17,
    409
End-point-type situations, 156–157, 163
Enlightenment period, 21, 24, 414
Environment
  adaptability to, 40, 76
  attempt to cope with, 6, 257, 375, 430–431
  changes in, 32, 34, 40
  conditions of, 69, 115, 163, 273, 302, 309,
    418, 420, 422
  influence of, 14, 32, 419
  internal and external, 33, 39, 305
  and personal characteristics, 11, 422
  psychological, 314
  responses to, 27, 257, 419
  social, 32, 34
  unfamiliar, 115–116
Envy, feelings of, 383
Equalitarianism and equality, 180, 187, 232
  and helpfulness, 129
  and justice, 24
  principles and ranking of, 267
  and rewards, 286
Equilibrium
  existence of in culture, 33
  tension disrupts, 314
Equity
  conceptions of, 201, 343
  concern with, 211, 223, 232, 302
  derogation establishes, 169, 182
  different systems of, 178, 187–188
  and harmdoing, 180–184, 192
  and hedonic balancing hypothesis, 302–
    308
  and inequity, 178–180
  interpretations of, 184, 187, 338
  justice represented by, 24
  and the Just World hypothesis, 57, 181
  maintaining of, 44, 345–347
  and personal values, 187, 419, 421
  principles of, 24, 180, 194
  psychological, 181–182
  restoration of, 169, 179–184, 192, 419
  sex differences and, 180
  standards of, 188–189, 193
  theorists in, 152, 169, 178–181, 190, 194

Escape
  opportunities for, 106–114, 203
  from unpleasant experiences, 240
Esteem, measure of, 131
Ethics
  authoritarian, 15, 21
  humanistic, 15, 47, 266
Ethnography, cross-cultural, 344–345
Evaluation-apprehension condition, 83–84,
    157
  of human nature, 52
  negative, 46, 80, 83–86, 103, 108, 153, 161,
    164, 169, 181, 297, 299
  by others, 86, 100, 164, 290, 297
  perception of, 296, 305
  and personality characteristics, 61, 280
  positive, 46, 166, 318
  and rewards, 288, 319
  of victims, 156, 161, 165–170
Events
  control over, 166, 296
  interpretation and ambiguity of, 86–88,
    305, 418, 425
  real-life, 278
Everyday life
  prosocial interactions in, 311–312
  reciprocity in, 371–374
Evil, perpetration of by man, 14–17, 153
Evolution
  biological, 18, 26–29, 32–34
  cultural, 34
  social course of, 4, 32–34
Exchange(s)
  acts and assets as commodities, 336
  commodities of, 337–338, 340, 353
  of kindness and intimacy, 338, 418
  positive, 29, 335, 338, 382
  reciprocal and nonreciprocal, 340–346,
    356, 369
  social principles of, 336–340, 418
  theories of, 24, 337–338, 412, 414
Expectations and expectancy
  cultural, 341
  of gains, 8, 226
  of reciprocity, 373, 418
  of reward, 199
  societal, 201, 207–208, 337
  of success, 295, 299
  value theories of, 50, 211, 214, 285, 311
Experiences
  anger-provoking, 143, 194–195, 263, 293
  cooperation in, 394

emotional, 5, 55, 110, 136, 140–143, 149–150, 177, 333, 423
empathic, 44–45, 136–140, 146, 148, 184, 420
of guilt and repentance, 184–185, 193, 305
of helpfulness, 240, 291
of needs, goals, and desires, 414
negative, 224, 232, 240, 291–297, 305–308
past or prior, 36, 187, 318–322, 332
personal and interpersonal, 136, 185–188, 206, 294, 399, 406, 425
positive, 138, 157, 190–191, 232, 290–296, 303, 328–330
psychological, 71, 295–297, 313
quality and nature of, 25, 33, 216, 251, 256, 283, 308
reminiscences about, 293
sad, 293, 306
shared, 393, 396
social, 18–19, 179, 395
subjective, 192, 417
unpleasant, 240
vicarious, 7, 37, 44, 143
Experimenters, 42, 226, 244, 364
outwitting, 260
sex of, 228, 232
Experiments
animal, 34–38
conditions of, 52, 67–68, 89
involving females in ESP projects, 78
misleading results in, 173
psychological, 186
treatments in, 80–81, 148, 378
volunteers for, 291
Exploitation(s)
and desires, 425
of others, 336, 389
tendencies of men toward, 3, 180, 341, 387, 389, 414
Exposure
positive effects of, 200, 395–398
public, 83–85, 164

F

Facial expressions, perception of, 136, 146–147, 298
Failure
effects of, 282–285, 290
experiences of, 296
feelings of, 287, 330

group, 283, 301
and success in maintaining a positive image, 278, 282–283, 287–295
Fairness, conceptions of, 155, 201
Family
close ties in, 27–29
in-group includes, 325
nature of, 328, 356
working class, 270, 368
Fate
responsibility for, 186
similarity in, 164
Favordoers and favordoing, 197, 335, 343, 364–369
Favors
for others, 352
reactions to, 365, 368
recipient-instigated, 362
Fear
of abuse or confrontation, 83, 325
of detection, 257
of disapproval, 83, 227
of punishment, 257
response-conditional, 35–37
therapy lessens, 15
Feedback, 191, 271, 311, 388, 430
continuous verbal, 319
false, 278
inconsistent, 222
negative or neutral, 217, 223
physiological reactions of, 222
positive, 223, 299
standard, 160, 349
value of in research, 67
Female(s), 31, 103–104, 156, 235
college students, 112, 268
competence in, 410
dependent, 233
experimenters, 76–80
and helpfulness, 91, 231, 253–255, 283
opportunities for, 34, 230
personality characteristics, 60–62, 65–66
and self-disclosing, 403–404
subjects, 76, 117, 158, 160, 169
victims, 159
Feudal system, serfs in, 23
First impressions, importance of, 395, 399
Food, scarcity and sharing of, 33, 38
Foolishness, appearance of, 75, 83
Foot-in-the-door technique, 219, 245
Foreigners, responsiveness to, 325–326
Fortitude and virtue, 12

Freedom
  of action, 214, 216, 225
  decisional, 215–216
  reduction in, 205, 215, 358, 366
  threat to, 216
  important value of, 379
Free speech movement, 127
Freudian theory, 1, 5
Friendliness, meanings of, 48, 390–393
Friends
  in-group includes, 325
  interactions among, 418
  obligation to help, 229, 384
  reciprocity between, 369–374
Friendship
  acts leading to, 1, 8, 164, 415
  concept of, 229
  desire for, 57, 229
  development of, 320, 396, 399, 402, 408
  mutuality of, 369–371
  responsibility inherent in, 418

G

Gain(s)
  expectation of, 8, 42–43, 226
  long-term, 386
  material, 7, 46, 383
  personal, 227
  and a reward, 46, 197, 234
  sacrifice of, 428
  of satisfaction, 271
Galvanic Skin Response (GSR), 137, 144, 279
Games
  behavior strategies' influence on, 266, 377, 385, 429
  mixed-motive, 351
  participants in, 388, 389
  prisoner's dilemma, 262, 384–388
  "trucking," 387
General orientations versus specific norms, 247–253
Generosity
  acts of, 262, 298, 361, 372, 429
  failure in competition reduces, 290
  measures of, 260, 286–287, 294
  negative experiences reduce, 296
  reciprocation of, 343
  studies and values of, 150, 254, 275
Genes and genetics
  and altruism, origins of, 25–38, 328
  behavioral influence of, 26–29, 32

Givers and receivers, 369–371
Goals
  achievement of, 48, 53, 61, 65, 88, 197, 226, 258, 335, 382
  activation of personality influences, 45–50, 54–58, 194, 314, 413
  awareness of, 391
  behavior factor, 20, 22, 39, 391, 413
  conflicts over, 49–53, 58, 71, 193
  cooperation in seeking, 329, 381
  fulfilled and unfulfilled, 4, 314–317
  future, 417–422
  gradients, 315–316
  hierarchy of, 51, 305
  identification with, 133, 277, 313, 384
  and moral objectives, 22
  motives and end states of, 39
  negative and nonaltruistic, 51, 248
  personal, 5, 45–51, 54–58, 69, 124, 145, 241, 268, 296, 305, 311, 323, 413, 420–424, 428–430
  positive, 51, 58, 197
  prosocial, 48–49, 53–54, 77, 194, 323, 421
  and the psychological environment, 314
  rank-order of, 51
  self-aggrandizement, 18
  self-related, 305, 420
  shared, 329, 381, 392, 396
  understanding of another's, 2, 264, 277, 313, 335, 338
  valued norm orientation of, 77, 145, 147, 241, 316, 327, 415
God
  authority of, 15, 23
  beliefs in, 21, 32, 166
  as morality source, 13
  rebellion against, 17
Good and goodness
  aspiration for, 12, 33, 306, 356
  beliefs about, 161, 300, 361
  of man, 14–15, 167, 248, 307, 375
  productive concept of, 15–16, 297
Goods and services, 300, 339–400
Goodwill, glow of, 282, 335–336
Gratitude and gratification, indications of, 295, 300, 343, 366, 372
Greed and greediness
  models of, 21, 203–204, 212
  therapy decreases, 15
Grodman's trust scale, 250
Group(s)
  achievement orientation (high and low) of, 63–68, 301, 310

antagonism and conflict within, 28, 391–392, 430
cohesion within, 389–390
control, 98, 104, 130, 173, 175, 184, 186, 208, 217, 222, 224, 238, 282–283, 292, 295, 312, 316, 318, 330, 345, 378, 391, 404
cultural and civic, 270, 328, 396
failure, 283, 301
identification with, 303, 320–323, 328, 333
indifference and inconsistency of, 82, 310
membership, 320, 325–326, 328, 332–333, 427
military, 390
minority, 322–323
and morality, 10–11
reference and religious, 383, 396
selection, 27, 31
sensitivity-training, 407
social, based on cooperation, 3, 10, 303, 335, 356, 381
socioeconomic, 343
success, 272, 283–284
survival value of, 4, 28
trustworthy and untrustworthy, 379
Guilt
anticipatory, 185, 430
children feel, 175, 177
circumstances producing, 186, 193–194
experiencing, 177, 184–185, 193, 305
feelings of, 12, 107, 161, 175–178, 184, 193, 307
and harmdoing, 176–178, 181
indications of, 159, 319, 361, 418, 424
reduction in, 184–185
sex differences in, 257
theory, advocates of, 177, 190
transgressions lead to, 176–177, 257

H

Happiness, feelings of, 5, 280, 296, 330
Harm
causing or inflicting on others, 158, 176, 184–195, 343, 427
physical acts of, 170–171, 183, 375
psychological consequences of, 176
responsibility for, 172, 186
Harmdoing and harmdoers
altrustic behavior following, 177
cognitive reactions to, 171, 194
ecological significance of, 33–34, 194, 241

effects of on prosocial behavior, 170–179, 191, 201, 350
emotional reactions of, 194–195
equity-based, 180–184, 192
guilt induced by, 176–178, 181
perceived intent of, 357–361
punishment of, 171, 361
studies on, 174–175
suffering of, 138
and transgression, consequences of, 170–192, 245
voluntary or accidental, 192
Harris's social-responsibility scale, 269
Hate, factor of, 412
Health and heart rates, 137, 144, 278
Hedonic balancing hypothesis, 57, 232, 302–308, 420, 424, 427
Hedonic state, 17–18, 305
Help, helping, and helpfulness, 149, 228, 240, 304, 314, 316, 335, 409
age factor in, 101, 253
altruistic basis of, 111, 135, 246–247, 260, 267–268, 307, 378, 381–382
behavior, 61, 96–100, 104, 133, 229, 277
cost of, 58, 101, 106–114, 122, 202, 215, 228, 230, 236–241, 299, 320, 417–418, 427
cost of not aiding, 111, 114, 122
decision making in, 242–253
dependence and independence, degrees of in, 82, 226, 351–352
desire and willingness to, 106, 232–233, 244, 278, 281–282, 306, 356, 420
and devaluation, 168–170
and distress, 4, 74, 76, 116, 121, 124, 127–129, 197
empathy in, 135, 140–146
failure decreases, 287–291
frequency of, 106, 108
impulsiveness in, 114–115
individual characteristics involved in, 253–270
inhibitions to, 83, 104, 121, 215, 233, 252, 299, 304
magnitude and measures of, 118–120, 130
motivation for, 186, 198, 309
need for, 74–76, 104–107, 112, 118, 122, 216, 230, 249, 283, 331, 423
offers of, 224, 261
opportunities for, 111, 127–128, 171, 186, 278–279, 292–293, 320, 324–326
personality and bystanders' characteris-

Help, *(cont.)*
  tics and, 101, 103, 117, 120–127, 131–133, 253
  personal values and beliefs in, 98, 242–253, 372
  racial and cross-racial, 253, 320–321, 324, 326
  recipients of, 70, 344–350, 365
  refusal of or unneeded, 2–3, 216, 365
  requests or calls for, 69, 74–78, 216, 322, 344–350, 375
  responsibility diffusion and normative explanations of, 88–105
  sex differences factor in, 90–91, 230–231, 253–255, 283, 325
  social determinants in, 101–105, 122, 369
  spontaneous or impulsive, 114–116
  stimulus for, 105–114, 122, 198, 224, 422
  voluntary, 167, 183, 234–235, 354–355, 359
Helplessness, sense of, 56, 118
Heredity and heritage, 18–19, 26, 29, 253–255
Heroism, examples of, 4, 91, 95
Hierarchy of personal goals, 51, 305
High school students, 309–310, 354
High threat status conditions and subjects, 236–237, 247, 279–280
Homeostatic-drive theory, 5, 20
Honesty, factor of, 21, 254
Hope, importance of, 56, 427
Hostility
  attribution of, 263
  autistic hypothesis, 338
  behavior, 414–415
  indirect, 367
  therapy lessens, 15
Human beings
  impulses of, 16–18
  morality and living together, 16, 22, 24
  purposefulness of, 46
  responsiveness to others, 256
  as self-seeking creatures, 17–18, 20
  sufferings of, 5
  welfare of, 21, 147, 267
Human interactions, complexity of, 41, 65–66, 188, 309, 412–415
Humanitarianism, condition of, 16, 21, 153–154, 167, 214, 323
Human life, sanctity of, 17, 124, 126
Human nature
  beliefs about, 388
  and biological needs, 20–21, 73, 400
  duality of, 32–33
  laws of, 13
  and morality, 10–38
  Platonian view of, 14
  psychological testing and philosophies of, 329, 377
  and self-examination, 13
Human relationships, continuity of, 24, 373, 429–430
Humanity, shared, and orientation toward others, 328–333
Humiliation, 320
Hunting and gathering societies, 3, 9, 30
Hypocrisy, inconsistency between words and deeds, 205

I

Ideals, changes in, 34, 43, 213
Identification
  degrees of, 165, 390–391
  and the emotions aroused, 110, 333
  and empathy with other people, 44–45, 144, 165, 317, 327, 332–333, 417–418
  and goals, 113, 277, 313–14, 384
  group, 303, 320–323, 328, 333
  racial, 321, 325–326
  sense of, 93, 97, 320, 328, 424
  theory and principle of, 49, 57, 309, 338, 414, 430
  with the victim, 108–109
Ignorance, pluralistic, 75–76, 106
Image
  improvement of, 288–290
  reparation of, 288, 298, 306
"Imagine him" orientations, 141–143
"Imagine self" instructions, 141–142, 163–164
Imitation, 204–206, 209
"Immorality" and "immoral" beliefs, 361
Impulses and impulsiveness
  adultery and incest, 19
  behavior, 56, 114–115, 263
  of children, 146
  gratification of, 5
  human restrictions of, 16–19, 21
Incompetence
  actions of, 75, 83, 278
  appearance of, 174–175
  diminishes helpfulness, 282–283
  feeling of, 109, 346–347
Inconsistency, sources of, 40, 231
Indebtedness
  feeling of, 352, 356, 359
  and receiving help, 344–350

Independence, effects of, 56, 82, 234, 257, 378
Individual characteristics and helping behavior, 253–270
Individualism and individuality
  and competition, 28, 391
  development of, 19
  differences in, 165–168, 418
  freedom stressed in, 215
  pressure created by, 336
  protection of, 2, 34
  sense of, 120, 385–390, 409
Inequality, status of, 232, 346–347
Inequity
  and equity, 178–180
  perception of, 3, 58
  responsibility for, 194
  sensitivity to, 302, 421
Influence(s)
  classes of, 69–72
  inhibiting, 75–76, 85, 100
  modeling, 237–238, 333
  normative conception of, 88–89
  and power and capacity exertions, 118, 427
  situational, 77–105, 121–122
  social, 85, 99, 225, 246, 266, 417
  stimulus on, 225–242
Information
  anecdotal, 151, 181, 272
  disclosure of, 399, 402
  empirical, 409
  extensiveness of, 426
  intimate, 399–401
  from questionnaires, 251
  reciprocal exchange of, 404
In-group solidarity, 28, 119, 325–327, 391
Inhibition and inhibiting factors
  effects of, 83–85, 104, 199
  on emotions, 147
  on empathy, 141, 145, 150, 187
  on helpfulness, 83, 104, 121, 215, 233, 252, 299, 304
  on other people, 75–76, 85, 100
Initiative
  kinds of, 94, 255, 300
  social, 200, 254–255
  taking of, 57, 94
Injustice
  anger over, 202
  causation of, 171
  evidence of, 152
  perception of, 58, 164
  sensitive reactions to, 23, 152, 157, 171

Innocent victims, 151–152, 159–161
Instinctive behavior, 26
Institutions
  changes in, 34
  pressures on, 336
  social, 23, 25
Instructions, permissive and verbal, 100, 163, 209, 216
Integration, racial and social, 24, 395
Intelligence and intellectualization
  the anthropological view, 144, 251
  and competence, 43, 354
  measured scores and tests in, 261, 298–299
Intentions
  attribution of prosocial, 361–366
  and motivation, 205, 379
  perception of, 358, 362
  prosocial, 6, 173
  selfish, 358–363
Interaction
  and the age factor, 285
  among children, 354
  human complexity in, 41, 65–66, 188, 409, 412–415
  principles of, 335, 394, 409–413
  real-life, 311, 385, 387
  reciprocity with, 41
  transactional, 69
Interests, shared, 277, 397
Intergroup conflict, 28, 391
Internal norms and values, 98, 256
  deviation from standards, 24, 181
  versus external sources of dependence, 233–236, 247, 272, 377–379
Interpersonal relationships
  behavior, 61, 69, 279
  model of, 412–415
  and trust, 375–376
Interpretation(s)
  equity, 184, 187, 338
  of events, 86–88, 305, 418, 423–426
  no-emergency, 78
  of stimulus, 75–76, 81
Intervention
  benefits of, 101, 403–404
  degrees of, 77, 82, 88, 95
  direct, 109–110
Interviews
  with bystanders, 116
  in depth, 41
  studies aided by, 132–133, 173, 312
Intimacy
  of information, 399–401

Intimacy, (*cont.*)
  levels of, 405–407
  and self-disclosure, 400, 404, 408
  social exchange in, 57, 384, 418
Intimate relationships
  development and maintenance of, 394–395
  positive acts within, 1–3
  and reciprocity, 371–374
Involvement, process of, 92, 112, 322, 425

J

Job-related responsibilities, 91
Jourard's scale, 376–377
Judgment(s)
  expression of, 136, 142, 326, 338, 376
  moral, 12, 125, 257–264, 275–276
  negative and positive, 142, 259
  personal, 353, 403
  and role taking, 258, 276
Justice, 21, 276, 338
  acts to maintain, 44, 169
  belief in, 17, 152
  conception and principles of, 24, 124, 152, 187, 262
  concern about, 8, 12, 193
  distributive, 260, 262, 343
  social, 24, 270, 427
Justification(s)
  (in high and low) conditions, 186, 220
  forms of, 135, 164, 183, 303, 398, 420, 427
  of inaction, 162, 301, 324
  processes of, 50, 58, 110, 126, 187, 193, 319
  self-disinhibiting, 154–155
Just World
  belief, differences of opinion, 162, 165–167, 193, 419
  desire to live in, 152, 421
  devaluation and aggression and belief in, 151–170
  equity concept in, 57, 159, 181, 186
  hypothesis, 151, 156–164, 182, 187, 189, 211
  research on, 156–164, 189
Juvenile delinquency, counsel for, 220

K

Kagan's Matching Familiar Figures Test, 115, 129
Kin and kinship selections and altruism, 27–31

Kindness
  as commodity of exchange, 338
  ideal of, 264, 372
  manifestations of, 1, 373
  to oneself, 293, 418
  to others, 293, 331
  reciprocation of, 340, 343
  therapy increases, 15
  value and understanding of, 150, 265, 348
Knowledge, limitations of, 13, 417–422
Kohlberg-type measures, 262–263, 266

L

Labor, divisions of, 3, 390
Laws
  religious, 21, 52
  scientific, 17
Leaders and leadership, positions of influence, 84, 93–94, 225
Learner–teacher situation, 136, 174, 193
Learning
  efficiency in, 80, 199
  role of, 36–37
  tasks, 158–160, 163
  theories of, 15, 20, 26
Lewinian perspective, 47, 121, 313
Liberation movement, women's, 118–119, 232
Lies and lying, factor of, 174, 177, 377
Life, philosophy of, and goodness, 14, 19
Likert-type scale, 59
Liking condition
  anticipated and genuine, 393
  mutual, 408–409, 411
  self-disclosure leads to, 404
Locus-of-control concept, 55, 116, 271–272, 295
Loneliness, negative emotion of, 306, 408
Love
  definition of, 338
  emotional, 15, 31
  versus hate, 412
  manifestation of, 1, 136, 373, 413
  need to give and receive, 15, 338, 348, 394
  therapy increases, 15
  unselfish, 15–16
Loyalty groups, 28–29

M

Machiavellianism, test and scale of orientation toward, 52, 66, 122, 129, 250, 379

Maladjustment, 40
Males, characteristics of, 31, 60, 230–233, 253, 256, 283, 325
Man
  behavior of, 21, 26
  biological makeup of, 15, 20
  pessimistic view of, 18–20
  science and the nature of, 16–17, 23
  and self-interest in social groups, 18, 21
Marginality, sense of, 49, 133
Married couples
  principles of infidelity, 373–374
  interactions, 409–411
  transactions within, 1, 382, 386, 402–403
Martyr condition, 156, 158, 161, 163
Masochistic self-effacing behavior, 413
Materialism, mechanistic, 2, 17, 27, 289
Maximum-positive-influence groups, 82
Memory, factor of, 15, 297
Mercy, capacity for, 166
Merit, function of performance, 179
Middle-class society, 270, 275, 343, 368, 372
Midpoint conditions, 156–158, 163
Minnesota Multiphasic Personality Inventory (MMPI) Pd (Psychopathic deviate) scale, 145
Minority groups and members of, 320–323
Mobs, influence of, 76
Models and modeling
  observations of, 198, 201
  theoretical, for predicting behavior, 45–54, 79
  and verbal communications, 203–205, 210
Money and monetary compensation, 190, 285, 351
Monkeys, experiments with, 35–38
Mood(s)
  and behavior, effects on, 291–294, 330, 384, 424
  of children, 293
  negative, 305–308
  neutral, 306–307
  positive, 290–295, 300–308
  variation in, 296–297, 308
Moral factors and tendencies, 22, 28, 49
  and behavior, 2–10, 273–275
  and cognitive-developmental theory, 13, 17, 25, 188
  and conduct and acts, 12, 154–155
  conflicts and dilemmas, 126, 259, 263
  issues, 125, 196
  judgment and helping behavior, 12, 125, 257–264, 275–276
  and obligation, sense of, 11, 242–251, 430

prescriptive and prohibitive, 2–3, 23
reasoning, 17, 55, 59, 124–126, 129–130, 156, 259–260, 263, 266
rules and authority, 10–12, 22–23, 267
situational influences, 264–267
and transgressions, 257, 358
values and development of, 5–6, 10, 23, 128, 256, 271, 276
views and principles, 52, 124–126, 257
Morality
  authoritarian, 21–22
  autonomous stage of, 10–11, 17, 22, 25, 257, 358
  configurative, 10–12
  and duty and discipline, 22, 267, 430
  Greek conception of, 12
  guide to, 15–16, 22
  and human nature, 10–38
  imposed internally and externally, 10, 17–21
  personal and individual development, 10, 25
  and positive behavior, 258, 273, 417
  scientific study of, 22–23, 33
  and social groups and institutions, 2, 23–24, 33
  societal changes in, 13, 21–25
  sources of, 13–17, 21
  standards and decisions, 21, 257
  types and stages of, 10–11
Motivation
  and achievement, 20, 61–62, 271
  altruistic, 6–10, 242, 332
  characteristics, 261–263, 425–426
  competitive, 309, 386, 390
  concepts and goals, 39, 45
  and cooperation, 381, 386, 390, 428–429
  and devaluation, 151, 162–163
  empathy theories of, 136, 146, 314–315
  and mixed/motive games, 415
  for helpfulness, 105, 186, 198, 309
  for image reparation, 288, 298, 306
  index of, 259, 265
  for love and affiliation, 20, 373
  mixed, 8
  orientation, 252, 385
  personal and extrinsic, 86, 132, 174, 237, 250
  positive, 136, 146
  and prosocial action, 5–10, 42–43, 115–117, 135, 205–206, 309, 420
  racist or sexual, 324–325
  for rewards, 45
  selfish, 6, 357–358, 381

Motivations, *(cont.)*
  suspect or repressed, 19–20, 341, 349
  variations and differences in, 8, 205, 230, 357, 379
  will as force, 12, 14
Motor skills and coordination, 139, 279, 283

N

Narcissistic behavior, 413
Naturalism and natural law, 14–15
Natural selection, Darwin's theory of, 18, 26–28, 32
Nazi Germany, 49, 133, 153, 182, 429,
Need(s)
  for achievement or power, 48, 58, 239
  ambiguity of, 106, 110–111
  for approval, 123, 132, 271–274, 290, 298
  for assurance, 2, 53, 314, 398
  biological and physical, 14, 215, 398
  complementarity in, 396–399
  concept of, 107, 169, 197
  (high or low) conditions of, 66, 223, 238
  for creativity, 15, 278
  degrees of, 106–114, 223–224, 227, 240, 246, 305
  and dependence, 225–230
  factor of, 45, 146, 251, 253
  for help, 74–76, 104–107, 112, 118, 122, 216, 230, 249, 283, 331, 423
  for kindness and affiliation, 59, 348
  for love and affection, 15, 338, 348–349, 394
  perceptions of, 237–238, 243
  psychological, 314
  satisfaction of, 306, 328, 337, 341, 413–415
  valid and invalid, 238, 242, 425
Negative-definition condition, 78–79
  goals, 51
  and hedonic imbalances, 305–308
  thoughts, 142, 297, 300, 312
Negative emotions, 43, 306, 328, 408
Negative evaluation, 46, 80, 83–86, 103, 108, 153, 161, 164, 181, 297, 299
Negative experiences, 224, 232, 240, 291–297, 302, 305–308
Neuroticism, 19
Neutral conditions, 154, 205–206, 223, 306–307
Noble savage and *noblesse oblige* ideas, 14, 279

No-information group, 102–104
Noncooperative moves, frequency of, 262, 390, 413
Nondisturbed couples, 410–411
Nonhelpers, 281, 359
Nonmoral characteristics, 11, 16
Nonphysical distress, 108, 253
Nonresponsiveness of children, 62–63, 90
Nonsharing by friends, 364, 384
Nonverbal communications, 62–63, 208, 355
Nurturance, factor of, 53, 61, 208, 328, 373, 398

O

Obedience to authority, 15, 22, 81–83
Obligation
  feeling of, 63, 187, 229, 242, 269, 356, 359, 384, 420
  fulfillment of an, 109, 306, 366
  gratitude leading to a sense of, 343
  kinds and types of, 52, 216, 341, 426
  moral, 11, 242–251, 430
  mutual, 70
  professional, 248
  sense of, 8, 11, 229, 242–251, 430
Observers and observation
  emotional reactions, 45, 137–138, 142–144, 146–148, 194, 422
  empathy created, 111, 140–142, 186
  as (line of) evidence, 143, 163, 198, 201, 392
  of harm, 158, 184–192, 194
  of pain and suffering, 138, 161, 168, 170, 185, 192
Oedipus complex, 256–257
Opinions and attitudes, 251–252, 314–315, 354
  similarity of, 316–317, 322
Opportunity and opportunism, 53, 69, 161, 386
  to donate, 205–209
  for escape, 106–114, 203
  for help, 111, 127–128, 171, 186, 278–279, 292–294, 320, 325
  to reciprocate, 344–347, 368
  self-disclosure and self-serving, 29, 405
  to win rewards, 172, 213
  for women, 34
Optimism, 299
Organization, societal, 335–336, 349
Orientation

interpersonal, 121, 129, 163, 167
perceptual–cognitive differences, 55, 141–145, 148, 163
prosocial, measuring of, 63–69, 124, 130, 167
sympathetic, 59
value, 8, 44–45, 52, 140, 166
"watch him," 141–142, 163
Ostracism, 40, 43, 160
Out-group, concepts in, 325–327, 391, 429
Overload, high and low, 118–119

P

Pain, effects of, 137–140, 144
Paper and pencil test measures, 121, 126, 144, 246, 255, 268, 295, 310, 312, 318, 410
Parental care, 29, 31, 34, 372–373
Particularism, terms of, 160, 284, 338
Passersby, 113, 120, 237, *see also* Bystanders
Peabody Picture Vocabulary test, 311
Peers
    approval by, 227
    in childhood, 41, 150
    interaction research on, 11, 262, 309
    ratings by, 100, 246, 249, 264
Perceptual–evaluative cognitive determinants of behavior, 54–55, 237–238, 296, 305, 333
Perceptual–interpretive tendencies, 144, 163–164, 243, 260, 282, 425
Performance
    arousal and differences in, 112, 147, 179, 260, 389
    children's, 288, 293
    poor, indicative of laziness, 155, 281, 289–290
    sexual differences in, 180
    standards and productivity of, 172, 226–229, 301
    tasks, 56, 185, 278, 300, 319
Permission, relevance of, 102–103, 129, 209
Personal factors
    beliefs, 273
    characteristics affect tendencies, 11, 41–42, 52–53, 71, 127–133, 163, 193, 259, 275, 306, 311, 321, 368, 376, 418, 421–422, 425
    and costs, 107
    emotional well-being, 33, 353
    experiences, 136, 185–188, 206, 399, 406

goals, 5, 45–51, 54–58, 69, 124, 145, 241, 268, 296, 305, 311, 323, 413, 420–424, 428–430
    judgments, 46, 353, 403
    morality and individual development, 10, 25
    motivation, 86, 132, 175, 237, 250
    norms, 140, 192, 419
    responsibility, 130–131
Personality
    bond between self and others, 315–323, 330–334
    characteristics, 41, 46, 58, 60–62, 65–66, 69–70, 92, 94, 96, 101, 103, 110, 117, 120–128, 131–135, 197, 231, 241–242, 252–253, 264–267, 274–276, 280, 317, 333, 367, 378, 388, 414, 418
    differences, 87, 194, 240, 255–258, 330, 367–369, 431
    ideographic approach to, 39, 252
    influences on, 76, 98, 428, 430
    and interactions, 42, 54, 124, 129, 144
    measures of, 121, 124, 141, 144, 165, 194, 246, 253, 403
    research and studies of, 41, 53, 264
    scales, 147, 378
    scores, 68, 123
    and self-attribution determination, 221–222
    similarity–dissimilarity in, 315–318, 331–332, 352
    stimulus conditions on, 418, 428
    tests, 60–62, 66–67, 123, 127–128
    traits, 40, 315
    and values activated, 88, 98, 107, 113, 140, 171, 187, 190, 242–253, 372, 419, 421
    variations in, 16, 64, 114, 276, 377
    and volunteering 60
Pessimism, man's views on, 18–20
Philanthropy, 372
Philosophy, moral and social, 11–12, 16, 19, 126
Physical capacities, 109, 278
    and acts of harm, 170–171, 183, 240, 375
    and distress, 1, 4, 54, 70, 73, 76, 99, 116, 118, 121, 124, 127, 132, 150, 197–198, 200, 227, 259
    and proximity, 322, 396–398
Physiological arousal, 136–138, 141, 144, 256
Physiological reactions to suffering, 141, 148, 222, 280
Pictures, responses to, 222, 280
Piliavin study, 320

Plans, execution of, 252, 413
Plato, conception of morality, 12–13, 17, 19
Pluralistic ignorance, 75–76, 106
Positive attitudes, 68, 82, 291, 305
Positive behavior, 2, 7, 172, 178, 217, 223, 225, 259, 422–429
Positive conditions
    definitions, 78–79, 82
    and empathy, actions, 136, 146
    and exchanges, 29, 198, 335, 338, 382
    and images of success or failure, 282–283, 287–295
    and (acts within) intimate relationships, 1–3, 132
    and morality, 258, 273, 417
Positive evaluations, 46, 156, 166, 312, 316
Positive experiences, 240, 290–295, 300–308
Positive feedback, 223, 299
Positive goals, 58, 197
Possessions, material, 2, 275, 289
Potency, sense of, 299–300, 306, 308, 356
Power, 167, 239
    appeal and acceptance of, 192, 265, 383, 385
    unilateral, 387
Praise, earning of, 284, 310
Prejudices, 320–324, 396, 398
Prescriptive and prohibitive morality, 2–3, 23
Pressure, conditions of, 220, 225, 237, 240, 301
Prestige, seeking of, 9, 178, 336, 383
Prisoner's dilemma game, 262, 384–388
Profits and losses, emphasis on, 336, 338, 383
Projective test (TAT), 310
Promotive tension, theory of, 314–317
Proximity, 399, 402
    physical, 322, 396–398
Psychedelic drugs, 125
Psychoanalysis, 18
Psychology and psychologists
    clinical, 5
    consequences of, 176, 296, 306
    and distress, 4, 48, 67–70, 150, 170, 215, 227, 235
    experiences and experiments, 71, 186, 295–296, 313–314
    and humanitarianism, 16, 21, 214, 323
    and human nature, 10, 336, 430
    processes, 70, 215
    reactance to, 214, 228, 349, 364–365

    and restoring equity, 181–182
    and sexual desire, 20
    social, 398, 417
Psychopaths, 145
Punishment
    concern about, 218, 263
    cooperation decreases, 389
    deserving of, 151, 153–155, 177
    external and unfair, 91, 152, 200, 224
    fear of, 257
    functional and dysfunctional, 154
    group, 154
    public exposure of, 83–84, 109, 167, 183, 200

Q

Questionnaires
    about attitudes, 244, 246
    and market research, 87
    postexperimental, 62–65, 68, 238, 404
    about public opinion, 315
    responses to, 269, 327
    self-disclosures in, 408
    use of, 85, 153, 166, 174, 228–230, 251, 379, 324, 347
Questions and problems, research and theoretical issues, 172–176

R

Racial and cross-racial relationships, 47, 253, 320–326, 333, 395, 397
Rank-ordering and random conditions, 51, 161
Ratings of attraction and attractiveness, 222, 301–302, 318, 331, 352, 364, 405
Rationalizations, 238, 427
Rats, studies on, 35–37, 100, 184–185
Reactance and reactions
    arousal of, 214–218, 366
    and attribution, 216–219, 366–367
    of bystanders, 97–99
    determinants of, 128, 135, 156–158, 194, 237, 354
    emotional, 45, 137–138, 142, 144, 146, 148, 194, 422
    empathic, 45, 57, 187, 189, 192, 233, 271, 276
    of helpfulness, 70, 217–219, 344–350, 365
    physiological, 141, 148, 222
    psychological, 214, 228, 349, 364–365

Reality and real-life interaction, 79–80, 311, 358, 385, 387

Reason and reasoning
authority of, 23
conventional and preconventional, 262–263
levels of, 12, 129
Mischel's analyses of, 40–41
moral, 55, 59, 124–126, 129–130, 156, 257–260, 263, 266
and self-examination, 14

Rebellious and distrustful behavior, 413

Reciprocity
and altruism, 27–30
attribution of intention and, 57–361
in behavior, 178, 251, 350–355
beliefs about, 343–344, 371–373
benefits of, 336, 341, 343, 369
class differences in, 45, 368–369
condition of, 335–336, 342, 344
in everyday life, 371–374
exchanges in, 340–346, 356, 404, 418
forms of, 338, 354
among friends, 369–374
generalized, 355–358, 360
and generosity, 343
and human interaction, 30, 41, 188
inadequacy of, 362–363
index of, 400
and intimate relationships, 371–374, 403
of kindness, 340, 343
norms of, 44, 220, 226, 360
opportunities for, 344–347, 368
and self-disclosure, 401–404

Reformers, social, 195

Regional differences, 166, 291

Regret, indications of, 195, 361

Reinforcement
activation and values of, 45, 301, 307, 312, 374
alternative forms and explanations of, 190, 212, 219
and altruism, 139
effects, 224, 389
empathic, 140
negative, 157
positive, 157, 190, 218
vicarious, 199, 211–212

Relatedness, primary levels of, 57, 121, 394

Relationships
formation and nature of, 96, 395–399
long-term, 408–412

minimal, 335, 342, 353, 369, 373, 394
positive, 390, 408
prior, 424
variable, 133, 164–165

Religion
belief in, 17, 166, 396
changes and differences in, 34, 275
laws of, 20–21, 52
and virtue and morality, 12, 21, 372

Reparation of image, 288, 298, 306

Repayment defined, 341, 373

Repentance and forgiveness, 177

Requests, moderate and difficult, 218, 319, 322

Research
and empathy
interpretation and value of, 41–42, 58, 67, 82
Just World and justification hypotheses, 156–164, 189, 257, 319
limitations of, 192–196
and self-disclosure, 371, 406
supporting, and validity of, 58–69, 241–242
and theoretical issues, 172–176
volunteering for, 60

Resolutions, conflict principles of, 24, 49–51, 115, 409

Responsibility
and ability and behavior, 76, 96, 261, 358, 413
ascription of (AR), 66, 129, 131, 243, 246–250, 267–268
assumption of, 5, 57, 76, 98, 194, 242, 423
attribution of, 159, 363
of children, 159, 209
commitment-induced, 92, 96
concept of, 91, 160–161, 189, 276, 417
denial of, 144, 182, 186, 243
diffusion of, and the normative explanation of helping behavior, 75, 88–105, 153–155, 324, 426
feelings of, 60, 92, 96–97, 128, 158, 187, 226, 417, 427
in friendship and in intimate relationships, 96, 418
Harris's scale of, 269
and helping others, 75, 88, 125, 159–164, 170, 186, 188
job-related, 91, 272
and justification, 172, 186, 417

Responsibility, (*cont.*)
    measures of, 124, 129–131, 153–154
    moral implications and leadership, 94, 228, 267
    personal sense of, 51, 96, 98, 130–131, 146, 155, 164, 268, 276, 338
    salience of, 244, 246, 351
    social, 66, 88, 122, 208, 225–230, 250–251, 267–272, 276, 356, 368
    variation and degrees in, 160, 184, 246, 268
    verbal focusing of, 89–91, 94–96, 139, 250, 423
Responsiveness and responses
    affectionate, 135, 338
    degrees of, 237, 243, 318, 328
    and distress conditions, 64, 128, 136, 235, 335
    empathic index of, 37–38, 145, 147, 256, 258
    and environment, 27, 257, 419
    to foreigners, 325–326
    nonverbal, 62–63, 90
    to questionnaires, 269, 327–328
Restoration of equity, 169, 182–184, 419
Retaliation and revenge, threat of, 181, 263, 387, 414
Reward(s)
    children received, 179, 210, 221, 260, 287, 300
    and costs, 292, 336
    and decision conditions, 156–158
    distribution or dividing of, 179–180, 254, 256, 327
    donations of, 204–208, 221
    earned or deserved, 210–211, 284–289
    and equitable or equal conditions, 152, 178–179, 286, 410
    evaluation of, 288, 319
    expectation of, 9, 199, 403
    group-administered, 158, 327, 389
    for helping, 109, 188, 212, 229–230, 296, 315, 383
    loss or withdrawal of, 389–390
    material or monetary, 10, 46, 107, 175, 190, 234, 255, 300
    and motivational and objective values, 45, 289
    and punishments, 10, 91, 200, 223–224
    receipt or winning of, 147, 152, 156, 172, 195, 210, 213, 327
    social, 10, 107
    undeserved or unearned, 231, 384–387

Right and wrong, thoughts on, 17, 126
Rights, individual, 2, 34
Rokeach's scale of values, 51, 56, 60, 66, 264, 379
Role taking and role playing
    capacity for, 54–56, 136, 145–148, 258–260, 367, 426
    levels of, 44, 96, 151, 157, 163, 248, 259, 276, 317
    measures of, 256, 260–264
Rotter's internal–external (I–E) Control scale, 247, 272, 377–379
Rules
    of correspondence, 54, 66
    on morality, 10–12, 22–23, 267
    societal, 11, 52, 167, 353
Rural areas, factor of, 120

S

Sacrifice
    degree of 128, 240, 350, 360
    of material possessions, 275, 289, 427–428
    substantial, 1, 316
    willingness to, 284
Sadism, 44, 138, 413
Sadness, role of, 143, 293, 297, 306, 308
Safety, personal and physical, 46, 58, 72 131–132
Sanctions of Evil (by Sanford and Comstock) cited, 152–153
Sanctity of human life, 17, 124, 126
Satisfaction
    feeling of, 5, 138, 221, 251
    mutual, 390, 399
    need of, 306, 328, 337, 341, 413, 415
    and self-disclosure, 409
    sources and goals of, 241, 271
Schwartz's decisional model, 242–247
Science and scientific laws, 16–17, 22–23, 33
Security
    economic, 373
    interpersonal, 414
    need for, 394
Self, 311, 319, 330, 333, 428
Self-abasement, 181
Self-absorption, 384
Self-acceptance, 301, 310
Self-actualization, 14–16
Self-aggrandizement, 18
Self-assertiveness, 94, 215, 220, 326, 357
Self-assured, 398

Self-attribution, 217–222, 324
Self-benevolent, 319, 330
Self-centered, 30, 261, 381, 389, 413
Self-competent, 309
Self-concept, 5, 181, 258, 311, 332, 348, 350, 414–415, 430
Self-concern, 94, 104–105, 115, 122, 191, 278–279, 283, 297–299, 306, 309, 330 347, 424, 426
Self-confidence, 132, 398
Self-control, 257
Self-criticism, 296–297
Self-derogation, 177
Self-description, 177, 363, 400
Self-destruction, 77
Self-determination, 215
Self-devaluation, 349
Self-discipline, 23–24
Self-disclosure, 371, 399–409, 376, 405
  intimate, 399–401
  reciprocal, 404
Self-disinhibiting, 154–155
Self-distraction, 311
Self-esteem, 300–302, 305, 308–312, 323, 331–332, 347–348, 383, 394, 398, 424
Self-evaluation, 57, 70, 116, 147, 191, 221, 278–281, 287, 290–298, 306, 310, 383
Self-examination, 13–14, 19
Self-expression, 185, 294
Self-fulfillment, 389
Self-gain, 9, 42–43, 226, 381, 424
Self-guidance, 333, 428
Selfhood, sense of, 15
Self-image, 43, 174, 306, 319, 383
Self-injury, 181
Self-interests, 2, 7, 18, 21, 24, 43, 178, 214, 263, 277, 297, 341, 414, 427
Selfishness, 208, 238, 320, 361
  of children, 370
  control of, 21, 262
  of friends, 369
  and intentions, 6, 357–363, 381
  manifestations of, 203–205, 374
Self-knowledge, 14
Selflessness, 268
Self-love, 15, 21
Self-mastery, 22
Self-monitoring and observation, 5, 222
Self–other relationship, 7, 57–58, 300–302, 330–333, 420, 428
Self-perception, 219–223, 319
Self-preoccupation, 116, 297, 299, 306, 311, 330

Self-presentation, 312, 363
Self-protection, 113, 361, 367
Self-punishment, 43, 107, 171, 177, 181–183, 361
Self-ratings, 350, 400
Self-regulation, 423, 428
Self-reinforcement, 212–213, 428
Self-reliance, 257
Self-reports, 48, 166, 177, 249, 251, 270
Self-reward, 7, 43, 211
Self-sacrifice, 2–3, 6, 27–29, 31, 38, 57, 117, 156, 211, 214–215, 303, 328–329, 415
Self-seeking, 17–18, 20
Self-selection, 92, 322
Self-serving, 28, 155, 357, 384
Self-sufficiency, 224, 372
Self-therapy, 287, 300, 306
Self-transcending, 15
Self-understanding, 18
Self-worth, 310
Sensation seeking, 60–61
Senselessness, element of, 236
Sensitivity and sensitive reactions, 152, 157, 171, 280
  to inequity and injustice, 23, 302, 421
  interpersonal, 61, 250
  measure of motivational, 36, 232, 310
  to other people in need, 224, 425
  training groups, 377, 407
Sensory deprivation studies, 234–235
Sex-typed activities and interactions, 65, 133, 160, 228, 239
  attitudes and discrimination, 166, 180, 410
  behavior and values, 255–257
  differences relating to helpfulness, 90–91, 230–233, 253–255, 283, 325
  impulses at work in, 18, 20, 394, 402
  sameness of workers, 234, 255
Shame, element of, 171, 306
Sharing
  age factor in, 287
  among animals, 35
  behavior with others, 1, 197, 204, 212, 253, 364
  in children's activities, 260–261, 286–287
  costs of, 299
  emotional responses to, 142, 146, 320
  experiences, 393, 396–397
  learning to participate in, 284–286
  of values and interests, 208, 211, 397
  willingness to, 38, 272
Shyness, factor of, 68, 147

Similar and similarity
  agreement on issues, 315–317, 395–398
  of attitudes, 315–318, 332, 352
  in attractiveness, 318, 331–332
  in belief, hypotheses, 327, 396–398
  of interests, 397, 409
  of opinions, 316–317, 322
  perception of, 164, 424
  racial, 397
Social and Societal activities
  agencies, 166, 349
  approval, 7, 122, 337
  behavior, 1, 27–29, 32, 86, 102, 202, 254–255, 273–274, 362
  class structure, 24, 270, 275, 343, 368–369, 372, 397
  comparison processes, 79–80, 84, 286–287, 312, 348, 384
  consequences, 166, 171, 181, 227, 258, 381
  convention, 14, 84
  Darwinism, 18, 28
  desirability tests, 269–270, 273
  disapproval, 7, 75, 113
  environment, 32, 34, 178, 325
  evolution, 4, 32–34
  exchange theory, 25, 57, 336, 340, 384, 418
  existence conditions, 34, 166, 178
  expectations, 201, 207, 337
  genetic basis of, 27–29
  groups and cooperation, 3, 10, 21–22, 24, 303, 335, 356, 381
  and helpfulness, 101–104
  ideals, 213, 427
  influences exerted, 70, 76, 85, 99, 105, 122, 162, 198–223, 225, 246, 257, 266, 417
  institutional changes in, 2, 22–25
  intelligence tests and, 298, 337
  interactions, 26–27, 376
  involvements in justice, 270, 322, 427
  living conditions, 21–25, 398, 417
  morality in, 2, 13, 21–25, 33
  motives and norms, 14, 28, 32, 42–43, 84, 89, 113, 146, 178, 207, 210, 228, 336, 419
  order and nature of, 15, 21–24, 167, 188, 195, 215, 221
  organization, 335–336, 349
  penetration theory and pressures, 206–207, 403
  progress in civil rights, 195, 326
  responsibility, 66, 88, 122, 208, 225–230, 250–251, 267–272, 276, 351, 356, 368

  responsiveness, 31, 190
  rewards, 10, 107
  rules of, 11, 52, 86, 167, 351, 353
  science and scientists, 23, 195
  sensitivity, 3, 298, 335, 381
  situations and stability, 21, 41, 85, 227
  standards, 11, 13, 18, 21, 178
  status and traditions in, 10–11, 25, 195, 337
  values, 43, 88, 101–104, 172, 174, 268, 270
Socialization and sociability, different techniques of, 34, 43, 179, 243–254, 257, 307, 324, 327–328, 395, 412
Sociobiology, proponent of, 29
Socioeconomic groups, 343
Sociometric ratings, 301, 392
Socratic method of virtue, 13, 17
Stability, 21, 41, 308
Standards
  of cultural conduct, 2, 25, 200, 206
  equity and self-interest, 188–189, 193
  feedback, 349
  morality in, 21, 257
  societal, 11, 13, 18, 21, 178
  violations of, 188–190, 193
Status
  achieved and ascribed, 230–232
  considerations of, 231, 279, 412
  social, 25, 195, 336–337
Status quo, acceptance of, 167
Stimuli
  ambiguous, 99, 104
  and anxiety (producing distress), 6, 100
  auditory and tactile, 281
  characteristics affecting helpfulness, 105–114, 122, 198, 224, 239, 422
  and children's memory, 294
  conditions identified, 121, 417–418
  definition of and exposure to, 82, 87, 114
  emotion-arousing, 147
  influences of, 225–242
  interpretation of, 75–76, 81, 101, 119
  nature of, 70, 121, 331
  physiological reactions to, 90
  positive and negative, 376
  stressful, 117–119
  unconditional, 137
Strangers
  behavior toward, 77, 411–412
  intimate information given to, 399–401
  liking for, and concern over welfare of, 384, 393
Students

high-school, 309–310, 354
college, 263, 268, 271, 278, 280, 283, 321
Subcultural groups, 97, 188
Subjects, control, 174, 190, 288, 292, 310, 329
Submission–dominance dimension, 412, 414, 429
Success
children donate less following, 289
effects of, 282–285, 290
expectation of, 71, 295, 299
feelings of, 287, 330
of groups, 272, 283–284
positive image of, 278, 282–283, 287–295
Suffering and sufferers
arousal and, 136–138, 141, 144, 256
circumstances leading to, 162, 320
dealing with, 5, 156–158
and derogation, 169, 186
empathy with, 107–108, 170, 189
of harmdoers, 138
of innocent people, 151–152, 171
justification of, 164
observation of, 138, 161, 168, 170, 185, 192
reduction in, 427
victims of, 186
Supervisors and supervisory abilities, paradigm, 226, 298, 351, 360
Surveillance
of children by adults, 209–210
conditions and effects of, 98, 172, 295, 322, 324, 430
mutual, 89, 188
Suspicion, mutual, 379, 393, 401
Sympathy
expressions of, 22, 62, 125, 149
manifestations of, 64, 80, 165

T

Taboos, cultural, 18, 398
Tasks
cooperative, 392
learning, 47, 158–163, 177
manual dexterity, 240
perceptual, 185, 279, 283
and performance effects, 56, 278, 300, 319
Taxonomy, of human behavior, 412–413
Teacher–learner selections, 174, 186, 193
Technology, changes in, 34

Tendencies, personal behavioral
perceptual–interpretive, 144, 163–164, 260, 282, 425
personality, 222, 247, 354, 422
reciprocal interactive, 30
self-serving, 28
Tension
arousal of, 47, 333
promotive, 47, 121, 314–317
sources of, 309, 314
Tests and testing
of competence, 272
intellectual aptitude, 310–311
of moral reasoning, 124–125, 130, 259
paper-and-pencil, 121, 126, 144, 246, 255, 268, 295, 310, 312, 318, 410
personality, 60–62, 66–67, 123, 127–128
reliance on, 332
sentence-completion, 131
sociometric, 301
supervisory ability, 226, 298
visual creativity, 280
Therapy, 15, 287, 300, 306
Time, factor of, 41, 270
Tolerance, lack of, 24
Tradition, patterns of, 10–11, 34, 372
Training sessions and trainees, 183, 217, 258, 377, 407
Traits, concept of, 39, 48, 60
Transgressions
consequences of, 170–175, 191–192, 245, 306
guilt following, 176–177
moral, 257, 358
private and public, 177
Trust and trustworthiness
and close relationships, 385, 401–402, 410
Grodman's scale of, 250
interpersonal, 375–378
mutual, 8, 386–388
in other people, 335, 374–379

U

Uncooperativeness, 263
Understanding, capacity for, 18, 262
Unhappiness, 296, 425
Unselfishness, 3, 15–16
Untrustworthiness and unjust world, 156, 378
Urban areas, factor of, 118–120, 390
Utility, law of diminishing marginal, 337

V

Values
changes and differences in, 34, 44–45, 333, 397
hierarchy of, 51
index of, 259
internalized, development of, 4–6, 10, 23, 128, 174, 256, 269, 271, 276
moral, 5–6, 10, 23, 128, 174, 256, 269, 271, 276
and orientations, 8, 52, 140, 166, 311
personal, 43–44, 55, 88, 98, 107, 113, 140, 171, 187, 190, 242–253, 273, 372, 417, 419, 421
similar, 395–398
Verbal expressions and effects, 147, 175, 241
agreements, 173, 245
and children, 207
communications, 62–63, 95, 173, 197, 201–205, 207–211, 214, 217, 225, 235, 244–245, 280
influences of, 198, 209–214, 246
as instructions, 100, 216
as reinforcement, 312
responses to, 64–65
responsibility focused by, 89–91, 94–96, 139, 250, 423
statements, 204–205, 215–216, 266–267, 363
Vicarious emotional responses, 111, 137, 146, 161, 211–212
Victim(s)
characteristics of, 107–109
derogation of, 183, 192, 249
devaluation of, 152, 159–160, 164–165
evaluation of, 156, 161, 165–170
and harmdoers, 183
identification with, 108–109
innocent, 159–161
(ascribed) responsibility of, 159–163, 186
Violation of beliefs and values, 189, 386
Violence, fear of, 195, 325, 368
Virtue, element of, 12–13, 17, 21, 372
Visual creativity, 280

Volunteers and volunteering
versus assignments, 160–161
experiments involving, 192, 291
of helpfulness, 167, 183, 234–235, 348, 354–355, 359
personality characteristics of, 60, 270, 278, 310
studies of, 247, 249

W

Warmth and the warm glow of success, 258, 284
"Watch him" orientation, 141–143, 163
Weaknesses of others, 387–389
Welfare
of other human beings, 7, 21, 44, 46, 88, 147, 164, 258, 267, 303
own state of, 384
physical, 2–4
psychological, 336
of society, 25, 303–305
of strangers, 384, 418
Well-being
sense of, 280, 298, 302–312
state of, 57–58, 300, 302, 304, 330, 425–426
White American attitudes toward blacks, 320–326
Will and willingness in aiding and sharing, 200, 224, 272, 284, 328, 376
"Winning," 383, 385
Women, *see also* Females
liberation movement, 118–119, 232
opportunities for, 34
personality characteristics of, 65–66, 403–404, 410
as victims, 159
Work and workers paradigm, 16, 233–235, 255, 351
"Wrong-number technique," 218, 291, 320, 331

Z

Zeigarnick effect, 47